THE BATTLE OVER BILINGUAL BALLOTS

Election Law, Politics, and Theory

Series Editor: David Schultz

Election Law, Politics, and Theory broadly examines election law at the national, subnational, and international or comparative levels. Titles in the series provide both empirical and theoretical analysis of topics and issues that affect voting, campaigns, and elections, and as such offer coverage of political as well as legal concerns and controversies. Useful for scholars, researchers, and practitioners in the field, volumes address such subjects as voting rights, reapportionment, ballot access, campaign finance reform, the courts and election regulation, and the role of actors including political parties and the media. The series' ultimate goal is to build scholarship in this key area by seeking to understand how elections function in an increasingly complex, technological, and global community, and the ways in which election law impacts outcomes, disputes, and eventually governance in particular nations and societies.

The Battle Over Bilingual Ballots

Language Minorities and Political Access Under the Voting Rights Act

JAMES THOMAS TUCKER

Routledge
Taylor & Francis Group
LONDON AND NEW YORK

First published 2009 by Ashgate Publishing

Published 2016 by Routledge
2 Park Square, Milton Park, Abingdon, Oxon OX14 4RN
711 Third Avenue, New York, NY 10017, USA

Routledge is an imprint of the Taylor & Francis Group, an informa business

British Library Cataloguing in Publication Data
Tucker, James Thomas.
The battle over bilingual ballots : language minorities and political access under the Voting Rights Act. -- (Election law, theory, and politics)
1. United States. Voting Rights Act of 1965. 2. Linguistic minorities--Suffrage--United States. 3. Linguistic minorities--Legal status, laws, etc.--United States. 4. Voting--United States. 5. Language policy--United States.
I. Title II. Series
342.7'3072-dc22

Library of Congress Cataloging-in-Publication Data
Tucker, James Thomas.
The battle over bilingual ballots : language minorities and political access under the Voting Rights Act / by James Thomas Tucker.
p. cm. -- (Election law, theory, and politics)
Includes index.
ISBN 978-0-7546-7572-3 (hardback)
1. Linguistic minorities--Suffrage--United States. 2. United States. Voting Rights Act of 1965. I. Title.

KF4896.L56T83 2009
342.73'072--dc22

2009020470

ISBN 9780754675723 (hbk)

For Product Safety Concerns and Information please contact our EU representative:
GPSR@taylorandfrancis.com
Taylor & Francis
Verlag GmbH, Kaufingerstraße 24, 80331 München, Germany

Contents

List of Figures

Dedicated to my wife, Sue, for her love and support, without which this book would not have been possible.

Preface[1]

Imagine that you are a registered voter and want to exercise your fundamental right to participate in the political process. You have trouble locating your designated polling site because you cannot read either the written instructions that accompanied your voter registration card or the posted signs directing you to the site. If you are fortunate enough to arrive at the correct destination, you encounter poll workers who are speaking incomprehensible words and are visibly irritated when you do not know how to respond to them. When you give them your name, the poll workers cannot find it in their registration books. Even if they find your name and give you a ballot, you do not know what to do with it. A look of embarrassment spreads across your face. You have not voted before. You cannot grasp any of the instructions the poll workers try to give to you, if they bother to make the effort. You walk into the voting booth but do not even know how to close the curtain. No one is allowed to accompany you inside the voting booth to help you out. You cannot read the ballot that is given to you. Alone and without any guidance, you attempt to cast a meaningful ballot.

The language assistance provisions of the Voting Rights Act (VRA) were enacted to remove language barriers to voting. A permanent requirement for bilingual voting materials and assistance was included in the original 1965 Act, but was limited to only Puerto Rican voters who were educated in Spanish (Chapter 2). In 1975, Congress added a temporary mandate that included Alaska Natives, American Indians, Asian Americans, and persons of Spanish heritage who had suffered from educational discrimination (Chapters 3–5, 8–9). That mandate, contained in Sections 4(f)(4) and 203, prohibits jurisdictions with prescribed levels of limited-English proficient (LEP) voting-age U.S. citizens from conducting English-only elections. Other sections of the VRA help secure equal access to elections for language minorities (Chapters 1–4). As of July 2002, the temporary language assistance provisions apply to five states in their entirety and portions of 26 additional states (Chapter 5). Where the VRA's bilingual requirements have been implemented properly, they have proven to be effective in providing LEP voters with equal opportunities to participate in the political process (Chapters 6–8, 11).

Despite the increasing importance of minority language assistance throughout the United States, the federal bilingual election requirements are probably the least known and most widely misunderstood provisions of the VRA. Many English-speaking voters cannot comprehend why it is necessary to provide election information in any language other than English. The Act's temporary language assistance provisions enjoyed strong bipartisan support in Congress when they were adopted and each time they were up for renewal (Chapters 3–4, 7). But they have also come under fire by opponents of the so-called "bilingual ballot" mandate. These critics advocate making English the "official" language of the United States and malign the use of language materials

1 Portions of this Preface originally were published in the New York University Journal of Legislation and Public Policy as James Thomas Tucker, *Enfranchising Language Minority Citizens: The Bilingual Election Provisions of the Voting Rights Act*, 10 N.Y.U. J. Leg. & Pub. Pol'y 195 (2006–2007). That article has been adapted to correspond with the discussion in the remainder of this book.

and assistance in elections in non-English languages.[2] Since 1981, they have introduced bills in Congress that would repeal federal requirements for bilingual materials or assistance in several areas including voting. The most significant challenge came in 1996, when the Bill Emerson English Language Empowerment Act of 1996 was adopted by the House of Representatives,[3] but died in a Senate committee.[4]

Opponents of the VRA's language assistance provisions insist that bilingual ballots and assistance are unnecessary and harmful to American society in several ways. They have cited a number of reasons for eliminating those provisions, including the perceived absence of voting discrimination against language minorities, lack of demand, ineffectiveness, cost, and a belief that the provisions are divisive and create a disincentive to learn English. Some of their criticism rests upon a misapprehension of the purpose of the federal bilingual election provisions and the effects of implementing language assistance requirements. Other arguments rest on the contention that the provisions divide American citizens along ethnic lines by creating a "modern-day Tower of Babel."[5] Those arguments are analyzed at length in Chapter 8.

Although the temporary language assistance provisions of the Act have been in effect since 1975 and the permanent protections for Puerto Rican-schooled voters since 1965, no comprehensive study of them has been published. The purpose of this book is to help fill that void. In addition, the book provides a factual response to arguments made by opponents of the provisions. Linda Chavez's viewpoint is typical of critics of bilingual ballots. She contends that the VRA "was originally intended to protect primarily one group" – southern Blacks – because "no other group had so systematically been denied the right to vote."[6] Chavez's assertion bears little semblance to the reality of the need for language assistance, what created that need, or the congressional response to remedy discrimination against language minority voters.

For language minority citizens denied equal schooling opportunities, English-only elections can be insurmountable barriers that victimize them again. While many aspire to have "our citizens with limited English skills speak and understand English proficiently,"[7] LEP citizens must be allowed to participate until the shackles of the crippling legacy of educational discrimination are removed. The language assistance provisions help overcome barriers posed by English-only elections to ensure that, in Senator Orin Hatch's words, citizenship is not "just an empty promise" for language minority citizens who want to be integrated into American society and the democratic process.[8]

---

2 *See* Spencer Overton, Stealing Democracy: The New Politics of Voter Suppression 131–47 (2006); Language Loyalties: A Source Book of the Official English Controversy (James Crawford ed., 1992).

3 *See* Bill Emerson English Language Empowerment Act of 1996, H.R. 123, 104th Cong., 2d Sess. (1996). The House adopted the bill by a vote of 259 to 169. *See* 142 Cong. Rec. H9769-H9771 (daily ed. Aug. 1, 1996).

4 *See* Language of Government Act of 1995, S. 356, 104th Cong., 1st Sess. (1995); S. 175, 104th Cong., 1st Sess. (1995).

5 H. Rep. No. 102–655 at 28 (1992) (dissenting views of seven congressmen).

6 Linda Chavez, Out of the Barrio 40 (1992).

7 H.R. Rep. No. 109–478 at 59–60 (2006).

8 *Voting Rights Act Language Assistance Amendments of 1992: Hearings on S. 2236 Before the Subcomm. on the Constitution of the Senate Comm. on the Judiciary*, 102d Cong., 2d Sess., S. Hrg. 102–1066, at 134 (1992) (statement of Sen. Hatch).

Acknowledgments

This book has its genesis in conversations I had with Danny Levitas in 2004 in the months leading up to reauthorization of the Voting Rights Act. At that time, little had been written on the Act's language assistance provisions. Danny, an Ira Glasser Racial Justice Fellow at the ACLU, suggested I write this book to help fill that void. Five years later, after completing a series of articles on reauthorization, the journey is now complete. I am grateful to Danny for gently prodding me to write this book.

Two of the chapters are the product of extensive contributions by Professor Rodolfo Espino and several students at Barrett, The Honors College at Arizona State University: Rebecca Amrani, Elizabeth Andrews, Linley Barney, Jessica Becker, Nicole Finch, Heather Hinderland (Owens), Karissa Kater, Kristine Kelley, Lauron Lovato, and Laura Thorson. Professor Espino's insight and humor carried all of us through the arduous task of completing a comprehensive national study of language assistance practices. The study would not have been possible without the support of Barrett's Dean, Mark Jacobs, as well as ASU's Political Science Department and several other departments on campus. To my former students, each of you showed that undergraduates can really make a difference in helping protect the crown jewel of civil rights laws.

Thanks to Jon Greenbaum for asking me in 2003 to work on reauthorization. Our many conversations ultimately led to the study I conducted with Dr. Espino. That was followed by my return to Washington, D.C., in early 2006 to work full-time on the VRARA.

Debo Adegbile, Kristen Clarke-Avery, Julie Fernandes, and LaShawn Warren encouraged commentators to make the reauthorization record more accessible to the general public, and greatly informed my approach in this book. Each stood by me over the past few years, providing words of encouragement and support along the way. They also helped me reconstruct the timeline of events surrounding the VRA's reauthorization in 2005–2006. Working with them has been one of the highlights of my professional career, along with Terry Ao, Kim Betz, Charlotte Burrows, Phil Kiko, Kristine Lucius, Stephanie Moore, Jeremy Paris, Paul Taylor, Jim Walsh, and Peter Zamora, among many others. Arturo Vargas, Rosalind Gold, and the National Association of Latino Elected and Appointed Officials (NALEO) made my participation on reauthorization possible.

Some chapters have evolved based upon feedback I received from law reviews that edited earlier publications excerpted throughout this book. I appreciate the extensive comments from editors at the New York University Law School's *Journal of Legislation and Public Policy*, the University of Notre Dame Law School's *Journal of Legislation*, and the University of Texas Law School's *Texas Journal on Civil Liberties and Civil Rights*.

Natalie Landreth of the Native American Rights Fund has been a great friend and colleague. I had the privilege of working with Natalie on the Bethel, Alaska, litigation for more than two years. Along with our ACLU co-counsel Brian Sutherland, Natalie provided a lot of feedback on the Alaska chapters. The story of voting discrimination in Alaska could not have been told without Natalie, who identified the problems in Bethel while preparing the Alaska report for the congressional record in 2005 and 2006.

Peyton McCrary, historian in the Civil Rights Division of the U.S. Department of Justice, offered suggestions on my discussion of literacy tests, as well as encouragement and unflagging support throughout the course of writing the book. Susan Nichols and Brian Landsberg also provided helpful information on North Carolina's literacy test. Jocelyn Friedrichs Benson offered many helpful comments on some of the book's chapters. I also appreciate Tim Mellett and Avner Shapiro for putting up with my discussion of the book for several years and emphasizing how important it was to write it.

Several people are responsible for the book's pictures. Thanks to Debo Adegbile and Nina Perales for providing personal photos from the Rose Garden ceremony from 2006. I also appreciate the assistance of Caroline Atuk-Derrick of the University of Alaska-Fairbanks, Julia Devore of the Anchorage Museum at Rasmuson Center, and Sandra Johnston at the Alaska State Library. A special thanks to Charles MacNulty, the Voter Outreach Manager for the San Francisco Department of Elections, who provided many of the examples of bilingual and multilingual voting materials that appear in Appendix A.

The book would be incomplete without the different perspectives of the five commentators who provided essays for Chapter 11: Terry Ao, Jocelyn Benson, Ana Henderson, Glenn Magpantay, and John Tanner. To each commentator, thank you for taking the time to share your experiences, which greatly enriched the discussion in the book.

Last, but certainly by no means least, I am indebted to Ashgate Publishing. Eric Levy, Ashgate's Commissioning Editor, has been terrific in helping a novice author navigate the publication process. David Schultz, the Series Editor, provided invaluable feedback to ensure that the book was accessible and told the story of language assistance so it was accessible to the general public. The book was a work in progress, and I commend David and Eric for bearing with me until it was completed. Sarah Wardill, Senior Editor in Ashgate's Social Sciences Department, and Phyllis Singer did a marvellous job editing the book. Sarah, in particular, worked wonders with the presentation of the manuscript, pictures, tables and appendices. The book is much stronger because of her efforts. Carolyn Court, Ashgate Social Sciences Editorial Administrator, made the entire publication process seamless from start to finish.

PART I
REMEDIES FOR LANGUAGE MINORITY VOTERS BEFORE 1975

Chapter 1

Literacy Test Bans before 1975

There are many common bonds that language minority and African-American voters share. The barriers posed by literacy tests, which require applicants to demonstrate their ability to read and write as a prerequisite to voting, are one. Discrimination in several areas, including schooling, is another. Non-English speaking citizens suffered from educational discrimination in the United States that often was as severe as the separate and unequal schooling provided to African-American children (Chapters 8–10). Like African-Americans, language minorities frequently were unable to pass English literacy tests when attempting to register to vote. But the effects of educational discrimination extended far beyond the voter registration. In most states, all election information was available only in English. That imposed a *de facto* requirement to be able to read even in places where literacy tests were not in effect or were later suspended. As a result, English-only elections themselves often functioned as literacy tests (Chapters 3–4, 9–10).

The Voting Rights Act (VRA), as originally enacted, mainly focused on remedying voting discrimination against African-Americans in the South.[1] Since Reconstruction, white segregationists had brutally suppressed efforts by African-American voters to register and participate in elections. On March 7, 1965, violence shocked the nation's conscience on what became known as "Bloody Sunday." A peaceful group of 600 men, women, children, and ministers were met with blows from clubs, the sting of tear gas, and the terror of armed state troopers on horseback as they attempted to cross the Edmund Pettus Bridge on a voting rights march from Selma, Alabama to Montgomery. Television coverage brought the brutal images into America's homes.[2] Selma Mayor Joseph Smitherman described the scene, noting that "When that beating happened at the foot of the bridge, it looked like war ... That went out all over the country. And the people, the wrath of the nation came down on us" (Williams 1987: 273). Eight days later, President Lyndon Johnson announced before a joint session of Congress that he intended to introduce a voting rights bill that would end, once and for all, disenfranchisement of southern Blacks (Williams 1987: 278). President Johnson signed the Act into law on August 6, 1965.

The "heart of the Voting Rights Act,"[3] Sections 4 through 9, were special temporary measures that only applied to states or political subdivisions that had used a literacy test or similar tests or devices as prerequisites to voting in a manner that had resulted in low registration or voting rates.[4] Section 4 temporarily suspended literacy tests or devices in a covered jurisdiction. Section 5 required a covered jurisdiction to obtain approval for voting changes before implementing them. To ensure that covered jurisdictions complied with those requirements, federal examiners were authorized to enroll and list eligible voters under Section 6, and federal observers were authorized to observe and document how elections were conducted and ballots were tabulated under Section 8. Application of the triggering formula was restricted primarily to seven southern states. Consequently, the 1965

1 *See South Carolina v. Katzenbach*, 383 U.S. 301, 308 (1966).

2 *See* Juan Williams, Eyes on the Prize: America's Civil Rights Years 1954–1965, at 251–87 (1987).

3 U.S. Comm'n on Civil Rts., The Voting Rights Act: Ten Years After 5 (Jan. 1975).

4 *See* Pub. L. No. 89–110, 79 Stat. 437 (1965).

Act initially had its greatest impact on African-American voters (U.S. Comm'n on Civil Rts. 1975: 13).

At the same time, language minority voters received some relief from their inability to participate in English-only elections. The VRA's temporary suspension of literacy tests in certain areas originally included some jurisdictions with large numbers of language minorities, including all of Alaska and parts of Arizona, Hawaii, and Idaho.[5] As discussed in Chapter 2, the 1965 Act included permanent bilingual election procedures that protected Puerto Rican voters educated in Spanish from being disenfranchised because of their language, as well as other federal remedies. This chapter explores the evolution of remedies aimed at literacy tests, which formed the basis for broader relief from English-only elections included in the 1975 VRA Amendments.

Discriminatory Origins of Literacy Tests

Literacy tests are commonly associated with disenfranchisement of African-Americans in the South, beginning in the late nineteenth century. But literacy tests were used much earlier against another group of Americans: the foreign born and other non-English speaking citizens. The tests also were used to deny voter registration applications by Alaska Natives and other native voters as they began to get the franchise in the early twentieth century (Chapter 9). Language minorities were the first to suffer the pernicious effects of what would become one of America's most successful disenfranchisement schemes.

Two developments in the 1840s fueled the cry for literacy tests. First, the franchise dramatically expanded during the rise of populism that followed the election of President Andrew Jackson. A majority of states removed restrictions such as property ownership, payment of taxes, and religion, which had limited voting primarily to white male Protestant landowners.[6] Universal manhood suffrage (at least among white males) became increasingly common. Second, the pace of immigration quickened, with nearly three million foreigners, or roughly 15 percent of the total population in 1845, arriving between 1845 and 1854.[7] These events offered fertile ground for the rise of Nativism and anti-immigrant groups that sought to restrict the right to vote to newer arrivals.

The Know-Nothings were the most prominent of those groups. According to Alexander Keyssar, the Know-Nothings avowed that they did not want to stop immigration altogether or to permanently disenfranchise immigrants. Instead, they sought "to restrict the political rights of immigrants until they had been 'nationalized' through prolonged immersion in the American way of life" (Keyssar 2000: 85). Literacy was an effective tool for limiting the vote of poor, illiterate new arrivals and non-English-speaking citizens. A commentator at the time explained, a voter "ought to be able to read and write with facility, so that he may inform himself, by study of the structure

5 Four counties in Arizona and one county each in Hawaii and Idaho met the triggering formula provided under the 1965 Act. Between 1965 and 1970, Alaska, three counties in Arizona, one county in North Carolina, and the one Idaho county were exempted from coverage after successful lawsuits under the bailout provisions of Section 4(a) of the VRA (U.S. Comm'n on Civil Rts. 1975: 13–14).

6 *See* Christian Collier, *The American People as Christian White Men of Property: Suffrage and Elections in Colonial and Early National America, in* Voting and the Spirit of American Democracy: Essays on the History of Voting and Voting Rights in America (Donald W. Rodgers, ed. 1992); Chilton Williamson, American Suffrage from Property to Democracy, 1760–1860 (Princeton University Press, 1960).

7 Alexander Keyssar, The Right to Vote: The Contested History of Democracy in the United States 82 (2000).

of our government… and so that he may learn from the common publications … the condition and wants of the country."[8] The literacy test was born. Figure 1.1 is illustrative of the racist treatment experienced by immigrants from disfavored countries, particularly those from southern and eastern European countries and Ireland.

Literacy tests suffered some early setbacks, including a rejection by New York at its constitutional convention in 1846.[9] But they quickly took hold in Connecticut, which adopted a literacy test in

THE WASHINGTON TIMES, SUNDAY, JUNE 19, 1904. 9

PROBLEM OF THE IMMIGRANT JUST NOW ESPECIALLY PRESSING

Cut Rates Across the Ocean Bringing Added Thousands.

How to Keep Out Undesirables a Very Serious Question

Health Requirements Are Now Enforced With Stringency.

Bureau of Immigration Makes Constant Study of Types.

From Northern Europe Come the Most Desirable Classes.

Latins in General Do Not Assimilate With the Americans.

A HUNGARIAN. One of the Middle Stand ard of Races Seeking Haven in This Country.

A PINK WOMAN. Her Sterling Character Is Clearly Shown in the Lineaments of Her Face.

A SWISS GIRL. No Need to Question the Desirability of Such Immigrants as She.

A RUSSIAN FARMER BOY. If All Russian Immigrants Were of This Type They Would Not Be Listed With the "Undesirables."

THE FAMILIAR ITALIAN TYPE. Such as Reside in Filthy Quarters and Remains Alien for Generations.

A SLAV. An Anarchist in the Making If Not Already Made—A Menace to American Institutions.

Figure 1.1 Press coverage of immigrants from Southern and Eastern Europe used racist themes

Source: *Washington Times* article, June 19, 1904, Magazine Features, p. 9, image 33. Reproduction courtesy of the Library of Congress, Prints & Photographs Division. Washington, D.C.

8 Samuel Jones, A Treatise on the Right of Suffrage 132–33 (1842).

9 Jones 1842: 143–44; Arthur W. Bromage, *Literacy and the Electorate*, 24 Am. Pol. Sci. Rev. 946, 950–51, 955–56 n.27 (Nov. 1930).

1855 by popular referendum. "Connecticut was the first state to comprehend the possibilities of the literacy test in discriminating against immigrants" (Bromage 1930: 951). The literacy test originally required an elector to read any portion of the state's constitution or a state statute. The *Connecticut Courant* (now the *Hartford Courant*) hailed the restriction and attacked its critics, stating this "miserable tribe of low, hack, partisan, demagogic, hollow, hypocritical democrats would give the state into the arms of foreigners or drunkards … or irresponsible grog-shop scoundrels and poorhouse rum-blossoms." The test did not initially achieve its intended effect because it failed to require literacy in English. Non-English-speaking voters passed the test by reading a clause of the state constitution translated into German, Hebrew, or Irish by sympathetic politicians or registrars (Bromage 1930: 951–52). In response, by a ten to one margin Connecticut voters amended the test in 1897, adding a requirement that electors be literate in English.[10]

Massachusetts followed the example of its sister state in 1857 (Bromage 1930: 952; Haynes 1898: 497–98). Irish-born immigrants poured into the state after the potato famines, accounting for 15 percent of the total population by 1860. Unlike other immigrants, however, the Irish were politically active in their new country, voting for Democrats and imperiling Whig hegemony over Massachusetts. Nativists and Whigs pushed a constitutional amendment through the state legislature that required a voter to be able to read the state constitution and to write his name. The amendment included a grandfather clause exempting those who already had the right to vote, persons 60 years and older, and the physically disabled (Bromage 1930: 952–53). The *Boston Herald* criticized the amendment, which was "aimed, as has been boldly avowed, against that class of foreigners who are presumed to be Catholics, and proceeds upon the impudent assumption that large numbers of them are unable to read and write," with its reach extending "to every emigrant from Protestant European states."[11] Nevertheless, Massachusetts voters adopted the literacy test by a nearly two to one vote. One observer would later write, "It was the ignorant, poverty-stricken, famished, unwashed Irish Catholic rowdy whom the country may thank for bringing forth literacy tests."[12]

Proponents of literacy tests justified them on several grounds. Non-English speakers needed to learn English in order to become fully assimilated (Bromage 1930: 961). The ability to read also was said to be necessary for voters to make informed decisions: "The voter who cannot read a newspaper or the election address of a candidate is ill equipped for voting."[13] Access to other forms of media, such as radio, was viewed as insufficient because "there still remains the need for literacy in casting the ballot." Likewise, it was argued that literacy tests minimized the possibility of vote fraud caused by voter assistance, in which "the designated assistant enters the voting booth, leaving the voter outside, and marks [the ballot] to suit himself."[14]

In truth, efforts to stem the tide of "ignorance and corruption" at the polls, which the former governor of Mississippi used to argue for literacy tests, often were euphemisms for taking away the vote from immigrants, language minorities, and African-Americans.[15] The impact was profound. In Mississippi, where African-Americans comprised about two-thirds of the population in 1890, it was estimated that the state's literacy test disqualified about 80 percent (Haynes 1898: 499–500,

10 Bromage 1930: 952; George H. Haynes, *Educational Qualifications for the Suffrage in the United States*, 13 Pol. Sci. Q. 495, 496–97 (Sept. 1898).

11 Bromage 1930: 953 (quoting Editorial, Boston Herald, Apr. 29, 1857).

12 Bromage 1930: 953 n. 20 (quoting Kirk H. Porter, Suffrage in the United States 118–19 (1918)).

13 Bromage 1930: 948 (quoting Lord James Bryce, Modern Democracies 71 (1921)).

14 Jerome G. Kerwin, *Electoral Administration in Chicago*, 21 Am. Pol. Sci. Rev. 830, 831 (Nov. 1927).

15 Haynes 1898: 500 (quoting former Mississippi Governor Alcorn in The Nation, Sept. 4, 1890).

506). Approximately 35,000 voters were disenfranchised by the literacy tests in Connecticut and Massachusetts. Nationwide, as many as a third of all Americans were illiterate in 1917–1918 (Bromage 1930: 953–54, 962). Illiteracy rates could have been even higher among recent immigrants, first-generation Americans, and Native American adults on reservations. Requiring proof of the ability to read and write was an effective tool to bar millions of Americans from the polls without explicitly singling out voters by their race, ethnicity, or language minority status.

Following the lead of Connecticut and Massachusetts, 16 more states enacted literacy tests between 1889 and 1924 (Keyssar 2000: 362–67). Eight southern states adopted the tests as "a very effective means for the control of the negro vote": Mississippi in 1890, South Carolina in 1895, Louisiana in 1898, North Carolina in 1900, Alabama in 1901, Virginia in 1902, Georgia in 1908, and Oklahoma in 1910. Not to be outdone, eight states in the Northeast and the West began requiring literacy to vote to exclude immigrants from the franchise: Wyoming in 1889, Maine in 1892, California in 1894, Washington in 1896, New Hampshire in 1902, Arizona in 1913, New York in 1921, and Oregon in 1924 (Bromage 1930: 954–55). States implemented literacy tests even when they did not have a significant number of immigrants. In Wyoming, only 2 percent of the population was foreign born, but the state took action "both to disenfranchise miners and guard against a future influx of immigrants" (Keyssar 2000: 145). Western states directed their literacy tests to bar voting by Indians, Mexicans, and particularly the Chinese (Figure 1.3).

The inequity of literacy tests was heightened when combined with another procedure that was nearly universally adopted in the United States at the end of the nineteenth century. The secret, or Australian, ballot required voters to cast in private a standard ballot prepared by local election officials. It replaced ballots prepared by political parties that did not require any literacy at all. Although the secret ballot reduced the possibility of corruption and voter intimidation, it could disenfranchise illiterate voters just as effectively as a literacy test did, unless a voter was allowed to receive assistance when casting a ballot. As later events would prove, illiterate African-Americans and language minorities were especially vulnerable to the discriminatory effects of English-only ballots that they could not understand without assistance (Keyssar 2000: 142–43). The secret ballot therefore could be just as effective at disenfranchising voters even in states that did not have literacy tests.

The Constitutionality of Some Literacy Tests

In 1959, six years before the VRA was enacted, the United States Supreme Court considered whether literacy was a legitimate qualification for voting. At that time, 19 states had some form of literacy test, with most implicitly or directly mandating that voters prove their English literacy. Five states required a voter to read a section of the State or Federal Constitution and write his or her own name.[16] Five states required a voter to read and write a section of the State or Federal Constitution, with Alabama also requiring proof of "good character" and the ability to "embrace the duties and obligations of citizenship."[17] Three southern states required demonstration of literacy and additional requirements similar to those of Alabama that were either mandatory for all voters, or in the case of Georgia, required only if a voter was physically incapable of reading a ballot.[18] Virginia required that

16 These states were Arizona, California, Delaware, Maine, and Massachusetts. *Lassiter v. Northampton Bd. of Elections*, 360 U.S. 45, 52 n.7 (1959).

17 These states were Alabama, New Hampshire, North Carolina, Oklahoma, and South Carolina. *Lassiter* 1959: 52 n.7.

18 These states were Georgia, Louisiana, and Mississippi. *Lassiter* 1959: 52 n.7.

the voting registration application be filled out in the voter's hand in front of the registrar without receiving any aid. Five states mandated demonstration of English literacy: New York and Oregon required a voter to show the ability to read and write English; Connecticut and Wyoming required voters to read a constitutional provision in English; and Washington required a voter to be able to read and speak the English language (*Lassiter* 1959: 52 n.7).

North Carolina's Literacy Test

North Carolina's law was typical of the background and requirements of literacy tests. Following ratification of the Fifteenth Amendment to the United States Constitution, Congress passed the Enforcement Act of 1870, which required that election officials provide all citizens with equal opportunities to register and vote.[19] In 1894, Congress repealed most of the provisions of the Enforcement Act.[20] Like other southern states, North Carolina responded by amending its constitution to prevent African-Americans from voting. An amendment to the state constitution that was adopted in 1899 and went into effect in 1902 provided:

> Every person presenting himself for registration shall be able to read and write any section of the Constitution in the English language. But no male person, who was, on January 1, 1867, or at any time prior thereto, entitled to vote under the laws of any State in the United States wherein he then resided, and no lineal descendant of any such person shall be denied the right to register and vote at any election in this State by reason of his failure to possess the educational qualifications herein described: Provided, he shall have registered in accordance with the terms of this section prior to December 1, 1908.[21]

North Carolina's constitutional literacy test did not expressly apply to only African-American voters, but that was plainly its purpose and effect. African-Americans who were victims of unequal schooling could not pass the literacy test. At the same time, the constitution's grandfather clause exempted only illiterate whites from the test. On January 1, 1867, well before ratification of the Fourteenth and Fifteenth Amendments to the United States Constitution, no former slaves in the state could vote.[22] Nationwide, only a handful of African-Americans were registered in six northern states that permitted them to vote, making the exemption inapplicable to nearly all African-Americans who moved to North Carolina (Tucker 1999: 471–72). That was made clear in the *Raleigh News and Observer*'s headline to a January 1900 article on the literacy test: "WHITE SUPREMACY MADE PERMANENT." As the article explained, whites registered before 1908 were exempt from the requirement, with the test being used solely to "eliminate the baneful and ruinous influence of irresponsible negro suffrage."[23] The constitutional provision ensured that 50,000 white voters (one-fifth of the white population) who were illiterate remained on voter registration lists, while 60,000

19 16 Stat. 140 (1870). In 1871, the Enforcement Act was amended to allow federal supervision of the electoral process, from registration to the tabulation of ballots and certification of election results. *See* 16 Stat. 433 (1871).

20 28 Stat. 36 (1894); Warren Christopher, *The Constitutionality of the Voting Rights Act of 1965*, 18 Stan. L. Rev. 1, 1–2 (1965).

21 N.C. Const. of 1902, art. VI, § 4 (1902).

22 *See* U.S. Const. amend. XIV; James Thomas Tucker, *Tyranny of the Judiciary: Judicial Dilution of Consent Under Section 2 of the Voting Rights Act*, 7 WM. & MARY BILL RTS. J. 443, 469–87 (1999).

23 *Gaston County v. United States*, 288 F. Supp. 678, 684 n.11 (D.D.C. 1968) (three-judge court), *aff'd*, 395 U.S. 285 (1969).

Black voters (half the Black population) who were literate were removed.[24] Despite the clear racial purposes and effects, the state's highest court upheld the constitutional literacy test.[25]

In practice, the constitutional provision's discriminatory impact was exacerbated by its arbitrary application. There was no uniform literacy test in North Carolina. In most counties, voting registrars exercised nearly unlimited discretion over whether an individual applicant was literate. That led to what the U.S. Commission on Civil Rights would later describe as "the haphazard administration of literacy tests" against Black registrants.[26] Registrars denied Black applicants for "reading deficiencies" or mispronouncing or misspelling a single word, while registering illiterate white applicants who were not required to take a literacy test (U.S. Comm'n on Civil Rts. 1961: 32–34). Some county registrars required Black applicants to write from dictation, a practice that the North Carolina Supreme Court subsequently found unlawful.[27] Henry Frye, who would go on to become the first African-American chief justice of the state's Supreme Court, was disenfranchised by the literacy test. Despite being a college graduate who had just been admitted to law school at the University of North Carolina, Frye failed the literacy test in 1956. He was unable to correctly name five signers of the Declaration of Independence and the twelfth president of the United States. Several weeks later, Frye was allowed to register after he complained to the local political boss.[28] Figure 1.2 is an example of a literacy test that complied with the requirements of North Carolina law.

In 1957, the state adopted a statutory literacy test that was substantially similar to the test in the state constitution. The statutory test required that "Every person presenting himself for registration shall be able to read and write any section of the Constitution of North Carolina in the English language" (*Lassiter* 1959: 46 n.1). Shortly after the law was enacted, Louise Lassiter, an African-American voter, challenged it. In 1956, Lassiter had failed a literacy test when the local registrar found that she mispronounced three words (U.S. Comm'n on Civil Rts. 1961: 34). When she reapplied in 1957, her registration application was denied after she refused to take the statutory literacy test (*Lassiter* 1959: 45). A three-judge federal court found the state constitution's grandfather clause unconstitutional in light of *Guinn v. United States*, in which the Supreme Court struck down a similar exception to a literacy test in Oklahoma that exempted many illiterate white voters.[29] Since the North Carolina statute did not have a grandfather clause, the federal court required the African-American voter to exhaust her remedies in state court. The North Carolina courts upheld the law, and she appealed (*Lassiter* 1959: 46).

Lassiter v. Northampton County Board of Elections

In *Lassiter*, the United States Supreme Court acknowledged that North Carolina had tremendous discretion in imposing a literacy requirement for voting. The Court's deference was grounded in the ability of states to set voter qualifications. The United States Constitution makes that explicit, providing that "the Electors in each State shall have the Qualifications requisite for Electors of

---

24 William R. Keech and Michael P. Sistrom, *North Carolina*, *in* Quiet Revolution in the South 155, 158 (Chandler Davidson & Bernard Grofman eds. 1994).

25 *See Allison v. Sharp*, 184 S.E. 27 (N.C. 1936).

26 U.S. Comm'n on Civil Rts., Book 1: Voting 32 (1961).

27 *See Bazemore v. Bertie County Bd. of Elections*, 119 S.E.2d 637, 644 (N.C. 1961).

28 Rob Christensen, The Paradox of Tar Heel Politics 263 (2008); N.C Museum of Hist., *Henry Frye, Chief Justice: An Interview*, 39 Tar Heel Junior Historian 1–3 (Spring 2000).

29 238 U.S. 347 (1915).

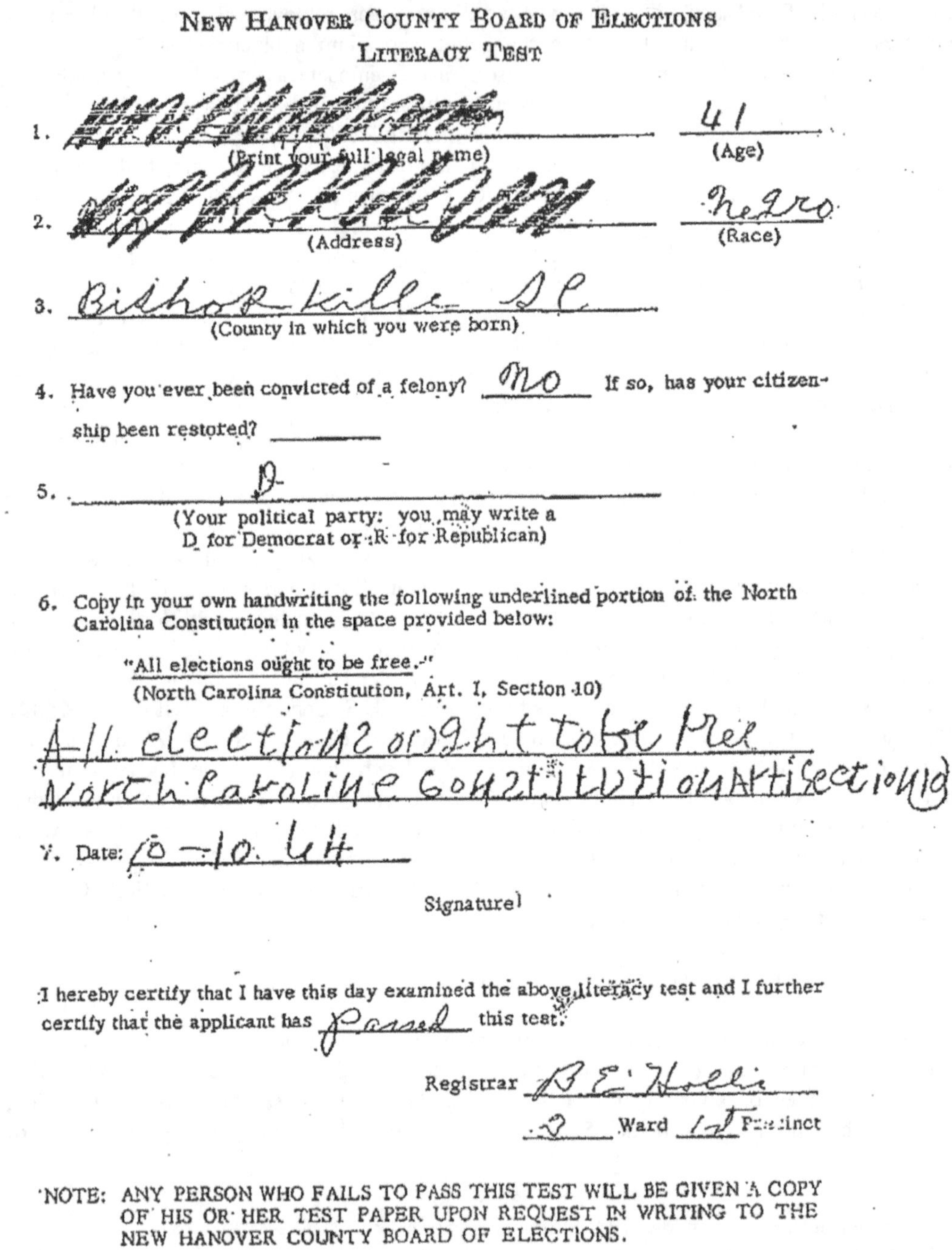

NEW HANOVER COUNTY BOARD OF ELECTIONS
LITERACY TEST

1. ______________________________ (Print your full legal name) 41 (Age)

2. ______________________________ (Address) Negro (Race)

3. Bishopville SC (County in which you were born)

4. Have you ever been convicted of a felony? no If so, has your citizenship been restored? ________

5. D (Your political party: you may write a D for Democrat or R for Republican)

6. Copy in your own handwriting the following underlined portion of the North Carolina Constitution in the space provided below:

"All elections ought to be free."
(North Carolina Constitution, Art. I, Section 10)

7. Date: 10-10-64

Signature

I hereby certify that I have this day examined the above literacy test and I further certify that the applicant has passed this test.

Registrar B. E. Hollis
2 Ward 1st Precinct

NOTE: ANY PERSON WHO FAILS TO PASS THIS TEST WILL BE GIVEN A COPY OF HIS OR HER TEST PAPER UPON REQUEST IN WRITING TO THE NEW HANOVER COUNTY BOARD OF ELECTIONS.

Figure 1.2 Example of a literacy test administered in North Carolina
Senator Ervin submitted this example to support his contention that the literacy test was not difficult to pass, notwithstanding evidence that it was arbitrarily applied to disenfranchise black voters.
Source: Reprinted from *Hearings on S.1564 to Enforce the Fifteenth Amendment to the Constitution of the United States Before the Senate Comm. on the Judiciary, Part 1*, 89th Cong., 1st Sess., at 795 (1975).

the most numerous branch of the State Legislature."[30] The Court interpreted the Constitution as permitting states to set voter qualifications as long as those requirements "are not discriminatory" and do not violate "any restriction that Congress, acting pursuant to its constitutional powers, has imposed" (*Lassiter* 1959: 51). Any voting requirements, including literacy tests, therefore had to be consistent with the Fourteenth and Fifteenth Amendments, as well as enforcement legislation passed by Congress.

The *Lassiter* decision recognized that many restrictions on the right to vote, including residency, age, and a criminal record, could provide a legitimate basis for voter qualifications (*Lassiter* 1959: 51). The Court reasoned that literacy also could be a prerequisite to voting:

> The ability to read and write likewise has some relation to standards designed to promote the intelligent use of the ballot. Literacy and illiteracy are neutral on race, creed, color, and sex. [I]n our society where newspapers, periodicals, books, and other printed matter canvass and debate campaign issues, a State might conclude that only those who are literate should exercise the franchise … [t]o insure an "independent and intelligent" exercise of the right of suffrage (*Lassiter* 1959: 52).

Therefore, the Court found that literacy tests such as North Carolina's were not automatically invalid because there were at least some legitimate reasons why they might be used. At the same time, the *Lassiter* Court sounded a cautionary note that literacy tests could be unconstitutional where they were used as racially discriminatory devices (*Lassiter* 1959: 52–54). Louise Lassiter had not presented evidence of "discrimination in the actual operation of the ballot laws in North Carolina," preventing the Court from addressing it for the first time on appeal (*Lassiter* 1959: 50, 53).

Successful Constitutional Challenges to Literacy Tests

Despite *Lassiter*, successful challenges to literacy tests in other states followed. On March 8, 1965, the day after Bloody Sunday, the Supreme Court issued rulings in cases challenging two state literacy tests that had been used to disenfranchise Black voters.

In *Louisiana v. United States*, the Court considered the constitutionality of Louisiana's test.[31] During Louisiana's constitutional convention in 1898, legislators intended to adopt a literacy requirement specifically to disenfranchise African-Americans. A commentator from the period observed that the legislature's "main cause" was to make "negro domination impossible by disenfranchising the blacks so far as this could be done without running foul of constitutional snags" (Haynes 1898: 503). Louisiana later adopted a statutory literacy test to stem the growing tide of Black voter registration in the aftermath of *Smith v. Allwright*, in which the Texas all-white primary system was found unconstitutional.[32] Louisiana had an all-white primary system that was nearly identical. The state responded with a series of new discriminatory measures. By the early 1950s, Louisiana had purged thousands of Black voters from the polls. It then adopted an interpretation test that "vested in the voting registrars a virtually uncontrolled discretion as to who should vote and who should not," allowing registrars in 21 predominately Black parishes to "deprive otherwise qualified Negro citizens of their right to vote" (*Louisiana v. U.S.* 1965: 150). The Court found that Louisiana's test violated the Fifteenth Amendment, describing it as "not a

30 *See* U.S. Const. art. I, § 2; U.S. Const. amend. XVII.

31 380 U.S. 145 (1965).

32 321 U.S. 649 (1944).

test but a trap, sufficient to stop even the most brilliant man on his way to the voting booth" (*Louisiana v. U.S.* 1965: 153).

Similarly, in *United States v. Mississippi*, the state used several discriminatory devices, including a literacy test, requirements to interpret the state constitution and the duties of citizenship, and a "good moral character" qualification.[33] Many of those restrictions came under the state's 1890 constitution, where the goal was clear. "Within the field of permissible action under the limitations imposed by the federal constitution, the convention swept the circle of expedients to obstruct the exercise of the franchise by the negro race."[34] In 1962, the state legislature adopted several new registration laws to facilitate the disenfranchisement of Black voters:

> [In the] package of legislation affecting registration, the purpose and effect … was to 'deter, hinder, prevent, delay and harass Negroes and to make it more difficult for Negroes in their efforts to become registered voters, to facilitate discrimination against Negroes, and to make it more difficult for the United States to protect the right of all its citizens to vote without distinction of race or color … [The laws gave] registrars even greater discretion to deny Negroes the right to register on formal, technical, inconsequential errors (Mississippi 1965: 134–35).

Mississippi's discrimination was very successful. Voter registration among African-Americans dropped from over 50 percent in 1899 to just 5 percent by 1954 (*U.S. v. Mississippi* 1965: 132). The Supreme Court did not reach the question of whether the laws were unconstitutional, limiting its opinion to the question of whether the federal government had stated a claim (*U.S. v. Mississippi* 1965: 143–44). The Court found that the government did, observing that the complaint "charged a long-standing, carefully prepared, and faithfully observed plan to bar Negroes from voting in the State of Mississippi, a plan which the registration statistics … would seem to show had been remarkably successful" (*U.S. v. Mississippi* 1965: 135–36). The case was remanded to the three-judge district court, which struck down the state's restrictions as violating the recently enacted Voting Rights Act.[35]

The *Louisiana* and *Mississippi* decisions highlighted that where there was evidence of actual discrimination, federal courts would overturn literacy tests or other state prerequisites to voting, notwithstanding *Lassiter*.

The VRA's Temporary Ban on Some Literacy Tests

In the 1965 Act, Congress focused on evidence of the discriminatory purpose and effect of literacy tests in its temporary suspension of some of those tests. Later, when that ban proved insufficient to remedy disenfranchisement for voters living in non-covered jurisdictions, Congress extended it nationwide in 1970 and made it permanent in 1975. The Supreme Court subsequently upheld the ban, even though it had found that literacy tests could be constitutional just a few years earlier.

Congressional Findings of Discriminatory Literacy Tests

When Congress enacted the VRA in 1965, it took *Lassiter* to heart by developing an extensive record of the discriminatory application of literacy tests. The primary focus of the Act was to

---

33 380 U.S. 128, 131–33 (1965).

34 *Ratliffe v. Beale*, 20 So. 865, 868 (Miss. 1896).

35 *See* 256 F. Supp. 344 (S.D. Miss. 1966) (three-judge court).

cure deficiencies of earlier civil rights legislation passed in 1957, 1960, and 1964 that had proven inadequate to prevent the discriminatory use of barriers to political participation by southern Blacks, including poll taxes, voter registration procedures, and literacy tests.[36] Of the nine states with voter turnout below 50 percent in the 1964 presidential election, seven had literacy tests that impacted the political participation of African-American and Alaska Native voters: Alabama, Alaska, Georgia, Louisiana, Mississippi, South Carolina, and Virginia. Forty predominately African-American counties in North Carolina also had turnout below 50 percent (U.S. Comm'n on Civil Rts. 1975: 13). The southern states had "a general public policy of racial segregation evidenced by statutes in force and effect in the areas of travel, recreation, education, and hospital facilities."[37] In addition, in Apache County, Arizona, a covered majority-American Indian county that included a large part of the Navajo Nation, fewer than 50 percent of eligible citizens voted because of the barriers posed by the state's English literacy test (H.R. Rep. No. 89–439, 1965: 2445).

Congress found that in each of those places, there was "overwhelming evidence that, where discrimination in voting has occurred, literacy tests have been an effective instrument of such discrimination" (H.R. Rep. No. 89–439, 1965: 2446). Prior to 1890, no southern state used a literacy test or similar device as a prerequisite to voting. However, southern states began using the tests to prevent African-American citizens from voting:

> It is significant that in 1890, 69 percent or more of the adult Negroes in seven southern states which adopted these tests were illiterate (Alabama, 78 percent; Louisiana, 77 percent; Georgia, 75 percent; Mississippi, 74 percent; South Carolina, 73 percent; North Carolina, 70 percent, Virginia, 69 percent). These percentages were much higher than comparable figures for white illiteracy (Alabama, 19 percent; Louisiana, 19 percent; Georgia, 17 percent; Mississippi, 13 percent; South Carolina, 18 percent; North Carolina, 25 percent; Virginia, 15 percent).[38]

The tests were especially pernicious for two reasons. First, before the Civil War, most of the slave states made it a crime to teach African-Americans how to read or write (*South Carolina v. Katzenbach* 1966: 310 n.9). Second, after emancipation, African-American voters bore the effects of the separate and unequal schooling they received following *Plessy v. Ferguson*,[39] which upheld the practice in 1896. *Plessy* remained the law of the land until it was abrogated by *Brown v. Board of Education*,[40] just 11 years before the VRA was enacted. To minimize the possible disenfranchisement of white citizens who were unable to pass a fairly administered literacy test, southern states combined those tests with grandfather clauses that would ensure illiterate whites could continue to vote.[41]

---

36 *See* H.R. Rep. No. 89–493 (1965), *reprinted in* 1965 U.S.C.C.A.N. 2437; S. Rep. No. 89–162 (1965), *reprinted in* 1965 U.S.C.C.A.N. 2508. For a summary of the social, economic, and physical pressures directed at suppressing the Black vote in the South, see James Thomas Tucker, *Affirmative Action and [Mis]representation: Part I – Reclaiming the Civil Rights Vision of the Right to Vote*, 43 How. L.J. 343, 343–48 (2000).

37 H.R. Rep. No. 89–439, 1965: 2445.

38 H.R. Rep. No. 89–439, 1965: 2540, 2542 (Joint views of 12 members of the Judiciary Committee relating to the Voting Rights Act).

39 163 U.S. 537 (1896).

40 347 U.S. 483 (1954).

41 H.R. Rep. No. 89–439, 1965: 2540, 2542 (Joint views of 12 members of the Judiciary Committee relating to the Voting Rights Act). For further discussion of such measures, *see* Armand Derfner, *Racial Discrimination and the Right to Vote*, 26 Vand. L. Rev. 523, 537–38 (1973).

Congress found that of all the lawsuits brought by the United States Department of Justice in Alabama, Louisiana, and Mississippi, it was "striking that no voting discrimination suit has ever been concluded without a judicial finding of racial discrimination by either the district court or the court of appeals." Evidence from those cases showed that in many places the tests were only applied to African-American voters, allowing illiterate whites to vote without taking the tests (H.R. Rep. No. 89–439, 1965: 2443–44). Even when white applicants took the tests, they were given easier versions, "received extensive help from voting officials," and were "registered despite serious errors in their answers." For example, one white applicant in Louisiana was found to satisfactorily demonstrate his interpretation of the state constitution by writing, "FRDUM FOOF SPETGH" (*South Carolina v. Katzenbach* 1966: 312).

Moreover, the tests were "vague, arbitrary, hypertechnical or unnecessarily difficult, and [had] little (if any) bearing upon the capacity to cast an intelligent ballot" (H.R. Rep. No. 89–439, 1965: 2444). In Panola County, Mississippi, African-American applicants were required to interpret the provision of the state constitution concerning "the rate of interest on the fund known as the 'Chickasaw School Fund.'"[42] Six African-American applicants were rejected in Forrest County, Mississippi, even though they each had a four-year college degree, including three who had Master's Degrees.[43] Consequently, Congress concluded "that these tests were not conceived as and are not designed to be bona fide qualifications in any sense, but are intended to deprive Negroes the right to register to vote. The only real function they serve is to foster racial discrimination" (H.R. Rep. No. 89–439, 1965: 2444).

The Temporary Suspension of Some Literacy Tests in 1965

Congress considered other options that would keep the literacy tests in place, but determined that they were not feasible for several reasons. First, the origins of the tests showed they were not legitimate, non-discriminatory voting qualifications. Second, the states had proven that the tests could not be fairly administered because they were arbitrary and subject to abuse of discretion by voting registrars. Third, even if the tests could be fairly administered, "following decades of discrimination when most whites were permanently registered without having to pass such tests, would simply freeze the present registration disparity created by past violations of the 15th amendment." Fourth, the continued use of literacy tests would undermine efforts to remedy voting discrimination in the VRA. The strong nexus between educational and voting discrimination, and the absence of a viable alternative, forced Congress to take decisive action by suspending the literacy tests (H.R. Rep. No. 89–439, 1965: 2446–47).

Sections 4(a) and (b) of the 1965 Act automatically suspended all literacy tests or other similar measures in jurisdictions meeting a coverage formula, or "trigger," tied to "tests or devices" and voter registration or turnout. The Act defined "test or device" to include any prerequisites to registering or voting that required demonstration of "the ability to read, write, understand, or interpret any matter," to prove education achievement or knowledge of any subject, possession of "good moral character," or to prove qualifications "by the voucher of registered voters, or members of any other class."[44] Jurisdictions were covered if they (1) maintained a test or device on November

42 *United States v. Duke*, 332 F.2d 759, 764 (5th Cir. 1964).

43 *United States v. Logue*, 344 F.2d 290, 292 (5th Cir. 1965).

44 42 U.S.C. § 1973b(c).

1, 1964, and (2) less than 50 percent of the voting age population was registered or voted in the presidential election of 1964.[45]

Congress adopted the formula because it found that "where these two factors are present there is a strong probability that low registration and voting are a result of racial discrimination in the use of such tests" (H.R. Rep. No. 89–439, 1965: 2444). Twenty-one states had used some form of test or device, including many outside the South. However, aside from the six southern states covered statewide by the formula, there were only two other states "which have had a similar policy of racial discrimination reflected by their laws." One of those, North Carolina, had several dozen counties with large African-American populations that were covered under the trigger. In the other, Delaware, Congress found that "recent enactments reflect an abandonment of that policy." Unlike the jurisdictions covered under the formula, Congress found that non-covered states "express, in so many areas, a public policy against racial discrimination," making it "reasonable to assume that voting discrimination on account of race does not exist" (H.R. Rep. No. 89–439, 1965: 2445). Congress left the question of how language minorities had been disenfranchised by literacy tests for another day.

Covered jurisdictions in which there had been no racial discrimination in violation of the Fifteenth Amendment could be exempted from coverage "by obtaining an adjudication that such tests or devices have not been used by it to accomplish substantial discrimination in the preceding 5 years." This five year "cooling-off" period was included "to permit dissipation of the long-established political atmosphere and tradition of discrimination in voting because of color" in those places where "literacy tests and low registration and voting have gone hand in hand" (H.R. Rep. No. 89–39, 1965: 2445–46). When a jurisdiction that had used literacy tests was able to demonstrate the absence of discrimination for the statutory period, it could file a request for exemption from the literacy test ban with the federal district court in the District of Columbia.[46]

The 1965 Act ensured that most jurisdictions with African-Americans who had suffered from racial discrimination in voting and education would be covered by the temporary suspension of literacy tests. On the other hand, few jurisdictions with language minorities were covered in 1965, notwithstanding congressional findings that literacy tests were subject to abuse in their administration and had a discriminatory impact on other minority groups who had suffered from disparate educational opportunities (H.R. Rep. No. 89–439, 1965: 2444–47). It would take later amendments to the VRA to remove the significant barriers that English literacy tests posed to millions of language minority citizens.

Constitutionality of the 1965 Act's Ban on Some Literacy Tests

The United States Supreme Court examined the constitutionality of the VRA's original ban on literacy tests in two cases decided between 1966 and 1970. A third case addressed a challenge to the VRA's suspension of literacy tests for Puerto Rican voters (Chapter 2). Each of those decisions focused on the power to pass legislation under the Reconstruction Amendments. Nearly 100 years earlier, in *Ex Parte Virginia*, the Court described broad congressional powers to enforce the guarantees in the Amendments:

45 *See* Pub. L. No. 89–110, § 4(a)-(b), 79 Stat. 437, 438 (1965).

46 *See* 42 U.S.C. § 1973b.

> [The Reconstruction Amendments were] intended to be ... limitations of the power of the States and enlargements of the power of Congress … Congress is authorized to enforce the prohibitions by appropriate legislation. Some legislation is contemplated to make the amendments fully effective. Whatever legislation is appropriate, that is, adapted to carry out the objects the amendments have in view, whatever tends to enforce submission to the prohibitions they contain, and to secure to all persons the enjoyment of perfect equality of civil rights …. if not prohibited, is brought within the domain of congressional power.[47]

That standard provided a strong basis for enacting the VRA to remedy voting discrimination. The Court's rulings in challenges to the Act's suspension of literacy tests, such as New York's English literacy test, confirmed Congress's power to later expand protections for language minorities in 1975.

South Carolina v. Katzenbach

Shortly after the VRA became law, the Supreme Court considered the constitutionality of the Act's protections, including the temporary suspension of literacy tests.[48] The challenge was brought by South Carolina, which had made the intent of its own literacy test clear during its state constitutional convention in 1895. Senator Ben Tillman, "the dominant political figure" in that convention, explained the relationship and effect of the test and its grandfather clause on African-American and white voters:

> The only thing we can do as patriots and as statesmen is to take from [the "ignorant blacks"] every ballot that we can under the laws of our national government … There is no particle of fraud or illegality in [an exemption for those who could understand and explain a section of the state constitution]. It is just simply showing partiality, perhaps [laughter], or discriminating … By means of the $300 clause [which exempted those who paid state property taxes] you simply reach out and take in some more white men and a few more colored men (*South Carolina v. Katzenbach* 1966: 310 n.9).

Five other southern states that had adopted their own literacy tests for similar reasons joined South Carolina in its opposition to the VRA.[49]

In *South Carolina v. Katzenbach*, the Court found that Section 2 of the Fifteenth Amendment, the Enforcement Section,[50] allowed Congress to "use any rational means to effectuate the constitutional prohibition of racial discrimination in voting" (*South Carolina v. Katzenbach* 1966: 324). According to the Court, the Enforcement Section provided Congress with "full remedial powers to effectuate the constitutional prohibition against racial discrimination in voting," similar

47 100 U.S. 339, 345–46 (1879).

48 I have explored the constitutionality of the language assistance provisions and the suspension of literacy tests in more detail elsewhere. *See generally* James Thomas Tucker, *The Battle Over "Bilingual Ballots" Shifts to the Courts*, 45 Harv. J. on Legis. 507 (2008).

49 The states included Alabama, Georgia, Louisiana, Mississippi, and Virginia. In contrast, 21 states supported the efforts of the Attorney General of the United States to uphold the VRA. *See South Carolina v. Katzenbach* 1966: 308 n.2.

50 *See generally* U.S. Const. amend. XV, § 2 ("The Congress shall have power to enforce this article by appropriate legislation").

to its powers under the Necessary and Proper Clause of the Constitution.[51] In other words, the power to legislate under Section 2, "like all others vested in Congress, is complete in itself, may be exercised to its utmost extent, and acknowledges no limitations, other than are prescribed in the Constitution."[52]

Turning to the constitutionality of the VRA, the Court reasoned that Congress could exercise its powers in an "inventive manner," as it did in suspending literacy tests. Congress properly implemented the remedies "without any need for prior adjudication" because a case-by-case approach in challenging discriminatory tests and devices had proven unworkable (*South Carolina v. Katzenbach* 1966: 327–28). Voting suits were "unusually onerous to prepare" and litigation of individual cases was "exceedingly slow." When the cases were successful, states would simply switch to a new discriminatory test, device, or procedure. Alternatively, local registrars would respond by defying court orders or close their registration offices to freeze the voting rolls and prevent new registrations by disenfranchised African-Americans (*South Carolina v. Katzenbach* 1966: 314). Therefore, the Court concluded that "Congress might well decide to shift the advantage of time and inertia from the perpetrators of the evil to its victims" (*South Carolina v. Katzenbach* 1966: 328).

Moreover, the remedies were limited to only those particular areas of the country "where immediate action seemed necessary." Use of a triggering formula was permissible because it identified jurisdictions where there was a "significant danger" of voting discrimination, as documented by "a low voting rate" caused by the application of literacy tests and other devices. The coverage formula therefore was "rational in both practice and theory" (*South Carolina v. Katzenbach* 1966: 328–30). It did not matter that the formula excluded localities that engaged in voting discrimination but did not use literacy tests or other devices. "Congress had learned that widespread and persistent discrimination in voting during recent years [had] typically entailed the misuse of tests and devices, and this was the evil for which the new remedies were specifically designed" (*South Carolina v. Katzenbach* 1966: 331). As Debo Adegbile explained during the 2006 reauthorization of the VRA, depressed voter registration and turnout were "a legislative proxy" for identifying "jurisdictions that had entrenched histories of discrimination" through the use of discriminatory devices such as literacy tests and were not "the evil that Congress sought to remediate."[53]

The Supreme Court likewise rejected South Carolina's argument that the literacy tests were constitutional under *Lassiter*. Congress had shown that the tests could be banned because the evidence showed their discriminatory purpose and effect. The Court reasoned, "[I]n most of the States covered by the Act, including South Carolina, various tests and devices have been instituted with the purpose of disenfranchising" African-Americans, they were drafted to facilitate that aim, and they had been discriminatorily administered (*South Carolina v. Katzenbach* 1966: 333–34). Consequently, the Court found that "the Fifteenth Amendment has clearly been violated" and unanimously found that the VRA's ban on literacy tests was constitutional (*South Carolina v. Katzenbach* 1966: 329–37).[54]

---

51 *South Carolina v. Katzenbach* 1966: 325–26 (citing *Ex Parte Virginia* 1879: 345–46).

52 *South Carolina v. Katzenbach* 1966: 325–26 (quoting *Gibbons v. Ogden*, 22 U.S. (9 Wheat.) 1, 196 (1824)).

53 *Reauthorizing the Voting Rights Act's Temporary Provisions: Policy Perspectives and Views from the Field: Hearing Before the S. Comm. on the Judiciary*, 109th Cong. 26 (2006).

54 Even Justice Black, who dissented with the Court's holding that the administrative preclearance requirements of Section 5 were constitutional, agreed that Congress had the authority to impose the ban on literacy tests. *South Carolina v. Katzenbach* 1966: 355–56 (Black, J., concurring and dissenting in part).

Gaston County v. United States

The North Carolina statutory literacy test that was upheld by the Supreme Court in 1959 in *Lassiter* was the subject of a second Supreme Court decision a decade later. Gaston County was one of 40 counties in North Carolina for which the state's literacy test was suspended in March 1966 as a result of coverage under Section 4 of the VRA.[55] In August 1966, the county filed a case in the federal district court in the District of Columbia seeking to be exempt from coverage so it could reinstate the literacy test in its voter registration process (*Gaston County v. U.S.* 1968: 681–82).

Even fairly administered, North Carolina's literacy test was difficult to pass. The Supreme Court of North Carolina explained, "It demands more than the mere ability to write one's own name and to recognize and read a few simple words." Instead, an applicant was required "to read and write any section" of the state constitution. The state's highest court concluded, "Admittedly, the standard is relatively high, even after more than a half-century of free public schools and universal education."[56]

Nevertheless, buoyed by evidence of how the county had impartially enforced the literacy test, Gaston County sought reinstatement of the test for its elections. The county pointed to its "considerable publicity" regarding its voter registration process that was "fairly directed to all persons residing in the county, regardless of race or color," which included meetings with local African-American leaders. Three of the county's five appointed deputy voting registrars were African-American. According to the county, no African-Americans had complained to the Board of Elections about the use of the literacy test. In addition, the county highlighted that it had allowed at least ten "illiterate or nearly illiterate" African-Americans to register to vote despite their inability to pass the test (*Gaston County v. U.S.* 1968: 682–84).

The United States opposed Gaston County's request for exemption. It introduced evidence that 29 "illiterate or nearly illiterate whites" were allowed to register without demonstrating their literacy, including 15 who told the registrar that they were illiterate. There was evidence that although the county might grant a waiver to any applicant, that policy was not publicized, causing African-Americans to justifiably believe that they would have to prove their literacy "or be embarrassed by being turned away." There was evidence that African-American leaders did not encourage illiterate African-Americans to try to register, and that several who had attempted were rejected when they failed the literacy test (*Gaston County v. U.S.* 1968: 683–84).

The trial court found it unnecessary to resolve the conflicting evidence of whether Gaston County had intentionally discriminated against African-American applicants in its administration of the literacy test. Instead, the court focused on evidence of the discriminatory effects of the test. African-American applicants had been subjected to segregated schooling until 1965. At that time, after "token integration was begun," 297 out of 300 white students zoned into a school with African-American students transferred out immediately. The schooling was of "appreciably inferior quality," with expenditures on white facilities and learning resources three times higher than for African-American students (*Gaston County v. U.S.* 1968: 685–86). The education provided "hardly reached the literacy level," causing African-Americans to have twice the rate as whites among those with no education or those with four years or less schooling (*Gaston County v. U.S.* 1968: 687–88). It was not surprising, then, that many illiterate African-Americans never tried to register to vote after they were told they had to be educated. The trial court reasoned, "It would be incongruous to allow a state or county to disenfranchise people for an inability to pass a literacy

55 *See* 31 Fed. Reg. 5080–5081 (Mar. 29, 1966).

56 *Bazemore v. Bertie County Bd. of Elections*, 119 S.E.2d 637, 641 (N.C. 1961).

test, when that ability was denied them as a result of discriminatory state action" (*Gaston County v. U.S.* 1968: 689–90). Therefore, the court denied Gaston County's petition to reinstate its literacy test and be removed from coverage under the special provisions of the VRA.

On appeal, the United States Supreme Court agreed, with only Justice Black dissenting.[57] Documented educational discrimination also allowed Congress to ban literacy tests that would disenfranchise the illiterate victims of unequal and segregated schooling. The Court found that even though educational discrimination itself could not be remedied under the Fifteenth Amendment, its effects on voters could be. Congress was "fully cognizant of the potential effect of unequal educational opportunities upon exercise of the franchise" when it temporarily suspended literacy tests in covered jurisdictions (*Gaston County v. U.S.* 1969: 289). There was "substantial evidence" that Gaston County "deprived its black residents of equal educational opportunities, which in turn deprived them of an equal chance to pass a literacy test" (*Gaston County v. U.S.* 1969: 291). Consequently, the continued suspension of the county's use of North Carolina's literacy test was constitutional.

The Court further determined that Congress could use a coverage formula derived from voting or registration data because a formula "based on educational disparities, or one based on literacy rates, would be administratively cumbersome: the designation of racially disparate school systems is not susceptible of speedy, objective, and incontrovertible determination," and the Census Bureau did not have the literacy data available (*Gaston County v. U.S.* 1969: 291–92). According to the Court, even if covered jurisdictions eliminated educational discrimination against current students, it did "nothing for their parents" who were voters and who continued to suffer from the effects of past discrimination. As a result, the *Gaston County* decision recognized congressional authority to impose a localized and temporary ban on literacy tests (*Gaston County v. U.S.* 1969: 293, 296–97).

The 1970 Nationwide Ban on Literacy Tests

In 1970, Congress enacted Section 201 of the VRA, which extended the suspension of literacy tests or other similar measures nationwide for five years.[58] Section 201 provides that "No citizen shall be denied, because of his failure to comply with any test or device, the right to vote in any Federal, State, or local election conducted in any State or political subdivision of a State."[59] It adopted the same definition of "test or device" used in the suspension of literacy tests included in Section 4 of the VRA in 1965.[60] According to Congress, the nationwide ban was justified because "there is insufficient relationship between literacy and responsible interested voting to justify such a broad restriction of the franchise."[61]

The 1970 amendments to the VRA provided other relief to language minorities.[62] Congress expanded the triggering formula under Section 4 to also include voter turnout in the 1968 Presidential election,[63] requiring many jurisdictions with large numbers of language minorities

57 *See Gaston County v. United States*, 395 U.S. 285, 297 (1969).

58 *See* Voting Rights Act Amendments of 1970, Pub. L. No. 91–285, § 6, 84 Stat. 314, 315 (1970).

59 42 U.S.C. § 1973aa(a).

60 *Compare* Pub. L. No. 91–285, § 6, 84 Stat. 314, 315, *with* Pub. L. No. 89–110, § 4(c), 79 Stat. 437, 438–39.

61 S. Rep. No. 94–295 at 23 (1975), *reprinted in* 1975 U.S.C.C.A.N. 774, 789 (citing 116 Cong. Rec. 5221 (1970)).

62 *See* Pub. L. No. 91–285, 84 Stat. 314 (1970), *reprinted in* 1970 U.S.C.C.A.N. 373.

63 *See* Pub. L. No. 91–285, § 64, 84 Stat. 314, 315, *reprinted in* 1970 U.S.C.C.A.N. 373.

to comply with the Act's special coverage provisions. Three counties in New York City, five counties in Arizona, two counties in California, one county in Wyoming, and several towns in New Hampshire were covered under the new triggering formula. In addition, some jurisdictions that had successfully sought exemption from the special provisions after initially being covered under the 1965 Act were covered again under the 1970 amendments, including four election districts in Alaska, three counties in Arizona, and the one county in Idaho (U.S. Comm'n on Civil Rts. 1975: 14–15). Furthermore, Section 4(a) was amended to provide that covered jurisdictions had to be free from discriminatory tests or devices for at least ten years before being eligible for exemption from coverage.[64]

Impact on States with Large Language Minority Populations

Unlike the original 1965 ban, which primarily focused on prohibiting literacy tests that disenfranchised African-Americans in the South, the 1970 nationwide ban also applied to states with large numbers of language minorities. As the Civil Rights Commission observed, the "requirement of English-language literacy disenfranchised many otherwise qualified voters in jurisdictions such as New York, California, and Arizona" (U.S. Comm'n on Civil Rts. 1975: 16–17). The impact of the ban in literacy tests on language minorities in New York is discussed in Chapter 2. Three other states with English literacy tests, Arizona, California, and Washington, also illustrate that impact.

Arizona's literacy test Arizona enacted its first English literacy test when it became a state in 1912. The statute only permitted an eligible resident to register to vote "if he … [i]s able to read the Constitution of the United States in the English language in such manner as to show he is neither prompted nor reciting from memory, unless prevented from doing so by physical disability" and is "able to write his name, unless prevented from doing so by physical disability."[65] According to historian David Berman, the literacy test was enacted "to limit 'the ignorant Mexican vote.' As recently as the 1960s, registrars applied the test to reduce the ability of blacks, Indians and Hispanics to register to vote."[66] Berman explained, "Anglos sometimes challenged minorities at the polls and asked them to read and explain 'literacy' cards. Intimidators hoped to discourage minorities from standing in line to vote" (Berman 1998: 76). Justice Rehnquist was said to have used the literacy test to challenge African-American and Latino voters during his participation in the Republican Party's ballot security program from 1958 to 1968.[67]

On August 7, 1965, Apache County, Arizona was included in the original list of jurisdictions covered by Section 5 of the Voting Rights Act.[68] On November 19, 1965, Navajo and Coconino Counties also became covered by Section 5.[69] As a result of these amendments, application of the literacy test was suspended in each of the three counties, where a majority of the voters were

64 *See* Pub. L. No. 91–285, § 3, 84 Stat. 314, 315 (1970).

65 Ariz. Rev. Stat. Ann. § 16–101(A)(4)-(5) (1956).

66 David R. Berman, Arizona Politics and Government: The Quest for Autonomy, Democracy, and Development 75 (Univ. of Neb. Press 1998).

67 *See* Chandler Davidson et al., *Vote Caging as a Republican Ballot Security Technique*, 34 Wm. Mitchell L. Rev. 533, 543–59 (2008); Paul Butler, *Rehnquist, Racism, and Race Jurisprudence*, 74 Geo. Wash. L. Rev. 1019, 1021–22 (2006).

68 *See* Determination of the Director of the Census Pursuant to Section 4(b)(2) of the Voting Rights Act of 1965, 30 Fed. Reg. 9897 (Aug. 7, 1965).

69 Determination of the Director of the Census Pursuant to Section 4(b)(2) of the Voting Rights Act of 1965, 30 Fed. Reg. 14,505 (Nov. 19, 1965).

American Indian. In 1966, the U.S. District Court for the District of Columbia held that Arizona's literacy test had not been discriminatorily applied on account of race or color in the preceding five years and, as a result, these three counties became the first jurisdictions to successfully bail out from coverage under Section 5.[70] As a result of the 1970 amendments to the VRA, Apache, Coconino and Navajo Counties were again covered by Section 5, along with five additional Arizona counties. Furthermore, the nationwide ban on literacy tests again preempted Arizona's literacy test.[71] Arizona did not repeal its English literacy test until two years later, in 1972.

California's literacy test California adopted an English literacy requirement as part of its state constitution. It provided that "no person who shall not be able to read the Constitution in the English language and write his or her name, shall ever exercise the privileges of an elector in this State."[72] The legislative history of the literacy test closely parallels the discriminatory purposes behind similar restrictions in the southern states.

California was a hotbed for Nativism in the late nineteenth century. It was home to several prominent members of the American Protective Association, "a powerful anti-immigrant political party which advocated an English literacy requirement as a method of disenfranchising voters of foreign ancestry."[73] In 1891, the English literacy requirement was introduced before the State Assembly. Its lead sponsor was Assemblyman A.J. Bledsoe, a past member of the "vigilante Committee of Fifteen which expelled every person of Chinese ancestry from Humboldt County." When Bledsoe introduced the provision, he stated:

> We look with alarm upon the increased immigration of the illiterate and unassimilated elements of Europe, and believe that every agency should be invoked to preserve our public lands from alien grasp, to shield American labor from this destructive competition, and to protect the purity of the ballot-box from the corrupting influences of the disturbing elements … from abroad (*Castro v. State* 1970: 248).

A separate provision of the state constitution adopted in 1879 excluded "natives of China" from voting. However, Bledsoe and other Nativists also wanted to ensure that the children of Chinese immigrants were excluded. A literacy test would have that effect because most Chinese-Americans retained their Chinese language and customs (*Castro v. State* 1970: 248 n.11).

Newspaper accounts from 1892 confirmed the discriminatory purpose of the literacy test. A Redlands paper urged adoption to "Wipe out the ignorant foreign vote." The *Anaheim Gazette* stated that the provision would prevent voting by "the increasing flood of debased and ignorant Europeans." The *San Bernardino Weekly Courier* was equally blunt, citing the "ignorant and vicious foreigners who are a constant menace to our free institutions" (*Castro v. State* 1970: 249 n.14). Chinese and Mexican-Americans remained the primary targets of the literacy test (Keyssar 2000: 145). The public hysteria against immigrants and non-English-speaking citizens led the California Assembly to adopt the constitutional English literacy test in 1893, which voters approved in a statewide vote in 1894 (*Castro v. State* 1970: 245–46). As Figure 1.3 shows, the press continued to play on racist fears of Chinese voters even after passage of the literacy test.

---

70 *See Apache County v. United States*, 256 F. Supp. 903 (D.D.C. 1966).

71 *See* Pub. L. No. 91–285, § 201, 84 Stat. 314, 315 (1970) (current version at 42 U.S.C. § 1973b (2000)).

72 Cal. Const. art. II, § 1 (1894).

73 *Castro v. State*, 466 P.2d 244, 247 n.8 (Cal. 1970).

The San Francisco Call.

VOLUME LXXXVII—NO. 144. SAN FRANCISCO, FRIDAY, APRIL 13, 1900. PRICE FIVE CENTS.

MAKING CHINESE CITIZENS BY WHOLESALE.

Collector Jackson Lands More Than Ten Thousand Mongols in Thirty-Four Months.

Startling Operations of a Gigantic Ring Organized in This City to Deal in the Importation of Coolies.

An Army of Native Sons and Voters Sent Into Chinatown by Fraud of the Grossest Kind.

George H. Pippy, Frank V. Bell and George A. McGowan, Aided by Powerful Friends, Cheat the Exclusion Act.

HOW THOUSANDS OF COOLIE CITIZENS ARE MADE.

CRIME IN THE NAME OF THE EXCLUSION ACT.

IMPORTERS OF

LOCAL FRIENDS

AN ARMY OF

SOME OF THEIR

CHINESE AND

Figure 1.3 Chinese voting was targeted in California even after the state adopted a literacy test

Source: *The San Francisco Call* front page, April 13, 1900, image 1. Reproduction courtesy of the Library of Congress, Prints & Photographs Division. Washington, D.C.

In 1967, U.S. citizens from Los Angeles County who were literate in Spanish but not in English sued the state to bar its use of the English literacy test. The trial court rejected their claims under *Lassiter*, concluding that English literacy was a rational state policy that served a compelling interest in an informed electorate (*Castro v. State* 1970: 245–47). In *Castro v. State*, the Supreme Court of California reached the opposite conclusion, holding that the English literacy test violated the Fourteenth Amendment (*Castro v. State* 1970: 258–59). The *Castro* Court distinguished *Lassiter* because it did not involve a claim by applicants who were literate in a language other than in English and had access to news media written in another language. It also observed that *Lassiter*'s deference to restrictions on the right to vote had been undercut by the United States Supreme Court's strict scrutiny on that right beginning with *Baker v. Carr* in 1962 (*Castro v. State* 1970: 250–51).

Castro assumed that promoting an informed electorate was a compelling state interest, but found that an English literacy test did not achieve that interest for applicants literate in other languages. The applicants showed that they had access to 17 Spanish language newspapers and 11 Spanish language magazines, which the Court determined provided ample access to information about "political candidates, events, and issues" (*Castro v. State* 1970: 253–55). The court found that exclusion of applicants literate in other languages "is hardly so compelling that it justifies denying the vote to a group of United States citizens who already face similar problems of discrimination ... and need a political voice if they are to have any realistic hope of ameliorating the conditions in which they live" (*Castro v. State* 1970: 256). *Castro* concluded that it would be "ironic" if the Spanish-speaking applicants, "who are heirs of a great and gracious culture, identified with the birth of California and contributing in no small measure to its growth, should be disenfranchised in their ancestral land, despite their capacity to cast an informed vote" (*Castro v. State* 1970: 259).

Section 201 of the VRA provided even broader protection to California's voters. *Castro* still permitted California to enforce its literacy test, but required that applicants be allowed to demonstrate their literacy in languages other than English. In contrast, Section 201 prohibited consideration of literacy in any language as a condition on voting. As a result, adult citizens were eligible to register and vote regardless of their native language or literacy.

Washington's literacy test When Congress enacted the VRA in 1965, Washington was one of just five states that explicitly required voter registration applicants to successfully demonstrate their English literacy (Lassiter 1959: 52 n.7). The state's constitution was amended in 1896 to provide that all applicants must "be able to read and speak the English language."[74] The state legislature also enacted an implementing law that required a voting registrar to "interrogate the applicant for registration, concerning his qualifications as a voter," and "requiring him to state":

> Whether the applicant ... is able to read and speak the English language so as to comprehend the meaning of ordinary English prose, and in case the registration officer is not satisfied in that regard, he may require the applicant to read aloud and explain the meaning of some ordinary English prose.[75]

The combined use of the English literacy test with an oral examination in English effectively disenfranchised thousands of language minority voters.

74 Wash. Const. art. VI, *as amended by* amend. 5, § 1 (1896).

75 Wash. Rev. Code § 29.07.070.

In 1968, four Spanish-speaking U.S. citizens, joined by a Mexican-American advocacy group, sued election officials in Yakima County for refusing to register them.[76] In each instance, the applicants were accompanied by a bilingual interpreter who informed the officials that the applicants wanted to register to vote and that he would act as an interpreter to ensure the officials obtained all of their essential information. The election officials declined to process the applications, telling the interpreter that the applicants had to present their own requests "in the English language" to comply with "the mandate of the Washington Constitution" (*Naff* 1969: 589–90).

A three-judge federal court rejected the applicants' constitutional challenge to Washington's registration requirements, citing *Lassiter*. The court observed that the state attorney general had advised all election officials not to administer the literacy test following the VRA's enactment in 1965. The court then determined that questioning the applicants' knowledge of English was not a literacy test. The court defined a test as "a series of questions or exercises or other means of measuring the schooling, knowledge, intelligence, capacities, or aptitudes of an individual." (*Naff* 1969: 590–92). According to the court, the applicants could not meet that definition, reasoning, "A simple inquiry by the registrar of the applicant … 'Can you speak and read English?' is not a test and could not conceivably result in discriminatory practices." In reaching that conclusion, the court downplayed evidence that an election official asked one of the applicants to read a list of candidates as part of the registration process, stating that it did not have any "discriminatory overtones" (*Naff* 1969: 592–3).

The *Naff* court narrowly construed literacy tests and the requirements imposed on the Spanish-speaking applicants. Asking applicants whether they speak and read English had precisely the same effect as administering a test requiring them to read an English-only ballot. Since each of the applicants admitted that they could not read English, they were not permitted to register (*Naff* 1969: 588–90). That is the very definition of a literacy test, particularly as defined by the VRA.[77] On appeal, the United States Supreme Court reversed the decision, directing the lower court to consider the effect of the VRA's nationwide ban on literacy tests on the applicants' claims.[78]

The Constitutionality of the Nationwide Ban

In *Oregon v. Mitchell*, the Court unanimously upheld Section 201's nationwide ban on literacy tests.[79] Arizona, Oregon, and Texas, argued that the ban could not be enforced to the extent that it was inconsistent with the state's registration and voting procedures. The Supreme Court rejected the states' argument and upheld the ban under the Enforcement Clause of the Fourteenth Amendment (*Oregon v. Mitchell* 1970: 132).

The Court observed that Congress enacted the ban because literacy tests were used to discriminate against voters on account of their race. Overwhelming evidence also showed that the VRA's ban on tests or devices substantially increased minority registration in the states where it had been applied (*Oregon v. Mitchell* 1970: 132–33). In contrast, other states like Arizona continued to suffer from depressed registration:

---

76 *See Mexican-Am. Fed'n-Wash. State v. Naff*, 299 F. Supp. 587 (E.D. Wash. 1969) (three-judge court), *vacated and remanded*, 400 U.S. 986 (1971).

77 *See* 42 U.S.C. § 1973b(c). For further commentary criticizing Naff's reasoning, *see* Note, *Constitutional Law – Voting Rights – State English Literacy Requirement Upheld*, 45 WASH. L. REV. 401 (1970).

78 *See Jimenez v. Naff*, 400 U.S. 986 (1971).

79 400 U.S. 112, 118 (1970).

> In Arizona, for example, only two counties out of eight with Spanish surname populations in excess of 15% showed a voter registration equal to the state-wide average. Arizona also has a serious problem of deficient voter registration among Indians. Congressional concern over the use of a literacy test to disfranchise Puerto Ricans in New York State is already a matter of record in this Court … And as to the Nation as a whole, Congress had before it statistics which demonstrate that voter registration and voter participation are consistently greater in States without literacy tests (*Oregon v. Mitchell* 1970: 132–33).

Justice Douglas similarly observed:

> [Congress] can rely on the fact that most States do not have literacy tests; that the tests have been used at times as a discriminatory weapon against some minorities, not only Negroes but Americans of Mexican ancestry, and American Indians; that radio and television have made it possible for a person to be well informed even though he may not be able to read and write. We know from the legislative history that these and other desiderata influenced Congress in the choice it made in the present legislation; and we certainly cannot say that the means used were inappropriate (*Oregon v. Mitchell* 1970: 147 (Douglas, J., dissenting)).

The Court concluded that American citizens could be informed in their own native language and responsibly and knowledgably cast a ballot.

Although the Justices disagreed on which enforcement section authorized Congress to legislate the ban,[80] they all agreed that Congress had broad discretion to impose it. Justice Black found the ban constitutional because of the discriminatory use of literacy tests, their impact on voter participation, and the "denial of equal protection [in conditioning] the political participation of children educated in a dual school system upon their educational achievement" (*Oregon v. Mitchell* 1970: 132–33). Justice Douglas reasoned that the ban was rational and did not require "findings as to the incidence of literacy" because "most [s]tates do not have literacy tests, … the tests have been used at times as a discriminatory weapon against some minorities, [and] radio and television have made it possible for a person to be well informed even though he may not be able to read and write."[81] Justice Harlan likewise deferred to Congress, concluding that "[w]hether to engage in a more particularized inquiry into the extent and effects of discrimination," either before or after suspending literacy tests, "was a choice for Congress to make."[82]

Justice Stewart explained in *Mitchell* that the justification for making the ban nationwide "need not turn on whether literacy tests unfairly discriminate against Negroes in every State," and Congress did not have to make "state-by-state findings" concerning educational equality and the impact of literacy tests on voting. Rather, Congress could choose to "paint with a much broader brush than may this Court, which must confine itself to the judicial function of deciding individual cases … upon individual

---

80 Justices Black, Marshall, and White concluded that the ban was a proper exercise under Section 5 of the Fourteenth Amendment, while the remaining justices concluded it was proper under Section 2 of the Fifteenth Amendment. *See Oregon v. Mitchell* 1970: 132 (plurality opinion of Black, J.); *Oregon v. Mitchell* 1970: 144 (Douglas, J., joined by White and Marshall, JJ., concurring in the judgment); *Oregon v. Mitchell* 1970: 216 (Harlan, J., concurring in the judgment); *Oregon v. Mitchell* 1970: 282 (Stewart, J., joined by Burger, C.J., and Blackmun, J., concurring in the judgment).

81 *Oregon v. Mitchell* 1970: 147 (Douglas, J., joined by White and Marshall, JJ., concurring in the judgment).

82 *Oregon v. Mitchell* 1970: 216 (Harlan, J., concurring in the judgment).

records." Congress therefore had great discretion in using the "[e]xperience gained under the 1965 Act" with a localized ban "to conclude it should go the whole distance."[83]

Conclusion

Literacy is one way to promote an informed electorate. Voters who are able to read can learn about candidates and issues appearing on the ballot through newspapers, campaign materials, and information pamphlets provided by local election officials. But English literacy is not the exclusive way for voters to decide how to cast their ballots, particularly with the growth of radio, television, and newspapers written in non-English languages. When racial, ethnic, and language minorities have been denied the opportunity to read English through unequal educational opportunities, the justification for using literacy as a prerequisite to voting becomes even more tenuous. As a result, although the U.S. Supreme Court initially upheld the use of literacy tests in 1959, within a few years it reversed course. The Court struck down tests in southern states that were discriminatory and upheld the ban on the tests in the Voting Rights Act of 1965.

There is a common misperception that literacy tests were only used to disenfranchise African-American voters in the South. However, the first literacy tests targeted non-English-speaking citizens in the Northeast. Later tests were adopted in the western states to bar language minorities from the polls. Congress and the courts soon found that English literacy tests had the same discriminatory purposes and effects of literacy tests that had been suspended primarily in the South. By 1970, Congress had expanded the ban on literacy tests nationwide, and the Supreme Court had upheld the ban. That marked an important first step in removing registration and voting barriers for millions of non-English-speaking U.S. citizens. More steps would follow.

83 *Oregon v. Mitchell* 1970: 284 (Stewart, J., joined by Burger, C.J., and Blackmun, J., concurring in the judgment).

Chapter 2
Language Assistance for Voters before 1975

The ban on literacy tests included in Section 4 of the VRA principally protected African-American voters in southern states, with some secondary benefits to language minorities. But southern Blacks who were disenfranchised by tests and devices were not the only focus of the original 1965 Act. Section 4(e) of the 1965 Act prohibited the use of English literacy tests as a condition for voting by Puerto Ricans. That provision was important in laying the foundation for the language assistance provisions that Congress added in 1975.

Other federal and state remedies also played a role. Section 2 of the VRA is a permanent anti-discrimination provision protecting all voters nationwide from qualifications or practices denying or limiting the right to vote. It offered some hope for language minority voters, though it initially was used sparingly. Successful challenges to state restrictions on voter assistance would inform the congressional record developed in mandating language assistance. Congress likewise considered the experience of states that provided assistance for non-English-speaking voters. This chapter discusses Section 4(e) and other pre-1975 remedies, which later shaped the contours of the VRA's broader relief from English-only elections.

Federal Barriers to Puerto Ricans' English Literacy

Most Puerto Rican adults were unable to read and write English as a result of federal educational policies. After its defeat in the Spanish-American War, Spain ceded Puerto Rico to the United States in the Treaty of Paris of 1899. Federal education commissioners tried to balance Americanization of Puerto Rican students with using the most effective language of instruction. Since nearly all students lived in a non-English environment, over time education policy evolved towards greater use of Spanish. In 1916, the Commissioner of Education, who was appointed by the President, directed that Spanish be the primary language of instruction through the fourth grade for Puerto Rican students, with English used after that. In 1930, Spanish was made the medium of instruction through the eighth grade. By 1947, it was apparent that even these steps were insufficient. A new Commissioner of Education appointed by the first popularly elected governor of Puerto Rico, implemented a policy requiring Spanish to be the medium of instruction for all grade levels. The increased use of Spanish in the schools ultimately promoted more effective learning opportunities for students.[1]

But it had an unintended consequence. American citizens from Puerto Rico who were encouraged by the government "to use Spanish as the means of communication in both public and private life" often were left unable to speak, understand, read, or write in English (*U.S. v. Monroe County* 1965: 319). The Jones Act of 1917, which conferred U.S. citizenship on Puerto Ricans, allowed anyone born

---

1 *See United States v. Bd. of Elections of Monroe County*, 248 F. Supp. 316, 318–19 (W.D.N.Y. 1965) (three-judge court), *appeal dismissed*, 383 U.S. 575 (1966).

in Puerto Rico to migrate to the Mainland.[2] Hundreds of thousands of Spanish-speaking American citizens soon moved to the States, especially during the Great Migration that followed the Second World War, peaking in 1953 with a net migration of more than 69,000 to the Mainland.[3] By 1970, about a million Puerto Ricans lived in New York City, comprising two-thirds of all Puerto Ricans residing on the Mainland; more Puerto Ricans lived in New York City than in San Juan.[4]

Disenfranchisement of Puerto Ricans in New York

Spanish-speaking Puerto Ricans educated in schools where Spanish was the predominant language faced a formidable barrier when they arrived in the United States: the literacy test. What resulted was a group of voting-age citizens "who, in an attempt to integrate their community into the mainstream of American life and to improve their economic and social position" through voting, were faced with state-imposed requirements "that one must read and write the English language in order to register to vote" (*U.S. v. Monroe County* 1965: 320). Without some relief, American citizens from Puerto Rico were effectively disenfranchised by English literacy tests. New York's onerous English literacy test would prove the biggest hurdle because the state had the largest concentration of Puerto Ricans on the Mainland.

New York's English Literacy Test

New York considered adopting a literacy test as early as the mid-nineteenth century, nearly a decade before Connecticut became the first state to do so in 1855. At New York's constitutional convention in 1846, several different limitations on voting were suggested.[5] One proposal offered by Delegate Alpheus Greene would have required electors to show they were "able to both read and write."[6] Delegate William Bouck introduced an amendment that "no person shall have the right of suffrage under this Constitution unless he can read the English language" (Bishop and Attree 1846: 309). Delegate George Simmons sponsored a similar restriction. The proposals were rejected.[7] A separate debate during the 1846 constitutional convention identifies one reason for the opposition. Several delegates decried the poor quality of education, noting "the insufficient number

2 Organic Act of Puerto Rico ("Jones-Shafroth Act" or "Jones Act"), 39 Stat. 461 (Mar. 2, 1917); *see also* 12 U.S.C. § 1402 (conferring U.S. citizenship on all persons born in Puerto Rico on or after April 11, 1899).

3 Thomas Sowell, Ethnic America: A History 231 (1981). Puerto Rican movement must be viewed in terms of net migration because of the large numbers of people moving freely between the Mainland and the island. For example, 343,720 people moved to the Mainland in 1955, compared to 297,706 who departed the Mainland, for a net migration of 45,464 people (Sowell 1981: 231).

4 Sowell 1981: 231; Clara E. Rodríguez, Puerto Ricans: Immigrants and Migrants, A Historical Perspective 9 (1990). By 2003, the number of Puerto Ricans living on the Mainland actually exceeded the number living in Puerto Rico. *See* Angelo Falcón, Atlas of stateside Puerto Ricans (2004).

5 At the same time, the convention delegates also considered lifting some restrictions, such as granting suffrage to women – some two years before the Seneca Falls Convention in July 1848. *See New York Constitutional Convention: Important Reports of Committees – Women's Rights – Convention of 1846*, N.Y. Times, June 12, 1867.

6 William G. Bishop and William H. Attree, Report of the Debates and Proceedings of the Convention for the Revision of the Constitution of the State of New York 91 (1846).

7 Arthur W. Bromage, *Literacy and the Electorate*, 24 Am. Pol. Sci. Rev. 946, 950–51 (Nov. 1930).

of qualified teachers and poor supervision of classrooms."[8] The principal cause for rejecting the proposals, however, was politics. "Though called by the Whigs, the 1846 convention was organized and dominated by the Democrats, who elected a narrow majority of the delegates."[9] Democrats, "backed by the Irish and later the Italian and Jewish communities," opposed suffrage restrictions directed at immigrants, who tended to support their party.[10]

Republicans, who were successors to the Whigs, introduced the literacy test at each of the state constitutional conventions that followed (Bromage 1930: 955–56 n.27).[11] A proposal during the 1867–1868 constitutional convention died in committee, with members finding that "men's relative capacity is not absolutely measured by their literary acquirements" (Galie 1996: 120, 164). Republicans dominated the constitutional convention in 1894, and again proposed a literacy test because of "Republican concerns about the growing immigrant population, with its potential impact on traditional Republican values and the likelihood that the immigrants would become affiliated with the Democratic Party." Moderate Republicans joined with Democrats to defeat the measure on the floor of the convention (Galie 1996: 160–61, 164). A similar result occurred in the 1915 convention, when Republicans reprised their success in securing a majority but remained unsuccessful in securing passage of a literacy test (Galie 1996: 188–89; Bromage 1930: 955–56 n.27).

The political environment changed considerably by 1920. "As immigration increased, support for a literacy requirement in English gained popularity, no doubt fueled by the patriotic fervor unleashed by World War I" (Galie 1996: 207). The 1921 legislature was so firmly in the hands of the Republicans and dominated by Republican Governor N.L. Miller that it was known as "Miller's Mill" (Bromage 1930: 956). In 1920, the New York legislature enacted a constitutional provision stating that "no person shall become entitled to vote by attaining majority, by naturalization or otherwise, unless such person is also able, except for physical disability, to read and write English."[12] The legislature passed the amendment again in 1921, securing enough support to get it on the ballot for a popular referendum.

There were "clear racial purposes" to use the literacy requirement to prevent immigrants and non-English speaking persons from political participation.[13] The evidence shows "that it was passed to specifically disenfranchise 1,000,000 Yiddish-speaking Jews,"[14] along with the growing Italian population. Indeed, in the 50 years between 1877 and 1927, the Jewish population in the United States increased "from less than 350,000 to over 4,000,000" with most of those immigrants coming from Russia and Eastern Europe.[15] Supporters did not try to conceal the purpose of the literacy test:

8 Josh Kagan, *A Civics Action: Interpreting "Adequacy" in State Constitutions' Education Clauses*, 78 N.Y.U. L. Rev. 2241, 2262 (2003).

9 Peter J. Galie, Ordered Liberty: A Constitutional History of New York 99 (Fordham Univ. Press 1996).

10 Alexander Keyssar, The Right to Vote: The Contested History of Democracy in the United States 145 (2000).

11 For a more thorough accounting of New York's racism against new arrivals, *see* Jim Crow New York: A Documentary History of Race and Citizenship 1777–1877 (N.Y.U. Press 2003).

12 N.Y. Const. art. II, § 1 (1921).

13 Juan Cartagena, *Latinos and Section 5 of the Voting Rights Act: Beyond Black and White*, 18 Nat'l Black L.J. 201, 204–205 (2005).

14 Sandra Del Valle, Language Rights and the Law in the United States: Finding Our Voices 92 (2003).

15 Carl Wittke, We Who Built America: The Saga of the Immigrant 330 (Prentice Hall 1939).

> More precious even than the forms of government are the mental qualities of our race. While those stand unimpaired, all is safe. They are exposed to a single danger, and that by constantly changing our voting citizenship through the wholesale, but valuable and necessary infusion of Southern and Eastern European races … The danger has begun … We should check it.[16]

Another proponent of literacy tests argued at the 1915 constitutional convention, that it was "a question of race," securing assimilation by fitting immigrants "to walk in the paths to which our Anglo-Saxon ancestry and our Anglo-Saxon traditions point as the paths in which lies our national destiny" (Del Valle 2003: 93).

Max Kohler derided the constitutional amendment in a lengthy *New York Times* editorial published two weeks before a November 1921 referendum. C.H. Young, the amendment's primary sponsor, had argued during the debate in the legislature that it targeted only new arrivals, a claim which Kohler called "unquestionably fallacious." Previous amendments were defeated because moderate Republicans and Democrats recognized that an English literacy test would disenfranchise thousands of native-born Americans who lived in non-English-speaking households. Moreover, 1910 census data confirmed that the amendment would have a disproportionate impact on the foreign born, among whom 13.7 percent were illiterate compared to 5.5 percent for the total population. Night schools reached only "a small fraction of those unable to speak English," effectively removing any incentive the amendment was said to create to learn English. The literacy test also deprived literate Yiddish speakers of the ballot, despite their ability to be well read from five major Yiddish newspapers with a circulation of over 500,000 in New York City alone.[17]

Kohler presciently analogized New York's English literacy test aimed at disenfranchising language minorities with similar tests in the South targeting African-Americans:

> We in the North emphatically decry the action of the South, in preventing the great majority of the negroes of the South from voting, though there much greater ignorance is involved, and a far greater menace, because of their theoretical balance of power. Should we rashly, for a mere whim, by reason of unconsidered dogmas, disenfranchise hundreds of thousands of foreign-born citizens in our own midst?

He explained, "Serious questions of public policy arise when large numbers of our citizens are denied the right to vote, particularly among the foreign-born, not yet sufficiently familiar with our American method of appealing to the ballot-box." Kohler urged voters to reject the constitutional amendment "as emanating from 'Know-Nothingism' propaganda" (Kohler 1921). Despite his pleas, New Yorkers adopted the measure by a 3 to 2 margin in November 1921, making the literacy test effective in 1922 (Bromage 1930: 956).

The state legislature separately enacted laws to implement the mandate. In 1922, the legislature provided that literacy could be established in one of two ways: "a new voter might either present to the board of inspectors a certificate of literacy signed by the principal of a public school or submit to an examination by the election board."[18] The State Board of Regents, which oversaw the public schools, was authorized to issue literacy certificates (Bromage 1930: 956 n.32). If a new voter instead was examined by the election board, he or she was required to "read aloud intelligently

16 *Katzenbach v. Morgan*, 384 U.S. 641, 656 n.17 (1966) (quoting III New York State Const. Conv. 2012 (Rev. Record 1916)).

17 Max J. Kohler, *New Test for Voters: Case Against the Proposed Amendment Requiring Knowledge of English*, N.Y. Times, Oct. 23, 1921.

18 Bromage 1930: 956 (citing N.Y. Laws chap. 588, § 166 (1922)).

from slips containing extracts from the state constitution, and write ten words from such slips as selected by the inspectors of election."[19] The implementing laws generally failed because "the illiterate foreigner and the politicians" soon recognized that many election officials treated the literacy test as optional or otherwise did not impose it at all on new voters (Bromage 1930: 956).

New York's legislature responded with a 1923 law that placed exclusive authority for making rules and regulations for obtaining literacy certificates in the State Board of Regents.[20] That gave New York "the distinction of being the only state in which this power is placed solely in the hands of the educational authorities" (Crawford 1925: 790). The new law required a new voter to present a certificate or diploma showing completion of "the work of an approved eighth-grade elementary school or of a higher school in which English is the language of instruction." Literacy tests were to be given as "only a last resort for those who can present no other acceptable proof of their literacy" (Bromage 1930: 959). There was some procedural regularity in the construction of the tests, which required a demonstration of reading and writing comprehension at the fifth-grade level. Topics on the tests included "America, Americanization, American history and government, citizenship and naturalization, civic duties and institutions, industries and occupations, [and] international relationships" (Bromage 1930: 958–59). Figure 2.1 is an example of one of the literacy tests administered by the State Board of Regents between 1923 and 1930. Nevertheless, the literacy test proved an insurmountable barrier for many language minority citizens.

New York's Board of Regents issued a report documenting some of the effects of the literacy test between 1923 and 1929. There were isolated instances in which the test was circumvented or ignored, but for the most part it was applied to all new voters. During that period, 14.9 percent of all applicants who took the test failed it.[21] But that figure does not include the thousands of citizens who, like southern Blacks, were discouraged from trying to register in the first place because of the test. According to the Staff Report on Suffrage prepared by the 1965 Temporary Commission on the Constitutional Convention, an estimated 100,000 applicants failed the test (Galie 1996: 207). The actual number disenfranchised by New York's English literacy test was doubtless much greater.

Although the English literacy test primarily targeted immigrants from Southern and Eastern Europe, its enforcement soon posed a significant barrier to Puerto Rican voters (Cartagena 2005: 204–05). In 1920, there were only 7,364 Puerto Ricans in New York City, a figure that grew nearly a hundredfold by 1960, when there were 612,574.[22] The arrival of hundreds of thousands of Puerto Ricans greeted with signs in restaurants proclaiming "No dogs or Puerto Ricans"[23] made the literacy test an expedient vehicle for their political exclusion. The statutory exception for voters who could produce a certificate of completion for eighth grade schooling in English would never exempt those educated in Puerto-Ricans public schools, where Spanish was the language of instruction. The U.S. Commission on Civil Rights documented this intentional disenfranchisement in a 1959 report, observing that "Puerto Rican American citizens are being denied the right to vote, and that these denials exist in substantial numbers in the State of New York."[24]

---

19 F.C. Crawford, *New York State Literacy Test*, 19 Am. Pol. Sci. Rev. 788 (Nov. 1925).

20 Bromage 1930: 957 (citing N.Y. Laws chap. 803, § 166 (1923)).

21 Finla G. Crawford, *Operation of the Literacy Test for Voters in New York*, 25 Am. Pol. Sci. Rev. 342, 345 (May 1931).

22 Carmen Teresa Whalen, *Colonialism, Citizenship, and the Making of the Puerto Rican Diaspora: An Introduction*, *in* The Puerto Rican Diaspora: Historical Perspectives 3 (Temple Univ. Press 2005).

23 Manuel Roig-Franzia, *A Terrorist in the House*, Wash. Post, Feb. 22, 2004, at W12.

24 Report of the U.S. Comm'n on Civil Rights 68 (1959).

Instructions for the Test

(To be read aloud by the examiner)

"On the other side of this paper is a test to see whether you can read and write English. It is a paragraph like this one you are reading now. Below it are some questions like those you see below this paragraph. When you turn over the paper, the first thing to do is to read the paragraph. Next, read the first question. Then, go back and read the paragraph until you find the answer to this question. When you find the correct answer, write it on the dotted line after the first question. You do not have to answer the question in a complete sentence unless you want to. Usually, one or two words will be enough for your answer to the question. Write the answer as plainly as you can, for this is a test of both reading and writing. Answer all the other questions in the same way. When you have answered every question, read the paragraph and all your answers over again. This is to make sure that you have made no mistakes."

New York State Regents Literacy Test

Read this and then write the answers. Read it as many times as you need to.

"Mary had been waiting for the Fourth of July. It was on this day that her father and mother were going to take her to the park. Because it was a holiday her father did not have to work. Mary had learned in school why we celebrate the Fourth of July. The Declaration of Independence was signed on July 4, 1776. It was written by Thomas Jefferson. It is called the Declaration of Independence because it declared the thirteen American colonies free from England. The Fourth of July is celebrated as a national holiday by all of the forty-eight states."

(The answers to the following questions are to be taken from the above paragraph.)

1. For what day had Mary been waiting?
2. Where were her father and mother going to take her?
3. Why did Mary's father not have to work?
4. Where had Mary learned why we celebrate the Fourth of July?
5. When was the Declaration of Independence signed?
6. Who wrote the Declaration of Independence?
7. From what country did the Declaration of Independence declare the thirteen American colonies free?
8. How many states celebrate the Fourth of July as a national holiday?

Figure 2.1 Example of a literacy test administered by the State of New York
Source: Arthur W. Bromage, *Literacy and the Electorate*, 24 Am. Pol. Sci. Rev. 946, 958 (Nov. 1930). Reprinted with permission of Cambridge University Press.

Challenges to New York's English Literacy Test Before 1965

Puerto Ricans unsuccessfully challenged New York's literacy requirement under the Fourteenth and Fifteenth Amendments and the federal Civil Rights Acts. In 1958, Jose Camacho sought an order in state court requiring the poll workers in his voting precinct to allow him to demonstrate his literacy, at his option, in either English or Spanish and to register him to vote until he learned to read and write in English. In that case, *Camacho v. Doe*, the court rejected the request even though it acknowledged that the petitioner was "a citizen of the United States by reason of his being a native of Puerto Rico."[25] The court found that New York's constitutional and statutory literacy requirements did not violate the United States Constitution because "[t]he petitioner is not denied the right to vote. Under the laws of this State, however, he must first learn to read and write English. This cannot be deemed an unreasonable requirement" (*Camacho v. Doe* 1958: 262–63).

Undeterred, Camacho filed a separate challenge in federal court that rested not only on the U.S. Constitution and the Civil Rights Act of 1957 and 1960, but also the United Nations Charter

25 *Camacho v. Doe*, 221 N.Y.S.2d 262 (Sup. Ct. 1958), *aff'd*, 163 N.E.2d 140 (N.Y. 1959).

and the Treaty of Paris, under which Puerto Rico became a United States territory.[26] The court dismissed the claims and found that the Treaty of Paris did not provide Puerto Rican citizens with "preferential treatment over a resident of a sister state who moves to New York" and also would have to take the literacy test (*Camacho v. Rogers* 1961: 158).

The court found the reasoning of *Lassiter* persuasive (Chapter 1), describing the Supreme Court's justifications for upholding North Carolina's literacy test as "just as apposite for a person literate in a foreign tongue." The court explained, "It is not unreasonable to expect a voter not only to be conversant with the issues presented for determination in choosing between candidates for election, but also to understand the language used in connection with voting" (*Camacho v. Rogers* 1961: 159). The court did not consider evidence of the discriminatory purpose and effect of New York's literacy test, concluding that the Fifteenth Amendment only prohibited the right to vote from being "denied because of race, creed, or color," and not "because of ... illiteracy in the English language" (*Camacho v. Rogers* 1961: 160). The court's decision in *Camacho v. Rogers* therefore suggested that *Lassiter*'s discussion of the discriminatory use of literacy tests would not provide any relief where the method of that discrimination was through an English language requirement.

Section 4(e)'s Permanent Ban on English Literacy Tests for Puerto Rican Voters

In 1965, Congress responded to the unsuccessful challenges by Comacho and others by enacting Section 4(e) of the VRA. Under that provision, no person who demonstrates he has successfully completed a sixth grade education in a school in the United States "in which the predominant classroom language was other than English, shall be denied the right to vote in any Federal, State, or local election because of his inability to read, write, understand, or interpret any matter in the English language."[27] Therefore, bilingual voting materials[28] and Spanish language assistance had to be provided for illiterate voters protected under Section 4(e).[29] Unlike most of the other provisions of the VRA, which were enacted pursuant to the Enforcement Section of the Fifteenth Amendment, Section 4(e) was adopted to enforce the guarantees of the Fourteenth Amendment.[30] Although there is no explanation for this difference in treatment between the VRA's provisions, it may have been at least in part a response by Congress to *Camacho v. Rogers*.

New York's congressional delegation, led by Senators Jacob Javits and Robert Kennedy and Representatives Jacob Gilbert and William Fitts Ryan, sponsored Section 4(e). During the floor debate on the VRA, Senator Kennedy noted that the English language disabilities faced by Puerto Ricans were not their fault. He explained, "That his schooling takes place in Spanish is not up to him, but is due to the fact that the U.S. Government has chosen to encourage the cultural autonomy of the Commonwealth of Puerto Rico, to make Puerto Rico a showcase for all of Latin America."[31] Representative Gilbert agreed, concluding it was "an anomaly for [Congress] to encourage the

26 *Camacho v. Rogers*, 199 F. Supp. 155 (S.D.N.Y. 1961).

27 42 U.S.C. § 1973b(e)(2).

28 *See Torres v. Sachs*, 381 F. Supp. 309 (S.D.N.Y. 1974).

29 *See Torres v. Sachs* 1974: 309; *Coal. for Educ. in Dist. One v. New York City Bd. of Elections* ("*Coalition v. NYC Bd. of Elections*"), 370 F. Supp. 42 (S.D.N.Y. 1974), *aff'd*, 495 F.2d 1090 (2d Cir. 1974); *Lopez v. Dinkins*, No. 73 Civ. 695 (S.D.N.Y. Feb. 14, 1973).

30 Warren Christopher, *The Constitutionality of the Voting Rights Act of 1965*, 18 Stan. L. Rev. 1, 24 (1965).

31 111 Cong. Rec. 10,675 (daily ed. May 20, 1965).

perpetuation of Puerto Rico's Spanish language culture and at the same time do nothing to protect the rights of citizenship of Puerto Ricans who move to other sections of the country."[32]

Section 4(e) of the VRA would solve the problem by enfranchising much of the Puerto Rican population in New York that was barred from voting by the state's English literacy requirement. "Throughout the congressional debate it was repeatedly acknowledged that § 4(e) had a particular reference to the Puerto Rican population in New York. That situation was the almost exclusive subject of discussion" (*Katzenbach v. Morgan* 1966: 645 n.3). Juan Cartagena has summarized the evidence of discrimination in New York that Congress considered in enacting the provision:

> Estimates were offered that of 730,000 Puerto Ricans in the city of all ages, 150,000 registered to vote but close to 330,000 were prevented from registering. Accounts were given about how literacy test certificates would "suddenly disappear" causing delays of hours, if not the entire day, to replace them, or how basic supplies like pencils would be missing whenever Puerto Ricans sought to take the test. Finally the witnesses sought to defuse the "myth in our State of New York that a citizen can be an intelligent, well-informed voter only if he is literate in English" (Cartagena 2005: 205).

Although Section 4(e) applied to students educated in languages other than English anywhere in the United States, its practical effect was "limited to enfranchising those educated in Puerto Rican schools." As the Solicitor General of the United States explained, outside of Puerto Rico, no other public schools in the United States had a "predominant language of instruction ... other than English" that "would have generally been attended by persons who are otherwise qualified to vote except for their lack of literacy in English" (*Katzenbach v. Morgan* 1966: 645 n.3).

Nevertheless, the provision gave solace to other language minority voters that if they established the discriminatory effect of English literacy tests in light of unequal or segregated schooling, it might be possible to receive language assistance to allow them to vote. At the same time, Section 4(e) proved to be too narrow: it did not secure the right to vote for other language minority groups and Spanish-speaking persons who were not educated in Puerto Rican schools. Moreover, the alternative remedy provided by the temporary suspension of all literacy tests or other similar "tests or devices" under Sections 4(a) and 4(b) of the 1965 Act applied to only those jurisdictions meeting the triggering formula. As a result, few jurisdictions with language minorities were covered in 1965, notwithstanding congressional findings that literacy tests were subject to abuse in their administration and had a discriminatory impact on minority groups who had suffered from disparate educational opportunities.[33]

Despite Section 4(e)'s passage in 1965, the New York literacy test would remain on the books for another dozen years. The state did not repeal its statutory literacy requirements until 1977 (Galie 1996: 207). New York's legacy of using English-only elections to disenfranchise language minority voters would last far longer.

Katzenbach v. Morgan and the Constitutionality of Section 4(e)

Registered voters in New York did not take the VRA's suspension of the state's literacy test lightly. Shortly following the enactment of Section 4(e), a group of those voters filed a challenge to the

32 111 Cong. Rec. 15,666 (1965).

33 *See* H.R. Rep. No. 89–439, *reprinted in* 1965 U.S.C.C.A.N. at 2444–2447.

provision, claiming that it "adversely affected" the "weight of their votes" by allowing Puerto Rican citizens who were only literate in Spanish "to vote in disregard of the State literacy test."[34] They further argued that Section 4(e) was unconstitutional because Congress exceeded its powers in enacting it in violation of the Tenth Amendment to the United States Constitution. A three-judge federal court in the District of Columbia agreed and struck down the provision in a 2 to 1 decision, relying upon *Lassiter* to conclude that states like New York could lawfully impose literacy requirements for registering to vote (*Morgan v. Katzenbach* 1965: 203–204).

The Majority Opinion

The Supreme Court reversed the lower court's ruling. In *Katzenbach v. Morgan*, the Court distinguished its earlier holding in *Lassiter* because no showing of an Equal Protection violation was necessary to sustain Section 4(e) under expansive congressional enforcement powers. Instead, the Court held that the Enforcement Section, "[c]orrectly viewed," constituted "a positive grant of legislative power authorizing Congress to exercise its discretion in determining whether and what legislation is needed to secure the guarantees of the Fourteenth Amendment" (*Katzenbach v. Morgan* 1966: 648–51). As long as Congress did not exceed its discretion, the Court had no authority to second-guess it:

> It was well within congressional authority to say that this need of the Puerto Rican minority for the vote warranted federal intrusion upon any state interests served by the English literacy requirement. It was for Congress, as the branch that made this judgment, to assess and weigh the various conflicting considerations – the risk or pervasiveness of the discrimination in governmental services, the effectiveness of eliminating the state restriction on the right to vote as a means of dealing with the evil, the adequacy or availability of alternative remedies, and the nature and significance of the state interests that would be affected by the nullification of the English literacy requirement as applied to residents who have successfully completed the sixth grade in a Puerto Rican school (*Katzenbach v. Morgan* 1966: 654).

The Court noted that "Section 2 of the Fifteenth Amendment grants Congress a similar power." The Court acknowledged that it could not micromanage and "review the congressional resolution of these factors. It is enough that we be able to perceive a basis upon which the Congress might resolve the conflict as it did" (*Katzenbach v. Morgan* 1966: 654).

Turning to the constitutionality of Section 4(e), the Court reasoned that Congress had made valid legislative choices to limit the scope of the provision to Puerto Ricans (*Katzenbach v. Morgan* 1966: 657–58). The Court explained:

> In the context of the case before us, the congressional choice to limit the relief effected in § 4(e) may, for example, reflect … a recognition of the unique historic relationship between the Congress and the Commonwealth of Puerto Rico, an awareness of the Federal Government's acceptance of the desirability of the use of Spanish as the language of instruction in Commonwealth schools, and the fact that Congress has fostered policies encouraging migration from the Commonwealth to the States (*Katzenbach v. Morgan* 1966: 654).

34 *Morgan v. Katzenbach*, 247 F. Supp. 196, 198 (D.D.C. 1965) (three-judge court), *rev'd*, *Morgan*, 384 U.S. at 641.

In reaching this conclusion, the Court rejected the assertion by the voters that New York's English language requirement was created to give language minorities an incentive to learn English. Instead, the Court found that Congress may have "questioned whether denial of a right deemed so precious and fundamental in our society was a necessary or appropriate means of encouraging persons to learn English, or of furthering the goal of an intelligent exercise of the franchise" (*Katzenbach v. Morgan* 1966: 658). Therefore, the Court determined that Section 4(e) was a valid exercise of the Enforcement Section of the Fourteenth Amendment. As a result, the requirement that the State of New York provide language assistance to Spanish-speaking Puerto Rican voters, like the VRA's ban on literacy tests, was constitutional (*Katzenbach v. Morgan* 1966: 657–58).

Justice Harlan's Dissent

Justice Harlan, joined by Justice Stewart, dissented. According to Justice Harlan, "Worthy as its purposes may be thought by many," he did not see how Section 4(e) could "be sustained except at the sacrifice of ... the separation between the legislative and judicial function and the boundaries between federal and state political authority."[35] He disagreed that restrictions on the right to vote were subject to "a different and broader equal protection standard," as the majority contended. Instead, he maintained that since voting was "essentially a matter of state concern," any restrictions on that right should be sustained as long as the state shows a "mere rational policy to justify classifications in this area." Applying that standard, Justice Harlan concluded that "New York has shown that its English literacy test is reasonably designed to serve a legitimate state interest," similar to the interest upheld in *Lassiter*.[36]

The crux of the Harlan dissent lies in his narrow construction of congressional power under Section 5 of the Fourteenth Amendment. He acknowledged that "Congress is of course empowered by Section 5 to take appropriate remedial measures to redress and prevent" any "recognized state violations of federal constitutional standards."[37] Nevertheless, he asserted that only the courts could make that determination, illustrated by the numerous judicial findings considered by Congress when it enacted the VRA. Reaching the opposite conclusion, as suggested by the majority, would give "Congress the power to define the substantive scope" of the Fourteenth Amendment. Justice Harlan reasoned, "If that indeed be the true reach of Section 5, then I do not see why Congress should not be able as well to exercise its Section 5 'discretion' by enacting statutes so as in effect to dilute equal protection and due process decisions of this Court."[38]

Justice Harlan argued Section 4(e) was based on merely "hypothesized discrimination" that had to give way to the state's interest in enforcing its literacy test.[39] In doing so, he ignored evidence of the discriminatory purpose and effect of New York's literacy test that was included in the congressional record, raising arguments later repeated by commentators who oppose the VRA's language assistance provisions. He acknowledged that "there is a difference between a totally illiterate person and one who is literate in a foreign tongue," but found that difference did not affect the constitutionality of New York's literacy test. According to Justice Harlan, voters literate in Spanish but not English had access to a smaller range of material about government, ballots were in English, and most candidates campaigned in English. He contended, "It is noteworthy that the Federal Government requires literacy in English as a prerequisite to naturalization, attesting to

35 *Katzenbach v. Morgan* 1966: 659 (Harlan., J., and Stewart, J., dissenting).

36 *Katzenbach v. Morgan* 1966: 660–62 (Harlan., J., and Stewart, J., dissenting).

37 *Katzenbach v. Morgan* 1966: 666 (Harlan., J., and Stewart, J., dissenting).

38 *Katzenbach v. Morgan* 1966: 666–68 (Harlan., J., and Stewart, J., dissenting).

39 *Katzenbach v. Morgan* 1966: 670 (Harlan., J., and Stewart, J., dissenting).

the national view of its importance as a prerequisite to full integration into the American political community." [40] He likewise found that New York's literacy test was fairly administered and not discriminatory, which was bolstered by the free English classes offered by the state. Justice Harlan reasoned that in light of the state's "legitimate concern with promoting and safeguarding the intelligent use of the ballot" and its "long experience … integrating non-English-speaking residents into the mainstream of American life," he did not see how the test could be unconstitutional.[41]

Justice Harlan's dissent rejected congressional authority under the Reconstruction Amendments, which the Court had recognized in *Ex Parte Virginia*.[42] However, the Amendments' legislative history refutes his position. Congress intended to limit the courts' power to restrict congressional legislation properly enacted under the Enforcement Sections.[43] Specifically, broad enforcement powers were added under the Reconstruction Amendments because "[f]rom at least *Dred Scott* onward the Court was in ill repute."[44] Given that the States refused to enforce the remedial legislation such as the Civil Rights Act of 1866, a majority in Congress felt that the federal legislative branch needed to have greater discretion to enact appropriate remedial legislation through the Enforcement Sections of the Fourteenth and Fifteenth Amendments (Tucker 1999: 474–77, 486–87 and 486 n.206).

The history that led to the passage of the VRA's broad protections also repudiates the Harlan dissent. Chapter 1 illustrated the shortcomings of the case-by-case approach suggested by Justice Harlan. That approach had proven unworkable and was more likely to lead to the perpetuation of the very discrimination that led to enactment of the Fourteenth and Fifteenth Amendments in the first place. It also ignored the Court's longstanding recognition that voting is a fundamental political right "preservative of all rights."[45] If the limits Justice Harlan suggested were imposed on Congress, it is difficult to envision what remedial legislation would be permissible under the Enforcement Sections. In short, the seven justices forming the majority in *Morgan* had the better of the arguments, with the weight of history on their side.

Enforcement of Section 4(e) as the Foundation for the 1975 VRA Amendments

It did not take long for voters to seek relief under the newly enacted Section 4(e). The first cases were brought in New York. In the early 1970s, cases were brought in other states and urban centers around the country with growing Puerto Rican populations. Enforcement of Section 4(e) would expand the remedies available for non-English-speaking language minority voters, including bilingual voting materials, language assistance at the polls, and requirements for improved outreach to minority communities. More than one million Spanish-speaking Puerto Rican voters would benefit from Section 4(e) cases brought in New York and other urban areas.[46] That experience

---

40 *Katzenbach v. Morgan* 1966: 662–63 (Harlan., J., and Stewart, J., dissenting).

41 *Katzenbach v. Morgan* 1966: 663–64 (Harlan., J., and Stewart, J., dissenting).

42 100 U.S. 339, 345–46 (1879).

43 *See* John Mabry Mathews, Legislative and Judicial History of the Fifteenth Amendment 97–126 (1909); James Thomas Tucker, *Tyranny of the Judiciary: Judicial Dilution of Consent Under Section 2 of the Voting Rights Act*, 7 Wm. & Mary Bill Rts. J. 443, 479–86 (1999).

44 Raoul Berger, The Fourteenth Amendment and the Bill of Rights 90 (1989).

45 *Yick Wo v. Hopkins*, 118 U.S. 356, 270 (1886); *accord Harper v. Virginia Bd. of Elections*, 383 U.S. 663, 667 (1966).

46 *See* Katherine Culliton-González, *Time to Revive Puerto Rican Voting Rights*, 19 Berkeley La Raza L.J. 27 (2008).

would play a crucial role in the broader requirements for language assistance that Congress enacted in 1975.

The First Section 4(e) Case: Monroe County, New York

In September 1965, the month after President Johnson signed the VRA into law, Maria Lopez sued her county Board of Elections after her voter registration application was denied because she could not pass New York's English literacy test. Lopez was represented by attorneys from the Justice Department's Civil Rights Division, headed by John Doar, the Assistant Attorney General. Doar was a legend in the Department. He gained fame in 1962 for confronting Ross Barnett over his efforts to exclude James Meredith from the then-segregated University of Mississippi. In 1965, he prosecuted and convicted Collie Leroy Wilkins for the murder of Viola Liuzzo in Alabama during the aftermath of the march from Selma to Montgomery. Doar was instrumental in drafting key provisions of the VRA. St. John Barrett, a Justice Department attorney who represented the United States at trial after the government intervened in *Katzenbach v. Morgan* to defend the constitutionality of Section 4(e), served as the lead trial counsel for Lopez.

The Justice Department's experience with literacy tests in the South proved useful in New York. Maria Lopez had successfully completed the ninth grade attending an American-flag public school in Puerto Rico. Since her schooling had been Spanish, she could not read or write in English sufficiently to satisfy the local election officials. Just as the literacy tests in the South barred African-Americans from voting, New York's English literacy test proved an insurmountable barrier to Spanish-speaking Puerto Ricans. Despite Section 4(e)'s mandate, officials refused to register Lopez because it conflicted with New York's constitutional and statutory literacy requirements (*U.S. v. Monroe County* 1965: 318).

Citing the VRA, a federal court granted Lopez's request to order election officials to stop applying the state literacy test to Lopez and other American citizens educated in Puerto Rico (*U.S. v. Monroe County* 1965: 323). The court noted that although the Act had focused primarily on disenfranchisement in the South, it "was not designed to remedy deprivations of the franchise in only one section of the country. Rather, it was devised to eliminate second-class citizenship wherever present" (*U.S. v. Monroe County* 1965: 317). That was evident in New York City, where the government had strengthened "the hold of Spanish as the native tongue" of Puerto Ricans by encouraging its employees to learn Spanish and issuing "many pronouncements to the general public in both the Spanish and English languages" (*U.S. v. Monroe County* 1965: 320). In the process, whatever tenuous justifications may have existed for excluding the language minorities who were originally targeted by New York's literacy test, they did not apply to Puerto Ricans:

"Spanish already has a much stronger official position in New York than either Italian or Yiddish ever had," with the result that "people active in politics and the leaders of the Puerto Rican community expect that Spanish will be the major language (after English) in use in the community for as long ahead as any one can see."[47]

Monroe County also was the first decision to specifically uphold the constitutionality of Section 4(e), anticipating the Supreme Court's ruling in *Katzenbach v. Morgan.* The court reasoned, "We believe that Congress acted well within its constitutional limits when it legislated to prevent New York from prohibiting or, at the very least, substantially impeding the integration of Puerto Rican emigrants into its political life through the imposition of an English language requirement for voter

47 *Monroe County* 1965: 320 (quoting Glazer and Moynihan, Beyond the Melting Pot 101 (M.I.T. and Harv. Univ. Press 1963)).

registration" (*U.S. v. Monroe County* 1965: 321). In reaching this conclusion, the court disagreed with the lower court's ruling in *Morgan* and adopted dissenting Circuit Judge Carl McGowan's view that Section 4(e) was properly enacted to make the right to vote equally available to Spanish-speaking citizens of Puerto Rican heritage (*U.S. v. Monroe County* 1965: 323).

Monroe County is important for two other reasons. It established that any adult citizen educated in Puerto Rico was entitled to the protection of Section 4(e) and could enforce its mandate. Monroe County, with Rochester as its county seat, is located in upstate New York some 250 miles from New York City. Notwithstanding the legislative history focusing on the plight of Puerto Ricans in New York City, the plain language of Section 4(e) applied without regard to geography. Furthermore, unlike the language assistance provisions that followed in 1975, no numerical threshold was required regardless of how many Puerto Ricans lived in a community. Maria Lopez successfully brought the case on her own behalf, without any proof of the size of the Spanish-speaking Puerto Rican community in Monroe County. In the end, the court enjoined application of New York's literacy test as to Lopez "and other American citizens educated in Spanish-language Puerto Rican schools" (*U.S. v. Monroe County* 1965: 320). *Monroe County* showed that Section 4(e) was a powerful remedy even when other provisions of the Voting Rights Act, including those later enacted in 1975, were unavailable (Culliton-González 2008).

Bilingual Election Requirements under Section 4(e)

In *Cardona v. Power*, decided the same day as *Katzenbach v. Morgan*, the Supreme Court suggested that other applications of New York's literacy statute might be invalid under Section 4(e) of the VRA, even if not expressly prohibited.[48] Martha Cardona was a Puerto Rican citizen who could not register to vote because she was literate in Spanish but could not pass the state's English literacy test. The Court recognized that Cardona might be covered by Section 4(e), making it unnecessary to address her constitutional challenge of the literacy test. Even if the section was inapplicable, the Court observed that "New York courts should ... determine whether, in light of this federal enactment, those applications of the New York English literacy requirement not in terms prohibited by § 4(e) have continuing validity" (*Cardona v. Power* 1966: 673–74).

Four members of the *Cardona* Court dissented from the opinion, stating that they would have reached the question of constitutionality. As we have already seen, Justices Harlan and Stewart would have upheld Section 4(e) as a proper exercise of state power under *Lassiter*.[49] In contrast, Justices Douglas and Fortas would have held the English literacy requirement unconstitutional as applied to those literate in Spanish.[50]

After *Cardona*, federal courts established that Section 4(e) required more than suspending English literacy tests. "Enfranchisement of Puerto Ricans [had] sharpened the focus on another aspect of the problem of helping voters use their ballots effectively."[51] By 1972, only 30 percent of Puerto Ricans in New York City were registered to vote, about half the percentage of the city as a whole (U.S. Comm'n on Civil Rts. 1975: 58). More was needed to implement Section 4(e) fully.

Materials written in Spanish were mandated. One court explained, "It is simply fundamental that voting instructions and ballots, in addition to any other material which forms part of the official communication to registered voters prior to an election, must be in Spanish as well as English, if

48 384 U.S. 672 (1966).

49 *Katzenbach v. Morgan* 1966: 659–71 (Harlan., J., and Stewart, J., dissenting).

50 *Cardona v. Power* 1966: 675–77 (Douglas, J., and Fortas, J., dissenting).

51 U.S. Comm'n on Civil Rts., The Voting Rights Act: Ten Years After 22 (Jan. 1975).

Figure 2.2 Hilda Hernandez, originally from Aguadilla, Puerto Rico, registers to vote in New York City in 1960

Source: Photo courtesy of the Library of Congress, Prints & Photographs Division, Washington, D.C., New York World-Telegram and the Sun Newspaper Photograph Collection (Library of Congress), Reproduction no. LC-USZ62-117551 (b&w film copy neg.).

the vote of Spanish-speaking citizens is not to be seriously impaired" (*Torres v. Sachs* 1974: 312). The broad interpretation was necessary because "[t]he right to vote means the right to effectively register the voter's political choice, not merely the right to move levers on a voting machine or to mark a ballot."[52]

Oral language assistance for illiterate Spanish-speaking voters also was necessary. After all, "Simple logic … requires that the assistance given to the … voters at the polls on election day by trained representatives of the Board of Elections be in a language they understand, in order that their vote will be more than a mere physical act void of any meaningful choice" (*Torres v. Sachs* 1974: 312). The rationale for providing effective Spanish assistance corresponded with one used in the South to provide redress for illiterate African-American voters under the VRA and the Equal Protection Clause.[53] Absent such oral language assistance, the English-only election materials,

52 *Puerto Rican Org. for Political Action v. Kusper*, 350 F. Supp. 606, 610 (N.D. Ill. 1972), *aff'd*, 490 F.2d 575 (7th Cir. 1973).

53 *See, e.g., Torres v. Sachs* 1974: 309 (invalidating city elections for failing to provide language assistance to Spanish-speaking voters); *Coalition v. NYC Bd. of Elections* 1974: 42 (invalidating school board elections for inadequate language assistance for Hispanic voters), *aff'd*, 495 F.2d 1090 (2d Cir. 1974); *Lopez v. Dinkins* 1973 (invalidating school board elections in Manhattan).

like the literacy tests used in the South, constituted mechanisms that "cannot withstand scrutiny under the Voting Rights Act."[54] That became clear when three New York counties that had bailed out under Section 4(a) of the Act in 1972,[55] became covered again in early 1974 after a federal court found that a New York City school board's use of an English-only requirement with no oral language assistance was a prohibited "test or device" (*Coalition v. NYC Bd. of Elections* 1974: 45 n.6).

In a seminal 1974 decision, *Torres v. Sachs*, the federal court ordered that violations of Section 4(e) in New York City's elections be remedied through several measures. The Board of Elections was required to provide all written voting materials offered to voters or prospective voters, including ballots, in both English and Spanish. Bilingual election workers fluent and literate in both Spanish and English had to be provided in every polling place and voter registration site "within a census tract containing 5 percent or more persons of Puerto Rican birth." Election officials had to post "conspicuous signs at all polling places and places of registration" where bilingual election workers were required "indicating in Spanish that election officials are available to assist Spanish-speaking voters or registrants, and that bilingual printed materials are available." Voter outreach and publicity in Spanish also was mandated (*Torres v. Sachs* 1974: 313). The *Torres* remedies provided much of the substance of the language assistance provisions that Congress added to the VRA in 1975.

Foreshadowing the 1975 VRA Amendments

Two other important developments came out of Section 4(e) enforcement actions. First, as *Monroe County* (*U.S. v. Monroe County* 1965: 316) and another case out of Buffalo highlighted,[56] lawsuits under the provision were not limited just to New York City. But application of Section 4(e) also was not confined just to the State of New York, even though it was enacted primarily to suspend the application of New York's English literacy test to Puerto Rican voters. In the early 1970s, Puerto Rican voters also brought successful cases in Chicago (*Kusper* 1972: 606), the New Jersey suburbs,[57] and Philadelphia (*Arroyo v. Tucker* 1974: 764). Those decisions anticipated the national scope of jurisdictions that would be required to provide language assistance after 1975.

Second, another federal court found that as a result of discrimination against African-American, Puerto Rican, and Asian American voters in a New York City school district, language materials and assistance had to be provided not just in Spanish, but Chinese as well.[58] Although Section 4(e) did not protect the Asian voters, widespread disenfranchisement deprived them of their rights to equal access to the electoral process in violation of Section 2 of the VRA and the Fourteenth and Fifteenth Amendments (*Coalition v. NYC Bd. of Elections* 1974: 54–56). The court's relief for the Chinese-speaking voters was essentially the same as that ordered in *Torres*: bilingual sample ballots and instructions, at least one bilingual Chinese election worker at every polling site in which more

54 *Arroyo v. Tucker*, 372 F. Supp. 764, 767 (E.D. Pa. 1974).

55 *See New York v. United States*, 65 F.R.D. 10, 12 (D.D.C. 1974) (per curiam) (three-judge court). The counties were Bronx, Kings, and New York (Manhattan) Counties, which were covered following the 1970 Amendments to the VRA. *See* 36 Fed. Reg. 5,809 (Mar. 27, 1971).

56 *See Ortiz v. New York State Bd. of Elections*, Civil No. 74–455 (W.D.N.Y. Oct. 11, 1974). The *Ortiz* litigation largely duplicated the relief sought in *Monroe County* to secure relief for Puerto Ricans statewide under Section 4(e), except for those already covered in New York City as a result of the *Torres* litigation (Culliton-González 2008).

57 *See Marquez v. Falcey*, Civil No. 1447–73 (D.N.J. Oct. 9, 1973).

58 *Coalition v. NYC Bd. of Elections* 1974: 42 (citing relief in *Lopez v. Dinkins* 1973).

than 5 percent of the students were Chinese, and outreach and publicity in Chinese (*Coalition v. NYC Bd. of Elections* 1974: 44–45). The case highlighted the need to provide language assistance not just for Spanish-speaking voters, but for other language minorities who also had suffered from educational and voting discrimination. The 1975 Amendments to the VRA would do precisely that.

The Permanent Nationwide Ban on Literacy Tests and Its Impact on Section 4(e)

In 1975, Congress relied on the evidence cited by Justice Douglas in *Oregon v. Mitchell* to make the nationwide ban on literacy tests permanent.[59] By that time, only 14 states still used some form of literacy test,[60] and none of the witnesses who testified during the Senate hearings opposed extending Section 201 of the VRA.[61] In addition, there was substantial evidence that literacy tests were subject to discriminatory uses against minority groups. In a similar vein, Congress deemed it "patently unfair" for states to require a certain level of literacy of the same minority citizens for whom the states had denied educational opportunities. Finally, Congress concluded that "[i]t is difficult to see why citizens who cannot read or write should be prevented from participating in decisions that directly affect their environment, particularly in an era when radio and television are primary sources of information" (S. Rep. No. 94–295, 1975: 23–24).

Section 201 had one immediate impact on language minority voters. It effectively removed the requirement in Section 4(e) of the Act that Puerto Rican voters had to prove they had completed the sixth grade in an American-flag school before obtaining relief (*Kusper* 1973: 579). The nationwide ban on literacy tests in Section 201 meant that no level of educational attainment in any language was necessary to secure a remedy under the VRA (U.S. Comm'n on Civil Rts. 1975: 22). As a result, Section 4(e) required Spanish-language materials and assistance to be provided to Puerto Rican voters regardless of their literacy in English or Spanish.

Although the ban on literacy tests under Section 201 of the VRA provided some relief for language minorities, it was designed specifically to address "[t]he problems of English-speaking illiterates – those citizens who can speak but can neither read nor write English" (S. Rep. No. 94–295, 1975: 23). Congress opted to address problems for language minorities without proficiency in spoken English through Sections 4(f)(4) and 203(c) of the 1975 amendments to the VRA. Those provisions are discussed in Chapters 3 and 4.

The narrow coverage of language minorities under the Section 4(e) and the different purpose of Section 201 of the VRA did not leave non-Puerto Rican-language minority voters without any recourse. Prior to 1975, other sources for language assistance were available. Although those sources provided some relief, they were insufficient remedies to state-sponsored discrimination in education and voting against language minority voters. Nevertheless, like Section 4(e), those provisions would lay the groundwork for the broader relief included in the 1975 amendments to the VRA (Chapters 3–4).

---

59 *See* 121 Cong. Rec. H4716 (daily ed. June 2, 1975) (statement of Rep. Edwards) (quoting Justice Douglas); Title I of the 1975 extension of the Voting Rights Act of 1965, Pub. L. No. 94–73, § 102, 89 Stat. 400, 400 (codified as amended at 42 U.S.C. § 1973aa (2000)).

60 *See Extension of the Voting Rights Act of 1965: Hearings on S. 407, S. 903, S. 1297, S. 1409, and S. 1443 Before the Subcomm. on Constitutional Rts. of the S. Comm. on the Judiciary*, 94th Cong. 666 (1975) (Ex. 24 to statement of Asst. Att'y Gen. J. Stanley Pottinger).

61 S. Rep. No. 94–295 at 23 (1975).

Other pre-1975 Sources for Language Assistance

The VRA's ban on literacy tests and requirement for Spanish assistance for Puerto Rican voters were not the only foundations for the subsequent passage of the VRA's language assistance provisions in 1975. At least three other sources were available. Section 2 of the VRA prohibits discrimination against voters on the basis of their race or color. In addition, courts held that illiterate voters had a right to receive assistance at the polls. Finally, some states had their own affirmative requirements for language materials or assistance for non-English-speaking voters. Each of these sources offered some precedent for mandating broader language assistance. Standing alone, however, they often proved to be insufficient and incomplete remedies for the barriers faced by language minority voters.

Section 2 of the VRA

The VRA of 1965 focused primarily on removing direct barriers to voting, such as literacy tests. Commentators have described these as "first generation" voting rights claims that directly impaired ballot access.[62] But the VRA's protection for language minority voters was not limited solely to the types of tests or devices encompassed by Section 4. Congress recognized it would have to be flexible in dealing with changes in "methods" of discrimination (H.R. Rep. No. 89–439, 1965: 2441), by "legislating not only for the immediacy of today's problems but for the requirements of the future as well."[63] Members had considered evidence of the extensive and persistent ability of many jurisdictions to exploit the limitations of the judicial process in seeking "new ways and means of discriminating" against African-Americans and other racial and ethnic minorities (H.R. Rep. No. 89–439, 1965: 2441). Therefore, the "new, strong legislation to protect voting rights" had to anticipate other barriers resulting in disenfranchisement of minority voters.[64]

Section 2 of the VRA received little attention in the legislative history when it was enacted in 1965. It provided, without elaboration, "No voting qualification or prerequisite to voting, or standard, practice, or procedure shall be imposed or applied by any State or political subdivision to deny or abridge the right of any citizen of the United States to vote on account of race or color."[65] The Act broadly defined the terms "vote" and "voting" as including, "all action necessary to make a vote effective in any primary, special, or general election, including, but not limited to, registration, ... casting a ballot, and having such ballot counted properly.."[66] Attorney General Nicholas Katzenbach testified that Section 2 was a general anti-discrimination provision that would prohibit "any kind of practice ... if its purpose or effect was to deny or abridge the right to vote on account of race or color."[67] In that manner, the VRA offered broad protection across the

62 *See, e.g.*, Samuel Issacharoff, *Polarized Voting and the Political Process: The Transformation of Voting Rights Jurisprudence*, 90 MICH. L. REV. 1833, 1839 (1992); Binny Miller, *Who Shall Rule and Govern? Local Legislative Delegations, Racial Politics, and the Voting Rights Act*, 102 YALE L.J. 105, 138–50 (1992).

63 H.R. Rep. No. 89–439, 1965: 2468 (Republican views of Rep. McCulloch et al.).

64 S. REP. NO. 89–162, *reprinted in* 1965 U.S.C.C.A.N. at 2540 (providing the joint views of 12 members of the Senate Judiciary Committee relating to the Voting Rights Act of 1965).

65 Pub. L. No. 89–110, § 2, 79 Stat. 437, 437 (1965) (codified as amended at 42 U.S.C. § 1973(a)).

66 42 U.S.C. § 19731(c)(1).

67 *Hearings on S. 1564 Before Sen. Comm. on the Judiciary*, 89th Cong. 191 (1965) (emphasis added); *see also* S. REP. NO. 97–417 at 17 and n.50 (1982) (quoting *Katzenbach*).

spectrum of the political process "to create a set of mechanisms for dealing with continuing voting discrimination, not step by step, but comprehensively and finally" (S. Rep. No. 97–417, 1982: 5).

A 1969 case illustrates Section 2's broad protection. In *United States v. Post*, election officials mistakenly printed erroneous information in a sample ballot in Madison Parish, Louisiana, in which a majority of the registered voters were African-American.[68] According to the sample ballot, pulling a party lever would cast votes for all of that party's nominees in a parish-wide general election and the special election being held for the election of a village marshal in Tallulah, one of the communities in Madison Parish. An African-American candidate geared his entire campaign around asking his supporters to pull the Democratic Party lever because he was the party's nominee for village marshal. Later, local election officials learned that because of limitations on the voting machine, pulling the party lever would only register voters in the parish election, but not the village election. The officials failed to effectively communicate that information to the African-American community or the African-American nominee. As a result, many voters who thought they voted for the African-American candidate by pulling the party lever failed to cast a ballot for him (*U.S. v. Post* 1969: 48–50). The federal court ordered a new election. The court reasoned that election officials had a duty under Section 2 of the VRA "to refrain from applying any voting procedure which will have the effect of denying Negro voters the right to cast effective votes for the candidate of their choice" (*U.S. v. Post* 1969: 50–51). The rationale from *Post* was applied to English-only materials, assistance, and procedures when they denied language minority voters an effective opportunity to register and vote (*Kusper* 1973: 579–80).

Some leading pre-1975 language cases included claims under Section 2, although those claims usually were secondary to those brought under Section 4(e) or the Fourteenth and Fifteenth Amendments (*Coalition v. NYC Bd. of Elections* 1974: 54–58; *Torres v. Sachs* 1974: 311). Section 2 offered relief for unequal treatment at the polls that exacerbated language barriers. There are many ways that could happen (U.S. Comm'n on Civil Rts. 1975: 97–98). A jurisdiction's failure to have poll workers proportionate to the number of language minority voters made it less likely that bilingual language assistance would be available.[69] Inconvenient polling places might require language minorities to vote at sites in predominately English-speaking areas of the community where no poll workers spoke their language.[70] Lack of bilingual poll workers could lead to eligible voters being turned away because of problems reading non-English names on registration lists.[71] Inadequate training resulted in poll workers denying voters language assistance from the person of their choice, even when they brought that person with them.[72] Poll workers could be "hostile and abusive to particular Puerto Rican" voters and even instruct "Puerto Rican and Chinese voters to

---

68 297 F. Supp. 46, 48–50 (W.D. La. 1969).

69 *See generally United States v. Morengo County Comm'n*, 731 F.2d 1546, 1552–53 (11th Cir. 1984); *Harris v. Graddick*, 593 F. Supp. 128, 132–33 (M.D. Ala. 1984) (finding Section 2 violations where a disproportionately small number of Black poll workers were used); U.S. Comm'n on Civil Rts. 1975: 114–17.

70 *See generally Perkins v. Matthews*, 400 U.S. 379, 387 (1971); *Brown v. Dean*, 555 F. Supp. 502, 504–506 (D.R.I. 1982) (finding that violations of Section 2 occurred where polling place locations constructively disenfranchised minority voters); U.S. Comm'n on Civil Rts. 1975: 104, 108.

71 *See generally Coalition v. NYC Bd. of Elections* 1974: 51–52 (describing disenfranchisement that occurred because poll workers could not read Chinese and Spanish names on registration cards); U.S. Comm'n on Civil Rts. 1975: 103–104.

72 *See Coalition v. NYC Bd. of Elections* 1974: 52–53 (Finding that lack of uniform training led to interpreters who were "unaware of their proper functions or of the proper way to offer assistance").

mark their ballots so as to render them invalid" (*Coalition v. NYC Bd. of Elections* 1974: 54). All of that discrimination could be stopped by Section 2.

Section 2 had some advantages for protecting language minority voters that were unavailable elsewhere in the original 1965 Act. Like Section 4(e), it is permanent and national in scope. But unlike Section 4(e), it applies to any voter who is the victim of discrimination on the basis of their race, ethnicity, or language minority status. It can be used by all language minority voters, not just Puerto Rican voters who received their education in Spanish. It provides relief for so-called "episodic violations," or those that may occur during just a single election but have the effect of denying equal access to the electoral process (S. Rep. No. 97–417, 1982: 30). It offers broader remedies any place discrimination occurs, whether that discrimination is intentional, has a discriminatory effect, or is the product of the denial of assistance at the polls.

On the other hand, Section 2 had many more disadvantages. Protection was not automatic. Although Section 4(e) required jurisdictions with Spanish-speaking Puerto Rican voters to take affirmative steps to make the registration and voting process equally accessible to them, Section 2 contained no such mandate. A voter had to demonstrate that the absence of language materials and assistance denied them equal access to the political process before a jurisdiction could be compelled to provide it. The process of meeting that burden could be time consuming and expensive and was typically achieved through litigation. It also generally required more detailed evidence of discrimination against a group of voters than Section 4(e), which only required proof that a single plaintiff was an adult U.S. citizen of Puerto Rican descent who was not provided with Spanish language information necessary to register or cast an effective ballot. Remedies could be limited in time and scope just to address the violations that occurred. Section 2 often could be impractical to use, particularly if other options such as Section 4(e) or Section 201 of the VRA were available to relieve the discrimination.

Assistance for Illiterate Voters

The VRA's suspension of literacy tests would do little good if illiterate voters did not receive assistance reading the ballot. Louisiana illustrates that point. Unlike most southern states, Louisiana always allowed illiterate adults to vote.[73] However, in 1960 the state legislature enacted a statute that provided, "The inability to read or write shall not entitle a voter to assistance in the casting of his vote." That prohibition, which was included in a package of segregation bills, imposed a *de facto* literacy requirement that would disenfranchise the growing number of African-American voters. A federal court struck down the law under the VRA and explained, "If an illiterate is entitled to vote, he is entitled to assistance … that will make his vote meaningful." Otherwise, the ban on literacy tests would be undercut by a "self-defeating notion that an illiterate has the right [to] pull the lever of a voting machine, but not the right to know for whom he pulls the lever" (*U.S. v. Louisiana* 1966: 708).

In Texas, which was not covered under Section 4 of the original 1965 Act, a federal court found that the denial of assistance to illiterate voters violated the Equal Protection Clause of the Fourteenth Amendment.[74] Three illiterate Mexican-Americans challenged a Texas voter assistance

---

73 *United States v. Louisiana*, 265 F. Supp. 703, 708 (E.D. La. 1966) (three-judge court), *aff'd*, 386 U.S. 270 (1967).

74 *Garza v. Smith*, 320 F. Supp. 131 (W.D. Tex. 1970) (three-judge court), *vacated and remanded for appeal to 5th Circuit*, 401 U.S. 1006 (1971), *appeal dismissed for lack of jurisdiction*, 450 F.2d 790 (5th Cir. 1971).

law similar to Louisiana's in *Garza v. Smith*.[75] The court recognized that if the right to vote only guaranteed "the right to enter the voting booth without hindrance or discrimination, perform the physical act of voting, and have the vote … counted, we cannot say that the challenged provisions have an impact on the illiterate voter's ability to exercise the right" (*Garza v. Smith* 1970: 136). But the court held that more than that was required to make voting a meaningful right for illiterates, who like physically disabled voters suffered from "an infirmity that prevents them from casting their vote"; namely, illiteracy. "[T]he 'right to vote' … includes the right to be informed as to which mark on the ballot, or lever on the voting machine, will effectuate the voter's political choice" (*Garza v. Smith* 1970: 137). The court found that the voter assistance law had "a substantial impact on the ability of the illiterate voter to exercise his franchise"; it discriminated against illiterate voters and could not be justified by the state's interest in preventing fraud (*Garza v. Smith* 1970: 137, 139).

The Louisiana and Texas decisions were cited as authority for providing language assistance in the leading cases enforcing Section 4(e) (*Arroyo v. Tucker* 1974: 767; *Torres v. Sachs* 1974: 312 n.5; *Kusper* 1973: 575). Allowing illiterate voters to receive assistance also paved the way for the 1982 addition of Section 208 to the VRA, which is discussed in Chapter 4. Removing restrictions on assistance offered some relief for language minority voters who brought someone with them to translate the ballot and other voting materials written in English. However, it did not require election officials to ensure that language assistance was available at the polls. That would have to come from another source. It also would prove to be an empty right in many states where it continued to be denied. Nevertheless, the *Garza* decision and the denial of assistance to illiterate voters was key evidence supporting passage of the language assistance provisions in 1975.

State Provisions for Language Assistance

Prior to 1975, bilingual assistance was available to voters in some states, although it was often very limited. A survey by the Department of Justice shortly before the 1975 VRA hearings found that parts of 15 states and the District of Columbia had some non-statutory practices for providing bilingual voting assistance, with most offered in Spanish.[76] The District of Columbia, Massachusetts, New Jersey, New Mexico, New York, and Pennsylvania printed bilingual sample ballots and instructions. Arizona offered bilingual ballot information. California provided ballots and voter information. Colorado produced bilingual voting instructions and voter registration pamphlets. Connecticut had bilingual voter materials and pamphlets, providing bilingual assistance in communities in which the Spanish-speaking population was 5 percent or greater (S. Rep. No. 94–295, 1975: 33 n.35). In 1973, Dade County, Florida began providing bilingual sample ballots, registration information, and voter pamphlets.[77] Idaho used a bilingual voter guide on its sample ballot, voting machines, and ballot questions. Illinois translated election materials in certain precincts located in Cook County, which includes metropolitan Chicago. Kansas produced a bilingual version of its voter information

---

75 *Garza v. Smith* 1970: 132 n.1 (providing that "no voter shall be entitled to any assistance in the marking of his ballot on the ground of illiteracy").

76 For a summary of some of the findings of that survey, *see Extension of the Voting Rights Act of 1965: Hearings on S. 407, S. 903, S. 1297, S. 1409, and S. 1443 Before the Subcomm. on Constitutional Rts. of the Senate Comm. on the Judiciary*, 94th Cong., 1st Sess., at 177, 288–89 (1975) (statement of Asst. Att'y Gen. J. Stanley Pottinger).

77 *See generally* 121 Cong. Rec. S13648 (daily ed. July 24, 1975) (statement of Sen. Stone) (quoting letter from the Dade County Supervisor of Elections regarding the county's bilingual voting program).

booklet. Washington included bilingual descriptions of all ballot issues and bilingual versions of its voter pamphlets. Blake County, Indiana even offered voting instructions in Polish.[78]

Since most of these bilingual materials and other voting information were the products of non-binding practices by state or local election officials, there was no legal recourse if they were not provided. Just five states expressly required bilingual elections through constitutional or statutory provisions: California, Hawaii, Massachusetts, New Jersey, and New Mexico. Only Hawaii and New Mexico, which historically were dominated by non-English-speaking cultures, and Massachusetts voluntarily adopted and maintained some requirements for bilingual elections.[79]

California In *Castro v. State*, the Supreme Court of California struck down the state's English literacy test but only for voters literate in other languages (Chapter 1).[80] It did not eliminate the literacy requirement altogether, although that later occurred as a result of the 1970 amendments to the VRA adding Section 201's nationwide ban on literacy tests. The court did not require California to provide a "bilingual electoral apparatus." Instead, *Castro* found the "state interest in maintaining a single language is substantial and the provision of ballots, notices, ballot pamphlets, etc., in Spanish is not necessary either to the formation of intelligent opinions on election issues" or casting a ballot (*Castro v. State* 1970: 258).

The California legislature responded to *Castro* with several laws requiring some bilingual election materials and assistance for non-English-speaking voters. County officials were required to make reasonable efforts to recruit bilingual registration officials in precincts in which there was a 3 percent or higher non-English-speaking voting age population.[81] They had to "make reasonable efforts" to appoint bilingual poll workers in precincts meeting or exceeding the 3 percent threshold and to publicize a list of those precincts and the languages being covered at least 14 days before an election.[82] Election officials needed to make a Spanish translation of a sample ballot and a voter's pamphlet available to any candidate who requested one, which could be distributed to voters upon request.[83] Finally, sample ballots and instructions were required to be printed in Spanish and could be translated only by approved translators or interpreters.[84]

Election officials failed to comply with state law. The Civil Rights Commission documented widespread violations in Monterey County, which had one of the state's larger percentages of Spanish-speaking voters. The county clerk made no special efforts to recruit bilingual officials, resulting in only two bilingual poll workers at a single polling site out of eight that were surveyed. In Soledad, bilingual Latinos either were not hired or were not given "positions of major responsibility" (U.S. Comm'n on Civil Rts. 1975: 114–15). Spanish sample ballots were unavailable, and many poll workers who failed to attend a voluntary training session were unaware

78 Some, but not all, of these state practices were identified during the hearings on the 1975 amendments to the VRA. *See* S. Rep. No. 94–295, 1975: 33 n.35 (New Jersey; Dade County, Florida; Massachusetts; Pennsylvania; and Connecticut).

79 All of these states except Hawaii would later be the subjects of successful lawsuits by the Justice Department and private litigants for their failure to provide effective language assistance to voters.

80 *Castro v. State*, 466 P.2d 244, 258–59 (Cal. 1970).

81 Cal. Election Code § 201 (West. Supp. 1974) (codified as amended at Cal. Election Code §§ 2103(c)-(d)).

82 Cal. Election Code § 1611 (West Supp. 1974) (codified as amended at Cal. Election Code § 12303).

83 Cal. Election Code § 10012.5 (West. Supp. 1974) (later renumbered as Cal. Election Code § 10012 and repealed by Stats. 1994, c. 920 (S.B.1547), § 1).

84 Cal. Election Code § 14201.5 (West. Supp. 1974) (later repealed by Stats. 1994, c. 920 (S.B.1547), § 1).

of the state's bilingual language requirements. Local election officials likewise failed to publicize the availability of bilingual materials and assistance, leaving many Spanish-speaking voters in the dark (U.S. Comm'n on Civil Rts. 1975: 118–19).

In addition to lack of enforcement, California's experience demonstrates another shortcoming of state laws. They were more susceptible than federal requirements to being repealed as a result of local pressures driven by English-only and anti-immigrant attitudes. Los Angeles County, California provides one such example. In 1975, the county became covered by the language assistance provisions of the VRA for Spanish. As a result of a change in the coverage formula in 1982, the county was removed from coverage in 1984. In response, on August 7, 1984, "the Board of Supervisors voted to discontinue providing election materials in Spanish."[85] A federal remedy was necessary to ensure that the fundamental right to vote of language minorities was not subject to being taken away at the whim of local officials.

Hawaii Historically, Hawaii has had a large non-English speaking population of native Hawaiians, other Pacific Islanders, and immigrants from far eastern countries including China, Japan, and the Philippines. In 1970, Hawaii adopted two laws facilitating language assistance in native Hawaiian. The names of candidates could be printed on ballots "with the Hawaiian … equivalent."[86] Voters who could not read English were allowed to receive assistance from two polling officials or from a qualified voter in Hawaiian.[87] In 1978, Hawaii made English and Hawaiian its two official languages but provided, "Hawaiian shall be required for public acts and transactions only as provided by law."[88]

Massachusetts Despite its notoriety as the second state to enact a literacy test that disenfranchised immigrants, the Bay State voluntarily adopted some bilingual election procedures. In 1943, the state added a provision directing the state secretary to "provide English and Spanish affidavits of voter registration to all registration agencies."[89] In 1962, the voter registration requirement was amended to also include "forms in such additional language as he deems necessary or as required by law."[90] In 1970, at the request of Senator Edward Kennedy, state election officials "voluntarily established bilingual election materials … to assist and to encourage Spanish-speaking citizens in their efforts to vote," as well as providing "Spanish-speaking assistants" at some registration and polling sites.[91]

Massachusetts repealed its statutory literacy test in 1971,[92] shortly after Section 201 of the VRA imposed a nationwide ban on the tests. The following year, the legislature amended its voter assistance law to permit assistance from any voter who informs the presiding election official of his or her "inability to read or to read in the English language."[93] At the time of the Justice

85 *Garza v. County of Los Angeles*, 756 F. Supp. 1298, 1341 (C.D. Cal.), *aff'd*, 918 F.2d 763 (9th Cir. 1990).

86 Haw. Sess. Laws 1970, ch. 26, § 2 (codified as amended at Haw. Rev. Stat. § 11–112(e)).

87 Haw. Sess. Laws 1970, ch. 26, § 2 (codified as amended at Haw. Rev. Stat. § 11–139).

88 Haw. Const. art. XV, § 4 (1978).

89 *See* 1943 Mass. Acts ch. 453, § 24 (approved June 7, 1943) (codified as amended at Mass. Gen. Laws Ann. ch. 51, § 36).

90 *See* 1962 Mass. Acts ch. 437, § 14 (approved May 11, 1962) (codified as amended at Mass. Gen. Laws Ann. ch. 51, § 36).

91 121 Cong. Rec. S13670 (daily ed. July 24, 1975) (statement of Sen. Kennedy).

92 *See* Mass. Gen. Laws Ann. ch. 51, § 1 (repealed 1971).

93 *See* Mass. Gen. Laws Ann. ch. 54, § 79 (1972).

Department survey, Massachusetts published Spanish sample ballots for statewide elections that were distributed in approximately 260 precincts throughout the state.

New Jersey A single city in New Jersey is largely responsible for the state's adoption of bilingual election procedures. Hoboken is located in Hudson County, which would become covered by the language assistance provisions in 1984. Hoboken experienced a dramatic growth in its Puerto Rican population following the Second World War. Between 1960 and 1970, the number of Puerto Ricans in the city doubled to about 10,000,[94] roughly one-quarter of the city's total population.[95] The new arrivals soon experienced widespread discrimination. During city elections in May 1973, there were numerous complaints of election irregularities, including the use of English-only procedures in the polls to disenfranchise Spanish-speaking Puerto Rican voters.

In 1974, before the federal government could act on the voter complaints, the state legislature enacted several remedial measures. "In election districts in which the primary language of 10% or more of the registered voters is Spanish"[96] the county was required to: (1) "appoint two additional members who shall be of Hispanic origin and fluent in Spanish";[97] (2) print sample ballots bilingually in English and Spanish and mail them to each registered voter;[98] and (3) post bilingual sample ballots or instructions in each polling place.[99] A separate law required preparation of bilingual primary sample ballots in all counties in which the primary language of 10 percent or more of the registered voters is Spanish.[100] These actions satisfied the Justice Department for the Hoboken complaints. However, in 1976 the State of New Jersey agreed to additional statewide relief to secure equal registration and voting opportunities for all Puerto Ricans under Section 4(e) of the VRA.[101]

New Mexico The broadest state protections for non-English-speaking citizens are a legacy of New Mexico's Spanish history. Following the Mexican-American War in 1848, Mexico ceded vast territory to the United States, including all of what is now California, Nevada, and Utah, most of Arizona, and parts of Colorado, New Mexico, and Wyoming. That territory included approximately 75,000 Spanish-speaking people, 60,000 of whom lived in what is now New Mexico. In the region, Spanish was the primary language, and the dominant culture was a combination of Indian, Mexican, and Spanish influences. As a result of the Treaty of Guadalupe Hidalgo of February 2, 1848, all Mexican nationals who remained were granted United States citizenship and were guaranteed certain civil, political, and religious rights.[102] By 1863, when Arizona and New Mexico became separate territories, about 50 percent of New Mexico's total population was Spanish-speaking (U.S. Comm'n on Civil Rts. 1972: 77).

---

94 *See* Manuel Maldonado-Denis, The Emigration Dialectic: Puerto Rico and the USA 137 (Int'l Publishers, New York 1980).

95 City of Hoboken, *Hoboken Today: How Do We Compare?* 1 (July 2002), *available at* http://www.cityofhoboken.com/July18factsheet.pdf (last visited Aug. 6, 2008).

96 S.B. 890 ch. 30 (approved May 28, 1974).

97 N.J. Stat. Ann. § 19:6–1 (1974).

98 N.J. Stat. Ann. §§ 19:14–21, 19:14–25 (1974).

99 N.J. Stat. Ann. § 19:49–4 (1974).

100 N.J. Stat. Ann. § 19:23–22.4 (1974).

101 *See Marquez v. Falcey*, Consent Order, Civil No. 1447–73 (D.N.J. June 29, 1976).

102 U.S. Comm'n on Civil Rts., The Excluded Student: Educational Practices Affecting Mexican Americans in the Southwest 76 (May 1972).

Protection of the dominant Spanish-language population proved to be a wedge for statehood. In 1906, Congress passed a joint statehood bill, requiring voters in the predominantly "American" Territory of Arizona and the predominately Spanish and Mexican Territory of New Mexico to agree to the same terms. Arizona protested, citing "[t]he decided racial difference between the people of New Mexico who are not only different in race and largely in language, but have entirely different customs, laws and ideals." Arizona declined to submit "to the probability of control of public affairs" by New Mexico's population, "many of whom do not speak the English language, and who outnumber the people of Arizona two to one." New Mexico had several other marked differences with its neighbor to the west. "[T]he New Mexico courts and legislature were conducted through interpreters; … New Mexico published its statutes in two languages; … and … the Spanish-speaking New Mexicans would not consent to the loss of their right to serve on juries" in which English was required (U.S. Comm'n on Civil Rts. 1972: 77). A 1910 enabling act passed by Congress would have required the state constitutions of both territories to eliminate bilingual education and make English a prerequisite for holding state office (U.S. Comm'n on Civil Rts. 1972: 78). New Mexico rejected both requirements.

In 1911, New Mexico completed its draft constitution, which included three sections guaranteeing the rights of Spanish-speaking citizens.[103] The most important of those provided:

> The right of any citizen of the state to vote, hold office, or sit upon juries, shall never be restricted, abridged, or impaired on account of religion, race, language or color, or inability to speak, read or write the English or Spanish languages as may be otherwise provided in this Constitution …[104]

Congress acquiesced to the section, deleting the conflicting provision of the enabling act. Representative George Legare of South Carolina explained:

> These people come to us from New Mexico, both Republicans and Democrats and say that in the Enabling Act passed last year we have taken them by the throat and told them that they must enact an irrevocable ordinance whereby no Spanish-speaking person can hold office in their State. They tell us, both factions, that some of the best people of their State and some of their most brilliant men are Spanish-speaking people (U.S. Comm'n on Civil Rts. 1972: 80).

The Constitution further required that for 20 years following its enactment, all state laws were to be published in Spanish and English.[105]

New Mexico enacted several laws to facilitate language assistance for elections. Prior to 1967, a law provided that notices of statewide and county elections "may be printed in Spanish."[106] Another provision required the use of bilingual ballots in English and Spanish for all state constitutional amendments.[107] In counties, cities, and towns in which the population was 75 percent or more Spanish-speaking, all official publications of the proceedings of public bodies

103 The other two constitutional provisions required teachers to become proficient in English and Spanish to be able to teach Spanish-speaking students and guaranteed children of Spanish descent would receive equal educations and would not be segregated from other students. *See* N.M. Const. art. XII, §§ 8, 10 (1912).

104 N.M. Const. art. VII, § 3 (1912).

105 N.M. Const. art. XX, § 12 (1912).

106 N.M. Stat. Ann. §§ 3-3-1, 3–11–15 (repealed by 1967 N.M. Laws ch. 98, § 30).

107 N.M. Stat. Ann. § 3–16–5 (1953) (codified as amended at N.M. Stat. Ann. § 1–16–5). The statute was amended to provide that all ballots proposing constitutional amendments "shall be in the form prescribed

were to be in Spanish. In communities with a Spanish-speaking population between 25 percent and 75 percent, the publications were to be in both English and Spanish.[108] Applicants "unable to read and write either the English or Spanish language" were entitled to assistance from voting registrars in the completion of a voter registration form.[109] A voter who "is a member of a language minority who has an inability to read well enough to exercise the elective franchise" was entitled to language assistance on Election Day.[110] Separate provisions authorized voter assistance for any voter requesting assistance who "is a member of a language minority."[111] According to the Justice Department survey, the Secretary of State's office provided, as a regular practice, sample bilingual ballots published in local newspapers in both English and Spanish and posted in each precinct throughout the state.

Conclusion

The VRA's ban on literacy tests for voting, which was extended nationwide in 1970, was an important step in removing barriers for many voters who could not read English. However, standing alone, the ban proved to be insufficient to provide millions of non-English-speaking language minority voters with equal access to the political process. The ban did not require election officials to undertake affirmative efforts to provide assistance in languages other than English. Although those voters were no longer barred from registering to vote because of their lack of English literacy, it was a hallow remedy because in most jurisdictions, all election materials were written in English.

Limited remedies were available prior to 1975. Courts increasingly required that illiterate and non-English-speaking voters be allowed to receive assistance if it was needed to allow them to cast an informed ballot. Section 2 of the VRA was applied in a handful of federal court cases to compel election officials to provide language assistance for language minority voters. Some states adopted their own language assistance statutes, but most of those laws were limited in scope and were only sporadically enforced. Section 4(e) of the VRA and the cases interpreting it would provide some of the strongest relief in terms of bilingual written materials and assistance. Although Section 4(e) is a permanent provision, it only applied to Spanish-speaking Puerto Rican voters and not millions of other language minority U.S. citizens who had experienced comparable discrimination or barriers to registering or voting.

Nevertheless, taken together, the experience of those remedies was essential to shaping the contours of the temporary language assistance provisions that would be included in the 1975 amendments to the VRA. The limitations of voter assistance would highlight the need for a separate federal law requiring language assistance. State laws using a numerical formula would provide the framework that would be used in the triggering formula for Section 203 coverage. Section 4(e) and the court decisions interpreting it identified the basic standards of oral and written language assistance that would be included in Section 203. Finally, pervasive discrimination against language minority voters in some jurisdictions would provide the impetus for modifying the formula under Section 4 of the VRA. Congress would use that evidence to revise the trigger for

---

by the secretary of state," removing an explicit requirement for bilingual ballots. *See* N.M. Stat. Ann. § 1–16–5.

108 N.M. Stat. Ann. § 14–11–11 (1915).

109 N.M. Stat. Ann. § 3–4–5 (1953) (codified as amended at N.M. Stat. Ann. § 1–4–5).

110 N.M. Stat. Ann. § 3–12–29 (1953) (codified as amended at N.M. Stat. Ann. § 1–12–12).

111 N.M. Stat. Ann. §§ 3–12–30, 3–12–31 (1953) (codified as amended at N.M. Stat. Ann. §§ 1–12–13, 1–12–15, respectively).

the special provisions of the Act to include use of English-only election procedures that resulted in depressed political participation. That will be discussed in the next chapter.

PART II
THE LANGUAGE ASSISTANCE AMENDMENTS TO THE VOTING RIGHTS ACT

Chapter 3
Special Protections for Language Minority Voters since 1975

The protections available to language minority voters before 1975 proved inadequate. The VRA's nationwide ban on literacy tests was temporary and did not fully remedy the effects of discriminatory schooling on non-English-speaking voters. Requirements for bilingual election materials and assistance under Section 4(e) of the Act were only available to citizens schooled in Puerto Rico. Court decisions requiring that voters be allowed to receive assistance at the polls did little to alleviate the situation. Instead, they shifted the burden to the victims of unequal educational opportunities to obtain the help they needed to cast an informed ballot. Moreover, election officials often denied the right to receive assistance because it conflicted with local procedures, they claimed it promoted vote fraud, or it simply was unavailable under state law. Of 17 states without voter assistance laws, 11 had substantial language minority populations and were among the first to be covered by the bilingual election provisions in 1975.[1]

State and local governments did not fill the gap in federal remedies. The Senate Judiciary Committee observed:

> Despite the evidence of high illiteracy rates for language minority citizens, states and local areas continue to adhere to uniform language assistance.... [T]he practice of conducting registration and voting only in English does impede the political participation of voters whose usual language is not English. The failure of states and local jurisdictions to provide adequate bilingual registration and election materials and assistance undermines the voting rights of non-English-speaking citizens and effectively excludes otherwise qualified voters from participating in elections (S. Rep. No. 94–295, 1975: 30).

Just a handful of jurisdictions offered bilingual materials and assistance. Some did so only under threat of federal action. New Jersey enacted its bilingual election procedures in 1974 to stave off a Justice Department investigation of discrimination against Puerto Rican voters in Hoboken. The Texas legislature passed a bilingual election bill "in great haste" right before Congress began holding hearings in 1975, "upon learning that Texas [might] be included under the Voting Rights Act of 1965."[2] In California, language assistance laws only came after a court order struck down the state's English literacy test in 1970.[3] Even in New Mexico, which adopted some bilingual election procedures, the laws were deficient. State election officials admitted that only a portion of the ballot was available in Spanish,[4] and there was no requirement for language assistance for the large native population. The state also decided in 1969 that it "did not need bilingual ballots," leaving

---

1 S. Rep. No. 94–295 at 39 (1975).

2 121 Cong. Rec. H4748 (daily ed. June 2, 1975) (statement of Rep. Conyers).

3 *See Castro v. State*, 466 P.2d 244 (Cal. 1970).

4 *See* 121 Cong. Rec. S13591 (daily ed. July 24, 1975) (statement of Sen. Domenici) (quoting statement of New Mexico Attorney General Toney Anaya).

Congress to "tell New Mexico that they have to have them."[5] More needed to be done to overcome the crippling effects of illiteracy in English on language minority voters, and the states were not up to the task.

The discriminatory effects of inadequate bilingual election laws were compounded by more direct forms of voting discrimination against non-English-speaking voters. Congress focused the 1975 reauthorization on solving the disenfranchisement of Spanish-speaking voters in Texas, particularly those of Mexican descent.[6] However, Congress also considered evidence of discrimination against other language minority groups.[7]

> Described were instances where the inability to speak English served to deter … the registration and voting efforts of language minority citizens. Election officials who speak only English and election materials printed only in the English language effectively exclude such citizens from the electoral process. Also related were instances of discriminatory districting plans, discriminatory annexations, and acts of physical and economic intimidation when language minority citizens do in fact attempt to participate. The entire situation in these uncovered jurisdictions is tragically reminiscent of the … problems experienced by blacks in currently covered areas.[8]

Congress found that "voting discrimination against citizens of language minorities is pervasive and national in scope" and was combined with educational discrimination "resulting in severe disabilities and continuing illiteracy in the English language."[9] Congress declared that, "in order to enforce the guarantees of the fourteenth and fifteenth amendments to the United States Constitution, it is necessary to eliminate such discrimination by prohibiting English-only elections, and by prescribing other remedial devices."[10]

Congress did so by broadening the VRA's special coverage to encompass language minorities (S. Rep. No. 94–295, 1975: 24), the "excluded citizens … waiting in the wings" since 1965.[11] Non-English-speaking voters were provided with "the same protection" already available for other citizens under the Act, including Spanish-speaking Puerto Ricans and African-Americans in the South.[12] As one member explained, "Extension of voting rights coverage to these minorities will enable them to begin achieving the same gains that blacks have begun to realize since the 1965 law."[13]

In 1975, Congress made the nationwide ban on literacy tests permanent and expanded the Act by including a temporary bilingual election mandate and special coverage for language minorities in jurisdictions meeting designated criteria.[14] The bilingual election provisions originally were to

---

5 121 CONG. REC. S13588 (daily ed. July 24, 1975) (statement of Sen. Domenici).

6 *See* David H. Hunter, *The 1975 Voting Rights Act and Language Minorities*, 25 CATH. U. L. REV. 250, 254–57 (1976); S. Rep. No. 94–295, 1975: 25–30.

7 *See* S. Rep. No. 94–295, 1975: 24–31, 37–39; 121 CONG. REC. H4709–13, H4716–18 (daily ed. June 2, 1975) (statement of Rep. Edwards).

8 121 CONG. REC. H4711 (daily ed. June 2, 1975) (statement of Rep. Rodino).

9 42 U.S.C. § 1973b(f)(1); *see also* 42 U.S.C. § 1973aa-1a(a) (stating the legislative intent for Section 203 of the Voting Rights Act).

10 42 U.S.C. § 1973b(f)(1).

11 121 CONG. REC. H4711 (daily ed. June 2, 1975) (statement of Rep. Rodino).

12 121 CONG. REC. H4737 (daily ed. June 2, 1975) (statement of Rep. Badillo).

13 121 CONG. REC. H4830 (daily ed. June 3, 1975) (statement of Rep. Kastenmeier).

14 *See* Voting Rights Act Amendments of 1975, Pub. L. No. 94–73, 89 Stat. 400 (codified as amended in scattered sections between 42 U.S.C. §§ 1973 to 1973bb-1).

be in effect for ten years, until August 6, 1985,[15] and were reauthorized in 1982, 1992, and 2006. This chapter begins the discussion of the VRA's remedies for language minority voters since 1975 by exploring the Act's special provisions.

The Nationwide Ban on Literacy Tests Is Made Permanent

In 1975, Congress relied on the evidence cited by Justice Douglas in *Oregon v. Mitchell* to make the nationwide ban on literacy tests in Section 201 of the Act permanent.[16] Congress rejected the main justification for the tests; namely, that literacy was necessary to promote an informed electorate. As the Senate Judiciary Committee explained, "It is difficult to see why citizens who cannot read or write should be prevented from participating in decisions that directly affect their environment, particularly in an era when radio and television are primary sources of information" (S. Rep. No. 94–295, 1975: 24). By 1975, only 14 states still used some form of literacy test. Six additional states repealed their tests following the enactment of the nationwide ban on literacy tests in 1970 (S. Rep. No. 94–295, 1975: 23).[17] None of the witnesses who testified during the Senate hearings opposed extending Section 201.

There were three reasons for making the nationwide ban on literacy tests permanent. First, there was substantial evidence that literacy tests were subject to discriminatory uses against minority groups (Chapters 1–2, 9). Second, Congress deemed it "patently unfair" for states to require a certain level of literacy of the same minority citizens for whom the states had denied educational opportunities (S. Rep. No. 94–295, 1975: 23):

> [U]nder the Supreme Court's decision in *Gaston County v. United States* ... any literacy test has a discriminatory effect if the State or county has offered its minority citizens inferior educational opportunities. It may be assumed that many minority citizens who have received inferior education in certain areas of the country migrate to Northern and Western States where literacy tests might be imposed. For this reason ... a nationwide test suspension would be appropriate to protect throughout the country the voting rights of minorities who had been unconstitutionally subjected to educational disparities.[18]

There was widespread educational discrimination outside the South, particularly in western states such as Alaska, Arizona, and California with large language minority populations. Finally, evidence developed since 1959, when the Supreme Court upheld North Carolina's literacy test in *Lassiter*, showed that literacy "tests are invalid under the Fourteenth Amendment because they are not justified by any compelling state interest" (S. Rep. No. 94–295, 1975: 23). During the House floor debate, an amendment offered to extend the literacy test ban for only ten years was defeated by a

15 *See* Pub. L. No. 94–73, § 301, 89 Stat. 402–03 (1975).

16 *See* 121 Cong. Rec. H4716 (daily ed. June 2, 1975) (statement of Rep. Edwards) (quoting Justice Douglas).

17 For a list of the 14 states, *see Extension of the Voting Rights Act of 1965: Hearings on S. 407, S. 903, S. 1297, S. 1409, and S. 1443 Before the Subcomm. on Constitutional Rts. of the House Comm. on the Judiciary, Part 1* (1975 House Hearings Part I), 94th Cong., 1st Sess., at 666 (1975) (Ex. 24 to statement of Asst. Att'y Gen. J. Stanley Pottinger).

18 121 Cong. Rec. H4715 (daily ed. June 2, 1975) (statement of Rep. Edwards).

vote of 89 to 318.[19] Section 201's permanent nationwide ban on literacy tests removed a substantial barrier to language minority voters.[20]

Language Groups Covered under the VRA's Special Provisions

The 1975 amendments expanded the VRA's special provisions to include language minority voters in addition to Puerto Ricans. Early on, the principal goal was to revise the triggering formula in Section 4 of the Act to include Texas. Unlike other southern states, Texas never used a literacy test to disenfranchise African-American and Spanish-speaking voters. As a result, it was not covered under Section 4 in either 1965 or 1970. Nevertheless, like its neighboring states, Texas had "a long history of discriminating against members of both minority groups in ways similar to the myriad forms of discrimination practiced against blacks in the South" (S. Rep. No. 94–295, 1975: 25). Those practices included the infamous White Primary, which excluded all non-white voters from the Democratic Party primary elections that effectively chose nearly all of the state's elected officials.[21] Texas officials also used other measures to bar minorities from voting, including the poll tax, "the most restrictive voter registration procedures in the nation" to replace the poll tax when it was struck down, and other obstacles to "frighten, discourage, frustrate, or otherwise inhibit" their political participation (S. Rep. No. 94–295, 1975: 25–26).

Although the record for Spanish-speaking voters in Texas was among the strongest, there was "substantial" evidence that other language groups likewise suffered from the twin burdens of English illiteracy and voting discrimination. Assistant Attorney General J. Stanley Pottinger, the head of the Justice Department's Civil Rights Division responsible for enforcing the VRA, testified about the problem's scope. The Civil Rights Division had participated in 97 civil suits and 14 criminal prosecutions on behalf of Spanish-speaking voters, American Indians, and Asian Americans (S. Rep. No. 94–295, 1975: 30–31). The U.S. Commission on Civil Rights[22] and other witnesses confirmed the problem's extent (S. Rep. No. 94–295, 1975: 24). Additional evidence is described in Chapter 9. Based upon that record, Pottinger asked that the VRA be amended to include "Asian Americans, native Americans, Puerto Ricans and Mexican-Americans, and other Americans of Latin American origin" (1975 House Hearings Part I: 289). Congress adopted Pottinger's recommendation.[23]

As part of the 1975 amendments, the VRA was modified to include "language minorities," defined as "persons who are American Indian, Asian American, Alaskan Natives or of Spanish heritage."[24] The same definition applied to both the special provisions under Section 4(f)(4) and the bilingual election provisions under Section 203, which are discussed later in this chapter and in

19 *See* Roll No. 253, 121 Cong. Rec. H4824 (daily ed. June 3, 1975).

20 *See* Title I of the 1975 extension of the Voting Rights Act of 1965, Pub. L. No. 94–73, 89 Stat. 400, § 102 (codified as amended at 42 U.S.C. § 1973aa (1975)).

21 *See Terry v. Adams*, 345 U.S. 461 (1953); *Smith v. Allwright*, 321 U.S. 649 (1944); *Grovey v. Townsend*, 295 U.S. 45 (1935); *Nixon v. Herndon*, 273 U.S. 356 (1927).

22 *See* U.S. Comm'n on Civil Rts., The Voting Rights Act: Ten Years After 22–25, 57–59, 85–87, 97–99, 103–04, 108–11, 114–21, 123, 144, 160, 166, 220–30, 242–48, 251–54, 331–32 (1975), *reprinted in Extension of the Voting Rights Act of 1965: Hearings on S. 407, S. 903, S. 1297, S. 1409, and S. 1443 Before the Subcomm. on Constitutional Rts. of the House Comm. on the Judiciary, Part II* (1975 House Hearings Part II), at 969–1466 (1975).

23 *See* 121 Cong. Rec. H4737 (daily ed. June 2, 1975) (statement of Rep. Badillo).

24 42 U.S.C. § 1973l(c)(3).

Chapter 4.[25] There were extensive debates in 1975 on three issues: the language groups that were covered, how that coverage was to be determined, and parochial efforts to exclude certain language minority groups. During the 2006 reauthorization of the VRA, there were unsuccessful efforts to expand coverage to include other language minority groups experiencing discrimination.

The Covered Language Groups

The four language minority groups were selected for several reasons. Each group suffered from voting discrimination and language barriers that limited participation in the political process. In most cases, "these language barriers were the result of unequal educational opportunities having been afforded these citizens."[26] The effect of that discrimination was profound:

> Of all Spanish heritage citizens over 25 years old, more than 18 percent have not completed 5 years of education – the level generally said to be necessary to achieve literacy in English – compared to 5.5 percent for the total U.S. population… In Texas, more than 33 percent of the Mexican-American population has not completed the fifth primary grade. American Indians, Alaskan Natives and Asian Americans have similar language difficulties. The illiteracy rate among Chinese-Americans is 16.2 percent; among American Indians, 15.5 percent; among Anglos, 4.5 percent …[27]

As much as 90 percent of Spanish heritage citizens in counties along the Rio Grande River in Texas and half of Spanish heritage citizens in Dallas, Fort Worth, and Houston only spoke and wrote in Spanish. Statewide in Texas, 90 percent of the Mexican-American population spoke Spanish at home. Nationwide, nearly half of all Spanish heritage citizens spoke Spanish with only a limited oral and written understanding of English. Among Alaska Natives, nearly all of the 17,000 Central Yup'ik Eskimos and over half of Inupiaq Eskimos spoke a non-English language at home. Similar percentages existed for many American Indian tribes, such as the Navajo, and for Asian American voters.

That data showed that members of the four language groups "generally suffer from severe language barriers" because of their high rate of English illiteracy.[28] Moreover, largely because of language barriers, members of the four language groups had depressed voter registration and turnout, as shown by data for Spanish heritage voters (S. Rep. No. 94–295, 1975: 30–31). In every presidential election between 1960 and 1972, voter turnout in Texas was consistently below 50 percent of the voting age population (S. Rep. No. 94–295, 1975: 25). In 1972, only 44.4 percent of Spanish heritage citizens were registered to vote, compared to 73.4 percent of non-Hispanic whites. Only 22.9 percent of Spanish heritage persons voted in the 1974 presidential election, less than half the rate for Anglos (S. Rep. No. 94–295, 1975: 30).

The 1975 amendments to the VRA were intended to remove these obstacles to voting. Father Robert Drinan, a Congressman from Massachusetts, described the Act's remedy. "While the ultimate solution for such language minorities is through the educational process, this bill would allow these citizens to vote now; they will not have to await some distant, indeterminate time when remedial

25 *See generally* 121 Cong. Rec. H4719 (daily ed. June 2, 1975) (statement of Rep. Edwards) (observing that Title III of the 1975 Amendments, which required bilingual voting materials and assistance, "covers the same language minorities as Title II" of the Amendments, which triggered the special provisions of the Act).

26 121 Cong. Rec. H4716 (daily ed. June 2, 1975) (statement of Rep. Edwards).

27 121 Cong. Rec. H4709 (daily ed. June 2, 1975) (statement of Rep. Young).

28 121 Cong. Rec. H4716 (daily ed. June 2, 1975) (statement of Rep. Edwards).

educational programs might furnish sufficient skills to comprehend the English-only elections."[29] Quoting *Katzenbach v. Morgan*, the Senate Judiciary Committee similarly concluded, "This bill rejects the notion that the 'denial of a right deemed so precious and fundamental in our society [is] a necessary or appropriate means of encouraging persons to learn English.'"[30] Congress provided a broader remedy than Section 4(e), "the provision sustained in *Morgan*, which was limited to one group." Instead, the 1975 Amendments "would enfranchise four principal language minorities: persons of Spanish heritage (including Puerto Ricans), American Indians, Alaskan Natives, and Asian Americans. These are the groups which, the evidence shows, have been subjected to voting discrimination" (S. Rep. No. 94–295, 1975: 36). It was estimated that more than six million language minorities would be protected under that definition.[31]

Efforts to limit coverage to Spanish During the House floor debate, Congressman Charles Wiggins of California offered a substitute bill that would have covered "only blacks and browns."[32] The Wiggins substitute also would have amended the Section 4 coverage formula by providing that the special provisions of the Act would be triggered where African-Americans or persons of Spanish heritage comprised more than 5 percent of the population, and 50 percent of those minorities did not vote in the previous federal election. Under the Wiggins substitute, the special provisions only would be in place until the next federal election. Wiggins claimed that there was "clear" evidence of discrimination against "Negroes and those of Spanish heritage," but that a "compelling case has not been made with respect to others."[33] Similarly, Congressman Robert McClory of Illinois claimed there was no evidence "that Asian Americans, Alaskan Natives, or other persons are unable to understand the English language."[34]

Other members rebuffed their arguments, citing the lack of English literacy and depressed registration and turnout rates of language minorities resulting from educational and voting discrimination. As Father Drinan explained, "the statistics with regard to Asian Americans, native Americans and Native Alaskans demonstrate precisely the same thing" as the "very significant facts indicating that blacks had not been allowed to vote."[35] Efforts to limit the amendment to Spanish did not reflect a sincere desire to provide language assistance to just one group, but to kill the entire bill. The Wiggins substitute was rejected by a vote of 134 to 269.[36] Congressman M. Caldwell Butler of Virginia announced his intention to remove American Indians and Asian Americans from coverage, but he did not introduce his amendment after it became clear that it would fail.[37]

Efforts to expand coverage to all languages Two Democratic members from New York attempted to expand coverage to all language minority groups. Congressman Mario Biaggi offered an amendment that would have applied to any group "whose principal spoken language is other than English." He argued against "a restrictive approach which leaves people outside" of the definition of language minority "to struggle for themselves," citing Albanians, Greeks, and Italians. Instead, Biaggi proposed a definition that would not "eliminate other groups in

29 121 Cong. Rec. H4734 (daily ed. June 2, 1975).

30 S. Rep. No. 94–295, 1975: 34 (quoting *Katzenbach v. Morgan*, 384 U.S. 641, 655 (1966)).

31 121 Cong. Rec. H4756 (daily ed. June 2, 1975) (statement of Rep. Clay).

32 121 Cong. Rec. H4739 (daily ed. June 2, 1975).

33 121 Cong. Rec. H4741 (daily ed. June 2, 1975).

34 121 Cong. Rec. H4747 (daily ed. June 2, 1975).

35 121 Cong. Rec. H4826 (daily ed. June 3, 1975).

36 Roll No. 250, 121 Cong. Rec. H4806 (daily ed. June 3, 1975).

37 121 Cong. Rec. H4884 (daily ed. June 4, 1975).

the future" by including "all Americans."[38] Congressman Stephen Solarz sponsored a similar amendment, which would have covered language minorities who were at least 5 percent of a jurisdiction's population with an illiteracy rate above the national average. Solarz argued that "fundamental fairness" required that other language minorities sought to receive "bilingual ballots," regardless of whether they were "French Americans in Louisiana, German Americans in Wisconsin, Italian Americans in Rhode Island, or Yiddish-speaking Americans in Brooklyn."[39] Both amendments were rejected.[40] During the Senate floor debate, Senator John Tunney explained that the bill would have no impact on non-covered language minority groups, such as the Yiddish-speaking community in New York, who might receive language assistance in areas other than voting.[41]

The Senate Judiciary Committee considered including other language groups, but declined to do so for three reasons. First, it found that the illiteracy of Alaska Natives, American Indians, Asian Americans, and persons of Spanish heritage was "a product of racially discriminatory educational systems" (S. Rep. No. 94–295, 1975: 38). Immigrants from European countries "did not confront these problems," except, perhaps, in isolated cases.[42]

Second, although the Committee had been presented with "substantial" evidence of "discrimination and non-responsiveness" towards the four language groups, it had not received any "evidence of difficulties for other language groups." That fact was borne out by voter participation rates in the 1972 presidential election. Only 44.4 percent of Latinos were registered to vote, compared to 79 percent of Germans, 77.5 percent of Italians, 76.7 percent of Irish, 72.7 percent of French, 79.8 percent of Polish, and 85.7 percent of Russians. A similar pattern emerged for voter turnout. Just 37.5 percent of registered Latinos voted, compared to 70.8 percent of Germans, 71.5 percent of Italians, 66.6 percent of Irish, 63.2 percent of French, 72 percent of Polish, and 80.5 percent of Russians. This "high degree of participation by other language groups" simply did not support their coverage. Nevertheless, the Committee "encourage[d] states and political subdivisions to assist other ethnic groups in voting and registration" (S. Rep. No. 94–295, 1975: 38).

Third, the Committee found that the "historical experience" of the four covered language groups was "far different from the European immigrants": For the most part, the Spanish heritage, American Indian and Alaska Native groups were living on territory suddenly annexed by the United States; in most cases their ancestors had been living on the same land for centuries. These groups stayed on their original lands after the annexation, and while mobility certainly existed within their own cultures, opportunity for mobility within the European-dominated American culture was often denied them, most frequently by poor educational institutions and unresponsive political institutions. Important decisions of direct consequence to them were often made without their participation.

Congress was "obligated to intervene" on behalf of the four language groups because state and local election officials had been "disturbingly unresponsive" to those problems (S. Rep. No. 94–295, 1975: 38–39). Other language groups were not included because there was no evidence that they experienced similar difficulties in voting (S. Rep. No. 94–295, 1975: 31).

Congress wisely limited the definition of "language minority" to only those groups that had been victimized by discrimination. Expanding coverage to all language groups likely would

38 121 Cong. Rec. H4893–94 (daily ed. June 4, 1975).

39 121 Cong. Rec. H4905 (daily ed. June 4, 1975).

40 *See* 121 Cong. Rec. H4896 (daily ed. June 4, 1975) (rejecting Biaggi amendment 156 to 253); 121 Cong. Rec. H4905 (daily ed. June 4, 1975) (rejecting Solarz amendment 36 to 73).

41 121 Cong. Rec. S13372 (daily ed. July 23, 1975).

42 121 Cong. Rec. H4895 (daily ed. June 4, 1975) (statement of Rep. Badillo).

have rendered the bilingual election provisions unconstitutional. The Supreme Court decisions upholding bans on literacy tests did so because they were the products of intentional discrimination, were unfairly administered, or had a discriminatory effect on minority voters. Unequal educational opportunities exacerbated disenfranchisement of racial, ethnic, and language minorities. Without that evidence, it was less apparent that Congress could exercise its powers under the Enforcement Sections of the Fourteenth and Fifteenth Amendments. Although a narrower definition was necessary, it did have one negative effect. It erected a barrier to later non-English-speaking groups, such as Arabic-speakers and Haitian-Creoles, who were victims of discrimination in education, voting, and other areas after 1975.

Application of the Language Minority Definition

Congress intended to use the Census Bureau's definitions for each of the four language groups.[43] When the 1975 amendments were enacted, the Bureau defined the language minority groups in the following manner:

> [T]he category of Asian American includes persons who indicated their race as Japanese, Chinese, Filipino, or Korean. The category of American Indian includes persons who indicated their race as Indian (American) or who did not indicate a specific race category but reported the name of an Indian tribe. The population designated as Alaskan Native includes persons residing in Alaska who identified themselves as Aleut, Eskimo or American Indian. Persons of Spanish heritage are identified as (a) "persons of Spanish language" in 42 States and the District of Columbia; (b) "persons of Spanish language" as well as "persons of Spanish surname" in Arizona, California, Colorado, New Mexico, and Texas; and (c) "persons of Puerto Rican birth or parentage in New Jersey, New York, and Pennsylvania."[44]

At the time, the Census Bureau also included Hawaiians in the Asian American category, but they were excluded as covered language minorities because "the Hawaiian language is seldom, if ever, used."[45] Effective for the 2000 Census, the Census Bureau placed Hawaiian in a separate category called "Native Hawaiian and Other Pacific Islander," which includes "Native Hawaiian," "Samoan," and "Guamanian or Chamorro."[46] The way the Census Bureau defines language minority groups and determines their numbers was subject to criticism from some members in 1975.[47] However, efforts to change the language minority definition were unsuccessful.[48]

Parochial Efforts to Exclude Alaska Natives

One of the most concerted efforts to change the scope of covered language minority groups in 1975 came from Alaska's lone representative in the House. Congressman Don Young proposed

---

43 *See* 121 Cong. Rec. H4716 (daily ed. June 2, 1975) (statement of Rep. Edwards).

44 S. Rep. No. 94–295, 1975: 24 n.14 (quoting Letter from Meyer Zitter, Chief, Population Division, Bureau of the Census, to House Judiciary Committee, Apr. 29, 1975).

45 *See* 121 Cong. Rec. H4716 (daily ed. June 2, 1975) (statement of Rep. Edwards).

46 *See* Bureau of the Census, Economics and Statistics Admin., U.S. Dep't of Commerce, The Native Hawaiian and Other Pacific Islander Population: 2002 (Dec. 2001).

47 *See* 121 Cong. Rec. H4738 (daily ed. June 2, 1975) (statement of Rep. Goldwater); 121 Cong. Rec. H4812 (daily ed. June 3, 1975) (statement of Rep. Frenzel).

48 *See* 42 U.S.C. §§ 1973b(b), 1973b(f)(3), 1973l(c)(3), 1973aa-1a(b)(4).

an amendment to delete the term "Alaska Natives" from the bill. As part of his efforts, Young misrepresented Alaska's discriminatory election practices. Alaska enacted its first English literacy test in 1925, when it was still a territory, after a candidate supported by Alaska Natives was elected in 1924. After statehood, Alaska adopted an English literacy test in its state constitution, which it did not repeal until August 1970, two months after Congress banned literacy tests nationwide (Chapter 9). That was hardly evidence of what Congressman Young characterized as a state that was "one of the most progressive in the Union, where voting rights are concerned."[49] Instead, like so many other states with English literacy tests, Alaska eliminated its discriminatory practice only after federal law required it to do so.

Young correctly noted that the Justice Department had twice consented to Alaska bailing out from coverage in 1966 and 1971. However, Assistant Attorney General Pottinger asked that Alaska Natives be included as covered language minorities following revelations of the extent of the State's educational discrimination.[50] The Senate Judiciary Committee found that Alaska Native students were not offered any secondary schooling by the state, citing the landmark *Molly Hootch* case in its Committee report (S. Rep. No. 94–295, 1975: 29; Chapter 9). Pottinger therefore suggested that the burden should be placed on Alaska to prove to a federal court that the Act's special protections should not apply to it based upon its actual record.[51] Following its renewed coverage in 1975, Alaska did not meet its burden, failing in two separate attempts to show the absence of discrimination against Alaska Natives.

Congressman Young also understated the need for language assistance in Alaska. He argued, "Although there are many Eskimo and Indian dialects, English is the only language spoken and understood by all minority groups." He further represented that the only people who spoke the Alaska Native dialects were "bilingualists and some people at the University of Alaska." In the process, Congressman Young suggested that providing language assistance in his state would "cause a burden upon the Alaska natives who themselves do not want to be included in the act."[52] His contentions were rebutted by another member of Alaska's congressional delegation, Senator Mike Gravel, who acknowledged that there were tens of thousands of non-English-speaking Alaska Natives.[53] The House rejected Congressman Young's parochial efforts to remove Alaska Natives from the definition of language minority by a vote of 145 to 264.[54]

Efforts to Broaden the Definition of Language Minorities in 2006

During the 2006 reauthorization of the VRA, some civil rights advocates asked Congress to broaden the definition of language minority to include two other language groups. Professor Jocelyn Friedrichs Benson and at least one student commentator proposed that Arab Americans

49 121 Cong. Rec. H4807–09 (daily ed. June 3, 1975).

50 *See* 1975 House Hearings Part I: 289 (testimony of Asst. Att'y Gen. J. Stanley Pottinger); 121 Cong. Rec. H4737 (daily ed. June 2, 1975) (statement of Rep. Badillo).

51 121 Cong. Rec. H4807 (daily ed. June 3, 1975) (statement of Rep. Young) (quoting letter from Asst. Att'y Gen. J. Stanley Pottinger).

52 121 Cong. Rec. H4807 (daily ed. June 3, 1975).

53 *See Extension of the Voting Rights Act of 1965: Hearings on S. 407, S. 903, S. 1297, S. 1409, and S. 1443 Before the Subcomm. on Constitutional Rts. of the Senate Comm. on the Judiciary* [1975 Senate Hearings], 94th Cong., 1st Sess., at 531 (1975).

54 *See* Roll No. 255, 121 Cong. Rec. H4829 (daily ed. June 3, 1975).

be included (Chapter 11).[55] The Census Bureau does not consider Arabic as an "Asian" language, instead classifying it as part of "All other languages."[56]

Benson made an especially strong case for Arab American citizens, citing evidence of education and voting discrimination against them. One example in particular stood out. In November 1999, Arabic U.S. citizens in Hamtramck, Michigan were targeted for disenfranchisement by partisan workers after an Arab American announced his candidacy for mayor. A group of non-Arab voters formed an organization called "Citizens for Better Hamtramck" to register individuals to be present in polling places to challenge the citizenship of voters who "looked" Arab, had dark skin such as Bengali voters, or who had distinctly Arab or Muslim names. Intimidation by the partisan workers resulted in substantially depressed voter participation by members of the Arab and Bengali communities, which was worsened by the lack of poll workers from those communities. After the Justice Department sued, the city was placed under federal oversight, including monitoring by non-partisan federal observers.[57] Even then, Hamtramck election officials failed to recruit Arabic-speaking poll workers as required by the consent decree (Benson 2007: 366; Chapter 11).

Similarly, Professor JoNel Newman described voting discrimination suffered by Haitian-Creole voters in south Florida.[58] Like Arabic-speakers, Haitian-Creoles were not included in one of the four categories of covered language minority groups. Instead, the Census Director includes them in the category of "Other Indo-European Languages," along with European languages like French, German, and Italian (Selected Appendixes 2000: B-30 to -31). But the differences between Haitian-Creole voters and other language groups classified as "European" is evident, particularly in terms of the tremendous disparity in voter participation rates. Congressional efforts in 1975 to ensure that the bilingual election provisions were constitutional unintentionally excluded language groups that could later show that discrimination impaired their political participation.

Attempts to correct this problem in 2006 were unsuccessful. House leadership rejected any proposed expansion to include new language groups because it would have jeopardized bipartisan support for the bill (Chapter 7). Arabic and Haitian-Creole voters were left to rely upon Section 2 of the VRA, the general non-discrimination provision, for any language assistance they received beyond what state and local election officials provided. While that offered some relief, it fell far short of the more comprehensive remedies available for the four covered language minority groups (Chapter 4).

Section 4(f)(4) and the VRA's Special Provisions

In 1975, there was overwhelming evidence of "a systematic pattern of voting discrimination and exclusion against minority group citizens who are from environments in which the dominant

---

55 *See* Jocelyn Benson, *Language Protections for All? Extending and Expanding the Language Protections of the Voting Rights Act*, *in* VOTING RIGHTS ACT REAUTHORIZATION OF 2006: PERSPECTIVES ON DEMOCRACY, PARTICIPATION, AND POWER 327, 353–73 (Ana Henderson ed. 2007); Brenda Fathy Abdelall, Note, *Not Enough of a Minority? Arab Americans and the Language Assistance Provisions (Section 203) of the Voting Rights Act*, 38 U. MICH. J. L. REFORM 911 (2005).

56 *See* U.S. CENSUS BUREAU, 2000 CENSUS OF POPULATION AND HOUSING, SELECTED APPENDIXES: 2000, at B-30 to -31, B-40 (June 2003) (SELECTED APPENDIXES 2000).

57 *See* Press Release, U.S. Department of Justice, *City of Hamtramck, Michigan to Revamp Election Procedures to Prevent Voter Discrimination Under Justice Department Settlement* (Aug. 4, 2000).

58 *See* JoNel Newman, *Unfinished Business: The Case for Continuing Special Voting Rights Act Coverage in Florida*, 61 MIAMI L. REV. 1, 32–37 (Oct. 2006)

language is other than English." Congress responded by modifying the VRA "to broaden its special coverage to new geographic areas in order to ensure the protection of the voting rights of 'language minority citizens'" (S. Rep. No. 94–295, 1975: 24). Coverage was added by applying "the Act's special remedies to jurisdictions where language minorities reside in greatest concentrations and where there is evidence of low voting participation" (S. Rep. No. 94–295, 1975: 32). The intent was "to maintain precisely the same structure," retaining a "trigger mechanism that is ... identical to the mechanism in the 1965 act."[59]

Congress did so through Title II of the 1975 Act, which expanded the existing triggering formula in Section 4 to apply to "those jurisdictions with the more serious problems" of voting discrimination against language minorities (S. Rep. No. 94–295, 1975: 31). Coverage was applied to areas "where severe voting discrimination was documented" (S. Rep. No. 94–295, 1975: 9). Specifically, "the more severe remedies ... are premised not only on educational disparities," like the less stringent provisions in Section 203 of the Act, "but also on evidence that language minorities have been subjected to 'physical, economic, and political intimidation' when they seek to participate in the political process."[60]

The Formula for Section 4(f)(4) Coverage

In the original 1965 Act, literacy tests or other devices were suspended in covered jurisdictions, primarily in the South, because they disenfranchised minority voters (Chapter 1). English-only elections had an effect similar to literacy tests on non-English-speaking voters. Language minorities were victims of longstanding and systemic educational discrimination. Asian Americans and Latinos in Arizona, California, and Texas received separate and unequal schooling.[61] Alaska Natives in Alaska and American Indians in the Desert Southwest often were denied schooling altogether (Chapter 9). In cases such as *Gaston County*, *Katzenbach v. Morgan*, and *South Carolina v. Katzenbach*, the United States Supreme Court acknowledged "the inextricable relationship between educational disparities and voting discrimination" (S. Rep. No. 94–295, 1975: 34; *see* Chapters 1–2). Language minority voters denied the opportunity to learn to speak and read English by state-sponsored educational discrimination were left unable to read English-only voting materials. Therefore, English-only elections barred language minority voters just as effectively as the English literacy tests that had been used to disenfranchise non-English speaking voters in states like Alaska, Arizona, California, and New York.

The formula for coverage under Section 4(f)(4) is "virtually identical" to the existing formula under Section 4(b), except that it expanded the term "test or device" to "also mean the use of English-only election materials in jurisdictions where more than 5 percent of the voting age citizen population is comprised of members of any single language minority group."[62] Like the VRA's existing bar on literacy tests and similar devices, "the purpose of suspending English-only and requiring bilingual elections is not to correct the deficiencies of prior educational inequality. It is to permit persons disabled by such disparities to vote now." The prohibition would "fill that hiatus until genuinely equal educational opportunities are afforded language minorities" that would allow

59 121 Cong. Rec. H4737 (daily ed. June 2, 1975) (statement of Rep. Badillo).

60 121 Cong. Rec. H4718 (daily ed. June 2, 1975) (statement of Rep. Edwards).

61 *See* James Thomas Tucker, *The Battle over Bilingual Ballots Shifts to the Courts: A Post-*Boerne *Assessment of Section 203 of the Voting Rights Act*, 45 Harv. J. on Legis. 507, 553–68 (2008).

62 121 Cong. Rec. H4716 (daily ed. June 2, 1975) (statement of Rep. Edwards).

them to understand election materials and information provided in English (S. Rep. No. 94–295, 1975: 34).

Adopting the existing formula in Section 4(b), coverage could be applied either statewide or to a political subdivision of a state. "Political subdivision" was defined as "any county or parish, except that where registration for voting is not conducted under the supervision of a county or parish, the term shall include any other subdivision of a State which conducts registration for voting."[63] When a political subdivision such as a county or parish is covered, "all political units that hold elections within that political subdivision (e.g., cities, school districts) are subject to the same requirements" under the Act as the political subdivision.[64]

The amended formula for language minorities provides that a state or political subdivision is covered if it meets three criteria: (1) more than 5 percent of the voting-age citizens on November 1, 1972, were members of a single language minority group;[65] (2) the Attorney General finds that "registration or voting notices, forms, instructions, assistance, or other materials or information relating to the electoral process, including ballots" were provided only in English on November 1, 1972;[66] and (3) the Director of the Census determines that fewer than 50 percent of voting-age citizens were registered to vote on November 1, 1972, or that fewer than 50 percent voted in the November 1972 Presidential election.[67]

During the 1975 debates, opponents attempted to scuttle the expanded protections for language minority voters. In an effort to render the VRA unconstitutional, some members proposed nationwide coverage. Others offered parochial amendments that would have removed their states entirely by raising the threshold for coverage. Alaska's congressional delegation attacked the application of "single language minority group" Alaska Natives, which resulted in statewide coverage there. Each of these efforts failed.

Efforts to Apply Coverage Nationwide

Congress adopted the triggering formula in Section 4(f)(4) to insure that the VRA's special temporary provisions only would apply to states and political subdivisions where "significant concentrations of minorities with native languages other than English reside" (S. Rep. No. 94–295, 1975: 9). But during congressional debates on the 1975 amendments, several members argued in favor of nationwide coverage rather than a triggering formula, which they viewed as arbitrary and resulted in covering jurisdictions with no history of discrimination against language minorities.

In the House, the defeated Wiggins substitute bill would have applied the VRA's special protections to any jurisdiction with voter turnout in a federal general election of less than 50 percent and an African-American or Spanish heritage citizen population of more than 5 percent.[68] That coverage would only last until the next federal general election. Congressman Wiggins asserted it was necessary to "improve" the VRA by providing that "the same law should apply elsewhere"

63 42 U.S.C. § 1973*l*(c)(2).

64 28 C.F.R. § 55.9.

65 *See* 42 U.S.C. § 1973b(f)(3).

66 *See* 42 U.S.C. §§ 1973b(b) and 1973b(f)(3); *see also* 42 U.S.C. § 1973b(b) (providing that coverage under the special provisions of the VRA requires a determination by the Attorney General that a state or political subdivision maintained on November 1, 1972 any "test or device").

67 *See* 42 U.S.C. § 1973b(b). Determinations by the Attorney General and Director of the Census under Section 4(f)(4) are not reviewable in any court and are effective upon publication in the Federal Register.

68 121 Cong. Rec. H4727 (daily ed. June 2, 1975) (statement of Rep. Butler).

regardless of whether a jurisdiction had ever used a test or device.[69] Members from southern states seeking to eliminate coverage in their own states, including Congressman Butler of Virginia, Walter Flowers of Alabama, and James Mann of South Carolina, supported his efforts.[70]

John Stennis of Mississippi offered a similar amendment in the Senate, saying it was supported by a request from President Ford "to extend the Voting Rights Act nationwide."[71] Supporters claimed that application of the Act's special protections to all jurisdictions was necessary "to protect, on a uniform basis, the rights of citizens to vote and not to have discrimination against them in the exercise of that right."[72] One of the amendment's most ardent supporters, Senator Strom Thurmond of South Carolina,[73] introduced other amendments to repeal the Section 4 trigger, eliminate the special protections of Section 5, and allow jurisdictions seeking to be removed from coverage to begin with a presumption of non-discrimination.[74] The primary purpose of the Stennis amendment was "to repeal section 4," thereby "gutting the Voting Rights Act."[75] Senator Kennedy explained that the proposal also was unconstitutional because it would "fail to reach down to meet the particular problems that have existed and do exist in the area of the right to vote."[76] The Stennis amendment was tabled by a vote of 58 to 38, despite support from every southern senator.[77] Similar amendments offered by the two senators from Georgia, Sam Nunn and Herman Talmadge, also were tabled.[78]

Congress rejected nationwide coverage for several reasons. As an initial matter, certain provisions of the VRA already applied nationwide. Section 2 of the Act could be enforced anywhere voters were the victims of discrimination on account of their race or language minority status (Chapter 2). In addition, a "pocket trigger" in Section 3(c) allowed a court to apply the Act's special provisions to any jurisdiction for an "appropriate time" if it found voting discrimination in violation of the Fourteenth or Fifteenth Amendments.[79] The pocket trigger later was applied to the states of Arkansas and New Mexico; Buffalo County, South Dakota; Escambia County, Florida, and Cicero, Illinois to stop voter disenfranchisement.[80] Section 3 therefore completed "the rest of the national coverage" by giving "the Attorney General the power to sue in situations which are not covered by the trigger" in Section 4 of the Act. In that way, the VRA "gives complete coverage to every person and every State."[81]

---

69 121 Cong. Rec. H4740 (daily ed. June 2, 1975).

70 *See* 121 Cong. Rec. H4727 (daily ed. June 2, 1975) (statement of Rep. Butler); 121 Cong. Rec. H4815 (daily ed. June 3, 1975) (statement of Rep. Mann); 121 Cong. Rec. H4902 (daily ed. June 4, 1975) (statement of Rep. Flowers).

71 121 Cong. Rec. S13379 (daily ed. July 23, 1975) (quoting letter from President Ford dated July 21, 1975).

72 121 Cong. Rec. S13393 (daily ed. July 23, 1975) (statement of Sen. Chiles).

73 *See* 121 Cong. Rec. S13398 (daily ed. July 23, 1975).

74 *See* 121 Cong. Rec. S13593, S13606, S13608 (daily ed. July 24, 1975). All of Thurmond's amendments were defeated.

75 121 Cong. Rec. S13395 (daily ed. July 23, 1975) (statement of Sen. Brooke).

76 121 Cong. Rec. S13389 (daily ed. July 23, 1975).

77 *See* Roll Vote No. 312, 121 Cong. Rec. S13399 (daily ed. July 23, 1975).

78 *See* Roll Vote No. 309, 121 Cong. Rec. S13363 (daily ed. July 22, 1975) (Talmadge amendment tabled by a vote of 46 to 38); Roll Vote No. 327, 121 Cong. Rec. S13662 (daily ed. July 24, 1975) (Nunn amendment tabled by a vote of 48 to 41).

79 42 U.S.C. § 1973a(c).

80 *See* Nat'l Comm'n on the Voting Rts. Act, Protecting Minority Voters: The Voting Rights Act at Work 1982–2005, at 34 (Feb. 2006).

81 121 Cong. Rec. S13394 (daily ed. July 23, 1975) (statement of Sen. Javits).

Furthermore, the formula for Section 4(f)(4) coverage used a trigger "essentially identical to the traditional trigger" found in Section 4(b), which already had proven effective in covering jurisdictions with a history of discriminating against African-Americans (S. Rep. No. 94–295, 1975: 32). Limited resources also made it impossible for the Attorney General to administer and enforce the Act effectively nationwide, which Senator Brooke explained would mean "we would not even have a Voting Rights Act."[82] Finally, nationwide coverage created the risk that the Section 4(f)(4) trigger would be unconstitutional because it would be broader than necessary to remedy discrimination against language minorities. Congressman Don Edwards of California, the House floor manager of the bill, observed that nationwide coverage "suffered from such a degree of overbroadness that it would destroy the bill" because it "would result in a coverage of over 40 States and 1,200 counties where there is no record of discrimination whatsoever."[83]

Despite the defeat of the Wiggins and Stennis proposals, similar attempts to impose nationwide coverage were made during subsequent reauthorizations of the VRA, including most recently in 2006 (Chapter 7). Efforts to modify coverage under the Act's special provisions to exclude specific states foundered, largely because the existing formula successfully identified jurisdictions that had discriminated against minority voters. The Supreme Court's decisions upholding the constitutionality of the formula also suggested no changes were needed.[84]

Proposed Local Changes to the Coverage Formula

During the Senate floor debate on the 1975 amendments, members from the Florida and New Mexico delegations offered two separate amendments to alter the Section 4(f)(4) formula. The proposals were intended to remove most, if not all, of the coverage in the senators' respective states.

The two senators from Florida proposed a change in the coverage formula for the language-assistance provisions from 5 percent to 10 percent. The senators were "aware that triggering percentages are common practices to be used in determining when there is a requirement for a bilingual ballot."[85] However, they maintained that a 10 percent formula was better, with Senator Richard Stone citing "the strength behind it of the New Jersey experience," where state law used that figure to target Spanish-language voting materials and assistance.[86] The proposal would have exempted four out of five Florida counties that would be covered by a 5 percent trigger, but the senators claimed it was necessary because there had not been any discrimination reported in those counties.[87] Senator Lawton Chiles further criticized the 5 percent trigger as being picked "out of the air" without any basis.[88]

Congress had adopted the 5 percent formula because it already was widely used among jurisdictions providing bilingual voting materials and assistance. The problem with a 10 percent

---

82 121 Cong. Rec. S13661 (daily ed. July 24, 1975).

83 121 Cong. Rec. H4895 (daily ed. June 4, 1975).

84 *See Lopez v. Monterey County*, 525 U.S. 266 (1999); *City of Rome v. United States*, 446 U.S. 156 (1980); *South Carolina v. Katzenbach*, 383 U.S. 301 (1966).

85 121 Cong. Rec. S13645–46 (daily ed. July 24, 1975) (statement of Sen. Chiles).

86 121 Cong. Rec. S13648 (daily ed. July 24, 1975) (statement of Sen. Stone); *see also* 121 Cong. Rec. S13646 (daily ed. July 24, 1975) (statement of Sen. Chiles).

87 The Florida jurisdictions that would have been exempted were Collier, Hardee, Hendry, and Hillsborough Counties. Monroe County would have remained as the only jurisdiction in Florida covered by Section 4(f)(4). *See* 121 Cong. Rec. S13645-6 (daily ed. July 24, 1975) (statement of Sen. Chiles).

88 121 Cong. Rec. S13645 (daily ed. July 24, 1975).

trigger was it failed to cover many areas where voting discrimination had occurred that would be covered under a 5 percent formula.[89] Senate Birch Bayh of Indiana explained that regardless of the numerical threshold used, "we are not going to be perfect. But in this area of trying to root out discrimination, I would rather go a little bit too far and be a little too protective than not protective enough."[90] The Chiles-Stone amendment was defeated by a vote of 28 to 58.[91]

Senator Pete Domenici made a similar effort to exclude all of New Mexico from coverage. Citing New Mexico's record of providing language assistance under state law and what he described as a lack of discrimination, he proposed a modified trigger to apply to all of the bilingual-election provisions. Domenici's amendment would have exempted from coverage any jurisdiction in which a single minority group comprised at least 25 percent of the membership of both houses of the state legislature, or 30 percent or greater aggregating all minority groups together. Senator Domenici acknowledged that New Mexico was the only state in which 30 percent or more of its legislators were minorities, meaning that the amendment effectively would only apply to his state.[92]

The senator's colleague from New Mexico, Joseph Montoya, opposed the Domenici amendment. Senator Montoya reasoned that "New Mexico and the three counties … included by the triggering formula have nothing to fear from inclusion" because if they were free from discrimination they could be removed by bailing out from coverage.[93] Senator Charles Mathias, Jr., of Maryland also tied his opposition to what he described as Domenici's "somewhat brittle test" to the effect it would have on other jurisdictions trying to bailout from coverage. According to Mathias, it improperly set up "a single criterion" for bailout, ignoring the Act's more comprehensive examination "of a State's political life … in terms of the broad purposes and the broad goals of the bill."[94]

The Domenici amendment was tabled by a vote of 68 to 27.[95] Senator Montoya's prediction proved accurate. Shortly after becoming covered under the newly enacted Section 4(f)(4) trigger, Curry, McKinley, and Otero Counties in New Mexico succeeded in being exempted from the VRA's special provisions, although they continued to be required to provide language assistance under Section 203.[96]

The Single Language Minority Requirement

Congressman Young's failed amendment to remove Alaska Natives from the definition of language minority group was not just an effort to eliminate coverage of Alaska. It also was a response to the modified formula for coverage under Section 4(f)(4)'s special provisions.[97] That formula applied if more than 5 percent of the voting-age citizens on November 1, 1972, were members of a "single language minority group."[98] Congressman Edwards described the meaning of that phrase:

---

89 121 Cong. Rec. S13649 (daily ed. July 24, 1975) (statement of Sen. Bayh).

90 121 Cong. Rec. S13651 (daily ed. July 24, 1975).

91 *See* Roll Vote No. 324, 121 Cong. Rec. S13652 (daily ed. July 24, 1975).

92 121 Cong. Rec. S13589–92 (daily ed. July 24, 1975).

93 121 Cong. Rec. S13449 (daily ed. July 23, 1975).

94 121 Cong. Rec. S13592 (daily ed. July 24, 1975).

95 *See* Roll Vote No. 317, 121 Cong. Rec. S13606 (daily ed. July 24, 1975).

96 *See New Mexico v. United States*, No. 76–0067 (D.D.C. July 30, 1976).

97 The Wiggins amendment, which would have eliminated Alaska Natives, American Indians, and Asian Americans from the definition of "language minority group," was offered for similar reasons. *See* 121 Cong. Rec. H4805 (daily ed. June 3, 1975) (statement of Rep. Wiggins).

98 *See* 42 U.S.C. § 1973b(f)(3).

> [T]he single language minority terminology is used to indicate that populations cannot be aggregated from among the four language minority groups in order to reach the over 5 percent criteria. For example, American Indian citizens and Asian American citizens cannot be added together to meet the criteria. Of course, subgroups within a single language minority group are to be aggregated for coverage determination purposes. So, Japanese, Chinese, and Filipino would be added together in arriving at any Asian American coverage. The same would be true with respect to adding together various tribal populations within a jurisdiction to arrive at American Indian coverage and adding together Aleut and Eskimo populations to arrive at Alaska Native coverage.[99]

Once a jurisdiction became covered for a single language minority group, it would be required to furnish bilingual voting materials and assistance in all of the subgroups of that group.

Alaska's congressional delegation derided the "single language minority group" formula because it resulted in statewide coverage of Alaska. Congressman Young contended that the definition's danger was that "if it is triggered, the ballots must be printed in all 20 dialects" of the various Alaska Native languages,[100] such as Inupiaq, Yup'ik, and Tlingit.[101] Senator Ted Stevens complained, "They are not interchangeable languages at all; they are as different as Chinese and Italian. Yet the Census Bureau has lumped them all together … Unless something is done … the Alaskan Natives become a single-language minority."[102]

The "single language minority group" phrase was retained in the Act. Alaska subsequently became covered statewide for Alaska Native languages. Although Senator Stevens disagreed with that decision, he acknowledged that there were between 60,000 and 70,000 Alaska Natives in Alaska,[103] or over 20 percent of the state's estimated population in 1970.[104] Aggregating the thousands of Alaska Natives together was supported by the state's well-documented history of educational and voting discrimination against them (Chapter 9). Later events would confirm that statewide coverage for Alaska Natives was essential to halt attempts by state election officials to resurrect their repealed literacy test through English-only elections (Chapter 10).

Requirements for Jurisdictions Covered under Section 4(f)(4)

A state or political subdivision covered under Section 4(f)(4) must provide all election materials, including assistance and ballots, in the language of the applicable language minority group.[105] Those requirements are described in greater detail below. In addition, a covered jurisdiction is subject to the special provisions of the VRA in Sections 5 and 8. The special provisions play a crucial role in protecting language minorities' right to vote.

Under Section 5 of the Act, a covered jurisdiction must demonstrate that a change affecting voting "neither has the purpose nor will have the effect" of denying or abridging the rights of

99 121 Cong. Rec. H4718 (daily ed. June 2, 1975).

100 121 Cong. Rec. H4807 (daily ed. June 3, 1975).

101 For a summary of the Alaska Native languages, *see* 1975 Senate Hearings: 531 (App. A to statement of Sen. Mike Gravel).

102 121 Cong. Rec. S13649 (daily ed. July 24, 1975).

103 121 Cong. Rec. S13655 (daily ed. July 24, 1975).

104 *See* Bureau of the Census, Economics and Statistics Admin., U.S. Dep't of Commerce, Table 16, *Population: 1790 to 1990.*

105 *See* 121 Cong. Rec. H4716 (daily ed. June 2, 1975) (statement of Rep. Edwards).

language minorities to vote.[106] The Supreme Court generally has construed Section 5 liberally, finding that it encompasses changes in voting laws, practices, and procedures, such as: changes resulting from redistricting; changes from single-member districts to at-large elections; changes from elected to appointed offices; changes in the methods of placing independent candidates on ballots; changes in procedures for casting write-in ballots; and changes in the manner of voting, such as the location of polling places.[107] Changes to comply with the language assistance requirements of the VRA are also covered by Section 5 (Chapter 10).[108]

A covered jurisdiction cannot implement a voting change without first obtaining "preclearance" from the Attorney General or a declaratory judgment from the United States District Court for the District of Columbia.[109] This administrative process allows the federal government to determine in advance whether covered changes "evade the remedies for discrimination contained in the Act itself" (*South Carolina v. Katzenbach* 1966: 335). Section 5 thus helps ensure that the progress made because of the availability of language assistance "shall not be destroyed through new procedures and techniques" that discriminate against language minorities (S. Rep. No. 94–295, 1975: 19).

Section 8 of the Act facilitates evaluation of a jurisdiction's language assistance practices through the use of federal election observers, who are non-lawyer employees of the United States Office of Personnel Management (OPM). Federal observers are authorized to observe the casting and tabulating of ballots.[110] "[T]he role of Federal observers can be critical in that they provide a calming and objective presence which can serve to deter any abuse which might occur. Federal observers can also still serve to prevent or diminish the intimidation frequently experienced by minority voters at the polls."[111] In 2006, several amendments were made to the federal-observer provisions that enhanced opportunities for coverage in jurisdictions where it is needed.[112]

The 2006 Amendments to Section 5

The Voting Rights Act Reauthorization Act (VRARA) amended the provisions for Section 5 preclearance in three ways. First, it reauthorized Section 5 for 25 years. Second, it confirmed that Section 5 barred voting changes that were intended to be discriminatory, even if they failed to achieve that goal. Third, Congress clarified that Section 5 protected the ability of minority voters to elect their preferred candidates of choice, regardless of whether they could influence the election of others they did not prefer.

Twenty-Five Year Extension

The VRARA reauthorized the provisions for 25 years from their effective date of July 27, 2006, when the bill was signed into law, or until July 27, 2031. This extension was accomplished

---

106 42 U.S.C. § 1973c.

107 *See Allen v. State Bd. of Elections*, 393 U.S. 544 (1969); *Presley v. Etowah County Comm'n*, 502 U.S. 491, 502–03 (1992).

108 *See* S. Rep. No. 94–295, 1975: 47; 28 C.F.R. § 55.22 (2006).

109 *See* 42 U.S.C. § 1973c.

110 *See* 42 U.S.C. § 1973f.

111 S. Rep. No. 94–295, 1975: 21; *see* Barry H. Weinberg and Lyn Utrecht, *Problems in America's Polling Places: How They Can Be Stopped*, 11 Temp. Pol. & Civ. Rts. L. Rev. 401 (2002).

112 *See* James Thomas Tucker, *The Power of Observation: The Role of Federal Observers under the Voting Rights Act*, 13 Mich. J. Race & Law 227 (Fall 2007).

by striking "Voting Rights Act Amendments of 1982" from Section 4(a) and replacing it with "Fannie Lou Hamer, Rosa Parks, and Coretta Scott King Voting Rights Act Reauthorization and Amendments Act of 2006."[113] Although this change was consistent with past amendments to the VRA, it created a shorter coverage period than for the reauthorized Section 203 (Chapter 4).

Intentionally Discriminatory Voting Changes

The VRARA clarified congressional intent to address the Supreme Court's decision in *Reno v. Bossier Parish School Board* ("*Bossier II*").[114] In Bossier Parish, Louisiana, African-Americans comprised 20 percent of the population but had never been elected to the 12-member school board, which was elected from single-member districts (*Bossier II* 2000: 323). After the 1990 Census, the school board refused to include any majority-Black districts, even though it admitted "it was obvious that a reasonably compact black-majority district could be drawn within Bossier City." It was undisputed that two of the white board members opposed "black representation" or a "black-majority district."[115] Nevertheless, in a 5 to 4 decision, the Supreme Court found that there was no basis for an objection under Section 5 (*Bossier II* 2000: 340–41). The Court held that Section 5 "prevents nothing but backsliding" that makes minority voters worse off than they were before the voting change under the statute's language "does not have the purpose and will not have the effect." Since African-American voters in Bossier Parish had never had a majority-Black district, the Court concluded an objection was improper, regardless of the presence of intentional discrimination (*Bossier II* 2000: 335–41).

Bossier II substantially curtailed the ability of the Attorney General and the District of Columbia court to object to voting changes with a discriminatory purpose. For example, the House Judiciary Committee noted that it would not have allowed the court to issue an objection to Georgia's 1980 congressional redistricting plan, in which redistricting chair Joe Mack Wilson proclaimed, "I don't want to draw nigger districts," because the existing plan did not have any majority-Black districts.[116] Section 5 objections based solely on discriminatory purpose comprised 25 percent of all objections in the 1980s and 43 percent of all objections in the 1990s.[117]

The VRARA addressed *Bossier II* in three ways. It struck "does not have the purpose and will not have the effect" from Section 5, replacing it with "neither has the purpose nor will have the effect." It added a subsection (b) to Section 5, providing that any voting change "that has the purpose or will have the effect of diminishing the ability of any citizens ... on account of race or color, or in contravention of ... section 4(f)(2) to elect their preferred candidates of choice denies or abridges the right to vote within the meaning of subsection (a) of this section." It also added a subsection (c), clarifying that the term "purpose" includes "any discriminatory purpose." In this manner, Congress clarified that a Section 5 objection could be made based upon discriminatory purpose, effect, or both.[118]

113 Pub L. No. 109–246 § 4, 120 Stat. 580 (2006).

114 528 U.S. 320 (2000).

115 *Bossier II* 2000: 348, 350 (Souter, J., dissenting).

116 *See* H.R. Rep. No. 109–478 at 67 (2006) (quoting *Busbee v. Smith*, 549 F. Supp. 495, 501 (D.D.C. 1982)).

117 *See* Peyton McCrary et al., *The End of Preclearance as We Knew It: How the Supreme Court Transformed Section 5 of the Voting Rights Act*, 11 Mich. J. Race & L. 275, 278 (2006).

118 VRARA, Pub L. No. 109–246 § 5, 120 Stat. 580–81 (2006).

Discriminatory Effects on Opportunity to Elect

The VRARA also restored the standard for determining discriminatory effects that had been in place for three decades. In the 1976 case of *Beer v. United States*, the Supreme Court held that a voting change had a discriminatory effect if it "would lead to a retrogression in the position of racial minorities with respect to their *effective exercise* of the electoral franchise."[119] Citing the VRA's legislative history, *Beer* explained that this standard required examining whether "the ability of minority groups ... to elect their choices to office is *augmented, diminished, or not affected*" by the voting change.[120]

Despite *Beer*'s straightforward test, in 2003 a narrow majority of the Court in *Georgia v. Ashcroft* adopted a new totality of the circumstances standard for determining discriminatory effect that did not rest on just the ability to elect.[121] Rather, the *Ashcroft* Court held that:

> [A]ny assessment of the retrogression of a minority group's effective exercise of the electoral franchise depends on an examination of all the relevant circumstances, such as the ability of minority voters to elect candidates of choice, the extent of the minority group's opportunity to participate in the political process, and the feasibility of creating a nonretrogressive plan (*Georgia v. Ashcroft* 2003: 479).

In the process, the Court indicated that no discriminatory effect was present if minority voters could influence election results, even if their preferred candidates of choice were defeated (*Georgia v. Ashcroft* 2003: 483).

The House Judiciary Committee was concerned that the amorphous *Ashcroft* standard "would encourage States to spread minority voters under the guise of 'influence' and would effectively shut minority voters out of the political process." Instead of having at least the same opportunity to elect their preferred candidates of choice under the *Beer* standard, under *Ashcroft*, minority voters would be turned "into second class voters who can influence elections of white candidates" (H.R. Rep. No. 109–478, 2006: 70). The VRARA restores the *Beer* test for discriminatory effect by adding subsection (d) to Section 5, clarifying that the purpose of Section 5 "is to protect the ability of such citizens to elect their preferred candidates of choice."[122]

Bailout from Section 4(f)(4) Coverage

Some members expressed concerns that the Act's special provisions would be applied in jurisdictions that did not have a history of voting discrimination against language minorities. Congress responded to these concerns in several ways. Under Section 4(d) of the Act, a jurisdiction can be removed from Section 4(f)(4) coverage if it shows that the uses of discriminatory "tests or devices" were few in number and were corrected promptly and effectively, the effects of such uses have been eliminated, and there is no reasonable probability of their recurrence.[123]

---

119 425 U.S. 130, 141 (1976) (emphasis added).

120 *Beer v. U.S.* 1976: 141 (quoting H.R. Rep. No. 96–196, at 60 (1975)) (emphasis in original).

121 *Georgia v. Ashcroft*, 539 U.S. 461, 480 (2003).

122 VRARA, Pub L. No. 109–246 § 5, 120 Stat. 580–81 (2006).

123 *See* 42 U.S.C. § 1973b(d) (2000).

The "bailout" provision in Section 4(a) likewise allows a state or political subdivision to be removed from coverage under Section 4(f)(4).[124] Under that provision, a covered jurisdiction may obtain a declaratory judgment from the District Court of the District of Columbia that it has not used English-only elections or any other "test or device" in a discriminatory manner against language minorities and other racial or ethnic groups for the preceding ten years.[125] Bailout helped ensure the constitutionality of the VRA's special provisions. "[T]he act acknowledges the possibility of the overbroadness of its trigger by providing for the bailout process for nondiscriminating jurisdictions which are caught under the act's application." Congressman Edwards described how the bailout provision would work for a jurisdiction covered by Section 4(f)(4):

> [I]t is expected that a successful bailout could typically be achieved if the jurisdiction can demonstrate factors such as high turnout and participation by its language minority population; and literacy in the English language among that group. It is clear that if factors such as these could be demonstrated, for the 10 years preceding the filing of the bailout action, then the jurisdiction's past use of English-only election procedures did not have a discriminatory effect.[126]

Where a jurisdiction is covered by both of the bilingual-election provisions of the VRA, Section 4(f)(4) and Section 203, termination of coverage under one of these sections does not have the effect of terminating coverage under the other section (S. Rep. No. 94–295, 1975: 46).

Finally, a covered jurisdiction may partially bail out from the special provisions where the jurisdiction can show that it has "not discriminated against one or more of the pertinent subgroups." For example, a jurisdiction that is covered for Asian American language minorities, may be able to bail out of coverage for bilingual election materials for Japanese, Chinese, Filipino, or Korean, if it can prove that it has not discriminated against one of those "subgroups" of Asian American languages.[127]

Jurisdictions Covered under Section 4(f)(4)

Following enactment of the 1975 amendments, the Director of the Census, in consultation with the Attorney General, determined the jurisdictions that were covered under Section 4(f)(4). Three states were covered in their entirety: Alaska for Alaska Natives, and Arizona and Texas for persons of Spanish heritage.[128] Each of those states had lengthy histories of discriminating against language minorities in virtually every facet of economic, social, and political life (Chapters 2, 8, 9; Hunter 1976). In addition, 24 political subdivisions of eight other states also were brought under Section 4(f)(4).

---

124 For further discussion of the "bailout" provisions, *see, e.g.*, Hunter 1976: 259–60; U.S. Comm'n on Civil Rights, A Citizen's Guide to Understanding the Voting Rights Act 13–14 (Oct. 1984); Paul F. Hancock and Lora L. Tredway, *The Bailout Standard of the Voting Rights Act: An Incentive to End Discrimination*, 17 Urb. Law. 379 (1985).

125 *See* 42 U.S.C. § 1973b(a); *see also* S. Rep. No. 94–295, 1975: 35 (describing "bailout" for areas covered by Section 4(f)(4) "where there has been no voting discrimination").

126 121 Cong. Rec. H4718–19 (daily ed. June 2, 1975).

127 121 Cong. Rec. H4718 (daily ed. June 2, 1975) (statement of Rep. Edwards); *see also* 121 Cong. Rec. H4886–87 (daily ed. June 4, 1975) (statement of Rep. Edwards) (describing bailout on a subgroup-by-subgroup basis).

128 *See* 28 C.F.R. pt. 55, app.

The determinations were made using a combination of Census data, voter participation data, and information obtained directly from the jurisdiction about its election practices, as required by the VRA.[129] McKinley County, New Mexico provides a good example. In October 1975, the county clerk sent the Justice Department a copy of its absentee ballot. Although it included Spanish translation of constitutional questions and bond issues, all of the remaining information on the ballot, including instructions, offices, and terms of office, was in English only. The county had a population of over 26,000 American Indians, including Navajo, Zuni, Keresan, Hopi, and several others. Nevertheless, no bilingual assistance of any kind was provided by the county in any American Indian languages. As a result of this information, a determination was made that McKinley County maintained a test or device in the form of English-only elections with respect to both the American Indian and Spanish heritage language groups. A similar process was used to make coverage determinations for the other jurisdictions.

Shortly after becoming covered in late December 1975, all five covered counties in two of the states successfully bailed out (Appendix B). In New Mexico, Curry, McKinley, and Otero Counties had been covered for Spanish heritage, and McKinley County had been covered for American Indian languages.[130] All were removed from coverage in July 1976.[131] In Oklahoma, Choctaw and McCurtain Counties had been covered for American Indian languages.[132] Both were removed from coverage in May 1978.[133] McKinley County's removal from Section 4(f)(4) coverage would prove to be premature. The Department of Justice subsequently engaged in extensive enforcement activities there as a result of the county's violations of Section 203 of the VRA.

The 19 jurisdictions that remain under Section 4(f)(4) today include four counties in Arizona covered for American Indian languages; three counties in California for Spanish heritage; five counties in Florida for Spanish heritage; two townships in Michigan for Spanish heritage; two counties in New York for Spanish heritage; Jackson County in North Carolina for American Indian languages; and two counties in South Dakota for American Indian languages (Figure 3.1). Since 1976, no further determinations have been made for coverage under Section 4(f)(4). Even though the Director of the Census periodically makes new coverage determinations under Section 203 of the VRA (Chapter 5), the existing determinations under Section 4(f)(4) remain in effect.[134]

Conclusion

Language assistance was insufficient to stop discrimination in every jurisdiction. Many language-minority voters would be effectively barred from participating in the political process without the same broad prophylactic relief that Congress implemented in southern states that disenfranchised African-American voters.

Efforts to secure that relief proved arduous. Debates during the 1975 reauthorization were marked by parochial efforts to block coverage of jurisdictions with records of discrimination against language minorities, attempts to render the VRA unconstitutional, and amendments to curtail enforcement of the Act. Opponents of extending and reauthorizing special protections for language

129 *See* 42 U.S.C. § 1973b(f)(3).

130 *See* 41 Fed. Reg. 784 (Jan. 5, 1976).

131 *See New Mexico v. United States*, No. 76–0067 (D.D.C. July 30, 1976).

132 *See* 41 Fed. Reg. 784 (Jan. 5, 1976).

133 *See Oklahoma v. United States*, No. 76–1250 (D.D.C. May 12, 1978).

134 *See* Voting Rights Act Amendments of 1992, Determinations Under Section 203, 67 Fed. Reg. 48,871 (July 26, 2002) (to be codified at 28 C.F.R. pt. 55).

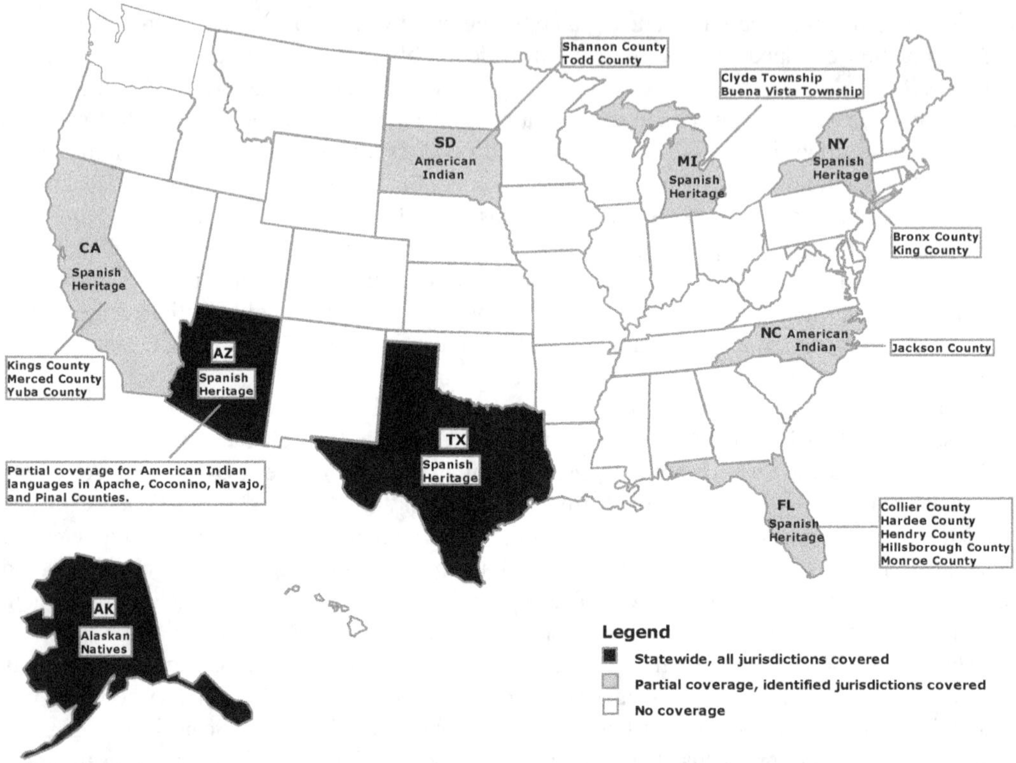

Figure 3.1 Jurisdictions covered by Section 4(f)(4) of the Voting Rights Act, by state and language

Source: 28 C.F.R. Part 55, Appendix (summarizing coverage determinations). Coverage determinations were published at 40 Fed. Reg. 43746 (Sept. 23, 1975), 40 Fed. Reg. 49422 (Oct. 22, 1975), 41 Fed. Reg. 784 (Jan. 5, 1976) (corrected at 41 Fed. Reg. 1503 (Jan. 8, 1976)), and 41 Fed. Reg. 34329 (Aug. 13, 1976).

minorities vilified some of the beneficiaries of language assistance, whom they mischaracterized as undeserving immigrants. Later struggles to expand coverage to other language groups in 2006 failed largely as a result of anti-immigrant sentiment (Chapter 7). In the end, coverage under the language assistance provisions was applied to the four language minority groups that suffered the most sustained patterns of educational and voting discrimination: Alaska Natives, American Indians, Asian Americans, and Spanish-speaking voters.

For those language groups, Section 4(f)(4) of the VRA applies the same special protections that were in place for African-American voters in places meeting a coverage formula tied to use of English-only elections and depressed political participation. In addition to mandating that registration and voting assistance be provided to covered language minorities in their native language (Chapter 4), Section 4(f)(4) requires that covered jurisdictions submit any changes affecting voting to the U.S. Attorney General or federal court in Washington, D.C. for approval before they are implemented and authorizes the Attorney General to deploy federal observers to ensure compliance with the VRA. These special protections are critical to stopping discrimination against language minorities before it takes place. Chapter 10 provides a more detailed example of how Section 4(f)(4) also facilitates compliance with the language-assistance mandate.

Chapter 4

Language Assistance and Voter Assistance since 1975

The Voting Rights Act included another important mandate to help non-English-speaking voters overcome the disabling effects of English-only elections. Title III of the 1975 amendments was "specifically directed to the problems of 'language minority groups.'"[1] Codified in Section 203, it differed from the special provisions in Section 4(f)(4) in a key respect. "The line between … [the two] is based upon the severity of voting discrimination against … language minorities. The evidence … demonstrates that the voting problems of language minority groups are not uniform in all parts of the country." Section 4(f)(4) included more severe restrictions based on evidence of both voting discrimination and the effects of educational discrimination.[2]

In contrast, Section 203 has "less stringent" requirements "based largely on the unequal educational opportunities which language minorities have suffered at the hands of State and local officials." Therefore, "those jurisdictions in which the evidence shows extensive discrimination against language minorities" were covered under Section 4(f)(4), while Section 203 was "designed to be both broader and narrower. It covers more areas but imposes less stringent requirements." For a jurisdiction covered under both sections, double coverage did not "impose any additional obligations." Instead, a jurisdiction that complies with Section 4(f)(4) "will invariably comply" with Section 203.[3]

Section 203 is grounded in the effects of discrimination against language minorities, including high illiteracy rates and depressed voter participation, which had "a close and direct correlation" with one another.[4] Those effects resulted from "the failure of state and local officials to afford equal educational opportunities" and a lack of adequate bilingual assistance at the polls (S. Rep. No. 94–295, 1975: 28). As Congress stated in Section 203:

> [T]hrough the use of various practices and procedures, citizens of language minorities have been effectively excluded from participation in the electoral process. Among other factors, the denial of the right to vote of such minority citizens is ordinarily directly related to the unequal educational opportunities afforded them, resulting in high illiteracy and low voting participation. The Congress declares that, in order to enforce the guarantees of the fourteenth and fifteenth amendments to the United States Constitution, it is necessary to eliminate such discrimination by prohibiting these practices, and by prescribing other remedial devices.[5]

Congressional action was necessary because election officials failed to address the effects of discrimination against language minorities in the voting process (S. Rep. No. 94–295, 1975: 39). Section 203 adopts a practical approach to those problems. Rather than attempting to "correct the deficiencies of prior educational inequality," it permits "persons disabled by such disparities to

1 S. Rep. No. 94–295 at 37–38 (1975).

2 121 Cong. Rec. H4718 (daily ed. June 2, 1975) (statement of Rep. Edwards); *see* S. Rep. No. 94–295, 1975: 9.

3 121 Cong. Rec. H4718–19 (daily ed. June 2, 1975) (statement of Rep. Edwards).

4 121 Cong. Rec. H4738 (daily ed. June 2, 1975) (statement of Rep. Badillo).

5 42 U.S.C. § 1973aa-1a(a).

vote now." It does that by requiring covered jurisdictions to provide "bilingual election materials and information in the language" of each group triggering coverage.[6] That mandate was "not new," but instead "simply affirm[ed] a growing number of … Federal court decisions requiring bilingual elections in Spanish speaking communities."[7]

Section 203's addition to the VRA in 1975 enhanced the existing but more limited remedies for language minorities already available under the Act.[8] In 1982, Section 203 was extended for 10 years and strengthened with the addition of voter assistance requirements.[9] In 1992, Congress renewed the requirements for 15 years, expanding coverage to correct infirmities in the existing law.[10] In 2006, the temporary language assistance requirements were reauthorized for 25 years.[11] This chapter describes the VRA's language and voter assistance remedies and how Section 203 has evolved since being enacted in 1975.

Evolution of Section 203's Coverage Formula

Coverage under Section 203 applies to jurisdictions "with less severe voting difficulties" than those covered by Section 4(f)(4) (S. Rep. No. 94–295, 1975: 31). Under Section 203, a state or political subdivision is covered if it has a sufficient number of "limited-English proficient"[12] (LEP) single language minority citizens who experience an illiteracy rate higher than the national average.[13] Today, the population standard is met in a state or political subdivision if the Director of the Census determines any one of the following: more than 5 percent of the voting-age citizens are members of a single language minority and are LEP;[14] more than 10,000 voting-age citizens are members of a single language minority and are LEP;[15] or, in a political subdivision containing any part of an Indian reservation, more than 5 percent of the American Indian or Alaska Native voting-age citizens are members of a single language minority and are LEP.[16] Section 203 uses the same definition of language minorities as Section 4(f)(4), discussed in Chapter 3.[17]

Statewide coverage for a language is only triggered if more than 5 percent of the voting-age citizens in the state are members of a single language minority and are LEP.[18] The other two population formulas are expressly limited to "political subdivisions" of a state.[19] Restricting the formula to only those places with substantial language minority populations makes the statute more narrowly focused to ensure it is constitutional.

6 121 Cong. Rec. H4719 (daily ed. June 2, 1975) (statement of Rep. Edwards); *see* 42 U.S.C. § 1973aa-1a(c).

7 121 Cong. Rec. H4744 (daily ed. June 2, 1975) (statement of Rep. Roybal).

8 *See* Voting Rights Act Amendments of 1975, Pub. L. No. 94–73, 89 Stat. 400 (1975).

9 *See* Voting Rights Act Amendments of 1982, Pub. L. No. 97–205, 96 Stat. 131 (1982).

10 *See* Voting Rights Language Assistance Act of 1992, Pub. L. No. 102–344, 106 Stat. 921 (1992).

11 *See* The Fannie Lou Hamer, Rosa Parks, and Coretta Scott King Voting Rights Act Reauthorization and Amendments Act of 2006 (VRARA), Pub. L. 109–246, 120 Stat. 577 (2006).

12 *See* 42 U.S.C. § 1973aa-1a(b)(3)(B).

13 *See* 42 U.S.C. § 1973aa-1a(b)(2).

14 42 U.S.C. § 1973aa-1a(b)(2)(A)(i)(I).

15 42 U.S.C. § 1973aa-1a(b)(2)(A)(i)(II).

16 42 U.S.C. § 1973aa-1a(b)(2)(A)(i)(III) (2000).

17 *Compare* 42 U.S.C. § 1973aa-1a(e) *with* 42 U.S.C. § 1973*l*(c)(3).

18 42 U.S.C. § 1973aa-1a(b)(2)(A)(i)(I); *see also* 28 C.F.R. § 55.6(a)(2) (describing the state approach to Section 203 coverage).

19 42 U.S.C. §§ 1973aa-1a(b)(2)(A)(i)(II)-(III).

Another exception to this formula also applies to statewide coverage. Under Section 203, a political subdivision within that state cannot independently be covered under the coverage formula if it "has less than 5 percent voting age limited-English proficient citizens of each language minority which comprises over 5 percent of the statewide limited-English proficient population of voting age citizens."[20] Typically, that means that in a county where there is statewide coverage, the county will only use whatever bilingual materials are provided by the state. For example, in Texas, a county with less than 5 percent Spanish-speaking voters would use bilingual materials prepared by the state, such as forms for voter registration or absentee voting, but not prepare its own ballot in Spanish. The 1975 Committee Report encouraged election officials in political subdivisions that are not independently covered to provide language assistance to voters who need it (S. Rep. No. 94–295, 1975: 38). Any efforts necessary to allow language minorities to participate equally with other voters should be undertaken.

The trigger for coverage under Section 203 has evolved over time. The formula originally targeted states or political subdivisions with 5 percent or more language minority voting-age citizens whose illiteracy rate exceeded the national average. In 1982, the formula was amended to require that the citizens triggering coverage be LEP. Because of the substantial decrease in coverage following the 1982 amendment, Congress modified the formula again in 1992 to also trigger coverage in political subdivisions with 10,000 or more LEP language minority voters or that included at least a portion of an Indian reservation that could satisfy the 5 percent trigger. Those changes had a dramatic impact on coverage (Figure 4.1; Appendix B).

The 1975 Coverage Formula

As originally enacted, Section 203 was triggered if the Director of the Census determined "(1) that more than 5 percent of the citizens of voting age of such State or political subdivision are members of a single language minority and (2) that the illiteracy rate of such persons as a group is higher than the national illiteracy rate."[21] Unlike Section 4(f)(4), the Section 203 formula did not "depend on overall low voting turnout for coverage" because it did not "impose any of the act's special remedies aside from a bilingual elections requirement."[22] Under the 1975 formula, a total of 385 political subdivisions in 30 states were covered (Figures 4.1 and 4.2; Appendix B).

Five percent formula Congress adopted the 5 percent formula because it had been established as a "relevant cut-off" in court decisions and state laws mandating bilingual election materials in areas with sufficient numbers of language minorities (S. Rep. No. 94–295, 1975: 32 n.31). The 5 percent trigger was ordered by courts to determine coverage for providing bilingual election materials in New York and Philadelphia under Section 4(e) of the Act.[23] In addition, state legislatures in California and Connecticut used a trigger of 5 percent or less (Chapter 2).[24] Therefore, the Committee Report recommended a 5 percent trigger (S. Rep. No. 94–295, 1975: 32–33).

---

20 42 U.S.C. § 1973aa-1a(b)(2)(B).

21 Voting Rights Act Amendments of 1975, Pub. L. No. 94–73, § 203(b), 89 Stat. 400, 403 (1975) (codified as amended at 42 U.S.C. § 1973aa-1a(b)(2)).

22 121 Cong. Rec. H4713 (daily ed. June 2, 1975) (statement of Rep. Edwards).

23 *See Torres v. Sachs*, 381 F. Supp. 309, 313 (S.D.N.Y. 1974); *Arroyo v. Tucker*, 372 F. Supp. 764, 768 (E.D. Pa. 1974).

24 121 Cong. Rec. S13647 (daily ed. July 24, 1975) (statement of Sen. Bayh); 121 Cong. Rec. S13650 (statement of Sen. Tunney); S. Rep. No. 94–295, 1975: 33 n.35.

State	1975–1977* (*excludes deleted coverage described in Appendix B)	1984	1992	2002
Alaska	14	7	16	14
Arizona	14	9	11	12
California	39	7	19	25#
Colorado	34	11	11	10
Connecticut	1	2	4	7
Florida	7	2	8	10
Hawaii	4	3	3	2
Idaho	2	1	4	5
Illinois	0	0	1	2
Iowa	0	0	1	0
Kansas	3	0	0	6
Louisiana	1	0	1	1
Maine	1	0	0	0
Maryland	0	0	0	1
Massachusetts	0	3	5	6
Michigan	9	3	3	1
Minnesota	2	0	0	0
Mississippi	1	0	6	9
Montana	7	1	0	2
Nebraska	2	0	0	2
Nevada	4	0	2	6
New Jersey	0	2	5	7
New Mexico	32	26	25	26#
New York	3	3	7	7
North Carolina	4	0	0	0
North Dakota	5	2	3	2
Oklahoma	25	1	1	2
Oregon	2	0	1	1
Pennsylvania	0	0	1	1
Rhode Island	0	0	1	2
South Dakota	7	4	7	18
Texas	143	106	99	104†#
Utah	4	1	1	1
Virginia	1	0	0	0
Washington	5	0	0	4
Wisconsin	4	3	1	0
Wyoming	5	0	0	0
TOTAL	385	197	247	296

Figure 4.1 Jurisdictions designated for Section 203 coverage, by state and year of Census determinations

Statewide coverage.

† Loving County, Texas was included by the Census Bureau in its 2002 coverage determinations as a jurisdiction covered for Spanish. The Census data used to make the 2002 determinations indicates Loving County is only flagged for statewide coverage for Spanish and is not separately covered under Section 203. Nevertheless, it has been counted because it was included in the 2002 determinations.

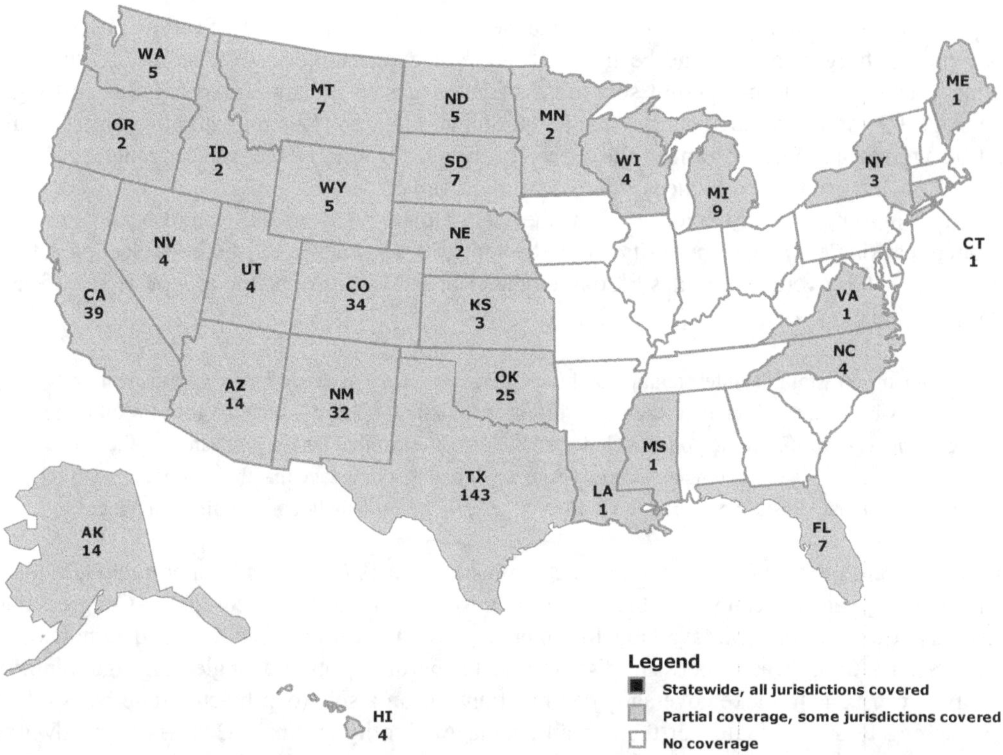

Figure 4.2 Jurisdictions designated for Section 203 coverage, by state (1977 Census determinations)

Source: Implementation of the Provisions of the Voting Rights Act Regarding Language Minority Groups: Interpretative Guidelines; Corrections and Amendments, 28 C.F.R. Pt. 55, App., 42 Fed. Reg. 35,970 (July 13, 1977). Figure 4.2 excludes all jurisdictions where coverage was deleted (Appendix B).

Citizenship requirement The formula was qualified further by including "a citizenship standard in the 5 percent population standard for coverage of language minorities."[25] Language minorities from Asian American and Spanish heritage groups included many more recent arrivals who were not yet U.S. citizens. For example, Congresswoman Patsy Mink of Hawaii complained that in her district, "we may very well have to have a ballot in five languages, if we count the aliens."[26] Congressman McClory responded by offering an amendment that substituted "citizens" for "persons" in the bill,[27] which was adopted by a vote of 311 to 103.[28] By excluding aliens, the formula limited coverage to only those language minority persons 18 years and older generally eligible to vote. Even after Section 203 was limited to citizens, critics continued to tie the language assistance provisions to illegal immigration by arguing that it could be used to allow aliens to vote (Chapters 7–8).

25 121 Cong. Rec. H4713 (daily ed. June 2, 1975) (statement of Rep. Edwards).

26 121 Cong. Rec. H4884 (daily ed. June 4, 1975).

27 121 Cong. Rec. H4884 (daily ed. June 4, 1975).

28 *See* Roll No. 261, 121 Cong. Rec. H4892–4893 (daily ed. June 4, 1975).

Single language minority requirement Like Section 4(f)(4) of the Act, Section 203 required that citizens triggering coverage be from a "single language minority."[29] Section 203 used the term differently. It did not permit subgroups of languages to be aggregated together to trigger coverage for the entire language group. For example, Chinese, Korean, and Vietnamese could not be aggregated together to meet the 5 percent trigger for Asian American language coverage. Instead, each language had to meet the trigger individually.

There is some contrary evidence from the 1975 House floor debate. Congressman Edwards implied that single language minority would be applied the same way for both the Section 4(f)(4) and Section 203 coverage formulas.[30] Congressman Robert Duncan of Oregon suggested a different interpretation:

> I think the only rational interpretation of this language is that if you have a 5-percent Asian minority group who speak a single language – 5 percent speak one language – then in order to fulfill the civil rights of those people you must have the ballot printed in that language. I cannot believe that if there are only two of the Asian minority who spoke a single language that this Congress wants to impose on that legislative district the burden of printing multiple ballots in multiple languages.[31]

Inadequate Census data caused some of the confusion. The 1970 Census did not track individual language usage and illiteracy with the level of precision it does today. According to Congressman Edwards, where that data was available for illiteracy, it was to be used. For coverage determinations under Section 203, "where there are distinct racial subgroups within a single language minority group … census is to make coverage determinations … on a subgroup-by-subgroup basis rather than aggregate one … figure for the overall language minority group."[32] Congressman Edwards later qualified his initial statement about aggregating to make it clear that he only intended it to be used in "making determinations under title II," or Section 4(f)(4) of the Act.[33]

Today, the manner in which Section 203 coverage determinations are made lies between the interpretations of Congressman Duncan and Congressman Edwards in 1975.[34] Language subgroups were aggregated for some of the earlier Alaska Native determinations using 1970 and 1980 Census data.[35] That is evidenced by certain coverage determinations listing only the language groups, like "Alaska Native," and not specific subgroups, such as "Athabascan" or "Inupiaq." Starting with the 1990 Census, more precise determinations were provided for all of the language subgroups, as defined by the Census. Even today, however, the Census does not track every single Alaska Native or American Indian language. While the determinations may be more precise now, they do not eliminate the need for jurisdictions to identify the specific native languages that are covered.[36]

The determinations do not base coverage on dialects within a specific language subgroup, as Congressman Duncan suggested. For instance, Chinese-speaking citizens are treated together, and are not divided further by whether they speak Cantonese or Mandarin. Nevertheless, under the Justice Department's regulations, a jurisdiction required to provide written voting materials to a language minority group with more than one language is only required to do so in the language

29 *See* 42 U.S.C. §§ 1973b(f)(3), 1973aa-1a(b)(2)(A).
30 121 Cong. Rec. H4718 (daily ed. June 2, 1975).
31 121 Cong. Rec. H4892 (daily ed. June 4, 1975).
32 121 Cong. Rec. H4719 (daily ed. June 2, 1975).
33 121 Cong. Rec. H4886 (daily ed. June 4, 1975).
34 *See* 28 C.F.R. § 55.6(c).
35 *See* 121 Cong. Rec. S13658 (daily ed. July 24, 1975) (statement of Sen. Stevens).
36 *See* 28 C.F.R. §§ 55.11, 55.13(a).

that is most widely used among those voters.[37] Conversely, for languages like Chinese with more than one dialect, "the jurisdiction's obligation is to ascertain the dialects that are commonly used by members of the applicable language minority group in the jurisdiction and to provide oral assistance in such dialects."[38] The net effect is that a covered jurisdiction generally must provide written voting materials in at least one version of the language triggering coverage, but must have bilingual interpreters available for all dialects of that language.

Illiteracy requirement Part of Section 203's coverage formula requires that the illiteracy rate of the language group triggering coverage be higher than the national rate,[39] which was 4.6 percent in 1970[40] and was 1.35 percent in 2000.[41] That requirement was included because "illiteracy is all too often a product of racially discriminatory educational systems" (S. Rep. No. 94–295, 1975: 38). In that manner, the coverage formula linked the need for bilingual voting materials and assistance with the educational discrimination that helped cause the language group's illiteracy in the first place.

"Illiteracy" was defined as "the failure to complete the 5th primary grade."[42] It was adopted to conform to the Census definition of that term.[43] Congressman McClory criticized that definition, arguing it was "determined arbitrarily" without any evidence that less than a fifth-grade education precluded someone from voting.[44] He is correct, but not in the way that he intended. A fifth-grade education falls far short of what is needed to understand a ballot proposition, typically drafted at the high school level or greater. Even simpler ballot questions require more advanced English skills, such as California's November 2005 Proposition 77, which was a 42-word sentence written at the twelfth-grade level.[45] If anything, limiting coverage to language groups that have illiteracy rates higher than the national average underestimates the actual need for language assistance.

The 1982 Amendments: the "Limited-English Proficient" Requirement

In 1975, Congress considered amendments to narrow the coverage formula by exempting language minorities "whose dominant language is English."[46] Congressman William Armstrong of Colorado, sponsor of the House amendment, argued that the Act did not intend "to include in the definition

37 *See* 28 C.F.R. § 55.12.

38 *See* 28 C.F.R. § 55.13.

39 *See* 42 U.S.C. § 1973aa-1a(b)(2).

40 Originally, the Census Bureau identified the national illiteracy rate from the 1970 Census as 5.5 percent. *See* S. Rep. No. 94–295 at 39, *reprinted in* 1975 U.S.C.C.A.N. at 806. However, that "was based on illiteracy of persons 25 years or older," prior to the voting age being lowered to 18, which produced the lower rate. *Doi v. Bell*, 449 F. Supp. 267, 270 n.14 (D. Haw. 1978).

41 Dr. James Thomas Tucker and Dr. Rodolfo Espino et al., Minority Language Assistance Practices in Public Elections 24, 29–30 and app. C (2006), *reprinted in Voting Rights Act: Evidence of Continued Need, Hearing Before the Subcomm. on the Constitution of the H. Comm. on the Judiciary*, 109th Cong. 2124, 2158, 2163–64, 2272–95 (2006).

42 42 U.S.C. § 1973aa-1a(b)(3)(E).

43 *See* 121 Cong. Rec. H4719 (daily ed. June 2, 1975) (statement of Rep. Edwards).

44 121 Cong. Rec. H4747 (daily ed. June 2, 1975).

45 Ana Henderson, *English Language Naturalization Requirements and the Bilingual Assistance Provisions of the Voting Rights Act* 3 (2006) (on file with author).

46 *See* 121 Cong. Rec. H4882 (daily ed. June 4, 1975) (statement of Rep. Armstrong); 121 Cong. Rec. S13405 (daily ed. July 23, 1975) (statement of Sen. Bellmon).

of language minorities those persons who in fact are fluent in English and who speak and read and write English."[47]

Senator Henry Bellmon of Oklahoma, sponsor of the Senate amendment, contended that Section 203 was based on "the false assumption that one automatically has a dominant language other than English" if that person was a member of a language minority group. Senator Bellmon made it clear his amendment would exempt Section 203 coverage from most of Oklahoma's counties where "it is absolutely not needed."[48] He was joined by senators from other states with large native and Spanish-speaking populations. Senator Ted Stevens claimed that the dominant language throughout Alaska "is, in fact, English."[49] Senator Pete Domenici argued that New Mexico's decision to make bilingual materials optional, rather than mandatory, supported the amendment.[50] Senator Barry Goldwater asserted that the dominant language among Arizona's American Indian tribes was English, but nevertheless said "we must come under this act."[51]

The Armstrong and Bellmon amendments would have created an impossible task for the Census Bureau, which had "no statistics and no category which would fall into the classification of the 'dominant language.'"[52] Senator Tunney explained that if adopted, the amendments would prevent any determinations from being made under Section 203.[53] The House rejected the Armstrong amendment by a vote of 122 to 292.[54] The Senate rejected the Bellmon amendment by a vote of 26 to 59.[55]

In 1982, Senator Bellmon's successor from Oklahoma, Don Nickles, resurrected Bellmon's amendment in a slightly different form. During the Senate floor debate on the VRA reauthorization bill, Senator Nickles proposed the "limited-English proficient" requirement to "more accurately target bilingual assistance to those who are truly in need of such assistance." According to Nickles, this change was necessary to ensure that the Director of the Census only counts those persons who are unable to understand English sufficiently to participate in the electoral process. The Nickles amendment was accepted without any debate[56] and was enacted as part of the 1982 amendments to the VRA.[57]

LEP is defined under the Act as the inability "to speak or understand English adequately enough to participate in the electoral process."[58] The 1992 House Report explains the manner in which the Director of Census determines the number of LEP persons:

> The Director of the Census determines limited English proficiency based upon information included on the long form of the decennial census. The long form, however, is only received by approximately 17 percent of the total population. Those few who do receive the long form and speak a language other than English at home are asked to evaluate their own English proficiency. The form requests that they respond to a question inquiring how well they speak English by

47 121 CONG. REC. H4882 (daily ed. June 4, 1975).
48 121 CONG. REC. S13405 (daily ed. July 23, 1975).
49 121 CONG. REC. S13406 (daily ed. July 23, 1975).
50 121 CONG. REC. S13406 (daily ed. July 23, 1975).
51 121 CONG. REC. S13407 (daily ed. July 23, 1975).
52 121 CONG. REC. H4883 (daily ed. June 4, 1975) (statement of Rep. Drinan).
53 *See* 121 CONG. REC. S13407 (daily ed. July 23, 1975).
54 *See* Roll No. 260, 121 CONG. REC. H4883 (daily ed. June 4, 1975).
55 *See* Roll No. 314, 121 CONG. REC. S13408 (daily ed. July 23, 1975).
56 128 CONG. REC. S7104 (daily ed. June 18, 1982).
57 *See* Voting Rights Act Amendments of 1982, Pub. L. No. 97–205, § 4, 96 Stat. 131, 134 (1982).
58 42 U.S.C. § 1973aa-1a(b)(2).

> checking one of the four answers provided – "very well," "well," "not well," or "not at all." The Census Bureau has determined that most respondents over-estimate their English proficiency and therefore, those who answer other than "very well" are deemed LEP.[59]

Although the Nickles amendment seemed innocuous, it dramatically affected Section 203 coverage. Prior to the 1982 reauthorization, it was estimated that more than 300 counties would be covered under the 1975 formula. Because of the LEP requirement, however, coverage was reduced to just 197 counties when Section 203 determinations were made in 1984 (Figure 4.3).[60] California decreased from 39 covered counties to seven, Colorado from 34 to 11, and Texas from 143 to 106 (Figure 4.1; Appendix B).

Nowhere were the effects of the 1982 amendments more obvious than in Nickles' own state. In 1976, Oklahoma had 25 covered counties, including 23 for American Indian languages and two for Spanish.[61] When the next coverage determinations were made in 1984, the first time the

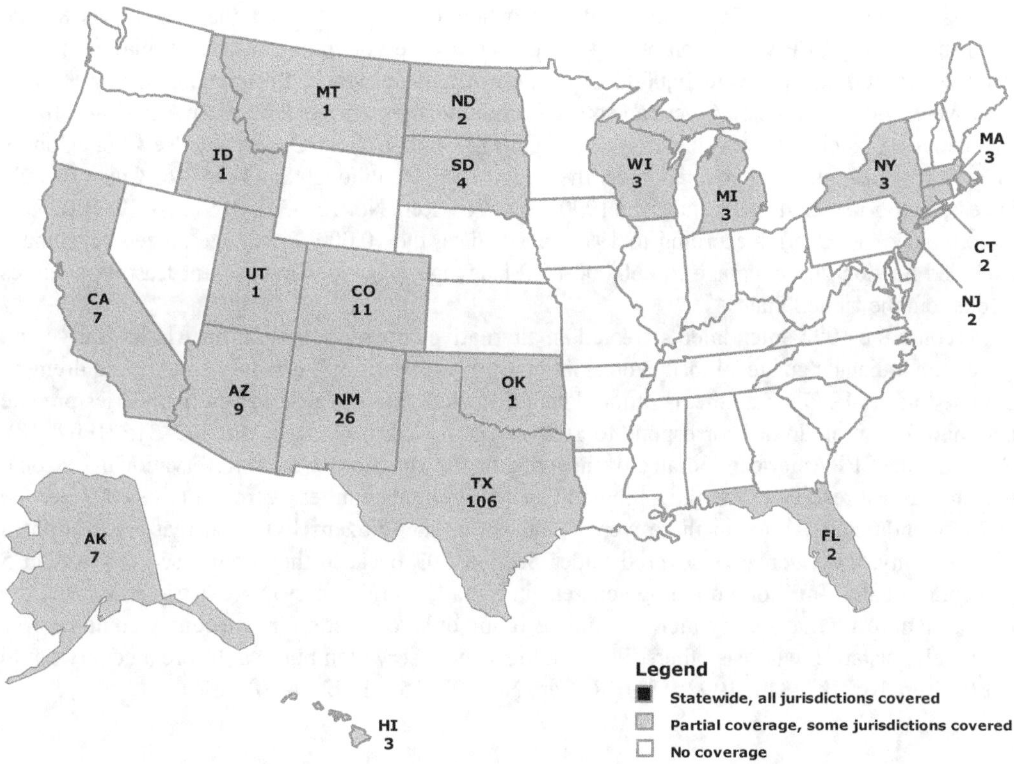

Figure 4.3 Jurisdictions designated for Section 203 coverage, by state (1984 Census determinations)

Source: 49 Fed. Reg. 25,887 (Jun. 25, 1984); U.S. Comm'n on Civil Rts., A Citizen's Guide To Understanding The Voting Rights Act 51–53 (1984).

59 H.R. Rep. No. 102–655 at 8 (1992), *reprinted in* 1992 U.S.C.C.A.N. 766, 772.

60 *See* S. Rep. No. 102–315 at 10 (1992).

61 *See* 42 Fed. Reg. 35,970, 35,972 (July 13, 1977).

LEP requirement was part of the formula, just one county was left covered, Adair County for Cherokee.[62] Senator Nickles' amendment achieved one of its primary goals: eliminating most of the Section 203 coverage in Oklahoma.

The 1992 Amendments: the Numerical and Reservation Triggers

Congress further modified the bilingual election trigger in 1992 in two ways to cure "serious flaws" created by the LEP requirement, which excluded large numbers of language minorities who comprised less than 5 percent of the voting-age citizen population.[63]

First, it added the 10,000 voting-age citizen population trigger[64] to cover "highly populated metropolitan areas" where "many language minority citizens in need of assistance are not covered because they do not make up a large enough percentage of the local population to trigger coverage" (S. Rep. No. 102–15, 1992: 16).

According to 1990 Census data, there were tens of thousands of LEP language minority citizens who lived in large metropolitan areas not covered under the trigger implemented in the 1975 Act and the 1982 amendments. In Cook County, Illinois, where Chicago is located, there were over 87,000 Spanish-speaking LEP voters comprising 2.5 percent of the voting-age citizen population. In Los Angeles, California, there were 39,000 LEP Chinese-Americans voters. In Honolulu County, Hawaii, there were 37,000 LEP Asian American voters. In addition, thousands of LEP Asian American citizens living in San Francisco County, California, and Queens County, Kings County, and New York County in New York also were not covered under the original trigger, although San Francisco County would have met the 5 percent trigger under the 1990 Census (S. Rep. No. 102–315, 1992: 16–17; H.R. Rep. No. 102–655, 1992: 8). According to 1990 census data, the 10,000 voting-age citizen benchmark extended Section 203 coverage to 860,000 LEP language minorities living in at least 34 counties throughout the United States.[65]

Second, the 1992 amendments created an alternative coverage formula for Alaska Native and American Indian language minority voters living on reservations.[66] The county-specific requirement included in the 1975 amendments ignored "the historical fact that reservation boundaries predate and therefore often do not correspond to State or county lines" (S. Rep. No. 102–315, 1992: 18). For example, LEP American Indian citizens living on the Tohono O'odham Reservation in Arizona, the fifth largest reservation in the nation and spanning three counties, were not covered under the 1975 amendments. Although there were 4,500 voting-age citizens living on that reservation in Pima County, they were not covered under Section 203 because they comprised fewer than 5 percent of the half-million voting-age citizens in Pima County. The 1975 Act's trigger created the inconsistent result that some American Indians living on a reservation in one county could receive bilingual assistance, whereas others living on the same reservation but in a different county could not (S. Rep. No. 102–315, 1992: 18; H.R. Rep. No. 102–655, 1992: 9–10).

62 *See* U.S. Comm'n on Civil Rts., A Citizen's Guide to Understanding the Voting Rights Act 52 (Oct. 1984).

63 H.R. Rep. No. 102–655, 1992: 7–8; 138 Cong. Rec. H6609 (daily ed. July 24, 1992) (statement of Rep. Torres).

64 *See* Pub. L. No. 102–344, § 2, 106 Stat. 921 (codified at 42 U.S.C. § 1973aa-1a(b)(2)(A)(i)(II)).

65 S. Rep. No. 102–315, 1992: 17 (estimating 34 counties); H.R. Rep. No. 102–655, 1992: 4 (estimating 38 counties); *see also* 57 Fed. Reg. 43,213 (Sept. 18, 1992) (making Section 203(c) coverage determinations).

66 *See* Pub. L. No. 102–344, § 2, 106 Stat. 921 (codified at 42 U.S.C. § 1973aa-1a(b)(2)(A)(i)(III)).

The reservation trigger covers any political subdivision "that contains all or any part of an Indian reservation" on which "more than 5 percent of the American Indian or Alaska Native citizens of voting age within the Indian reservation are members of a single language minority and are limited-English proficient."[67] An "Indian reservation" was defined as "any area that is an American Indian or Alaska Native area, as defined by the Census Bureau."[68] In Alaska, there are at least 229 federally recognized tribes, including many villages with 100 people or less.[69] The 1992 Senate Report indicates that this alternative standard "is intended to supplement, not supplant, the coverage triggers under current law" and therefore a "county may be covered for Native Americans under any of [the] three coverage formulas" (S. Rep. No. 102–315, 1992: 18).

Congresswoman Nancy Pelosi of California said that maintaining the LEP requirement helped make Section 203 "well-targeted" to calculate "coverage by counting only those citizens who do not speak English well enough to make an informed vote."[70] But the 1992 amendments proved critical to improving the Section 203 trigger by giving "a voice to those citizens who [had] been left out" under the existing coverage formula.[71] Shortly after Congress amended Section 203 to include the two additional population triggers, the Census Bureau made its new determinations. Fifty counties were added to coverage, increasing the number of covered political subdivisions from 197 to 247 (Figure 4.4; Appendix B). Tens of thousands of LEP American Indian and Asian language minority voters received relief from English-only elections. Under the 2002 determinations as a result of Section 203, the number of covered political subdivisions increased to 296 (Figures 4.1 and 5.1; Appendices B and C).

Oklahoma's Failed Effort to Change the Formula in 2006

In 2006, another senator from Oklahoma tried to roll back the expanded coverage that followed the 1992 amendments. Senator Tom Coburn was elected in 2004 to fill the vacancy created when Senator Nickles retired. During the markup of the VRA reauthorization bill in the Senate, Coburn offered an amendment to change the definition of LEP to include only persons who speak English "not well" or "not at all."[72] Like the Nickles amendment, the Coburn amendment would have had a devastating impact, reducing Section 203 coverage by more than two-thirds. It would have eliminated statewide coverage for Spanish in two states, reducing the number of covered counties from 58 to 10 in California and from 33 to one in New Mexico.

Senator Coburn's amendment wrongly assumed that persons who speak English "well" do not need language assistance. Since Section 203 does not define which responses to the Census language question qualify as LEP,[73] the Census Director has discretion to make that determination. The Census Bureau found "[t]hose who indicated they spoke English 'Well,' 'Not well,' or 'Not at all' were considered to have difficulty with English – identified also as people who spoke English less than 'Very well.'"[74] In a follow-up study, the Bureau determined that "persons reporting ability

67 42 U.S.C. § 1973aa-1a(b)(2)(A)(i)(III).

68 42 U.S.C. § 1973aa-1a(b)(3)(C); *see also* H.R. Rep. No. 102–655, 1992: 10 (describing the definition of American Indian and Alaska Native areas used by the Census Bureau in the 1990 decennial census).

69 *See* 67 Fed. Reg. 46,328 (July 12, 2002).

70 138 Cong. Rec. H6595 (daily ed. July 24, 1992).

71 138 Cong. Rec. H6595 (daily ed. July 24, 1992) (statement of Rep. Kennelly).

72 *See* S. Rep. No. 109–295 at 4 (2006).

73 *See* 42 U.S.C. § 1973aa-1a(b)(3)(B).

74 U.S. Census Bureau, Census 2000 Brief, Language Use and English-Speaking Ability: 2000 2 (Oct. 2003).

Figure 4.4 Jurisdictions designated for Section 203 coverage, by state (1992 Census determinations)

Source: 57 Fed. Reg. 43,213 (Sep. 18, 1992); 28 C.F.R. Pt. 55, App. (1993).

levels as 'well' or worse had significantly higher levels of failure" than the English-speaking control group.[75] The Director concluded that because people overestimated their language skills, LEP should be defined as anyone speaking English less than "very well." The high level of English proficiency needed to understand voting materials fully, and ballot questions in particular, support that conclusion. Senator Coburn's amendment failed on a voice vote in committee (S. Rep. No. 109–295, 2006: 4).

Coverage Determinations by the Director of Census

Prior to 2006, the Census Director updated Census data and published Section 203 coverage determinations on a discretionary basis as new data became available, typically following each decennial Census (*Doi v. Bell* 1978: 272). The Director did so in 1975–1977, 1984, 1992, and 2002 (Figure 4.1; Appendices B and C). In future censuses, the existing method of collecting data used for the determinations, the decennial long-form data, will be replaced by the American

75 Robert Kominski, U.S. Census Bureau, Population Division, *How Good is "How Well"? An Examination of the Census English-Speaking Ability Question* 1 (1989).

Community Survey (ACS), which will "provide long-form type information every year instead of once in ten years." Because the American Community Survey is part of the Census, responding to it is required by law.[76] During the 2006 reauthorization, Congress amended the VRA to reflect that change. Section 203 now provides that coverage determinations will be made using "the 2010 American Community Survey census data and subsequent American Community Survey data in 5-year increments, or comparable census data."[77] The Director will continue to have discretion to make more frequent determinations, but must do so at least every five years beginning with the 2010 ACS data.

Section 203 is unique in another way. Ordinarily, determinations made by an administrative agency like the Census Bureau only have to be accepted if they are "based on a permissible construction of the statute."[78] However, Section 203 provides that the Director's determinations are not reviewable in any court and are effective upon publication in the Federal Register.[79] When the Supreme Court was confronted with similar language pertaining to Section 5 determinations, it unanimously held that federal courts had no jurisdiction to consider the challenge.[80] The Court noted that "the finality of determinations … like the preclearance requirements of section 5, may well be 'an uncommon exercise of congressional power.'" Nevertheless, the Court reasoned that "there can be no question that in attacking the pervasive evils and tenacious defenders of voting discrimination, Congress acted within its 'power to enforce' the Fourteenth and Fifteenth Amendments 'by appropriate legislation.'"[81]

A federal court confirmed the Director's broad authority under the VRA. Less than two months after Section 203 was enacted in 1975, the Director issued coverage determinations for 11 states. Hawaii was covered statewide and in Honolulu County for Chinese and Filipino, and for Filipino and Japanese in Hawaii, Kauai, and Maui Counties.[82] "Hawaii received the news that it might have to conduct its elections for the next 10 years in four languages with less than joy" (*Doi v. Bell* 1978: 270). It responded by filing a bailout lawsuit.

In *Doi v. Bell*, the court rejected Hawaii's challenge to the Director's illiteracy determinations for the state and its request to accept its own alternative illiteracy data (*Doi v. Bell* 1978: 272–74). The United States stipulated to the bailout of Maui County for Japanese because the illiteracy rate for that language group no longer exceeded the national average. However, the *Doi* court denied relief for all other language groups based upon the Census determinations. The state's approach using its own "adjusted illiteracy rate" raised considerable evidentiary problems, including the scientific validity of its adjustment and problems trying to compare it with a national rate determined by the Census Bureau using different methodology. The *Doi* court suggested that Hawaii's more arbitrary approach raised potential questions of "man's ingenuity in seizing upon every possible technicality to circumvent the Congressional intent" (*Doi v. Bell* 1978: 272–74).

---

76 U.S. Census Bureau, American Community Survey: A Handbook for State and Local Officials 1 (Dec. 2004).

77 VRARA § 8, *enacted as* Pub L. No. 109–246 § 8, 120 Stat. 581.

78 *Chevron U.S.A., Inc. v. Natural Resources Defense Council*, 467 U.S. 837, 843 (1984).

79 42 U.S.C. § 1973aa-1a(b)(4).

80 *See Briscoe v. Bell*, 432 U.S. 404, 410 (1977).

81 *Briscoe v. Bell* 1977: 414 (quoting *South Carolina v. Katzenbach*, 383 U.S. 301, 334 (1966)).

82 *See* Fed. Reg. 43,044, 43,045 (Sept. 18, 1975).

Requirements for Written Bilingual Election Materials

The absence of election materials written in the native languages of covered language minority groups imposed a barrier to their participation. Congresswoman Cardiss Collins of Illinois, the first African-American woman to represent the Midwest in Congress, explained, "The right to vote is meaningless – for practical purposes – if the potential voter is unable to comprehend voting notices and materials."[83] In 1975, there was extensive evidence that "a lack of bilingual materials at the polls for non-English-speaking persons" has "severely limited participation."[84] The committee hearings left "no question but that bilingual election materials would facilitate voting on the part of language minority citizens and would at last bring them into the electoral process on an equal footing with other citizens" (S. Rep. No. 94–295, 1975: 32). Therefore, bilingual voting materials had to be provided where needed.

Mandating bilingual materials was "certainly not a radical step." Under Section 4(e) of the VRA, many Spanish-speaking Puerto Rican voters had obtained orders requiring bilingual ballots and other election information and materials. The seminal decisions in *Torres v. Sachs* and *Arroyo v. Tucker* provided the framework for the bilingual remedies included in the 1975 amendments to the VRA. The incomplete steps taken by state and local election officials also played a role in remedying the exclusion of language minority voters (S. Rep. No. 94–295, 1975: 32–34; Chapter 2). Therefore, "in mandating bilingual elections," Section 203 "affords a remedy implicit in the provisions sustained in *Morgan*" (Section 4(e) of the VRA) and "required by later court decisions" (S. Rep. No. 94–295, 1975: 36).

Under Section 203, a covered jurisdiction is prohibited from providing English-only "voting materials" in any election it administers.[85] Voting materials are defined as "registration or voting notices, forms, instructions, assistance, or other materials or information relating to the electoral process, including ballots."[86] With some narrow exceptions, all voting materials provided in English must be provided in the language of all applicable minority groups or sub-groups that triggered coverage.[87]

The Justice Department's regulations elaborate on the requirement. According to the Department, Section 203 encompasses "voter registration through activities related to conducting elections, including, for example, the issuance, at any time during the year, of notifications, announcements, or other informational materials concerning the opportunity to register, the deadline for voter registration, the time, places and subject matters of elections, and the absentee voting process."[88] It also includes materials provided by mail, public notices, registration materials, polling place activities and materials, and publicity concerning the availability of minority language materials.[89] The Justice Department advises that the definition of voting materials "should be broadly construed to apply to all stages of the electoral process."[90]

---

83 121 Cong. Rec. H4829 (daily ed. June 3, 1975).

84 121 Cong. Rec. H4830 (daily ed. June 3, 1975) (statement of Rep. Kastenmeier).

85 *See* 42 U.S.C. § 1973aa-1a(b)(1); *see also* 42 U.S.C. § 1973*l*(c)(1) and 28 C.F.R. § 55.10 (describing elections covered by Section 203).

86 42 U.S.C. § 1973aa-1a(b)(3)(A).

87 42 U.S.C. § 1973aa-1a(c) (2000).

88 28 C.F.R. § 55.15.

89 28 C.F.R. § 55.18.

90 28 C.F.R. § 55.15.

Covered jurisdictions must provide the same materials offered in English in each covered language.[91] All materials provided in minority languages must be "clear, complete and accurate."[92] If the covered language minority group uses more than one language, dialect, or written form, voting materials and assistance should be in the form most commonly used among the voting-age citizens in that group.[93] Also, jurisdictions must publicize the availability of minority language materials and assistance through methods most likely to reach language minority citizens, including outreach with language minority organizations and citizens.[94] Providing written translations of some, but not all, of the election information and materials available in English to language minority voters is insufficient.[95] Appendix A provides examples of bilingual voting materials and explains how they can help facilitate effective language assistance.

The responsibility for determining what materials must be provided in a minority language ultimately rests with the covered jurisdiction.[96] That does not mean that whatever a jurisdiction determines is needed, if anything, is conclusive. Rather, it reflects the reality that the needs of language minority groups can differ, and can even vary within the same language from place to place. Each jurisdiction is required to work with the covered language groups to determine what is needed to comply with Section 203. Failing to do that makes it likely the jurisdiction will violate Section 203.

Even good faith efforts to comply with Section 203 are actionable if they are ineffective. In California, a federal court found a city violated Section 203 despite having little time to come into compliance after becoming covered and presenting some evidence of its efforts to offer limited bilingual election information.[97] In that sense, then, Section 203 functions like a strict liability statute. A jurisdiction failing to provide effective materials and assistance in each covered language, as determined by the actual practices of its election officials and the needs of the language minority voters, will violate the statute.

There are three special circumstances that have arisen with bilingual written materials. Section 203 provides that if a language is oral or unwritten, or in the case of Alaska Natives and American Indians "historically unwritten," certain written bilingual voting materials may not be required. In addition, some courts have held that materials created by private citizens that are part of the election process, such as initiative and recall petitions, are not covered. Finally, translating voting materials into certain languages pose unique challenges. For Chinese, it is necessary to use transliteration, which phonetically approximates the names of candidates using Chinese characters. Some election officials and courts have applied these special circumstances in a manner that does not reflect the letter or the spirit of Section 203. In certain instances, they have been used by election officials as a pretext for denying language assistance altogether and reinstituting English-only election practices.

---

91 *See* 28 C.F.R. § 55.15.

92 *See* 28 C.F.R. § 55.19(b).

93 *See* 28 C.F.R. §§ 55.12–55.13.

94 *See* 28 C.F.R. § 55.18(e).

95 *See United States v. Metropolitan Dade County*, 815 F. Supp. 1475 (S.D. Fla. 1993) (holding that Section 203 applied to a voter information pamphlet that explained changes in election format, registration and voting times and voting places, and that publication of the same information in two Spanish language newspapers was insufficient).

96 *See* 28 C.F.R. § 55.19(a).

97 *See Chinese for Affirmative Action v. Leguennec*, 580 F.2d 1006 (9th Cir. 1978), *cert. denied*, 439 U.S. 1129 (1979).

Oral, Unwritten, and Historically Unwritten Languages

During the House floor debates in 1975, some members raised concerns that language assistance would be required even when unneeded. Two counties in Oklahoma that would be covered under Section 4(f)(4) illustrated the point. There was evidence indicating "that the American Indians in these two counties, mainly Choctaws, use English as their dominant language and continually have had high rates of voter participation." In addition, it appeared "that the members of the Choctaw Tribe no longer currently use the Choctaw language." Congressman Edwards concluded that the bill reported out of the House Judiciary Committee addressed this issue in two ways. First, "If the Choctaw Indians in these counties do, indeed, speak English and have had generally high voter participation, then it would surely seem that these two counties would be able to easily" bail out from coverage. To the extent those counties were covered under Section 203, Edwards explained, "if an American Indian language is historic in nature and is not used by the population of the relevant tribes, then it is obvious that not even oral assistance in such nonspoken language cases will be required."[98]

The debates made it clear that there was no categorical exemption for Alaska Native or American Indian languages from the requirement for written bilingual election materials. The languages for those two language minority groups were "generally oral only," making it possible to fulfill the bilingual election procedures "primarily by the providing of bilingual oral assistance at each stage of the election process."[99] But that did not mean that there were no circumstances under which bilingual election materials would be provided. Congressman Wiggins inquired whether the VRA would "require the ballot to be printed in the dialect of the Indian,"[100] to which Congressman Badillo replied, "If the other conditions were met, yes."[101] Congressman Edwards noted, "most," but not all, "Alaskan Native and American Indian languages have no written form."[102] Section 203 merely mandates that a covered jurisdiction provide written language materials or oral assistance based upon the actual needs of the applicable language groups or sub-groups.[103]

Adoption of the McClory amendment in the House Some members desired to exempt jurisdictions covered for languages that were unused or that did not have a written form. Congressman McClory introduced an amendment to Section 203 providing, "That where the language of the applicable minority group is oral or unwritten, the State or political subdivision is only required to furnish oral instructions, assistance, or other information relating to registration and voting." He stated that the amendment merely memorialized the members' understanding that "we will not require the reduction of the unwritten language into written form." The McClory amendment was agreed to without objection.[104]

The Senate Report explained the purpose for exempting certain covered languages from Section 203's requirements: "Nor does Title III require the impossible. A jurisdiction with a minority group whose language is oral is, of course, required only to provide oral assistance. And, obviously, a jurisdiction is not required to provide materials or assistance in an extinct language" (S. Rep. No.

98 121 Cong. Rec. H4908 (daily ed. June 4, 1975).

99 121 Cong. Rec. H4718 (daily ed. June 2, 1975) (statement of Rep. Edwards); *see* 121 Cong. Rec. at H4719.

100 121 Cong. Rec. H4738 (daily ed. June 2, 1975).

101 121 Cong. Rec. H4738 (daily ed. June 2, 1975).

102 121 Cong. Rec. H4886 (daily ed. June 4, 1975).

103 *See* 121 Cong. Rec. H4718 (daily ed. June 2, 1975) (statement of Rep. Edwards).

104 121 Cong. Rec. H4893 (daily ed. June 4, 1975).

94–295, 1975: 39). Congressman Edwards concurred, stating "if an American Indian language is historic in nature and is not used by the population of the relevant tribes, then ... not even oral assistance in such nonspoken language cases will be required."[105] The clarification offered by the McClory amendment and in the Senate Report did little to mollify parochial efforts by some members of Congress seeking to exempt their own states from Section 203.

Charles City County, Virginia, and defeat of Scott amendment Senator William L. Scott complained about an issue "of concern to the people of Virginia"[106] regarding coverage of Charles City County, Virginia, for the Chickahominy language. According to an affidavit Scott produced from a tribal member, "Chickahominy is a dead language. It is not reduced to written form, nor is it spoken by members of the Chickahominy tribe. There are only a few members of the tribe left who understand even a few words." Senator Scott offered an amendment that would have provided that language assistance was inapplicable "if the language of the minority is extinct. For the purposes of this provision, a language is extinct if there are no individuals known to have been raised with it as the primary language."[107] Senator Tunney, the floor manager of the Senate bill, opposed the Scott amendment because it was "unnecessary" in light of the McClory amendment, which would exempt Charles City County because the covered American Indian language was no longer used.[108] The Scott amendment was tabled by a vote of 59 to 34.[109]

Charles City County was subsequently covered by Section 203.[110] According to the 1970 Census, the county had 556 Powhatan Indians of the Chickahominy Tribe and 30 other Indians from unreported tribes. The county had a voter participation rate below 50 percent in the 1972 presidential election and conducted English-only elections. Although the county met the trigger for Section 4(f)(4) coverage, the Attorney General concluded that the evidence showed the Chickahominy language was extinct. As a result, it was impossible to conduct elections in any language other than English, excusing the county from Section 4(f)(4) coverage. Although the county remained covered under Section 203, it was never required to provide election materials and assistance in any language other than English. When the next determination was made under Section 203 using 1980 census data, Charles City County dropped from coverage. The exemption for extinct languages worked exactly as intended.

Adoption of Senator Stevens' historically unwritten amendment Two members of Alaska's congressional delegation mounted a vigorous challenge to get their state removed from coverage altogether. Congressman Young unsuccessfully attempted to delete Alaska Natives from the definition of "language minority" for both Section 4(f)(4) and Section 203 (Chapter 3). Senator Stevens supported the defeated Bellmon amendment, which would have exempted coverage for single language groups "whose dominant language is English." According to Senator Stevens, the "dominant language throughout my State is, in fact, English," and if that requirement was applied, Alaska would be exempted.[111] Even after the McClory amendment was adopted, they persisted in their efforts.

105 121 Cong. Rec. H4908 (daily ed. June 4, 1975).
106 121 Cong. Rec. S13048 (daily ed. July 18, 1975).
107 121 Cong. Rec. S13340 (daily ed. July 22, 1975).
108 121 Cong. Rec. S13341 (daily ed. July 22, 1975).
109 *See* Roll No. 308, 121 Cong. Rec. S13357 (daily ed. July 22, 1975).
110 *See* 40 Fed. Reg. 49587, 49588 (Oct. 23, 1975).
111 121 Cong. Rec. S13406 (daily ed. July 23, 1975).

Senator Stevens proposed amending the coverage formula to apply only to languages in which "the 5 percent would be those who would be relying upon primarily the written form of the minority language."[112] He would require "that the members of the language minority be able to read their written language before being included under the bilingual provisions."[113] Senator Tunney rejected his suggestion, noting, "We do, after all, have a serious problem for some of these language groups."[114] Tunney reasoned, "If the person is illiterate … he will get oral assistance in a language other than English. We want to give to people who are language minorities an opportunity to know for whom they are voting and on what they are voting."[115] Alaska Natives suffered from some of the highest illiteracy rates of all covered language minorities because of state-sponsored educational discrimination (Chapter 9). It would have been a strange result, indeed, if the VRA's remedies afforded to illiterate language minorities were denied to those who needed it most because of their inability to read. The primary reason for Alaska's amendments was stated by Senator Stevens, who admitted, "we do want to print our election materials in English only."[116]

To achieve that purpose, Stevens and other members made statements about Alaska Natives that were contradictory, not based on any evidence, and were factually inaccurate. Congressman Edwards erroneously stated that "the languages of Alaska are similar and they require only one interpreter."[117] Stevens repudiated that point by observing that among Aleuts, Eskimos, and American Indians, the state had "some 18 languages and some 35 dialects among those languages"[118] that "are not interchangeable languages at all; they are as different as Chinese and Italian."[119] While Stevens repeatedly argued that "no one can read the language" of the Alaska Natives,[120] he also conceded that he had no factual basis for his conclusion. "We have no studies, to my knowledge, which show any statistics as to the number of people in Alaska who would be capable of using the written form of any of these minority dialects."[121]

Furthermore, Stevens was dismissive of "making written materials available in languages other than English" in his state because it allegedly was "not going to assist those who are illiterate; that is self-evident, by definition."[122] Though that is true, the same logic applies to all language minorities who are, under Section 203's formula, covered in part because of their illiteracy. But a voter's inability to read in any language does not obviate the need for bilingual election materials. Alaska Natives have a tradition of having educated tribal members, typically younger people, read to elders who are illiterate. Senator Stevens acknowledged, "The younger people, who are learning now to read the language as it has been developed by the University of Alaska and certain missionary groups, are very much bilingual."[123] Election materials written in Alaska Native languages plainly would be widely used and helpful, even to illiterate voters.

Senator Stevens ultimately proposed a modification to the McClory amendment that added an exception to providing bilingual election materials for "historically unwritten" languages:

112 121 Cong. Rec. S13369 (daily ed. July 23, 1975).
113 121 Cong. Rec. S13367 (daily ed. July 23, 1975).
114 121 Cong. Rec. S13369 (daily ed. July 23, 1975).
115 121 Cong. Rec. S13407 (daily ed. July 23, 1975).
116 121 Cong. Rec. S13655 (daily ed. July 24, 1975).
117 121 Cong. Rec. H4827 (daily ed. June 3, 1975).
118 121 Cong. Rec. S13655 (daily ed. July 24, 1975).
119 121 Cong. Rec. S13649 (daily ed. July 24, 1975).
120 121 Cong. Rec. S13407 (daily ed. July 23, 1975).
121 121 Cong. Rec. S13369 (daily ed. July 23, 1975).
122 121 Cong. Rec. S13655 (daily ed. July 24, 1975).
123 121 Cong. Rec. S13367 (daily ed. July 23, 1975).

> [W]here the language of the applicable minority group is oral or unwritten or in the case of Alaskan Natives and American Indians, if the predominant language is historically unwritten, the State or political subdivision is only required to furnish oral instructions, assistance, or other information relating to registration and voting.[124]

Stevens introduced his amendment after consulting with other senators and members of the House. It was adopted without objection.[125] The same proviso was added to both Section 4(f)(4) and Section 203.[126] If a covered language is "historically unwritten," the jurisdiction still must provide oral translations of all voting materials in that covered language at the same time those voting materials are disseminated to voters in English.[127]

Section 203 does not define "historically unwritten." Members were ambivalent about the term. Senator Stevens suggested it meant a language had to be written for longer than 15 years,[128] while Senator Tunney suggested it meant longer than 25 years.[129] But the purpose of the amendment is clear. Senator Tunney reasoned that "one cannot expect the State to publish a language that has never been written except by a few anthropologists and is not read or understood by any of the natives. That was not intended by this section."[130] Congressman Edwards explained the effect of the proviso on bilingual election procedures under Sections 4(f)(4) and 203(c) of the Act:

> Languages recently developed by anthropologists, which are obviously not used or widely used by citizens of voting age within the language group, have always been, for our purposes, "oral" or "unwritten" languages. Therefore, the mandate imposed under such circumstances was not one for printed bilingual election materials but rather one for bilingual oral assistance in registration and voting.. [A]lthough the language of the Stevens amendment has been placed only in [Section 203], ... this is in no way to imply that a contrary interpretation is to be given to the bilingual elections mandate as it appears in [Section 4(f)(4)].[131]

To summarize, the Stevens amendment simply exempted certain written materials for any language that was unwritten or not commonly used by the covered language minority. That is consistent with the VRA's intent to provide effective language assistance. Written bilingual voting information that even literate voters cannot read or understand obviously would not achieve that result.

The Justice Department confirmed that the Stevens amendment did not implement a categorical exemption for providing written bilingual materials in Native languages. Instead, Assistant Attorney General Pottinger explained:

> It has been the understanding of the Department of Justice that this proviso, which was added to the Act on the floor of the House, should be read broadly to include languages of protected language minority groups which are not in fact written by the language minority group itself. Thus, it has been our interpretation of this proviso, together with the related portions of the Act, that if a written language has been developed linguistically, but has little or no relevance to the persons who speak

124 121 Cong. Rec. S13658 (daily ed. July 24, 1975).
125 121 Cong. Rec. H4893 (daily ed. June 4, 1975).
126 *See* 42 U.S.C. §1973b(f)(4); 42 U.S.C. § 1973aa-1a(c).
127 *See* 42 U.S.C. §§ 1973aa–1a(b)(1), (c); Apache County v. United States, Civil Action No. 77-1515, mem. op. (D.D.C. June 12, 1980) (three-judge court).
128 121 Cong. Rec. S13367 (daily ed. July 23, 1975).
129 121 Cong. Rec. S13369 (daily ed. July 23, 1975).
130 121 Cong. Rec. S13651 (daily ed. July 24, 1975).
131 121 Cong. Rec. H7631 (daily ed. July 28, 1975).

> the language, a jurisdiction would not be required to print election and registration materials in that language, but instead would be required to provide oral assistance to registrants and voters.[132]

The Department's regulations reflect that understanding as well, indicating that languages used "by some American Indians and Alaskan Natives are unwritten." The focus under the regulations is on the written language's usage among language minorities: "Even though a written form for a language may exist, a language may be considered unwritten if it is not commonly used in a written form."[133] In addition, "materials and assistance should be provided in a way designed to allow members of applicable language minority groups to be effectively informed of and participate effectively in voting-connected activities."[134] If bilingual written materials achieve that goal for a covered Alaska Native or American Indian language, they should be provided.

In practice, many jurisdictions create and use some bilingual written materials for Native languages. Senator Stevens contemplated that would happen even to the extent he maintained (inaccurately, as shown in Chapter 10) that all Alaska Native languages were unwritten and not commonly used. He inserted a letter from a State of Alaska elections supervisor, who wrote:

> Perhaps printing "sample" bilingual ballots would be a plausible solution. Sample ballots printed in all those languages which are in written form could be effectively disseminated to the public through a number of ways -- the news media, posted in public gathering places, election offices, registrars, city and borough clerk's offices, village and minority leaders, as well as the candidates themselves. Here would be a means whereby the voter would have the opportunity to study, discuss, and decide, prior to all elections in the privacy and leisure of his own time and language, what and how he will vote ... Sample bilingual ballots can be the only logical means of reaching this small percentage of our population, without implementing a burdensome, unnecessary and somewhat more confusing feature to our voting system -- and still obtain the same objective![135]

In 1997, the General Accounting Office (GAO) reported that four out of 34 responding jurisdictions provided bilingual written materials to American Indian voters.[136] In a 2005 study, two jurisdictions reported that they provided written materials in an American Indian language (Chapter 6).[137] Figure 4.5 is an example of a public information pamphlet on Arizona's voter identification requirements disseminated in Navajo.

Even jurisdictions that contend their Native languages are unwritten often use written materials in covered languages such as bilingual election glossaries, sample ballots, polling place signs, translator training materials, voter information pamphlets, and "I voted" stickers. In 2008, a federal judge ordered Alaska to prepare a sample ballot and provide certain other materials written in Yup'ik for Eskimos in the Bethel region, notwithstanding his finding that Yup'ik was "historically unwritten." Until that time, Alaska had relied upon the exception to conduct largely English-only

---

132 121 Cong. Rec. H7632 (daily ed. July 28, 1975) (statement of Rep. Edwards) (quoting Letter from Pottinger to Edwards).

133 28 C.F.R. § 55.12(c).

134 28 C.F.R. § 55.2(b)(1).

135 121 Cong. Rec. S13368 (daily ed. July 23, 1975) (statement of Sen. Stevens) (quoting letter dated May 28, 1975 from Lory B. Leary, Southeast Election Supervisor, State of Alaska).

136 *See* U.S. Gen. Accounting Office, Bilingual Voting Assistance: Assistance Provided and Costs 13 (1997).

137 *See* James Thomas Tucker and Rodolfo Espino, *Government Effectiveness and Efficiency? The Minority Language Assistance Provisions of the VRA*, 12 Tex. J. C.L. & C.R. 163, 190 (2007).

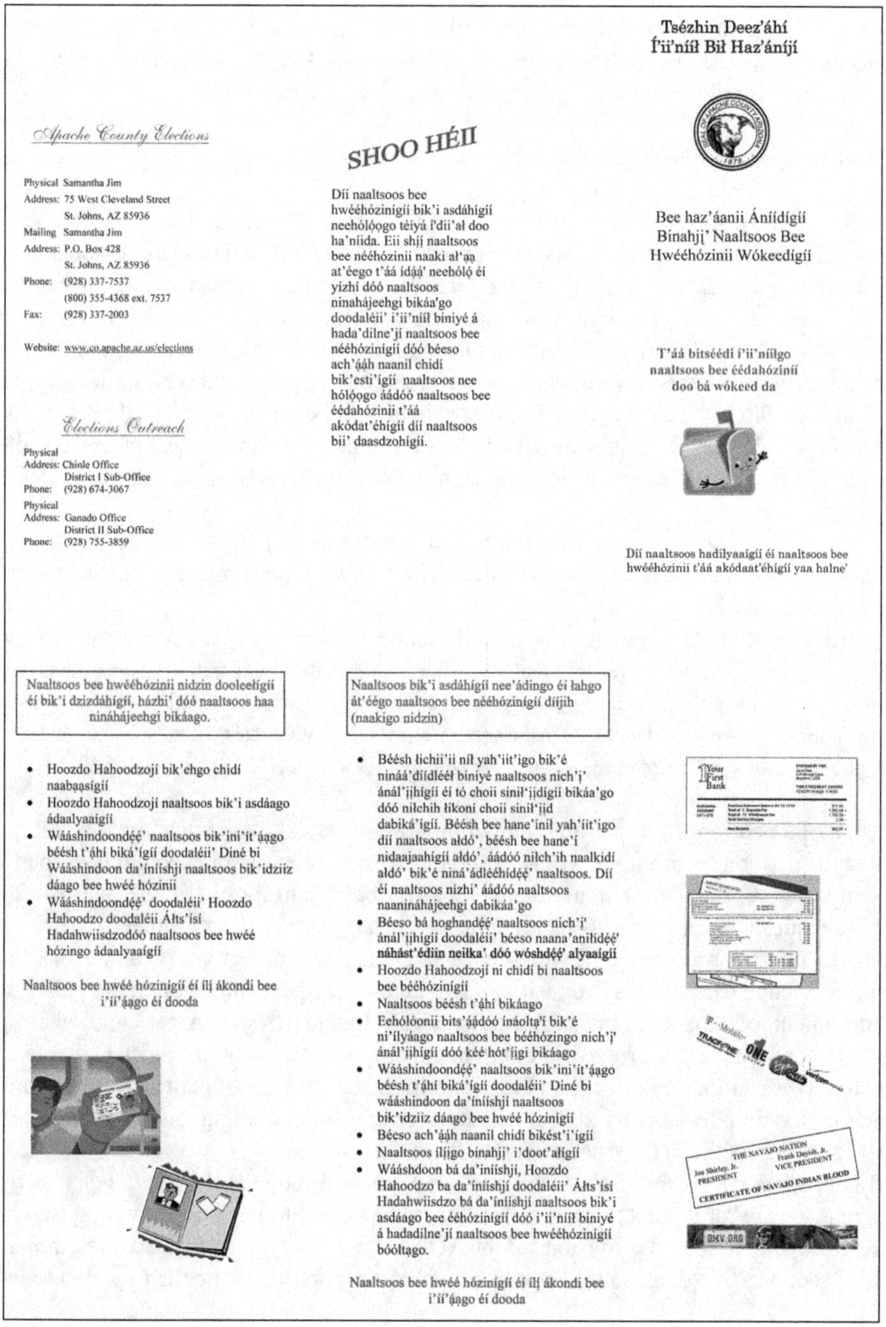

Apache County Elections

Physical Address: Samantha Jim
75 West Cleveland Street
St. Johns, AZ 85936

Mailing Address: Samantha Jim
P.O. Box 428
St. Johns, AZ 85936

Phone: (928) 337-7537
(800) 355-4368 ext. 7537

Fax: (928) 337-2003

Website: www.co.apache.az.us/elections

Elections Outreach

Physical Address: Chinle Office
District I Sub-Office
Phone: (928) 674-3067

Physical Address: Ganado Office
District II Sub-Office
Phone: (928) 755-3859

SHOO HÉII

Díí naaltsoos bee hwééhózinigíí bik'i asdáhígíí neehólǫǫgo téíyá í'dii'ał doo ha'níida. Eii shįį naaltsoos bee nééhózinii naaki ał'ąą at'éego t'áá ídąą' neehólǫ éí yízhí dóó naaltsoos ninahájeehgi bikáa'go doodaléii' i'ii'nííł biniyé á hada'dilne'jí naaltsoos bee nééhózinígíí dóó béeso ach'ąąh naanil chidí bik'esti'ígíí naaltsoos nee hólǫǫgo áádóó naaltsoos bee éédahózinii t'áá akódat'éhígíí díí naaltsoos bii' daasdzohígíí.

Tsézhin Deez'áhí
Í'ii'nííł Bił Haz'áníjí

Bee haz'áanii Áníídígíí
Binahjį' Naaltsoos Bee
Hwééhózinii Wókeedígíí

T'áá bitséédi í'ii'níilgo
naaltsoos bee éédahózinií
doo bá wókeed da

Díí naaltsoos hadilyaaígíí éí naaltsoos bee hwééhózinii t'áá akódaat'éhígíí yaa halne'

Naaltsoos bee hwééhózinii nidzin dooleełígíí éí bik'i dzizdáhígíí, házhi' dóó naaltsoos haa ninááhájeehgi bikáago.

- Hoozdo Hahoodzojí bik'ehgo chidí naabąąsígíí
- Hoozdo Hahoodzojí naaltsoos bik'i asdáago ádaalyaaígíí
- Wááshindoondę́ę́' naaltsoos bik'ini'ít'ąągo béésh t'ąhí biká'ígíí doodaléii' Diné bi Wááshindoon da'íníishjí naaltsoos bik'idziiz dáago bee hwéé hózinii
- Wááshindoondę́ę́' doodaléii' Hoozdo Hahoodzo doodaléii Áłts'ísí Hadahwiisdzodóó naaltsoos bee hwéé hózingo ádaalyaaígíí

Naaltsoos bee hwéé hózinigíí éí íłį ákondi bee i'íí'ąągo éí dooda

Naaltsoos bik'i asdáhígíí nee'ádingo éí łahgo át'éégo naaltsoos bee nééhózinígíí díįjih (naakigo nidzin)

- Béésh łichii'ii nił yah'iit'igo bik'é ninââ'díídléél biniyé naaltsoos nich'į' ánál'įįhígíí éí tó choii siniłʻįįdígíí bikáa'go dóó niłchih łikoní choii siniłʻįįd dabiká'igíí. Béésh bee hane'ínił yah'íít'igo díí naaltsoos ałdó', béésh bee hane'í nidaajaahígíí ałdó', áádóó niłch'ih naalkidí ałdó' bik'é niná'ádlééhídę́ę́' naaltsoos. Díí éí naaltsoos nízhi' áádóó naaltsoos naanináhájeehgi dabikáa'go
- Béeso bá hoghandę́ę́' naaltsoos nich'į' ánál'įįhígíí doodaléii' béeso naana'aniłídę́ę́' **náhást'édiin neiłka' dóó wóshdę́ę́' alyaaígíí**
- Hoozdo Hahoodzojí ni chidí bi naaltsoos bee bééhózinígíí
- Naaltsoos béésh t'ąhí bikáago
- Eehólóonii bits'ąądóó ínáoltą'í bik'é ni'ílyáago naaltsoos bee bééhózingo nich'į' ánál'įįhígíí dóó kéé hót'įįgi bikáago
- Wááshindoondę́ę́' naaltsoos bik'ini'ít'ąągo béésh t'ąhí biká'ígíí doodaléii' Diné bi wááshindoon da'íníishjí naaltsoos bik'idziiz dáago bee hwéé hózinígíí
- Béeso ach'ąąh naanil chidí bikést'i'ígíí
- Naaltsoos íłįįgo binahjį' i'doot'ałígíí
- Wááshdoon bá da'iníishjí, Hoozdo Hahoodzo ba da'íníishjí doodaléii' Áłts'ísí Hadahwiisdzo bá da'íníishjí naaltsoos bik'i asdáago bee ééhózinígíí dóó i'ii'nííł biniyé á hadadilne'jí naaltsoos bee hwééhózinígíí bóóltągo.

Naaltsoos bee hwéé hózinígíí éí íłį ákondi bee i'íí'ąągo éí dooda

Figure 4.5 Navajo information pamphlet on Arizona's voter identification requirements
Source: Apache County, Arizona, Elections Department.

elections with little language assistance offered at any stage of the voting process (Chapter 10). Figure 10.5 depicts a sample ballot written in Yup'ik prepared by Alaska's election officials as one remedy for their violations of the language assistance provisions.

Initiative and Referenda Petitions

Participation in the political process is not limited to casting a ballot on Election Day. Voters also play an important role in direct democracy procedures, most of which were adopted during the so-called Progressive Era.[138] Initiatives or referenda, or similar mechanisms, sometimes known as "ballot measures," "propositions," or "questions," differ from the usual process of electing legislators to pass laws. They allow citizens to vote directly on proposed legislation. Typically, state and local governments have adopted procedures requiring anyone seeking to get a question on the ballot to file a petition containing a specified number of signatures of registered voters (Magleby 1994: 225–26). The question of whether those petitions are "voting materials" that must be provided in each covered language has been one of the most litigated issues under Section 203.

There are strong policy reasons to require citizen-initiated petitions to be translated into a jurisdiction's covered languages. It is consistent with the VRA's expansive definition of voting:

> The terms "vote" or "voting" shall include all action necessary to make a vote effective in any primary, special, or general election, including, but not limited to, registration, listing pursuant to this Act, *or other action required by law prerequisite to voting*, casting a ballot, and having such ballot counted properly and included in the appropriate totals of votes cast with respect to candidates for public or party office and propositions for which votes are received in an election.[139]

Submission of a petition is an "action required by law prerequisite to voting" on a ballot question. Excluding the petition requirement would exempt a growing process for enacting laws, particularly in western states. In the 1990s alone, there were 353 ballot questions (Magleby 1994: 230–32). Many ballot questions have a substantial impact on language minority voters. Alaska has had several ballot questions affecting the subsistence and land rights of Natives (Chapter 10). Arizona's Proposition 203 and California's Proposition 227 banned bilingual education in the public schools, to the detriment of tens of thousands of American Indians, Asian Americans, and Spanish-speaking persons. Arizona's Proposition 200, mandating identification to register to vote and cast a ballot, has a discriminatory effect on language minority citizens.[140] If petitions are unavailable in languages covered under Section 203, it has the potential for excluding language minority voters from participating on the very issues affecting them the most.

Early on, some courts found that petitions were covered. The court in *Zaldivar v. City of Los Angeles* rejected the "argument that a recall notice is only a preliminary step to voting and therefore is unaffected by the bilingual provisions of the Act" as "without merit." Instead, the *Zaldivar* court found that Section 203 "does not exempt information or material, compelled by statute, which is

---

138 *See* David B. Magleby, *Direct Legislation in the American States*, *in* Referendums Around the World: The Growing Use of Direct Democracy 218–19 (David Butler and Austin Ranney eds. 1994).

139 42 U.S.C. § 1973*l*(c)(1) (emphasis added).

140 *See* James Thomas Tucker and Rodolfo Espino et al., *Voting Rights in Arizona 1982–2006*, 17 S. Cal. Rev. L. & Soc. Just. 283, 354–58 (2008).

preliminary to voting, but essential if an election is to occur."[141] The court in *Montero v. Meyer* agreed, finding that petitions circulated for purposes of placing a constitutional initiative on the ballot were covered "voting materials." The *Montero* court reasoned that the Colorado government played a key role in the initiative process and access to that information was essential to effective participation.[142]

However, neither court's ruling was binding. *Zaldivar*'s discussion was merely explanatory dictum and not part of its ruling, and was later rejected by the court of appeals.[143] *Montero*'s holding was reversed on appeal.[144] More recently, courts have tended to exclude actions such as publication of an English-only notice to seek a recall[145] or circulation of an English-only initiative petition from Section 203 if neither the state nor the political subdivision created the materials (*Delgado v. Smith* 1988: 1489; *Montero v. Meyer* 1988: 603).

Those decisions have found some support in congressional materials. The 1975 Senate Report implied that private citizen actions would not qualify as voting materials: "Whenever any *jurisdiction* covered under this title provides *official* registration or election materials, those materials must be provided in the language of the applicable language minority group as well as in English."[146] In 2006, the House Judiciary Committee bowed to the pressure of Orange County, California, which was being sued for failing to provide its petitions in languages covered by Section 203 (Chapter 7). In a successful effort to undercut that litigation, the 2006 House Report stated, "However, language assistance that facilitates equal participation in the voting process so language minority citizens are able to cast effective ballots does not require private citizens to make privately prepared and distributed materials available in the covered languages."[147]

The exclusion of petitions from "voting materials" has impeded the political participation of many language minority voters. Section 203's protections ring hollow if they can be circumvented by citizens through the petition process. State and local governments impose many requirements on those seeking to place a question on a ballot. Any minor inconvenience of providing those same written materials to language minorities impacted by the questions is a small price to pay.

Transliteration of Bilingual Voting Materials

Translation of candidates' names into Chinese is one of the more interesting issues under Section 203. Chinese is not an alphabetic language, so it is not possible to spell out the names of candidates appearing on ballots. Instead, names and other proper nouns are translated "by the process of 'transliteration,' in which the sounds that compose the English word are represented by Chinese

---

141 780 F.2d 823, 833 n.11 (9th Cir. 1986), *abrogated on other grounds*, *Coopter and Gell v. Hartmarx Corp.*, 496 U.S. 384 (1990).

142 696 F. Supp. 540 (D. Colo.), *rev'd*, 861 F.2d 603 (10th Cir. 1988), *cert. denied*, 492 U.S. 921 (1989).

143 *See Delgado v. Smith*, 861 F.2d 1489 (11th Cir. 1988), *reh'g denied*, 865 F.2d 1274, *cert. denied*, 492 U.S. 918 (1989).

144 *See* 861 F.2d 603 (10th Cir. 1988), *cert. denied*, 492 U.S. 921 (1989).

145 *See Padilla v. Lever*, 463 F.3d 1046 (9th Cir. 2006) (en banc); *Gerena-Valentin v. Koch*, 523 F. Supp. 176 (S.D.N.Y. 1981); *Zaldivar v. City of Los Angeles*, 590 F. Supp. 852 (C.D. Cal. 1984), *rev'd in part on other grounds*, 780 F.2d 823, 833 n.11 (9th Cir. 1986) (in dictum, disagreeing with district court's conclusion).

146 S. Rep. No. 94–295, 1975: 49 (emphasis added).

147 H.R. Rep. No. 109–478, at 60 (2006).

characters."[148] Former Assistant Attorney General Deval Patrick explained that "a candidate's name is one of the most important items of information sought by a voter before casting … [a] ballot for a particular candidate … For voters who need Chinese-language materials, the translation of candidates' names is important because Roman characters are completely different from Chinese characters." Stated another way, it would be like an American driver attempting to navigate "the streets of Beijing while trying to read street signs written only in Chinese characters" – completely incomprehensible.[149] Transliteration makes English names and other proper nouns appearing on a ballot understandable to anyone reading voting materials written in Chinese.[150]

Dictionaries carry standard translations for most names. More uncommon names are transliterated using "[s]tandard phonetic transliterations of vowels and consonants … to devise the Chinese characters" (Brief of Chinese Progressive Ass'n 2007: 9). This process allows an entire ballot, including candidates' names, to be translated in a way that is understandable to Chinese voters. "LEP Chinese American voters typically know the candidates by their translated/transliterated names, and not by their English names. These names appear in Chinese-language media outlets, advertising, public notices, and campaign literature" (Brief of Chinese Progressive Ass'n 2007: 6). In September 1994, New York City began transliterating its ballots into Chinese for 54,000 LEP Chinese in three of its boroughs.[151] San Francisco County, California, first used transliterated ballots in November 1999.[152] Other jurisdictions using Chinese transliterations include Alameda County, Los Angeles County, Orange County, and Santa Clara County in California (Lee and Wong 2007).

Despite common usage of transliteration and its approval by Chinese voters, some election officials oppose it. In 2005, Boston entered into a consent decree with the Justice Department and private litigants to resolve language claims brought against the city under Section 2 of the VRA.[153] A three-judge federal court entered the decree in October 2005. The next month, the number of Chinese-speaking poll workers citywide increased from nine to 68. In May 2006, Massachusetts enacted legislation providing that in Boston's elections, officials would offer bilingual ballots in both Chinese and Vietnamese in designated precincts with at least 35 Chinese-surnamed voters or 30 Vietnamese-surnamed voters through December 2008.[154] The city separately agreed to provide transliterated Chinese ballots for city elections and did so for the April and May 2007 city elections.[155]

148 Brief of Chinese Progressive Ass'n et al., at 2, *United States v. City of Boston*, Case No. 05–11598 (D. Mass. July 24, 2007) (three-judge court).

149 Suzanne Lee and Ann Har-Yee Wong, *Chinese Americans deserve full voting rights*, Boston Globe, July 11, 2007, at A9.

150 For a more detailed explanation of transliteration, *see* Yin Binyong, Chinese Romanization: Pronunciation and Orthography (translated and edited by Mary Felley 1990).

151 *See* Ashley Dunn, *Board Agrees on Ballots in Chinese*, N.Y. Times, Aug. 25, 1994.

152 *See* Julie Chao, *Elections Board to Hire Bilingual Coordinator, S.F. Department to Boost Number of Chinese-Speaking Poll Workers*, S.F. Exam'r, July 27, 1999, at A3.

153 *See* Consent Decree, *United States v. City of Boston*, Case No. 05–11598 (D. Mass. July 24, 2007) (three-judge court).

154 Mass. Acts of 2006, ch. 111, § 2.

155 *See* Chinese Progressive Ass'n, *Historical Overview of Chinese Bilingual Ballots in Boston* ("Historical Overview"), available at http://www.cpaboston.org/.

The state initially provided transliterated names as well, including them on partially translated ballots used statewide and in Middlesex and Suffolk Counties in 2006.[156] However, Secretary of State William Galvin subsequently balked at continuing the practice, which he considered imprecise. According to Galvin, the transliterated Chinese names for candidates would include: "Imbecile," "Sun Moon Rainbow Farmer," or "Barbarian Mud No Mind of His Own" for Boston mayor Tom Menino; "Stickey Rice" or "Uncooked Rice" for Governor Mitt Romney; "Triumphant Wheat" for Senator John McCain; "Upset Stomach" or "Tired Forest" for Senator Hillary Rodham Clinton; and "Oh Bus Horse" or "Profound Horse" for Senator Barack Obama.[157] Galvin criticized transliteration of proper names saying it would be create chaos and confuse voters and refused to include transliteration on ballots produced by the state (Phillips 2007). Despite several requests from Asian American voters and community organizations, the Secretary of State declined to meet with them to discuss the issue (Historical Overview).

The Justice Department and city sought to end the impasse by asking the federal court to clarify that the consent decree required transliteration. In August 2007, the court declined, leaving it to the parties.[158] In May 2008, hundreds of Chinese voters attended a city council hearing to urge passage of a home-rule petition mandating transliteration and continued use of Chinese and Vietnamese bilingual ballots beyond December 2008. A little more than a week later, the city council passed the petition unanimously and forwarded it to the state legislature (Sacchetti 2008). However, the legislative session closed in July 2008 without enacting Boston's home-rule petition (Historical Overview).

A Chinese community group described Galvin's examples as "a false construction created for the entertainment of *Boston Globe* readers" (Transliteration FAQ). The Asian American Legal Defense and Education Fund (AALDEF) explained:

> Although each character used to develop a translated/transliterated name individually has a meaning, together the characters of a translated/transliterated name *do not* convey meanings and are certainly not understood to be characteristics of a particular person. Just as an English-speaking voter would not believe that Mr. Green is a green man and therefore undeserving of his/her vote, a Chinese-speaking person would not think that Mitt Romney (transliterated as Rice Clear Nun) is a nun who eats clear rice and thus undeserving of his/her vote. Chinese is read contextually and each character is read in light of other characters surrounding it. A string of words that have no meaning when read together, followed by an English name in parenthesis, would be read by a Chinese-speaking individual to be just that – a name (Brief of Chinese Progressive Ass'n 2007: 8–9).

Working together with the Justice Department, AALDEF, and other Asian groups, Boston implemented a four-step transliteration procedure successfully used elsewhere. First, a qualified translation company transliterated the candidate names. Second, it used "at least two linguistic liaisons to check the transliterations for accuracy or conflicts with any existing transliterations." Third, the city provided

156 *See* Chinese Progressive Ass'n, *Frequently Asked Questions about Chinese Bilingual Ballots and Transliteration* ("Transliteration FAQ"), *available at* http://www.cpaboston.org/ftp/pressFAQs.doc.

157 Frank Phillips, *Boston translations could mean too much*, Boston Globe, June 26, 2007; Maria Sacchetti, *Fresh fight over bilingual ballots; Council to pursue state law ordering names in Chinese*, Boston Globe, May 14, 2008; David Schoetz, *Lost in Translation or Chinese Food for Thought? Justice Department vs. Massachusetts Ballot Issue Could Land in Court*, ABC News, June 28, 2007; Andrea Stone, *Candidates lost in Chinese translation*, USA Today, July 10, 2007.

158 *See* Order, *United States v. City of Boston*, Case No. 05–11598 (D. Mass. Aug. 3, 2007) (three-judge court).

the transliterated names to all candidates early in the process, giving them one week to alter their transliterated name. Fourth, the transliterated names were then released "to all candidates, campaigns, Chinese language media sources, and Chinese community groups" (Transliteration FAQ).

Boston's approach worked well for the city's large LEP Chinese population. There were 6,545 voters with Chinese surnames in the city, including 1,563 who were elderly and struggled most with the English language (Sacchetti 2008). In the region, Chinese media used transliterated names, including the Chinese language newspaper *World Journal*, which had a Boston-area circulation of 30,000 readers (Brief of Chinese Progressive Ass'n 2007: 8–9). According to the Justice Department, when candidate names were written in English using Roman characters, there were reports of poll workers "mis-marking ballots of Chinese voters" that did not reflect the voter's intent (Phillips 2007). Tse Ngar Cho, an 83-year-old who only speaks and reads Chinese observed, "With the ballot translated, your chance of making a mistake is really small. You know what candidate you're voting for" (Sacchetti 2008). AALDEF counsel Glenn Magpantay explained, "We are looking to make sure Asian Americans are able to vote for their candidates of choice ... That is difficult to do when voters with limited-English proficiency cannot find those candidates" (Phillips 2007). Transliterated ballots dramatically impacted voter participation. In two city elections held in spring 2007, Boston's Chinatown had record turnout, exceeding the city's general voter turnout rate for the first time in history (Historical Overview).

The Boston example illustrates why transliteration is necessary. Section 203 prohibits providing voting materials, including ballots, "only in the English language."[159] There is no exception for any portion of those materials, such as the candidates' names, which are one of the most important parts of a ballot. Moreover, bilingual voting materials should be provided in a way allowing covered language minorities to "be effectively informed of and participate effectively in" elections.[160] That requires candidate names be transliterated to ensure that the information Chinese-speaking voters receive is clear, complete, and accurate. The preparation of transliterated ballots in consultation with Chinese community groups facilitates compliance with that requirement.[161] Transliterated ballots allow Chinese voters to understand the complete ballot and cast an effective vote. Without a ballot providing a complete translation of all information, including the candidates' names, LEP Chinese voters are "effectively excluded from participation in the electoral process."[162]

Requirements for Oral Language Translations

Section 203 also was needed because of "the almost total absence of bilingual registrars and election officials in areas having a substantial percentage of Spanish speaking and other language minority voters."[163] This "underrepresentation of minority persons as poll workers" contributed to "the unavailability or inadequacy of assistance." (S. Rep. No. 94–295, 1975: 26). There was nothing new about mandating bilingual poll workers. Cases brought under Section 4(e) of the Act resulted in orders requiring "extensive bilingual assistance to voters" in election districts with large language minority populations, such as through "bilingual media" and "use of bilingual election inspectors" (S. Rep. No. 94–295, 1975: 32–33). Many state and local governments implemented election practices to provide oral translations (Chapter 2). The 1975 amendments to the VRA filled

159 42 U.S.C. § 1973aa-1a(b)(1).

160 28 C.F.R. § 55.2(b).

161 28 C.F.R. § 55.19(b).

162 42 U.S.C. § 1973aa-1a(a).

163 121 Cong. Rec. H4743 (daily ed. June 2, 1975) (statement of Rep. Roybal).

gaps in existing laws and procedures. Under Section 203, oral translations must be provided at every stage of the voting process.

Effective Bilingual Assistance before Election Day

Covered jurisdictions must ensure they provide effective bilingual assistance for voting information and registration before Election Day. One method of accomplishing that objective is to provide bilingual registration materials to all prospective registrants and to have only bilingual persons working as registrars. Alternatively, it may be sufficient to use some bilingual registrars who are members of the covered language group, establish registration sites in areas heavily populated by language minorities, and have bilingual registration materials available at those sites.[164] Regardless of the method, registration sites should be kept open at times convenient for language minorities to register, bilingual registrars need to be accessible for telephone inquiries, and signs should be displayed at the central registration office and at sites in language minority communities "advertising the availability of bilingual assistance" (U.S. Comm'n on Civil Rts. 1984: 16).

Failure to provide language minorities with equal access to registration and voter information violates Section 203 in covered jurisdictions. For instance, in Cook County, Illinois, a federal court found that election officials did not provide effective pre-election language assistance when they only offered voter registration materials written in Spanish. The court ordered the officials to provide oral language assistance for voter registration including "public service announcements in the Spanish language … providing assistance in Spanish under the fail safe provisions of the Act, as well as providing oral and written assistance at all registration sites."[165] The Senate Committee Report explained, "If a language minority person is not permitted to register … that person is obviously denied full participation in the political process" (S. Rep. No. 94–295, 1975: 27).

A jurisdiction that does not provide equal pre-election voter opportunities can be liable under Section 2 of the VRA, regardless of Section 203 coverage. A federal court in Illinois held that Latino voters could challenge a local practice of appointing only two deputy election registrars from any civic organization, even though Latinos comprised less than 5 percent of the county's eligible voters.[166] In Montana, a vote dilution claim brought by American Indian voters under Section 2 was supported by "irregularities in distribution of registration cards," such as limiting the number of cards that they could pick up to conduct voter registration drives.[167] Federal courts have broadly construed Section 2 to find liability for any election practice that fails to provide information in an effective manner to a group of racial, ethnic, or language minority voters (Chapter 2).[168]

164 *See* 42 U.S.C. § 1973aa-1a(c); 28 C.F.R. § 55.18(c).

165 *Association of Community Orgs. for Reform Now v. Edgar*, 1995 WL 532120, at *3 (N.D. Ill. 1995).

166 *Hernandez v. Woodard*, 714 F. Supp. 963 (N.D. Ill. 1989).

167 *Windy Boy v. County of Big Horn*, 647 F. Supp. 1002, 1008 (D. Mont. 1986).

168 *See United States v. Post*, 297 F. Supp. 46, 50–51 (W.D. La. 1969).

Effective Bilingual Assistance at Polling Places

Language assistance likewise must be available at polling places on Election Day.[169] In most cases, all written materials at the polls needs to be in the language of each covered language[170] and be "readily accessible and in a conspicuous place," along with signs advertising the availability of bilingual assistance (U.S. Comm'n on Civil Rts. 1984: 16). Oral language assistance must be provided to the extent necessary to allow language minority citizens to participate effectively.[171] Justice Department guidelines require covered jurisdictions to determine the number of "helpers" necessary to provide oral assistance in the minority language.[172] Jurisdictions should be proactive in recruiting bilingual poll workers who are members of covered language minority groups to ensure oral language assistance is available (U.S. Comm'n on Civil Rts. 1984: 16).

There are many ways that the absence of bilingual poll workers can result in disenfranchisement. Language minority voters may be turned away because monolingual English-speaking poll workers cannot "locate voters' names on precinct lists." Latino voters often have more than one surname (using the surname of their mother, father, or both), and poll workers may not ask them if they registered under a different name. Voters casting challenged or provisional ballots may not be given instructions that they can understand, causing them to void their vote by filling out their ballot incorrectly. Even if a non-English-speaking voter receives a regular ballot, that person may be unable to understand it or the written instructions accompanying it without language assistance. If the poll worker providing assistance is not fluent and literate in both English and the covered language, the voter will receive incomplete and inaccurate information that may cause him or her to vote the wrong way. "What is done at the local level by local officials has the most impact upon the ability of these minorities to vote and the effectiveness of that vote" (S. Rep. No. 94–295, 1975: 26).

Failure to hire sufficient language minorities for Election Day also can violate Section 2 of the VRA, which prohibits discriminatory poll official appointment policies or practices.[173] The absence of minority language poll officials may discourage language minority citizens from voting because they do not feel welcome at polling places, particularly if they were mistreated at the polls in the past or no language assistance is available for them.[174] The "people in charge are frequently the same ones who so recently excluded minorities from the political process" (S. Rep. No. 94–295, 1975: 26). Often, LEP voters are greeted by poll workers with ethnic epithets or are taunted for requesting language or voter assistance.[175]

Proactive Language Assistance Programs

Effective language assistance typically is not possible without the cooperation of local election officials (U.S. Comm'n on Civil Rts. 1981: 82–83). It is insufficient for a covered jurisdiction to merely translate election materials and hire bilingual poll workers. Election officials frequently

169 *See* 42 U.S.C. § 1973aa-1a(c) (2000); 28 C.F.R. § 55.20 (2006).

170 *See* 42 U.S.C. § 1973aa-1a(c).

171 28 C.F.R. § 55.20; *see also* 42 U.S.C. § 1973aa-1a(c).

172 28 C.F.R. § 55.20(c).

173 *See Harris v. Graddick*, 593 F. Supp. 128, 132–33 (M.D. Ala. 1984).

174 *See Harris v. Graddick* 1984: 131–32; U.S. Comm'n on Civil Rts., The Voting Rights Act: Unfulfilled Goals 79–80 (1981).

175 *See* James Thomas Tucker, *The Power of Observation: The Role of Federal Observers under the Voting Rights Act*, 13 Mich. J. Race & Law 227, 259–60 (Fall 2007).

violate the language assistance provisions because they do not understand them, are following inconsistent state law, or refuse to comply. Therefore, all election officials should be provided with effective training and be informed of consequences if they do not comply. That is true for both new poll workers and "veteran poll officials."[176] If election officials fail to comply, they not only might be dismissed, they may face criminal penalties under the VRA.[177]

Furthermore, election officials must work closely with members of the language minority community to determine the most effective way to implement their bilingual election program. The Justice Department's regulations observe that a "jurisdiction is more likely to achieve compliance ... if it has worked with the cooperation of and to the satisfaction of organizations representing members of the applicable language minority group."[178] Outreach should not be limited to minority leaders.

By talking to a broad range of people in the minority community – educators, business groups, labor groups, [English as a Second Language] programs, parent-teacher organizations, senior citizen groups, church groups, social and fraternal organizations, veterans groups, and the like – election officials will be able to identify the most effective and most efficient program possible (U.S. Dep't of Justice 2002).

Local members of minority language groups likewise are a good source for bilingual election officials and can confirm the accuracy of translations.

Election officials also must be prepared for contingencies, such as poll workers failing to appear, problems with distribution of language materials, and unexpected LEP voters showing up at polling sites. Some ways to address these problems include proper training, back-up communication, and extra language materials and bilingual poll workers. Effective bilingual election programs cannot be static, but instead must evolve with the changing realities of the local language minority communities (U.S. Dep't of Justice 2002).

Anomalies Caused by the 25-Year Extension of Section 203 in 2006

The Voting Rights Reauthorization Act of 2006 (VRARA) provided for a straight reauthorization of language assistance provisions by substituting "2032" for "2007" in the sunset date specified in Section 203(b)(1) of the Act (Chapter 7).[179] However, the revised expiration date of August 6, 2032 for Section 203 coverage inadvertently created three anomalous results. First, it adopted a later sunset date than the one for Section 5 coverage, which expires 25 years from the date of enactment, or July 27, 2031 (Chapter 3).

Second, the later date only applies to jurisdictions covered under Section 203 and not jurisdictions covered for language assistance under Section 4(f)(4). Instead, those jurisdictions will only remain covered after July 27, 2031 if they independently meet the coverage formula in Section 203.[180] In 2006, one of the three Section 4(f)(4) covered states, Texas, and 14 of the 19

---

176 U.S. Dep't of Justice, Civil Rights Div., Voting Section, Minority Language Citizens: Section 203 of the Voting Rights Act (2002), *available at* http:www.usdoj.gov/crt/voting/sec_203/203_brochure.htm.

177 *See generally* 42 U.S.C. § 1973aa-3 (providing that violations of Sections 201, 202, or 203 of the Act are punishable by a fine of up to $5,000 and up to five years imprisonment).

178 28 C.F.R. § 55.16.

179 *See* VRARA § 7, Pub. L. No. 109–246 § 7, 120 Stat. 581 (2006); 42 U.S.C. § 1973aa-1a(b)(1) (2000).

180 *See* 42 U.S.C.A. § 1973aa-1a(b)(2) (West 2003).

Section 4(f)(4) covered counties or townships also were covered under Section 203. Two states (Alaska for Alaska Natives and Arizona for Spanish) and five counties and townships (Spanish in Yuba County in California, Collier and Monroe Counties in Florida, and Buena Vista Township in Michigan and American Indian coverage in Jackson County in North Carolina) were covered under Section 4(f)(4), but not Section 203 (Tucker and Espino 2006: 6, App. C).

Third, unless the sunset date for Section 4 is changed from July 27, 2031, during the last year Section 203 is in effect, federal observer coverage only will be available in jurisdictions certified by a federal court for coverage under Section 3(a) of the Act.[181] These anomalies are consistent with the 1982 amendments, when Section 203 was extended for 10 years and Section 4(f)(4) was extended for 25 years.[182]

Bailout and Removal from Section 203 Coverage

Section 203(d) of the Act provides that a covered jurisdiction may bail out from coverage if it can demonstrate "that the illiteracy rate of the applicable language minority group" that triggered coverage "is equal to or less than the national illiteracy rate."[183] "Having found that the voting barriers experienced by these citizens [are] in large part due to disparate and inadequate educational opportunities," this bailout procedure rewards jurisdictions that are able to remove these barriers.

Since illiteracy is determined by language subgroups, such as Chinese and Filipino, and not language groups, such as Asian American, bailout under Section 203 can be done on "a subgroup-by-subgroup basis."

So, if coverage of a jurisdiction is triggered by both Chinese and Filipino, when its Chinese illiteracy rate has dropped to equal to or below the national illiteracy rate, it can seek bailout from its Chinese bilingual procedures. It need not wait until the illiteracy rate of all of its triggering groups has improved before it can attempt to bail out.

If a jurisdiction is covered by both Section 4(f)(4) and Section 203, it "must satisfy the requirements of each, including the differing provisions for bailing out." As Congressman Edwards explained, "the remedial devices" in the two sections "are different. It is not the intention of Congress to merge them for bailout or any other purpose."[184]

The bailout procedure is straightforward. A jurisdiction seeking to be removed from Section 203 coverage may file an action in any federal court for a declaratory judgment.[185] That differs from bailout actions for jurisdictions covered under Section 4(f)(4) of the Act, which must be brought in the U.S. District Court for the District of Columbia.[186] Originally, a similar limitation was included for Section 203, but Congressman Edwards agreed to an amendment during the House floor debate that changed it to any federal court.[187]

---

181 *See generally* 42 U.S.C.A. § 1973d (West 2003) (providing that observer coverage certifications are to be made by a federal court pursuant to Section 3(a) or by the Attorney General pursuant to Section 4(b) of the Act).

182 *See* Pub. L. No. 97–205, 96 Stat. 131 (1982).

183 42 U.S.C. § 1973aa-1a(d).

184 121 Cong. Rec. H4719–21 (daily ed. June 2, 1975) (statement of Rep. Edwards).

185 42 U.S.C. § 1973aa-1a(d).

186 *See* 42 U.S.C. § 1973b(a)(1).

187 *See* 121 Cong. Rec. H4897 (daily ed. June 4, 1975) (agreeing to an amendment offered by Rep. Johnson).

As part of a bailout lawsuit, the jurisdiction cannot challenge the Census Director's coverage determination,[188] but instead is limited to showing that the illiteracy rate of the language group has dropped below the national rate since that determination was made. To do so, the jurisdiction may rely upon scientifically reliable and accepted data showing its illiteracy rate even if it not gathered by the Census Bureau. However, there will be a strong presumption of the validity of any updated illiteracy data that is provided by the Census Bureau (*Doi v. Bell* 1978: 272–73). In response to a bailout action, "members of the language minority which triggered coverage, or their organizational representative, or any other aggrieved person, may intervene … in appropriate circumstances."[189]

Some members criticized Section 203's bailout provision, arguing it "would be almost impossible" to meet the standard.[190] Their fears proved to be unfounded, as demonstrated by Maui County, Hawaii's successful bailout for Japanese (*Doi v. Bell* 1978: 272–74). Moreover, coverage may be terminated without any action by the jurisdiction because of an automatic "bailout" mechanism in place under the Section 203 formula. Jurisdictions can be removed from coverage because of changing demographics revealed during the more frequent Census determinations using ACS data. When the need for language assistance drops below the population threshold or the illiteracy rate of a language group no longer exceeds the national average, coverage ends.

Like the Section 4(f)(4) bailout procedure, the bailout provision and coverage formula in Section 203 limits coverage to where it is needed, namely, areas where language minority voters suffer from the effects of educational discrimination through illiteracy rates exceeding the national rate. The U.S. Supreme Court has found that the bailout procedure makes the VRA's special provisions constitutional. It ensures "that the reach of the [VRA is] limited to those cases in which constitutional violations were most likely (in order to reduce the possibility of overbreadth)," by terminating coverage where voting and education discrimination and their effects have subsided.[191]

Voter Assistance under Section 208 of the VRA

State laws did not adequately protect many voters, including LEP language minority citizens, who needed assistance at the polls. Although the permanent ban on literacy tests and the language assistance provisions filled some of that gap, more was needed:

> Certain discrete groups of citizens are unable to exercise their rights to vote without obtaining assistance in voting including aid within the voting booth. These groups include the blind, the disabled, and those who either do not have a written language or who are unable to read or write sufficiently well to understand the election material and the ballot. Because of their need for assistance, members of these groups are more susceptible than the ordinary voter to having their vote unduly influenced or manipulated. As a result, members of such groups run the risk that they will be discriminated against at the polls and their right to vote in state and federal elections will not be protected.

188 42 U.S.C. § 1973aa-1a(b)(4).

189 121 Cong. Rec. H4720 (daily ed. June 2, 1975) (statement of Rep. Edwards).

190 121 Cong. Rec. H4890 (daily ed. June 4, 1975) (statement of Rep. Talcott).

191 *City of Boerne v. Flores*, 521 U.S. 507, 533 (1997); *see also South Carolina v. Katzenbach*, 383 U.S. 301, 331–32 (1966) (making a similar statement).

The solution was to allow voters who needed assistance to be able "to bring into the voting booth a person whom the voter trusts and who cannot intimidate him."[192]

Congress responded by adding a general voter assistance provision to the VRA in 1982.[193] Section 208 provides, "Any voter who requires assistance to vote by reason of blindness, disability, or inability to read or write may be given assistance by a person of the voter's choice, other than the voter's employer or agent of that employer or officer or agent of the voter's union."[194] The employer limitation "does not apply to cases of voters who must select assistance in a small community composed largely of language minorities whose language is primarily unwritten or oral, such as those residing in an Alaskan native village [or] a New Mexico pueblo or reservation." The ban on assistance by an agent "does not extend to assistance by a voter's co-worker, or fellow union-member." Some federal court decisions already recognized that illiterate voters and disabled voters had the right to receive voting assistance from the person of their choice (Chapter 2). Section 208 therefore did not "create a new right … to receive assistance; rather it implements an existing right by prescribing minimal requirements as to the manner in which voters may choose to receive assistance" (S. Rep. No. 97–417, 1982: 63–64).

Like the language assistance provisions, voter assistance under Section 208 must be allowed at every stage of the voting process, from registration through casting a ballot. Under Section 208, "a procedure could not deny assistance at some stages of the voting process during which assistance was needed" (S. Rep. No. 97–417, 1982: 63). Unlike Section 203, however, Section 208's requirements are permanent and apply nationwide, mandating that election officials permit voters to receive assistance from the person of their choice.[195] State laws, such as those permitting only poll officials, relatives, or registered voters to provide assistance (U.S. Comm'n on Civil Rts. 1984: 6), are preempted if they are inconsistent with Section 208 (S. Rep. No. 97–417, 1982: 63).

Provisions Facilitating Enforcement of the VRA

In 1975, Congress added two amendments to the VRA to facilitate enforcement. In Section 3(a) of the Act, "any aggrieved person" was authorized to obtain federal court authorization for examiners and observers in "a proceeding under any statute to enforce the voting guarantees of the fourteenth or fifteenth amendment in any State or political subdivision."[196] As a result, private parties may secure application of the Act's special provisions, including Sections 4(f)(4), 203, and 208.[197] In Section 14 of the VRA, private parties have an incentive to enforce the Act.[198] Under this "private attorneys general" provision (S. Rep. No. 94–295, 1975: 40), private parties who have prevailed in "any action or proceeding to enforce the voting guarantees of the fourteenth or fifteenth

192 S. Rep. No. 97–417 at 62 (1982).

193 *See* Voting Rights Act Amendments of 1982, Pub. L. No. 97–205, § 5, 96 Stat. 131, 134–35.

194 42 U.S.C. § 1973aa-6 (2000).

195 *See* 42 U.S.C. § 1973aa-6.

196 Pub. L. No. 94–73, § 402, 89 Stat. at 404 (codified as amended at 42 U.S.C. §1973l (2000)); *see* § 401, 89 Stat. at 404 (adding the words "or an aggrieved person") (codified as amended at 42 U.S.C. § 1973a(a) (2000)).

197 *See* S. Rep. No. 295, 1975: 40 ("The amendment proposed by S. 1279 would authorize courts to grant similar relief to private parties in suits brought to protect voting rights in covered and non-covered jurisdictions").

198 *See* Pub. L. No. 94–73, § 402, 89 Stat. 400 at 404 (codified as amended at 42 U.S.C § 1973l (2000)).

amendment" may be awarded a reasonable attorney's fee.[199] Congress recognized the importance of dual enforcement by the Attorney General and private parties who would "assist the process of enforcing voting rights" of language minorities.[200]

Even with these changes, the VRA failed to explicitly authorize recovery of expert witness fees. In 1991, the United States Supreme Court held that absent such express authority under federal civil rights laws, expert fees could not be recovered as part of reasonable attorneys' fees.[201] That same year, Congress responded by amending the Civil Rights Act of 1964 to provide for recovery of expert witness fees, recognizing "employment discrimination victims very often cannot win their cases without the help of costly statisticians and other experts."[202] However, the VRA was unaffected by the amendment.

In 2006, Congress corrected the oversight.[203] It amended Section 14(e) of the Act by providing for recovery of "reasonable expert fees, and other reasonable litigation expenses" in addition to reasonable attorneys' fees.[204] There was "substantial testimony indicating that much of the burden associated with either proving or defending a Section 2 vote dilution claim is established by information that only an expert can prepare" (H.R. Rep. No. 109–478, 2006: 64). Senator Patrick Leahy explained that this simple amendment would "have a significant impact on the ability of litigants to successfully combat discrimination in court."[205]

Conclusion

The 1975 amendments to the VRA removed language barriers to voting for non-English-speaking citizens. Congress considered substantial evidence of the effects of English-only elections on language minority voters denied equal educational opportunities. The failure of election officials to provide language assistance forced voters to cast ballots using materials written in English that they could not understand. Those practices were the functional equivalent of literacy tests, which had been banned nationwide in 1970 (Chapter 1). Although there was some relief available to language minority voters prior to 1975, it was limited in scope and effect (Chapter 2).

Congress enacted Section 203 to provide broad relief for those barriers. That remedy did not come easily. From the time that Section 203 was first enacted in 1975, opponents of bilingual materials and assistance have fought to curtail its scope. Chapter 3 described unsuccessful efforts to remove several language minority groups from coverage. Those efforts continued during subsequent reauthorizations, with the geographical extent of coverage being determined by the political ebb and flow of the triggering formula. In 1984, Senator Don Nickles of Oklahoma prevailed in amending Section 203 to include the LEP requirement in the trigger, virtually eliminating all coverage in his state and curtailing coverage in most others. Congress responded by adding numerical (10,000 LEP voting-age U.S. citizens) and reservation-based triggers in 1992. The data source for coverage

199 42 U.S.C. § 1973l(e) (2000). For an additional discussion of this provision, *see* Martha S. Davis, *Attorney Fee Awards in Voting Rights Litigation*, 34 S.D. L. Rev. 303 (1989).

200 S. Rep. No. 94–295, 1975: at 40; 121 Cong. Rec. S13374 (daily ed. July 23, 1975) (statement of Sen. Tunney).

201 *See West Virginia Univ. Hosps., Inc. v. Casey*, 499 U.S. 83, 101–02 (1991).

202 H.R. Rep. No. 102–40, at 77 (1991).

203 *See* H.R. Rep. No. 109–478, 2006: 64; 152 Cong. Rec. H5149 (daily ed. July 13, 2006) (statement of Rep. Chabot).

204 VRARA § 6, Pub L. No. 109–246, § 6, 120 Stat. 581 (2006).

205 152 Cong. Rec. S3988 (daily ed. May 3, 2006).

determinations was updated in 2006 to rely upon ACS data, which allows determinations to be made more frequently. But Congress made that change only after Section 203 survived several attempts to repeal it during the 2006 reauthorization process (Chapter 7).

The requirements for providing language assistance under Section 203 are straightforward. All covered jurisdictions must provide oral language assistance at every stage of the voting process, including voter registration, outreach and publicity, and at polling places on Election Day. Jurisdictions covered for Asian languages or Spanish must provide bilingual written election materials. Places covered for Alaska Native or American Indian languages also must provide bilingual written materials if the covered language is "historically written," which focuses on whether providing those materials would be useful to the particular language group.

There is some disagreement in the courts over the extent of the written material requirement, such as whether it applies to certain Alaska Native tribes (Chapter 10), encompasses initiative or referenda petitions circulated by private citizens, or mandates transliteration. That is unfortunate. Section 203 adopts a bottom-up view of assistance. The standard does not rest on what assistance election officials deem best, but rather what provides LEP voters with effective and equal access to registration and voting opportunities. Section 203 makes the promise of American democracy a reality for millions of LEP citizens unable to vote without assistance in their native tongue. The need for assistance is the subject of the next chapter, which describes the Section 203 coverage determinations made by the U.S. Census Bureau in 2002.

PART III
THE NEED FOR LANGUAGE ASSISTANCE AND ITS AVAILABILITY, QUALITY AND COST

Chapter 5
The July 2002 Determinations and Section 203 Coverage[1]

Chapter 4 explained how coverage determinations are made under Section 203. In July 2002, the Director of the Census Bureau issued a notice of determination identifying the jurisdictions covered by Section 203.[2] Those determinations are important for several reasons. As of 2009, they are the most recent determinations available. Congress considered evidence from jurisdictions covered under those determinations when reauthorizing Section 203 for another 25 years (Chapter 7). The 2002 Determinations provide a wealth of data showing the need for assistance and the impact of the existing triggering formulas on coverage.

This chapter explores the 2002 Determinations. It describes data for each covered language minority group and identifies where they are located. The coverage formulas are placed into context, examining how they have impacted each group. The strong correlation between Section 203 coverage and lack of English learning opportunities also is described to show why language groups suffer from high illiteracy rates. The chapter concludes by examining a 2005 survey of election officials in covered jurisdictions, which shows a divergence between officials' perceptions and the need for language assistance. Other findings are discussed in Chapter 6.

The Number of Jurisdictions Covered by Section 203

Following the 2002 Determinations, the number of states covered in whole or in part by Section 203 increased from 27 to 31. Section 203 covers three states in their entirety (California, New Mexico, and Texas for Spanish heritage), in addition to two states covered statewide under Section 203 because of Section 4(f)(4) determinations (Alaska for Alaska Natives and Arizona for Spanish heritage).[3] Nationwide, 296 political subdivisions located in 30 states were identified for Section 203 coverage (Figure 4.1; Appendix B).

Two states previously covered in part, Iowa and Wisconsin, no longer were covered under the 2002 Determinations. Section 203 coverage was extended to five new states: Kansas, Maryland, Montana, Nebraska, and Washington. Demographic changes led to 27 political subdivisions losing their coverage under Section 203 and the addition of 73 new political subdivisions (Appendix B). Figure 5.1 is a map graph depicting coverage following the 2002 Determinations.

The scope of coverage under the language-assistance provisions is even broader. Although the Director of the Census periodically makes new coverage determinations under Section 203,

---

1 Published originally in the *Texas Journal on Civil Liberties & Civil Rights*. *See* James Thomas Tucker and Rodolfo Espino, *Government Effectiveness and Efficiency? The Minority Language Assistance Provisions of the VRA*, 12 TEX. J. C.L. & C.R. 163 (2007). In certain places, the content of this chapter has been modified from the original article to reflect the discussion included elsewhere in this book.

2 *See* Voting Rights Act Amendments of 1992, Determinations Under Section 203 ("2002 Determinations"), 67 FED. REG. 48,871 (July 26, 2002) (to be codified at 28 C.F.R. pt. 55).

3 Texas also is covered statewide under Section 4(f)(4) for Spanish heritage (Appendix B).

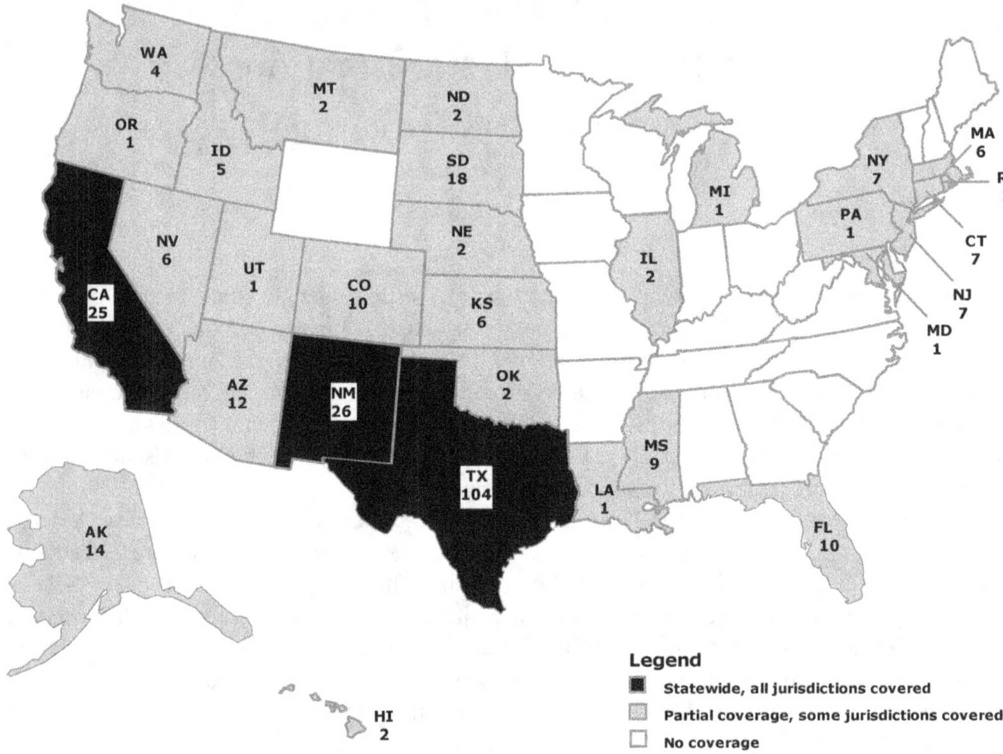

Figure 5.1 Jurisdictions designated for Section 203 coverage, by state (2002 Census determinations)

The numbers for the three states in Figure 5.1 that have statewide coverage only include jurisdictions independently covered by Section 203. If all counties in those three states are included, California has a total of 58 covered counties, New Mexico has 33, and Texas has 254.
Source: 2002 Census Determinations.

the existing determinations under Section 4(f)(4) remain in effect (Chapter 3). A total of 505 political subdivisions now are covered by one or both of the provisions. Figure 5.2 is a map graph depicting the combined coverage under the existing Section 4(f)(4) determinations and the 2002 Determinations for Section 203. Unless otherwise indicated, the number of political subdivisions includes all jurisdictions covered because of Section 4(f)(4) or Section 203 and all county-level political subdivisions in states that are covered in their entirety.

Spanish language assistance is the most common with coverage in 425 jurisdictions. It applies to 84.2 percent of all covered jurisdictions, including statewide coverage in Arizona, California, New Mexico, and Texas and 224 political subdivisions in 20 states. Assistance in American Indian languages is the next most common, encompassing 16 percent of all covered jurisdictions, including 81 political subdivisions of 18 states. Language assistance in Alaska Native languages is required statewide in Alaska and in 13 separately covered political subdivisions; the 27 covered jurisdictions in Alaska comprise 5.3 percent of all covered jurisdictions. Asian American language

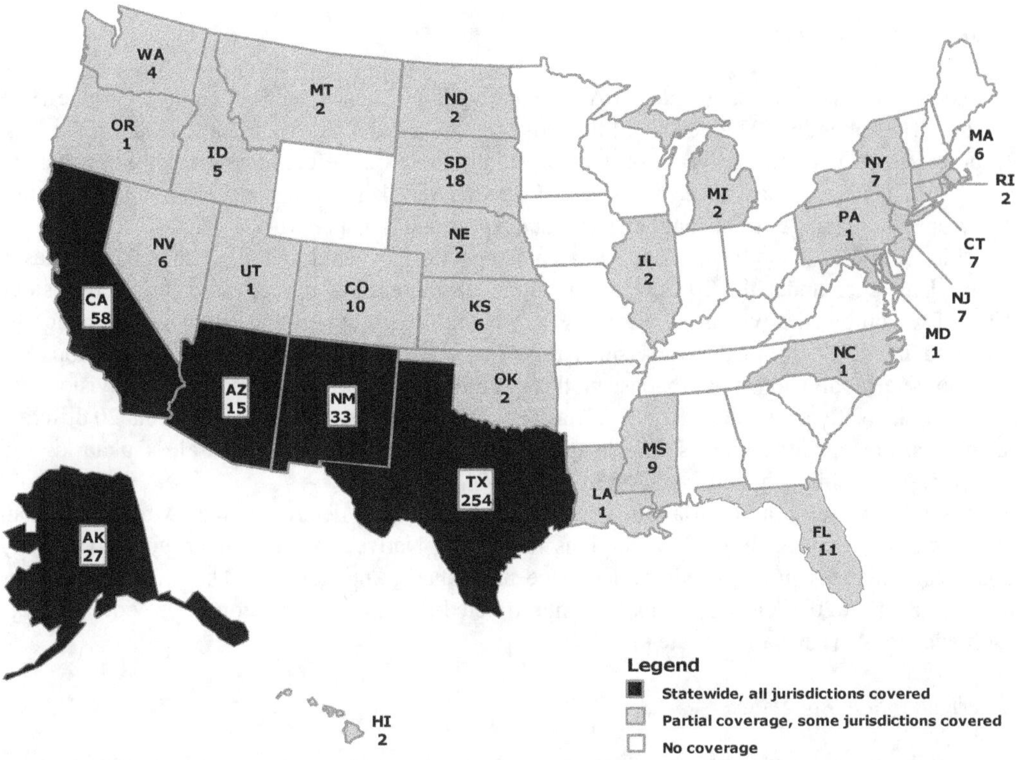

Figure 5.2 Jurisdictions designated for coverage under Sections 4(f)(4) or 203, by state (2002 Census determinations)

Figure 5.2 includes Section 4(f)(4) covered jurisdictions that were designated for coverage in 1975 and have not bailed out. See Figure 3.1 and Appendix B. Section 203 coverage resulting from the 2002 Determinations is depicted in Figure 5.1.
Source: 2002 Census Determinations.

assistance must be provided in 3.2 percent of all covered jurisdictions, including coverage in 16 political subdivisions of seven states (Figures 5.3, 5.5, 5.6; Appendix C).

Forty-eight covered political subdivisions have to provide assistance in more than one language: 31 in two languages; 14 in three languages; two in four languages; and one, Los Angeles County, California, in six languages (Spanish, Chinese, Filipino, Japanese, Korean, and Vietnamese). Appendix C lists the covered languages by state and political subdivision including the number of limited-English-proficient (LEP) U.S. citizens of voting age (citizen voting-age population, or CVAP) for each language and their illiteracy rate, as well as the formula triggering the jurisdiction's coverage under Section 203.

Alaska Native Languages

Alaska has been covered statewide for Alaska Native languages under Section 4(f)(4) since 1975 (Figure 3.1; Appendix B).[4] Because of that coverage, Alaska must obtain approval from the U.S. Attorney General or the federal court in Washington, D.C., before it implements any voting changes (Chapter 3). Alaska's coverage under Section 4(f)(4) is a key consideration in the state's enforcement of changes to its language assistance program (Chapter 10).

Thirteen political subdivisions of Alaska are separately covered under Section 203 for Alaska Native languages under the 2002 Determinations, an increase of one covered jurisdiction since 1992. The combined coverage of Sections 4(f)(4) and 203 requires that language assistance be provided in all 27 political subdivisions for Alaska Native languages, eight subdivisions for Eskimo, five subdivisions for Athabascan, three subdivisions for Aleut, and three subdivisions for Other Alaska Native languages. The five Alaska Native language groups include about 20 different languages. For example, the Eskimo language group includes Alutiiq; Central, Naukanski, and Siberian Yup'ik; Inupiaq, and Sirenikski.[5]

There have been minor variations in coverage from earlier determinations. Most result from changes in the Census Bureau's definitions for Alaska Native language subgroups and not any underlying changes in the need for language assistance (Appendix B). The slight differences between Section 203 determinations have not affected the state's obligation to provide language assistance for Alaska Natives statewide.

American Indian Languages

Three states are partially covered for American Indian languages under Section 4(f)(4). Arizona has four counties covered for American Indian languages: Apache, Coconino, Navajo, and Pinal Counties. In addition, Jackson County, North Carolina, is covered for an American Indian language. Two counties in South Dakota, Shannon and Todd Counties, are covered for the Sioux language (Figure 3.1; Appendix B). Each Section 4(f)(4) covered jurisdiction must obtain preclearance for voting changes that impact it before those changes are implemented, including statewide redistricting plans and statewide changes in registration and voting procedures (Chapter 3).

Following the 2002 Determinations, American Indian language assistance must be provided in political subdivisions of 18 states, a net increase of two states since 1992. South Dakota had the largest number of political subdivisions added under American Indian coverage, more than doubling from eight under the previous determinations to 18 under the new determinations. Two states that did not have to provide language assistance to any American Indian groups under the 1992 determinations, Montana and Nebraska, must now do so following the 2002 Determinations. Two states previously covered for American Indian languages, Iowa and Oklahoma, no longer are covered as a result of the 2002 Determinations (Appendix B). Figure 5.3 is a map graph depicting the number of political subdivisions in each of the 18 states that are covered in whole or in part for Alaska Native or American Indian languages under either Section 4(f)(4) or Section 203 following the 2002 Determinations.

Figure 5.4 identifies the number of political subdivisions in each state covered for the 18 languages encompassed by the American Indian language group in the 2002 Determinations.

4 *See* 40 Fed. Reg. 49,422 (Oct. 22, 1975); 28 C.F.R. § 51, App.

5 *See* Alaska Native Languages Center, University of Alaska-Fairbanks, *Alaska Native Languages (Eskimo Family Tree)*, *available at* http://www.uaf.edu/anlc/languages.html.

Figure 5.3 Jurisdictions designated for coverage under Sections 4(f)(4) or 203 for Alaska Native or American Indian languages, by state (2002 Census determinations)

Figure 5.3 includes Section 4(f)(4) covered jurisdictions that were designated for coverage in 1975 and have not bailed out. *See* Figure 3.1 and Appendix B.

Source: 2002 Census Determinations.

Language assistance must be provided in more than the 18 identified languages. American Indian languages can include several different languages or dialects. For example, the Pueblo group includes the Havasupai, Hopi, Keres, Tiwa, and Towa Indian languages. The Sioux group includes Dakota, Lakota, and Nakota.[6] Many descriptions for language minority groups changed under Census Bureau definitions used in the 2000 Census. Election officials must work with the Justice Department and local tribes to identify the specific American Indian languages for which language assistance must be provided (Chapter 4).

Asian Languages

Under the 2002 Determinations, 16 political subdivisions of seven states are covered for Asian languages. Chinese language assistance must be provided in 12 political subdivisions, including coverage of six urban counties in California, Honolulu County in Hawaii, Cook County in Illinois (encompassing metropolitan Chicago), three counties in the New York City metropolitan area, and

6 *See* S.D. Codified Laws § 12–3-9 (1976).

Language	Political Subdivisions Covered	Affected States
Sioux	21	NE, ND, SD
Other American Indian Languages	16	AK, ID, LA, NC, NV, OR, TX
Navajo	13	AZ, CO, NM, UT
Pueblo	13	AZ, NM, TX
Choctaw	9	MS
Apache	5	AZ
Unspecified American Indian Languages	4	AK
Ute	4	CO, NM, UT
Seminole	3	FL
Shoshone	3	NV
Tohono O'Odham	3	AZ
Central/South American Indian	2	CA
Cheyenne	2	MT
Yuman	2	AZ, CA
Chickasaw	1	AK
Paiute	1	NV
Yacqui	1	AZ
Zuni	1	NM

Figure 5.4 Jurisdictions designated for coverage under Sections 4(f)(4) or 203 for American Indian languages, by language and state (2002 Census determinations)

Figure 5.4 includes Section 4(f)(4) covered jurisdictions that were designated for coverage in 1975 and have not bailed out. *See* Figure 3.1 and Appendix B.

Source: 2002 Census Determinations.

King County in Washington State (encompassing metropolitan Seattle). Filipino language assistance must be provided in the Kodiak Island Borough of Alaska, three urban counties in California, and two counties in Hawaii. Vietnamese language assistance must be provided in three urban counties in California and in Harris County, Texas (encompassing metropolitan Houston). Japanese language assistance must be provided in Los Angeles County, California, and Honolulu County, Hawaii. Figure 5.5 is a map graph depicting the number of political subdivisions of the seven states that are partially covered for Asian languages under Section 203.

No jurisdictions are covered under Section 4(f)(4) for an Asian language. Nevertheless, Asian American voters obtain benefits from preclearance in jurisdictions that were covered for another language group or that were covered by one of the other triggers in Section 4 of the Act. For example, the Act's special protections encompass tens of thousands of LEP Chinese and Korean voters in the metropolitan New York City region because of the Section 4(f)(4) coverage for Spanish-speaking voters in Bronx County and Kings County. Similarly, Filipino voters in Kodiak, Alaska, and Vietnamese voters in Harris County, Texas, benefit from statewide coverage of their states for Alaska Native languages and Spanish, respectively. Asian language voters in those covered jurisdictions are protected by the preclearance requirements from voting changes that have a discriminatory purpose or effect. The Attorney General also has discretion to designate federal observers for those areas, which likewise can prevent voting discrimination (Chapter 3).

Figure 5.5 Jurisdictions designated for coverage under Section 203 for Asian American languages, by state (2002 Census determinations)

No jurisdictions have been designated for Section 4(f)(4) coverage for Asian American languages. See Figure 3.1 and Appendix B.

Source: 2002 Census Determinations.

Spanish

Spanish language assistance must be provided statewide in Arizona, California, New Mexico, Texas, and an additional 224 political subdivisions in 20 states. Under the 2002 Determinations, political subdivisions of five states are required to provide Spanish language assistance for the first time: six counties in Kansas, Montgomery County (metropolitan Washington, D.C.) in Maryland, Colfax County in Nebraska, Clark County (metropolitan Las Vegas) in Nevada, Harmon and Texas Counties in Oklahoma, and three counties in Washington. In addition, Spanish is covered in several municipalities, including two townships in Michigan, and larger urban populations in Connecticut, Massachusetts, and Rhode Island. Wisconsin, which previously was covered for Spanish in a township in Clark County, no longer is covered (Appendix B).

Figure 5.6 is a map graph depicting the number of political subdivisions of the 20 states covered in whole or in part for Spanish under either Section 4(f)(4) or Section 203. Of the four states covered statewide, Arizona is covered under Section 4(f)(4); California and New Mexico are covered under Section 203; and Texas is covered under both Section 4(f)(4) and Section 203. Eight of the 12 political subdivisions covered under Section 4(f)(4) also are covered under Section 203 because of the 2002 Determinations: Kings and Merced Counties in California; Hardee, Hendry, and Hillsborough Counties in Florida; Clyde Township in Michigan; and Bronx and Kings Counties in New York. The remaining four counties are covered under Spanish because of Section 4(f)(4): Yuba County in California; Collier and Monroe Counties in Florida; and Buena Vista Township in Michigan (Figure 3.1; Appendix B). Each jurisdiction covered under Section 4(f)(4) must comply with the preclearance requirements in addition to providing language assistance in Spanish (Chapter 3).

Formulas Triggering Section 203 Coverage

Under Section 203, a jurisdiction is covered if the Director of the Census determines that two criteria are met. First, the LEP citizens of voting-age in a single language group: (a) number more than 10,000; (b) comprise more than 5 percent of all citizens of voting-age; or (c) comprise more than 5 percent of all American Indians of a single language group residing on an Indian reservation. Coverage for persons living on Indian reservations can be based upon a reservation that is either entirely within a political subdivision (the whole reservation trigger) or split between two or more political subdivisions (the partial reservation trigger). Second, the illiteracy rate of the LEP language minority citizens must exceed the national illiteracy rate.[7] A person is LEP if he or she speaks English "less than very well" and would need assistance to participate in the political process effectively (Chapter 4).[8]

In the 367 covered political subdivisions,[9] on average 8,403 citizens of voting-age were LEP in the 464 language groups triggering coverage,[10] or 13.1 percent of the VAP.[11] Nearly one-third (N = 147) of covered language groups in these political subdivisions had LEP rates exceeding 20 percent. In 15.5 percent (N = 72) of the 464 language groups, more than one-half of the VAP was LEP in the covered language. Nearly 19 percent (N = 87) of the covered language groups in these political subdivisions could not meet the 5 percent trigger and were covered under either the 10,000-person or reservation triggers.

The overwhelming majority of the 116 jurisdictions with more than 5,000 voting-age LEP citizens were urban areas covered for Spanish or Asian languages. Among the 77 covered jurisdictions falling into this category for which Census data was available, 54.5 percent (N = 42) were covered for Spanish and 33.8 percent (N = 26) were covered for Asian languages. Only 11.7 percent (N = 9) of those jurisdictions were covered for American Indian languages, and none were covered for Alaska Native languages. As a result, the 10,000-person trigger had the greatest impact on Spanish and Asian language groups, just as Congress expected when it added the trigger in 1992 (Chapter 4).[12]

7 *See* 42 U.S.C. § 1973aa-1a(b)(2).

8 *See generally* 42 U.S.C. § 1973aa-1a(b)(3)(B) (defining LEP as the inability "to speak or understand English adequately enough to participate in the electoral process").

9 "Political subdivision" refers to the subdivisions of states that are covered by Section 203. The term excludes the three states (California, New Mexico, and Texas) that are covered statewide, but includes all of the subdivisions of those states that are covered in their own right as a result of the 2002 Determinations.

10 The 464 languages include each instance in which a jurisdiction is covered for a distinct language group. Several of the 367 political subdivisions are covered by more than one language under Section 203.

11 The average of 13.1 percent is calculated from the 403 language groups for which Census data is available. The Census Bureau has suppressed some of the data used in the 2002 Determinations.

12 *See* 42 U.S.C. § 1973aa-1a(b)(2)(A)(i)(II).

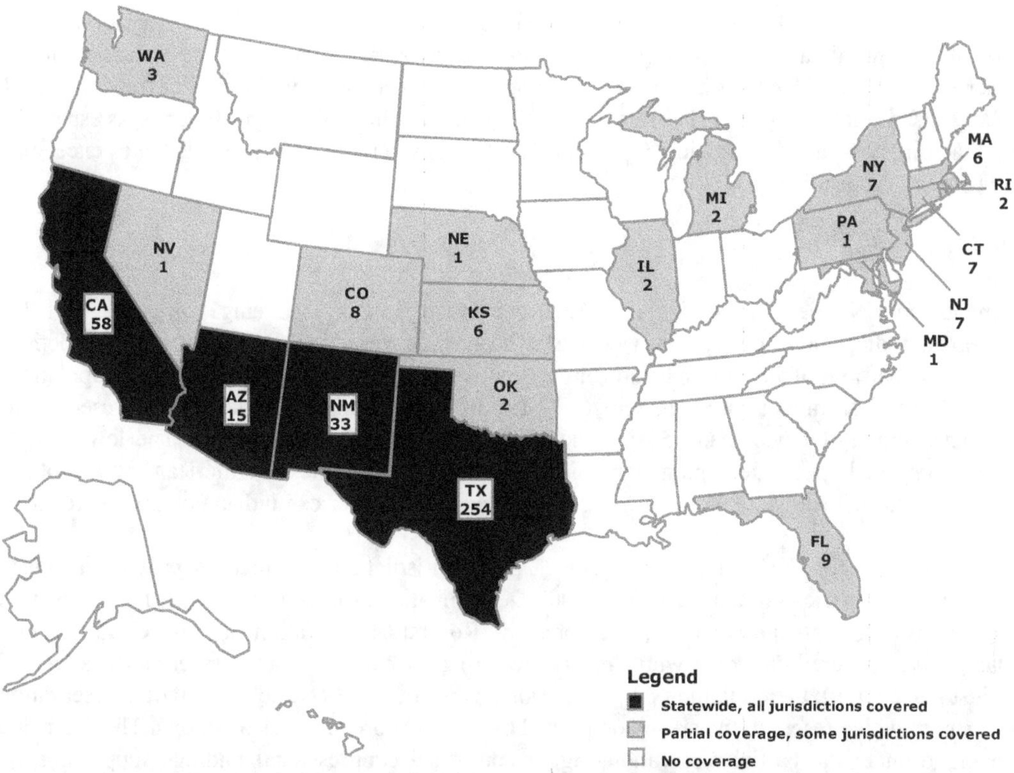

Figure 5.6 Jurisdictions designated for coverage under Sections 4(f)(4) or 203 for Spanish, by state (2002 Census determinations)

Figure 5.6 includes Section 4(f)(4) covered jurisdictions that were designated for coverage in 1975 and have not bailed out. See Figure 3.1 and Appendix B.
Source: 2002 Census Determinations.

Alaska Native and American Indian coverage was based almost entirely on the reservation trigger for the small number of American Indian voters in most covered jurisdictions.[13]

Alaska Native Languages

There are 21 political subdivisions covered for Alaska Native languages for which at least some Census data is available. All were covered under the partial reservation trigger.[14] The jurisdictions included portions of 90 Alaska Native reservations with an average of 86 Alaska Native voting-age LEP citizens. Several Alaska political subdivisions are covered for multiple language groups. The low number reflects very sparsely populated and geographically isolated communities of Alaska Native voting-age citizens. There are at least 6,934 covered LEP Alaska Native voters (Figure 5.8).

13 *See* 42 U.S.C. § 1973aa-1a(b)(2)(A)(i)(III).

14 Alaska is covered statewide for Alaska Native languages under Section 4(f)(4) of the VRA.

Complete census data was only available for 50 of the 90 Alaska Native reservations under the 2002 Determinations. Data is suppressed for several reservations with small populations. In reservations for which data is available, an average of 22.6 percent of voting-age citizens were LEP in an Alaska Native language. The rate of non-English speaking voting-age citizens was especially high among Alaska Natives, with 40 percent (N = 36) of reservations having LEP rates exceeding 50 percent (Appendix C).

American Indian Languages

Among the 129 reservations triggering American Indian language coverage, an average of 721 American Indian voting-age citizens were LEP. The average was raised dramatically by jurisdictions containing portions of the Navajo Nation or the Sioux reservations, which had the largest populations of LEP American Indian voting-age citizens. Most of the remaining American Indian reservations had an average of fewer than 251 American Indian voting-age LEP citizens. The low number reflected sparsely populated and geographically isolated communities of American Indian voting-age citizens. There are a total of at least 56,679 covered LEP American Indian voters (Figure 5.8).

The importance of the reservation trigger All 81 jurisdictions required to provide language assistance to American Indians under the 2002 Determinations were covered under the reservation trigger. Among those jurisdictions, only one, the Rosebud Reservation in Todd County, South Dakota, was covered under the whole reservation trigger (that is, the entire reservation is located in just one county); the remaining 80 jurisdictions were covered because of the partial reservation trigger (in which reservations are encompassed by two or more counties or states). The extensive coverage under the partial reservation trigger confirmed congressional findings supporting the addition of the reservation trigger in 1992 (Chapter 4). Every covered American Indian reservation except the Rosebud Reservation was divided among multiple political subdivisions and, in many cases, among several states (Appendix C).

Only 8.9 percent (N = 9) of American Indian covered counties also met the 5 percent trigger. Six of those counties were covered for the Navajo language, including: Apache, Coconino, and Navajo counties in Arizona; McKinley and San Juan counties in New Mexico; and San Juan County in Utah. The remaining three counties were located in South Dakota and were covered for a Sioux language: Shannon, Todd, and Ziebach counties (Appendix C).

Apache County, Arizona was the only jurisdiction covered for an American Indian language (Navajo) under the 10,000 person trigger. It also was covered under the 5 percent trigger and the partial reservation trigger. The Navajo Nation has its capital in Window Rock, Arizona, located in northern Apache County near the New Mexico border. According to the 2000 Census, there were 11,245 Navajo voting-age citizens who were LEP, comprising 26.5 percent of all voting-age citizens in the county. Apache County also was covered for the Apache and Hopi (Pueblo) languages under the partial reservation trigger (Appendix C).

Covered jurisdictions without any LEP voters Some jurisdictions covered for American Indian languages did not have any voting-age citizens who were LEP in the covered language. For example, Bernalillo County, New Mexico, was covered for the Pueblo (Keres and Tiwa) language because it contained a portion of the Laguna Pueblo and off-reservation trust land, which met the 5 percent trigger.[15] However, the Census Bureau reported that Bernalillo County did not contain any voting-age citizens who were LEP in the Pueblo language. By comparison, Cibola County, New Mexico, which also was covered for the Pueblo language because of the Laguna Pueblo, had 430 voting-age citizens who were LEP on the portion of the reservation in the county (Appendix C).

Jurisdictions covered under the partial reservation trigger that did not contain any LEP voting-age citizens in the covered language, such as Bernalillo County, were not required to provide language assistance. Instead, targeting would allow the jurisdiction to determine that no assistance was needed (Chapter 8). Only a handful of jurisdictions with no LEP voters were covered under the partial reservation trigger, which was necessary for the reasons discussed in Chapter 4.

Asian Languages

There are a total of 672,750 covered LEP Asian American voters (Figure 5.8). Chinese has the largest number of covered voters among the five covered Asian languages: over a third of a million LEP voters comprising over half of all covered LEP Asian voters and nearly 10 percent of all covered LEP voters. Vietnamese is the next most commonly used Asian language, including nearly 125,000 LEP voters, or nearly one-fifth of covered LEP Asian American voters. The remaining three covered Asian languages include 94,020 LEP Tagalog-speaking voters, 66,465 LEP Korean-speaking voters, and 26,375 LEP Japanese-speaking voters. Altogether, covered LEP Asian voters comprise about 16.71 percent of all covered LEP voters (Figure 5.7).

Figure 5.7 depicts the number of LEP voters in each of the covered five Asian language groups.

Triggering formulas for coverage Most jurisdictions required to provide Asian language assistance were covered under the 10,000-person trigger. That trigger was added in 1992 to cover "highly populated metropolitan areas" where "many language minority citizens in need of assistance are not covered because they do not make up a large enough percentage of the local population to trigger coverage."[16] Of the 27 jurisdictions covered for Asian languages, 88.9 percent (N = 24) were covered because of the 10,000-person trigger and only 7.4 percent (N = 2) because of the 5 percent trigger. Only one jurisdiction, San Francisco County for Chinese, was covered under both the 10,000-person and 5 percent triggers (Appendix C).

The importance of the 10,000-person trigger The 2002 Determinations confirmed the 1992 congressional finding that a numerically based trigger, such as the 10,000-person trigger, was necessary to cover Asian languages in populous urban counties (Chapter 4). Without that trigger, only three jurisdictions would have been covered under the 5 percent trigger: Kodiak Island Borough, Alaska, for Filipino; San Francisco County, California, for Chinese; and Maui County, Hawaii, for Filipino. The number of Asian voters who need language assistance is tremendous. The 27 jurisdictions covered for Asian languages had the highest average number of voting-age citizens who were LEP in the covered language among all four principal language groups, with an average of 24,917. Only two jurisdictions covered for Asian languages, Kodiak Island Borough in Alaska and Maui County in Hawaii, had Asian voting-age citizen LEP populations of less than 10,000.

---

15 See the table in 28 C.F.R. Part 55, which indicates that the covered Pueblo languages in Bernalillo County are Keres and Tiwa (Appendices B–C). The Census Bureau aggregated these and other American Indian languages for Pueblo tribes, such as the Hopi, into a single "Pueblo" language group.

16 S. Rep. No. 102–315 at 16 (1992).

Language	Number of Covered LEP Voters	% of All Covered Asian Language Voters	% of All Covered Voters
Chinese	361,585	53.75	8.97
Filipino/Tagalog	94,020	13.97	2.34
Japanese	26,375	3.92	.66
Korean	66,465	9.88	1.65
Vietnamese	124,305	18.48	3.09
Totals	672,750	100.00	16.71

Figure 5.7 LEP voters covered under Section 203, by Asian American language group (2002 Census determinations)

Source: 2002 Census Determinations. *See* Appendix C.

Nearly half (N = 13) of jurisdictions covered for Asian languages had more than 20,000 voting-age citizens who were LEP in the language triggering coverage (Appendix C).

On the other hand, on average only 2.4 percent of all voting-age citizens in the covered Asian languages were LEP. This low percentage masks the widespread need for language assistance in jurisdictions covered for Asian languages. For example, in Los Angeles County, California, none of the five covered Asian language groups had LEP voting-age citizens comprising more than 2 percent of the county's voting-age citizens. At the same time, there were nearly a quarter-million LEP Asian voting-age citizens in the county, including: 95,700 Chinese-speaking citizens; 42,930 Korean-speaking citizens; 34,985 Filipino-speaking citizens; 30,340 Vietnamese-speaking citizens; and 12,510 Japanese-speaking citizens. The large population of urban centers such as Los Angeles County prevented nearly all groups of Asian voting-age citizens who were LEP from meeting the 5 percent trigger (Appendix C). Plainly, the 10,000-person trigger has been critical to extending Section 203 coverage to provide language assistance to LEP Asian American voters who need it.

Spanish

There are nearly 3.3 million covered LEP Spanish-speaking voters (Figure 5.8). Spanish is by far the largest of the four covered language groups, comprising more than 81 percent of the four million LEP voters covered nationwide. Spanish is the only language group with a single language, although it has many different dialects. For example, the Cuban dialect has variations from the Puerto Rican dialect of Spanish, and there can be considerable differences in pronunciation and grammar with South American dialects.

The importance of statewide coverage Spanish is most greatly impacted by statewide coverage. Among the five states covered statewide under either Section 4(f)(4) or Section 203, only Alaska (for Alaska Native languages) is not covered for Spanish (Figure 3.1; Appendix B). Statewide Spanish language coverage is a product of the millions of LEP voters who live in the states bordering Mexico. According to the 2000 Census, a majority of all LEP Spanish-speaking voters were born in the United States.

Three states, California, New Mexico, and Texas, were covered in 2002 under Section 203 for Spanish under the 5 percent trigger. The three states had an average of 632,345 Spanish-speaking LEP voting-age citizens, or 5.8 percent of all voting-age citizens. Although California barely met the 5 percent trigger at 5.02 percent, it had over one million LEP Spanish heritage voting-age citizens. In New Mexico, more than 6 percent (N = 74,855) of Spanish heritage voting-age citizens were LEP. Texas had the highest LEP rate among the three states at 6.15 percent, which included 818,185 Spanish heritage voting-age citizens (Appendix C).

Arizona is covered statewide for Spanish under Section 4(f)(4), but not under Section 203 (Figure 3.1; Appendix B).[17] In the six Arizona counties covered for Spanish under Section 203, an average of 3.4 percent of all voting-age citizens are LEP Spanish-speaking persons. Two Arizona counties with large urban centers, Maricopa (Phoenix) and Pima (Tucson), do not meet the 5 percent threshold and are covered by Section 203 under the 10,000-person trigger. The remaining four Arizona counties are covered by the 5 percent trigger with Spanish-speaking LEP persons comprising approximately 9 percent of the combined voting-age citizen populations in those counties (Appendix C).

Political subdivisions covered under the 5 percent triggering formula Among the 217 political subdivisions covered under Section 203 for Spanish for which Census data was available,[18] 85 percent (N = 188) were covered under the 5 percent trigger and 28 percent (N = 62) under the 10,000-person trigger.[19] Those political subdivisions had an average of 14,335 Spanish heritage LEP voting-age citizens, comprising an average of 10.4 percent of all voting-age citizens (Appendix C).

Nearly two-thirds (N = 136) of the 217 covered political subdivisions had more than 1,000 LEP Spanish heritage voting-age citizens. The remaining 82 jurisdictions had 1,000 or fewer LEP Spanish-heritage voting-age citizens because they were located in sparsely populated rural areas. However, the percentage of LEP Spanish-speaking voting-age citizens remained high even among these jurisdictions. Over one-third (N = 81) of covered political subdivisions had more than 5,000 LEP Spanish heritage voting-age citizens (Appendix C).

Nearly half (N = 106) of the 217 political subdivisions covered for Spanish heritage had Spanish LEP percentages among voting-age citizens between 5 and 10 percent. Approximately one-quarter (N = 52) had a Spanish LEP percentage among voting-age citizens between 10 and 20 percent. The remaining 12.4 percent (N = 27) had Spanish LEP percentages among voting-age citizens of over 20 percent, including five with over 35 percent (Appendix C). The 5 percent trigger has played a key role in covering rural counties and more sparsely populated counties for Spanish.

The importance of the 10,000-person trigger Only 15.2 percent (N = 33) of the 217 political subdivisions had 5 percent or less Spanish heritage voting-age citizens who were LEP. The 33 jurisdictions were covered as a result of the 10,000-person trigger and were located in populous urban centers. For example, although Spanish heritage voting-age citizens who were LEP comprised only 3.84 percent of all voting-age citizens in Cook County (metro Chicago), Illinois, the county was covered because there were 131,530 Spanish heritage voting-age citizens who were LEP (Appendix C). Ten jurisdictions in large urban areas had more than 75,000 LEP Spanish heritage voting-age citizens: Los Angeles County, California; Miami-Dade County, Florida; Cook County (metro Chicago), Illinois; Bronx, Kings, New York, and Queens counties in metropolitan New York City; Bexar County (San Antonio), Texas; El Paso County, Texas; and Harris County (Houston), Texas.

The 2002 Determinations highlight why the 10,000-person trigger has been critical to covering Spanish-speaking voters in large urban centers. Without it, despite their large populations, they

---

17 *See* 28 C.F.R. pt. 55, App.

18 Census data for Borden County, Texas, has been suppressed by the Census Bureau.

19 The percentages add up to more than 100 percent because 13.1 percent (N = 29) of all jurisdictions are covered because of both the 5 percent and 10,000-person triggers.

Language	Number of Covered LEP Voters	% of all Covered Voters
Alaska Native	6,934	.17
American Indian	56,679	1.41
Asian American	672,750	16.71
Spanish	3,290,018	81.71
Totals	4,026,381	100.00

Figure 5.8 LEP voters covered under Sections 4(f)(4) or 203, by language group (2002 Census determinations)
Source: 2002 Census Determinations. See Appendix C.

would be unable to meet the 5 percent trigger in metropolitan areas where there may be millions of voting-age citizens (Chapter 4).

The Number of Language Minority Voters Covered by Section 203

Taken together, the coverage data depicts the large need for language assistance. Nationwide, there are over four million LEP citizens of voting-age in the four language groups who are specifically covered by Sections 4(f)(4) or 203.[20] Spanish is the most common, with nearly 3.3 million LEP voters comprising over 81 percent of all covered voters. Asian American languages are the next most commonly spoken with over two-thirds of a million LEP voters, or over 16 percent of all covered voters. Alaska Native and American Indian languages include the smallest numbers, together comprising about 63,500 LEP voters who constitute less than 2 percent of all covered voters.

Figure 5.8 is a table summarizing the number of LEP voters from each of the four language groups covered by Sections 4(f)(4) or 203.

Unequal Learning Opportunities in the Covered Jurisdictions

When Congress enacted Section 203, it found that unequal educational opportunities result "in high illiteracy and low voting participation" among language minority voters.[21] Despite some progress, educational barriers still impede equal political participation for many LEP voters today (Chapters 2, 8–10). As Congressman James Sensenbrenner explained during the 2006 reauthorization:

> Now I think that probably the need for continuation of bilingual ballots is perhaps an indictment as to the lack of effectiveness of bilingual education … Should we close the door to understanding a ballot because of a failure of our educational system or because of the fact that people have moved

20 The Census determinations indicate there are 4,026,381 LEP CVAP voters who are specifically covered by Sections 4(f)(4) or 203. The actual number is slightly higher because Census data has been suppressed in some of the more sparsely populated covered jurisdictions.

21 42 U.S.C. § 1973aa-1a(a).

> to a place where English is commonly used in the United States from a place in the United States where English is not commonly used? I would answer that question no ...[22]

In addition to past discrimination, educational and literacy barriers to language minorities come in two other forms: more recent educational discrimination and the lack of opportunities for adults to learn English.

Educational Discrimination

As early as the turn of the twentieth century, the Supreme Court found that language minorities have a right under the Fourteenth Amendment to an equal education addressing their unique language needs. In *Meyer v. Nebraska*, the Court struck down a prohibition of teaching languages other than English in the public schools, reasoning "the protection of the Constitution extends to all, to those who speak other languages as well as those born with English on the tongue."[23] In another case just a few years later, the Court struck down a Hawaii law that restricted private foreign language schools, such as a Japanese school attended by the plaintiffs.[24]

In *Lau v. Nichols*, the Court held that an English-only curriculum violated Title VI of the Civil Rights Act of 1964[25] where it deprived Chinese-speaking students in San Francisco of equal educational opportunities.[26] Many cases brought since 1975 have been under the authority of *Lau* and other appellate court decisions.[27]

Educational discrimination against language minority students has been most severe in jurisdictions covered by either Section 4(f)(4) or Section 203. In 2002, the top six states with English Language Learner (ELL) students were California with 1,511,646, Texas with 570,022, Florida with 254,517, New York with 239,097, Illinois with 140,528, and Arizona with 135,248.[28] Arizona, California, and Texas are covered statewide under the language assistance provisions of the VRA, while Florida, Illinois, and New York are partially covered for the hundreds of thousands of LEP voters who live there (Figure 5.2). Twenty-seven of the 28 school districts with 10,000 or more ELL students in 2004–2005 were in Section 203-covered jurisdictions, including all of the top 25. School districts with more than 50,000 ELL students included: Los Angeles with 328,684; New York with 122,840; Chicago with 82,540; Miami-Dade with 62,767; Houston with 61,319; Clark County (Las Vegas), Nevada, with 53,517; and Dallas with 51,328.[29]

Educational discrimination and inadequate funding for ELL programs in public schools persisted when the VRA was reauthorized in 2006. Between 1975 and 2006, ELL students brought

---

22 H.R. Rep. No. 109–478 at 135 (2006) (statement of Rep. Sensenbrenner).

23 262 U.S. 390, 401 (1923).

24 *Farrington v. Tokushige*, 273 U.S. 284 (1927).

25 *See generally* 42 U.S.C. § 2000d (providing that "No person in the United States shall, on the ground of race, color, or national origin, be excluded from participation in, be denied the benefits of, or be subjected to discrimination under any program or activity receiving Federal financial assistance").

26 414 U.S. 563 (1974).

27 *See Castañeda v. Pickard*, 648 F.2d 989 (5th Cir. 1981); *Serna v. Portales Mun. Sch.*, 499 F.2d 1147 (10th Cir. 1974).

28 U.S. Department of Education, Office of English Language Acquisition, Language Enhancement and Academic Achievement for Limited English proficient Students (OELA), Survey of the States' Limited English Proficient Students and Available Educational Programs and Services 4, 19 (Oct. 2002).

29 Clearinghouse for English Language Acquisition and Language Instruction Educational Programs, FAQ No. 2, *available at* http://www.ncela.gwu.edu/faq/02districts.htm.

at least 24 successful educational discrimination cases in 15 states, 14 of which were covered in whole or in part by Section 4(f)(4) or Section 203. Between 1992 and 2006, at least 10 successful ELL cases were brought, or plaintiffs had additional relief granted under existing court decrees.[30] Other cases brought on behalf of ELL students were pending when Section 203 was reauthorized in 2006, including one in Alaska[31] and one in Illinois.[32] Consent decrees or court orders were in effect for ELL students statewide in Arizona and Florida, and in the covered cities of Boston, Denver, and Seattle. Those cases likely represented only a fraction of the successful litigation because so many court decisions are unpublished.

Lack of English-as-a-Second-Language (ESL) Programs

Insufficient adult English-as-a-Second-Language (ESL) programs in most of the covered jurisdictions added to the lack of English literacy and spoken proficiency.[33] A 2006 survey of 184 ESL providers from 22 cities in 16 states covered by Section 203 demonstrated the problem's scope (Tucker 2007: 36). Almost three out of five ESL providers had waiting lists. Adult students seeking to enroll in ESL classes could wait three years or longer, depending on their location (Tucker 2007: 30, 35, 37).

For example, in Phoenix, Arizona's largest ESL provider had a waiting list of over 1,000 people, who waited up to 18 months for the highest-demand evening classes (Tucker 2007: 30, 35, 37). In Albuquerque, the largest provider reported waiting times of 12 to 14 months. In Boston, where Massachusetts had mandated class sizes of no more than 20 students, there were at least 16,725 adults on ESL waiting lists, with waiting times as long as three years. In New York City, where an estimated one million adults needed ESL, only 41,347 adults were able to enroll in 2005 because of limited availability. In Rhode Island, more than half of all adults seeking ESL classes were on a waiting list for a year or longer (Tucker 2007: 35–37). The number of surveyed ESL providers and the average waiting times in the 22 cities is summarized in Figure 5.9.

In 2006, many ESL providers reported that they no longer used waiting lists because of the extreme demand. Instead, they used lotteries in which at least three of four applicants were turned away, and the waiting time could be several years. ESL providers without waiting lists often suffered from overcrowded classrooms and insufficiently trained instructors. Frequently, they placed ESL students in the wrong level of English class, and even turned adults away because of insufficient resources (Tucker 2007: 35, 37). "[O]f 3 million nonparticipating adults who were interested in taking ESL classes 58.8 percent 'reported that they did not know of any classes they could have taken in the past 12 months.'"[34]

Even adults enrolled in an ESL class were left without the English language skills they needed to vote without assistance. The waiting time data provided in Figure 5.9 is for classes at the most basic level of English; "the system is too overwhelmed to provide more than

30 *See* Testimony of Dr. James Thomas Tucker, Voting Rights Consultant for the National Association of Latino Elected and Appointed Officials (NALEO) Educational Fund, Before the Subcomm. on the Const. of the House Jud. Comm., *Fannie Lou Hamer, Rosa Parks, and Coretta Scott King Voting Rights Act Reauthorization and Amendments Act of 2006 (Part II)*, H. Hrg. 109–19, at 85–92 (May 4, 2006).

31 *See Moore v. State of Alaska*, Case No. 3AN-04–9756-CIV (Alaska Superior Ct.).

32 *See Leslie v. Board of Educ. for Ill. Sch. Dist. U-46*, 379 F. Supp.2d 952 (N.D. Ill. 2005).

33 *See* James Thomas Tucker, *The ESL Logjam: Waiting Times for ESL Classes and the Impact on English Language Learners*, 96 Nat'l Civic Rev. 30 (Mar. 2007).

34 Tucker 2007: 34 (quoting Richard Venezky and Daniel Wagner, Supply and Demand for Literacy Instruction in the United States 6 (National Center on Adult Literacy, Philadelphia, 1994)).

State and City	Number Surveyed	Number offering ESL classes	Number with ESL waiting list	Maximum waiting time
Arizona (Phoenix)	11	10	9	36
California	42	41	17	12
Anaheim	4	4	1	12
Los Angeles	9	9	3	.5
San Diego	7	7	2	3
San Francisco	22	21	11	12
Colorado (Denver)	7	6	4	3
Connecticut (New Haven)	8	6	3	12
Florida (Miami)	5	5	1	Unknown
Hawaii (Honolulu)	5	5	0	N/A
Illinois (Chicago)	13	12	8	6
Massachusetts (Boston)	6	6	6	36
Nevada (Las Vegas)	6	6	4	4
New Jersey (Newark)	4	4	3	3
New Mexico (Albuquerque)	4	4	3	14
New York (New York City)	12	12	8†	18‡
Pennsylvania (Philadelphia)	13	10	5	12
Rhode Island (Providence)	6	6	5	12
Texas	29	29	14	12
Dallas	4	4	2	2
El Paso	5	5	5	12
Houston	7	7	5	2
San Antonio	13	13	2	6
Washington (Seattle)	13	13	10	4
STATE TOTALS	184	175	100	36‡

Figure 5.9 Waiting times for adult English-as-a-second-languages (ESL) classes, by state and city (2006)

† Many ESL providers in New York City hold lotteries for classes instead of using waiting lists.
‡ The waiting time for ESL classes in New York City can be five years or more for students not selected by lotteries.
Source: Tucker 2007.

a few advanced classes" (Tucker 2007: 30). More comprehensive programs providing advanced English learning were in the highest demand and had the longest waiting lists (Tucker 2007: 35). According to the 2003 Assessment of Adult Literacy:

> Only 3 percent of adults with basic English literacy were able to correctly answer a simple prose literacy question; only 4 percent of adults with basic English literacy were able to correctly answer a simple document literacy question; and only 40 percent of adults with basic English literacy were able to correctly answer a simple quantitative literacy question (Tucker 2007: 33).

Among those enrolled in advanced English classes, it could take several years for them "to acquire spoken English language and literacy skills equal to those of a person with a fifth grade education – and that level is still functionally illiterate" (Tucker 2007: 35). Understanding written voting materials (especially complex ballot questions) requires an even higher level of English proficiency that most adult ESL students will never acquire (Chapter 4). The lack of ESL opportunities in jurisdictions covered under Sections 4(f)(4) and 203 highlights the continuing need for the VRA's language-assistance provisions. That need is identified in the 2002 Determinations.

Illiteracy Rates in the Covered Jurisdictions

Because of unequal educational and English learning opportunities, illiteracy rates among language minority voting-age citizens were extremely high in political subdivisions covered under the 2002 Determinations. The Census Bureau defines "illiteracy" as those persons having less than a fifth-grade education.[35] According to the 2000 Census, the illiteracy rate of the CVAP in the United States was 1.35 percent. Section 203 applies to a jurisdiction if a single-language group meets at least one of the triggers described above and "the illiteracy rate of the citizens in the language group is higher than the national illiteracy rate."[36]

Among the 464 covered language groups in the covered political subdivisions, only 10.3 percent (N = 48) had illiteracy rates of 2.5 percent or less among LEP voting-age citizens. By comparison, approximately three-quarters (N = 345) of LEP voting-age citizens in the covered language groups had illiteracy rates over seven times higher than the national illiteracy rate. Over 15 percent (N = 70) of covered language groups had illiteracy rates among LEP voting-age citizens exceeding 50 percent, or more than 37 times the national illiteracy rate. Among the 403 language groups for which complete Census data was available, the average illiteracy rate of voting-age citizens in the covered language groups was 18.8 percent, nearly 14 times the national illiteracy rate. The combination of limited-English proficiency and high illiteracy rates resulted in a particularly acute need for language assistance among these groups. Availability of oral language assistance at every stage of the election process was especially important for illiterate LEP voters.

Alaska Native Languages

According to the 2002 Determinations, an average of 28.3 percent of Alaska Native LEP voting-age citizens on those reservations were illiterate, nearly 21 times the national illiteracy rate. Forty percent (N = 36) of Alaska Native reservations had illiteracy rates exceeding 50 percent.

American Indian Languages

Among the 100 American Indian reservations for which complete Census data was available in the 2002 Determinations, 11.7 percent of the LEP American Indian voting-age citizens were illiterate, nearly nine times the national illiteracy rate. Over one-quarter (N = 33) of covered American Indian reservations had illiteracy rates exceeding 50 percent. The illiteracy rates were even higher on some reservations. For example, four of the six counties covered in Arizona for the Navajo and Tohono O'Odham languages had illiteracy rates of at least 25 percent among LEP voting-age

35 *See* U.S. Bureau of the Census, Voting Rights Output File Documentation (Sept. 2, 2004).

36 42 U.S.C. § 1973aa-1a(b)(2)(A)(ii).

citizens, over 18 times the national illiteracy rate. In Apache County, Arizona, the illiteracy rate among LEP Navajo voting-age citizens was 25.4 percent, nearly 19 times the national illiteracy rate. Similarly, Maverick County, Texas, which was covered for the Kickapoo language, had an illiteracy rate of 86.2 percent among LEP voting-age citizens.

Asian Languages

The 27 jurisdictions covered for Asian languages had the lowest average illiteracy rates among the four language groups in the 2002 Determinations. Nevertheless, Asian-covered jurisdictions still had an average illiteracy rate of 8.5 percent for LEP Asian voting-age citizens, more than six times the national illiteracy rate.

Spanish

The three states covered statewide for Spanish under the 2002 Determinations had an average of 16.3 percent of LEP Spanish heritage voting-age citizens who were illiterate, 12 times the national illiteracy rate. The illiteracy rate for political subdivisions covered for Spanish also was very high. Among the 217 covered political subdivisions, an average of 20.8 percent of LEP Spanish heritage voting-age citizens were illiterate, over 15 times the national illiteracy rate. Over half (N = 110) had illiteracy rates greater than 20 percent. Fifteen political subdivisions had illiteracy rates among LEP Spanish heritage voting-age citizens greater than 35 percent.

Only two jurisdictions had illiteracy rates for LEP Spanish heritage voting-age citizens that were less than 5 percent; in both cases, the illiteracy rates still far exceeded the national illiteracy rate. Greenlee County, Arizona, had an illiteracy rate of 4.76 percent among Spanish heritage voting-age citizens, over three times the national rate. Bergen County, New Jersey, had the lowest illiteracy rate of Spanish heritage voting-age citizens, which at 3.76 percent was still nearly three times the national rate. The high illiteracy rates among Spanish heritage voting-age citizens confirmed congressional findings that educational disparities continued to result in barriers to political participation by those citizens.[37]

Election Officials' Perceptions about the Need for Language Assistance

In a 2005 study of all jurisdictions covered by Sections 4(f) and 203, election officials were asked to estimate the number of voters in their jurisdiction who needed language assistance.[38] The purpose of the question was to determine whether the perceptions of election officials corresponded to the 2002 Determinations. Of 361 jurisdictions providing complete responses to the survey, three-quarters (N = 271) estimated that an average of 5.5 percent of their jurisdiction's voters required oral language assistance in the covered language. However, according to the 2000 Census, the average number of LEP voters in those jurisdictions was actually double that number, or 10.9 percent.

This divergence between perception and reality was the same regardless of how much language assistance the jurisdiction provided, if any. Of the 271 responding jurisdictions, 67.2 percent (N = 182) indicated that they provided both oral and written assistance to voters; they estimated the

37 *See* 42 U.S.C. § 1973aa-1a(a); Pub L. No. 109–246 § 2(b), 120 Stat. 577–78.

38 The survey and its respondents are described in more detail in Chapter 6.

average assistance need at 6.5 percent, compared to the actual need of 12.8 percent. Approximately 14 percent (N = 39) indicated that they provide neither oral nor written assistance to voters; they estimated the average need for assistance at 2.5 percent, compared to the actual need of 4.5 percent. Slightly more than 11 percent (N = 31) indicated that they provided only written language materials to voters; they estimated the need for assistance at 2.5 percent, compared to the actual need of 4.5 percent. The 7 percent (N = 19) of responding jurisdictions providing only oral language assistance estimated the need for assistance at 4.6 percent, compared to the actual need of 7.6 percent. It appeared that the acknowledged failure of many jurisdictions to provide language assistance in the covered languages may have been attributable to the misperception of election officials about the need for that assistance.

There may be several reasons for these misperceptions. Nearly two-thirds of covered jurisdictions reported they did not engage in outreach with covered language minority groups and voters. Similarly, election officials may have misunderstood how voters were determined to be LEP and in need of language assistance for public elections. Some election officials appeared to perceive that voters who spoke some English did not need language assistance, even if they spoke English less than "very well." For example, one election official noted that language assistance was not needed in their jurisdiction because "[e]veryone in the community speaks English."[39] Another election official reported a lack of need for assistance because "[t]he majority of our voters speak English fluently, even those with Spanish surnames" (Respondent 624).

Other election officials apparently relied upon the absence of requests for language assistance as evidence that such assistance was not needed.[40] One election official reported an "[e]xtremely low use of both oral and written mediums" of assistance (Respondent 357). In some cases, the absence of requests could be an indication that assistance is not needed. However, often the absence of requests was the result of LEP voters failing to participate in the election process because of the lack of language assistance or the failure to publicize that it was available.

At least some election officials appeared to underestimate the need for language assistance because of confusion over what Section 203 required. As one election official reported, "[h]ave had no experiences in providing language assistance to voters" (Respondent 1029). Indeed, one-third of all election officials reported that they either provided no language assistance or only written language materials in the covered language despite the identified need for assistance. Training and information about Section 203 could have dispelled their misconceptions.

Some election officials may have underestimated the need for language assistance because of their ideological opposition to that assistance. There appeared to be very few election officials who fell into that category. Only 12 jurisdictions expressly advocated English-only elections. Conversely, nearly three-quarters of responding jurisdictions indicated that they believed the federal language-assistance provisions should remain in effect for public elections. The divergence between perception and the actual need for language assistance under the 2002 Determinations reaffirms why Sections 4(f)(4) and 203 remain necessary to break down language barriers for non-English speaking voters.

---

39 Respondent 269 to survey described in DR. JAMES THOMAS TUCKER AND DR. RODOLFO ESPINO ET AL., MINORITY LANGUAGE ASSISTANCE PRACTICES IN PUBLIC ELECTIONS (2006), *reprinted in Voting Rights Act: Evidence of Continued Need, Hearing Before the Subcomm. on the Constitution of the H. Comm. on the Judiciary*, 109th Cong. 2124 (2006). All references to Respondents in the text refer to responses to the Tucker and Espino survey.

40 *See* Respondents 364, 412, 639, 706, 758, 854, 987 and 1029.

Conclusion

The 2002 Determinations are instructive for several reasons. They demonstrate the nationwide scope of Section 203, covering states from Alaska to Florida. Coverage has expanded to some jurisdictions and been removed from others, consistent with changing demographics. The various triggering formulas have impacted the four covered language minority groups in different ways. Language minority groups in covered jurisdictions have very high levels of limited-English proficiency. Illiteracy rates vary considerably between language minorities, but all language groups experience rates far above the national rate because of the impact of unequal opportunities to learn to speak and read English. The 2002 Determinations show the continuing vitality of Section 203 as a mechanism for accurately targeting jurisdictions where the need for language assistance in voting is greatest.

Chapter 6

Implementation and Cost of Language Assistance in Covered Jurisdictions[1]

There have been few studies examining how covered jurisdictions have implemented Sections 4(f)(4) and 203. Congress commissioned the General Accounting Office (now the General Accountability Office, or GAO) in 1986, 1997, and 2008 to determine the costs associated with language materials and assistance under Section 203. The 1986 GAO study obtained information from 318 political subdivisions and 19 state governments.[2] The 1997 GAO study reported data from 292 covered jurisdictions in 26 states.[3] The 2008 GAO study evaluated how language assistance was provided in 14 jurisdictions in 12 states.[4] Both the 1986 and 1997 GAO studies were limited by the inability of many jurisdictions to report the costs of bilingual voting assistance. A study I conducted with Dr. Rodolfo Espino and students at Arizona State University in 2005 encountered similar problems. Nevertheless, for jurisdictions reporting complete expense data, the costs of compliance comprised only a small fraction of total election expenses.

The purpose of our study was to update cost data collected by the 1986 and 1997 GAO studies and to determine how public officials provided language assistance under the Act. Our survey assessed the availability and quality of assistance in several areas: use of bilingual coordinators as liaisons between the election office and covered language groups; recruitment and training of Election Day poll workers; telephonic assistance; oral language assistance; written language materials provided to limited-English-proficient (LEP) voters; outreach and publicity; and the ability of voters to receive assistance from the person of their choice. The survey concluded with questions about the respondent's views of reauthorization, the federal government's role in providing language assistance, and the jurisdiction's experiences under Section 203.[5] This chapter summarizes the results of our study.

---

1 Published originally in the *Texas Journal on Civil Liberties & Civil Rights*. *See* James Thomas Tucker and Rodolfo Espino, *Government Effectiveness and Efficiency? The Minority Language Assistance Provisions of the VRA*, 12 TEX. J. C.L. & C.R. 163 (2007). In certain places, the content has been modified from the original to reflect the discussion elsewhere in this book.

2 *See* U.S. GEN. ACCT. OFF. ("GAO"), BILINGUAL VOTING ASSISTANCE: COSTS OF AND USE DURING THE 1984 GENERAL ELECTION 11–12 (1986) ("1986 GAO STUDY").

3 *See* GAO, BILINGUAL VOTING ASSISTANCE: ASSISTANCE PROVIDED AND COSTS 1, 33 (1997) ("1997 GAO STUDY").

4 *See* GAO, BILINGUAL VOTING ASSISTANCE: SELECTED JURISDICTIONS' STRATEGIES FOR IDENTIFYING NEEDS AND PROVIDING ASSISTANCE (2008). The GAO cited our study in deciding not to evaluate the cost efficiency of providing language assistance (GAO 2008: 2–3, 11).

5 For a copy of the survey, *see* DR. JAMES THOMAS TUCKER AND DR. RODOLFO ESPINO ET AL., MINORITY LANGUAGE ASSISTANCE PRACTICES IN PUBLIC ELECTIONS Appendix D (2006), *reprinted in Voting Rights Act: Evidence of Continued Need, Hearing Before the Subcomm. on the Constitution of the H. Comm. on the Judiciary*, 109th Cong. 2124, 2296–2307 (2006).

Jurisdictions Surveyed

A total of 810 jurisdictions in 33 states were surveyed (Tucker and Espino 2006: App. E). The surveyed jurisdictions included: all jurisdictions covered under Section 4(f)(4) or Section 203; all counties in the five states covered statewide under either Section 4(f)(4) or Section 203; all cities in covered jurisdictions that the 2000 Census reported as having 50,000 or more people; a handful of jurisdictions that no longer were covered following the July 2002 Census determinations under Section 203 ("2002 Determinations");[6] and the chief elections officer in each surveyed state.

More than half of surveyed jurisdictions responded. Complete responses were received from 361 jurisdictions in 31 states, making this one of the most comprehensive studies of language assistance practices under the Voting Rights Act (VRA). A response was considered "complete" if the responding jurisdiction answered at least half the survey questions. Responses were received from 50 additional jurisdictions that did not complete the survey because they reported that other surveyed jurisdictions handled their elections. The number of responses varied because some questions did not apply to all respondents, and some respondents chose not to answer certain questions.

Responses came from elections officials in 93.9 percent of the 33 states surveyed (N = 31). Two states with a single covered county or parish, Louisiana and Pennsylvania, did not respond. Seventy-two percent of responding jurisdictions were counties, 26 percent were cities or boroughs, and 2 percent were states. Responding jurisdictions had populations ranging from 67 people to over eight million people, with a mean population of 33,627 people. Among the respondents, 57.9 percent (N = 209) were required to make Section 5 submissions because of coverage under Section 4(f)(4) or Section 4(b) of the VRA. Texas and California had the most responses, comprising 62.9 percent (N = 227) of all responding jurisdictions. However, the percentage of responses from these two states was proportionate to the number of surveys they received, which comprised 62.1 percent (N = 503) of the 810 surveys. Figure 6.1 depicts the number of responses received from each state covered in whole or in part by the language assistance provisions of the VRA.

Responding jurisdictions were covered for an average of 1.4 languages, with the mean jurisdiction covered for one language. Fourteen responding jurisdictions were in Los Angeles County, California, where six languages are covered (Spanish, Chinese, Filipino, Japanese, Korean, and Vietnamese). Fifteen respondents had no covered language because they were either previously covered jurisdictions that lost coverage following the 2002 Determinations or were states not covered in their own right but with covered political subdivisions (such as counties, boroughs, cities, or towns).

The percentage of responding jurisdictions covered by the four language groups approximated the percentage of all jurisdictions covered for those languages. Among the respondents, 85.9 percent (N = 310) were covered for Spanish, 14.7 percent (N = 53) for American Indian languages, 10.8 percent (N = 39) for Asian languages, and three percent (N = 11) for Alaska Native languages. In comparison, of jurisdictions covered by Section 4(f)(4) or Section 203 of the VRA, 84.2 percent (N = 425) are covered for Spanish, 16 percent (N = 81) for American Indian languages, 3.2 percent (N = 16) for Asian languages, and 5.3 percent (N = 27) for Alaska Native languages (Chapter 5).

Respondents included jurisdictions covered by 89.7 percent of the 29 languages (N = 26) identified for coverage in the 2002 Determinations. Only three American Indian languages, each

6 Jurisdictions covered by Section 203 immediately prior to the release of the 2002 Determinations were surveyed to determine whether they continued to provide language materials and assistance in the absence of a requirement that they do so.

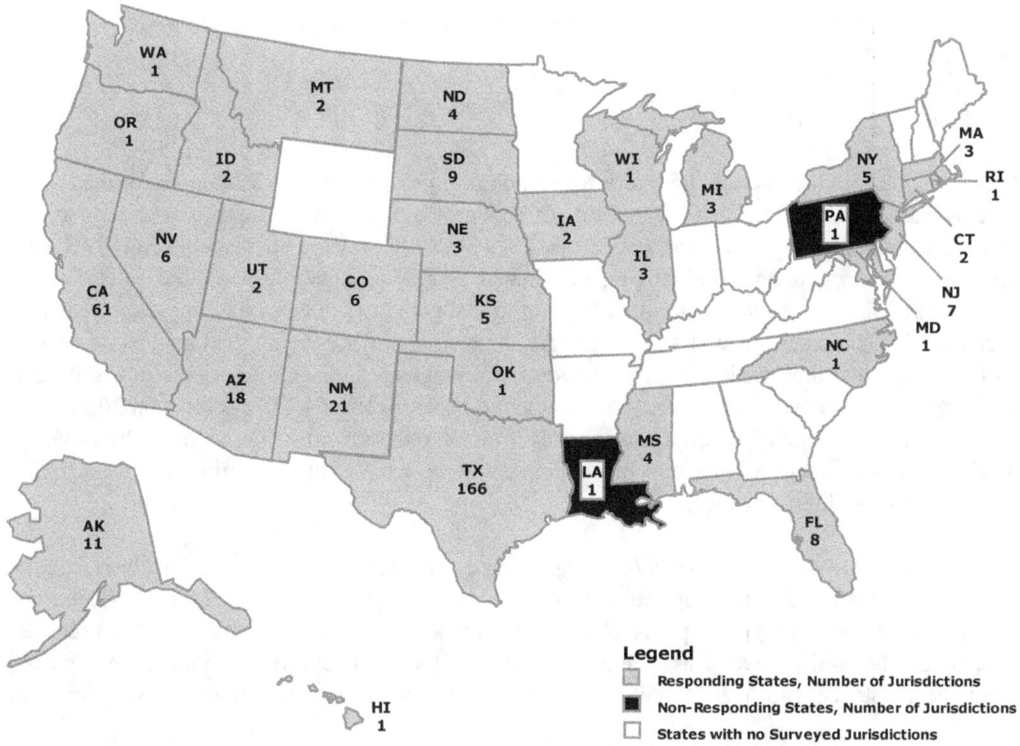

Figure 6.1 Section 4(f)(4) or Section 203 covered jurisdictions responding to survey, by state

Source: Responses to 2005 ASU/BHC Survey of Minority Language Assistance Practices in Public Elections (on file with authors).

covered in a single jurisdiction, Chickasaw, Paiute, and Yacqui (Figure 5.4), were not encompassed by the responses. Chinese was the most common language among the 39 responding jurisdictions covered for an Asian language, at 89.7 percent (N = 35), consistent with being the most frequently covered Asian language. Vietnamese was the next most common, at 66.7 percent (N = 26), followed by Korean at 56.4 percent (N = 22), Filipino at 51.3 percent (N = 20), and Japanese at 38.5 percent (N = 15). At least one response was received from jurisdictions covered by each of the five Alaska Native languages.[7]

Availability of Language Assistance in Covered Jurisdictions

Many covered jurisdictions reported election practices that fell short of complying with the VRA's language assistance provisions. Approximately 80 percent (N = 287) provided some type of language assistance to voters: 60.4 percent (N = 215) provided both oral and written assistance;

7 For more information on the survey respondents, *see* Tucker and Espino 2006: Chapter 2 and App. E, *reprinted in* H. Hrg. 109–103, at 2308–32.

14 percent (N = 50) provided only written materials; and 6.2 percent (N = 22) provided only oral language assistance.

Availability by Language Group

Figure 6.2 depicts the average LEP rate for responding jurisdictions, by language, for the type of language assistance offered. The availability of both oral and written language assistance increased as the Spanish-speaking LEP increased. Jurisdictions with the lowest Spanish-speaking LEP were more likely to provide only oral language assistance or no language assistance. Jurisdictions with the highest Asian language-speaking LEP reported that generally only written language assistance was available. Jurisdictions with the highest Alaska Native or American Indian language-speaking LEP reported that they typically only provided oral language assistance. Jurisdictions providing language assistance were more likely to be covered under Section 4(f)(4) or Section 203 in their own right than those that did not, which tended to be covered political subdivisions such as counties or cities. There was no relationship between the jurisdiction's total population and whether that jurisdiction provided assistance.

Alaska Native and American Indian languages Sixty-two responding jurisdictions were covered for an Alaska Native or American Indian language, among other languages. Of those jurisdictions, 30.7 percent (N = 19) reported providing no language assistance, 24.2 percent (N = 15) reported providing only oral language assistance, 3.2 percent (N = 2) reported providing only written language assistance, and 41.9 percent (N = 26) reported providing both. Among the 34 responding

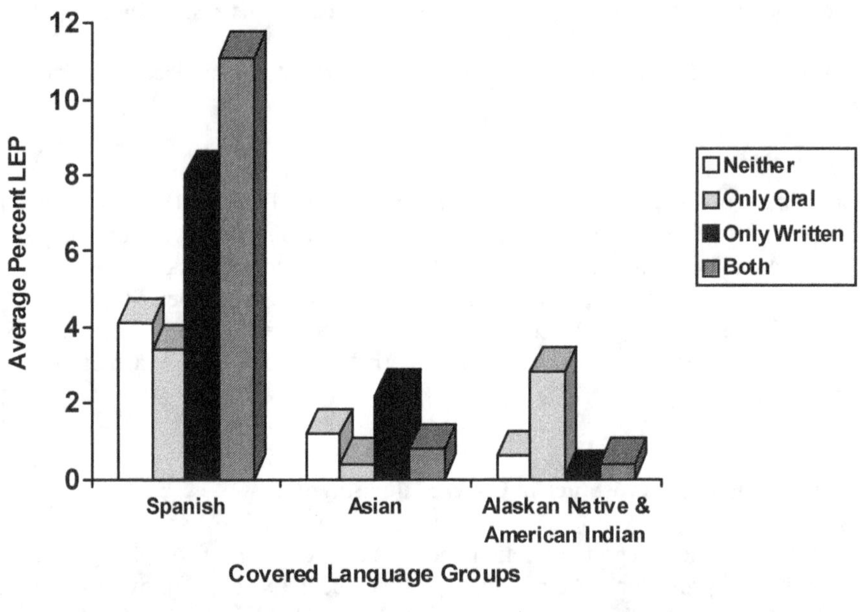

Figure 6.2 Types of language assistance available, by LEP of covered language group
Source: Responses to 2005 ASU/BHC Survey of Minority Language Assistance Practices in Public Elections, Questions E-4 and F-1 and 2000 Census, Summary Tape Files 3 and 4 (on file with authors).

jurisdictions covered only for Alaska Native or American Indian languages, 55.9 percent (N = 19) reported providing no language assistance, 38.2 percent (N = 13) reported providing only oral language assistance, and 5.9 percent (N = 2) reported providing both. None of the jurisdictions reported providing only written language assistance.

Asian Languages Thirty-seven responding jurisdictions were covered for an Asian language. Of those jurisdictions, 18.9 percent (N = 7) reported providing no language assistance, 2.7 percent (N = 1) reported providing only oral language assistance, 35.1 percent (N = 13) reported providing only written language assistance, and 43.2 percent (N = 16) reported providing both. All responding jurisdictions covered for Asian languages also were covered by another language, generally Spanish. It therefore is not possible to provide data for jurisdictions covered only for Asian languages.

Spanish Three hundred eight responding jurisdictions were covered for Spanish, among other languages. Of those jurisdictions, 13.3 percent (N = 41) reported providing no assistance, 2.9 percent (N = 9) reported providing only oral language assistance, 15.3 percent (N = 47) reported providing only written language assistance, and 68.5 percent (N = 211) reported providing both. The percentages were slightly different when jurisdictions covered only for Spanish were considered. Excluding Spanish covered jurisdictions that also were covered for Asian or American Indian languages, 14 percent of the 243 responding jurisdictions (N = 34) reported providing no language assistance, 2.5 percent (N = 6) reported providing only oral language assistance, 13.2 percent (N = 32) reported providing only written language assistance, and 70.4 percent (N = 171) reported providing both.

Amount of Language Assistance Offered

The amount of language assistance offered varied greatly. Many jurisdictions did not provide any language assistance. Among those that did, the assistance offered often failed to provide assistance for all voting materials and information.

No Assistance Every covered language group was affected by the lack of assistance available in the 69 jurisdictions reporting no assistance. According to the 2000 Census, 59.4 percent (N = 41) were covered for Spanish with an average Hispanic voting-age population (VAP) of 18.8 percent, of whom 39.4 percent were LEP. Approximately 27.5 percent (N = 19) were covered for Alaska Native or American Indian languages with an average Alaska Native or American Indian VAP of 17.4 percent, of whom 6 percent were LEP. About 10 percent (N = 7) were covered for Asian American languages with an average Asian VAP of 13.8 percent, of whom 40.7 percent were LEP. A few jurisdictions that reported they did not provide any assistance were no longer covered under either Section 4(f)(4) or Section 203.

Among jurisdictions providing no language assistance, the mean Hispanic VAP was 12.7 percent with a mean LEP of 32 percent, yielding a Hispanic LEP of 4.1 percent of all VAP. The mean Asian VAP was 3.2 percent with a mean LEP of 37.3 percent, yielding an Asian LEP of 1.2 percent of all VAP. The mean Alaska Native/American Indian VAP was 6.7 percent with a mean LEP of 8.7 percent, yielding an Alaska Native/American Indian LEP of 0.6 percent of all VAP.

Oral language assistance only More than two-thirds of the 22 jurisdictions (N = 15) that offered only oral language assistance were covered for Alaska Native or American Indian languages, which in some cases will not require written materials (Chapter 4). But that is not always true. In Bethel, Alaska, the jurisdiction's determination that no written materials are required is contradicted by the widespread and common usage of the written Alaska Native language, Yup'ik (Chapter 10).

The 15 jurisdictions offering only oral language assistance had an average Alaska Native/American Indian VAP of 27.7 percent, of whom 15 percent were LEP. Only one of the 63 respondents covered for Alaska Native or American Indian languages reported receiving voter requests for bilingual election materials. However, the absence of requests often is the product of insufficient outreach and does not necessarily mean there is no need for written materials (Chapters 4, 10).

Jurisdictions providing only oral language assistance also included: 40.9 percent (N = 9) covered for Spanish with an average Hispanic VAP of 23.5 percent, of whom 37.2 percent were LEP; and 4.5 percent (N = 1) covered for Asian languages with an Asian VAP of 7.6 percent, of whom 48.5 percent were LEP. According to the 2000 Census, of jurisdictions providing only oral language assistance, the mean Hispanic VAP was 12.4 percent with a mean LEP of 27.7 percent, yielding a Hispanic LEP of 3.4 percent of all VAP. The mean Alaska Native/American Indian VAP was 19.1 percent with a mean LEP of 14.9 percent, yielding an Alaska Native/American Indian LEP of 2.8 percent of all VAP. The mean Asian VAP was 1.4 percent with a mean LEP of 24.1 percent, yielding an Asian LEP of 0.4 percent of all VAP.

Bilingual written materials only Fourteen percent of responding jurisdictions (N = 50) reported providing only bilingual written materials.[8] Those jurisdictions generally had large numbers of LEP voters in one or more covered languages. Ninety-four percent (N = 47) were covered for Spanish, with an average Hispanic VAP of 18.3 percent, of whom 45.4 percent were LEP. Twenty-six percent (N = 13) were covered for Asian American languages, with an average Asian VAP of 17 percent, of whom 44.6 percent were LEP.

According to the 2000 Census, the 50 jurisdictions providing only bilingual written materials had a mean Hispanic VAP of 17.5 percent and a mean LEP of 45.7 percent, yielding a Hispanic LEP of 8 percent of all VAP. The mean Asian VAP was 5.5 percent with a mean LEP of 39.6 percent, yielding an Asian LEP of 2.2 percent of all VAP. The average percentages of both Spanish heritage and Asian voting-age citizens in all 50 jurisdictions were high enough to require full compliance with Section 203. The absence of bilingual oral language assistance in these jurisdictions could be a significant deterrent to LEP voters.

Both oral and written language assistance Among the 60.4 percent of jurisdictions (N = 215) that reported providing both oral and written language assistance, 98.1 percent (N = 211) were covered for Spanish with an average Hispanic VAP of 29 percent, of whom 39 percent were LEP; 12.1 percent (N = 26) were covered for Alaska Native or American Indian languages with an average VAP of 12.4 percent, of whom 20.5 percent were LEP; and 7.4 percent (N = 16) were covered for Asian American languages with an average VAP of 13.8 percent, of whom 43.3 percent were LEP. According to the 2000 Census, of the jurisdictions providing both oral and written language assistance, the mean Hispanic VAP was 28.6 percent with a mean LEP of 38.7 percent, yielding a Hispanic LEP of 11.1 percent of all VAP. The mean Alaska Native/American Indian VAP was 2.2 percent with a mean LEP of 17.2 percent, yielding an Alaska Native/American Indian LEP of 0.4 percent of all VAP. The mean Asian VAP was 2.2 percent with a mean LEP of 35.7 percent, yielding an Asian LEP of 0.8 percent of all VAP.

8 Two responding jurisdictions were covered for Alaska Native or American Indian languages, but were excluded because they indicated that the bilingual materials were provided in other covered languages.

Election Activities for Which Language Assistance Was Offered

To accurately assess the availability of language assistance, respondents were asked whether they offered assistance for several common election activities. This assessment included the availability of oral language assistance, bilingual written election materials, bilingual election workers, and bilingual telephone assistance.

Oral language assistance Slightly more than two-thirds of the 328 responding jurisdictions (N = 237) reported providing at least some oral language assistance. However, the scope of that assistance was limited. Respondents were asked to identify whether they provided oral language assistance for 14 common election activities, including voter registration, voter purges, polling place information, absentee and early voting, and casting a ballot on Election Day (Tucker and Espino 2006: App. D). Nearly all acknowledged not providing oral language assistance at every stage of the election process. Only 32.9 percent (N = 108) reported providing language assistance for more than half of all election activities. Jurisdictions translating more than half of all election materials were more likely to provide oral language assistance for election activities than those translating less than half of all election materials.

The absence of oral language assistance at all stages of the election process is inconsistent with Justice Department guidelines, which provide:

> [Language assistance] should be broadly construed to apply to all stages of the electoral process, from voter registration through activities related to conducting elections, including for example the issuance … of notifications, announcements, or other informational materials concerning the opportunity to register … the time, places and subject matters of elections, and the absentee voting process.[9]

Nevertheless, less than one-third of responding jurisdictions did so. Figure 6.3 summarizes election activities for which jurisdictions reported providing oral language assistance. Only four of the 14 activities were provided in the covered languages by at least half of the jurisdictions: reading the ballot, Election Day information, explaining ballot questions, and absentee voting. No activity was provided in the covered language by more than two-thirds of the jurisdictions. Even worse, three-quarters of jurisdictions indicated they did not recruit poll workers in the covered languages.

A majority of responding jurisdictions reported that oral language assistance was unavailable for activities likely to have the greatest impact upon first-time voters. Only 40.9 percent indicated assistance was available for voter registration. Similarly, only 46.4 percent provided oral language assistance on polling place locations and changes, 45.2 percent for checking in at the polling place, and 32.2 percent for voting machine instructions. Few jurisdictions reported providing oral language assistance for candidate qualification. Of responding jurisdictions, only 19.5 percent (N = 63) provided language assistance for potential candidates. Nearly the same number of jurisdictions indicated that election results were provided only in English (Figure 6.3).

Only 7.1 percent reported providing oral language assistance for voter purges (Figure 6.3). The absence of assistance may remove minority language voters who are not informed of what they must do to remain on the active voter registration list. Lack of notice for purges is inconsistent with

9 28 C.F.R. § 55.15.

Election Activity	Number Providing	Percent
Reading the ballot	199	61.6
Election Day information	194	60.1
Explaining ballot questions	164	50.8
Absentee voting	163	50.5
Early or mail-in voting	156	48.3
Polling place locations and changes	150	46.4
Checking in at the polling place	146	45.2
Voter registration	132	40.9
Voting machine instructions	104	32.2
Poll worker recruitment	79	24.5
Election results	69	21.4
Candidate qualification	63	19.5
Voter purges	23	7.1
Other (specify)	15	4.6

Figure 6.3 Election activities for which jurisdictions reported providing oral language assistance

Source: Responses to 2005 ASU/BHC Survey of Minority Language Assistance Practices in Public Elections, Question E-2 (on file with authors).

Section 203 and may violate the National Voter Registration Act (NVRA) or federal "motor-voter" law.[10]

High illiteracy rates may make it impossible for many minority language voters to read bilingual written materials unless someone reads to them. The absence of oral language assistance for these voters may prevent them from getting help and casting a meaningful ballot. Moreover, requiring an illiterate voter to rely upon written materials may constitute a "test or device" violating Section 201 of the VRA (Chapters 1, 3).[11]

Bilingual written materials Approximately three-quarters of the 361 jurisdictions giving complete responses (N = 265) reported providing at least some bilingual written materials for public elections. Respondents were asked to identify whether they provided bilingual written materials for 18 types of common election materials. Generally, jurisdictions provided bilingual versions of most election materials. A majority of the 279 jurisdictions that provided information on their written election materials indicated that they provided bilingual versions of 13 types of written election materials. However, less than one-fifth of responding jurisdictions (N = 55) reported that they used bilingual poll worker recruitment materials. Figure 6.4 summarizes the percentage of responding jurisdictions that reported providing the identified bilingual election materials. The failure to provide bilingual poll worker publicity materials may exacerbate lack of oral language assistance. Examples of bilingual election materials that are frequently part of an effective language program are included in Appendix A.

10 42 U.S.C. §§ 1973gg, *et seq.*
11 *See* 42 U.S.C. § 1973aa(b).

Election Material	Number Providing	Percent
Sample ballots	254	91.0
Ballots	229	82.1
Early voting or mail-in voting materials	224	80.3
Absentee ballots	222	79.6
Instructions on provisional ballots	218	78.1
Polling place signs	213	76.3
Instructions on using voting machine or ballot	211	75.6
Voters' rights or other information pamphlets	205	73.5
Voter registration materials	201	72.0
Election day information	196	70.3
Election day forms (challenge paperwork, etc.)	185	66.3
Publicity regarding polling place locations	172	61.7
Communications from elections office	141	50.5
Check-in information	96	34.5
Internet or web-based information	59	21.2
Election results	58	20.8
Poll worker recruitment	55	19.7
Other (please specify)	15	5.4

Figure 6.4 Types of bilingual written materials jurisdictions reported providing
Source: Responses to 2005 ASU/BHC Survey of Minority Language Assistance Practices in Public Elections, Question F-2 (on file with authors).

Four jurisdictions reported they did not offer ballots, sample ballots, or provisional ballots in covered languages.[12] Four jurisdictions did not offer instructions, polling place signs, and other Election Day materials.[13] Two jurisdictions did not offer voter registration and materials required by the NVRA (Respondents 350 and 672). One jurisdiction with an election office webpage acknowledged the page was not translated (Respondent 441). Seven jurisdictions reported they did not offer candidate-qualifying information and forms in the covered languages.[14] Six jurisdictions did not provide election results in the covered languages.[15]

Two-thirds of respondents (N = 189) reported they translated more than half of all election materials (Figure 6.4). The jurisdiction's population had no relationship to whether bilingual materials were provided. Some jurisdictions reported that they intended to provide required bilingual written materials in the future (Respondents 431 and 839). Others said they would not provide bilingual materials for reasons including cost,[16] technological issues (Respondents 709 and 786), the failure of vendors to offer translation services (Respondents 672 and 833), and redundancy due to bilingual poll workers who translated materials for voters (Respondent 421). Eighteen respondents reported that only Alaska Native or American Indian languages were covered in their respective jurisdictions and that they believed no bilingual written materials were needed. One respondent reported that

12 Respondents 350, 395, 412, and 714 to survey described in Tucker and Espino 2006. All references to Respondents in the text refer to responses to the Tucker and Espino survey.

13 Respondents 395, 441, 451, and 639.

14 Respondents 350, 571, 760, 833, 839, 857, and 901.

15 Respondents 299, 441, 639, 709, 786, and 987.

16 Respondents 486, 561, 760, and 888.

bilingual materials had been requested for an American Indian language. Again, however, bilingual written materials may be needed for certain Alaska Native or American Indian languages that are commonly used (Chapters 4, 10). Figures 4.5 and 10.5 illustrate examples of ballots provided in Native languages.

Full-time bilingual election workers Respondents were asked whether their jurisdiction employed at least one full-time employee fluent in a language besides English, regardless of whether it was a covered language. Of the jurisdictions responding to this question, 57.1 percent (N = 192) reported having no full-time employees fluent in another language. The percentage of jurisdictions with at least one full-time worker in a covered language was less than 42.9 percent. Of 391 responding jurisdictions covered for one or more languages, 39.1 percent (N = 153) reported having at least one full-time worker who was fluent in at least one covered language.[17]

Among the 299 responding jurisdictions covered for Spanish, 55.8 percent (N = 167) did not employ a Spanish-speaking full-time worker.[18] Among the 61 jurisdictions covered for Alaska Native or American Indian languages, 81.9 percent (N = 50) had no full-time employees fluent in the covered language.[19] Fifty-two respondents were covered for an American Indian language but not an Alaska Native language. Among those 52 jurisdictions, 81.8 percent (N = 42) did not employ a full-time worker fluent in an American Indian language. Of the 10 responding jurisdictions covered for an Alaska Native language, only 10 percent (N = 1) reported having a full-time employee fluent in a covered language.[20] The lack of bilingual employees in Alaska is consistent with the evidence in the *Nick* litigation (Chapter 10). Among 31 responding jurisdictions covered for at least one Asian language, more than two-thirds (N = 21) had no full-time employees fluent in an Asian language.[21]

There was a strong positive relationship between the percentage of LEP voters and whether jurisdictions employed bilingual full-time workers in the covered languages. Jurisdictions employing at least one full-time, Spanish-speaking employee had a higher average LEP than jurisdictions that do not. Among respondents with at least one full-time Spanish-speaking employee, the mean Spanish VAP was 31.5 percent, with an average LEP of 37.9 percent, meaning that approximately 11.9 percent of all VAP was LEP in the covered language. By contrast, of respondents not employing at least one full-time Spanish-speaking employee, the mean Hispanic VAP was 17.4 percent with an average LEP of 37.5 percent, meaning that approximately 6.5 percent of all VAP was LEP in the covered language.

17 The 391 jurisdictions are the aggregate of all data. If a jurisdiction was covered for two distinct language groups (e.g., Spanish heritage and American Indian), it was counted for each of those language groups. This approach was used to better depict whether a bilingual full-time worker was available for each of the covered language groups. It did not depict whether a bilingual full-time worker was available in each language in the covered language group (e.g., Chinese, Filipino, Japanese, Korean, and Vietnamese for Asian language coverage), and therefore still may have overestimated the extent of full-time bilingual workers available.

18 Among the 48 jurisdictions not covered for Spanish, 6.2 percent (N = 3) employed at least one full-time worker fluent in Spanish.

19 One non-covered jurisdiction employed a full-time worker fluent in an Alaska Native or American Indian language.

20 One responding jurisdiction was covered for both Alaska Native and American Indian languages.

21 Seven jurisdictions not covered for an Asian language reported having a full-time worker fluent in one or more of those languages.

A similar pattern emerged for Alaska Native and American Indian-covered jurisdictions. Among respondents employing at least one full-time American Indian or Alaska Native-speaking employee, the mean Native language-speaking VAP was 31.3 percent with an average LEP of 20.9 percent, meaning that approximately 6.5 percent of VAP was LEP in the covered language. In comparison, among respondents not employing at least one full-time American Indian language-speaking employee, the mean Alaska Native or American Indian language-speaking VAP was 3 percent with an average LEP of 14.3 percent, meaning that approximately 0.4 percent of VAP was LEP in the covered language. That trend did not hold true in Alaska. The percentages of LEP voters were extremely high (more than 10 percent of the VAP) in several Alaska Native areas in which there was no full-time elections employee, offering strong evidence of Alaska's failure to provide effective language assistance (Chapter 10).

Likewise, jurisdictions employing at least one full-time Asian language-speaking employee had higher LEP rates than jurisdictions that did not. Respondents employing at least one full-time Asian language-speaking employee had a mean Asian-language VAP of 9.8 percent with an average LEP of 38.8 percent, meaning that approximately 3.8 percent of VAP was LEP in the covered language. Among respondents not employing at least one full-time Asian language-speaking employee, the mean Asian-language VAP was 2.1 percent with an average LEP of 35.2 percent, meaning that 0.7 percent of the VAP was LEP in the covered language.

Part-time bilingual election workers Respondents estimated the percentage of part-time election workers fluent in a language besides English. Respondents reported an average of 12.2 percent of part-time workers was fluent in Spanish, 0.6 percent were fluent in an Alaska Native or American Indian language, and 0.1 percent were fluent in an Asian language. However, the median percentages for part-time workers fluent in those language groups were substantially lower. Among responding jurisdictions, the median percentage of part-time workers fluent in Spanish was 2 percent, and the median percentages for Alaska Native/American Indian and Asian languages were 0 percent.

It appears that the lower median percentages were caused by a small group of jurisdictions. The outlying 1 percent of Spanish-covered jurisdictions reported that 90 to 100 percent of their part-time employees were fluent in Spanish. Similarly, the outlying 1 percent of Alaska Native and American Indian covered jurisdictions reported that 15 to 25 percent of their part-time employees were fluent in a covered language. For Asian languages, the outlying 1 percent reported having 3.3 to 8 percent of part-time employees fluent in an Asian language.

There was a strong relationship between the availability of bilingual part-time employees and coverage under either Section 4(f)(4) or Section 203. Among jurisdictions covered for Spanish, the mean percentage of part-time employees fluent in Spanish was 14 percent, compared to 0.5 percent for jurisdictions not covered for Spanish. Among jurisdictions covered for Alaska Native or American Indian languages, 2.7 percent of part-time employees spoke a covered language fluently, in contrast to 0.1 percent in jurisdictions not covered for those languages. Jurisdictions covered for an Asian language reported that 1 percent of their part-time employees were fluent in an Asian language, compared to 0 percent for jurisdictions not covered for Asian languages.

There also was a strong positive relationship between the percentage of LEP voters and whether jurisdictions employed bilingual part-time workers in the covered languages. Jurisdictions employing at least one part-time Spanish-speaking employee had a higher average LEP than jurisdictions that did not. Among respondents with at least one part-time Spanish-speaking employee, the mean Spanish VAP was 29 percent with an average LEP of 38.9 percent, meaning that approximately 11.3 percent of all VAP was LEP in the covered language. Among respondents not employing at least one part-time Spanish-speaking employee, the mean Hispanic VAP was 19.5 percent with an average LEP of 41.9 percent, meaning that approximately 8.2 percent of VAP was LEP in the covered language.

A similar pattern emerged for Alaska Native and American Indian covered jurisdictions. Among responding jurisdictions employing at least one part-time Alaska Native or American Indian language-speaking employee, the mean Native language-speaking VAP was 29.7 percent with an average LEP of 15.5 percent, meaning that approximately 4.6 percent of VAP was LEP in the covered language. Among respondents not employing at least one part-time Alaska Native or American Indian language-speaking employee, the mean Native language-speaking VAP was 7.4 percent with an average LEP of 13.7 percent, meaning that approximately 1 percent of all VAP was LEP in the covered language.

Likewise, jurisdictions employing at least one part-time Asian language-speaking employee had a higher LEP than jurisdictions that did not. Respondents employing at least one part-time Asian language-speaking employee had a mean Asian-language VAP of 17.2 percent with an average LEP of 44.1 percent, meaning that approximately 7.6 percent of VAP was LEP in the covered language. Among respondents not employing at least one full-time, Asian language-speaking employee, the mean Asian-language VAP was 13.1 percent with an average LEP of 40.2 percent, meaning that 5.3 percent of the VAP was LEP in the covered language.

Language assistance for telephone inquiries Less than half of the responding 326 jurisdictions reported providing assistance for telephone inquiries from voters in all the covered languages: 39 percent (N = 127) provided assistance in all covered languages; 26.4 percent (N = 86) in some covered languages; and 34.7 percent (N = 113) in none of the covered languages. Although two-thirds of jurisdictions provided some oral language assistance for telephone inquiries, only one-half did so for all covered languages. Spanish-language assistance was the most available, but one-quarter of all Spanish-covered jurisdictions did not provide telephone assistance to voters in Spanish.

The percentage of jurisdictions providing no telephone assistance decreased as the jurisdiction's population increased. Generally, the percentage of jurisdictions providing telephone assistance in all of their covered languages slowly increased with population size until the population was greater than 100,000, when there was a large increase in the availability of telephone assistance. Jurisdictions with a higher percentage of LEP voters were more likely to provide telephone assistance in the covered languages.

Among jurisdictions not providing telephone assistance, the Spanish LEP was lower than the Spanish LEP for jurisdictions that provided at least some telephone assistance. The same effect was not as notable for Asian-speaking LEP and American Indian-speaking LEP. Instead, while Asian-speaking LEP increased only slightly as the availability of telephone assistance increased, American Indian LEP decreased. No telephone assistance was available in any of the covered Alaska Native languages when Alaska was sued for violating Section 203 in 2007 (Chapter 10).

Quality of Language Assistance in Covered Jurisdictions

Each covered jurisdiction must "determine what actions by it are required for compliance with the requirements of Section 4(f)(4) and Section 203(c)."[22] Compliance is assessed by an "effectiveness" standard, which ensures that a language assistance program "is designed and implemented in such a way that language minority group members who need minority language materials and assistance

22 28 C.F.R. § 55.14(c).

receive them."[23] Covered jurisdictions need to make certain that election information, materials, and announcements are as readily available in the covered language(s) as they are in English and must ensure public awareness about the jurisdiction's minority language assistance program.[24] Assessing the quality of language materials, assistance, outreach, and publicity is essential to determine whether jurisdictions are in compliance (Chapter 4).

The Justice Department offers guidance on Section 203 compliance. Because election systems and minority language needs vary widely, the Department "has identified both guiding principles and practical suggestions for local election officials to pursue with their local language minority communities to serve them effectively and efficiently."[25] These guidelines suggest election officials talk to a broad range of organizations and individuals in the minority community to identify what will make the assistance effective. There are several common ways to assess and improve the quality of language assistance.

Bilingual Coordinators

Bilingual coordinators act as liaisons between election officials and covered language groups to improve the availability and quality of language assistance. They often train election officials and poll workers about the jurisdiction's language assistance program and federal, state, and local requirements for providing assistance. They recruit bilingual voters to serve as poll workers and confirm their spoken and written language abilities. They identify locations where voters require language assistance and ensure adequate bilingual poll worker staffing on Election Day. They engage in outreach and publicity with LEP voters about the jurisdiction's language assistance program. Bilingual coordinators can be volunteers or paid employees. They typically are fluent in both English and the covered language. It is helpful if they have established contacts in the covered language groups. As the liaison with the local elections office, they should be fully trained on all federal, state, and local election procedures.

Bilingual coordinators are not required by statute or regulation. However, jurisdictions using them are more likely to comply with the VRA's language assistance provisions than jurisdictions that do not. Therefore, bilingual coordinators are routinely required in consent decrees and as part of judicial remedies for Section 203 violations.[26]

Availability Among 338 responding jurisdictions, 38.2 percent (N = 129) reported that they used bilingual coordinators, while 61.8 percent (N = 209) did not. Of those using bilingual coordinators, 91.5 percent (N = 118) were covered for Spanish, 19.4 percent (N = 25) for American Indian languages, and 12.4 percent (N = 16) for Asian languages. Among jurisdictions not using bilingual coordinators, 82.3 percent (N = 172) were covered for Spanish, 16.8 percent (N = 35) for Alaska Native or American Indian languages, and 7.7 percent (N = 16) for Asian languages. The *Nick* litigation established that as of 2007, Alaska did not have bilingual coordinators for any Alaska Native languages (Chapter 10).

---

23 28 C.F.R. § 55.17.

24 42 U.S.C. § 1973aa-1a(c); 28 C.F.R. §§ 55.18-.20.

25 U.S. Dep't of Justice, Civil Rights Division, Voting Section, *About Language Minority Voting Rights*, http://www.usdoj.gov/crt/voting/sec_203/activ_203.htm#langguide.

26 For examples of bilingual coordinator requirements in Azusa and Ventura, California, and Osceola County, Florida, *see* http://www.usdoj.gov/crt/voting/litigation/caselist.htm#sec203cases.

There was little difference between the LEP of jurisdictions using bilingual coordinators and those that did not. In jurisdictions using coordinators, the average percent of voters LEP in the covered languages was 38.4 percent among Hispanic voters, 15.4 percent among Alaska Native and American Indian voters, and 34.6 percent among Asian voters. By comparison, in jurisdictions not using coordinators, the average percent of LEP voters was 37 percent among Hispanic voters, 14.4 percent among Alaska Native and American Indian voters, and 36.7 percent among Asian voters.

There was a positive correlation between the population of covered jurisdictions and whether they used bilingual coordinators. Generally, jurisdictions with larger populations were more likely to use bilingual coordinators than those with smaller populations. Bilingual coordinator use was highest among jurisdictions with populations of more than one million. Of 17 responding jurisdictions with more than one million people, 52.9 percent (N = 9) used a bilingual coordinator. By contrast, of the 50 smallest jurisdictions with populations of 5,000 people or less, only 30 percent (N = 15) used bilingual coordinators.

Employment status Of 129 jurisdictions using a bilingual coordinator, 89.1 percent (N = 115) identified the coordinator's employment status. While slightly more than one-third (38.2%) of jurisdictions reported using bilingual coordinators, 49 percent (N = 57) of those jurisdictions used full-time employees instead of part-time employees or volunteers. The use of full-time employees may have resulted from several factors, such as: election offices with more full-time staff, particularly in more populous jurisdictions; requirements to employ full-time bilingual coordinators under consent decrees or other court orders; requirements under state or local law; or jurisdictions searching for professionally trained bilingual coordinators who have the time to manage language assistance programs.

Among the remaining jurisdictions, 20.9 percent (N = 24) used part-time employees, 12.2 percent (N = 14) used bilingual coordinators appointed to the position, 11.3 percent (N = 13) used unpaid volunteers, 7 percent (N = 8) used bilingual coordinators who were elected to the position, and 1.7 percent (N = 2) used unpaid students. In addition, 22.6 percent (N = 26) of jurisdictions marked "other" to describe the status of their bilingual coordinators.

Recruitment Jurisdictions recruited bilingual coordinators through several methods.[27] Direct solicitation and use of community organizations were the most common methods at 41.4 percent (N = 48) and 25.9 percent (N = 30), respectively. Community-based recruitment made it more likely that hired coordinators understood the needs of LEP voters. Furthermore, recruiting with the assistance of community organizations facilitated work with those organizations after retention. Other recruitment methods included: government or school employees by 19.8 percent (N = 23); political parties by 18.1 percent (N = 21); newspaper advertisements by 15.5 percent (N = 18); election materials mailed to voters by 6 percent (N = 7); television advertisements by 3.5 percent (N = 4); translation agencies and temporary services each at 2.6 percent (N = 3); and radio advertisements at 1.7 percent (N = 2). No jurisdictions recruited bilingual coordinators through flyers.

27 Jurisdictions were given 12 choices for methods of recruiting their bilingual coordinators. Among the 116 responding jurisdictions, 72 selected one recruitment method, 23 selected two, 12 selected three, six selected four, two selected five, and one jurisdiction selected six. Seventeen jurisdictions did not report any method of recruiting bilingual coordinators.

Responsibilities Jurisdictions with bilingual coordinators identified several responsibilities for their coordinators.[28] In approximately two-thirds, coordinators provided voter instruction (N = 87), Election Day troubleshooting (N = 84), or translated written election materials (N = 84). However, approximately one-third or fewer jurisdictions used coordinators to prepare written election materials (N = 43), recruit poll workers (N = 42), engage in community outreach (N = 37), train poll workers (N = 35) or other election officials (N = 24). Most jurisdictions underutilized the knowledge, experience, and contacts of their coordinators.

Bilingual Poll Workers

Poll workers are the only election officials with whom most voters have contact. They typically are part-time contractors who only work on Election Day and a few hours before to prepare for the election. Their compensation is usually set by statute at little more than minimum wage for what can be a 14 to 16-hour workday. Low wages and long hours can make it difficult to recruit people. Yet, poll workers are on the frontline of elections and frequently are the weak link in providing effective language assistance.

Confirmation of language abilities Even where oral language assistance is provided at the polls, it may be impaired if bilingual election workers are not actually fluent in the covered languages. Respondents were asked how they confirmed the language abilities of part-time election workers. Approximately 90 percent (N = 324) of respondents providing complete responses to the survey responded.[29] Nearly two-thirds (N = 210) did not require any confirmation of language abilities of part-time poll workers. Part-time workers may overestimate or inaccurately report their oral or written language abilities.[30] Where this occurs, language assistance may be unavailable at polling places where it is supposed to be provided. That is what happened in the Bethel region of Alaska when state election officials failed to implement basic quality controls including confirmation of English and Yup'ik speaking and reading skills (Chapter 10).

Among the minority of responding jurisdictions confirming language abilities, conversations with the worker in the covered language was the most common method used. Of 114 jurisdictions confirming language abilities, 48.2 percent (N = 55) employed this method. Bilingual full-time election workers and bilingual coordinators may use this confirmation method at no additional expense other than the time that it takes them to do so. Nevertheless, 83 percent of jurisdictions failed to use this confirmation method.

A small number of jurisdictions confirmed language abilities through an oral or written exam (N = 11 for each), outside agency (N = 9), community organization (N = 8), or through an education requirement (N = 4). Approximately 10 percent of the 324 jurisdictions (N = 32) used some "other"

28 Jurisdictions were given 11 choices for bilingual coordinator responsibilities. Among the 115 responding jurisdictions, 26 selected one option, 21 selected two options, 21 selected three options, 12 selected four options, nine selected five options, 11 selected six options, 10 selected seven options, six selected eight options, four selected nine options, and five selected ten options.

29 Respondents were offered eight options and were instructed to select all that applied. Among the 324 responding jurisdictions, all but 22 selected only one option. Of the 22 respondents that checked more than one method of confirming language abilities, 16 selected two methods, five selected three methods, and one selected five methods.

30 There are several problems relying on self-reported language ability. *See* Paul Siegal et al., U.S. Census Bureau, *Language Use and Linguistic Isolation: Historical Data and Methodological Issues* 6–8 (Feb. 12, 2001).

method of confirmation. Among respondents checking "other," 11 confirmed language abilities of part-time election workers by asking the election worker about his or her language abilities or what they told other poll workers.[31] One respondent replied, "They tell me (if I ask) if they can speak [the covered language]" (Respondent 272). Relying upon self-reported information is not a valid form of confirmation and places these 11 jurisdictions in the same category as the 210 jurisdictions reporting that no confirmation was required. As a result, two-thirds (N = 221) of jurisdictions required no confirmation.

Seven respondents indicated that other jurisdictions or offices were responsible for confirming the workers' language abilities.[32] Six respondents reported that language abilities were confirmed by their personal knowledge of the election workers' language abilities.[33] Two respondents reported that other election officials tested part-time election workers to confirm their language abilities (Respondents 691 and 909). Two respondents indicated that a tribal government or organization confirmed the language abilities of part-time election workers fluent in American Indian languages (Respondents 347 and 706).

Content and frequency of training Responding jurisdictions generally provided regular training for poll workers. Of 316 responding jurisdictions, 67.4 percent (N = 221) required a training session before each election, 19.2 percent (N = 63) required annual training sessions, 7.6 percent (N = 25) "other," and 6.4 percent (N = 21) did not provide any training. Most jurisdictions trained part-time election workers before each election.[34] Most respondents (N = 328) identified the content of poll-worker training.[35] Nearly all covered basic information about setting up polling places and most forms of voter assistance in English. Ninety percent (N = 295) provided written materials, 83.5 percent (N = 274) instructions on voter assistance, 81.7 percent (N = 268) on polling place setup, and 78.7 percent (N = 258) on ballot instructions. Alaska provides an example of the impact that a jurisdiction's failure to provide mandatory training can have on the quality of language assistance offered (Chapter 10).

On the other hand, two-thirds (N = 217) reported their poll-worker training did not include information on the languages covered in their jurisdiction. That may be due to the lack of information included about language assistance in instructional videos, which were used by 63.8 percent (N = 208) of all respondents. In several cases, jurisdictions reported that videos were provided by the state's chief elections officer and did not include information about language assistance. Furthermore, lack of training might be attributable to the failure of two-thirds of jurisdictions with coordinators to include those coordinators in election-official training to describe how to offer language assistance.[36]

Furthermore, two-thirds of respondents (N = 110) did not use role-playing demonstrations as part of their training. Role-playing can provide an effective way to educate poll workers on common problems experienced by LEP voters, such as difficulty checking in, locating their name

---

31 Respondents 234, 272, 306, 322, 334, 418, 672, 859, 869, 887, and 926.

32 Respondents 729, 812, 861, 886, 905, 968, and 1009.

33 Respondents 245, 664, 714, 821, 889, and 940.

34 Of the 316 responding jurisdictions, 95.9 percent (N= 303) selected one option, 3.8 percent (N = 12) selected two options, and 0.3 percent (N = 1) selected three options.

35 Respondents were presented nine options and were asked to select all that applied. Most of the 328 responding jurisdictions selected more than one option: eight selected one option, 15 selected two options, 12 selected three options, 33 selected four options, 73 selected five options, 69 selected six options, 59 selected seven options, 30 selected eight options, and 10 selected nine options.

36 *See* Tucker and Espino 2006: Figure 5.5, *reprinted in* H. HRG. 109–103, at 2210.

on the voter registration list (a common problem for LEP voters using more than one surname or for Asian voters), voting machine instructions, and assistance. Role-playing also allows poll workers to observe first hand the proper way to treat voters and respond to inquiries.

A little more than half of jurisdictions (N = 174) provided training on how to use the voting machine. The absence of such training can make it difficult for poll workers, including bilingual poll workers, to provide assistance to first-time voters or voters using new voting equipment. Thirty jurisdictions provided some "other" form of training, including 10 using Power Point presentations,[37] six using hands-on exercises,[38] and two using audio tapes, CDs, or other media (Respondents 460 and 862).

Voter assistance training Although 83.5 percent of jurisdictions (N = 274) provided training to poll workers on voter assistance, that training was not necessarily accurate about federal requirements. Respondents were asked, "Who of the following may accompany voters who need assistance in the voting booth?" Jurisdictions could select one or more of the nine choices provided.[39] A total of 263 jurisdictions responded.

Section 208 of the VRA provides that "[a]ny voter who requires assistance to vote by reason of blindness, disability, or inability to read or write may be given assistance by a person of the voter's choice," except for the voter's employer or union representative.[40] Section 208 applies nationwide, independent of the language assistance provisions. Unlike Section 203, Section 208 does not require that a jurisdiction provide language assistance to voters who need it.[41] On the other hand, Section 208 complements the language assistance provisions by requiring jurisdictions to permit voters to receive assistance, regardless of whether the jurisdiction has an affirmative obligation under Section 203 to offer assistance itself (Chapter 4).

No responding jurisdiction selected the "none" option, indicating that all allowed at least some form of assistance in the voting booth. However, only 10.3 percent (N = 27) reported voter assistance practices at least as protective as Section 208: 1.9 percent (N = 5) correctly stated the federal standard; and 8.4 percent (N = 22) permitted voters to receive assistance from their person of choice, even if it fell into one of the two exceptions in Section 208.

It appears that in many cases, limiting voter-assistance practices resulted from jurisdictions complying with more restrictive state laws. More than half of respondents did not permit voters to receive assistance from their own children because of state requirements that only eligible voters were qualified to be poll workers. Nevertheless, minors frequently can provide effective assistance (whether language or otherwise) to their parents.

Only 11 percent (N = 29) permitted voters to receive assistance from campaign workers. The reluctance of many jurisdictions may have resulted from concerns about voting fraud or electioneering by campaign workers in the polls. Nonetheless, under Section 208, a voter is entitled to receive assistance from a campaign worker as long as that person is the voter's choice.[42] Concerns about assistance from campaign workers can be addressed by observing the manner in which assistance is provided.

---

37 Respondents 234, 334, 600, 767, 831, 839, 857, 883, 884, and 887.

38 Respondents 224, 299, 311, 384, 386, and 920.

39 Of the 263 responding jurisdictions, 39 jurisdictions selected one option, 28 selected two options, 40 selected three options, 53 selected four options, 47 selected five options, 18 selected six options, 18 selected seven options, and seven selected eight options.

40 42 U.S.C. § 1973aa-6.

41 *Compare* 42 U.S.C. § 1973aa-6 (Section 208) *with* 42 U.S.C. § 1973aa-1a (Section 203).

42 42 U.S.C. § 1973aa-6.

Approximately 30 percent (N = 81) indicated that bilingual poll workers were not permitted to provide assistance to voters in the voting booth. About one-half of respondents (N = 130) did not allow a voter to receive assistance in the voting booth from a translator. In some cases, the failure to permit assistance from these individuals was due to requirements that assistance only be provided by certain election officials such as a presiding judge.[43]

Approximately 90 percent of election officials identified voter assistance measures more restrictive than Section 208. It is likely that poll workers in those jurisdictions did not receive voter assistance training that accurately stated federal requirements. Restrictions on voter assistance under Section 208 have a correspondingly negative impact on the ability of voters to receive language assistance under Section 203.

In the Alaska litigation, the failure of election officials to ensure that poll workers received proper training and instructions on voter assistance requirements resulted in the state's violation of Section 208 and denied language assistance in violation of Section 203. Ultimately, a federal court entered an injunction against Alaska's election officials, directing them to comply with Section 208 and to correct their violations (Chapter 10).

Language Assistance Programs in Covered Jurisdictions

Effective language assistance requires that language minorities have the same opportunities to participate in elections as English-speaking voters. An effective program cannot rest just on bilingual election officials and poll workers. Jurisdictions that must provide bilingual written materials need to ensure that materials are translated properly into the language and dialect of covered languages. The availability of language assistance and need for bilingual poll workers must be publicized. Outreach also must be done to local language groups to ensure that effective language assistance is being provided.

Translation of Written Election Materials

Justice Department guidelines describe the importance of quality translations:

> It is essential that material provided in the language of a language minority group be clear, complete and accurate. In examining whether a jurisdiction has achieved compliance with this requirement, the Attorney General will consider whether the jurisdiction has consulted with members of the applicable language minority group with respect to the translation of materials.[44]

The Department further explains: "Poor translations can be misleading for voters and embarrassing for local officials. Beyond quality control, there can be significant differences in dialect within a given language group, and it is the responsibility of local [election] officials to provide a translation that local voters actually can use."[45] The failure to heed the Department's warning was evident in the poor quality of translations produced by Alaska in the *Nick* litigation (Chapter 10).

---

43 Respondents 308, 448, 691, and 888.

44 28 C.F.R. § 55.19(b).

45 U.S. Dep't of Justice, Civil Rights Division, Voting Section, *Minority Language Citizens: Section 203 of the Voting Rights Act*, http://www.usdoj.gov/crt/voting/sec_203/203_brochure.htm.

Respondents were asked about the persons or groups involved in translating written election materials.[46] Nearly half (N = 122) reported using election-office employees to translate written materials. Approximately 40 percent (N = 104) reported that professional services translated their election materials. About 15 percent (N = 38) reported that translations were received from the Secretary of State's office. Although 51 respondents selected "other,"[47] most provided responses that fell into one of the options included in the survey.[48] Six jurisdictions used computer or Internet translation programs. Four jurisdictions used newspapers for translations. Three jurisdictions used advisory committees or outreach to members of the covered language groups. One jurisdiction used school employees.

Less than a quarter of respondents (N = 59) reported that bilingual coordinators (N = 50) or community organizations (N = 9) were involved in translating written materials. Election officials may be more familiar with election requirements than others involved in translating election materials. Similarly, professional translation agencies routinely provide certified translations for many government functions, including elections. However, the failure of most jurisdictions to include members of the covered language group in the translation process likely has a negative impact on the quality of written translations. It also can lead to liability under Section 203 (Chapter 10).

Language Program Publicity

The Justice Department's guidelines emphasize the importance of publicizing the availability of language assistance:

> The Attorney General will consider whether a covered jurisdiction has taken appropriate steps to publicize the availability of materials and assistance in the minority language. Such steps may include the display of appropriate notices, in the minority language, at voter registration offices, polling places, etc., the making of announcements over minority language radio or television stations, the publication of notices in minority language newspapers, and direct contact with language minority group organizations.[49]

It is difficult for language minority voters to use language assistance if they are unaware it is available.

Respondents were asked how voters were informed about the availability of oral language assistance, and 257 jurisdictions provided that information.[50] Polling place signage was the most common method, with 70.4 percent of respondents (N = 181) doing so. Jurisdictions also informed

---

46 Respondents were presented with six options and asked to check all that applied. Most of the 256 responding jurisdictions selected two or fewer options: 135 jurisdictions selected one option, 82 selected two options, 25 selected three options, 13 selected four options, and one selected five options.

47 Thirty-eight jurisdictions indicated in response to the "other" option that the Secretary of State's office was involved in translating written election materials. Those jurisdictions are not included in the 51 jurisdictions.

48 Twenty-two jurisdictions reported that vendors are involved in the translation of written materials, 10 reported using employees to translate written election materials, nine reported using another office or jurisdiction's employees, and four reported using paid translators or certified translation services.

49 28 C.F.R. § 55.18(e).

50 Respondents were presented seven options and asked to check all that applied. Three-quarters of the 257 responding jurisdictions selected two or fewer options: 127 selected one option, 64 selected two options,

voters about the availability of language assistance through web advertisements or the Internet,[51] community organizations or community centers,[52] public service announcements,[53] and in election materials provided in the covered languages (Respondents 575, 693, and 940).

A majority of jurisdictions did not inform voters about the availability of assistance in the covered languages prior to elections. Forty-one percent (N = 105) did so through mailing election materials, 36.6 percent (N = 94) through newspaper advertisements, 17.9 percent (N = 46) through radio advertisements, 11.7 percent (N = 30) through flyers, and 9.7 percent (N = 25) through television advertisements. Several respondents indicated that voters were not told about language assistance until they arrived at their polling place on Election Day.[54]

Many jurisdictions did not publicize the availability of language assistance. Eight jurisdictions provided oral language assistance upon voter request.[55] One respondent wrote, "They either come in or are on the phone and say they cannot speak English, and we get the person who speaks [the covered language] to help them" (Respondent 272). Two jurisdictions reported that voters "are not" (Respondent 766) informed except by "word of mouth" (Respondent 725). Two jurisdictions stated no publicity was necessary because it is "common knowledge" (Respondents 550 and 820). One jurisdiction only publicized the availability of language assistance in "election worker training," and did not inform voters who did not serve as poll workers (Respondent 987). Jurisdictions that did not inform voters of the availability of oral language assistance likely decreased participation among language minority voters who are unaware they can receive help at the polls.

Language Minority Outreach

The Justice Department stresses the importance of engaging in outreach to community organizations and members of the covered language groups to ensure that effective language assistance is provided:

> The cornerstone of every successful [language assistance] program is a vigorous outreach program to identify the needs and communication channels of the minority community. Citizens who do not speak English very well, often rely on communication channels that differ from those used by English-speakers. Each community is different. The best-informed sources of information are people who are in the minority community and those who work with it regularly. Election officials should talk to them (U.S. Dep't of Justice, *Minority Language Citizens*).

Jurisdictions consulting with community organizations about language assistance are more likely to understand the needs of LEP voters. Consulting also may indicate whether a jurisdiction has taken steps to comply with Section 203.[56] Where that consultation and outreach is lacking, there is a good chance that the jurisdiction has failed to provide effective language assistance (Chapter 10).

---

27 selected three options, 13 selected four options, 14 selected five options, 10 selected six options, and two selected seven options.

51 Respondents 224, 306, 357, 461, 486, 715 and 857.

52 Respondents 393, 461, 462, 767, 810 and 857.

53 Respondents 311, 334, 563 and 600.

54 Respondents 319, 347, 394, 441, 449, 460, 526, 807, 871, and 1012.

55 Respondents 238, 272, 277, 416, 500, 581, 616, and 870.

56 28 C.F.R. § 55.19(b).

Respondents were asked whether they consulted with community organizations and individuals from covered groups about their language assistance program. Among the 322 responding jurisdictions, only 37.3 percent (N = 120) consulted with community organizations, while the remaining 62.7 percent (N = 202) did not. For those consulting with local groups, 50 worked with schools, 53 with clubs, 47 with churches, 43 with civil rights groups, and 31 with the League of Women Voters.[57] Other methods of community outreach included consulting with tribal governments (N = 15), election officials or other governmental employees (N = 9), office holders or leaders from the covered language group (N = 8), community activists (N = 6), political parties (N = 4), bilingual advisory committees (N = 4), the Chamber of Commerce (N = 3), a state agency (N = 3), media outlets (N = 3), senior citizen groups (N = 2), contractors (N = 2), employers (N = 1), and homeowners associations (N = 1). The variety of responses demonstrates the extent to which outreach must be tailored for each community. The failure of nearly two-thirds of covered jurisdictions to engage in any community outreach likely had a negative effect on the quality of the language assistance they offered.

Cost of Providing Language Assistance

Some commentators criticize language assistance because they say it is costly (Chapter 8). Their assertion is unsupported. The costs of compliance are modest if there are any costs at all. A majority of respondents reporting the cost of conducting elections in their jurisdiction indicated that they only incurred expenses either for oral language assistance or bilingual written materials, but not for both.

Among 154 jurisdictions reporting oral language assistance expenses, 59.1 percent (N = 91) incurred no extra costs. Of 144 jurisdictions reporting written language material expenses, 54.2 percent (N = 78) did not incur any additional costs. Of 158 jurisdictions reporting complete election expenses, 39.5 percent (N = 60) did not incur any added costs for either oral or written language assistance. Other jurisdictions provided narrative responses indicating no additional expenses for the following: 23 for oral language assistance; 13 for written language materials; and six for both.

Determining the Cost of Language Assistance

A majority of respondents were unable to provide the costs of their language assistance programs. Of 361 respondents providing complete responses to the survey, 42.7 percent (N = 154) were able to provide complete cost data for oral language assistance and 39.9 percent (N = 144) were able to provide complete cost data for bilingual written materials. The GAO encountered similar problems. The GAO reported in its 1986 study that, "nearly two-thirds (191) of the 295 responding jurisdictions that reported providing written assistance did not know their additional costs for the assistance" (GAO 1986: 16). Likewise, the GAO reported in its 1997 study that, "About 76 percent of the jurisdictions and 42 percent of the states that provided bilingual voting assistance were unable to determine the costs of doing so" (GAO 1997: 16).

57 Respondents were presented with six options and asked to check all that applied. Of the 113 respondents, 30.1 percent (N = 34) selected one option, 24.8 percent (N = 28) selected two options, 21.2 percent (N = 24) selected three options, 6.2 percent (N = 7) selected four options, 13.3 percent (N = 15) selected five options, and 4.4 percent (N = 5) selected all six options.

A total of 175 respondents reported they could not provide any cost data. Many did not have a language assistance program and therefore had no costs. Some indicated they were not required to provide language assistance to voters.[58] Others stated that they had few, if any, voters who needed assistance (Respondents 585 and 646). The remaining respondents indicated they did not provide assistance,[59] with one respondent reporting, "We do our best to muddle through if services are requested" (Respondent 854). Some jurisdictions did not provide cost data because they do not incur costs for their language assistance programs. Approximately 19 percent (N = 33) did not have any costs for their oral language assistance programs. Nearly 17 percent (N = 29) did not have any added costs for providing bilingual written materials. The reasons that these jurisdictions did not incur additional expenses are discussed below.

Other respondents reported a variety of reasons why their cost data was unavailable. "Costs are not separated" in many jurisdictions' budgets (Respondent 750). Nearly a third (N = 54) did not track the costs in their budgets. One respondent explained: "Many costs related to elections are not itemized separately from other activities. Oral language costs are not tracked separately or itemized. All election items are printed in English and [the covered language] in the same document. No estimates are available for one language only" (Respondent 693). About 15 percent (N = 26) reported that their vendors printed written language materials on the same forms as English materials and did not break out the costs attributed to the covered languages. Approximately the same number (N = 24) indicated another office provided the assistance, incurred any costs, or had the cost information. Three percent (N = 5) did not incur any additional costs by providing language assistance under the VRA because they were required to provide it under state law. One respondent observed: "It does not cost any extra [money] … [O]ur state law requires everything to be in [the covered language] as well as English" (Respondent 773). Four respondents could not provide estimates of their language assistance costs because they varied too much between elections. One explained, "Each election is different and there are various factors in place based on the number of polling places used, the number of staff used, and the assistance that we may get from a contracting entity that provides their own translators or material already in [the covered language" (Respondent 474). The remaining respondents provided a variety of other reasons for the unavailability of their cost data.

These reasons are consistent with the GAO's earlier findings. In the 1997 study, the GAO reported that jurisdictions could not identify the costs of their language assistance programs for the following reasons: they were not tracked because assistance had been provided for several years; printers did not provide itemized statements; their accounting systems or budgets did not itemize costs; and the inability to separate federal from state assistance requirements (GAO 1997: 16–18). The GAO reached the same conclusions in its 1986 study, observing that there "are no federal requirements that such information be collected and maintained" (GAO 1986: 17).

Oral Language Assistance Costs

The 59.1 percent of jurisdictions reporting no oral language assistance expenses attributed the lack of additional costs to several factors. Jurisdictions in New Mexico and Texas reported that state laws had language assistance requirements similar to Section 203, resulting in no additional cost for federal compliance. Many jurisdictions reported hiring bilingual poll workers paid the same wages as other poll workers. One respondent explained, "The bilingual poll workers we hire are

58 Respondents 207, 232, 279, 353, and 810.

59 Respondents 421, 561, 854, and 1029.

filling positions that would have to be filled by another individual" (Respondent 615). Another jurisdiction indicated, "We do not pay any extra … if you are bilingual and helping with the election" (Respondent 822). Some respondents reported that full-time employees often were bilingual and available to provide oral language assistance.[60] Other jurisdictions used unpaid volunteers to provide oral language assistance whenever necessary (Respondent 725).

Among 154 jurisdictions reporting complete data for oral language assistance, the average cost was 4.9 percent of all election expenses with the mean jurisdiction incurring no additional costs. However, the top 10 percent of respondents (N = 16) skewed this result by reporting average costs of 34 percent. By contrast, the remaining 138 jurisdictions reported average costs of only 1.5 percent. Two factors contributed to the disparate results. Some of the 16 jurisdictions attributed all their election expenses, including costs for hiring permanent staff and Election Day poll workers who have to be hired regardless of Section 203, to oral language assistance. Second, those 16 jurisdictions were less populated, with an average total population of 40,262 compared to an average total population of 170,439 in the remaining jurisdictions. When these factors were taken into consideration, oral language costs actually were close to the average of 2.9 percent reported by the GAO in 1986 (GAO 1986: 20).

Figure 6.5 depicts that the average cost of providing oral language assistance (the black line) remains approximately the same regardless of the responding jurisdiction's population. A majority of all jurisdictions reporting no oral assistance costs is depicted on the very bottom of Figure 6.5, with the mean jurisdiction incurring no additional costs. Approximately 10 percent of all

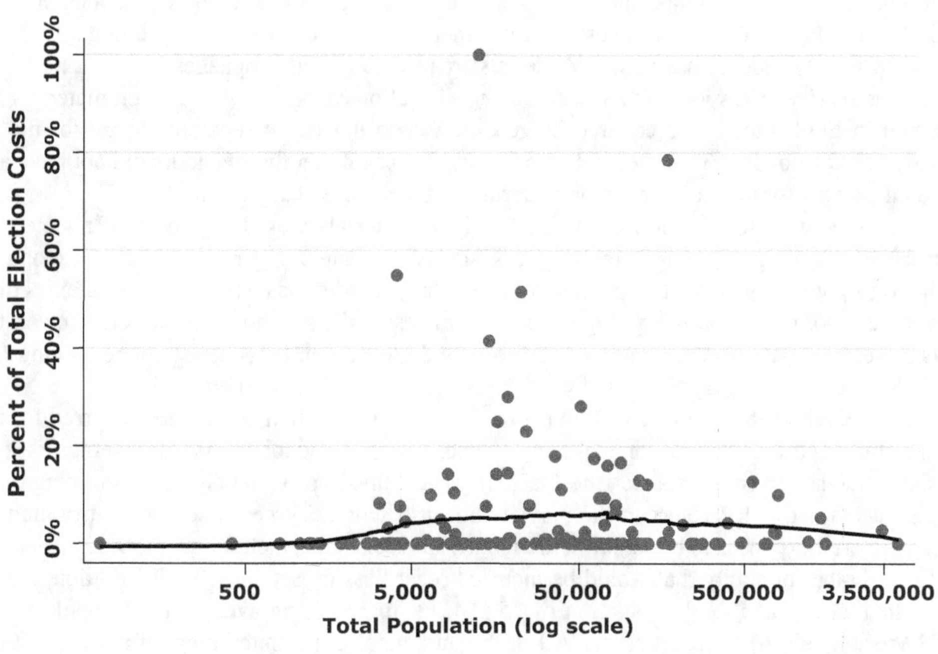

Figure 6.5 Reported cost of oral language assistance, by population of responding jurisdiction

Source: Responses to 2005 ASU/BHC Survey of Minority Language Assistance Practices in Public Elections, Question G-2a and 2000 Census, Summary Tape File 1 (on file with authors).

60 Respondents 280, 317, 488, 710, 742, 749, 767, 790, 816, 915, and 925.

responding jurisdictions reported costs far in excess of the average cost reported by the remaining 90 percent of respondents. These 16 outliers are depicted at the top of Figure 6.5. One jurisdiction reported that 100 percent of its total election costs are attributable to oral language assistance.

The average cost of oral language assistance remained approximately the same, regardless of the percentage of voters needing language assistance. Similarly, the average cost of providing oral language assistance remained approximately the same regardless of the percentage of LEP voters. Generally, there was no relationship between the percent of LEP voters in the responding jurisdiction and the costs the jurisdiction incurred to provide oral language assistance. Respondents indicated that the low cost of providing oral language assistance was attributable to using bilingual election workers paid at the same rate as other election workers.

Bilingual Written Material Costs

Among 144 jurisdictions reporting bilingual written material expenses, 54.2 percent (N = 78) incurred no extra costs. Thirteen additional jurisdictions provided narrative responses indicating they did not incur any additional costs for providing bilingual written materials. Respondents reported several reasons for not incurring costs. Jurisdictions with Alaska Native and American Indian voters reported that bilingual materials were not provided because the covered languages were unwritten.[61] Chapter 10 shows that conclusion is not necessarily accurate, particularly where there is evidence of widespread use of the written Native language.

Some jurisdictions providing bilingual written materials reported they used election officials or community volunteers to translate materials, resulting in no additional costs (Respondents 238 and 889). In many cases, printing costs did not increase as a result of having bilingual written materials. One respondent observed, "[M]aterials are printed in both languages – there is no added cost for this service" (Respondent 284). Another jurisdiction reported, "All election materials are preprinted in English and [the covered language]. We do not pay a separate charge for the … translations" (Respondent 306). Several respondents indicated that their vendors did not have any additional charges for providing election materials in the covered languages.[62]

The average cost for providing bilingual written materials was 8.1 percent of all election expenses. The average cost remained approximately the same regardless of the responding jurisdiction's population. About 10 percent of responding jurisdictions reported costs far exceeding the average reported by the remaining 90 percent of respondents. Those 15 outliers skewed the results by reporting average bilingual written costs of 51.8 percent. By contrast, the remaining 129 jurisdictions reported average bilingual written material costs of only 3 percent.

Figure 6.6 demonstrates the disparate results for bilingual written costs were occurred for the same reasons reported for oral language assistance. Figure 6.6 depicts that the average cost of providing oral language assistance (the black line) remains approximately the same regardless of the percentage of LEP voters in the responding jurisdiction. Three jurisdictions attributed all election material expenses to bilingual written materials assistance, including ballots, signs, public notices, and other publicity that would be incurred regardless of Section 203. In addition, the 15 outliers had an average total population of 35,664, compared to an average total population of 180,529 for the other 129 jurisdictions. All of the outliers also attributed most, if not all, of their total written costs to bilingual election materials.

61 Respondents 319, 347, 349, 395, 402, 453, 460, 617, 652, 690, 862, 881, 887, and 993.

62 Respondents 284, 306, 339, 340, 418, 488, 933, and 938.

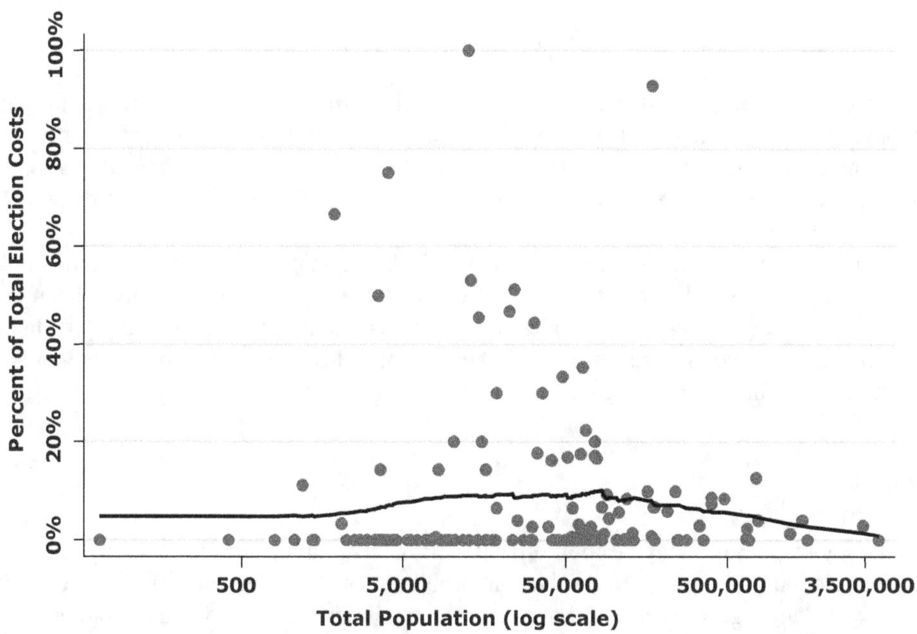

Figure 6.6 Reported cost of bilingual written materials, by population of responding jurisdiction

Source: Responses to 2005 ASU/BHC Survey of Minority Language Assistance Practices in Public Elections, Question G-2b and 2000 Census, Summary Tape File 1 (on file with authors).

When these factors were taken into consideration, the average cost of providing written language materials was substantially below the 7.6 percent reported by the GAO in 1986 (GAO 1986: 17). Overall, the average cost of providing bilingual written materials remained approximately the same regardless of the percentage of LEP voters in the responding jurisdiction. Generally, there was no relationship between the percent of LEP voters in the responding jurisdiction and the costs the jurisdiction incurs to provide bilingual written materials.

Approximately 40 percent of respondents (N = 145) reported their annual written language assistance expenses. Among those respondents, 93.8 percent (N = 136) reported costs for translating materials, two-thirds (N = 90) of whom incurred no translation costs. Reported costs for translating materials ranged from no cost at all to $300,000. The average translating cost was $4,981.29, with a median cost of $0.

Ninety-one percent of the 145 jurisdictions (N = 132) reported costs for printing bilingual materials. Over half (N = 71) incurred no additional printing costs. Reported costs for printing materials ranged from no cost at all to $1,092,000. The average printing cost was $23,957.17, with a median cost of $0.

Over 81 percent of the 145 jurisdictions (N = 118) reported other costs that might be incurred in translating and printing bilingual written materials. Of those respondents, 85.6 percent (N = 101) incurred no other costs. Reported costs for other bilingual material expenses ranged from no cost at all to $493,000. The average cost was $9,848.86, with a median cost of $0.

Miscellaneous Language Assistance Costs

Seventy-two respondents reported costs for a bilingual coordinator program. The small number of responses was attributable, at least in part, to the absence of a bilingual coordinator program in approximately two-thirds of responding jurisdictions. Reported costs for bilingual coordinators ranged from no cost at all to $464,000. The average reported cost for bilingual coordinators was $29,099.86 with a median cost of $1,300.

One hundred sixteen jurisdictions providing telephonic language assistance reported their costs. Ninety-five submitted complete cost data, for which the average cost was only 0.6 percent of total election expenses. Seventy-four percent (N = 86) incurred no costs at all. Many jurisdictions reported that their low costs were attributed to their use of full-time election workers or volunteers who were fluent in the covered languages.

Conclusion

In their survey responses, many election officials misunderstood the need for language assistance in their jurisdiction (Chapter 5). To resolve that problem, the chief elections officer for each state should provide language assistance training to covered political subdivisions and monitor Section 203 compliance. Likewise, election officials should disseminate more information about language assistance needs to all political subdivisions of their jurisdictions. To provide effective language assistance, it is first necessary for election officials to become better informed about the need for language assistance in their jurisdictions among voting age citizens who are LEP in the covered languages. Then, they will be better positioned to identify what language assistance is necessary in covered areas.

Inadequate information about the need for language assistance can result in the lack of available assistance. Once an accurate assessment of needs is completed, covered jurisdictions should provide oral language assistance at every stage of the election process where necessary. They should ensure that all English election materials are available in covered Asian and Spanish languages. In addition, they must work with any Alaska Native or American Indian language groups to determine whether those languages are written and commonly used. To facilitate the availability of Election Day assistance, poll worker recruitment should be done in the covered languages, in addition to English. Covered jurisdictions also should promote hiring and retention of full-time workers who are bilingual in English and one or more of the covered languages. Since many prospective voters only communicate with the elections office by phone, language assistance for telephone inquiries should be available in all covered languages.

Even where language assistance is available, it frequently is inadequate because of the lack of quality control. More covered jurisdictions should utilize bilingual coordinators to implement effective assistance programs in all of the covered languages. Election officials must confirm the language abilities of employees and volunteers who provide language assistance. In addition, election worker training must include information about language assistance and the needs of LEP voters. States should provide election officials with proper training on the voter assistance requirements in Section 208 of the VRA to facilitate compliance. Election officials should consult with language minority community organizations and individuals to ensure their language assistance programs are effective. They also must advertise the availability of language assistance at every stage to voting age citizens in the covered languages through appropriate outreach and publicity.

Jurisdictions can comply with the language assistance provisions in a cost effective manner, contrary to what detractors argue. Covered jurisdictions should recruit and retain bilingual individuals to fill full-time and part-time election worker positions to provide oral language assistance at no added cost. Volunteers from the covered language groups can be used to assist in translating written election materials to minimize costs and improve the accuracy of translations. State elections offices could provide common forms, signs, and other written election materials in all languages that are covered in political subdivisions to minimize duplication of costs. Where some costs are incurred, they can be reduced through effective targeting in consultation with local language minority groups (Chapter 8). Covered jurisdictions should partner with other local jurisdictions to reduce any common costs. A price tag should not be placed on the fundamental right to vote. Nevertheless, any costs incurred for providing language assistance can be reduced through proactive engagement with language minority citizens and other covered jurisdictions.

PART IV
THE DEBATE OVER REAUTHORIZATION OF THE VRA'S LANGUAGE ASSISTANCE PROVISIONS IN 2006

Chapter 7
Passage of the Voting Rights Act Reauthorization Act of 2006[1]

The Voting Rights Act (VRA) is one of the most successful civil rights statutes ever enacted. It has made the dream of political participation a reality for millions of minorities in the United States. Many of the Act's most important protections are temporary measures that prevent and remedy discrimination in states with histories of voter disenfranchisement. Some have argued that renewal of these provisions, which had been scheduled to expire on August 6, 2007,[2] was non-controversial. For example, according to Katherine Tate, "The extension of the temporary provisions of the 1965 Voting Rights Act sailed through Congress and was signed into law by President George Bush on July 27, 2006 without any major turbulence."[3]

Political reality painted a far different picture. Conservatives ideologically opposed to the VRA's broad protections mobilized to end them. Southerners covered by the Act's preclearance provisions argued their states no longer needed federal review of voting changes. Republicans, deeply divided over immigration reform, splintered on whether language assistance should continue. Partisanship threatened to derail efforts to renew an Act that increased participation by minority voters who tended to favor Democrats.

Against this backdrop, a broad coalition of civil rights groups, grassroots organizations, and voting rights advocates sought not only to renew the VRA's expiring provisions, but to strengthen them. With some unlikely allies, a few lucky breaks, and a little help from the White House and the Supreme Court, they achieved their goal. This chapter explores the long journey towards the 25-year reauthorization of the revitalized Act. Landslide votes in the House and Senate and accolades for the VRA conceal the long, strange trip towards passage of the Voting Rights Act Reauthorization Act of 2006 (VRARA).[4] In the end, the politics of persuasion, buttressed by a strong record and key allies, carried the day.

Prelude to Reauthorization: Building Bipartisan Support

Reauthorization could not be achieved without support from both political parties. Historically, the VRA received strong bipartisan backing, including renewal under four Republican Presidents.[5] But

1 Published originally in the *Journal of Legislation* at Notre Dame School of Law. *See* James Thomas Tucker, *The Politics of Persuasion: Passage of the Voting Rights Act Reauthorization Act of 2006*, 33 J. Legis. 205 (2007). In certain places, the content of this chapter has been modified from the original article to reflect the discussion included elsewhere in this book.

2 *See* 42 U.S.C. §§ 1973b(a)(8), 1973aa-1a(b)(1).

3 *See* Katherine Tate, *Black Politics, the GOP Southern Strategy, and the Reauthorization of the Voting Rights Act*, 4 The Forum 1, 2 (2006).

4 Pub L. No. 109–246, 120 Stat. 577 (2006).

5 *See generally* Pub. L. No. 91–285, 84 Stat. 314 (signed into law by President Nixon on June 22, 1970); Pub. L. No. 94–73, 89 Stat. 402 (signed into law by President Ford on August 6, 1975); Pub. L. No. 97–205,

it was unclear a similar broad-based political coalition could be assembled before several provisions of the Act expired in 2007. Achieving consensus on a bill that Republicans, Democrats, and the civil rights community could support was no small feat. The politics would be challenging, but there were several hopeful signs.

Politics and Pitfalls

At first glance, the political landscape did not appear favorable for reauthorization in 2006. The Republicans held the White House after President Bush's narrow re-election in 2004. Republicans held comfortable majorities with 55 seats in the Senate and 232 seats in the House of Representatives. Across the country, voters were deeply divided along party lines. The highly charged political environment was reflected in Washington, with the 109th Congress described as "one of the most partisan and polarized ever."[6] Although the Republican Party had been instrumental in the enactment of the VRA and subsequent reauthorizations, it was unclear that politicians would set aside partisan differences to renew the Act's expiring provisions.

The VRA itself seemed likely to deepen this political divide. Many conservatives criticized the Act's special provisions for benefiting Democrats. There was some evidence to support their conclusion. Black voters were the primary beneficiaries of the 1965 Act, with most southern states covered by Section 5 of the Act to prevent discrimination against them.[7] In 2004, few of the 14 million Black voters supported Republicans.[8] According to the National Exit Poll (NEP), 88 percent of Black voters voted for Democratic candidate John Kerry.[9] In 2004, President Bush received a lower percentage of the Black vote (which comprised 11 percent of the total vote) than Presidents Nixon, Ford, candidate Dole, and President Reagan when he was first elected in 1980.[10]

Voters covered by the Act's language assistance provisions were more of a mixed bag for Republicans. Native American voters, like Black voters, tended to vote overwhelmingly for Democratic candidates. In 2000, Native American voters in Washington turned out in large numbers against Republican Senator Slade Gordon, who lost to Maria Cantwell by about 2,000 votes.[11] In 2002, the Native vote made the difference in two closely watched campaigns. Strong Navajo support helped elect Democrat Janet Napolitano Governor of Arizona by 11,819 votes, less than 1 percent of the votes cast.[12] In South Dakota, Democratic Senator Tim Johnson won re-election by an even narrower margin of 524 votes over former Congressman John Thune, with heavy Lakota

---

96 Stat. 134 (signed into law by President Reagan on June 29, 1982); Pub. L. No. 102–344, 106 Stat. 921 (signed into law by President Bush on August 26, 1992).

6 Debra Rosenberg et al., *Firmly in Control, Holding the Line: The Republicans Kept their Lead in the Congress, Doesn't Mean Bush Will Have an Easy Time of It*, Newsweek, Nov. 15, 2004, at 30.

7 *See* U.S. Comm'n on Civil Rts., A Citizen's Guide to Understanding the Voting Rights Act 7–10, 47–50 (1984).

8 U.S. Census Bureau, Table 4a, Reported Voting and Registration of the Total Voting-Age Population by Sex, Race and Hispanic Origin: November 2004.

9 *See* CNN.com Election Results (2004), http://www.cnn.com/ELECTION/2004.

10 *See* Bob Wing, *Race, Racism and the Law: Race and Election 2004*, http://academic.udayton.edu/Race/04needs/politics02.htm.

11 *See* Daniel Kraker, *Tribal Poll Power: American Indians Could Decide Tight Races in Key Western States, Including Arizona*, Tucson Weekly, Sept. 9, 2004.

12 First American Education Project, Native Vote 2004: A National Survey and Analysis of Efforts to Increase the Native Vote in 2004 and the Results Achieved 13, 19 (2005).

Sioux turnout on the Pine Ridge Reservation providing the difference.[13] Although the NEP did not measure the Native vote in the 2004 election, county-level vote totals indicated it was "largely Democratic" (Wing 2004).

On the other hand, Republicans had made substantial inroads among other language minority voters. In the 2004 election, estimates of support for President Bush among the 2.7 million Asian voters ranged from one estimate of 24 percent to 44 percent in the NEP (Wing 2004). Asian support varied widely by ethnicity. Chinese, Asian Indian, and Hmong voters supported Democrat John Kerry, while Vietnamese and Filipino voters supported President Bush. Japanese, Korean, and Pacific Islander voters were evenly split between the two parties.[14] Neither party could ignore the growing political power of Asian voters, who had the highest percentage increase of new voter registrations between 1996 and 2004,[15] although they still lagged about 25 percent behind the registration rates of non-Hispanic whites (U.S. Census Bureau 2004: Table 4a).

Republican efforts to win the rapidly increasing Latino vote also paid dividends. Between 2000 and 2004, the number of eligible Latino voters increased 20 percent to 16 million, six times faster than for the non-Hispanic population.[16] Between 1996 and 2004, Latino turnout increased by more than one-third, from 4.9 million to 6.7 million,[17] although Latino registration still trailed non-Hispanic whites by about 20 percent (U.S. Census Bureau 2004: Table 4a). President Bush recognized the importance of the Latino vote and actively courted it in 2004, just as he had when he was Governor of Texas.[18] According to the NEP, he was rewarded for his efforts by receiving 44 percent of the Latino vote (Wing 2004). Other estimates gave Bush a slightly lower percentage. If Republicans wanted to win over Asian and Latino voters, it seemed apparent they would have to support reauthorization.

Nevertheless, some Republicans were divided over the VRA, with the greatest resistance directed at voter assistance in non-English languages – especially Spanish. Since 1981, Republicans introduced legislation to repeal the language assistance provisions. They came closest to succeeding in 1996 when the House passed an English-only bill that died in the Senate. In 2006, opposition to Section 203 was expected because of the immigration debate. The Republican Party bitterly divided over whether it should seek gains among Latinos by promoting a guest-worker program or taking more dramatic steps to deport and prosecute illegal immigrants. The immigration debate divided some minorities, with reports of growing resentment among Blacks who perceived that Latino immigrants were taking their job opportunities. If language assistance was tied to pending immigration legislation, it would be an uphill battle.

Finally, some conservatives were at best skeptical, and at worst hostile, towards Justice Department oversight under Section 5 of the Act. Abigail Thernstrom, who criticized Section 5 as "an instrument

---

13 *See* Carson Walker, *GOP Eyes American Indian Vote in Traditional Democratic Stronghold*, Rapid City J., Mar. 5, 2004, at *1.

14 New California Media, Executive Summary, *Poll of Asian Pacific Islanders on the 2004 Presidential Election* (Sept. 14, 2004).

15 Asian American Legal Defense and Education Fund, Asian Americans and the Voting Rights Act: The Case for Reauthorization vi (May 2006).

16 Pew Hispanic Center, Fact Sheet: The Hispanic Electorate in 2004, http://pewhispanic.org/files/factsheets/8.pdf.

17 *See* U.S. Census Bureau, Voting and Registration in the Election of November 1996, at 5 (July 1998).

18 *See* R.G. Ratcliffe, *Campaign 98: Upbeat Bush Predicting Win in El Paso Area*, Hous. Chron., Oct. 30, 1998, at A1.

for affirmative action in the electoral sphere,"[19] was appointed by President Bush as Vice Chair of the United States Commission on Civil Rights. Along with other conservative members who formed a majority on the Commission, Thernstrom urged Congress to "let these emergency provisions expire"[20] months before the Commission examined any evidence of the continued need for them.[21]

President Bush reportedly expressed similar reservations when he was Governor of Texas. In 1997, Bush's Secretary of State, Antonio Garza, Jr., wrote that it was "an affront to the integrity of Texans and their state lawmakers that the Texas election process is continuously thwarted by Section 5 of the federal Voting Rights Act" because of "the heavy hand of federal bureaucracy, resulting in a micromanagement mess."[22] Add to that claims by civil rights groups that the Bush Administration's Justice Department was reluctant to enforce Section 5, and it seemed reauthorization would be an uphill battle.

Republican Support for the Voting Rights Act

Despite the partisan political landscape, there were positive indications that Republican leadership would support reauthorization. President Bush repeatedly signaled approval of the language assistance provisions. In 1996, then-Governor Bush opposed the Bill Emerson English-only bill.[23] Bush described his approach as "English-plus," or the reciprocal obligation of Spanish-speaking Latinos to learn English and Americans to learn a second language.[24] He explained in his 1999 biography: "Those who advocate 'English-only' poke a stick in the eye of people of Hispanic heritage. 'English-only' says me, not you. It says I count, but you do not. That is not the message of America."[25] President Bush also opposed dismantling bilingual education, if it allowed students to become proficient in English.[26] His views were consistent with Section 203's purpose, which was "to permit persons disabled by [educational] disparities to vote now."[27] Shortly after taking office, President Bush affirmed his commitment to maintain Executive Order 13,166, a Clinton Administration initiative to "improve access" to federal programs "for persons who, as a result of national origin, are limited in their English proficiency (LEP)."[28]

Early on, President Bush publicly supported the VRA. In August 2005, President Bush issued a proclamation to mark the fortieth anniversary of the Act by acknowledging it "remains essential

19 Abigail Thernstrom, Whose Votes Count? Affirmative Action and Minority Voting Rights 27 (1987).

20 Abigail Thernstrom and Edward Blum, *Voting Rights Act: After 40 Years, It's Time for Virginia to Move On*, Richmond Times-Dispatch, Aug. 1, 2005; *see* Editorial, *Abigail Thernstrom on Why Congress Would be Wise to Let Part of the Voting Rights Act Expire*, N.Y. Sun, July 29, 2005, at 10.

21 *See* U.S. Comm'n on Civil Rights, Reauthorization of the Temporary Provisions of the Voting Rights Act: An Examination of the Act's Section 5 Preclearance Provision vi (2006).

22 Antonio O. Garza, Jr., opinion, *Fed Meddling in Texas Elections Must End*, San Antonio Bus. J., Nov. 17, 1997.

23 *See* Robert D. King, *Should English be the Law?*, Atlantic Monthly, Apr. 1, 1997, at 55.

24 Claudia Kolker, *Partial to Gov. Bush's Style, Latinos Look for Substance*, L.A. Times, Aug. 30, 1999, at 1.

25 George W. Bush, A Charge to Keep: My Journey to the White House 237 (1999).

26 *See* Frank Trejo, *Bush, Gingrich Address LULAC: Many Say GOP Beginning to Recognize Hispanics' Clout*, Dallas Morning News, July 2, 1998, at A25.

27 S. Rep. No. 94–295 at 34 (1975).

28 Exec. Order No. 13,166, 65 C.F.R. § 289 (2000). President Bush reaffirmed the policy in a letter from the Assistant Attorney General of the Civil Rights Division. *See* Letter from Ralph F. Boyd, Jr., Asst. Att'y Gen., Civil Rts. Div., U.S. Dept. of Just., to Jim Boulet, Jr., Exec. Dir. of English First, (Oct. 3, 2001).

as we continue our progress toward a society in which every person of every background can realize the American dream."[29] During a December 2005 bill signing to place a statue of civil rights heroine Rosa Parks in the Capitol he stated, "Congress should renew the Voting Rights Act."[30] The President made similar comments to mark the Martin Luther King, Jr. holiday in January 2006.[31] Administration officials, including Alberto Gonzales, the first Latino to serve as Attorney General of the United States, likewise acknowledged the continuing need for the Act. The Attorney General touted the Administration's efforts to enforce Section 203, resulting in more cases filed than the first 26 years it was in effect.[32]

Other Republican leaders agreed. In early 2004, Republican Senate Majority Leader Bill Frist introduced an amendment to a gun immunity bill to make the temporary provisions of the VRA permanent.[33] The amendment caught civil rights groups off guard, with Representative John Lewis asking Frist to withdraw the amendment as "premature" before a record had been developed (Stohlberg Feb. 27, 2004: A18).[34] Theodore Shaw, Director of the NAACP Legal Defense and Education Fund (LDF) explained: "If they are permanent, it is a trap ... They will be struck down as illegal and unconstitutional."[35] Others were less charitable. Reverend Jesse Jackson maintained that "Frist ... and House Majority Leader Tom DeLay ... are maneuvering to use the courts to gut the Voting Rights Act."[36] Nevertheless, with some education about how to proceed, Senator Frist was receptive to renewing the Act's expiring provisions. The press reported in June 2005 that House Republican leaders likely would join Frist in his support, though it was unclear if they would offer their own language in place of a Democratic bill.[37]

Republican National Committee (RNC) Chairman Ken Mehlman also came out early in favor of reauthorization. In April 2005, during an interview on National Public Radio, he stated that Section 5 "requires renewal," and "we look forward to working with both parties to make sure that's renewed."[38] Mehlman's support derived from his efforts to reach out to Black and Latino voters to bring them into the Republican Party. After becoming RNC Chairman in January 2005, he traveled to Black churches and organizations, describing Republicans as "the party of Lincoln and Frederick Douglass."[39] He actively recruited Black Republicans for statewide offices, including candidates for governor in Ohio and Pennsylvania and for Senate in Maryland. He described the importance of making Republicans

29 The White House, *40th Anniversary of the Voting Rights Act of 1965: A Proclamation by the President of the United States of America*, Aug. 5, 2005.

30 The White House, *President Signs H.R. 4145 to Place Statue of Rosa Parks in U.S. Capitol*, Dec. 1, 2005.

31 *See* James Gerstenzang, *President Urges Extension of the Voting Rights Act*, L.A. Times, Jan. 17, 2006, at 8.

32 *See* Att'y Gen. Alberto R. Gonzales, Prepared Remarks at the Anniversary of the Voting Rights Act, Aug. 2, 2005.

33 Sheryl Gay Stohlberg, *Senate Votes to Require Safety Locks on Guns*, N.Y. Times, Feb. 27, 2004, at A18.

34 *See* 152 Cong. Rec. S7965 (daily ed. July 20, 2006) (statement of Sen. Frist).

35 *Voting Rights Activists Want Law Extended, But Not Permanently*, Charleston Gazette, June 27, 2005, at 5C.

36 Jesse Jackson, *Republicans Maneuvering to Get Voting Rights Act Killed; Making It National and Permanent Would Set the Act Up for Being Ruled Unconstitutional*, Chi. Sun-Times, Mar. 8, 2005, at 31.

37 *See* Lynn Sweet, Editorial, *Hastert Lashes Dems on Race; Hastert Went Too Far in Ascribing a Motive to Their Blocking Tactics*, Chi. Sun-Times, June 16, 2005, at 41.

38 GOP Chairman Ken Mehlman Speaking on National Public Radio on Apr. 1, 2005, News & Notes, http://www.npr.org/templates/story/story.php?storyId=4571305.

39 Adam Nagourney, *Lost Horizons*, N.Y. Times, Sept. 24, 2006, at 632.

"whole again" by bringing Black voters "back home" to the party that supported reauthorization of the VRA and ended slavery.[40] In July 2005, Mehlman spoke at the NAACP's annual convention, publicly apologizing for the Republican's "Southern strategy" in which "[s]ome Republicans gave up on winning the African American vote, looking the other way or trying to benefit politically from racial polarization." President Bush agreed with his comments.[41] While Democratic National Committee (DNC) Chairman Howard Dean dismissed Mehlman's outreach to minorities,[42] his efforts resonated with many Black voters.[43] Civil rights groups had powerful Republican allies.

Strange Bedfellows

Renewal of the Act's expiring provisions would not have been possible without an unlikely alliance between a liberal Democrat and two conservative Republicans. Mel Watt served as Chairman of the Congressional Black Caucus (CBC) and was a member of the House Judiciary Committee that would consider any proposed reauthorization bill. A graduate of Yale Law School, in 1992 Representative Watt joined Eva Clayton as the first African-Americans elected to Congress from North Carolina since 1901. Months after taking office, Representative Watt's Twelfth Congressional District was struck down in *Shaw v. Reno*,[44] in which the United States Supreme Court "sidestepped" its precedent to allow white voters in a majority Black district to bring a claim for representational harm (*Shaw v. Reno* 1993: 657). Between 1993 and 2001, Representative Watt endured no less than four Supreme Court decisions[45] that resulted in his district being redrawn into a majority-white district. Representative Watt responded by establishing the Judge A. Leon Higginbotham, Jr. Memorial Voting Rights Braintrust of the CBC to respond to threats to minority voting rights.[46]

Although Representative John Conyers of Michigan was the ranking Democrat on the Committee, Representative Watt secured his approval to conduct direct negotiations with Republican leadership on VRA reauthorization. The Leadership Conference on Civil Rights (LCCR) agreed to have Representative Watt represent the single position of civil rights groups. Representative Watt was the right man for the job. A self-described "policy 'wonk,'" he would do "'the heavy lifting'" behind the scenes to get a good bill.[47] Representative Watt further recognized that reauthorization was impossible without Republican support that would evaporate if Democrats claimed the bill as their own. He also understood that he would have to restrain the impulse of DNC Chairman

40 Marjory Raymer, *Republican Honcho Woos Black Voters*, Flint J., July 21, 2005, at 3.

41 Edwin Chin, *GOP Rejects Its Past in Courting Black Support*, L.A. Times, July 15, 2005, at 22.

42 *See* Brendan McCarthy and Jeff Zeleny, *Dean Blasts GOP Over Voting Rights*, Chi. Trib., June 13, 2005, at 8.

43 *See* Nagourney Sept. 24, 2006: 632, Jim Wooten, Editorial, *Our Opinion: GOP's Appeal Gains Ground Among Backs*, Atl. J. & Const., July 17, 2005, at E6.

44 509 U.S. 630, 659 (1993) (White, J., dissenting). *Shaw* ignored longstanding precedent in *United Jewish Organizations of Williamsburgh, Inc. v. Carey*, 430 U.S. 144 (1977), in which the Court denied a challenge by Hasidic Jews who alleged that the creation of non-white majority-minority districts violated the Fourteenth Amendment.

45 *See Shaw v. Reno* 1993: 630; *Shaw v. Hunt*, 517 U.S. 899 (1996); *Hunt v. Cromartie*, 526 U.S. 541 (1999); *Easley v. Cromartie*, 532 U.S. 234 (2001).

46 *See* Webcast, Comments of Representative Mel Watt, Chairman, (CBC Voting Rights Braintrust) (Sept. 8, 2006), http://www.broadcasturban.net/webcast/cbcf2006/fri_voting.htm.

47 Tim Funk, *Watt Brokers Extension of Voting Rights Act: Charlotte Democrat in Spotlight as Bipartisan Support Announced*, Charlotte Observer, May 3, 2006.

Howard Dean and other Democrats to push the VRA bill by attacking with "partisan vitriol" any Republicans slow in their support.[48]

Representative Watt found his ally in James Sensenbrenner, the conservative Republican from Wisconsin who was Chairman of the House Judiciary Committee. In many ways, Chairman Sensenbrenner was an improbable partner. During prior efforts to extend the Act, he expressed reservations about Section 203. In the 1981 House hearings he stated, "I must express one concern with the administration of the present law and that is with the application of bilingual ballot provisions in certain jurisdictions where there has not been much of a demand for ballots printed in a language other than English."[49] In 1992, he joined six Republicans in filing dissenting views on the 15-year extension of the language assistance provisions, arguing they would "turn this country, blessed with a common language, into a modern-day Tower of Babel."[50] He also supported the Bill Emerson English-only legislation.[51] In 1996, Sensenbrenner argued the provisions were "unnecessary and costly," and the rationale for using them was "perplexing" because "only citizens may vote."[52]

Still, there were signs that Chairman Sensenbrenner would support reauthorization. At the start of the 1981 hearings, he was "an admitted skeptic" of the other expiring provisions of the VRA, including Section 5.[53] However, his attendance at extensive House hearings, including field hearings in Austin, Texas, and Montgomery, Alabama, and observations of more than 100 witnesses who described widespread voting discrimination, caused him to become a leader in the 1982 extension. During his February 1982 testimony before the Senate Judiciary Committee, he acknowledged to laughter, "I am not the most civil-righteous individual in the House of Representatives."[54] However, he willingly took on the Reagan Administration, which initially opposed renewing Section 5 and amending Section 2 to restore the "effects" test. Chairman Sensenbrenner explained,

> [A]fter sitting through the extensive hearings and seeing the abuses that were attempted to be perpetrated up to the present time in many of the covered jurisdictions, I ... reached the conclusion that section 5 has been a successful law and the bilingual preclearance and ballot provisions also have been very successful ... Without an effective section 2, there would be no way of catching the abuses that were enacted prior to 1965 in covered jurisdictions, as well as the abuses that might have happened in noncovered jurisdictions up until the present time.[55]

Having successfully championed the 1982 VRA extension, he proudly displayed a signed copy of the bill in his office with the pen President Reagan used to sign it into law (Yachnin Mar. 2, 2006). He also had refrained from co-sponsoring any of the post-1996 bills to repeal the language assistance

48 Erin P. Billings and Ben Pershing, *If the first four months of the year are an indicator, the next five weeks of Congressional business promise even more partisan vitriol, legislative gridlock and yes, even chatter about a post-election, lame-duck session*, Roll Call, Apr. 25, 2006, at 60; 2006 Braintrust.

49 *Hearings before the Subcomm. on Civil and Constitutional Rts. of the House Comm. on the Judiciary*, 97th Cong. 5 (1981) ("1981 House Hearings") (statement of Rep. Sensenbrenner).

50 *See* H.R. Rep. No. 102–655, at 28 (1992) (dissenting views of Reps. Hyde, Sensenbrenner, McCollum, Coble, James, Ramstad, and Allen).

51 *See* 142 Cong. Rec. H9772 (daily ed. Aug. 1, 1996).

52 142 Cong. Rec. H9740 (daily ed. Aug. 1, 1996) (statement of Rep. Sensenbrenner).

53 Jennifer Yachnin, *VRA's Unlikely Patron Keeps Fighting*, Roll Call, Mar. 2, 2006.

54 *Hearings before the Subcomm. on the Const. of the Senate Comm. on the Judiciary*, 97th Cong. 890 (1982) ("1982 Senate Hearings") (testimony of Rep. Sensenbrenner).

55 1982 Senate Hearings: 891.

Figure 7.1 Congressman Steve Chabot (R, OH-1) with key civil rights advocates from the 2006 VRA Reauthorization

Pictured from left to right: Caroline Fredrickson, American Civil Liberties Union (ACLU) Washington Legislative Office; James Thomas Tucker, National Association of Latino Elected and Appointed Officials (NALEO); LaShawn Warren, ACLU Washington Legislative Office; Congressman Steve Chabot, Chairman of the House Subcommittee on the Constitution; Debo Adegbile, National Association for the Advancement of Colored People Legal Defense Fund (NAACP LDF); Julie Fernandes, Leadership Conference on Civil Rights (LCCR); and Terry Ao, Asian American Justice Center (AAJC).

Source: Photo courtesy of Debo Adegbile, Director of Litigation, NAACP Legal Defense Fund.

provisions. Although many Democrats disagreed with Chairman Sensenbrenner's positions on legislation, they held him in "high regard" for being "evenhanded" and not "foreclosing debate."[56] Chairman Sensenbrenner would champion reauthorization if the record supported it.

Chairman Sensenbrenner was assisted by Republican Steve Chabot of Ohio, who served as Chairman of the House Judiciary Subcommittee on the Constitution. Representative Chabot shared many common traits with Sensenbrenner. He had solid conservative credentials, having served as a House Manager during the Senate impeachment trial of President Clinton. He supported the 1996 effort to repeal Section 203,[57] but like the Chairman did not co-sponsor subsequent efforts. He was widely praised for his work in the highly partisan impeachment trial. The strengths of Chairman Sensenbrenner and Representative Chabot complemented one another perfectly to navigate the treacherous waters of reauthorization.

56 Craig Gilbert, *Iron Will Brings Perils, Payoffs for Sensenbrenner*, Milwaukee J. Sentinel, July 10, 2005, at A1.

57 *See* 142 Cong. Rec. H9772 (daily ed. Aug. 1, 1996).

In late spring and early summer 2005, Representative Watt met with Chairman Sensenbrenner about reauthorization (2006 Braintrust). There was a sense of urgency to begin the process early because Representative Lamar Smith, a conservative Texas Republican who opposed the expiring provisions, likely would replace Chairman Sensenbrenner if Republicans maintained control of the House. Furthermore, an extensive record was needed to support, requiring significant committee time in both the House and Senate. In addition, it was likely there would be extended negotiations with LCCR over the bill's language. Equally important, a personal relationship built on trust had to be developed between Republicans, Democrats, and the civil rights community. Chairman Sensenbrenner later explained, "If there is partisanship that enters into the Voting Rights Act reauthorization, it will not be done either by myself or by Congressman Watt ... This is too important a law to allow it to fall off the edge into a partisan abyss" (Yachnin Mar. 2, 2006).

Before the July 4, 2005 recess, Republican Speaker of the House Dennis Hastert said that VRA renewal was among his priorities.[58] Despite Speaker Hastert's statement, many were surprised by Sensenbrenner's announcement on July 10, 2005, about his plans to push for early reauthorization. Speaking at the NAACP's annual convention near his home outside Milwaukee, Sensenbrenner stated:

> I am here to tell you publicly what I have told others privately, including the head of the Congressional Black Caucus, Representative Mel Watt—during this Congress we are going to extend the Voting Rights Act ... Soon I will be introducing legislation to extend the Voting Rights Act. Just like its enactment and its 1982 extension, this bipartisan effort will succeed ... [W]hile we have made progress and curtailed injustices thanks to the Voting Rights Act, our work is not yet complete. We cannot let discriminatory practices of the past resurface to threaten future gains. The Voting Rights Act must continue to exist—and exist in its current form.[59]

The next day, Speaker Hastert, joined by Republican Majority Leader Tom DeLay, Majority Whip Roy Blunt, and Chief Deputy Whip Eric Cantor, commended Sensenbrenner "for moving expeditiously to take up this important legislation."[60] Hilary Shelton, Director of the NAACP's Washington office, praised Sensenbrenner, encouraging him to "strengthen"[61] the VRA to "guarantee as broadly as possible that every American vote is going to be counted."[62] Several Democratic leaders met a few weeks later to discuss strategy and were cautiously optimistic about the prospects of reauthorization.

That optimism was buoyed in anticipation of the VRA's fortieth anniversary. Sensenbrenner and Chabot co-sponsored a resolution introduced by Representative Lewis expressing the sense of Congress that "it will advance the legacy of the Voting Rights Act of 1965 by ensuring the continued effectiveness of the Act to protect the voting rights of all Americans."[63] Although the resolution was symbolic, it sent an important message. While there had been "noteworthy progress" under the Act, Republican leadership on the Judiciary Committee agreed that "voter inequities, disparities, and obstacles still remain for far too many voters and serve to demonstrate the ongoing importance" of the VRA. It was vital the Act's

58 151 Cong. Rec. E1684 (daily ed. June 29, 2005) (extended remarks of Rep. Lewis).

59 *Rep. Sensenbrenner to Introduce 25-Year Voting Rights Extension Legislation, Calls for Bipartisan Approach to Civil Rights Issues*, U.S. Fed. News, July 10, 2005.

60 *House Leadership Commends House Judiciary Committee for Plans to Take up Voting Rights Act Reauthorization*, U.S. Fed. News, July 11, 2005.

61 Mike Allen, *Washington – House Judiciary Committee*, Contra Costa Times, July 10, 2005, at F4.

62 India Autry, *Voting Act Gets Early Lift from House*, Newsday, July 19, 2005, at A35.

63 H.R. Con. Res. 216, 109th Cong. (2005); *see* H. Rep. 109–195, 109th Cong. (2005).

provisions be "fully effective to prevent discrimination and dilution of the equal rights of minority voters."[64] A companion Senate resolution sponsored by Senator Ted Kennedy drew the support of Sensenbrenner's Republican Senate counterpart, Arlen Specter of Pennsylvania.[65]

The Bill: Renewing and Restoring the Voting Rights Act

Chairman Sensenbrenner delegated to Chabot the task of building a record supporting reauthorization. Between October 2005 and April 2006, the House Subcommittee on the Constitution held ten oversight hearings "examining the effectiveness of the temporary provisions of the VRA over the last twenty-five years." The Subcommittee received testimony from 39 witnesses, "including State and local elected officials, scholars, attorneys, and other representatives from the voting and civil rights community." The hearings produced over 12,000 pages of testimony and documentary evidence.[66] Key reports included findings from ten field hearings of the National Commission on the Voting Rights Act,[67] a summary of the ACLU's 293 voting cases since 1982,[68] LCCR's 14 state reports documenting voting discrimination in states covered by the Act's special provisions,[69] and a report by Arizona State University researchers identifying the need, availability, quality, and cost of language assistance under the VRA (Chapters 5–6).[70] Sensenbrenner noted the voluminous record gathered by Chabot represented "quality, rather than quantity."[71]

The House record showed "the extent to which discrimination against minorities in voting has and continues to occur," which supported "the continued need for the expiring provisions." It demonstrated that despite progress under the VRA, there was a substantial basis for renewing the expiring provisions for 25 years. But there also was a need "to update the VRA's temporary provisions, and to restore the VRA to its original intent," to effectively remedy the "continuing vestiges of racial discrimination" (H.R. Rep. No. 109–478, 2006: 5). After extensive negotiations between Sensenbrenner, Chabot, Conyers, and Watt, the House Judiciary Committee assembled a consensus bipartisan bill to address those findings.

64 H.R. Con. Res. 216, 109th Cong. (2005).

65 *See* S. Res. 232, 109th Cong. (2005); 151 Cong. Rec. S9541 (July 29, 2005) (statement of Sen. Kennedy).

66 Fannie Lou Hamer, Rosa Parks, and Coretta Scott King Voting Rights Reauthorization and Amendments Act of 2006, H.R. Rep. No. 109–478 at 5 (2006) (VRARA).

67 *See* Nat'l Comm'n on the Voting Rts. Act, Protecting Minority Voters: The Voting Rights Act at Work, 1982–2005 (2006), *reprinted in Voting Rights Act: Evidence of Continued Need* ("Continued Need"), H.R. Rep. 109–103 at 104 (2006).

68 *See* Voting Rts. Project of the Am. Civ. Liberties Union, VOTE: The Case for Extending and Amending the Voting Rights Act, Voting Rights Litigation 1982–2005 (2006), *in* Continued Need 2006: 378.

69 *See* Appendices to the Statement of Wade Henderson, Executive Director of the Leadership Conference on Civil Rights, *in* Continued Need 2006: 1308. Eleven of the reports were entered into the record during the House oversight hearings (H.R. Rep. No. 109–478, 2006: 5). The remaining three reports were entered into the Senate record.

70 Dr. James Thomas Tucker and Dr. Rodolfo Espino et al., Minority Language Assistance Practices in Public Elections 5–13 (Mar. 2006), *in* Continued Need 2006: 2094.

71 *Renewing the Temporary Provisions of the Voting Rights Act: An Introduction to the Evidence*: *Hearing Before the Senate Jud. Comm.*, 109th Cong. 2d Sess., S. Hrg. No. 109–555 at 6 (2006) ("Introduction Senate Hearing") (testimony of Rep. Sensenbrenner).

Section 2 of the VRARA summarized the congressional purpose and findings supporting the Act's constitutionality.[72] In *City of Boerne v. Flores*, the U.S. Supreme Court set the parameters for congressional exercise of its remedial powers under the Fourteenth and Fifteenth Amendments.[73] According to the Court, "[w]hile preventive rules are sometimes appropriate remedial measures, there must be a congruence between the means used and the ends to be achieved" considered "in light of the evil presented." *Boerne* cited evidence of racial discrimination supporting the VRA as meeting the congruence standard (*City of Boerne v. Flores* 1997: 530, 532–33). Where that record is established, Congress has "wide latitude" in determining appropriate deterrent or remedial legislation, "even if in the process it prohibits conduct which is not itself unconstitutional and intrudes into 'legislative spheres of autonomy previously reserved to the States'" (*City of Boerne v. Flores* 1997: 518). That is particularly true for legislation like the VRA in which "the possibility of overbreadth" is reduced by limiting its applications "to those cases in which constitutional violations were most likely" and terminating it when the danger subsided (*City of Boerne v. Flores* 1997: 533). Following *Boerne*, the Court confirmed that congressional power is at its apex for legislation protecting fundamental rights afforded heightened constitutional scrutiny.[74]

The House Judiciary Committee noted the "substantial volume of evidence" of racial discrimination from its ten oversight hearings far exceeded the records in the two post-*Boerne* decisions, *Lane* and *Hibbs* (H.R. Rep. No. 109–478, 2006: 57). That evidence included "vestiges of discrimination" such as "second generation barriers" to minority voting. It also encompassed "continued evidence of racially polarized voting in each of the jurisdictions covered by the expiring provisions" that made racial and language minorities "politically vulnerable." In jurisdictions covered by the temporary provisions, there was substantial non-compliance with Section 5, many had been denied bailout, minorities continued to file Section 2 cases, and the Justice Department actively enforced the language assistance provisions. Federal observers were widely used to document and prevent voting discrimination. In addition, the Court's misconstruction of Section 5 in *Bossier II* and *Ashcroft* had greatly weakened the VRA's effectiveness (Chapter 3).

Despite progress under the Act, 40 years was insufficient "to eliminate the vestiges of discrimination following nearly 100 years of disregard" for the Constitution.[75] Absent reauthorization, "significant gains" by minorities would be undermined. Congress reaffirmed existing statutory findings of discrimination.[76] Those findings presented a compelling basis to reauthorize the Act for 25 years under *Boerne*. The bill's substantive amendments to the VRA are described in greater detail in Chapters 3 and 4.

The Debate: Navigating a Treacherous Path to Reauthorization

On April 27, 2006, the late Coretta Scott King's birthday, reauthorization appeared likely. Chairman Sensenbrenner and Representative Conyers repeated their 1982 appearance before the Senate

72 *See* VRARA § 2, Pub L. No. 109–246, § 2, 120 Stat. 577–78 (2006).

73 *See City of Boerne v. Flores*, 521 U.S. 507, 517–19 (1997).

74 *See generally Tennessee v. Lane*, 541 U.S. 509, 533–34 (2004) (upholding congressional abrogation of state sovereign immunity under Title II of the Americans with Disabilities Act because it protected the fundamental right of access to the courts); *Nev. Dept. of Human Res. v. Hibbs,* 538 U.S. 721, 740 (2003) (upholding the congressional abrogation of state sovereign immunity under the Family Medical Leave Act because the Act prevented sex discrimination).

75 VRARA § 2(b), Pub L. No. 109–246, § 2(b)(2), 120 Stat. 577 (2006).

76 VRARA § 2(b)(9), Pub L. No. 109–246, § 2(b)(9), 120 Stat. 577 (2006).

Judiciary Committee,[77] joined by Representatives Lewis and Watt.[78] Sensenbrenner introduced the House record into the Senate's record, laying a strong foundation for Senate consideration of the bill. He stated he fully supported the VRARA, including reauthorization of Section 5 and the language assistance provisions. Conyers acknowledged Sensenbrenner's bipartisan leadership, agreeing that reauthorization would "ensure the continuing vitality" of the VRA (Introduction Senate Hearing 2006: 8). Not everyone concurred. Republican Senator John Cornyn of Texas extolled "marked progress" under the Act that required crafting "future national policy accordingly" (Introduction Senate Hearing 2006: 4). Republican Senator Arlen Specter of Pennsylvania, Chairman of the Senate Judiciary Committee, committed to a "joint introduction, bicameral introduction" and to timetables to expedite consideration of the VRARA (Introduction Senate Hearing 2006: 10).

On May 2, 2006, the die was cast. With great fanfare, the VRARA was introduced bicamerally in the House and the Senate. A bipartisan group of more than two dozen members from both chambers joined together in a press event on the steps of the Capitol. The group was led by Representative Lewis and included leaders from both parties: Senate Majority Leader Bill Frist, Senate Minority Leader Harry Reid, House Speaker Dennis Hastert, and House Minority Leader Nancy Pelosi. Representative Watt observed:

> [L]ike other landmark civil rights bills, the renewed and restored bill that we introduced today is good for all Americans. It is not a Republican bill, it is not a Democratic bill, it is not a House bill or a Senate bill. And it is not a bill solely for minorities. This is a bipartisan, bicameral bill that unites us as a country by ensuring that all Americans may have their voices heard.[79]

The VRARA was titled "The Fannie Lou Hamer, Rosa Parks, and Coretta Scott King Voting Rights Act Reauthorization and Amendments Act of 2006."[80] Representative Watt explained that although the three African-American civil rights "pioneers have left us, this bill allows us to ensure that rights they fought for remain for future generations."[81]

The leadership's bipartisan commitment was evident at the bill's introduction. Sensenbrenner said he would hold two legislative hearings within two days, followed by a committee markup the next week. House Majority Leader John Boehner hoped to have the bill on the House floor before Memorial Day. Senator Specter expected to complete six committee hearings by mid-May, with a markup immediately following the Memorial Day recess. According to Representative Watt, supporters had not "sensed" any significant opposition to the bill.[82]

The bipartisan bicameral introduction ensured the bill considered in the Senate was the same as the one in the House, avoiding a protracted battle over language in conference. With the benefit of a substantial House record, the Senate had the evidence it needed to support the bill's findings. Equally important, it sent the message of inevitability of passage of a clean bill, unencumbered by parochial interests. The Hill photo opportunity committed party leadership to the bipartisan

77 *See 1982 Senate Hearings*: 876–97 (Feb 4. 1982) (testimony of Rep. Sensenbrenner); 1982 Senate Hearings: 1650–52 (Mar. 1, 1982) (testimony of Rep. Conyers).

78 *See* Introduction Senate Hearing 2006: 2 (statement of Chairman Specter).

79 *Rep. Watt Comments on Introduction of Bicameral/Bipartisan Voting Rights Act Reauthorization Bill*, U.S. Fed. News, May 2, 2006.

80 *See* H.R. 9 § 1, 109th Cong. (2006) (enacted); S. 2703 § 1, 109th Cong. (2006) (enacting H.R. 9, as amended).

81 Gary Martin, *Lawmakers Unite in Push to Renew Voting Rights Act*, San Antonio Express-News, May 3, 2006, at A9.

82 Jennifer Yachnin, *Parties Show Unity on VRA*, Roll Call (Wash., D.C.), May 3, 2006.

agreement reached on the VRARA. Republican leadership would be held accountable if they broke their promise.

House Markup and Defeat of the King Amendments

The bipartisan commitment was soon put to the test in the House. On May 4, 2006, Constitution Subcommittee Chairman Chabot held two legislative hearings examining H.R. 9 (H.R. Rep. No. 109–478, 2006: 5, 85). Two of the seven witnesses at those hearings alluded to the political challenges the VRARA would face. Roger Clegg, General Counsel for the conservative Center for Equal Opportunity, testified that the expiring provisions were no longer needed.[83] Quoting from Representative Lewis's affidavit in *Ashcroft*, Clegg argued that people in Georgia and "in the American South ... are preparing to lay down the burden of race" (Clegg Testimony 2006: 14). Representative Lewis disagreed noting, "We have come a great distance, but we still have a great distance to go before all Americans have free and equal access to the ballot box" (House Legislative Hearing I 2006: 76). Clegg also tried to link the language assistance provisions to immigration, contending that they said "you can be a full participant in American democracy without knowing English – which is a lie" (Clegg Testimony 2006: 14).

Supervisor Chris Norby from Orange County, California, agreed.[84] Norby was trying to remove his county from Section 203 coverage for four languages (Appendices B-C) and to defeat a lawsuit against the county by the Mexican American Legal Defense and Education Fund seeking to translate recall petitions.[85] He claimed the provisions "perpetuate negative stereotypes, are outdated, vague, and violate the spirit of assimilation that holds our country together." Norby suggested that providing election materials in other languages would "create an anti-immigrant backlash" and create "Minutemen."[86] The themes raised by Clegg and Norby resonated with a small group of conservative Republicans.

Clegg and Norby found their closest ally in Steve King, a Republican Congressman from Iowa. King was an outspoken critic of the Bush Administration's immigration policy. He argued that illegal immigrants killed more Americans than Al Qaeda, referring to illegal immigration as "a slow motion holocaust on our hands."[87] He was widely criticized for suggesting use of electric fences to stop immigration from Mexico saying, "We do that with livestock all the time."[88] King contended that civil rights groups promoted bilingual ballots to create "cultural enclaves" to "control the

83 *Fannie Lou Hamer, Rosa Parks, and Coretta Scott King Voting Rights Reauthorization and Amendments Act of 2006 (Part I): Hearing on H.R. 9 Before the Subcomm. on the Constitution of the H. Comm. on the Judiciary* ("House Legislative Hearing I"), 109th Cong. 13–37 (May 4, 2006) (testimony of Roger Clegg).

84 *See* Abraham Mahshie, *O.C. Supervisor Lobbies to Limit Bilingual Ballots*, ORANGE COUNTY REG., Apr. 1, 2006.

85 In November 2005, the Ninth Circuit held that Orange County violated Section 203 by failing to translate the recall petitions. *Padilla v. Lever*, No. 03–56259 (9th Cir. Nov. 25, 2005). In September 2006, an en banc panel of the Ninth Circuit reached the opposite conclusion, holding that recall petitions were not covered "voting materials" under Section 203. *See Padilla v. Lever*, 463 F.3d 1046 (9th Cir. 2006) (en banc).

86 *Fannie Lou Hamer, Rosa Parks, and Coretta Scott King Voting Rights Reauthorization and Amendments Act of 2006 (Part II): Hearing on H.R. 9 Before the Subcomm. on the Constitution of the H. Comm. on the Judiciary*, 109th Cong. 14, 94–95 (May 4, 2006) (testimony of Chris Norby).

87 *Iowa Pol: I Said Holocaust, Not the Holocaust*, THE JEWISH DAILY FORWARD, July 7, 2006.

88 *They're People Too*, L.A. TIMES, July 26, 2006, at 10.

immigrants" and give the groups political power.[89] On February 3, 2006, he sent a letter signed by 56 Congressmen to Chairman Sensenbrenner opposing Sections 4(f)(4) and 203, claiming they "are a serious affront to generations of immigrants ... that have made great sacrifices to learn English in order to become naturalized citizens."[90] The letter cited unfounded allegations about language assistance, including its purported cost, lack of use, and that it promoted voter fraud (Chapter 8). ProEnglish, a group actively lobbying to repeal the language assistance provisions, drafted the King letter.[91]

On May 10, 2006, the House Judiciary Committee marked up H.R. 9. The Committee considered several amendments to the bill. Representative Darrell Issa of California offered an amendment requiring the Comptroller General to "study the implementation, effectiveness, and efficiency" of Section 203 and "alternatives to the current implementation consistent with that section" (H.R. Rep. No. 109–478, 2006: 124–25). The amendment was similar to previous studies conducted by the General Accounting Office (GAO) in 1984 and 1996, as well as a 2005 Arizona State University study submitted into the record during the House's oversight hearings (Tucker and Espino Mar. 2006). Chairman Sensenbrenner and Representative Conyers both accepted the amendment as "non-controversial," and it was adopted by voice vote. However, the amendment created what Representative Watt described as a "challenge ... to convince the Senate to put this in their bill" to ensure that a conference would not be necessary (H.R. Rep. No. 109–478, 2006: 126–27).[92]

Representative Sheila Jackson Lee offered an amendment that would make any mid-decade redistricting after adoption of an earlier plan in a Section 5 covered jurisdiction a "per se violation" requiring denial of preclearance. The amendment was a response to the mid-decade Texas redistricting by former House Speaker Tom DeLay, which the Justice Department precleared. Representative Conyers opposed the amendment because the Texas redistricting case was before the U.S. Supreme Court, and the legislative record did not support the change. Chairman Sensenbrenner was more direct, saying, "This bill is the subject of lengthy negotiations and it is an agreed upon bill, and this amendment is a deal breaker, and I will be very blunt in saying that." Mr. Watt acknowledged that Representative Jackson Lee and others would have "individual ... interests that go beyond the scope" of the bill, but asked that they "keep the balance" achieved through the VRARA to avoid a "divisive fight." Representative Jackson Lee reluctantly agreed and withdrew her amendment (H.R. Rep. No. 109–478, 2006: 127–32).

Representative Dan Lungren of California offered an amendment focusing on local interests. He proposed modifying the bailout requirements in Section 4(a) of the Act to exempt jurisdictions covered by Section 5 preclearance because of nonvoting military personnel and their families. He explained, in "certain small jurisdictions in my State, Merced County, Kings County, Yuba County ... voter turnout narrowly fell below the 50 percent rule because military personnel often voted in their home States by absentee ballot." Representative Lungren contended that these jurisdictions were "accidentally swept into coverage" for reasons Congress never intended, making the Act

89 Brian DeBose, *Lawmakers Push Official English*, Wash. Times, Apr. 3, 2006, at A6.

90 *See* Letter of 56 Congressmen to Rep. James Sensenbrenner, Chairman, House Judiciary Committee (Feb. 3, 2006).

91 *See* Duke Falconer, *Who Really Stalled the Voting Rights Act Renewal*, E Pluribus Media, July 12, 2006. K.C. McAlpin, the Executive Director of ProEnglish, testified against renewing the language assistance provisions. *See Voting Rights Act: Section 203 – Bilingual Election Requirements (Part II): Hearing Before the Subcomm. on the Constitution of the H. Comm. on the Judiciary* ("Bilingual Election Hearing Part II"), 109th Cong. 63–76 (2005) (testimony of K.C. McAlpin, Executive Director, ProEnglish).

92 The Issa Amendment became Section 9 of the VRARA. *See* Pub. L. No. 109–246, § 9, 120 Stat. 577, 581 (2006).

constitutionally vulnerable. He further argued that under Section 5, counties were held accountable for compliance by independent political bodies over which they had no control (H.R. Rep. No. 109–478, 2006: 151–56, 159–60).

Representative Watt described the amendment as a "back-door attempt to circumvent the existing bailout requirements" supported solely by materials submitted by lawyers lobbying for the covered counties (H.R. Rep. No. 109–478, 2006: 157). Chairman Sensenbrenner observed that one of the three California counties affected by the amendment had a Section 5 objection, and it was inappropriate to give it a "get-out-of-jail-free card." He also noted that the Supreme Court had upheld the trigger for Section 5 coverage on three occasions (H.R. Rep. No. 109–478, 2006: 162). Representative Lungren withdrew his amendment after several members requested more information, but suggested he might try to offer it during the floor debate.

Representative King offered the two most contentious amendments. His first amendment would strike Sections 7 and 8 of the VRARA, allowing the language assistance provisions to sunset in August 2007.[93] He injected immigration into the debate by arguing, "Reauthorizing the multilingual voting mandate contradicts our immigration law because English is a condition for naturalization." Representative Lamar Smith echoed King's concerns by maintaining "if you were born in America, you should know English. If you are a naturalized citizen, you should have passed an English proficiency test." Smith also stated his opposition to reauthorization of Section 5, which he claimed "overly burden many jurisdictions" that "no longer disenfranchise minority or other voters" (H.R. Rep. No. 109–478, 2006: 132–34, 137).

Chairman Sensenbrenner disagreed, noting "we are not dealing with illegal immigrants, we are dealing with United States citizens, and they are people who have either attained citizenship by reason of birth in the United States ... or have been naturalized." He pointed out it was unfair to "close the door to understanding a ballot because of the failure of our educational system" or because people move from a place where English is not commonly used (H.R. Rep. No. 109–478, 2006: 135). Members of the CBC and Congressional Hispanic Caucus (CHC) demonstrated their unity by unanimously reaffirming the continued need for language assistance. The King Amendment was defeated by a vote of 26 to nine, with a majority of Republicans opposing it (H.R. Rep. No. 109–478, 2006: 85–86, 149–51). Representative King offered a separate amendment to change the sunset date for the language assistance provisions from 2032 to 2013, a six-year reauthorization to "get ... through the next census ... to see the effect on reauthorization." It was defeated 24 to 10 (H.R. Rep. No. 109–78, 2006: 86–87, 165–70).

Following the debate on the amendments, the Judiciary Committee voted 33 to one to report the VRARA out favorably as modified by the Issa Amendment, with only Representative King opposing it (H.R. Rep. No. 109–478, 2006: 87, 171–73). There were two casualties from the debate. Efforts to lower the numerical trigger for coverage under the language assistance provisions failed after English-only forces mobilized to express their opposition. Furthermore, the House committee report agreed with Supervisor Norby's argument that petitions were not "voting materials" that had to be translated under Section 203. The reported provided:

> [L]anguage assistance that facilitates equal participation in the voting process so language minority citizens are able to cast effective ballots does not require private citizens to make privately prepared and distributed materials available in the covered languages ... To impose Section 203's requirements on private citizens whose actions are outside governmentally administered voting systems would

93 *See* VRARA §§ 7–8, *enacted as* Pub L. No. 109–246, §§ 7–8, 120 Stat. 577, 581 (2006).

have the effect of penalizing private citizens for injuries caused by States (H.R. Rep. No. 109–478, 2006: 59).

However, these concessions did little to mollify the bill's detractors, who continued to build their opposition and were waiting for the next chance to strike. The immigration debate in the Senate offered them their opportunity.

Immigration and English-Only in the Senate

During the year before introduction of the VRARA, there were growing efforts to address immigration reform. The Republican Party was bitterly divided over the issue. Some Republicans called for forced deportation of illegal aliens who would be declared felons,[94] while others joined a bipartisan coalition led by Republican Senator John McCain and Democratic Senator Ted Kennedy and supported by President Bush that proposed a path to earned citizenship.[95] On April 10, 2006, immigration was thrust into the national headlines when hundreds of thousands of protestors marched throughout the country, including large rallies in Atlanta, Houston, New York, Phoenix, and Washington. Three weeks later the rallies were repeated when more than one million immigrants and supporters marched in a national "day without immigrants."[96] The timing could not have been worse for the VRARA. The immigration debate threatened to spill over into reauthorization of the language assistance provisions.[97] Chairman Sensenbrenner managed to disentangle the provisions from immigration during the VRARA markup, but the threat had not subsided.

Decidedly mixed signals from the Bush Administration on English-only efforts did not help. In late April 2006, a Spanish-language pop version of "The Star Spangled Banner," "*Nuestro Himno*," was released in preparation for the immigration rallies.[98] The Spanish version included lines not in the national anthem, such as "My people keep fighting. It's time to break the chains." President Bush denounced the release saying, "I think the national anthem ought to be sung in English and I think people who want to be a citizen of this country ought to learn English, and they ought to learn to sing the national anthem in English."[99] He further stated the anthem would not "hold the same

94 *See* Comprehensive Enforcement and Immigration Reform Act of 2005, S. 1438, 109th Cong. (1st Sess. 2005) (sponsored by Sens. Cornyn and Kyl); Employers that Abide by the Law and Guaranteeing Uniform Enforcement to Stop Terrorism (REAL GUEST) Act of 2005, H.R. 3333, 109th Cong. (1st Sess. 2005) (sponsored by Rep. Tancredo).

95 *See* The Secure America and Orderly Immigration Act, S. 1033, 109th Cong. (1st Sess. 2005) (sponsored by Sens. McCain and Kennedy); H.R. 2330, 109th Cong. (1st Sess. 2005) (sponsored by Reps. Kolbe, Flake, and Gutierrez); *George W. Bush Delivers Remarks on Immigration, as Prepared for Delivery*, FDCH Cap. Transcripts, May 15, 2006.

96 *See* Mike Colias, *Immigration: "Marching Not Enough," Organizers of Rallies Say*, Miami Herald, May 3, 2006, at A3; *Jubilant Marchers Grab Nation's Attention: Immigration Rallies*, Seattle Times, May 2, 2006, at A10.

97 *See, e.g.*, Craig Gilbert, *Sensenbrenner Backs Keeping Bilingual Ballots; Immigration Fire Feeds on Mandate Extension*, Milwaukee J. & Sentinel, May 5, 2006, at 3; Brian DeBose, *Language Rules Impede Extension of Voter Rights Act*, Wash. Times, May 5, 2006, at A6; Nicole Gaouette, *House GOP Group Targets Bilingual Ballots; The 56 Lawmakers Want to Let Language Assistance Provisions in the Voting Rights Act Expire*, L.A. Times, May 6, 2006, at 9.

98 Mark Silva, *Bush Thinks National Anthem Should Be Sung in English*, Chi. Trib., Apr. 29, 2006, at 3.

99 Joyce Howard Price, *President Supports Anthem in English; Spanish Version Called an Insult*, Wash. Times, Apr. 29, 2006, at A1.

value" if it was sung in Spanish.[100] The President's statement conflicted with reports that in 2000 he would sometimes sing the national anthem in Spanish and that he had Jon Secada perform the anthem in Spanish in 2001.[101] Some notable people in the Administration publicly disagreed with the President, including Secretary of State Condoleezza Rice and First Lady Laura Bush.[102] In a speech on May 15, 2006, the President reaffirmed the need for newcomers to "assimilate into our society" by learning English.[103]

Three days later and for the first time in 23 years, the Senate considered an amendment to make English the national language.[104] An amendment offered by Senator James Inhofe of Oklahoma to the Comprehensive Immigration Reform Act declared, "English is the national language of the United States." It purported to "preserve and enhance the role of English as the national language" by providing that:

> Unless specifically stated in applicable law, no person has a right, entitlement, or claim to have the Government of the United States or any of its officials or representatives act, communicate, perform or provide services, or provide materials in any language other than English. If exceptions are made, that does not create a legal entitlement to additional services in that language or any language other than English.

The Inhofe Amendment required that immigrants seeking to become U.S. citizens "must, among other requirements, demonstrate an understanding of the English language, United States history and Government." Additionally, it directed the Department of Homeland Security to redesign the citizenship test to reflect those requirements.[105] U.S. English, which sponsored the 1983 English-only amendment, applauded the measure as "the right thing to do for our immigrants and for our society."[106] Senator Inhofe quoted President Bush's May 15th speech and noted he previously had stated, "Every new citizen of the United States has an obligation" to learn "the English language."[107]

Supporters of the Inhofe Amendment claimed it was "not an English-only amendment."[108] Senator Inhofe acknowledged his amendment would make English the "official" or "national" language.[109] Senator Lamar Alexander claimed, "The Inhofe amendment is not an official English amendment."[110] Although some supporters suggested the amendment would not apply to executive orders, Senator Inhofe made it clear that it repealed Executive Order 13166. He argued that "there is no legal basis for Executive Order 13166 that purported to direct services in languages other

100 Lesley Clark, *Anthem Song Sparks Debate in the 'Land of the Free,'* Miami Herald, Apr. 29, 2006, at 1A.

101 Peter Baker, *Singing U.S. Praises in Spanish Nothing New*, Fort Worth Star-Telegram, May 5, 2006, at A23.

102 Baker May 5, 2006: A23; Editorial, *Pandering with the Anthem*, Chi. Trib., May 8, 2006, at 22.

103 Address to the Nation on Immigration Reform, 42 Wkly. Comp. Pres. Doc. 931, 934 (May 15, 2006).

104 *See* The Comprehensive Immigration Reform Act, S. 2611, 109th Cong. (2d Sess. 2006).

105 The Comprehensive Immigration Reform Act, S. 4064, 109th Cong. (2006) (amendment to S. 2611), *available at* 152 Cong. Rec. S. 2723–24 (daily ed. May 17, 2006).

106 *Sen. Inhofe to Introduce Official English Amendment in Senate*, U.S. Fed. News, Mar. 30, 2006.

107 152 Cong. Rec. S4686 (daily ed. May 17, 2006).

108 152 Cong. Rec. S4736 (daily ed. May 18, 2006) (statement of Sen. Kyl).

109 152 Cong. Rec. S4686 (daily ed. May 17, 2006).

110 152 Cong. Rec. S4758 (daily ed. May 18, 2006).

than English" under Title VI of the Civil Rights Act, citing several court decisions. Senator Inhofe therefore contended that the amendment's exception for other requirements "provided by law" did not apply.[111] Senator Durbin argued that notwithstanding the contrary statements of some supporters of the Inhofe Amendment, "I believe what he is really aiming for is an Executive Order by President Clinton."[112]

The amendment's supporters admitted that the VRA's language assistance provisions were unaffected, but signaled their intent to repeal those provisions. Senator Inhofe stated, "Maybe it should be changed, but that should take special legislation that addresses the Voting Rights Act."[113] Senator Alexander agreed, noting, "We can have those discussions at another time." He explained, "In my opinion, I don't think there should be [bilingual ballots] because you have to be a citizen to vote and you have to demonstrate an eighth grade understanding of English to be a citizen."[114] Senator Inhofe likewise decried "an entitlement to have the Federal Government provide for language, services, and materials."[115]

Debate on the Inhofe Amendment highlighted a deep ideological divide. Senator Sessions argued that providing government materials and services in languages other than English threatened to tear the country apart.[116] Senator Graham described the Inhofe Amendment as a response to "Mexican flags" in the immigration demonstrations saying, "I am not going to sit on the sidelines and watch demonstrations that destroy national unity."[117] Opponents criticized the amendment as threatening democracy, including the right to vote,[118] failing to provide funding for English language instruction,[119] encouraging constitutional violations,[120] and dividing and stigmatizing non-English speaking Americans denied basic government services.[121] Senator Reid opined, "I really believe this amendment is racist. I think it is directed basically to people who speak Spanish." [122]

The Inhofe Amendment passed the full Senate by a vote of 62 to 35.[123] However, the amendment was substantially diluted by the subsequent passage of an alternative amendment by Senator Ken Salazar of Colorado. The Salazar Amendment declared, "English is the common and unifying language of the United States," and purported "to preserve and enhance the role of the English

111 152 Cong. Rec. S4753–55 (daily ed. May 18, 2006). Senator Inhofe cited Justice Scalia's opinion in *Alexander v. Sandoval*, 532 U.S. 275 (2001), in which the Court held that there was no private cause of action to enforce Executive Order 13166. 152 Cong. Rec. S4753 (daily ed. May 18, 2006).

112 152 Cong. Rec. S4765 (daily ed. May 18, 2006).

113 152 Cong. Rec. S4686 (daily ed. May 17, 2006).

114 152 Cong. Rec. S4736, 4759 (daily ed. May 18, 2006).

115 152 Cong. Rec. S4768 (daily ed. May 18, 2006).

116 152 Cong. Rec. S4736 (daily ed. May 18, 2006).

117 152 Cong. Rec. S4739 (daily ed. May 18, 2006).

118 152 Cong. Rec. S4756–57 (daily ed. May 18, 2006) (statement of Sen. Akaka).

119 152 Cong. Rec. S4758 (daily ed. May 18, 2006) (statement of Sen. Salazar); 152 Cong. Rec. S4763 (daily ed. May 18, 2006) (statement of Sen. Kennedy).

120 152 Cong. Rec. S4760 (daily ed. May 18, 2006) (statement of Sen. Bingaman); 152 Cong. Rec. S4767 (daily ed. May 18, 2006) (statement of Sen. Reid).

121 *See* 152 Cong. Rec. S4756 (daily ed. May 18, 2006) (statement of Sen. Akaka); 152 Cong. Rec. S4762, S4769 (daily ed. May 18, 2006) (statement of Sen. Leahy); 152 Cong. Rec. S4763 (daily ed. May 18, 2006) (statement of Sen. Kennedy); 152 Cong. Rec. S4767 (daily ed. May 18, 2006) (statement of Sen. Reid).

122 152 Cong. Rec. S4766 (daily ed. May 18, 2006).

123 *See* 152 Cong. Rec. S4769–70 (daily ed. May 18, 2006).

language," without making English the national language.[124] Although both amendments failed to become law when the immigration bill died, they were nevertheless problematic. Eleven Democrats crossed party lines to vote for the Inhofe Amendment, including many co-sponsors of the VRARA. Equally troubling, President Bush continued to send mixed messages by expressing support for both amendments while the Attorney General said the President opposed them. Reauthorization appeared to be in trouble.

Hijinks in the House and Slogging in the Senate: the Bill Is Hijacked

That message was not lost on a small group of House Republicans who jumped on the Inhofe Amendment. Representative King argued, "The Senate demonstrated their overwhelming support for English as our official language" and therefore supported his efforts to eliminate Section 203.[125] Emboldened by their Senate victory, opponents of the language assistance provisions formed a coalition with conservative Republicans from Georgia and Texas who opposed reauthorization of Section 5.

Republican Majority Leader John Boehner proposed bringing the VRARA to the House floor for a vote before Memorial Day. His plan quickly evaporated. Part of the delay was because of Boehner's efforts to bring the bill up under suspension of the House rules, which would have barred all amendments and required a two-thirds majority for passage. Boehner used the strategy to facilitate passage of a clean bill without the possibility of divisive amendments that might fracture the fragile coalition. He also recognized it would expedite enactment of the same bicameral bills introduced in the House and the Senate.[126] However, the growing rebellion within the ranks made it impossible to seek suspension of the rules.

Two days before the Senate passed the Inhofe and Salazar amendments, Republican Representative Lynn Westmoreland of Georgia circulated a "Dear Colleague" letter opposing suspension. Westmoreland argued, "We must have the opportunity to consider this important bill under regular order ... because amendments are needed." He contended that the Section 5 trigger needed to be "updated" because it unfairly targeted states such as Georgia.[127] Westmoreland suggested that in place of the existing trigger based upon registration and turnout in the 1960s and 1970s, Section 5 coverage should be determined by "recent elections."[128] Westmoreland participated during Judiciary Committee hearings on the VRARA, even though he was not on the committee. Despite his participation, his proposed amendment was never offered in committee. A separate amendment by Representative Charlie Norwood of Georgia to change the Section 5 trigger also had not been offered. Westmoreland later explained, "A lot of it looks as if these are some old boys from the South who are trying to do away" with the VRA. "But these old boys are trying to make it constitutional enough that it will withstand the scrutiny of the Supreme Court."[129]

---

124 The Comprehensive Immigration Reform Act, S. 4073, 109th Cong., 2d Sess. (2006) (amendment to S. 2611), *available at* 152 Cong. Rec. S. 4761 (daily ed. May 18, 2006).

125 Press Release, Congressman Steve King, King Comments on English as the Official Language Amendment Passes in Senate, May 18, 2006.

126 *Amendment to Voting Rights Act Extension Has Dim Prospects on House Floor*, CQ Today, June 16, 2006.

127 *See VRA Renewal Runs Into Delays*, U.S. Fed. News, May 17, 2006.

128 Seth Stern and Susan Ferrechio, *Not So Fast: Republicans Want Chance to Amend Extension to Voting Rights Act*, CQ Today, May 16, 2006.

129 Carl Hulse, *Rebellion Stalls Extension of Voting Act*, N.Y. Times, June 22, 2006, at A1.

On June 20, 2006, the House Rules Committee took up consideration of the VRARA.[130] Representative King resurrected his amendment to strike the language assistance provisions, arguing that voters should be proficient enough to vote in English. Chairman Sensenbrenner opposed King's efforts, again trying to disentangle the bill from the immigration debate. The Rules Committee agreed with Sensenbrenner and rejected consideration of the King Amendment, which already had been debated and lost during the markup. However, to placate Georgia and Texas Republicans seeking to "get the federal government's foot off our neck," the committee agreed to allow the Norwood and Westmoreland amendments to proceed to the floor.[131] No one was satisfied with this result. Republican Representative Jack Kingston of Georgia derided the rule, stating, "[P]eople are very concerned that we're not having the bilingual ballot issue in there" (Perine June 20, 2006). Democratic Representative Artur Davis of Alabama also criticized the arrangement, asserting, "My preference would have been that it come on suspension. There were good reasons for [leadership] to make that commitment ... instead of accommodating the concerns of a very small group of Members."[132]

The Republican leadership's concessions proved to be insufficient to quell the growing rebellion within their ranks. The next day, King presented Sensenbrenner with a letter signed by 79 Representatives stating that they would not support reauthorization until the language assistance provisions were removed from the bill.[133] During the weekly Republican Conference meeting held in anticipation of the floor vote on the VRARA later that afternoon, things quickly got out of control. A vocal group of the rebels chanted "in unison for the legislation to be dropped from consideration," with cries of "pull the bill, pull the bill."[134] There were at least four reasons for the delay. First, the rebels raised concerns about the *Ashcroft* and *Bossier II* fixes to Section 5 after intense lobbying by Michael Carvin, a Washington lawyer who represented Bossier Parish and wanted to preserve the *Bossier II* ruling permitting intentional discrimination. Second, the group argued that no action should occur on the bill until the Supreme Court issued its opinion in the Texas redistricting case. Third, they were upset that the King Amendment was not included under the rule for the bill. Finally, they were angry about Chairman Sensenbrenner's process for developing the bill.[135]

The rebels posed a significant dilemma for House leadership. Republican leaders applied a rule that no bill would proceed to the floor for a vote without the support of a "majority of the majority."[136] The opposition suggested that leadership might not be able to pass a clean bill after all. If that happened, then they would violate the agreement reached by Chairman Sensenbrenner and Representative Watt, turning a positive issue for the Republican Party into one that could very well cost them the 2006 election. The civil rights community would never forgive them if

---

130 *See* H. Rep. 109–516 at 1–3 (2006); *see also* H.R. 878, 109th Cong. (2006) (providing for the rule).

131 Keith Perine, *House Expected to Pass Bipartisan 25-Year Voting Rights Act Extension*, CQ Today, June 20, 2006; *see* H. Rep. 109–516 (2006).

132 Jennifer Yachnin, *VRA Set for Floor Vote This Week*, Roll Call, June 19, 2006.

133 *See Rep. King Applauds Decision to Give Americans Another Chance to End Bilingual Voting*, U.S. Fed. News, June 21, 2006.

134 Mark Halperin et al., ABC News, *The Note: Strategy of Necessity*, *available at* http://abcnews.go.com/Politics/TheNote/story?id=2110847; 2006 Braintrust.

135 *See* Johanna Neuman, *GOP Halts Extension of Voting Rights Act*, L.A. Times, June 22, 2006, at 9; Charles Babington, *GOP Rebellion Stops Voting Rights Act*, Wash. Post, June 22, 2006, at A7.

136 *See U.S. Representative John Boehner Holds a News Conference*, FDCH Cap. Transcripts, July 13, 2006.

that happened, laying waste to Republican efforts to court African-American and Latino voters. Speaker Hastert and Majority Leader Boehner therefore acceded to the rebels' demands, pulling the bill in hopes of mollifying the rebels with a compromise ensuring passage at a later date. Boehner was noncommittal out of concern that setting the bill's timeframe would "come back and bite me."[137] Instead, Republican leadership issued a joint statement pledging to "offer members the time needed to evaluate the legislation."[138]

The response from the civil rights community and Democrats was tempered by the understanding that attacks on Republican leadership would scuttle reauthorization. Two incidents demonstrated that point. In May 2006, DNC Chair Howard Dean attacked Sensenbrenner for trying to eliminate the VRA's language assistance provisions. Sensenbrenner angrily responded, "It's outrageous that the DNC would attempt to blowup the broad bipartisan support" the VRA enjoyed "by launching false attacks."[139] In June 2006, Democratic congressional candidate John Cranley falsely accused Representative Chabot of trying to "gut" the VRA.[140] Recognition that Sensenbrenner was "sensitive" to being "publicly criticized" kept most of the responses to the setback subdued (Gilbert July 10, 2005: 1). Instead, the bill's supporters depicted the rebels as extremists isolated from their own party. Wade Henderson, Executive Director of LCCR, described them as "a small band of miscreants" who "at the last moment, hijacked this bipartisan, bicameral bill" (Babington June 22, 2006: A7). National Urban League head Marc Morial made similar comments.[141] The VRARA would not be derailed by partisanship, despite the efforts by a small band of House Republicans.

Delays in the House carried over to the Senate, and Senator Specter's commitment to conclude six hearings by mid-May quickly disappeared. In contrast to the industrious House schedule, which held nine hearings in less than one month, the Senate took nearly three months for the same number of hearings. Senator Patrick Leahy, the Democratic manager for the bill in the Senate, described the hearings as plagued "by repeated cancellations and postponements."[142] Conservative senators were behind the delays. Senator Tom Coburn said he would "like to see some changes,"[143] later identified by Senator John Cornyn as the same proposals offered by House rebels. Senator Cornyn also asked Senator Specter to defer markup of the VRARA until after the Texas decision was issued. He subsequently called for a hearing to examine the impact of the case on the bill.

Senator Specter conducted the hearings fairly, readily acceding to requests by conservatives for "an opportunity for a wide variety of witnesses to appear."[144] Twelve of the 46 witnesses who testified in the Senate hearings also testified in the House, with most supplementing evidence already in the extensive House record.

Instead of trying to build a record, conservatives concentrated on calling witnesses opposed to reauthorization. They called the three most conservative members of the U.S. Commission on Civil Rights seeking to eliminate Section 5, Chair Gerald Reynolds, Vice-Chair Abigail Thernstrom (who testified twice), and Peter Kirsanow, without calling the remaining Commission members

---

137 152 Cong. Rec. H4494 (daily ed. June 22, 2006).

138 Laurie Kellman, *GOP Fails to Renew Voting Rights Act*, Orlando Sent., June 22, 2006, at A6.

139 *See Rep. Sensenbrenner Requests Retraction by Chairman Dean for Democratic National Committee's False Attack on his Voting Rights Act Effort*, U.S. Fed. News, May 11, 2006.

140 Michael Collins, Editorial, *Cranley Admits Mistake*, Cin. Post, July 15, 2006, at A14.

141 Hazel Trice Edney, *Voting Rights Act Extension "Hijacked" in Congress*, New Am. Media, June 30, 2006, at 8.

142 152 Cong. Rec. S7745 (daily ed. July 18, 2006).

143 Laurie Kellman, *Senators Set to Vote on Voting Rights Act*, Cin. Post, July 14, 2006, at A7.

144 *An Introduction to the Expiring Provisions of the Voting Rights Act and Legal Issues Relating to Reauthorization*: *Hearing Before the Senate Comm. on the Judiciary*, 109th Cong. at 4 (2006).

who supported it. They called Michael Carvin, who worked with House rebels to stall movement of the VRARA. Others called included Linda Chavez, Chairman of the Center for Equal Opportunity, and Mauro Mujica, Chairman of U.S. English, who vigorously opposed the language assistance provisions, as well as longstanding opponents of Section 5, such as Professor Carol Swain, author of *Black Faces, Black Interests: The Representation of African-Americans in Congress*, and Roger Clegg, General Counsel for the Center for Equal Opportunity.[145] Questions from conservatives demonstrated their hostility towards the Act and the substantial record of discrimination, which they dismissed as mere "anecdotes."[146] Although Senator Specter labored to get the bill out of committee, his conservative staff counsel actively undermined his efforts by working with conservative senators to delay and try to kill the bill. Their efforts were apparent during the Senate floor debate and what followed.

Momentum Shift: Texas, the Stearns Amendment, and Voices from the Past

The pivotal date for reauthorization came on June 28, 2006. The Supreme Court issued its opinion in *LULAC v. Perry*, in which the plaintiffs challenged a mid-decade Texas congressional redistricting plan as an unconstitutional partisan gerrymander and for violating Section 2 of the VRA.[147] The Court rejected the gerrymander claim, but found that the plan diluted the votes of Latinos because of racially polarized voting throughout the state (*LULAC v. Perry* 2006: 2607–23). The Court recognized that the VRA prohibited the elimination of districts where minority voters had an opportunity to elect their preferred candidates, or so-called "opportunity districts," even where minorities were not in the majority. According to the Court, although Latino voters had not elected their candidate of choice in the challenged district, District 23, they were "poised" to do so. In response, the state divided the cohesive Latino community in Webb County, moving 100,000 Latinos into an adjacent "Latino opportunity district" and leaving the others in District 23 where they now had "little hope of electing their candidate of choice" (*LULAC v. Perry* 2006: 2621). Significantly, Chief Justice Roberts and Justices Scalia, Thomas, and Alito concluded that the intentional creation of majority-minority or opportunity districts to comply with Section 5 of the VRA could be a compelling state interest.[148] They strongly implied that a majority of justices would reaffirm the constitutionality of Section 5 where it applied to "jurisdictions with a history of official discrimination" (*LULAC v. Perry* 2006: 2594, 2667). When combined with the majority holding that the Texas plan diluted Latino voting power, the *LULAC* decision was powerful evidence supporting reauthorization.

The Texas victory was bolstered by the decisive defeat of an amendment to the Commerce, State, and Justice (CJS) appropriations bill in the House. Representative Cliff Stearns of Florida proposed cutting off funding for Justice Department enforcement of the language assistance provisions. The amendment provided, "None of the funds made available in this Act may be used to carry out any provision of section 203 of the Voting Rights Act of 1965 …"[149] Supporters of the Stearns Amendment argued that Section 203 divided the nation, discouraged assimilation of

145 *See* S. Rep. 109–295 at 2–4 (2006).

146 *See, e.g., The Continuing Need for Section 5 Pre-Clearance: Hearing before the Senate Comm. on the Judiciary*, 109th Cong., at 98–104 (2006) (written questions to Prof. Pamela Karlan).

147 *LULAC v. Perry*, 126 S.Ct. 2594 (2006).

148 *See LULAC v. Perry* 2006: 2667 (Scalia, J., concurring in part and dissenting in part).

149 *See* Science, State, Justice, Commerce, and Related Agencies Appropriations Act for FY 2007, H.R. 1145, 109th Cong. (2006) (amendment to H.R. 5672).

immigrants, and violated the states' rights to conduct their elections.[150] However, they overplayed their hand. Stearns conceded, "If one faces a language barrier to voting, then I suspect that he or she is secluded from enjoying all the full rights and privileges of democracy in the United States."[151] King acknowledged that the amendment was a backdoor attempt to eliminate the language assistance provisions,[152] noting, "It ends the Federal foreign language mandate, at least for a year."[153] In short, the amendment was a referendum on reauthorization of the VRA and the continuing need for the Act's protections.

A unified bipartisan group, led by Republican Representative Lincoln Diaz-Balart, urged that immigration be removed from the debate on Section 203.[154] Representative John Lewis seized on Stearns' admission saying, "These are our neighbors. They are taxpayers. They are Americans. We should be opening up the process to each and every American. Let them come in and participate."[155] Representative Mike Honda likewise observed that the Stearns Amendment "would undermine the Voting Rights Act reauthorization process and effectively disenfranchise language minority voters through the appropriations process."[156] House members responded to their pleas, defeating the Stearns Amendment 254 to 167.[157]

The House rebels had suffered two defeats from which they would not recover. There was no longer any reason for House leadership to delay a vote because of the Texas decision. Furthermore, *LULAC* strongly supported the VRA's constitutionality. Additionally, the vote against the Stearns Amendment was the fourth time that the House had repudiated English-only efforts, following three prior defeats during the House markup of the VRARA. House leadership could adopt a more open-ended rule to allow a floor vote on the King Amendment, with some confidence that it would fail. There was no longer any reason to delay.

Moreover, Republican leadership was under increasing pressure to get the VRARA back on track. Newspapers in Georgia and Texas, home to the rebels, called for immediate passage. Corporations, including Coca-Cola, Disney, and Wal-Mart, among many others, followed suit. Leading Republicans joined in, along with civil rights leaders. Sensenbrenner authored an op-ed with LCCR Executive Director Wade Henderson calling for extension of Section 5 "and other key protections of the VRA for another 25 years."[158] The most powerful message came from Luci Baines Johnson and Lynda Johnson Robb, the daughters of President Lyndon Johnson, who signed the VRA into law in August 1965. They observed, "In his own era, our father faced powerful opposition to the Voting Rights Act, including from members of his own party. Nevertheless,

150 *See* 152 Cong. Rec. H4744 (daily ed. June 28, 2006) (statement of Rep. Stearns); 152 Cong. Rec. H4746 (daily ed. June 28, 2006) (statement of Rep. Rohrabacher); 152 Cong. Rec. H4746 (daily ed. June 28, 2006) (statement of Rep. King).

151 152 Cong. Rec. H4744 (daily ed. June 28, 2006).

152 *See* Seth Stern, *Second Markup Fails to Revive Bill Barring Constitutional Challenges to Pledge*, C.Q. Today, June 29, 2006, *available at* 2006 WLNR 11541668.

153 152 Cong. Rec. H4746 (daily ed. June 28, 2006).

154 *See, e.g.*, 152 Cong. Rec. H4744–45 (daily ed. June 28, 2006) (statement of Rep. Diaz-Balart); 152 Cong. Rec. H4746 (daily ed. June 28, 2006) (statement of Rep. Scott); 152 Cong. Rec. H4746 (daily ed. June 28, 2006) (statement of Rep. Sanchez).

155 152 Cong. Rec. H4745 (daily ed. June 28, 2006).

156 152 Cong. Rec. H4748 (daily ed. June 28, 2006).

157 *See* Science, State, Justice, Commerce, and Related Agencies Appropriations Act for FY 2007, H.R. 1145, 109th Cong. (2006) (amendment to H.R. 5672); *see also* 152 Cong. Rec. H4664 (daily ed. June 27, 2006) (reporting the vote on the Stearns Amendment).

158 Representative James Sensenbrenner and Wade Henderson, *Protecting Rights*, Roll Call, June 21, 2006.

he pushed forward with the legislation because he knew it was desperately needed. It was the right thing to do then. It still is."[159] With the weight of history against the rebels and all eyes on Washington, Republican leadership had to act quickly to get the bill to the House floor.

That would present some challenges. On June 29, 2006, intense lobbying by Michael Carvin at a meeting of the Republican Conference succeeded in confusing members about the Court's *LULAC* decision and the impact it had on the bill's *Ashcroft* fix. Mark Braden, who represented a group of interveners in the *Ashcroft* litigation, strongly disagreed with Carvin's conclusions. Majority Leader Boehner explained:

> The Texas case ... didn't have any direct impact on the reauthorization of the Voting Rights Act, but it has raised some questions ... And at least as of this morning, the confusion over the language over influence districts has escalated, because there are lawyers on both sides of this issue—Republican lawyers on both sides of this issue who have differing opinions as to what it means, the language in the Voting Rights Act.[160]

Despite a quarter-century under the pre-*Ashcroft* standard, the House rebels claimed they were confused over the VRARA's clarification that Section 5 protected "the ability of such [minority] citizens to elect their preferred candidates of choice."[161]

On July 11, 2006, Republican leaders met again with their rank-and-file in a heated two-hour meeting. Two weeks of wrangling over the issue had done nothing to placate the rebels. As one senior leadership aide observed, "[T]here are a lot of people who don't agree with how to remedy this." Representative Watt was incensed with this latest delay saying, "Now it sounds like Republicans would like to get some political advantage out of this. They think this doesn't benefit them in some way." Boehner was discouraged with the "complete disagreement" in the Conference (Ferrechio July 11, 2006). He and other Republican leaders discussed several alternatives to get the bill to the floor. One compromise was to keep the bill's language intact, but shorten the reauthorization from 25 years to six years. Another proposal would have an open rule on the bill, which would lead to a free-for-all permitting numerous amendments to be offered. There was a sense of urgency to bring the bill to the floor before thousands of members of the NAACP converged on Washington for their annual convention at the end of the week.

Republican leadership decided to stop the rebellion in its tracks. On July 12, 2006, the House Rules Committee again took up consideration of the VRARA.[162] Some concessions were made to the Republican dissidents, with a broader range of amendments allowed to come to the floor. The Norwood and Westmoreland amendments under the original rule were included in the new rule. In addition, the rule included consideration of an amendment by Representative Louie Gohmert of Texas to limit reauthorization of the VRA's temporary provisions to ten years. To placate the vocal contingent of English-only Republicans, Representative King's amendment to strike the language assistance provisions from the bill also would be considered.

Democrats were upset by the expanded rule, with Representative Lewis decrying it as "a big surprise" and "a step backwards." Representative James McGovern called the amendments "poison

159 *See* Luci Baines Johnson and Lynda Johnson Robb, *Don't Dismantle the Voting Rights Act*, N.Y. Times, July 7, 2006, at A17.

160 *U.S. Representative John Boehner Holds a News Conference*, FDCH Cap. Transcripts, June 29, 2006.

161 VRARA § 5, *enacted as* Pub. L. No. 109–246 § 5, 120 Stat. 581; *see* Susan Ferrechio, *Another Set of Meetings for Another Try at Voting Rights Act Reauthorization*, C.Q. Today, July 11, 2006.

162 *See* H.R. Rep. 109–554 (2006); *see also* H.R. 910, 109th Cong. (2006) (providing for the rule).

pills" and asserted that allowing votes on them threatened the "careful bipartisan coalition."[163] House Minority Leader Nancy Pelosi agreed. She maintained that the bipartisan agreement was "not being honored" and that "Democrats would not be able to vote for the bill if any one of those amendments is passed."[164] There would be a lively floor debate on the VRARA after all.

Passage of a Clean House Bill with No Amendments

For several months, the Bush Administration expressed general support for renewing the VRA, without any firm commitment of whether it supported the House bill. That commitment finally came the morning of the House floor vote on July 13, 2006. The White House issued a Statement of Administration Policy (SAP) stating, "The Administration is strongly committed to renewing the Voting Rights Act, and therefore supports passage of H.R. 9." The Administration explicitly rejected the seeds of division the House rebels were trying to plant on the fixes to Section 5. The SAP continued, "The Administration supports the legislative intent of H.R. 9 to overturn the U.S. Supreme Court's 2003 decision in *Georgia v. Ashcroft* and its 2000 decision in *Reno v. Bossier Parish School Board*."[165] President Bush's unambiguous statement deflated the hopes of the House rebels.

Three common themes quickly emerged during a floor debate "punctuated by shouting matches between white Republicans and black Democrats from Georgia."[166] First, there was strong bipartisan support for the VRARA.[167] Speakers from both parties commended Chairman Sensenbrenner, Representative Chabot, Representative Conyers, and Representative Watt for their substantial work to achieve a compromise bill.[168] The House Tri-Caucus, which includes the CBC, CHC, and the Congressional Asian Pacific American Caucus (CAPAC), spoke with a single voice in favor of a clean bill free of any amendments.[169] A coalition of leading governmental organizations including the Council of State Governments, the National Conference of State Legislatures, the National Association of Secretaries of State, the National Association of Counties, the National League of Cities, and the U.S. Conference of Mayors, urged swift reauthorization.[170] Republican and former

---

163 Basil Talbott, *Rules Panel Allows More Amendments to Voting Rights Act*, Congress Daily, July 13, 2006.

164 *U.S. Representative Nancy Pelosi Holds a News Conference*, FDCH Cap. Transcripts, July 13, 2006.

165 Executive Office of the President, *Statement of Administration Policy: H.R. 9 – Fannie Lou Hamer, Rosa Parks, and Coretta Scott King Voting Rights Act Reauthorization and Amendments Act of 2006* (July 13, 2006); *see also* 152 Cong. Rec. H5144 (daily ed. July 13, 2006) (providing a copy of the SAP introduced during the House floor debate).

166 Bob Kemper, *Voting Act Ok'd in Tense House*, Atlanta J. & Const., July 14, 2006, at A1.

167 *See, e.g.*, 152 Cong. Rec. H5143–44 (daily ed. July 13, 2006) (statement of Rep. Sensenbrenner); 152 Cong. Rec. H5162 (daily ed. July 13, 2006) (statement of Rep. Pelosi).

168 *See, e.g.*, 152 Cong. Rec. H5135 (daily ed. July 13, 2006) (statement of Rep. Hoyer); 152 Cong. Rec. H5146 (daily ed. July 13, 2006) (statement of Rep. Conyers); 152 Cong. Rec. H5147–48 (daily ed. July 13, 2006) (statement of Rep. Watt); 152 Cong. Rec. H5162 (daily ed. July 13, 2006) (statement of Rep. Pelosi); 152 Cong. Rec. H5165 (daily ed. July 13, 2006) (statement of Rep. Sensenbrenner).

169 *See, e.g.*, 152 Cong. Rec. H5135 (daily ed. July 13, 2006) (statement of Rep. Hoyer); 152 Cong. Rec. H5152 (daily ed. July 13, 2006) (statement of Rep. Napolitano); 152 Cong. Rec. H5152 (daily ed. July 13, 2006) (statement of Rep. Sanchez).

170 *See* 152 Cong. Rec. H5146 (daily ed. July 13, 2006).

Representative J.C. Watts did the same.[171] As Representative Corrine Brown of Florida explained, "That says it all. Bipartisan support. Democrats, Republicans, and the Administration. This is an American bill."[172]

The bill's supporters also invoked the history of discrimination against minorities. Watt described how he stood "on the shoulders" of George H. White, the last African-American elected to Congress after Reconstruction, who lost his election in 1900 through disenfranchisement of Black voters. He noted that it took nearly 30 years following passage of the VRA for African-Americans to be elected to Congress again in North Carolina. Watt concluded, "The successes have been gradual and of very recent origin."[173] John Lewis, "the conscience of the Congress,"[174] poignantly described the evidence underlying the VRA. He noted, "[A]ll across the American South very few African-Americans were registered to vote ... In Lowndes County, Alabama, more than 80 percent of that county was African-American, but not a single African-American was registered to vote." According to Representative Lewis,

> We cannot separate the debate today from our history and the past we have traveled. When we marched from Selma to Montgomery in 1965, it was dangerous. It was a matter of life and death. I was beaten, I had a concussion at the bridge. I almost died. I gave my blood, but some of my colleagues gave their very lives.[175]

Representative Conyers explained, "[W]e have to remember one historical fact. For 400 years, we have been dealing with the problem of discrimination and racism in America. I think it would

Figure 7.2 Congressman Mel Watt (D, NC-12)
Source: Photo courtesy of Debo Adegbile, Director of Litigation, NAACP Legal Defense Fund.

171 152 Cong. Rec. H5146 (daily ed. July 13, 2006) (letter from J.C. Watts to Chairman Sensenbrenner dated June 21, 2006).

172 152 Cong. Rec. H5190 (daily ed. July 13, 2006).

173 152 Cong. Rec. H5148 (daily ed. July 13, 2006).

174 152 Cong. Rec. H5162 (daily ed. July 13, 2006) (statement of Rep. Pelosi).

175 152 Cong. Rec. H5164 (daily ed. July 13, 2006).

be simplistic ... that we would think, after 40 years, we do not need to worry about it that much anymore."[176]

The Act's history showed that despite progress, the special provisions were still needed. The bill's supporters focused on recent voting discrimination in Georgia and Texas, home to most of the Republican dissidents. Several members described the discriminatory voter identification requirements in Georgia, which a federal court had struck down.[177] Others referred to the discriminatory Texas redistricting plan struck down by *LULAC*[178] and the VRA's success in stopping the blanket rejection of voter registration applications from Black students at Prairie View A&M.[179] Representative Scott pointed out that since the 1982 reauthorization, Georgia had at least 83 Section 5 objections by the Justice Department, 38 discriminatory voting changes withdrawn after it became clear there would be an objection, 17 successful Section 5 enforcement actions, and the deployment of federal observers on at least 55 occasions.[180] Chairman Sensenbrenner noted that Texas had at least 105 Section 5 objections since 1982, along with 14 Section 5 submissions that had been withdrawn since 2002 because they were discriminatory.[181] There were more Section 5 objections between 1982 and 2005 than there had been between 1965 and 1982.[182] Recent examples of voting discrimination from the rebels' own states sent a powerful message.

Chairman Sensenbrenner and his staff whipped the Republican rank-and-file to do "the right thing" and support a clean bill without amendments[183] after Majority Whip Roy Blunt of Missouri defected to side with the House rebels.[184] Sensenbrenner attempted to diffuse lingering doubts of southern conservatives about the *Ashcroft* fix. He first engaged in a colloquy with Representative Price of Georgia to clarify that "nothing in this legislation should be construed to allow the Supreme Court to say who is or who is not a minority community's candidate of choice simply because of a candidate's party affiliation."[185] Sensenbrenner subsequently engaged in a similar colloquy with Watt to confirm that determination of the retrogression standard was to be made "without consideration of political party control," and that the bill restored the pre-*Ashcroft* standard articulated in *Beer v. United States*.[186] Despite these clear statements, Representative John Shadegg continued to protest that the *Ashcroft* fix potentially would require "that a minority candidate must be of a particular party."[187]

---

176 152 Cong. Rec. H5189 (daily ed. July 13, 2006).

177 *See, e.g.*, 152 Cong. Rec. H5141 (daily ed. July 13, 2006) (statement of Rep. Jones); 152 Cong. Rec. H5141 (daily ed. July 13, 2006) (statement of Rep. Scott).

178 *See, e.g.*, 152 Cong. Rec. H5137 (daily ed. July 13, 2006) (statement of Rep. Doggett); 152 Cong. Rec. H5167 (daily ed. July 13, 2006) (statement of Rep. Roybal-Allard); 152 Cong. Rec. H5167 (daily ed. July 13, 2006) (statement of Rep. Blumenauer); 152 Cong. Rec. H5173 (daily ed. July 13, 2006) (statement of Rep. Serrano); 152 Cong. Rec. H5174 (daily ed. July 13, 2006) (statement of Rep. Ortiz).

179 *See* 152 Cong. Rec. H5161–62 (daily ed. July 13, 2006) (statement of Rep. Johnson).

180 152 Cong. Rec. H5151 (daily ed. July 13, 2006).

181 *See* 152 Cong. Rec. H5164–65 (daily ed. July 13, 2006).

182 *See* 152 Cong. Rec. H5160 (daily ed. July 13, 2006) (statement of Rep. Van Hollen).

183 152 Cong. Rec. H5165 (daily ed. July 13, 2006) (statement of Rep. Sensenbrenner).

184 Representative Blunt voted in favor of all four amendments to the VRARA offered by the dissident Republicans. *See* 152 Cong. Rec. H5204–07 (daily ed. July 13, 2006).

185 152 Cong. Rec. H5160 (daily ed. July 13, 2006) (colloquy between Reps. Price and Sensenbrenner).

186 152 Cong. Rec. H5163 (daily ed. July 13, 2006) (colloquy between Reps. Sensenbrenner and Watt).

187 152 Cong. Rec. H5166 (daily ed. July 13, 2006).

The debate on the four amendments proved contentious. Representative Norwood first offered his amendment, which would alter the Section 5 coverage formula to use a voter registration and turnout "rolling test based off of the last three presidential elections,"[188] in place of the 1964, 1968, and 1972 presidential elections.[189] Representative Phil Gingrey of Georgia claimed that "a lot has changed in 40-plus years" requiring "a law that fits the world of 2006" to ensure Section 5's constitutionality.[190] The amendment's supporters argued that Georgia was different, illustrated by improved Black voter registration and turnout rates and Representative Lewis's statements in his *Ashcroft* affidavit.[191] Representative Norwood decried that Georgia had been "put in the penalty box of Section 5" under "the heavy hand of the Justice Department." He said his modified coverage formula would ensure that Section 5 applied nationwide, so "whether you are from Tennessee, whether you are from Wisconsin, [you] have the same equal rights that minorities in Georgia have." According to Representative Norwood, his amendment would result in Section 5 coverage in 1,010 jurisdictions in 39 states. The coverage formula in the Norwood Amendment was devised, at least in part, by Ronald Keith Gaddie, a political science professor at the University of Oklahoma.[192] Representative Linder concluded, "[I]f this Voting Rights Act is good for Georgia and the 15 other states, it ought to be wonderful for the country."[193]

Sensenbrenner responded forcefully, "The amendment not only guts the bill, but turns the Voting Rights Act into a farce." Under the Norwood Amendment, only Glacier County would be covered in Montana, despite evidence of voting discrimination against American Indians in other counties.[194] Additionally, Hawaii, which had no history of voting discrimination against minorities and had some state protections for non-English languages even before the enactment of Section 203 (Chapter 2), would become the only state covered in its entirety by Section 5.[195] Sensenbrenner explained that these results occurred because the amendment was based upon "the constitutional flaw" that Section 5 coverage was determined "exclusively on voter participation, and not on any other factors." It ignored "the past history of discrimination and discriminatory voting practices."[196] The Chairman also observed that the existing Section 5 trigger had been upheld by the Supreme Court three times, including as recently as 1999.[197] According to Representative Watt, the Norwood Amendment merely resurrected previous efforts by southerners to render the Section 5 coverage formula unconstitutional.[198] The House rejected the Norwood Amendment by the widest margin of all the amendments, 318 to 96.[199]

---

188 H. Rep. 109–554 at 2 (2006) (providing the language for the Norwood Amendment).

189 *See* 42 U.S.C. § 1973b(b) (2006).

190 152 Cong. Rec. H5135 (daily ed. July 13, 2006).

191 *See, e.g.*, 152 Cong. Rec. H5135, H5151–52, 5184 (daily ed. July 13, 2006) (statement of Rep. Gingrey); 152 Cong. Rec. H5184 (daily ed. July 13, 2006) (statement of Rep. Deal); 152 Cong. Rec. H5185 (daily ed. July 13, 2006) (statement of Rep. Gohmert); 152 Cong. Rec. H5187 (daily ed. July 13, 2006) (statement of Rep. Westmoreland).

192 *See* 152 Cong. Rec. H5140, H5153, H5179–81 (daily ed. July 13, 2006).

193 152 Cong. Rec. H5183 (daily ed. July 13, 2006).

194 152 Cong. Rec. H5181 (daily ed. July 13, 2006).

195 *See* 152 Cong. Rec. H5179–80 (daily ed. July 13, 2006) (depicting coverage under the Norwood Amendment); 152 Cong. Rec. H5184 (daily ed. July 13, 2006) (statement of Rep. Sensenbrenner); 152 Cong. Rec. H5175–76, H5184 (daily ed. July 13, 2006) (statement of Rep. Case).

196 152 Cong. Rec. H5185 (daily ed. July 13, 2006) (statement of Rep. Sensenbrenner); *see also* 152 Cong. Rec. H5183 (daily ed. July 13, 2006) (statement of Rep. Chabot) (making a similar argument).

197 152 Cong. Rec. H5161 (daily ed. July 13, 2006).

198 152 Cong. Rec. H5182 (daily ed. July 13, 2006).

199 *See* 152 Cong. Rec. H5204 (daily ed. July 13, 2006).

Representative Gohmert of Texas next introduced an amendment to limit reauthorization of the VRA until 2016.[200] He explained, "Congress was getting a little more lazy in their obligation to continually monitor this act," when there was "empirical evidence" showing the Act had to be reviewed more often.[201] Representative Dan Lungren concurred, saying the amendment would "save" the VRA from being struck down.[202] Chairman Sensenbrenner disagreed, citing the number of Section 5 objections since 1982. He maintained that it would deny Congress sufficient data to consider the continuing need for Section 5 when it expired. Chairman Sensenbrenner further contended the nine-year reauthorization would nullify the incentive for jurisdictions to have a clean record for 10 years to be eligible for bailout.[203] Representative Chabot explained that the hearing process was time-consuming and developed a substantial record supporting a 25-year reauthorization.[204] Representative Watt elaborated, observing that the Supreme Court had upheld similar time frames for actions to remedy discrimination.[205] The Gohmert Amendment was defeated 288 to 134, though it was the only one of the four amendments that Majority Leader Boehner supported.[206]

The King Amendment, identical to the one defeated in the committee markup,[207] proved the most divisive. Representative King argued that to "improve" the VRA, it was necessary to "lift the Federal mandate imposing foreign language ballots on localities by allowing [the mandate] to sunset." He asserted that naturalized citizens "have no claim to a foreign language ballot" because they were required to demonstrate English proficiency, and that LEP native-born citizens could bring an interpreter with them.[208] Supporters of the King Amendment decried the Census definition of LEP persons and methods such as surname analysis and outreach used to target language assistance.[209] They contended that as a result of "flawed" data, bilingual ballots and other translated election materials were unused at great expense to covered jurisdictions.[210] Although Representative King denied the amendment was an immigration measure,[211] his supporters disagreed, saying it was necessary to ensure "that all of these immigrants learn to speak English"[212] and would help immigrants "to assimilate in our melting pot, truly to become Americans."[213]

Sensenbrenner responded by stating, "[W]e are dealing with United States citizens. Illegal immigrants ... are not eligible to vote." He added, "According to the 2000 Census, most of the people who are potential beneficiaries of section 203 assistance are native-born legal citizens" who were illiterate because of educational discrimination and lack of opportunities to learn English. The Chairman cited Supervisor Norby's testimony that ballot complexities required greater English

200 H. Rep. 109–554 at 2–4 (2006) (providing the language for the Gohmert Amendment).

201 152 Cong. Rec. H5186 (daily ed. July 13, 2006).

202 152 Cong. Rec. H5189 (daily ed. July 13, 2006).

203 152 Cong. Rec. H5190–91 (daily ed. July 13, 2006).

204 152 Cong. Rec. H5188 (daily ed. July 13, 2006).

205 152 Cong. Rec. H5188 (daily ed. July 13, 2006).

206 152 Cong. Rec. H5205, 5204, 5206 (daily ed. July 13, 2006).

207 *See* H. Rep. 109–554 at 2, 4 (2006) (providing the language for the King Amendment).

208 152 Cong. Rec. H5191 (daily ed. July 13, 2006).

209 *See* 152 Cong. Rec. H5191–93 (daily ed. July 13, 2006) (statement of Rep. King); 152 Cong. Rec. H5192 (daily ed. July 13, 2006) (statement of Rep. Gingrey); 152 Cong. Rec. H5197 (daily ed. July 13, 2006) (statement of Rep. Miller).

210 *See* 152 Cong. Rec. H5192 (daily ed. July 13, 2006) (statement of Rep. Gingrey); 152 Cong. Rec. H5193 (daily ed. July 13, 2006) (statement of Rep. Campbell).

211 *See* 152 Cong. Rec. H5192–93 (daily ed. July 13, 2006).

212 152 Cong. Rec. H5195–96 (daily ed. July 13, 2006) (statement of Rep. Stearns).

213 152 Cong. Rec. H5194 (daily ed. July 13, 2006) (statement of Rep. Istook).

proficiency than many Americans had mastered. He argued that eliminating Section 203 would eliminate the "incentive" jurisdictions had to be removed from coverage by teaching LEP citizens "how to read English." Bringing assistance to the polls was "not feasible" for millions of Americans who lived in linguistically isolated households. Citing strong support for language assistance in voting, Chairman Sensenbrenner further reminded members, "2 weeks ago ... the House soundly rejected on a bipartisan basis ... an effort to defund ... efforts to enforce Section 203."[214]

The Chairman was not alone in his past ambivalence towards the language assistance provisions,[215] which divided Republicans more than other amendments. The King Amendment's strongest supporters came from three groups of Republicans: members from the heartland;[216] California members from Orange County,[217] home to Supervisor Norby; and southern dissidents.[218]

Several Republicans opposed the amendment. Representative Lincoln Diaz-Balart observed that the language assistance provisions benefited voters in Florida.[219] Representative Christopher Shays stated, "These are American citizens who own the right to vote, but may need the assistance provided in Section 203."[220] Representative Shadegg, who supported the other three "poison pill" amendments[221] explained, "Whether an individual is Hispanic, Navajo, or any other background, [they] should be able to seek help when it comes to casting their vote."[222] Representative Mike Pence flatly rejected efforts to tie Section 203 to cultural assimilation arguing, "[L]anguage requirements belong in immigration law, not in the ballot box."[223] Reflecting the deep ideological divide among Republicans, the King Amendment failed 238 to 185. A total of 181 Republicans and four Democrats voted in favor of the King Amendment, compared to 193 Democrats, 44 Republicans, and one Independent who voted against it.[224]

Finally, Representative Westmoreland offered an amendment "for an expedited, proactive procedure" for jurisdictions to bail out from coverage under Section 5. The Westmoreland Amendment required that, within three years, the Justice Department begin an annual review of "jurisdictions eligible for bailout," notify them, and "consent to entry of a declaratory judgment

214 152 Cong. Rec. H5191–92, 5197–98 (daily ed. July 13, 2006).

215 *See generally* 152 Cong. Rec. H5200–01 (daily ed. July 13, 2006) (statement of Rep. Norwood) ("Mr. Chairman, in 1982 you voted against section 203. Today you are promoting section 203. You are against the King amendment. What happened?").

216 *See* 152 Cong. Rec. H5165 (daily ed. July 13, 2006) (statement of Rep. Paul); 152 Cong. Rec. H5194 (daily ed. July 13, 2006) (statement of Rep. Istook).

217 *See* 152 Cong. Rec. H5193 (daily ed. July 13, 2006) (statement of Rep. Campbell); 152 Cong. Rec. H5197 (daily ed. July 13, 2006) (statement of Rep. Miller); 152 Cong. Rec. H5196 (daily ed. July 13, 2006) (statement of Rep. Rohrabacher). Representative David Dreier, who represented parts of Los Angeles and San Bernardino Counties, joined the Orange County Republicans in supporting the King Amendment. *See* 152 Cong. Rec. H5142 (daily ed. July 13, 2006) (statement of Rep. Dreier).

218 *See* 152 Cong. Rec. H5192, H5201 (daily ed. July 13, 2006) (statement of Rep. Gingrey); 152 Cong. Rec. H5194 (daily ed. July 13, 2006) (statement of Rep. Brown-Waite); 152 Cong. Rec. H5195 (daily ed. July 13, 2006) (statement of Rep. Stearns); 152 Cong. Rec. H5200–01 (daily ed. July 13, 2006) (statement of Rep. Norwood).

219 *See* 152 Cong. Rec. H5133 (daily ed. July 13, 2006).

220 152 Cong. Rec. H5137 (daily ed. July 13, 2006).

221 *See* 152 Cong. Rec. H5166, 5207, 5204–07 (daily ed. July 13, 2006).

222 152 Cong. Rec. H5166 (daily ed. July 13, 2006).

223 152 Cong. Rec. H5194 (daily ed. July 13, 2006).

224 152 Cong. Rec. H5205–06 (daily ed. July 13, 2006).

allowing bailout."[225] Westmoreland claimed his amendment would "help save" the VRA,[226] although he previously stated he would "feel fine" if Section 5 were eliminated.[227] He claimed the existing bailout procedure was too onerous, and that some liberal law professors believed it needed to be amended.[228] Chairman Sensenbrenner criticized the proposal as "the worst amendment," saying tongue-in-cheek that "the liberal law professors that instructed me at ... law school about 40 years ago did not make very much impact then." He explained, "It would redirect limited resources away from voting rights enforcement, give the executive branch unprecedented and unfettered authority to remove crucial voting rights protections ... and impermissibly lock an executive branch agency into a litigation position."[229] Representative Chabot elaborated that the amendment "would render the Department of Justice ineffective in performing any of its responsibilities" under the VRA.[230] The Westmoreland Amendment was defeated 302 to 118.[231]

The House enacted the VRARA, 390 to 33. In the process, the vote exposed the roots of the Republican dissidents, with all but three coming from states covered in whole or in part by Section 5 or Section 203, led by six members each from California, Georgia, and Texas.[232] Although the dissenters were intent on rendering the VRA unconstitutional, their actions had the opposite effect. By debating a variety of amendments to the Act, they made it more likely it would be upheld through a very detailed record. They also galvanized Republican leadership, which praised reauthorization of the VRA and encouraged swift passage by the Senate.[233]

The Political End Game: the NAACP Convention and Senate Markup

The House floor vote came just days before the NAACP's convention in Washington. For months, RNC Chairman Ken Mehlman had been pleading with President Bush to speak at the convention, after refusing invitations. Mehlman's request was part of his efforts to reach out to Black voters (Nagourney Sept. 24, 2006: 36). The President relented after days of "ambivalence" about the Act following the House vote.[234] However, he could not commit to appearing while the Senate passage of the bill was still in doubt. Republicans also did not want to face the fury of thousands of NAACP members converging on the Capitol. President Bush's efforts to get movement in the Senate were bolstered by the House passage of a clean bill. Following the vote, the Senate bill finally had support from a majority of senators. On July 13, 2006, 51 senators joined Senator Specter in supporting the bill, with six more senators signing on as co-sponsors before final passage.[235]

---

225 *See* H. Rep. 109–554 at 2, 4 (2006) (providing the language for the Westmoreland Amendment).

226 152 Cong. Rec. H5198 (daily ed. July 13, 2006).

227 Peter Wallsten and Johanna Neuman, *Voting Rights Act Renewal Divides GOP*, L.A. Times, July 12, 2006, at 15.

228 152 Cong. Rec. H5198–5200, H5204 (daily ed. July 13, 2006).

229 152 Cong. Rec. H5200, H5204 (daily ed. July 13, 2006).

230 152 Cong. Rec. H5201 (daily ed. July 13, 2006).

231 *See* 152 Cong. Rec. H5206–07 (daily ed. July 13, 2006).

232 *See* 152 Cong. Rec. H5207 (daily ed. July 13, 2006).

233 *See Speaker Hastert Comments on Reauthorization of Voting Rights Act*, U.S. Fed. News, July 13, 2006; *Rep. Boehner Issues Statement on House Passage of Voting Rights Act*, U.S. Fed. News, July 13, 2006; *Republican National Committee Chairman Mehlman Issues Statement on House Vote to Renew the Voting Rights Act*, U.S. Fed. News, July 13, 2006.

234 Seth Stern, *Senate Clears Voting Rights Extension*, C.Q. Wkly., July 24, 2006, at 2038.

235 *See* S. 2703, 109th Cong. (2006), *available at* The Library of Congress, Thomas, http://thomas.loc.gov.

On July 19, 2006, the Senate Judiciary Committee marked up the bill after Senator Specter persuaded Senate Majority Leader Bill Frist to go through regular order. Specter said he made the request "to ensure a full record in case of court challenges later" (Stern July 24, 2006: 2039). Senator Leahy offered a technical amendment to add the name of César E. Chávez to the bill's title, which was accepted by voice vote. The amendment was later dropped from the final bill, when the Senate passed H.R. 9 as the House had enacted it.

Senator Coburn offered an amendment to change the definition of "limited-English proficient" to include only persons who speak English "not well" or "not at all," (S. Rep. No. 109–295, 2006: 4). The amendment would have further narrowed the definition added in 1982 by Senator Don Nickles of Oklahoma to restrict the scope of Section 203 coverage, reducing that coverage by more than two-thirds. The Senate Judiciary Committee rejected the Coburn Amendment by voice vote (Chapter 4). Senator Coburn planned to offer two additional amendments, but refrained when it became apparent they would not pass. He indicated the amendments would have limited VRA reauthorization to seven years and required photo identification in federal elections.[236] Senator Sessions expressed the Committee's sentiment for a clean bill saying, "[T]here's no interest in the Senate in making amendments to the House version."[237] The bill was reported favorably out of committee 18 to 0 (S. Rep. No. 109–295, 2006: 4).

On July 20, 2006, the Senate debate on the VRARA began. That morning, President Bush spoke at the NAACP convention. He recognized the event "as a moment of opportunity." He noted, "[M]any African Americans distrust my political party." The President thanked the House for reauthorizing the VRA saying, "Soon the Senate will take up the legislation. I look forward to the Senate passing this bill promptly, without amendment, so I can sign it into law."[238] Later, the President issued a statement describing the Act as "one of the most important pieces of legislation in our Nation's history" to allow millions of Americans to "enjoy the full promise of freedom."[239] The struggle to get a clean bill through both houses of Congress was concluding. And the NAACP played a key role at the beginning and end of reauthorization, as several senators acknowledged.[240]

Final Senate Passage and the Bill-Signing

The Senate debate was characterized by conservatives trying to undermine the constitutionality of Section 5 despite their expressed support for the bill. Senator Specter emphasized his efforts "to compile a very extensive record in order to avoid having the act declared unconstitutional" through nine hearings with 46 witnesses that built on the 12 House hearings.[241] Senator Cornyn acknowledged that Senator Specter readily acceded "to requests that were made to have a complete

236 *See* 152 Cong. Rec. S7989 (daily ed. July 20, 2006).

237 Seth Stern, *Voting Rights Act Renewal Advances in Committee*, CQ Comm. Coverage, July 19, 2006.

238 President's Remarks at the NAACP Annual Convention, 42 Wkly. Comp. Pres. Doc. 1366–67, 1371 (July 20, 2006).

239 President's Statement on Legislation to Reauthorize the Voting Rights Act, 42 Wkly. Comp. Pres. Doc. 1366 (July 20, 2006).

240 *See, e.g.*, 152 Cong. Rec. S7964 (daily ed. July 20, 2006) (statement of Sen. Leahy); 152 Cong. Rec. S7975 (daily ed. July 20, 2006) (statement of Sen. McConnell); 152 Cong. Rec. S7976 (daily ed. July 20, 2006) (statement of Sen. Pryor); 152 Cong. Rec. S7999 (daily ed. July 20, 2006) (statement of Sen. Dodd); 152 Cong. Rec. S8003 (daily ed. July 20, 2006) (statement of Sen. Lieberman).

241 152 Cong. Rec. S7950 (daily ed. July 20, 2006).

record" through "a sufficient number of fair and balanced hearings." Yet, he argued that the "act's language was a bit of a foregone conclusion" that precluded a "serious, reasoned deliberation over some of the suggested possible improvements."[242] Senator Coburn went further, criticizing the hearings as characterized by "political fear and perceived intimidation" that prevented consideration of amendments.[243] Democratic senators disagreed, emphasizing the depth of the record and the bipartisan way in which the hearings were conducted.[244] Senator Durbin explained that the hearings "were contentious. People were debating whether we needed a Voting Rights Act or whether this was some vestige of America's past which had no relevance today."[245]

Like the House rebels, a few Senate Republicans attacked Section 5. Senator Specter described a "different America" with a "different political reality." He attempted to substitute his conservative staff's politicized characterizations for the record, which he claimed showed "discrimination has become more incidental and less systematic." Despite *Boerne*'s broad protections for voting, Senator Specter argued "only six cases" of "unconstitutional discrimination" against minorities supported reauthorization.[246] His argument was contrary to Section 2's purpose, which allowed federal judges to find voting rights violations based solely on a voting practice's discriminatory effects.

Specter mischaracterized the record, claiming that only "39 court cases ended with a finding that one of the 880 covered jurisdictions had violated Section 2," in contrast to 40 such cases in non-covered jurisdictions since 1982. His assertion excluded hundreds of unpublished decisions. According to the National Commission on the Voting Rights Act report, between mid-1982 and the end of 2005, at least 653 successful Section 2 cases had been brought in nine of the jurisdictions covered by Section 5 – some 614 more than Senator Specter cited (Nat'l Comm'n on the Voting Rts. Act 2006: Table 5).[247]

A handful of conservative senators agreed with Specter, emphasizing the gains of African-Americans in voter registration and turnout under the Act.[248] Senator Cornyn argued that the "continual decline – almost to the point of statistically negligible numbers – of objections issued by the Department of Justice" illustrated why preclearance was unnecessary.[249] Senator Sessions argued the Norwood Amendment should be adopted "to update the coverage trigger" for Section 5 to apply nationwide.[250] He also claimed the Westmoreland Amendment's "proactive bailout"

---

242 152 Cong. Rec. S7981 (daily ed. July 20, 2006).

243 152 Cong. Rec. S7989–90 (daily ed. July 20, 2006).

244 *See* 152 Cong. Rec. S7963–64, S8009 (daily ed. July 20, 2006) (statement of Sen. Leahy); 152 Cong. Rec. S7970 (daily ed. July 20, 2006) (statement of Sen. Feinstein); 152 Cong. Rec. S7974 (daily ed. July 20, 2006) (statement of Sen. Durbin); 152 Cong. Rec. S8009–10 (daily ed. July 20, 2006) (statement of Sen. Kennedy).

245 152 Cong. Rec. S7974 (daily ed. July 20, 2006).

246 152 Cong. Rec. S7950–63 (daily ed. July 20, 2006).

247 *See* Ellen Katz, Documenting Discrimination in Voting: Judicial Findings Under Section 2 of the Voting Rights Act Since 1982, Final Report of the Voting Rights Initiative of the University of Michigan Law School, *reprinted in Hearing to Examine the Impact and Effectiveness of the Voting Rights Act*, H. Hrg. 109–70, at 964 (2005).

248 *See* 152 Cong. Rec. S7980 (daily ed. July 20, 2006) (statement of Sen. Cornyn); 152 Cong. Rec. S7985 (daily ed. July 20, 2006) (statement of Sen. Graham); 152 Cong. Rec. S7989 (daily ed. July 20, 2006) (statement of Sen. Coburn).

249 152 Cong. Rec. S7980–81 (daily ed. July 20, 2006).

250 152 Cong. Rec. S7986–87 (daily ed. July 20, 2006) (statement of Sen. Sessions); *see also* 152 Cong. Rec. S7981 (daily ed. July 20, 2006) (statement of Sen. Cornyn) (contending the Senate should have

was needed because existing bailout requirements were too onerous.[251] Senator Chambliss praised Georgia House Republicans for raising "legitimate concerns" and advancing "positive amendments which I believe would have strengthened this bill."[252]

A bipartisan group of senators rejected their claims. Senator Leahy, the Democratic Floor Manager of the bill, submitted extensive summaries of the "robust record" of "voluminous evidence of recurring discrimination" in jurisdictions covered by Section 5 and Section 203.[253] He cited the last minute cancellation of an election by the white mayor and all-white board of Kilmichael, Mississippi, in 2001 when several African-Americans declared their candidacies in the majority-Black community. Following a Section 5 objection, voters in Kilmichael elected the first Black mayor and three Black aldermen.[254]

Senator Kennedy described Georgia's unconstitutional voter identification law struck down by federal courts in 2006 along with the discriminatory Texas redistricting plan.[255] He commented that the "so-called updated trigger" under the Norwood Amendment would essentially exclude Louisiana, despite "substantial evidence" of ongoing voting discrimination there.[256] Senator Feinstein explained how a Section 5 objection to a redistricting plan in Monterey County, California, resulted in the election of the first Latino Supervisor in more than 100 years.[257] Senator Durbin observed that in 2004 South Dakota's redistricting plan was struck down for discriminating against Native voters, including evidence that a state official did not want them to vote.[258] Senator Brownback concluded, the VRA "is central in getting everybody participating in the democracy and a true opportunity to register to vote and to actually vote ... It is critical that we extend it."[259] Passing amendments to "gut" the Act would not achieve that.[260]

The bill's supporters noted that 56 percent of the 1,100 Section 5 objections had been issued since 1982[261] in states such as Georgia[262] and Mississippi, which had twice as many objections during that period as it did during the Act's first 17 years. Senator Kennedy offered several reasons for the recent drop in objections: the *Bossier II* limitation on purpose objections; discriminatory voting changes withdrawn after the Justice Department indicated it would object; and discriminatory submissions the Department wrongfully precleared. He argued that conservatives improperly discounted "the discriminatory changes the Act has deterred ... and the dialogue the Act promotes

---

considered the Norwood Amendment to "update the coverage formula"); 152 Cong. Rec. S7989–90 (daily ed. July 20, 2006) (statement of Sen. Coburn) (same).

251 152 Cong. Rec. S7987 (daily ed. July 20, 2006).

252 152 Cong. Rec. S7983 (daily ed. July 20, 2006).

253 152 Cong. Rec. S7745–49, S7902–05 (daily ed. July 19, 2006).

254 152 Cong. Rec. S8008 (daily ed. July 20, 2006).

255 152 Cong. Rec. S7967 (daily ed. July 20, 2006) (statement of Sen. Kennedy); *see also* 152 Cong. Rec. S7974 (daily ed. July 20, 2006) (statement of Sen. Durbin) (discussing the Georgia voter identification case).

256 152 Cong. Rec. S8010 (daily ed. July 20, 2006).

257 152 Cong. Rec. S7969 (daily ed. July 20, 2006).

258 152 Cong. Rec. S7974 (daily ed. July 20, 2006).

259 152 Cong. Rec. S7965 (daily ed. July 20, 2006).

260 152 Cong. Rec. S8010 (daily ed. July 20, 2006) (statement of Sen. Kennedy).

261 152 Cong. Rec. S7984 (daily ed. July 20, 2006) (statement of Sen. Obama); *see also* 152 Cong. Rec. S8002 (daily ed. July 20, 2006) (statement of Sen. Reid); 152 Cong. Rec. S8003 (daily ed. July 20, 2006) (statement of Sen. Lieberman) (describing the number of Section 5 objections).

262 152 Cong. Rec. S7974 (daily ed. July 20, 2006) (statement of Sen. Durbin).

... to ensure consideration of minority communities' concerns in the legislative process."[263] The number of Section 5 objections was compelling, but it did not tell the whole story.

Senators from both parties responded to contentions the Westmoreland Amendment was needed for meaningful bailout. Republican Senator George Allen stated, "Some will argue that counties and cities and States cannot be removed from 'bailout' or preclearance if they so desire and have a good record. The facts are that there are 11 counties and cities in Virginia that have been able to 'bailout'" by showing the absence of voting discrimination.[264] Senator Kennedy elaborated, "[E]very jurisdiction that has sought a bailout has succeeded," referring to letters from two such jurisdictions that did not find the process "onerous." The defeat of the Norwood and Westmoreland amendments, after a "full airing" in the House in light of the record, likewise demonstrated why the Section 5 trigger and bailout provisions needed to be retained.[265]

Finally, conservative Republicans attacked the VRARA's *Bossier II* and *Ashcroft* fixes for their "perceived potential to put a partisan thumb on the scale."[266] Senator Kyl argued the fixes would be "abused by the Justice Department to require creation of the maximum number of black majority districts possible or the maximum number of so-called coalition or influence districts" for partisan gains.[267] In a colloquy with other conservatives,[268] Senator Kyl claimed: Section 5 only applied to "protection of naturally occurring" majority-minority legislative districts;[269] it only barred departing from "normal rules of decision" that required such districts; it did not require maximization; purpose objections could not be based upon "partisan advantage" or incumbent protection; and the fixes were "importing the constitutional test in Section 5"[270] that required discriminatory purpose and effect.[271]

Democratic senators flatly rejected conservatives' claims. Senator Leahy said conservatives' statements "reflected their individual views" and were unsupported by evidence that informed the Judiciary Committee's vote.[272] Senator Kennedy explained:

> Contrary to the suggestions of Senator Cornyn and Senator Kyl on the floor, while the standard rejects the notion that "ability-to-elect" districts can be traded for "influence" districts, it also recognizes that minority voters may be able to elect candidates of their choice with reliable crossover support and, thus, does not mandate the creation and maintenance of majority-minority districts in all circumstances. The test is fact-specific, and turns on the particular circumstances of each case. As both Senator Cornyn and Senator Kyl noted, the Voting Rights Act is not about electing

263 152 Cong. Rec. S7967 (daily ed. July 20, 2006).

264 152 Cong. Rec. S7972 (daily ed. July 20, 2006).

265 152 Cong. Rec. S7968, 8010 (daily ed. July 20, 2006).

266 152 Cong. Rec. S7979 (daily ed. July 20, 2006) (statement of Sen. Kyl).

267 152 Cong. Rec. S7978 (daily ed. July 20, 2006).

268 *See* 152 Cong. Rec. S7978–79 (daily ed. July 20, 2006) (statement of Sen. Cornyn); 152 Cong. Rec. S7979–80 (daily ed. July 20, 2006) (statement of Sen. McConnell); 152 Cong. Rec. S7979 (daily ed. July 20, 2006) (statement of Sen. Hatch); 152 Cong. Rec. S7980 (daily ed. July 20, 2006) (statement of Sen. Cornyn).

269 152 Cong. Rec. S.7978 (daily ed. July 20, 2006) (statement of Sen. Kyl); *but see* James Thomas Tucker, *Redefining American Democracy: Do Alternative Voting Systems Capture the True Meaning of "Representation"?*, 7 Mich. J. Race & Law 357, 362–63 (2002) (noting that "all districting is gerrymandering" because districting criteria are "far from neutral").

270 152 Cong. Rec. S7978–79 (daily ed. July 20, 2006).

271 *See Washington v. Davis*, 426 U.S. 229, 239–42 (1976).

272 152 Cong. Rec. S8004–07 (daily ed. July 20, 2006).

> candidates of particular parties. It's about enabling minority voters to participate effectively and equally in the political process.[273]

Statements by conservative Republicans therefore were entitled to no weight.

Unlike the southern House rebels, none of the half-dozen conservative Republican dissenters opposed the bill on final passage. The Senate passed H.R. 9 unanimously by a vote of 98 to 0.[274] The Senate voted on H.R. 9 to avoid a conference because of slight differences between the House and Senate bills. After the bicameral introduction of H.R. 9 and S. 2703, H.R. 9 was amended during markup to include the Issa study on effective implementation of the language assistance provisions and S. 2703 had a technical amendment added in markup to add the name of César E. Chávez to the title of the bill. As Senator Leahy explained, he did not want "to complicate final passage of the Voting Rights Act so I urge the Senate to proceed to the House-passed bill and resist amendments so it can be signed into law without having to be reconsidered by the House."[275]

One week later, President Bush signed the VRARA into law. The President observed, "[W]e've made progress toward equality, yet the work for a more perfect union is never ending." He committed the Administration to "vigorously enforce the provisions of this law" and to "defend it in court."[276] The long battle for reauthorization was over.

After Game: Senate Conservatives Attempt to Rewrite Legislative History, Post-Enactment

A strange episode occurred after the VRARA passed the Senate and hours before it was signed into law. On July 26, 2006, Senator Specter and eight conservative Republicans filed the Senate Judiciary Committee's Report on the bill (S. Rep. No. 109–295, 2006: 1). The report parroted Specter's remarks during the Senate floor debate suggesting that the Act had achieved its purposes and was unneeded. He qualified any need for the VRA stating, "These types of anecdotes, and the others in the record, demonstrate … the type of behavior that *may* warrant oversight by federal officials." He cited Thernstrom's claim about the number of whites who are now "good friends" with African-Americans and appointments of four Blacks to two federal offices, despite its lack of relevance to evidence of voting discrimination. He argued "covered jurisdictions that once sponsored violence against minority voters now elect hundreds of minorities to elected office" (S. Rep. No. 109–295, 2006: 14, 19).

Senator Specter cited increased Black voter registration and turnout data, which he suggested showed minorities had equal political access (S. Rep. No. 109–295, 2006: 11). The data he used was replete with errors rendering it unworthy of any credibility. It lowered white registration and turnout by lumping in severely depressed data for Latinos with non-Hispanic whites. According to Census data, Black voters only registered at a higher rate than the national average for non-Hispanic whites in one covered state, Mississippi. Additionally, Black registration and turnout in the 2004 election was higher than for non-Hispanic whites in only Mississippi and North Carolina (U.S. Census Bureau 2004: Table 4a). Senator Specter's views were not supported by a majority of the Judiciary Committee.[277]

---

273 152 Cong. Rec. S8010 (daily ed. July 20, 2006).

274 152 Cong. Rec. S7949, 8012 (daily ed. July 20, 2006).

275 152 Cong. Rec. S7964 (daily ed. July 20, 2006).

276 President's Remarks on Signing The Fannie Lou Hamer, Rosa Parks, and Coretta Scott King Voting Rights Act Reauthorization and Amendments Act of 2006, 42 Wkly. Comp. Pres. Doc. 1392 (July 27, 2006).

277 Senator Mike DeWine of Ohio was the sole Committee Republican who declined to join the report, saying it was not "indicated in this case." Seth Stern, *Senate Democrats Suggest Republicans Tried to Undercut Voting Rights Act*, C.Q. Today, July 27, 2006.

Figure 7.3 President George W. Bush signing the Reauthorized VRA in the Rose Garden on July 27, 2006

Pictured from left to right immediately behind President Bush: Congressman Mel Watt (D, NC-12); Senator Patrick Leahy (D, VT), Ranking Minority Member of the Senate Judiciary Committee; Senator Arlen Specter (R, PA), Chairman of the Senate Judiciary Committee; Congressman John Conyers, Jr. (D, MI-14), Ranking Minority Member of the House Judiciary Committee; Congressman James Sensenbrenner, Jr. (R, WI-5), Chairman of the House Judiciary Committee; Congresswoman Nancy Pelosi (D, CA-8), House Democratic Leader; Senator Harry Reid (D, NV), Senate Minority Leader; and Senator Bill Frist (R, TN), Senate Majority Leader.

Source: Photo courtesy of Nina Perales, Southwest Regional Counsel, Mexican American Legal Defense and Educational Fund (MALDEF).

Three conservative Republicans supported Senator Specter's efforts. Senator Kyl repeated his personal views on how to interpret the *Bossier II* and *Ashcroft* fixes.[278] Senators Cornyn and Coburn reaffirmed their floor statements. They claimed the record did not support keeping the existing Section 5 trigger, describing it as "anecdotal accounts" that "implicate only a portion" of covered jurisdictions. The two senators denounced the "seemingly rushed, somewhat incomplete legislative process" that prevented "consideration of numerous suggested improvements." They admitted their views were filed "post-enactment" and that the committee report was not filed "until several days after passage of the legislation and just before it [was] signed into law."[279]

278 S. Rep. 109–295 at 22–24 (2006) (additional views of Sen. Kyl).

279 S. Rep. 109–295 at 25–53 (2006) (additional views of Sens. Cornyn and Coburn).

The eight Democratic senators on the Judiciary Committee unanimously objected to the post-enactment committee report and additional views. They criticized the report and views for failing to reflect the views of the bill's co-sponsors, the record, and the endorsement the bill had when reported favorably out of committee. They pointed out that the report could not have informed the floor debate because it was unavailable to senators. The eight senators argued, "Nothing written ... after final passage can diminish the force of those findings contained within the enacted legislation itself or the Member's vote supporting them." They concluded, "Any after-the-fact attempts to re-characterize the legislation's language and effects should not be credited."[280]

It is unlikely that federal courts will credit the post-enactment report or additional views as part of the VRA's legislative history. As the U.S. Supreme Court explained in *Chapman v. United States*, subsequent legislative history is "an unreliable guide to legislative intent."[281] Justice Scalia described "*post-enactment* legislative history" as a "contradiction in terms."[282] Other courts found it is "an oxymoron" raising separation of power concerns because statutory interpretation is the role of the courts, not Congress.[283]

Conclusion

Passage of the VRARA is not the end of the road, but a new beginning. While the politics of persuasion carried the day, civil rights advocates must remain vigilant for efforts to undermine the Act. One week after President Bush signed the VRARA into law, a bill was introduced in the Senate that would declare English the official language and would repeal the Act's language assistance provisions.[284] The next day, a constitutional challenge to Section 5 was filed in a municipal utility district in Austin Texas, Lamar Smith's district.[285] Linda Chavez has promised a similar challenge for the language assistance provisions (Bilingual Elections I 2006: 44–45). The U.S. Census Bureau's ability to make future Section 203 determinations is in doubt because of budget shortfalls for the annual American Community Survey.[286] The Stearns Amendment highlights the need to monitor appropriations to ensure they do not promote discrimination. Finally, the reauthorized Act does little good if it is not vigorously enforced.

Despite these challenges, there is evidence that the Act's revitalized provisions are working. In September 2006, the Justice Department made its first objection under the restored pre-*Bossier II*

280 *See* S. Rep. 109–295 at 54–55 (2006) (additional views of Sens. Leahy, Kennedy, Biden, Kohl, Feinstein, Feingold, Schumer, and Durbin).

281 500 U.S. 453, 464 n.4 (1991); *see Consumer Prod. Safety Comm'n v. GTE Sylvania, Inc.*, 447 U.S. 102, 118, n.13 (1980); *Oscar Meyer and Co. v. Evans*, 441 U.S. 750, 758 (1979).

282 *Sullivan v. Finkelstein*, 496 U.S. 617, 631 (1990) (Scalia, J., concurring).

283 *Strickland v. Commissioner*, 48 F.3d 12, 18 (1st Cir. 1995).

284 *See* National Language Act of 2006, S. 3828, 109th Cong. § 2 (2006). Representative Peter King previously introduced a companion bill in the House. *See* National Language Act of 2005, H.R. 4408, 109th Cong. § 3 (2005).

285 *See Northwest Austin Mun. Util. Dist. v. Gonzales*, No. 1:06-cv-01384-PLF (D.D.C. Aug. 8, 2006) (three-judge panel). Gregory Coleman, a former Solicitor General of Texas who testified against reauthorizing Section 5, represents the Municipal Utility District (MUD). *See Modern Enforcement of the Voting Rights Act, Hearing Before the Senate Jud. Comm.*, 109th Cong. 20–21 (2006) (testimony of Gregory Coleman).

286 *See* D'Vera Cohn, *Census Bureau Fears Budget Fallout: Proposed Cuts Said to Hurt Preparations for 2010 Count*, Wash. Post, July 15, 2006, at A10.

purpose prong of Section 5 to a submission from Randolph County, Georgia.[287] The objection is in stark contrast to the claims of Georgia Republicans that the Act is unnecessary. It also shows that while our nation has come a long way, it still has far to go. Thanks to the VRARA, the Department and private citizens continue to have powerful tools at their disposal to eradicate the blight of voting discrimination.

---

287 *See* Letter from Asst. Att'y Gen. Wan J. Kim to Tommy Coleman, Attorney for Randolph County, GA (Sept. 12, 2006).

Chapter 8
Debunking Ten Myths about Language Assistance[1]

Advocates of making English the "official" language of the United States malign the use of non-English materials and assistance in elections. They insist that bilingual ballots and assistance are unnecessary and harmful. They maintain that language assistance is "a great threat to our national unity" that risks breaking our country up "into many ethnic enclaves"[2] of non-English speaking communities.[3] Congressman Steve King of Iowa asserted in 2006, "Multilingual ballots divide our country, increase the risk of voter error and fraud, and burden local taxpayers. The multilingual ballot mandate encourages the linguistic division of our nation and contradicts the 'Melting Pot' ideal that has made us the most successful multi-ethnic nation on earth."[4]

Phrases like "balkanization" and "ethnic enclaves" detract from any meaningful debate with King and other critics about the merits of language assistance in voting. Balkanization is "a loaded term of mythical proportions that has absolutely no basis in fact, and is used as a divisive measure."[5] Such words play upon the raw emotions of those who disapprove of difference. Under the linguistic model advanced by opponents of language assistance, only those who speak English are authentic Americans. Typical of that viewpoint, U.S. English has argued that "Bilingual ballots are un-American."[6]

This chapter provides a factual response to ten myths about bilingual elections used by English-only advocates. It highlights the need for the language assistance provisions, particularly where unequal schooling and lack of English learning opportunities contribute to high rates of limited-English proficiency and illiteracy. It also shows the impact the requirements have on millions of non-English speaking citizens.

Myth 1: Knowledge of English Is a Requirement for Citizenship

A common myth is that bilingual voting assistance is unnecessary because English is a requirement for citizenship. Linda Chavez has asked, "If you can't read an English-language ballot, how can

1 Portions of this chapter originally were published in the *New York University Journal of Legislation and Public Policy* as James Thomas Tucker, *Enfranchising Language Minority Citizens: The Bilingual Election Provisions of the Voting Rights Act*, 10 N.Y.U. J. Leg. & Pub. Pol'y 195 (2006–2007). That article has been adapted to correspond with the discussion in the remainder of this book.

2 142 Cong. Rec. H9739 (daily ed. Aug. 1, 1996) (statement of Rep. Roukema).

3 Brian DeBose, *Lawmakers Push Official English*, Wash. Times, Apr. 3, 2006, at A6.

4 *Rep. King Applauds Decision to Give Americans Another Chance to End Bilingual Voting*, U.S. Fed. News, June 21, 2006.

5 *Continuing Need for Section 203's Provisions for Limited English Proficient Voters: Hearing Before the S. Comm. on the Judiciary*, 109th Cong. 66 (June 13, 2006) (response of John Trasviña, Interim President and General Counsel, Mexican American Legal Defense and Education Fund, to written questions).

6 David B. Caruso, *Bilingual Ballots Increasingly Requested*, Az. Daily Star, Mar. 28, 2003.

you pass the citizenship test in the first place?"[7] Similar arguments have been made each time Congress has considered Section 203 (Chapter 7). Chavez's rhetorical question is based upon a false premise about citizenship requirements. The Fourteenth Amendment to the Constitution "put it beyond doubt that all persons … born or naturalized in the United States, and owing no allegiance to any alien power, should be citizens of the United States and of the state in which they reside."[8] It says nothing about language abilities. A further response to the myth requires a brief examination of citizenship for those born here and those born abroad.

Native-Born Americans

Native-born Americans are not required to speak English. Indeed, federal law takes the opposite approach for some voters. The Native American Languages Act of 1990 recognizes the special status of Native Americans, Native Hawaiians, and Native American Pacific Islanders.[9] It declares a federal policy to "preserve, protect, and promote" the use of their native languages.[10] It further provides that the "right of Native Americans to express themselves through the use of Native American languages shall not be restricted in any public proceeding, including publicly supported education programs."[11] Federal law likewise acknowledges the unique position of Spanish-speaking Puerto Ricans, who are American citizens from birth (Chapter 2).

Congressman Lamar Smith claims, "[I]f you were born in America, you should know English."[12] However, millions of American citizens by birth have limited-English language skills. According to the 2000 Census, among Puerto Ricans, who comprise the second largest group of Latinos in the U.S., 26.7 percent are limited-English proficient (LEP) because they speak English less than "very well" (Chapter 4).[13] Pacific Islanders, including Native Hawaiians, American Samoans, and inhabitants of Guam, have lower levels of English attainment. Of the 600,000 Pacific Islanders who are U.S. citizens by birth, approximately 44 percent speak a language other than English at home and one-third are LEP.[14]

Many of the 4.1 million Alaska Natives and American Indians (AIAN) do not speak English.[15] Approximately 63,500 AIAN voters are LEP (Figure 5.8). Navajos comprise the largest number of LEP American Indians. According to the 2000 Census, Navajo-speaking persons comprise nearly half of the 380,000 persons who speak an American Indian language.[16] Alaska Natives also suffer from high LEP and illiteracy rates (Chapters 5, 10; Appendix C). Lack of English proficiency often results from educational discrimination and insufficient English learning opportunities (Chapters 5, 9).

7 Testimony of Linda Chavez, President of the Center for Equal Opportunity, *Hearing Before the Subcomm. on the Const. of the House Jud. Comm.* (Apr. 18, 1996).

8 *Elk v. Wilkins*, 112 U.S. 94, 101 (1884).

9 Pub. L. No. 101–477, 104 Stat. 1153 (codified at 25 U.S.C. §§ 2901 to 2905 (1990)).

10 25 U.S.C. § 2903.

11 25 U.S.C. § 2904.

12 H.R. Rep. No. 109–478 at 137 (2006) (statement of Rep. Smith).

13 Bureau of the Census, U.S. Dep't of Commerce, We the People: Hispanics in the United States 1, 10 (2004).

14 Bureau of the Census, U.S. Dep't of Commerce, We the People: Pacific Islanders in the United States 11 (2005).

15 Bureau of the Census, U.S. Dep't of Commerce, The American Indian and Alaska Native Population: 2000 3, 7 (2002).

16 Bureau of the Census, U.S. Dep't of Commerce, Census 2000 Summary File 3, at tbl. PCT10.

Naturalized Americans

George Will argues that federal naturalization law is a "barrier" between "people who cannot read English language ballots" and citizenship.[17] He claims, "[I]f someone needs a ballot written in a language other than English, that need proves the person obtained citizenship because the law was not enforced when he or she sought citizenship."[18] Similarly, John Miller contends that "immigrant voters should not even need bilingual ballots. We have required naturalization applicants since 1907 to demonstrate English-language proficiency."[19] Their arguments mischaracterize citizenship requirements.

The Immigration and Naturalization Act does not require a naturalized citizen to possess fluency in English sufficient to participate in elections. Applicants generally must demonstrate they "can read or write simple words and phrases" with "no extraordinary or unreasonable condition" imposed upon them. They must possess a third- or fourth-grade knowledge of English.[20] Voting, however, requires a much higher level of English proficiency. It is common for voting materials and ballot questions to be written at a twelfth-grade level or higher (Chapter 4). Therefore, many naturalized citizens who pass the English test as part of the citizenship application require language assistance to cast a meaningful ballot.

Older applicants comprise a majority of naturalized citizens.[21] Many do not have to satisfy any form of language proficiency to become citizens. Federal law exempts any person who, on the date of filing their application, is either over 50 years of age and a lawful resident alien for at least 20 years or over 55 years of age and a lawful resident alien for at least 15 years.[22] Consequently, fluency in English is not a prerequisite to citizenship, even among naturalized citizens.

Myth 2: Most LEP Voters Are Immigrants Denied Schooling Outside the U.S.

Opponents of bilingual elections also attempt to tie them to the immigration debate, arguing that most voters using language assistance are naturalized citizens denied educational opportunities elsewhere (Chapter 7). The Executive Director of ProEnglish contends that the "driving factor behind the literacy rate of the two largest of these groups, Asians and Hispanics, has little to do with educational opportunities in this country."[23] Another critic agrees.[24] The evidence refutes both parts of their argument.

17 George Will, *Discomforting Truths About Bilingual Ballots*, The Soc. Cont. 262 (Summer 1996).

18 George F. Will, *A Vote for English*, Wash. Post, May 25, 2006, at A29.

19 John J. Miller, *English Is Broken Here: Bilingual Ballots Are Bad for Democracy*, 79 Pol'y Rev. 54 (1996).

20 8 U.S.C. § 1423(a)(1).

21 Ana Henderson, *English Language Naturalization Requirements and the Bilingual Assistance Provisions of the Voting Rights Act*, at 6 (2006).

22 *See* 8 U.S.C. § 1423(b)(2) (2000).

23 Testimony of K.C. McAlpin, Executive Director of ProEnglish, Before the Subcomm. on the Const. of the House Jud. Comm., *Voting Rights Act: Section 203 – Bilingual Election Requirements (Part II): Hearing Before the Subcomm. on the Constitution of the H. Comm. on the Judiciary*, H. Hrg. 109–78, at 64 (Nov. 9–10, 2005).

24 Testimony of Roger Clegg, General Counsel of the Center for Equal Opportunity, Testimony (Nov. 8, 2005), *reprinted in Voting Rights Act: Section 203 – Bilingual Election Requirements (Part I): Hearing Before the Subcomm. on the Const. of the H. Comm. on the Judiciary*, 109th Cong., 1st Sess. 50 (2005).

Most LEP Voters Were Born in the U.S.

A majority of voters who need language assistance were born in this country. Alaska Natives and American Indians are citizens by birth.[25] According to the 2000 Census, 98.6 percent of Puerto Ricans are native born (We the People Hispanics 2004: 8). A majority of U.S. citizens of Japanese, Cambodian, Hmong, and other Asian ethnicity are native born.[26]

The same holds true for Spanish-speaking Americans. Spanish language assistance accounts for 81 percent of coverage under Section 203 (Figure 5.8). Hispanics comprise 35.2 million persons, about 12.5 percent of the U.S. population. According to the 2000 Census, 84.2 percent of Hispanic U.S. citizens are native born. Among all Hispanic persons in the U.S. (citizen and non-citizen alike), 59.8 percent are native born. Seventy-one percent of all Latinos in the U.S. are citizens (We the People Hispanics 2004: 1, 8). The GAO's 1986 study is the most comprehensive of its kind detailing the demographics of voters using language assistance. The GAO found that of 283,000 Hispanic voters it surveyed in Texas in 1984, "The typical bilingual voter was a native-born U.S. citizen, was older, and lacked a high school education." Seventy-seven percent of Hispanic voters using a bilingual ballot were born in the U.S.[27]

The Impact of Educational Discrimination on LEP Voters

LEP voters born in the U.S. typically require language assistance because of educational discrimination in this country. Unequal schooling has played a large role in disenfranchising language minorities (Chapters 6, 9), the effects of which Congress has remedied through the VRA's bilingual election requirements (Chapters 2–4). Evidence of discrimination against the group of voters studied by the GAO, Spanish-speaking LEP citizens in Texas, makes that clear.

Texas discriminated against Latinos in schooling from its earliest days as a republic, and later, a state.[28] Discrimination took two forms. First, the educational system "was to reproduce the caste society of the Southwest, with Anglos at the top and Mexicans, Indians, and Blacks at the bottom."[29] One school superintendent remarked, "Most of our Mexicans are of the lower class. They transplant onions, harvest them, etc. The less they know about everything else the better contented they are ... If a man has very much sense or education either, he is not going to stick to this kind of work."[30] Consistent with that policy, the state exempted Latino children from mandatory school attendance

25 Bureau of the Census, U.S. Dep't of Commerce, The American Indian and Alaska Native Population: 2000, at 1 (Feb. 2002).

26 Bureau of the Census, U.S. Dep't of Commerce, We the People: Asians in the United States 9 (Dec. 2004).

27 U.S. Gen. Acct. Off. (GAO), Bilingual Voting Assistance: Cost of and Use During the November 1984 General Election 61 (1986).

28 Nina Perales, Luis Figueroa, and Criselda G. Rivas, *Voting Rights in Texas*, 17 S. Cal. Rev. L. & Soc. Just. 713, 722–27 (2008).

29 Juan F. Perea, *Buscando América: Why Integration and Equal Protection Fail to Protect Latinos*, 117 Harv. L. Rev. 1420, 1439 (2004).

30 Perea 2004: 1439 (quoting from Herschel T. Manuel, The Education of Mexican and Spanish-Speaking Children in Texas 77 (1930)).

laws.[31] Second, state officials intentionally segregated Latinos from Anglos in the schools.[32] By 1930, their efforts were so successful that 90 percent of Texas schools were segregated.[33] State courts initially sanctioned discrimination through decisions such as *Independent School District v. Salvatierra*, claiming Latinos needed a separate education in their own language.[34]

Texas took an incremental step to integrate Latinos into Anglo schools in 1948 (Salinas and Kimball 2007: 223–24). Full integration did not begin until after 1970. That year, a federal court held that Latinos were "an identifiable ethnic minority" under the desegregation mandate in *Brown v. Board of Education*.[35] Latinos later brought successful desegregation cases in communities throughout Texas, including Midland[36] and Dallas.[37]

In *United States v. Texas*, a federal court rejected the 1930 state court ruling in *Salvatierra* endorsing segregation on the pretext of providing separate schools for Spanish-speaking students.[38] To remedy that discrimination, the court ordered Anglos and Latino students alike to receive bilingual and bicultural education (*U.S. v. Texas* 1971: 28). In 1981, the defendants "were found to have violated the constitutional and statutory rights of Mexican-American children throughout … Texas."[39] The court determined the state did not monitor and enforce compliance with requirements for non-English speaking students, was understaffed, and needed to "commit substantial additional resources" to English-language learners (*U.S. v. Texas* 1981: 427–28).

In 1981, Texas passed the Bilingual and Special Language Programs Act.[40] That Act, which tracked the federal court's remedy, marked the first time Texas provided bilingual education through the elementary grades, mandated bilingual education in districts with 20 or more LEP students in the same grade, and required the state to actively monitor implementation to ensure compliance.[41] However, Texas did not mandate bilingual education and ESL programs in all state schools until 1995.[42]

Educational discrimination against Latinos in Texas played a key role in the passage of Section 203 in 1975.[43] The Senate report described high dropout rates among Latinos resulting in an illiteracy rate of 18.9 percent among those 25 years and older, including a third of Mexican-American adults in Texas. More than half of all Mexican-American children in Texas never finished high school. The U.S. Civil Rights Commission found "a systemic failure of the educational process, which not only ignores the educational needs of Chicano students but also suppresses their hopes and ambitions,"

31 *See* Lupe S. Salinas and Dr. Robert H. Kimball, *The Equal Treatment of Unequals: Barriers Facing Latinos and the Poor in Texas Public Schools*, 14 Geo. J. on Poverty L. & Pol'y 215, 222 (2007).

32 *See United States v. Texas*, 506 F. Supp. 405, 412 (E.D. Tex. 1981), *rev'd and remanded on different grounds*, 680 F.2d (5th Cir. 1982); Jorge C. Rangel and Carlos M. Alcala, *Project Report: De Jure Segregation of Chicanos in Texas Schools*, 7 Harv. C.R.-C.L. L. Rev. 307 (1972).

33 Rubén Donato, Martha Menchaca, and Richard R. Valencia, *Segregation, Desegregation, and Integration of Chicano Students: Problems and Prospects*, *in* Chicano School Failure and Success 35 (Richard R. Valencia ed. 1991).

34 33 S.W.2d 790 (Tex. Civ. App. 1930), *cert. denied*, 284 U.S. 580 (1931).

35 *Cisneros v. Corpus Christi Indep. Sch. Dist.*, 324 F. Supp. 599, 606 (S.D. Tex. 1970).

36 *United States v. Midland Indep. Dch. Dist.*, 519 F.2d 60 (5th Cir. 1972).

37 *Tasby v. Estes*, 517 F.2d 92 (5th Cir. 1975).

38 *See* 342 F. Supp. 24 (E.D. Tex. 1971).

39 *United States v. Texas*, 523 F. Supp. 703, 709 (E.D. Tex. 1981).

40 Tex. Educ. Code §§ 21.451, *et seq.* (Vernon Supp. 1981).

41 *United States v. Texas*, 680 F.2d 356, 372 (5th Cir. 1982).

42 Tex. Educ. Code §§ 29.051, *et seq.* (Vernon Supp. 1995).

43 *See* David H. Hunter, *The 1975 Voting Rights Act and Language Minorities*, 25 Cath. U. L. Rev. 250 (1976).

making "the Chicano ... the excluded student."[44] The Senate Judiciary Committee concluded that "these high illiteracy rates are not the result of choice or happenstance. They are the product of the failure of state and local officials to afford equal educational opportunities ..."[45]

Opponents of Section 203 argue educational discrimination is in the past, eliminating the need for language assistance. However, even after educational discrimination is cured, its long-term effects remain in its victims:

> Texas and other states maintained segregated public school systems well into the 1970s. The pervasive impact of *de jure* segregation in public schools persists: many language minority citizens who attended segregated schools have never been able to gain the skills in English reading comprehension necessary to cast an informed ballot in an English-only election (Trasviña 2006: 55).

The next two chapters examine the continuing impact of unequal schooling on Alaska Natives (Chapters 9–10). The effects of educational discrimination are not limited to past litigation, but also include cases brought by a new generation of language minority citizens who experience discrimination today (Chapter 5).

Myth 3: Bilingual Ballots Can Be Limited to Native-Born Americans

Some commentators claim that only native-born citizens, and not naturalized citizens, should be covered by the language assistance provisions. One critic argues that American Indians have a "unique history and status" requiring that "their rights should not be confused or conflated with those of non-English-speaking naturalized citizens" (McAlpin 2005: 74). Opponents of bilingual elections hoped to divide AIAN groups, whose citizens are all native-born, from Asian and Latino groups that include some citizens born abroad. The strategy foundered in the face of a united coalition in 2006 (Chapter 7).

Moreover, limiting language assistance to native-born voting-age citizens is unconstitutional. The U.S. Supreme Court has rejected the argument, "[C]itizenship obtained through naturalization is ... a second-class citizenship."[46] There can be no distinction between native-born and naturalized citizens, with one exception. Article II of the U.S. Constitution limits eligibility to serve as President to citizens who are "natural born." Any effort to impose different protections for native-born citizens would be unconstitutional.[47]

The Supreme Court concluded that "it is plain that citizenship obtained through naturalization carries with it the privilege of full participation in the affairs of our society" (*Knauer v. United States* 1946: 658). That holds true, even though a minority of the beneficiaries of Section 203 are naturalized citizens whose illiteracy may be attributable to "the lack of educational opportunities they experienced in their Native countries" (McAlpin 2005: 64). The policy choice to include all illiterate LEP voters is a reasonable exercise of congressional power (Chapters 1–2), especially given evidence of educational discrimination in this country (Chapters 1–2, 5, 9–10).

44 U.S. Comm'n on Civ. Rts., The Excluded Student, Mexican American Education Study, Report III, 23 (May 1972).

45 S. Rep. No. 94–295 at 28 (1975).

46 *Knauer v. United States*, 328 U.S. 654, 658 (1946).

47 *Knauer v. United States* 1946: 658; *Schneider v. Rusk*, 377 U.S. 163, 165 (1964); *Luria v. United States*, 231 U.S. 9, 22 (1913); *Osborn v. Bank of the United States*, 22 U.S. 738, 827–28 (1824).

Moreover, treating Americans differently depending upon their place of birth is disingenuous. It is more likely to create the very sort of separatism that critics of bilingual ballots decry. Congress enacted the VRA's bilingual election requirements to facilitate civic participation by language minorities. As Senator Orin Hatch explained:

> Far from threatening the primacy of English in America, it is precisely tools such as Section 203 which facilitate the integration of immigrants into the diverse culture of this nation. Bilingual elections do not promote cultural separatism, but instead help to integrate non-English speaking citizens into our system of democracy.[48]

The way to bridge the linguistic divide is not by widening that gap further by denying language minorities the tools they need to vote. It also is not to create separate tiers of citizenship, bestowing assistance only for those born in this country. There are no first- and second-class citizens. The path to a unified nation requires making remedies for discrimination available to covered language minorities on an equal footing, without regard to their place of origin. "The right to vote is one of the most fundamental of human rights. Unless government assures access to the ballot box, citizenship is just an empty promise." The bilingual election requirements are "an integral part of our government's assurance that Americans do have such access."[49]

Myth 4: Bilingual Elections Create a Disincentive to Learn English

Opponents of bilingual elections cite a corollary to their argument that language assistance leads to balkanization. "By receiving such assistance they are receiving a disincentive to become proficient in English" (Will 2006: A29). Congressman King even claims that civil rights groups promote bilingual ballots to keep immigrants from learning English to control their votes (Chapter 7). However, there is no evidence that providing language assistance in voting discourages LEP citizens from learning English, much less that it is done to control immigrants.

Immigrants Continue to Acquire English Skills

Today's immigrants lose their native language by the second or third generation, and most are speaking English on a daily basis within ten years of their arrival.[50] Latinos provide the strongest evidence of English acquisition. English fluency, defined as persons who speak English "very well," increases among Latino immigrants from one generation to the next. According to a Pew Research Center study of more than14,000 Latinos, 23 percent of first-generation immigrants to the U.S. speak English fluently and 88 percent of their second-generation native-born children speak English fluently. By the third generation, their assimilation into English-speaking society is

---

48 *Voting Rights Act Language Assistance Amendments of 1992: Hearings on S. 2236 Before the Subcomm. on the Constitution of the Senate Comm. on the Judiciary* (S. 2236 Hearings), 102d Cong., 2d Sess., S. Hrg. 102–1066, at 25 (1992) (statement of Rep. Serrano).

49 S. 2236 Hearings, 102d Cong., 2d Sess., S. Hrg. 102–1066, at 134 (1992) (statement of Sen. Hatch).

50 Nat'l Council of La Raza, State of Hispanic America 1991: An Overview (1992), *reprinted in* S. 2236 Hearings, 102d Cong., 2d Sess., S. Hrg. 102–1066, at 99–100 (1992).

complete, with 94 percent speaking English "very well" and only one in four reporting that they speak Spanish at home.[51]

Latinos recognize the need to learn English better than any other surveyed group of Americans. In a separate study, Pew found that 92 percent of Latinos believe that teaching English to the children of immigrant families is "very important," compared to 87 percent of whites and 83 percent of Blacks. That percentage is even higher among foreign-born Latinos, 96 percent of whom identified learning English as "very important."[52] Immigrants from Latin America and elsewhere understand that English fluency is the key to their economic success. Congressman James Sensenbrenner made that point clear:

> If immigrants want to achieve the American dream, they better learn how to read and function in English. But this deals with the right to vote, and these people are United States citizens; they are not illegal immigrants. It seems to me these people should not be confused because they don't have proper instruction about how to vote on ballots for the candidates of their choice.[53]

LEP citizens recognize the importance of learning English. They should not be denied their fundamental right to vote until they do so.

Bilingual Elections Remove Language Barriers

Detractors of bilingual elections suggest that denying language assistance creates an incentive for "all of these immigrants [to] learn to speak English."[54] Similar statements frequently are made on Election Day by poll workers who tell LEP voters seeking assistance, "[M]y parents came over here and learned how to speak English before they could vote, you should too."[55] It is a fundamentally flawed argument intended to disenfranchise language minority voters. Congress has rejected the notion that voting rights should be denied as "a necessary or appropriate means of encouraging persons to learn English,"[56] instead opting to assist LEP voters (Chapters 1–4).[57]

Elderly, uneducated, and poor immigrants face substantial impediments to attaining English proficiency because their circumstances often make it impracticable.[58] "Older learners have a higher dropout in most programs because the pace is too fast and the programs contain too much content, and elderly learners are often illiterate and suffer from memory impairment."[59] That is why federal immigration law provides broad exemptions for them. A survey of non-participating adults

---

51 Shirin Hakimzadeh and D'Vera Cohn, Pew Hispanic Center, English Usage Among Hispanics in the United States ii (Nov. 2007).

52 *Pew Hispanic Center, Fact Sheet: Hispanic Attitudes Toward Learning English* (June 7, 2006).

53 Nicole Gaouette, *House GOP Group Targets Bilingual Ballots*, L.A. Times, May 6, 2006, at A9.

54 152 Cong. Rec. H5195–96 (daily ed. July 13, 2006) (statement of Rep. Stearns).

55 James Thomas Tucker, *The Power of Observation: The Role of Federal Observers under the Voting Rights Act*, 13 Mich. J. Race & Law 227, 259 (Fall 2007).

56 S. Rep. No. 94–295, 1975: 34 (quoting *Katzenbach v. Morgan*, 384 U.S. 641, 655 (1966)).

57 *See* Asian Am. Legal Def. & Educ. Fund (AALDEF), Asian Americans and the Voting Rights Act: The Case for Reauthorization 7 (2006).

58 *See* Mexican Am. Legal Def. & Educ. Fund, Bilingual Elections: Latinos, Language and Voting Rights 26–28 (1992), *reprinted in* S. 2236 Hearings, 102d Cong., 2d Sess., S. Hrg. 102–1066, at 32, 60–62 (1992).

59 James Thomas Tucker, *The ESL Logjam: Waiting Times for ESL Classes and the Impact on English Language Learners*, 96 Nat'l Civic Rev. 30, 32 (Mar. 2007).

interested in taking English classes found that time was cited as a barrier by 40 percent, money by 26 percent, and child care or transportation by 23 percent (ESL Logjam 2007: 32). Frequently, even the most basic English-learning classes are unavailable, much less those providing fluency sufficient to understand complex voting information written in English (Chapter 5).

State-sponsored educational discrimination against LEP citizens has contributed to lack of English proficiency (Myth 2). Congress found, "Among other factors, the denial of the right to vote of such minority citizens is ordinarily directly related to the unequal educational opportunities afforded them, resulting in high illiteracy and low voting participation."[60] Bilingual elections protect LEP voters from being victimized a second time at the polls by eliminating English literacy as a prerequisite to political participation (Chapters 1–4). The VRA provides state and local governments with incentives to eliminate unequal schooling and its effects. Jurisdictions covered by Section 203 may bailout by showing "that the illiteracy rate of the applicable language minority group" that triggered coverage "is equal to or less than the national illiteracy rate"[61] (Chapter 4). As Congressman Sensenbrenner explained, eliminating bilingual elections would create a disincentive for jurisdictions to remedy educational discrimination by teaching LEP voters "how to read English" (Chapter 7).[62]

Myth 5: Language Assistance Is Not Used

English-only groups claim that bilingual election requirements are unused. English First argues, "[T]here is little evidence that bilingual ballots were needed by many people."[63] In 2006, Congressman King and 79 other U.S. Representatives likewise argued that multilingual ballots "are a waste of taxpayer funds because they are mandated by the VRA without regard to whether they are actually used." That argument is contrary to their assertion that "Multilingual ballots divide our country."[64] It does not logically follow that bilingual election procedures could create a disincentive to learn English and balkanize our country unless they are actually used. Leaving aside the internal inconsistency of this myth, the facts also demonstrate it is untrue.

Use of Language Assistance among Covered Groups

"It is well documented that language assistance is needed and used by voters."[65] Bilingual materials and assistance are in demand wherever offered. According to a November 2000 exit survey of language minority voters in Los Angeles and Orange Counties in California, 54 percent of Asian and Pacific Islander voters and 46 percent of Hispanic voters reported they would be more likely to vote if they received language assistance. Those numbers are consistent with other exit surveys in March 2000 and November 1998.[66] In 2006, Deborah Wright, Acting Assistant Registrar-Recorder and County Clerk for Los Angeles County, testified:

---

60 42 U.S.C. § 1973aa–1a(a).

61 42 U.S.C. § 1973aa–1a(d).

62 152 Cong. Rec. H5191–92, 5197–98 (daily ed. July 13, 2006) (statement of Rep. Sensenbrenner).

63 English First Foundation, *Bilingual Ballots: Election Fairness or Fraud?* (2000).

64 Letter of 79 Congressmen to Speaker of the House Dennis Hastert and Majority Leader John Boehner (June 16, 2006).

65 152 Cong. Rec. H5143 (daily ed. July 13, 2006) (statement of Rep. Baca).

66 Statement of Eugene Lee, Staff Attorney, Voting Rights Project, Asian Pacific American Legal Center, Before the National Commission on the Voting Rights Act, Western Regional Hearing at 4 (Sept. 27, 2005).

> Language minority citizens in Los Angeles County have consistently demonstrated use of translated materials. Evidence of use includes continuous requests via voter registration forms for materials in languages other than English, tally cards prepared by poll workers on Election Day enumerating the number of voters who requested multilingual materials, and feedback from community-based organizations.

According to Los Angeles County data, bilingual material requests increased from 6,227 in 1993 to 137,091 by April 2006.[67] Between December 1999 and August 2005, the total number of voters in Los Angeles County requesting language assistance increased by 38 percent because of outreach efforts (Lee 2005: 4). The demand for language assistance is high for all covered language groups.

Alaska Natives and American Indians Native Americans often rely upon language assistance to participate in elections, as "many Native Americans – particularly older individuals – continue to speak their traditional languages and live in isolation from English-speaking society."[68] Surveys of tribes confirmed that language differences depress Native American political participation. Thirty-seven percent of 319 tribal leaders identified "language differences" and 25 percent identified "English language ballots" as significant barriers. A separate survey of Navajo and Pueblo Indians in northwestern New Mexico found that 48 percent were "more comfortable" speaking their own language than English.[69] The need for oral language assistance for Native American voters is acute for ballot questions. Federal observers found that during the 1988 and 1990 elections in southwestern states, many American Indians had no access to translations, and "even when translators were available, the message conveyed to minority language voters often did not resemble the issue on the ballot and it was impossible for a minority-language individual to cast an informed vote."[70]

In 2004, a survey in Coconino County, Arizona, found that 20 percent of Navajo voters required language assistance when they voted. Among voters whose primary language is Navajo, 81 percent needed language assistance to cast an effective ballot. One quarter of Navajo voters provided language assistance to LEP Navajo-speaking voters.[71]

Oral language assistance and information in voters' own languages are keys to Native American political participation. In the 1988 general election in Sandoval County, New Mexico, although 62.7 percent of ballots included votes on referendum issues, only 7.4 percent of American Indian ballots included votes for those issues. In the county's 1984 election, only 4 percent of eligible American Indian voters cast absentee ballots, compared to 26 percent of eligible white voters.[72] Similar problems have arisen in Alaska, where lack of language assistance prevents Alaska Natives from casting effective votes, particularly on complicated ballot questions (Chapter 10).

---

67 *Continuing Need for Section 203's Provisions for Limited English Proficient Voters: Hearing Before the S. Comm. on the Judiciary*, 109th Cong. 95, at 96 (response of Deborah Wright, Acting Assistant Registrar-Recorder, Dep't of Registrar-Recorder, Los Angeles, California, to written questions) ("Wright Response").

68 S. 2236 Hearings, 102d Cong., 2d Sess., S. Hrg. 102–1066, at 159 (1992) (statement of John Dunne, Assistant Att'y Gen.).

69 S. 2236 Hearings, 102d Cong., 2d Sess., S. Hrg. 102–1066, at 328 (1992) (joint testimony of Native Am. Rts. Fund and Nat'l Cong. of Am. Indians).

70 S. 2236 Hearings, 102d Cong., 2d Sess., S. Hrg. 102–1066, at 156–57 (1992) (statement of John Dunne, Assistant Att'y Gen.).

71 James Thomas Tucker and Rodolfo Espino, et al., *Voting Rights in Arizona: 1982–2006*, 17 S. Cal. Rev. L. & Soc. Just. 283, 316–19 (2008).

72 S. Rep. No. 102–315, at 9 (1992).

Asian language voters There is widespread demand for language assistance among Asian American voters. In New York, 80 percent of Chinese-American voters in Chinatown and Queens County stated that they would vote more often if bilingual assistance were provided. A 1991 survey of non-English-speaking Chinese voters in San Francisco found that nearly 90 percent believed the availability of bilingual materials was important to participate in elections, and one-third actually requested bilingual assistance. A survey of Asian American voters in Los Angeles County found that 84 percent indicated bilingual ballots would be helpful, with 56 percent of all registered voters stating that they would be more likely to vote if bilingual assistance were available (S. Rep. No. 102–315, 1992: 12).

More recent evidence is consistent with high usage among Asian language voters. Between December 1999 and August 2005, requests for language assistance among specific language groups in Los Angeles County increased as follows: Tagalog (Filipino) by 63 percent, Chinese by 49 percent, Vietnamese by 40 percent, Spanish by 37 percent, Korean by 26 percent, and Japanese by 25 percent (Lee 2005: 4).

A November 2004 exit poll of 11,000 Asian American voters found almost one-third needed language assistance to vote, including 46 percent of first-time voters. Of 7,247 Asian American voters surveyed in New York City, 46 percent reported that they were LEP. Thirty-seven percent of Chinese voters and 42 percent of Korean voters needed language assistance to vote. Among first-time voters, 68 percent used a bilingual interpreter to vote, and 53 percent used translated voting materials.[73]

Spanish-speaking voters In the 1984 GAO study (Myth 2), out of more than a quarter-million Hispanic voters surveyed, 69,000 used bilingual voting materials, and 85,000 used oral assistance (GAO 1986: 27–33). Use of language assistance was greatest among LEP Hispanic voters (GAO 1986: 28–29). Hispanics who were elderly or who had less than a high school education were the most likely voters to use language assistance. Seventy-three percent of voters using a Spanish language ballot had less than a high school education (GAO 1986: 61). The same patterns were present in other states.

In the 1988 general election, 20 percent of Hispanic voters in New Mexico, 19 percent of Hispanic voters in Texas, and 10 percent of Hispanic voters California reported using bilingual voting assistance. In the 1990 general election, 25 percent of Hispanic voters in Texas and 18 percent of Hispanic voters in California used bilingual election services.

In 1990, 18 percent of Hispanic voters in California used language assistance. Nationwide, one-fifth of all Spanish-speaking voters require Spanish language materials and assistance to cast an effective ballot (S. Rep. No. 102–315, 1992: 11–12).

The experience of Hispanics in Arizona has been similar. In a survey of Spanish-speaking Hispanic voters in Maricopa County who voted in 2004, 76 percent received some type of language assistance when they voted. Among all Hispanic voters, including LEP and non-LEP voters alike, approximately 10 percent needed language assistance (Tucker and Espino 2008: 318). That finding is roughly comparable to the need for language assistance among Latinos in Maricopa County that the Census Bureau identified in its July 2002 determinations under Section 203 (Chapter 5; Appendix C).

---

73 Asian Am. Leg. Def. and Educ. Fund, Asian Americans and the Voting Rights Act: The Case for Reauthorization, *attached to Continuing Need for Section 203's Provisions for Limited English Proficient Voters: Hearing Before the S. Comm. on the Judiciary*, 109th Cong. 229 (2006) (Testimony of Margaret Fung, Executive Dir. of the Asian Am. Legal Def. and Educ. Fund).

Causes of Low Use of Language Assistance

Critics argue that "low use" of language assistance demonstrates that bilingual election requirements are overbroad. In 2006, Mauro Mujica, Chairman of U.S. English, urged that jurisdictions covered by Section 203 be allowed to opt out if they could show that few voters used bilingual materials and assistance. He pointed to King County, Washington, where Seattle is located. According to Mujica, after the county became covered for Chinese language assistance in 2002, only 24 Chinese ballots were used.[74]

Even if there appears to be "low use" of bilingual election materials, the materials still may be needed. "Low use" could suggest a jurisdiction is conducting insufficient outreach. In a 2005 survey of Section 203 jurisdictions, nearly two-thirds admitted they did not engage in any community outreach to covered language groups (Chapter 6). King County illustrates the impact outreach has on language assistance usage. After the low use in the first election following the county's coverage, election officials worked with Chinese-American community organizations and increased publicity about bilingual election materials. According to the County Elections Office:

> Thanks to increased outreach efforts, King County had a record number of requests for elections materials in Chinese during the 2005 Primary and enlisted more bilingual poll workers than ever. The number of registered voters requesting election materials in Chinese for this year's General Election has increased more than 26 percent over last year's General Election. The pool of bilingual poll workers has increased 60 percent from 60 in the 2004 General Election to 96 so far this year.[75]

In 2005, just three years after the county became covered, the number of requested Chinese ballots increased by more than 5,800 percent (Trasviña 2006: 65).

"Low use" also results from the failure of covered jurisdictions to provide language materials and assistance. Of the covered jurisdictions that responded to a 2005 survey, 19.4 percent provided no language assistance and 14 percent provided only bilingual written materials. Sixty-one percent failed to provide language assistance to voters making telephonic inquiries. More than half did not have at least one full-time worker in the covered languages, and two-thirds failed to provide oral language assistance for more than half of all common election activities. More than two-thirds did not confirm the language abilities of their poll workers, and nearly two-thirds did not provide any training on Section 203 (Chapter 6). Language assistance cannot be used if it is not provided and the covered language minority voters do not know that it is available.

Myth 6: Language Assistance Must Be Offered Even Where It Is Unneeded

ProEnglish contends that Section 203's coverage formula "means that every municipality within a covered jurisdiction must provide multilingual election materials – even if everyone there speaks

---

74 *Continuing Need for Section 203's Provisions for Limited English Proficient Voters: Hearing Before the S. Comm. on the Judiciary*, 109th Cong. 304–05 (statement of Mauro E. Mujica, Chairman of the Board, U.S. English, Inc.).

75 King County (WA) Elections, Dep't of Exec. Servs., *Gary Locke helps Kings County recruit bilingual poll workers*, Oct. 25, 2005, *available at* http://www.metrokc.gov/elections/news/2005_10_25.htm.

English."[76] The English-only group has referred to a city in Florida as an example. Opponents of "bilingual ballots" therefore imply that the coverage formula is unconstitutionally overbroad. The facts do not support ProEnglish's example.

Assistance Only Is Required Where Needed

ProEnglish maintains that "the Justice Department ordered Briny Breezes, Florida to print notices for a local election in Spanish" even though 99 percent of residents speak English "very well." Briny Breezes is located in Palm Beach County, which is covered for Spanish under Section 203.[77] Justice Department regulations provide that when a county is covered under Section 203, "all political units that hold elections within that political subdivision (e.g., cities, school districts) are subject to the same requirements" as the county.[78] Therefore, according to ProEnglish, Briny Breezes must provide "bilingual ballots" in Spanish, even if no one requires them.

The Justice Department sends coverage notices to jurisdictions like Briny Breezes, when a county becomes covered.[79] But that does not mean the Department mandates "bilingual ballots" there. As the Department wrote in a notice letter following the 2002 determinations, Section 203 "does not require that information in minority languages be provided to people who have no need for it."[80]

The Section 203 coverage formula does occasionally lead to some anomalies. For example, the reservation trigger has resulted in coverage of some places where there are no members of the covered language group (Chapter 4). A handful of jurisdictions are covered for AIAN languages because they contain a portion of a reservation that satisfies the 5 percent trigger, even though there are no voters in those counties who speak the covered languages (Chapter 5). However, an isolated instance where coverage is unneeded does not invalidate Section 203's formula. Like Briny Breezes, locations covered for languages where there is no need for assistance are not required to provide it. "Targeting" helps a jurisdiction determine when that is the case.

Bilingual language assistance may be terminated in two instances. Section 203's bailout provision allows a jurisdiction to be removed from coverage where voting and educational discrimination and their effects have subsided. In addition, when the need for language assistance drops below the triggering threshold or the illiteracy rate no longer exceeds the national average, coverage ends. The language assistance requirements are thereby only applied where they are needed (Chapter 4).

Use of Targeting to Provide Assistance Where Needed

"Targeting" can help identify the location of LEP voters who need language assistance. Targeting allows a covered jurisdiction to comply with the bilingual election requirements by providing bilingual materials and assistance "only to the language minority citizens and not to every voter in

76 ProEnglish, *A Nation Divided: The Consequences of Bilingual Ballots; Five Reasons Why Congress Should Not Renew the Bilingual Voting Provisions of the Voting Rights Act*, *available at* http://www.proenglish.org.

77 McAlpin 2005: 71 (quoting a Washington Times story).

78 28 C.F.R. § 55.9.

79 *See* U.S. Dept. of Just., Civ. Rts. Div., Voting Section, Section 203 correspondence, *available at* http://www.usdoj.gov/crt/voting/sec_203/activ_203.htm#correspondence.

80 Letter from Ralph F. Boyd, Jr., Assistant Attorney General, Civil Rights Division, to Ms. Nadine Parkhurst, Clerk of the Board, Cochise County, Ariz. (July 26, 2002).

the jurisdiction" (S. Rep. No. 94–295, 1975: 39). It is not "illegal," as some critics claim (English First Foundation 2000). Although the VRA does not expressly provide for targeting, the Act's legislative history shows Congress intended to give jurisdictions flexibility in devising appropriate methods to provide assistance.[81]

Targeting is permissible if it provides language minorities with effective assistance (S. Rep. No. 94–295, 1975: 69). The Justice Department regulations explain "that a targeting system will normally fulfill the Act's minority language requirements if it is designed and implemented in such a way that language minority group members who need minority language materials and assistance receive them."[82] Even opponents of bilingual election requirements, like the former Chairman of U.S. English, acknowledge that targeting is cost-effective.[83]

Identifying the need for assistance The first step in targeting is to identify the location of covered LEP citizens eligible to vote. There are several ways to do this. New voters can be asked their language preference when they register, and existing voters can be sent a postcard in the covered language asking them to identify their preferred language, to ensure that written materials and oral assistance are available where necessary (S. Rep. No. 94–295, 1975: 68). A similar method can be used to identify voters to receive bilingual voting materials by mail.[84]

Election officials can rely upon existing data sources. The starting point should be the Census determinations (Chapter 5; Appendix C). If officials are unsure of LEP and illiteracy rates for their jurisdiction, they can contact the Census Bureau and request that data through a special tabulation. Despite its precision for making Section 203 coverage determinations, the utility of Census data sometimes can be limited.[85] Accurate local Census data may be unavailable if Census blocks are split between two or more election precincts. The data may be stale, particularly in places experiencing changing demographics. Language minorities may be undercounted. Sparsely populated Census blocks may preclude accurate sampled data from being available. Census data also may be suppressed for less populated jurisdictions where disclosure would reveal the sources of information and violate the respondents' rights to confidentiality. The 2006 amendments cured staleness problems through more frequently updated American Community Survey (ACS) data, which will be used to make coverage determinations in five-year increments starting in 2010 (Chapter 4).

Voter registration lists also can be used, particularly where data on the race or ethnicity of registered voters is available or surname analysis is possible (discussed below). Registration data will not necessarily identify precincts where large numbers of unregistered language minority citizens reside (U.S. Comptroller General 1978: 40). Jurisdictions may rely upon assessments by precinct officials, understanding that officials often downplay the need for language assistance (U.S. Comptroller General 1978: 39–40). The most effective way to target is to use some combination of these methods, along with input from language minority communities. Covered jurisdictions must update this information regularly, particularly if the demographics are changing.

---

81 121 Cong. Rec. S13,650 (daily ed. July 24, 1975) (statement of Sen. Tunney).

82 28 C.F.R. § 55.17.

83 *See* S. 2236 Hearings, 102d Cong., 2d Sess., S. Hrg. 102–1066, at 300 (statement of Stanley Diamond, Chairman of U.S. English).

84 *See* 28 C.F.R. § 55.18(a).

85 *See* Comptroller General of the United States, Voting Rights Act: Enforcement Needs Strengthening 39–40 (1978).

Providing the assistance in targeted areas After determining where bilingual materials and assistance should be targeted, a covered jurisdiction can reduce its costs by focusing its efforts on those areas. Mailings of bilingual written materials can be directed to only those "persons who are likely to need them or to residents of neighborhoods in which such a need is likely to exist, supplemented by a notice of the availability of minority language materials in the general mailing (in English and in the applicable minority language)," along with separate publicity regarding those materials.[86] As one congressman explained, "English language mailings sent to registered voters will obviously not assist language minority voters unless, at a minimum, the mail includes information in that minority language regarding how to request help."[87]

Minority language materials do not need to be provided at polling sites with a small number of language minority registered voters if the jurisdiction has targeted assistance through "an alternative system enabling those few to cast effective ballots."[88] Section 203 does "not demand the unreasonable from jurisdictions." Therefore, "[J]urisdictions with small language minority communities may not need to implement language assistance measures identical to those provided in larger jurisdictions" (Trasviña 2006: 74–76).

It may be unnecessary to have bilingual election officials at polling places where LEP voters receive assistance from a person of their choice.[89] Frequently, however, language minority voters are accompanied to the polls by assisters of their choice because no language materials or assistance are available (Trasviña 2006: 74–76). Therefore, covered jurisdictions typically cannot rely upon voters' use of outside assisters to justify their failure to provide language assistance (Myth 9). Also, jurisdictions often enforce voter assistance practices violating federal law (Chapter 6). Care must be taken to comply with Section 208, the federal voter assistance provision. Language assistance must comply with an "effectiveness" standard, in which the extent of assistance available is tailored to ensure that language minority voters can participate effectively in elections (Chapter 4).[90]

Bilingual poll workers can lower costs Another form of targeting is hiring and training bilingual language minorities to serve as election officials. Hiring bilingual poll workers is often overlooked as a way to lower costs. In some cases, the failure to hire bilingual poll workers may be intentional. During the 1992 reauthorization, the Idaho Attorney General testified that efforts by the Shoshone-Bannock Tribes to provide language assistance for elderly Native American voters by hiring bilingual Native American poll workers initially were rebuffed by local election officials.[91]

Covered jurisdictions generally are not required to hire additional poll workers if they use poll workers who can communicate effectively in covered languages.[92] In most cases, bilingual poll workers are paid the same as other poll workers. Rather than hiring bilingual poll workers for every polling place, some jurisdictions use standby poll workers who are "available to come to the polling place, if called, to provide assistance" (GAO 1986: 20). Use of on-call bilingual translators may be appropriate for covered jurisdictions with very few LEP voters at a particular precinct, but they cannot be used in every instance. States such as California, New Jersey, and Texas require in-

---

86 28 C.F.R. § 55.18(a).

87 138 Cong. Rec. H6605 (daily ed. July 24, 1992) (statement of Rep. Brooks).

88 28 C.F.R. § 55.18(d).

89 28 C.F.R. § 55.20(c).

90 28 C.F.R. § 55.20(c).

91 *See* S. 2236 Hearings, 102d Cong., 2d Sess., S. Hrg. 102–1066, at 197–98 (statement of Larry Echohawk, Att'y Gen., Idaho).

92 138 Cong. Rec. H6606 (daily ed. July 24, 1992) (statement of Rep. Pelosi).

person staffing during all poll hours in voting precincts with a designated number or percentage of registered voters who are LEP or have a Spanish surname (Chapter 2; Myth 7).

Use of volunteers may be acceptable if language minority voters have the same opportunities as other voters to serve as paid election officials (GAO 1986: 20). However, if equal opportunities are not provided, that practice violates Section 2, in addition to Section 203. If their exclusion is intentional, the jurisdiction also may be held liable under the Fourteenth and Fifteenth Amendments to the U.S. Constitution (Chapter 2).

Language recordings can be used if effective If a language recording provides oral instructions and assistance effectively to voters who need it, bilingual poll workers may be unnecessary. Maricopa County, Arizona, uses audio recordings to provide oral language assistance to some LEP voters from the Pima Indian community.[93] Nevertheless, language recordings tend to be less common than other forms of assistance, with just 5.7 percent of 227 surveyed jurisdictions reporting their use (Chapter 6).

While audio recordings can be effective under certain circumstances, they suffer from several defects. Instructions on how to complete voter registration forms and other materials can be so long that they are unusable. Audio translations of ballot questions can last for ten minutes or more, especially in AIAN languages. They can be difficult to understand if the recorded voice is in a different dialect or does not reflect the proper inflections for the covered language. Recordings can be cumbersome for voters who miss part of a translation and are unable to rewind it to a specific place, particularly with lengthy digital recordings. Typically, recordings cannot be taken into a voting booth with the voter, making it difficult to remember information when casting a ballot. Recordings also may be inappropriate for voters unaccustomed to technology, such as elderly voters or many AIAN voters. The greatest limitation of audio recordings is that they are not interactive and cannot answer any questions a voter might have.

Use of targeting to address voting machine limitations Targeting sometimes can address voting machines that "cannot mechanically accommodate a ballot in English and in the applicable minority language."[94] In 1992, Los Angeles County was required to provide election materials in six languages and was expected to have the greatest costs of any jurisdiction covered by Section 203. Faced with more languages than its voting machines could handle, Los Angeles County was forced to implement alternative voting methods allowing it to provide language assistance without relying on a bilingual ballot on a voting machine.

Congress recognized that under those circumstances, jurisdictions may use sample ballots in polling booths to minimize expenses.[95] Sample ballots are replicas of the official ballots that are provided in advance to allow voters to become familiar with the candidates and issues before Election Day. As long as sample ballots and voting machine instructions in the covered minority languages are distributed effectively and language minority voters are permitted to bring the sample ballots with them into the voting booth, it may be unnecessary for voting machines to have ballots printed in each of the covered languages.[96]

93 *See* Christina Leonard, *Translator Finds Words for Pima-Speaking Voters*, Ariz. Republic, Aug. 13, 2002, at 7B.

94 28 C.F.R. § 55.19(d).

95 H.R. Rep. No. 102–655 at 9, 12 (1992); S. Rep. No. 102–315, 1992: 20–21.

96 *See* 28 C.F.R. § 55.19(d).

Increasingly, voting machine technology facilitates the availability of assistance in multiple languages.[97] However, even the latest-generation audio-equipped electronic voting machines that produce a verifiable paper record are not a panacea. They do little good if no one uses them. In Alaska, only 1 percent of all ballots were cast on electronic voting machines. Cultural barriers and discomfort using the machines caused LEP Alaska Natives, particularly elders, to prefer paper ballots. In many Native villages, the machines were never turned on (Chapter 10).

Methods of targeting vary, depending upon the needs of the covered language minority group and the jurisdiction's resources. The touchstone for targeting is whether "it is designed and implemented in a manner that ensures that all members of the language minority who need assistance, receive assistance" (H.R. Rep. No. 102–655, 1992: 9).

Myth 7: Targeting by Surname Is Racial Profiling

Opponents of "bilingual ballots" also attack the use of surname analysis to identify where to offer language assistance. Critics call the practice "racial profiling,"[98] decrying it as a "stereotype" that language ability is determined from last names.[99] According to Peter Kirsanow, a conservative member of the U.S. Commission on Civil Rights, it "implicates constitutional issues of Section 203's proportionality and congruence" (Kirsanow 2006: 12). Chris Norby, a member of the Board of Supervisors in Orange County, California, contends that "English fluency assumptions must never be based on a voter's surname."[100] The evidence does not support their arguments. Surname analysis is used to target language assistance and to provide a reliable measure for compliance with federal and state bilingual election requirements.

Surname Analysis Is Not Racial Profiling

Under surname analysis, the number of registered voters may be determined by examining the last name of registered voters. Surname analysis is used to identify persons of certain ethnicities, particularly those of Spanish or Filipino heritage. In some cases, it also may be used to locate members of other ethnic or language minority groups.

Spanish surname analysis employs a four-step process. First, the number of registered voters with an identifiable Spanish surname is matched with the Census list of surnames from that group. Second, for each Census tract within a jurisdiction, the proportion of voting-age citizens who are "both Spanish surnamed and of Spanish origin among all persons with Spanish surnames" is

---

97 *See* Michael Amedeo, *Some voting machines will speak Navajo this election*, ALBUQUERQUE TRIB., Oct. 19, 2006.

98 Statement of Sen. Specter, *reprinted in Continuing Need for Section 203's Provisions for Limited English Proficient Voters: Hearing Before the S. Comm. on the Judiciary*, S. HRG. 109–669, at 24 (June 13, 2006).

99 Testimony of Peter Kirsanow, Member, United States Civil Rights Commission (June 13, 2006), *reprinted in Continuing Need for Section 203's Provisions for Limited English Proficient Voters: Hearing Before the S. Comm. on the Judiciary*, S. HRG. 109–669, at 17, 25 (June 13, 2006).

100 Testimony of Chris Norby, Supervisor, Orange County, California Board of Supervisors, Before the Subcomm. on the Const. of the House Jud. Comm., *Fannie Lou Hamer, Rosa Parks, and Coretta Scott King Voting Rights Act Reauthorization and Amendments Act of 2006 (Part II)*, H. HRG. 109–119, at 14–17 (May 4, 2006).

"applied to the number of Spanish-surnamed registered voters whose residences lay within that tract." That provides an estimate of the number of Spanish-surnamed registered voters who are of Spanish origin. Third, within each Census tract, the proportion of voting-age citizens without a Spanish surname but who are of Spanish origin "is applied to the number of registered voters without Spanish surnames." What results is "an estimate of the number of registered voters who did not have Spanish surnames" (often through marriage) but are of Spanish origin. Fourth, the "two estimates of Spanish origin voters resulting from steps 2 and 3 [are] added together to derive the total number of registered voters of Spanish origin."[101]

Surname analysis plays no role in Section 203 coverage determinations (Chapter 4). Rather, it is one of many tools commonly used to identify areas within covered jurisdictions where language assistance is likely needed, after coverage determinations have been made.[102] As the Assistant Attorney General explained:

> While a particular surname tells a county nothing about the language skills of a particular voter, a county that seeks to locate registered voters who speak Vietnamese logically could most effectively look among those precincts with substantial numbers of Vietnamese-surnamed voters. From that starting point, the local election officials can efficiently conduct further inquiry to determine the actual needs of the voters in those particular precincts. The surname – or ethnicity or place of birth analysis – is a tool that may help election officials comply with Sections 203 and 4(f)(4).[103]

In other words, "surname analysis should be one of the tools that is used, but not the only tool, and there should be much greater reliance placed on outreach to community groups that can help to identify where [LEP] voters are located" (Fung 2006: 25–26). Congress identified surname analysis as an accepted method for identifying persons of Spanish heritage (Chapter 3). Federal courts also have approved surname analysis to help locate where language assistance is needed.[104]

Surname Analysis Is Commonly Used in Settlements and under State Law

A former Justice Department attorney has criticized use of surname analysis in agreements to settle the Department's Section 203 lawsuits. He says it "suggests that having a certain surname imparts LEP status and lack of English-language ability on particular voters." He contends that is unreliable and does not necessarily provide effective language assistance. He implies that the Department's

---

101 *Garza v. County of Los Angeles*, 756 F. Supp. 1298, 1325–26 (C.D. Cal.), *aff'd*, 918 F.2d 763 (9th Cir. 1990), *cert. denied*, 408 U.S. 1028 (1991).

102 *See* Statement of Rena J. Comisac, Principal Deputy Assistant Attorney General, Civil Rights Division, Before the Subcomm. on the Const. of the House Jud. Comm., *Fannie Lou Hamer, Rosa Parks, and Coretta Scott King Voting Rights Act Reauthorization and Amendments Act of 2006 (Part II)*, H. Hrg. 109–19, at 12 (May 4, 2006).

103 Written Answers of Wan J. Kim, Assistant Attorney General, *Hearing Before the Committee on the Judiciary of the United States Senate, Modern Enforcement of the Voting Rights Act*, S. Hrg. 109–562, at 55, 59 (May 10, 2006).

104 *See Hernandez v. Texas*, 347 U.S. 745, 480 n.12 (1954); *Ely v. Klahr*, 403 U.S. 108, 118 (1971) (Douglas, J., concurring); *Aranda v. Van Sickle*, 600 F.2d 1267, 1269 (9th Cir. 1979); *Perez v. Pasadena Indep. Sch. Dist.*, 958 F. Supp. 1196, 1212 n. 21 (S.D. Tex. 1997); *Terrazas v. Slagle*, 789 F. Supp. 828, 836 (W.D. Tex. 1992); *Garza v. County of Los Angeles* 1990: 1325–28.

reliance on surname analysis to identify the number of bilingual poll workers required in voting precincts for certain jurisdictions only has occurred since 2004.[105]

It is true that surname analysis should be used as one tool, among many, to help identify where language assistance needs to be targeted. However, that does not make its use in settlement agreements improper. Like any contracting party, the Justice Department needs to include requirements to measure the covered jurisdiction's compliance. A general requirement of providing "effective" assistance, the standard used under Section 203, does not accomplish that (Chapter 4). Instead, for each voting precinct, it is necessary to identify the exact number of bilingual poll workers that are required. Although LEP rates of eligible voters may be available from the Census Bureau for a covered jurisdiction, that same data usually is unavailable for each voting precinct (Myth 6).

Surname analysis provides a verifiable standard. A settlement agreement might require that if a precinct has between 200 and 350 registered voters with a Spanish surname, there shall be at least one bilingual Spanish-speaking translator; if there are more than 350 such voters, there shall be at least two translators. If the jurisdiction does not staff voting precincts with the required number of translators, that fact will be easy to establish. A federal court overseeing the settlement agreement will know whether the jurisdiction is complying with the requirement. Covered jurisdictions often agree to include staffing tied to surname analysis because it provides clear guidelines. Similar provisions have been included in Justice Department settlement agreements long before 2004. The 1999 settlement agreement between the Department and Passaic County, New Jersey, required the county to "target the language assistance to those voting precincts in which 10 percent or more of the registered voters had Spanish surnames" (Tucker Fall 2007: 261).

The contention that targeting bilingual poll workers based upon surname "belies federal regulations' 'effectiveness' standard" improperly conflates two distinct standards to reach a false conclusion (Adelson 2007: 3). Targeting is not required to provide effective language assistance, but instead is used to allow a jurisdiction to reduce costs by ensuring that assistance is available only where it is needed (Myth 6). In litigation, targeting by surname is commonly used to facilitate compliance with court orders and settlement agreements. Like other components of a language assistance program, surname analysis does not ensure that assistance is effective. Staffing bilingual translators in polling places does little good if the language, reading, and translation skills of the translators are not confirmed, the translators are untrained, and they do not proactively offer language assistance. However, surname analysis facilitates identification of polling places where language assistance is needed. That assistance may be effective if the other necessary steps are taken (Chapters 4, 6).

Surname analysis is not limited to settlement agreements for Section 203 cases. Some states voluntarily use it to target assistance under their own laws. New Jersey requires at least two bilingual poll workers of Hispanic origin fluent in Spanish present in each designated Spanish Election District, which are those voting precincts "in which the primary language of 10% or more of the registered voters is Spanish," as determined by Spanish surname (Chapter 2). Texas "provides Spanish surname analysis to each county elections office in the State to assist local officials in compliance with State law, which requires a bilingual poll worker where five percent or more of registered voters have Spanish surnames" (Kim 2006: 59).

---

105 Bruce L. Adelson, *Minority-Language Election Rules and the Public Lawyer*, 15 Pub. Lawyer 1, 3 (2007).

Myth 8: Language Assistance Is Costly

In 1975, some Congressmen opposed Section 203 because of the high cost they believed it imposed on federal, state, and local governments.[106] Similar arguments were made in subsequent reauthorizations of the provisions, including in 2006 (Chapter 7). Their fears have not materialized.

The bilingual election requirements have imposed minimal costs on the federal government (S. Rep. No. 94–295, 1975: 64). Most federal expenditures resulted from the "modest" $45 to $55 million costs for surveys mandated under the 1975 VRA amendments. Because Section 203's definitions track existing Census definitions, those expenses have not recurred. Remaining federal expenditures have been for enforcing Section 203.[107] During a four-year period between 1993 and 1997, those costs only totaled $1 million (H.R. Rep. No. 102–655, 1992: 12; S. Rep. No. 102–315, 1992: 20–21). In part because of the low costs to the federal government and the importance of protecting the fundamental right to vote, efforts by opponents to cut off funds to enforce the bilingual election requirements have failed (Chapter 7).

The cost to state and local governments for the federal mandate also tends to be low. Many covered jurisdictions already have to comply with state bilingual election procedures (Chapters 2, 6), at "relatively little cost." In 1975, Congress found New York City had been holding elections in compliance with Section 203 at an additional cost of approximately $100,000 per year for 345,800 Spanish-speaking citizens (S. Rep. No. 94–295, 1975: 39). Therefore, federal funds have not been needed to implement Section 203 (Trasviña 2006: 59–60; H.R. Rep. No. 102–655, 1992: 12; S. Rep. No. 102–315, 1992: 20–21). Some minority languages are unwritten or no longer spoken, thereby reducing costs further (Chapter 4). Targeting and use of bilingual poll workers are perhaps the best ways to provide effective language assistance inexpensively.

Cost Savings from Targeting

The experience of covered jurisdictions demonstrates that targeting significantly reduces costs. The GAO conducted studies in 1986 and 1997 to determine costs associated with language assistance under Section 203.[108] While most responding jurisdictions failed to track the costs of providing bilingual voting assistance, the data suggested minimal costs. Overall, the costs of compliance generally comprised only a small portion of total election expenses, usually because of effective targeting (GAO 1986: 17; GAO 1997: 16, 18).

1986 GAO study According to the GAO's 1986 study, an estimated 18 states incurred no additional costs to provide language assistance. Of 295 responding jurisdictions, the average cost of providing written bilingual language materials or assistance was 7.6 percent of the total election expenditures. By comparison, of 259 jurisdictions providing oral language assistance, 205 reported no cost at all, and 39 reported a total cost of only $30,000, about 2.9 percent of election expenditures.

---

106 *See, e.g.*, 121 Cong. Rec. H4740 (daily ed. June 2, 1975) (statement of Rep. Wiggins); 121 Cong. Rec. H4828 (daily ed. June 3, 1975) (statement of Rep. Young); 121 Cong. Rec. H4890–91 (daily ed. June 4, 1975) (statement of Rep. Talcott); 121 Cong. Rec. H4901 (daily ed. June 4, 1975) (statement of Rep. Ashbrook); 121 Cong. Rec. H4912 (daily ed. June 4, 1975) (statement of Rep. Lagomarsino); 121 Cong. Rec. H3011–12 (daily ed. June 10, 1975) (statement of Rep. Kindness); 121 Cong. Rec. S13,367 (daily ed. July 23, 1975) (statement of Sen. Stevens); 121 Cong. Rec. S13,405 (daily ed. July 23, 1975) (statement of Sen. Bellmon); 121 Cong. Rec. S13,590 (daily ed. July 24, 1975) (statement of Sen. Domenici).

107 42 U.S.C. § 1973aa-5; S. Rep. No. 94–295, 1975: 64.

108 *See* GAO 1986; GAO, Bilingual Voting Assistance: Assistance Provided and Costs (1997).

The GAO concluded that low costs for oral language assistance could be attributed to targeting assistance to where it was needed and using bilingual poll workers. The GAO further determined that the cost of bilingual materials and assistance likely would decrease over time, because bilingual election materials could be reused and election officials would become more familiar with how to comply with Section 203 (GAO 1986: 16–20). The Congressional Budget Office relied upon the GAO's 1986 findings in estimating that the total costs incurred by the 140 jurisdictions affected by the triggering formula included in the 1992 amendments were "likely to be less than $5 million a year" (H.R. Rep. No. 102–655, 1992: 12; S. Rep. No. 102–315, 1992: 20–21).

1997 GAO study The GAO's 1997 study, reporting data from 26 states and 292 covered jurisdictions, also found cost-effective compliance with Section 203. Most jurisdictions reported providing written and oral assistance (GAO 1997: 1–3). Of 28 jurisdictions reporting complete data for 1996, bilingual costs averaged 4.9 percent of total election costs. Bilingual written materials comprised the largest percentage of bilingual costs, about 3.8 percent, but still comprised only a fraction of total election expenses (GAO 1997: 20–22). Nearly all responding jurisdictions incurred little or no additional costs for providing oral assistance (GAO 1997: 11–12, 20–22, 24–26, 27).[109]

Los Angeles County, which provided language materials and assistance to six different language groups, including English, in 5,632 polling places, reported bilingual costs of only 3.6 percent of its total election budget (GAO 1997: 20–22). Hawaii and Florida reported total bilingual costs of only $23,328 and $7,900, respectively (GAO 1997: 3–4). Bilingual election expenses varied greatly, depending upon the number of covered languages, the number of polling sites, the type of covered languages, and the jurisdiction's ability to use targeting to reduce costs (GAO 1997: 3–4, 8–9, 20–29).

2005 Arizona State University study A 2005 study by researchers at Arizona State University reported low costs for language assistance consistent with the two GAO reports. Where implemented properly, language assistance accounts for only a small fraction of total elections costs, if any at all. Among 411 responding jurisdictions in 31 states covered by Section 203, a majority reported no additional costs for either oral or written language assistance. Most of the remaining jurisdictions incurred expenses of less than 1.5 percent for oral language assistance and less than 3 percent for written language assistance (Chapter 6).

Low costs result from several factors. Many jurisdictions hired bilingual poll workers paid the same wages as other poll workers. Some jurisdictions reported that bilingual voting materials were not provided because the written languages were not commonly used. Several jurisdictions providing bilingual written materials used election officials or community volunteers to translate materials, resulting in no additional costs. In many cases, printing costs did not increase even with bilingual materials (Chapter 6).

Other cost evidence presented to Congress Election officials presented evidence in 2006 corroborating low costs to provide language assistance. The Secretary of State of New Mexico testified that Section 203 costs "are really minimal. The printing of ballots, the hiring of translators

109 Of the 227 jurisdictions reporting oral language assistance, 187 hired bilingual workers, 35 used volunteers, 30 hired interpreters, and 13 used language recordings. Thirty-four jurisdictions reported providing radio announcements, telephone hotlines, and use of bilingual officials in other offices to provide assistance (GAO 1997: 12).

to translate the issues – the bond issues, the constitutional amendment issues, the various offices that people are running for – in Spanish, for example it's [sic] a minimal cost to the State of New Mexico."[110]

Los Angeles County provided similar evidence. Los Angeles County has the highest number of language minority voters in the greatest number of languages (Wright Response 2006: 97). The county spends just below 10 percent of total election costs on language assistance in six languages to LEP citizens comprising 12.9 percent of the electorate.

The costs of Los Angeles County's multilingual (ML) program are reasonable in light of the challenges the county faces. Only eight states have more registered voters than Los Angeles County's nearly four million registered voters. The 2000 Census reported that Los Angeles County has approximately five million voting-age citizens, 12.9 percent of whom (644,505) are LEP in one of the six covered languages: 428,580 Spanish speakers, 95,700 Chinese speakers, 42,390 Korean speakers, 34,985 Tagalog speakers, 30,340 Vietnamese speakers, and 12,510 Japanese speakers.

A county official concluded, "Considering all of these challenges, the percentage of election expenses for language assistance is reasonable and is virtually the same as the percentage of voters who need assistance."[111]

Targeting is responsible for keeping the costs for LEP voters comparable to those for voters who do not require language assistance in Los Angeles County. "In recent years we have been able to realize cost savings in providing multilingual materials by analyzing the cost components and restricting printing to the exact precincts within the County where written materials are needed." The county does not incur additional costs for bilingual poll workers, who "are paid the same stipend as other election day staff, and of course perform regular duties of a poll worker as well" (Wright Testimony 2006: 386–87). Contrary to what critics like Linda Chavez have argued,[112] Los Angeles County's experience proves that language assistance can be offered cost-effectively.

Federal Assistance with Costs

Despite the modest expenses associated with the bilingual election provisions, some members of Congress have decried the provisions as an unfunded federal mandate.[113] In 1975, Congress considered and rejected an amendment offered by Congressman John Krebs of California that would have required the federal government to pay for all the costs of the bilingual elections

---

110 *Voting Rights Act: Section 203 – Bilingual Election Requirements (Part I): Hearing Before the Subcomm. on the Constitution of the H. Comm. on the Judiciary*, 109th Cong. 37 (2005) (statement of Rebecca Vigil-Giron, Sec'y of State, New Mexico).

111 *Continuing Need for Section 203's Provisions for Limited English Proficient Voters: Hearing Before the S. Comm. on the Judiciary*, 109th Cong. 384 (2006) (Testimony of Deborah Wright, Acting Assistant Registrar-Recorder, Dep't of Registrar-Recorder, Los Angeles, California) ("Wright Testimony").

112 *See* Linda Chavez, *Let Bilingual Voting Requirements of Voting Rights Act Die*, Human Events, Nov. 14, 2005.

113 *See, e.g.*, 152 Cong. Rec. H5165 (daily ed. July 13, 2006) (statement of Rep. Paul); 152 Cong. Rec. H5192 (daily ed. July 13, 2006) (statement of Rep. Gingrey); 152 Cong. Rec. H5193 (daily ed. July 13, 2006) (statement of Rep. Campbell); 152 Cong. Rec. H5193 (daily ed. July 13, 2006) (statement of Rep. Hayworth); 152 Cong. Rec. H5194 (daily ed. July 13, 2006) (statement of Rep. Brown-Waite).

mandate.[114] A similar amendment offered by Congressman Gary Condit of California was rejected when Section 203 was reauthorized in 1992.[115]

Although the VRA does not fund the bilingual election requirements, the Help America Vote Act of 2002 (HAVA) made substantial federal funding available for language assistance.[116] Section 101 of HAVA allocates funding for states "providing assistance to Native Americans, Alaska Native citizens, and to individuals with limited proficiency in the English language." The Act does not limit payments to Section 203-covered jurisdictions, providing a financial incentive to non-covered jurisdictions to take steps to make voting more accessible to LEP voters.[117] Total funding for programs directly assisting voters, including accessibility for minority language and disabled voters, amounted to $3.75 billion from Fiscal Years 2003 to 2005.[118]

Following passage of HAVA, jurisdictions could recover some of the modest costs resulting from compliance with the federal bilingual election requirements. Even if federal funds were unavailable, however, it would be reasonable to expect covered jurisdictions to absorb the minimal expenses required to make the fundamental right to vote fully accessible to language minorities. The benefits of such expenses greatly outweigh the costs. Senator Patrick Leahy explained: "[A]lthough there are costs associated with implementing the minority language assistance provisions, they are reasonable … Ensuring full access to American[s'] right to vote certainly is worth this reasonable cost."[119]

Myth 9: Private Assistance Makes Bilingual Elections Unnecessary

Section 203 opponents contend that LEP voters can provide their own assistance. John Miller suggests, "Perhaps we should allow voters to bring a friend or relative into the booth, just as blind voters can do" (Miller 1996). Linda Chavez argues, "Ethnic organizations have a long history of providing such benefits to their community without help from the government" (Chavez 1996). Congressman King made similar statements (Chapter 7). Their argument is flawed for several reasons.

Linguistic Isolation of Many LEP Voters Prevents Self-Help

Requiring LEP voters to bring interpreters with them incorrectly assumes that voters have access to people fluent and literate in their language and English. Many do not. According to the 2000 Census, 4.4 million households with 11.9 million people are "linguistically isolated," in which all household members 14 years and older are LEP. Many covered voters are linguistically isolated: 5 percent of AIAN households, 29.2 percent of Asian American and Pacific Islander households, and 23.9 percent of Spanish-speaking households with 10.7 million people.[120] Congressman James

114 *See* 121 Cong. Rec. H4901 (daily ed. June 4, 1975) (statement of Rep. Krebs); 121 Cong. Rec. at H4902 (daily ed. June 4, 1975) (rejecting the amendment).

115 *See* 138 Cong. Rec. H6600–6604 (daily ed. July 24, 1992) (rejecting the Condit amendment 186 to 184).

116 *See* Pub. L. No. 107–252, 116 Stat. 1666 (codified at 42 U.S.C. §§ 15301–545).

117 42 U.S.C. § 15301(b)(1)(G).

118 *See* 42 U.S.C. §§ 15304, 15407, 15424.

119 152 Cong. Rec. S7904 (daily ed. July 19, 2006) (statement of Sen. Leahy).

120 Bureau of the Census, Economics & Statistics Admin., U.S. Dep't of Commerce, Language Use and English-Speaking Ability: 2000, at 10 (Oct. 2003); 2000 Census, Summary Tape File 3 (STF-3), Tables QT-P17 and P20.

Sensenbrenner concluded that data showed bringing assistance to the polls was "not feasible" for millions of LEP Americans (Chapter 7).[121]

Election Officials Often Deny Voter Assistance

Even when LEP voters know someone who can provide language assistance, poll workers frequently do not allow it. With a few exceptions, Section 208 of the VRA requires that voters be allowed to receive assistance from the person of their choice (Chapter 4). However, nearly 90 percent of election officials responsible for training poll workers in Section 203-covered jurisdictions reported voter assistance practices that violate Section 208. One explanation for the widespread denial of voter assistance is that election officials follow their own state assistance laws, even when those laws are less protective than Section 208 (Chapter 6). Another is lack of training (Chapter 10).

In *United States v. Berks County, Pennsylvania*, the federal court described the discriminatory impact of such practices: "When Defendants deny Spanish-speaking voters in Reading the right to bring their assistor of choice into the voting booth, voters feel uncomfortable with the process, do not understand the ballot, do not know how to operate the voting machine, and cannot cast a meaningful ballot ..."[122] Before Congress enacted Section 203, illiterate LEP voters were routinely denied assistance. In a 1970 Texas case, election officials construed state voter assistance laws narrowly to exclude all forms of language assistance, resulting in the disenfranchisement of more than 300,000 illiterate Mexican-American U.S. citizens (Chapter 3).

Section 203 and Section 208 Remedy Different Problems

There is some overlap between Sections 203 and 208. Each allows voter assistance throughout the voting process, from registration through casting a ballot inside a voting booth. LEP voters illiterate in their native language and in English are permitted to get assistance from the person of their choice to overcome their illiteracy. However, the two provisions were enacted to remedy distinct problems.

Section 208 allows a voter to receive assistance because of blindness, disability, or illiteracy. It applies nationwide and is permanent. It does not require a jurisdiction to provide any assistance at the polls, except that any election officials or poll workers on duty should provide assistance if asked. Section 208 does not require that a jurisdiction provide language assistance. Instead, it is intended to remedy the failure of state laws to allow assistance for voters who want it (Chapters 2, 4).

Conversely, the federal bilingual election provisions mandate that effective language assistance be provided to LEP voters. Sections 4(f)(4) and 203 are temporary and only apply to covered jurisdictions.[123] Congress enacted the provisions to remedy educational and voting discrimination that denied LEP voters access to the political process. The bilingual election mandate was modeled on court remedies and state laws intended to overcome language barriers to voting. Eliminating that mandate would reward state and local governments for failing to address the effects of their discrimination (Chapter 4). It is inconsistent with American law to place the burden on LEP victims to remedy the effects of state-sponsored discrimination.

---

121 152 Cong. Rec. H5192 (daily ed. July 13, 2006) (statement of Rep. Sensenbrenner).

122 277 F. Supp.2d 570, 580 (E.D. Pa. 2003).

123 Section 4(e) of the VRA is permanent and applies nationwide (Chapter 2).

Myth 10: Language Assistance Does Not Increase Voting

Critics charge that language assistance does not increase registration and turnout among language minorities. The English Language Political Action Committee says that since the federal bilingual election requirements were enacted, "Hispanic voter participation has declined ... and the gap between white voting participation and Hispanic citizens' voting participation has widened."[124] This myth is not cited as much as the others, suggesting it is not as widely shared. Political participation data shows why.

Alaska Natives and American Indians

Among American Indians, registration and turnout have increased between 50 percent and 150 percent following enactment of the language assistance requirements.[125] Voter turnout in precincts on seven Arizona Indian reservations rose from 11,789 in 1972 to 15,982 in 1980, with voter registration increasing by 87 percent in Navajo County, Arizona, and 165 percent in Coconino County, Arizona (H.R. Rep. No. 102–655, 1992: 6–7). Turnout among American Indians in Navajo County increased by 120 percent between 1972 and 1990, while Apache County, Arizona, experienced an 88 percent increase during the same period (S. Rep. No. 102–315, 1992: 12). American Indians in New Mexico and Utah experienced similar improvements.[126]

Increases also follow enforcement efforts by the Justice Department. After Apache County, Arizona, entered into a consent decree with the Justice Department, over time the availability and quality of language assistance improved dramatically (Tucker and Espino 2008: 297–308, 320–34). Navajo voter turnout increased by 26 percent between 2000 and 2004, from 14,277 to 17,955.[127]

It is too early to judge the impact of Alaska's recent first-time efforts to provide language assistance after Yup'ik-speaking voters successfully sued the state for violating Sections 203 and 208. However, turnout data shows the impact of the state's violations on political participation. Between 2000 and 2006, voter turnout in the predominately Native area around Bethel trailed statewide turnout by more than 20 percent (Chapter 10).

Asian Language Voters

Following the 1992 amendments to Section 203, the number of Asian Americans registered to vote increased dramatically. Between 1996 and 2004, Asian Americans had the highest increase of new voter registrations, approximately 58.7 percent. During that same period, Asian Americans turnout increased by 71 percent (Asian American Legal Defense and Education Fund [AALDEF] 2006: vi). Those increases resulted from expanded coverage after the addition of the 10,000 person trigger (Chapter 4; Fung 2006: 231).

---

124 English Language Political Action Committee, *Language In America: Declaring English the Official Language of the United States Government – A Candidate's Briefing Paper* (5th ed. 2000).

125 *Voting Rights Act: Section 203 – Bilingual Election Requirements (Part II): Hearing Before the Subcomm. on the Constitution of the H. Comm. on the Judiciary*, 109th Cong. 17 (2005) (statement of Jacqueline Johnson, Executive Director, National Congress of American Indians).

126 S. 2236 Hearings, 102d Cong., 2d Sess., S. Hrg. 102–1066, at 181–89 (1992) (statement of Marshall Plummer, Vice-President of the Navajo Nation).

127 *Voting Rights Act: Sections 6 and 8 – The Federal Examiner and Observer Program: Hearing Before the Subcomm. on the Constitution of the H. Comm. on the Judiciary*, 109th Cong. 12–14 (2005) (statement of Penny Pew, Elections Director, Apache County, Arizona).

Enforcement by the Justice Department also has had an impact. In areas where the Department brought Section 203 enforcement actions, more Asian candidates have run for office after language assistance increased turnout. After the Department obtained an agreement in Harris County, Texas, Vietnamese-American voter turnout doubled and the first Vietnamese-American candidate in history, Hubert Vo, was elected to the Texas legislature. Vo defeated the incumbent chair of the Appropriations Committee by 16 votes out of more than 40,000 cast.[128] Today, at least 346 Asian Americans have been elected to office, including six to federal offices, an increase from 120 elected officials in 1978.[129]

Spanish-Speaking Voters

The link between the language assistance provisions and Latino political participation is evident because the increases far outpaced the increase in the number of Latinos who became naturalized citizens. The Hispanic voter registration rate, which was 34.9 percent in 1974, has nearly doubled since Sections 4(f)(4) and 203 have been in effect.[130] Between 1980 and 1990, Hispanic voter participation increased five times the national rate (H.R. Rep. No. 102–655, 1992: 6). Although Hispanic registration still lags far behind non-Hispanic registration, increased enforcement of Section 203 contributed to the increase of registered Hispanic voters from 7.6 million in 2000 to 9.3 million in 2004.[131] The year after the Justice Department brought a Section 203 lawsuit in San Diego County, Hispanic voter registration increased more than 24 percent (Scholzman 2005: 4).

A study of 1996 and 2000 turnout data established that "residing in an area offering voting materials in the respondent's language of origin" had a significant and positive correlation with Latino turnout. "Latinos living in California were 6 percent more likely to report voting than respondents living in other states." In addition, "Latinos living in an area covered by the language provisions of the Voting Rights Act were 4.4 percent more likely to have voted in 1996 and 2000 than their counterparts residing elsewhere."[132]

Increased voter registration and turnout have contributed to an increase in Hispanic representation at all levels of the government. Between 1973 and 2006, the number of Hispanic elected officials in six covered states, Arizona, California, Florida, New Mexico, New York, and Texas, increased more than 347 percent from 1,280 to 4,532.[133] By January 2006, there were more than 5,600 Hispanic elected officials (NALEO Educ. Fund 2006: 7). Following the November

---

128 *Voting Rights Act: Section 203—Bilingual Election Requirements (Part I): Hearing Before the Subcomm. on the Constitution of the H. Comm. on the Judiciary*, 109th Cong. 12 (2005) (statement of Bradley J. Schlozman, Acting Assistant Att'y Gen., Civil Rights Div., Dep't of Justice).

129 *See Fannie Lou Hamer, Rosa Parks, and Coretta Scott King Voting Rights Act Reauthorization and Amendments Act of 2006 (Part II): Hearing on H.R. 9 Before the Subcomm. on the Constitution of the H. Comm. on the Judiciary*, 109th Cong. 43 (2006) (statement of Karen K. Narasaki, President and Executive Director, Asian American Justice Center).

130 *Continuing Need for Section 203's Provisions for Limited English Proficient Voters: Hearing Before the S. Comm. on the Judiciary*, 109th Cong. 347 (2006) (statement of John Trasviña, Interim President and General Counsel, Mexican American Legal Defense and Education Fund).

131 Bureau of the Census, U.S. Dep't of Commerce, Current Population Reports, Series P20–542, Voting and Registration in the Election of November 2000, tbl.4a.

132 Michael Jones-Correa, *Language Provisions Under the Voting Rights Act: How Effective Are They?*, 86 Soc. Sci. Q. 549, 558 (Sept. 2005).

133 Nat'l Ass'n of Latino Elected and Appointed Officials (NALEO) Educ. Fund, 1985 National Roster of Hispanic Elected Officials xiii (1985); NALEO Educ. Fund, 2006 Latino Election Handbook 11, 15, 25, 37, 41, 45 (2006).

2006 election, Hispanic elected officials included three U.S. Senators, 23 U.S. Representatives, at least a half-dozen statewide officials (including three from New Mexico), approximately 60 state senators, and 180 state representatives.[134] Bilingual language assistance makes a difference in increasing voter registration and turnout among all covered language groups.

Conclusion

An examination of the realities of language assistance explains why critics of "bilingual ballots" rely upon myth. The facts do not support their contentions. Congress relied upon a rich and detailed record of the impact and need for language assistance when it reauthorized Sections 4(f)(4) and 203 in 2006. Section 203 adopts a practical remedy for language barriers, giving election officials in covered jurisdictions the flexibility to provide language assistance in only those places where it is needed, as long as it is effective for voters. Language assistance can be provided at little cost. The voter assistance protections in Section 208 of the VRA have proven to be a wholly insufficient substitute for language assistance. Taken together, these facts prevailed over the rhetoric offered by detractors in 2006. The fabric of American democracy is much stronger by making elections more accessible for LEP voters who need assistance in their native tongue to exercise their first right of citizenship.

---

134 *See* NALEO Educational Fund, *Press Release: Latinos Achieve New Political Milestones in Congress and State Houses* (Nov. 9, 2006).

PART V
A CASE STUDY OF DISCRIMINATION: ALASKA NATIVES

Chapter 9
Discrimination against Alaska Natives

The plight of Alaska Natives parallels that of American Indians in many respects. Despite being the first Americans, both were not fully admitted to citizenship until 1924. They were viewed by many whites as uncivilized. If any education was provided to them, it was through separate and inferior schools designed to destroy their culture and force them to assimilate into the white world.[1] Their lands were stolen from them. Their rights to valuable natural resources were taken away with little, if any, compensation. Both groups were ravaged by epidemics brought by explorers and traders.

There are two notable differences between Alaska Natives and their brethren in the lower 48 states. Unlike American Indians, the federal government never waged a war of extermination against Alaska Natives. However, the effects of the government's cultural war on Native customs, language, and lifestyle were nearly as great. Although the federal government had entered into about 370 treaties with American Indian tribes by 1871 and confined them to reservations, it took a different path with Alaska's tribes. Few reservations were created in Alaska before passage of the Indian Reorganization Act of 1934.[2] The impact of the Alaska Native Settlement Act (ANSA) in 1971 has been preeminent. Today, there are at least 231 federally recognized tribes in Alaska, 13 for-profit ANSA corporations, and 12 regional non-profit ANSA corporations.[3]

This chapter describes discrimination against Alaska Natives. Chapter 10 concludes the discussion with an example of how discrimination and English-only policies have denied the voting rights of Yup'ik-speaking voters in the Bethel region of Alaska.

Jim Crow Practices

For much of Alaska's history prior to statehood, Natives were victims of the same sort of Jim Crow policies pervasive in the South. A war correspondent noted in 1943 that "the social position of Indians and Eskimos in Alaska 'is equivalent to that of a Negro in Georgia or Mississippi.'"[4] For that reason, Territorial Governor John G. Brady "preferred to refer to Alaskan Indians as Natives or 'Alaskans,' because 'for too many whites *Indian* was synonymous with *nigger*'" (Cole 1996: 316). The distance between towns and isolated Native villages caused some separation between Natives and non-Natives. But in communities where geography was not a barrier, segregation and discriminatory practices against Alaska Natives were common.

---

1 *See* Special Subcomm. on Indian Education, Comm. on Labor and Public Welfare, *Indian Education: A National Tragedy – A National Challenge*, S. Rep. No. 501, 91st Cong., 1st Sess. (1969).

2 *See* Kenneth R. Philip, *The New Deal and Alaskan Natives, 1936–1945*, *in* An Alaska Anthology: Interpreting the Past 267 (Stephen W. Haycox and Mary Childers Mangusso eds. 1996).

3 *See* Natalie Landreth and Moira Smith, *Voting Rights in Alaska 1982–2006*, 17 S. Cal. Rev. L. & Soc. Just. 79, 83–85 (2007).

4 Terrence M. Cole, *Jim Crow in Alaska: The Passage of the Alaska Equal Rights Act of 1945*, *in* An Alaska Anthology, *in* An Alaska Anthology 1996: 314, 315.

Nome, "the spot where the people of the Arctic mingle with the invaders from the Temperate zone,"[5] provides an example of that discrimination. Historian Preston Jones documented the "paradox" that existed in Nome: "Nomeites both supported racial segregation and, generally speaking, were friendly toward Natives." The town had segregated "sleeping, eating, and worshipping quarters," but was otherwise tolerant of Natives. However, tolerance had its limits. After an editorial in the *Nome Nugget* about Natives "hanging about the stores and saloons, learning plenty of vice and little good," a reservation was established 20 miles west of town (Jones 2005: 47–49). Jim Crow practices in Nome would later play a critical role in the passage of the territory's first anti-discrimination law in 1945.

Segregation was present in every aspect of cultural, political, and social life in Alaska. Restrictive covenants were included in deeds to prevent property from being conveyed to Natives.[6] Restaurants and stores placed signs in their windows saying "No Natives Allowed" or "No Natives or Dogs Allowed."[7] Movie theaters restricted Natives to seats in the balcony, and communities established segregation in other public places such as hotels, playgrounds, and swimming pools (Cole 1996: 316–21). Natives were excluded from all-white schools and shut out of political life.

The federal government also discriminated against Natives. The commanding officer of the Alaska Defense Command was a southerner who barred Natives from participating in the USO. He separated whites from Natives by encouraging "soldiers to patronize restaurants, stores, and hotels that denied access to Natives" and by placing off limits businesses "that welcomed all races, simply because they did not discriminate against Natives" (Cole 1996: 322). Roy Peratrovich, head of the Alaska Native Brotherhood (ANB), complained of the treatment. He described the discrimination in the context of the war against fascism noting, "Native boys are already in the armed forces and are making the same sacrifices as their white friends ... One of the reasons this war is being fought is because of race discrimination and our nation has preached equality of all races ..."[8] Secretary of War Henry L. Stimson and President Roosevelt ultimately ordered the army to stop the discrimination (Cole 1996: 322–23). During World War II, the federal government also forcibly relocated Aleuts from the island of Attu to camps in southeast Alaska, where they suffered from high mortality rates because of deplorable conditions that destroyed their way of life.[9]

The beginning of the end of Jim Crow practices came in 1944, when 17-year-old Alberta Schenck, an Inupiaq, was arrested in Nome. Schenck had sat in the whites-only section of the Dream Theater, instead of the Eskimo-only section in the balcony nicknamed "Nigger Heaven." Despite assurances from the mayor of Nome to Governor Ernest Gruening that the discrimination would stop, the theater continued to enforce its policy of segregation. When the territorial legislature met in early 1945, it took up legislation that would ban the discrimination in Nome (Cole 1996: 325–32).

Supporters of the bill were confronted by skepticism from the press and racist statements by their opponents. The *Juneau Empire* agreed that discrimination existed in Alaska but argued that a law was unnecessary "because this disease of the mind is being cured gradually" by increasing

5 Preston Jones, *Yankees in Parkas: Native Influence at Nome, 1900–1920*, 20 Alaska Hist. 42, 49 (Fall 2005).

6 Restrictive covenant dated May 10, 1948 and Warranty deed dated March 12, 1953, *available at* http://www.alaskool.org.

7 Donn Liston, *Gruening Rights Fight Recalled*, Anchorage Daily News, June 28, 1974.

8 Letter from Roy Peratrovich, Grand President of the Alaska Native Brotherhood, to Commanding Officer of U.S. Army Camp in Juneau, June 19, 1942, *available at* http://www.alaskool.org.

9 *See* Report of the Commission on Wartime Relocation and Internment of Civilians, Personal Justice Denied 317–59 (1997).

Figure 9.1 Restaurant in Juneau, Alaska, advertising its segregated service in 1908
Source: Photo reprinted with permission of the Alaska State Library, Winter and Pond Photograph Collection, 1893-1943, ASL-PVA-87-1050.

numbers of businesses that allowed Natives (Cole 1996: 330). Senator Allen Shattuck of Juneau asked, "Who are these people, barely out of savagery, who want to associate with us whites with 5,000 years of recorded civilization behind us?"[10] Among those who spoke in favor of the legislation, none was more powerful than Elizabeth Peratrovich, a diminutive Tlingit Native who decried Jim Crow laws fostered by people including "the great superman who believes in the superiority of the white race." When asked by Senator Shattuck if the bill would eliminate discrimination, she answered, "No law will eliminate crimes but at least you as legislators can assert to the world that you recognize the evil of the present situation and speak your intent to help us overcome discrimination"[11] (CCTHITA 1991: 12).

The territorial legislature responded to Peratrovich's plea for equality by passing the Alaska Equal Rights Act of 1945. The Act provided that "All citizens ... shall be entitled to the full and equal enjoyment of accommodations, advantages, facilities, and privileges" of public places. Violations of the Act, which included posting a "sign indicating discrimination on racial grounds" was made a crime punishable by jail and a fine.[12] The Act marked an important first step in eliminating discrimination against Alaska Natives that would continue to persist in other areas.

---

10 Cent. Council of Tlingit and Haida Indian Tribes of Alaska (CCTHITA), *A Recollection of Civil Rights Leader Elizabeth Peratrovich, 1911–1958*, at 11 (1991).

11 *See Superior Race Theory Hit in Hearing: Native Sisterhood President Hits at Rights Bill Opposition*, Alaska Daily Empire, Feb. 6, 1945, at 8.

12 Territory of Alaska, H.B. 14 (approved Feb. 16, 1945), *available at* http://www.alaskool.org.

Figure 9.2 Governor Gruening signs the Alaska Equal Rights Act of 1945
Territorial Governor Ernest Gruening, seated, signs the territorial anti-discrimination act recognizing the equal rights of Alaska Natives. Witnessing the bill-signing are, from left to right: O.D. Cochran, Elizabeth Peratrovich, Edward Anderson, Norman Walker, and Roy Peratrovich.
Source: Photo reprinted with permission of the Alaska State Library, Alaska Territorial Governors Photograph Collection, ASL-PCA274-1-2.

Discriminatory Schooling

Segregated schooling was prevalent in Alaska for more than one hundred years. Initially, the only schooling available to Natives was provided by missionaries and private companies. Later, "a dual school system emerged unofficially in Alaska as resentment among the relatively few whites over emphasis on education for Natives and a belief that integrated schools would give only inferior education."[13] The dual system was born under federal laws governing the territorial government, which Alaska subsequently used as an excuse to repudiate public schooling for Alaska Natives. It remained in place until the early 1980s. Vestiges of educational discrimination remain even today.

13 Settlement Agreement, *Hootch v. State Operated Sch. Sys. ex rel. Tobeluk v. Lind*, Case No. 72–2450-CIV (Alaska Super. Ct. Sept. 3, 1976), at ¶ 9 ("Hootch Settlement").

Missionaries Step In for the Government

Nearly two decades following Russia's cession of Alaska to the United States in 1867, the government did not offer any schooling to Alaska Natives. This early failure was the product of federal indifference. The Department of Interior explained that "for a long time after cession … Congress took no particular notice of these natives … and no special provision was made for their support and education …"[14]

Limited educational opportunities were available in some places. The Alaska Commercial Company offered schooling for Native children on the Pribilof Islands.[15] Missionaries were the primary source of education. Between 1794 and 1887, Russian Orthodox missionaries based out of Kodiak worked with Natives to advance literacy in Aleut, Central and Siberian Yup'ik, and Tlingit.[16] Beginning in the 1870s, the Presbyterian Church established mission schools for Natives in Haines, Sitka, Wrangell, and other locations in southeastern Alaska. Elsewhere, mission schools were operated by Baptist, Episcopalian, Methodist, Moravian, and Roman Catholic missionaries (Alton 2005: 24–26). By 1890, Jesuit and Moravian missionaries had established themselves in Bethel and in villages along the Kuskokwim and lower Yukon Rivers, where they worked on the development of literacy in written Yup'ik (Chapter 10; Alton 2005: 26). Several missionary schools were later subsidized by the federal government. As late as 1949, missionary schools enrolled 600 Natives (Ray 1973: 7–8). In many villages, missionaries provided the only schooling. For Natives in villages without missionary schools, no meaningful educational opportunities existed for secondary schooling until the 1980s.

Federal Laws Fostering Segregation

Seventeen years after cession, Congress enacted the first legislation establishing a civilian government in Alaska. The Organic Act of May 17, 1884 excluded legislation and control over the Native schools from the territorial government. Instead, the Act reserved to the Secretary of the Interior the power to "make needful and proper provision for the education of children of school age in the Territory of Alaska, without reference to race, until such time as permanent provision" was made for them.[17] In 1885, Congress made a Commissioner of Education in the Department of Interior responsible for the education of Alaska Natives (Alton 2005: 20). Like American Indians in the lower 48 states, Alaska Natives were treated as wards of the federal government.

Segregated schools were established by settlers before the turn of the century in towns with larger non-Native populations, such as Douglas, Juneau, and Sitka.[18] That trend accelerated when the population of non-Natives exploded during the Gold Rush era. Non-Natives comprised less than 20 percent of the population in 1890, numbering 4,298 compared to 25,354 Natives. Just 10 years later, non-Natives made up roughly half the population, growing to 30,450 non-Natives compared to 29,542 Natives.[19] The effect of this dramatic growth was immediate: "[A]gitation grew for the

---

14 U.S. Dep't of Interior (DOI), *Status of Alaskan Natives*, 53 Interior Dec. 593, 594 (Feb. 24, 1932).

15 Charles K. Ray, *Alaskan Native Education: An Historical Perspective* 1 (Oct. 1973).

16 *See* Thomas Alton, *Politics, Economics, and the Schools: Roots of Alaska Native Language Loss Since 1867*, 20 Alaska Hist. 18, 20 (Fall 2005).

17 Organic Act of May 17, 1884 § 13, 23 Stat. 24, 27–28 (1884).

18 Stephen E. Cotton, *Alaska's "Molly Hootch Case": High Schools and the Village Voice*, 8 Educ. Res. Q. 30–43 (1984).

19 James H. Ducker, *Gold Rushers North: A Census Study of the Yukon and Alaskan Gold Rushes, 1896–1900, in* An Alaska Anthology 1996: 206.

establishment of a separate system of schools for the non-Native population" (Hootch Settlement 1976: ¶ 9).

In 1900, Congress responded by providing for the establishment and local control of all-white schools within incorporated towns. Native schools continued to be run by the Secretary of Interior.[20] In 1901, Congress amended the law to provide that half of license money collected on businesses outside incorporated towns be used for support of Native schools.[21] By 1903, nine incorporated towns established all-white schools (Cotton 1984).

In January 1905, Congress enacted the Nelson Act, which provided for the establishment of schools in Alaska. The law was written in stark racial terms:

> That the schools specified and provided for in this Act shall be devoted to the education of white children and children of mixed blood who lead a civilized life. The education of the Eskimos and Indians in the district of Alaska shall remain under the direction and control of the Secretary of the Interior, and schools for and among the Eskimos and Indians of Alaska shall be provided for by an annual appropriation, and the Eskimo and Indian children of Alaska shall have the same right to be admitted to any Indian boarding school as the Indian children in the States or Territories of the United States.[22]

The requirement that children of mixed blood "lead a civilized life" to attend white schools tracked the language of existing law prescribing how an Indian could become a U.S. citizen.[23] The Nelson Act relieved the Department of Interior "of responsibility for the education of white and mixed blood children, while the education of these children was provided by the Territory and local municipal authorities." The number of what became known as Nelson schools, "for children of white or mixed blood leading 'a civilized life' in communities outside of incorporated towns – grew from 10 in 1907 to 46 in 1918" (Hootch Settlement 1976: ¶ 10).

In 1912, Congress created the Territory of Alaska. The enabling act authorized the territorial legislature to enact laws consistent with federal law. However, schooling for Eskimos and Indians was excluded from the purview of the legislature, remaining under the control of the Secretary of the Interior.[24] Five years later, Congress passed enabling legislation authorizing the legislature to segregate schooling along racial lines.[25] The Uniform School Act of 1917 reaffirmed the dual system put into effect in 1905. That Act permitted the territorial government to enact its own laws governing schools for all non-Natives without congressional approval (DOI 1932: 598). The Act also allowed local school boards to admit Native children, but few did. Common reasons for rejecting Natives "included having infectious or communicable diseases, possessing vicious or immoral habits, being habitually unclean in person or dress, or having parents who refused to make them conform." Often, school boards exercised their discretion to exclude Native children whose "presence is detrimental to the best interests of the school."[26] By 1930, segregated schools existed in at least 19 communities – "white schools and Native schools in the same tiny villages" (Cotton 1984). Figure 9.3 is a photograph of the segregated school for Eskimo children in Nome.

20 *See* Act of June 6, 1900, 31 Stat. 321, 330 (1900).

21 *See* Act of March 3, 1901, 31 Stat. 1438 (1901).

22 Act of January 27, 1905 § 7, 33 Stat. 616, 619 (1905).

23 *See* Dawes Act of February 8, 1887, cl. 119, § 6, 24 Stat. 390 (1887).

24 *See* Act of August 24, 1912 § 3, 37 Stat. 512 (1912).

25 Act of March 3, 1917, 39 Stat. 1131 (1917).

26 Jim and Nancy Lethcoe, *Changes Affecting Native Communities: 1917–1941*, *in* A History of Prince William Sound, Alaska (1994).

Figure 9.3 Eskimo school in Nome, circa 1896–1913
Source: Photo reprinted with permission of the Anchorage Museum at Rasmuson Center, O.D. Goetze Collection, AMRC-b01-41-400.

Davis v. Sitka School Board

The pernicious effects of racist educational policies are illustrated in a 1908 court decision. The Sitka School Board rejected a request from six Native children who sought admission to a Nelson school. Each had a parent who was at least part-white. They previously had been included by the school district's enumerator as "children of mixed blood who live a civilized life."[27] The children, through their guardians, sued the school board.

Judge Royal Arch Gunnison began by exploring why Congress included the requirement that mixed blood children live "a civilized life." He explained that the qualification arose because the "Indian in his native state has everywhere been found to be a savage, an uncivilized being, when measured by the white man's standard" (*Davis* 1908: 484). As wards of the state, Natives were not entitled to citizenship, except in exceptional circumstances. First, an Indian had to "renounce the independent condition in which he had been since the adoption of the Constitution," and take up the life of a white person and become "civilized."[28] Alaska Natives, like Indians, were "uncivilized" until that occurred (*Davis* 1908: 485–86).

According to Judge Gunnison, "mixed blood" applied to any gradation of Native blood, regardless of the amount or "whether it comes from the father or mother" (*Davis* 1908: 486). He

27 *Davis v. Sitka Sch. Bd.*, 3 Alaska 481, 489–90 (D. Alaska Terr. 1908).

28 *Davis* 1908: 484–85 (quoting *United States v. Boyd*, 83 Fed. 547, 553 (4th Cir. 1897).

applied the "one drop" rule used by southern states in their Jim Crow laws: anyone with any trace of African ancestry was considered "Black" unless they could establish another basis for their non-white ancestry.[29] Therefore, he concluded, "As ordinarily understood by white people, a person of white and Indian parentage is deemed to be of mixed blood without regard to the source of the Indian blood" (*Davis* 1908: 486). Consistent with that racist approach, he determined the Native ancestry of a mother of two children by inspecting her features in a photograph (*Davis* 1908: 490).

Judge Gunnison further contended that a person's "civilization" was not just the product of parentage, but geography and relationship to a tribe. "A necessary deduction to be drawn from this is that the mixed blood is presumed to partake of the character of the tribe with which he lives, whether it be civilized or otherwise." His explanation detailed the extent of the racist views that sustained the rise of Alaska's segregated schools:

> [W]here mixed bloods live among and associate with the uncivilized, they become subject to and influenced by their environment as naturally as water seeks its level. It was, in my opinion, the intention of Congress that only such of the mixed bloods were to be admitted to those schools as had for themselves … put off the rude customs, modes of life, and associations, and taken up their abode and life free from an environment which retarded their development in lines of progressive living, systematic labor, individual ownership and accumulation of property, intellectual activity, and well-defined and respected domestic and social relations. For the children of those families which preferred the other life, without its attendant responsibilities and obligations to society at large, was provided a system of education under the control of the Secretary of the Interior, more appropriate to their undeveloped mental condition, and through which they could, in view of their surroundings, be better instructed (*Davis* 1908: 487).

Judge Gunnison described his test for whether children lived a "civilized life": have they "exchanged the old barbaric, uncivilized environment for one changed, new, and so different as to indicate an advanced and improved condition of mind, which desires and reaches out for something altogether distinct from and unlike the old life" (*Davis* 1908: 488). Applying his test, he noted that none of the children sought admission to the white school until their own Native school closed. He did not consider the impact the school closing would have. He also did not indicate how a Native could become "civilized" under his test if they were denied the educational opportunities provided to non-Native students.

Instead, Judge Gunnison found excuses why the six children could not qualify as living a "civilized life." The parents of two disqualified children lived in a house separate from Natives, owned a business, paid taxes, used a cash register in their store, had "adopted the white man's style of dress," and spoke, read, and wrote English. Three children were disqualified because they continued to play and fish with other Native children (*Davis* 1908: 491–93). The sixth child did not pass his test either, suggesting in his description of the child's parents that no child of mixed blood would qualify:

> It appears that his wife is a good housekeeper, so far as their means and station in life will allow her to be; that the pots and kettles and frying pans are not left upon the floor, after the native fashion, but are hung up, and that curtains drape the windows of their house. This indicates progress; but does it satisfy the test? It is urged that Allard and his wife have been entertained at the home of a former

29 *See* STATES' LAWS ON RACE AND COLOR (Pauli Murray, ed. 1997).

> Governor of this Territory. Savages, ere this, have been entertained by white men of culture and refinement; but that cannot be considered as a criterion of civilization. To me it is an evidence of the kindliness and of the interest and effort of the hosts in behalf of a people among and for whom they have labored long and assiduously, not an evidence of the civilization of the guests.

Any association between children of mixed blood with Natives who were "an uncivilized or semi-civilized people" could not, in Gunnison's opinion, "be classed those who live a civilized life" (*Davis* 1908: 494). *Davis* remained Alaska law for over two decades. Its implications for the education of Alaska Natives would linger much longer.

Natives Required to Pay for All-White Schools

Under the Uniform School Act of 1917, the territorial legislature could levy taxes to pay for schools. However, that power did not extend to Natives, who were not permitted to attend the all-white schools. Nevertheless, often the tax collectors required Natives to pay the territorial school tax of five dollars a year. According to one account,

> On 25 April 1922, L.M. Churchill, sitting as an election judge, refused to let George Mason vote, because, he said George was an Indian and consequently a ward of the government. On 26 April 1922, the same L.M. Churchill, disguised as a school tax collector, approached the same George Mason and demanded the school tax of $5.00 and threatened him with the strong arm of the law.[30]

Mason paid the tax to avoid going to jail. When other Natives were asked to pay the tax, they complained to Louis Fredrick "Fred" Paul, who with his brother William Lewis Paul led the ANB. Located in Sitka, the ANB was a self-help organization for Natives, which the Pauls politicized to advance Native rights in the territory.[31] Fred Paul advised them to pay the tax. Seeking to enfranchise Natives, Paul explained, "We take the position that we are full citizens and so we must carry the burdens like any other citizen. The strongest argument which you can make that you are a full citizen is that you pay taxes …" (Paul 2006: 59).

Desegregation Begins... Slowly

Alaska Natives sought to end the territory's segregated schooling. At least since 1906, there had been complaints, illustrated in *Davis*, that children who had become assimilated into the white culture could not attend all-white schools. In 1920, the ANB convention "adopted a resolution instructing ANB officials to 'carry the matter forward to the federal courts as a test case' if necessary to achieve satisfaction" (Haycox 1986–87: 19). Despite the ANB's efforts, it would be another nine years before a Native child was successful in being admitted to a local school.

In 1929, a Native child in Ketchikan sued to gain admission to the city's all-white schools. Unlike the children in *Davis*, the defendants stipulated that Irene Jones was "a child of mixed blood who leads a civilized life."[32] Nevertheless, the school board denied Jones admission because

---

30 Fred Paul, Then Fight for It 59 (2006).

31 Stephen Haycox, *William Paul, Sr., and the Alaska Voters' Literacy Act of 1925*, 2 Alaska Hist. 16, 19 (1986–1987).

32 *Jones v. Ellis*, 8 Alaska 146, 147 (D. Alaska Terr. 1929).

it claimed that the sixth grade was overcrowded. Despite the alleged overcrowding, the board had admitted four white students who, unlike Jones, lived outside the city. The board rationalized its disparate treatment of Jones by arguing that unlike the white students, "she could attend the school for Indian children" operated by the Department of Interior in Ketchikan (*Jones* 1929: 147–48).

Judge Justin W. Harding rejected the school board's argument. He observed that despite the widespread practice of segregated schooling in Alaska, there was no authority for it. The 1917 educational enabling act made "no provision as to the segregation of races, nor does it refer to the race or color of the children to be provided for in the municipal schools." Instead, the act merely limited the legislature's authority "to provide for white and colored children and children of mixed blood." Since Irene Jones was a child of mixed blood, she "had a legal right to attend the territorial schools in Ketchikan" (*Jones* 1929: 147).

The city schools were not so overcrowded that any child had to be excluded from the sixth grade. It appeared that every seat in the classroom was taken. "However, a closer inspection of the floor showed holes from which screws holding down desks and seats recently had been removed." The city's pretext for denying Jones a seat in the classroom became obvious while her case was pending. A white family with a child in the sixth grade moved to the city, and "the school at once made room for him" (Paul 2006: 62).

Judge Harding did not mention that evidence. Instead, he determined that even if the schools were overcrowded, the city could not admit the non-resident white students over a mixed blood child who lived in Ketchikan. He explained that any right of non-resident children to attend the city's public schools "must necessarily be secondary to that of any child living within the corporate limits who has a right to attend [the] schools." Since the school board failed to show why Irene Jones should not be admitted to the public schools, Judge Harding ordered them to do so (*Jones* 1929: 148–49).

Segregation Remains after Jones

Jones v. Ellis was viewed by some commentators as ending segregated schooling in Alaska.[33] Reality paints a different picture. In 1931, responsibility for Native schooling was transferred to the Office of Indian Affairs and became known as the Alaska Indian Service, which was renamed the Alaska Native Service (ANS) in 1945. Many of the smaller ANS schools went through the sixth grade, with most of the larger schools going through the eighth grade.[34] A 1949 census of ANS schools revealed fewer than 20 white children out of a total enrollment of 4,073 (BIA 1950: 5). About 1,800 Native children lacked any schooling facilities. Although the Bureau of Indian Affairs (BIA) acknowledged the "segregation," it claimed that it was "due to geographical reasons and not to who has jurisdiction of the school" (BIA 1950: 1–2). However, local school boards continued to deny Native children access to all-white schools even when they lived in incorporated towns. In 1939, a witness testified before Congress of a case in Valdez in which "an eighth-grade Native girl 'wanted to attend high school, but the school board didn't see fit to take her'" (Cole 1996: 319).

In 1956, 27 years after the *Jones* decision, the territorial attorney general requested an opinion from the Secretary of the Interior whether Alaska could create school districts in Native areas. The Secretary advised him that the territorial government could. He explained "the record shows

33 *See* Robert A. Leflar and Wylie H. Davis, *Segregation in the Public Schools – 1953*, 67 Harv. L. Rev. 377, 378 n. 3 (1954).

34 Bureau of Indian Affairs (BIA), *Answers to Your Questions on Alaska Native Service Educational Activities* 6 (Feb. 1950), *in* Ray 1973: Appendix A.

that Congress at all times attempted to encourage and support the establishment of a Territorial school system which would reach out and be available for all the children of Alaska, including the Indian and native children."[35] He pointed out that the *Jones* decision "directed the Territorial school officials to admit both white and Native children. This decision indicates a directive by the court requiring the Territorial legislature to expand its school system" (DOI 1956: 334–36).

Despite the Secretary's opinion, it would be another quarter-century before Alaska fully integrated Alaska Natives into its public schools, especially for secondary schooling. By 1958–1959, out of 34 public secondary schools operated by the territorial government, just six were in communities in which at least half the population was Native. At the same time, most of the secondary schools in non-Native communities had small enrollments: "Only 5 had enrollments exceeding 100; 24 had enrollments under 50, and 12 had enrollments of 10 or fewer" (Hootch Settlement 1976: ¶ 12). Villages with far greater numbers of Native children had no high schools. By the mid-1970s, there were 2,783 secondary school age children who lived in villages with a public or BIA elementary school but without a secondary school or daily access to such a school. More than 95 percent of those children were Native; statewide, only 120 white children of secondary school age had no ready access to a secondary school (Hootch Settlement 1976: ¶ 19).

Boarding Schools and the Boarding Home Program

Alaska's dual school system was pronounced for secondary education. While the territorial government provided local secondary schools for white and mixed-blood children, the federal government assumed responsibility for providing some secondary education for select full-blooded Natives. The federal government, through the U.S. Bureau of Education, selected only "the most intellectually advanced youth" for a basic vocational education that focused on trade schools, who then returned to the villages to use those trades. A traditional college-preparatory curriculum was unavailable. Natives selected for the program were removed from their villages and sent to boarding schools in the lower 48 states, often thousands of miles away from their homes. This early boarding program proved disastrous, with Native students experiencing "health hazards and sociological maladjustments" (Hootch Settlement ¶ 11).

In 1925, the federal government began establishing vocational boarding schools in Alaska. Initially, the Department established three schools in Eklutna, near Anchorage; at Kanakanak, on Bristol Bay; and at White Mountain, on the Seward Peninsula. In 1947, with the existing schools in disrepair, the BIA opened Mt. Edgecumbe, a single consolidated boarding school on a converted World War II naval base near Sitka (Hootch Settlement ¶ 11). For the next two decades, Mt. Edgecumbe was the only public boarding school available for Natives in Alaska (Ray 1973: 17). However, "only the best students" were "encouraged to go to Mt. Edgecumbe," with "more applications than can be favorably considered" (BIA 1950: 14–15). Each year, hundreds of Native students had no opportunity for secondary schooling. By 1960, just 1,832 out of 5,365 Native children between the ages of 14 and 19 were enrolled in high school.[36]

The BIA responded to the overcrowding at Mt. Edgecumbe by reviving the earlier program of sending Natives to Indian boarding schools in the lower 48 states. Students were uprooted thousands of miles from their villages and sent to Chemawa, Oregon, and Chilocco, Oklahoma.

35 U.S. Dep't of Interior (DOI), *Organization of School Districts on Indian Reservations in Alaska*, 63 Interior Dec. 333, 335 (Sept. 17, 1956).

36 State of Alaska, Governor's Comm. on Educ., *An Overall Education Plan for Rural Alaska* 2 (rev. Feb. 26, 1966), *in* Ray 1973: Appendix E.

Figure 9.4 Alaska Natives prepare to leave from the Native village of Shungnak to attend high school in the 1960s

The State's failure to provide schooling in native villages meant that only a handful of Alaska Native children could attend high school if they chose to leave their villages to attend boarding schools that could be thousands of miles away. The caption for this photo reads: "Dressed in their mail order catalogue finery, these self-confident Eskimo teenagers board a Wien Air bush plane to head south to attend high school. Students leaving for school from a sand bar airport of the Kobuk river. Shungnak village in background." Because of unequal schooling, by 2002, 43 percent of all voters in Shungnak were LEP and one-third were illiterate.
Source: Photo reprinted with permission of the Kay J. Kennedy Aviation Photograph Collection, UAF-1991-98-682, Archives, University of Alaska Fairbanks.

By 1969–1970, the BIA enrolled 876 secondary school students from Alaska at Chemawa and Chilocco. Professor Charles Ray described the effects of the out-of-state boarding school program on Natives. "[I]t is doubtful that any educational decision generated more public outcry from native and non-native citizens alike than the practice of sending secondary school students out of the State for their high school education." According to Ray, "concern was expressed about the deleterious effects of isolating children from their families and communities." In addition, "the practice of transporting students out of the State was psychologically offensive to the vast majority of Alaska's populace" (Ray 1973: 17–18).

Beginning in 1966, Alaska undertook two approaches to in-state secondary schooling for Natives. First, it began constructing regional secondary boarding schools closer to the villages. The state relied upon a report prepared by consultants from Virginia, who recommended building six boarding schools with at least 500 students each. The consultants were candid about their objective of eliminating Native villages altogether, arguing that movement to urban centers was essential "in the adjustment and acculturization of the Alaskan Native." They explained, "Residence in urban areas appears to accelerate the breakdown of old village patterns, patterns which may retard the development of rural folk into a disciplined and reliable workforce." Alaska ultimately opened three boarding schools in Nome (1966), Kodiak (1967), and Bethel (1972), but abandoned the program before completing the last three schools.[37]

Second, in 1967, the state Department of Education created a "Boarding Home Program" in which children from rural communities (mainly Natives) were paired to live with families in larger cities and towns to attend local secondary schools. Families received monthly stipends for boarding the students. Although it was supposed to be a temporary program, by 1971–1972, there were a total of 32 boarding home programs enrolling more than 1,200 students (Ray 1973: 19–20; Hootch Settlement 1976: ¶ 15).

As a result of the two programs, an entire generation of children was missing from their villages, forcing families living on subsistence fishing and hunting to work even harder to survive.[38] There were many reasons why Native students did not want to go to boarding school:

> The wrenching experience of going so far from home and family. The pressure to drink. The loneliness. Boarding home parents who themselves drank, abused students and treated them like servants. The lost opportunity to speak their own language, to learn traditional skills, just to be at home. Entire villages echoed with the silence of a whole generation of teenagers gone, for 9 months out of the year. It was a rotten system. And a lot of policymakers in Juneau and Anchorage just didn't get it (Cotton 2004: 7).

Those who attended the boarding schools suffered from high dropout rates – 42 percent in one year in Bethel and 65 percent during a two-year period in the Anchorage Boarding Home program (Cotton 2004: 6). Many Native children transferred so frequently they did not attain "discernable educational benefits from any program" (Hootch Settlement 1976: ¶ 20). By 1972, 96 percent of entering freshman in Bethel and 67 percent of the freshmen at the Nome-Beltz boarding school were failing (Cotton 1984).

The Molly Hootch Case and Its Aftermath

Kivalina is a small Eskimo village located north of the Arctic Circle. The state board operated a day school there that provided classes through the eighth grade, but no secondary education. To get a high school education, one Native child briefly attended Mt. Edgecumbe, located 1,000 miles away, and three other Native children participated in the Fairbanks Home Boarding Program, located 500 miles away. The children dropped out of school and returned to the village after experiencing chronic homesickness and unsatisfactory living conditions. Initially, a teacher in the day school offered them high school coursework through correspondence, but that stopped when he was transferred. In 1971, the parents of the students sued, and the state quickly settled.[39] The state agreed to provide correspondence courses until it built a high school in Kivalina.[40] Villages throughout the state learned of the result and clamored for high schools of their own.

Molly Hootch was a 15-year-old Eskimo from Emmonak, a Yup'ik village of about 400 people near the mouth of the Yukon River. She was sent 500 miles away to Anchorage for the ninth grade,

---

37 Stephen E. Cotton, *Thirty Years Later: The Molly Hootch Case*, Sharing Our Pathways vol. 9, issue 4, at 4, 6 (Sept./Oct. 2004) (speech to University of Alaska symposium on February 27, 2004).

38 *See* Diane Olthuis, *The Molly Hootch Case: 1972, Emmonak, in* It Happened in Alaska 126 (2006).

39 *See* Complaint and Memorandum in Support of Application for Temporary Restraining Order, *Sage v. State Bd. of Educ.*, Case No. 71–1245-CIV (Alaska Super. Ct. Apr. 27, 1971).

40 *See* Stipulation and Order, *Sage v. State Bd. of Educ.*, Case No. 71–1245-CIV (Alaska Super. Ct. May 5, 1971); Cotton 1984.

where she suffered from culture shock, loneliness, and mistreatment by her classmates and the family that boarded her (Olthuis 2006: 125–26). The lack of secondary schooling for Natives had a dramatic effect. By the early 1970s, just 2,200 out of more than 51,000 Alaska Natives had a high school education.[41] In 1972, Hootch and 27 other Native children from Emmonak and five Yup'ik villages joined in a class action filed by the Alaska Legal Services to secure secondary schools for Native villages statewide (Hootch Complaint 1972).

The court dismissed the claim brought under the education clause of the Alaska Constitution, which required that the state "establish and maintain a system of public schools open to all children of the state."[42] On appeal, the state supreme court upheld that ruling.[43] However, the children were allowed to proceed on their claim that the state's failure to provide secondary schools in the villages was racially discriminatory. The case was settled in 1976, 22 years after *Brown v. Board of Education*,[44] when Alaska agreed for the first time to establish a public secondary school in all 126 Native villages that wanted one (Hootch Settlement 1976). The settlement ultimately cost Alaska $137 million to provide secondary education in 105 villages, including building 92 new high schools (Cotton 1984; Cotton 2004: 9). Construction of the last of the so-called "Molly Hootch" high schools was completed in the mid-1980s (Olthuis 2006: 129).

Even after the Molly Hootch case concluded, Alaska still provided Native children with unequal educational opportunities. In 1999, a state court found that Alaska continued to use a dual, arbitrary, unconstitutional, and racially discriminatory system for funding school facilities.[45] As a result of that discrimination, Alaska Natives and American Indians have the lowest level of educational attainment in the state. More than 80 percent of Alaska Native graduating seniors are not proficient in reading comprehension, have failure rates on standardized tests more than 20 percent higher than non-Native students, and graduation rates that lag more than 15 percent behind the statewide average (Landreth and Smith 2006: 108–09). In 2007, another court found that Alaska had violated its "constitutional responsibility to maintain a public school system" by failing to sufficiently oversee the quality of secondary education in many Alaska Native villages and to provide a "meaningful opportunity to learn the material" on a graduation exam. As a result, it concluded that the state violated the due process rights of Alaska Native students when it conditioned high school graduation on passing that exam.[46] Today, many Native adults require language assistance when they vote because of their illiteracy and limited-English proficiency rates caused by the state's educational discrimination.

Voting Discrimination

Disenfranchisement was the rule for Natives for most of Alaska's history. Initially, Alaska Natives could not vote because they were denied citizenship. Those attempting to vote were prosecuted. When Natives finally became "Americans" through the Indian Citizenship Act of 1924, the territorial legislature responded by imposing a literacy test preventing most Natives from voting. Later, a less burdensome test would be included in the state constitution, disproportionately

41 *See* Landreth and Smith 2007: 108; George W. Rogers, *Alaska Native Population Trends and Vital Statistics, 1950–1985*, at table 1 (Nov. 1971).

42 Alaska Const. art. VII, § 1.

43 *See Hootch v. Alaska State Operated Sch. Sys.*, 536 P.2d 793 (Alaska 1975).

44 347 U.S. 483 (1954).

45 *Kasayulie v. State of Alaska*, Case No. 3AN–97–3782-CIV (Alaska Super. Ct. 1999).

46 Decision and Order, *Moore v. State of Alaska*, Case No.3AN–04–9756-CIV (Alaska Super. Ct. June 21, 2007) (unpublished opinion), at 194–95.

affecting non-English-speaking Native voters. Alaska's discriminatory literacy test would remain in place until 1970.

Alaska Natives as Aliens in Their Own Land

In Alaska's early years as a territory, most Natives were disenfranchised because they were not considered U.S. citizens. The cession treaty of 1867 formalized their exclusion. It provided that inhabitants of Alaska who chose to remain rather than return to Russia, "with the exception of uncivilized native tribes, shall be admitted to the enjoyment of all the rights, advantages, and immunities of citizens of the United States …" Alaska Natives therefore were treated like American Indians. They were subject to the burdens of United States laws, but could have no say in their enactment because they were not citizens.

A limited exception was available under the Dawes Act, an 1887 federal law relating to the allotments of land to Indians. It provided that "every Indian born within the territorial limits of the United States who has adopted the habits of civilized life, is hereby declared to be a citizen of the United States and is entitled to all the rights, privileges, and immunities of such citizen."[47] As the *Davis* case made clear in the context of a similar provision for attendance at white schools, few Natives in Alaska qualified for citizenship.

In 1915, the territorial legislature enacted a law based on the Dawes Act entitled an "Act to define and establish the political status of certain Native Indians within the Territory of Alaska."[48] The 1915 law established a complex procedure for becoming a citizen and voter. First, Native applicants had to go to a local school to be examined by a majority of the teachers. The examination had to "broadly cover the general qualifications of the applicant as to an intelligent exercise of the obligations of suffrage, a total abandonment of any tribal customs or relationship, and the facts regarding the applicant's adoption of the habits of a civilized life." The purpose was to assess whether the applicant had become assimilated into the white culture. The applicant next had to obtain an endorsement by at least five white U.S. citizens who were "personally acquainted with the life and habits of such Indian for a period of at least one year." They were supposed to assess whether the "Indian has abandoned all tribal customs and relationship, has adopted the ways and habits of a civilized life, and is duly qualified to exercise the rights, privileges, and obligations of citizenship." If the applicant was able to secure the five endorsements, he or she would have to apply to the federal court for a certification that the applicant "forever renounces all tribal customs and relationships." After the hearing notice and application was posted in the local post office to allow white citizens to object, only then would the applicant obtain a certificate of citizenship from a federal judge.

Natives in southeastern Alaska were the most active in seeking citizenship under the territorial law. However, the ANB and its counterpart for women, the Alaska Native Sisterhood (ANS) resisted complying with the stringent requirements. At the ANB's annual meeting in 1919, Louis Paul "contended that the right of the franchise was granted the Indian Americans by the Constitution of the United States" and argued "that the certificate demanded of the Indian voter … did not make him any more a citizen than he is now" (Paul 2006: 43). The ANB's leadership encouraged Natives to attempt to vote without obtaining a citizenship certificate by challenging election judges who tried to exclude them (Paul 2006: 41).

47 Dawes Act of February 8, 1887, cl. 119, § 6, 24 Stat. 390 (1887).

48 1915 Alaska Sess. Laws 52 (Apr. 1915).

United States v. Jones

In 1922, Charlie Jones, a Tlingit chief who lived in southeastern Alaska, was turned away from the local polling place when he tried to vote. He told Matilda (Tillie) Paul Tamaree, a Tlingit Native active in the ANS, what had happened. She accompanied Jones back to the polling place and demanded that he be allowed to challenge the decision of the election judges. Jones then swore that he was a citizen and voted (Paul 2006: 41).

In March 1923, the U.S. Attorney obtained an indictment against Jones for unlawful voting and for perjury for swearing he was a citizen and against Tamaree for aiding and abetting him. When they were tried later that year, William Paul, Tameree's son who was an attorney, represented them. Paul presented evidence that Jones owned a house, lived like a white person, paid taxes, gave money to charity, and his children attended school. The jury acquitted Jones of unlawfully voting, and the remaining charges against Jones and Tamaree were dropped at the request of the U.S. Attorney.[49] During the trial, Judge Thomas Reed determined that Alaska's 1915 citizenship act was preempted by the Dawes Act, and struck it down. He found that the territorial legislature had no authority to add procedures such as testing, vouching by white citizens, and obtaining a certificate of citizenship. If a Native met the requirements under the Dawes Act, he or she would be recognized as a citizen and be allowed to vote (Paul 2006: 44).

Partially in response to the *Jones* case, the next year Congress enacted the Indian Citizenship Act, which conferred citizenship on "all noncitizen Indians born within the territorial limits of the United States."[50] At long last, all of the first Americans in Alaska were recognized as U.S. citizens. However, the territorial and later the state government would erect other obstacles to the voting rights of Alaska Natives.

Alaska Voters' Literacy Act of 1925

With the removal of citizenship as a barrier, the ANB increased its efforts to organize Native voters, especially in southeastern Alaska, where the Tlingit and Haida Tribes were located. Paul was Tlingit himself, and he and his family had worked with the ANB and ANS to encourage members of the local tribes to learn English, attend school, and demand their rights as U.S. citizens. Starting in 1922, his efforts began to pay off when Native villages significantly increased their voting turnout (Haycox 1986–87: 18–19).

Paul had aligned himself with progressive Republican James Wickersham, "the major force in Alaskan electoral politics" whose supporters were called "Wickites." However, organizing Native voters to support Wickite candidates posed considerable difficulty. Despite longstanding efforts by Presbyterian missionaries, the ANB, and others to provide education to Natives excluded from territorial schools, progress was slow. Most Native voters were illiterate and could not read a ballot (Haycox 1986–1987: 18–20).

Earlier campaigns between white candidates provided Paul with the solution. In 1916, a white candidate had used a ballot cutout that covered up everything except the boxes that the campaign wanted checked. Working with other leaders in the ANB, ANS, and local tribes, Paul prepared similar sample ballots and cardboard cutouts that were widely used by Native voters in the 1922 election. The cutouts proved to be very successful, with Native voters in southeastern Alaska

49 Paul 2006: 41; Haa Kysteeyi, Our Culture: Tlingit Life Stories 495 (Nora Marks Dauenhauer and Richard Dauenhauer eds. 1994).

50 Indian Citizenship Act of June 2, 1924, 43 Stat. 253 (codified at 8 U.S.C. § 1401(b)).

overwhelmingly voting for the candidate supported by Paul and the ANB (Haycox 1986–1987: 20–21).

Anti-Wickites responded by introducing a literacy bill in the House during the opening days of the 1923 session of the territorial legislature. Representative Frank Foster sponsored the bill, which provided that "no person who is unable to read the Constitution of the U.S. and to write the English language shall be eligible to vote." Representative H. Royal Shepard filed a statement that highlighted the bill's discriminatory purpose. He argued that Natives were "practically all the illiterate voting population of the Territory" and held "the balance of power" in elections. According to Shepard, Native voters were being manipulated to cast ballots that did not reflect their own choices and erroneously pointed to the "illegality of large numbers of Indian votes" in earlier elections (Haycox 1986–1987: 21–22).

In the second week of the session, two days of hearings were held on the bill. Historian Stephen Haycox explained that "supporters of the literacy measure focused on the issue of race" charging that Paul and the ANB "used the Indian vote as their pawn." Representative Joseph Murray said that the "question of whether illiterates should vote 'resolves itself into whether or not the Senate and House and the Territory shall remain white.'" The bill passed the House by a vote of 10 to 6 (Haycox 1986–87: 21–23).

Similar arguments were raised during the Senate debate on the bill. Some senators argued that they supported Native voting, but a literacy test would benefit them because it would force them to learn English first. The *Alaska Daily Empire* ran an editorial maintaining that without the bill, "the Republic itself would fall" because "of ignorance, illiteracy, or failure to comprehend the meaning of the Constitution." However, the most forceful arguments in favor of the test were made unequivocally in racial terms. Senator Fred Ayer echoed the reports of many newspapers by saying, "We do not want to be ruled by an inferior race, nor dominated by an illiterate one." Representative Shepard testified in favor of the bill, proclaiming that Alaska was "white man's country" and that "the man who curries favor with the Indian vote by opposing this bill" would not be re-elected to office. Despite the racial appeals, the bill failed when the Senate tied 4 to 4 (Haycox 1986–1987: 23–24).

In 1924, the passage of the Indian Citizenship Act and William Paul's candidacy for the territorial legislature made a literacy bill one of the key issues in the campaign. The *Daily Empire* ran a large political ad paid for by Senator Shepard and other anti-Wickite candidates. The ad encouraged organization of those opposed "to having Indians in the Legislatures" and asked for support of a "law to prevent the mass voting of illiterate Indians" that would provide "an opportunity to keep the Indian in his place." A later ad decried "a real danger; for if illiterate Indians control nominations and election of candidates for the legislature, serious trouble is bound to result to all, both whites and Indians" (Haycox 1986–1987: 25–27). When Paul won his primary election, the *Daily Empire* ran a vigorous campaign against him. The newspaper charged that if Indians voting as a bloc had their way, "they will create a chasm between the races in Alaska that will … make this either a white man's country or an Indian's country for many years to come." The day before the election, proponents of the literacy test ran the ad depicted in Figure 9.5. Despite those racial appeals, the *Daily Empire* described accusations of fostering "racial hatred between the white and Indian races in Alaska" as "baseless." In the end, Paul won handily, aided by record turnout by Native voters (Haycox 1986–1987: 28). He became the first Native elected to state office in Alaska (Paul 2006: 45–46).

The first day of the 1925 legislative session, the literacy test bill was reintroduced. A compromise bill exempting anyone who previously had voted was proposed in the House and moved rapidly to a vote. The bill ensured that Paul's Native supporters in southeastern Alaska could continue to

ILY EMPIRE, MONDAY, NOV. 3, 1924.

Keep Alaska and Its Schools Free From Indian Control

PLATFORM

Full Territorial Government for Alaska.

A Literacy Test for all voters alike.

Extension of the Federal Highway Act to Alaska.

An equitable share of the proceeds of the seal industry for Alaska.

Real representation of Alaska in Congress capable of making an honest effort to get for Alaskans what they want.

FRANK A. BOYLE
CANDIDATE FOR DELEGATE TO CONGRESS

The establishment of a Literacy Test for voters of all races alike is the big issue in Tuesday's election. Without it, the Government of the Territory of Alaska, its institutions, its schools, the government of some of its towns, their institutions and the public schools, will inevitably pass into the hands of those controlling the votes of thousands of illiterates. In this Division this illiterate vote is organized and its bosses admit it was organized tory of Alaska, its institutions, its schools, the government of some of its towns, their institutions and the public schools, will inevitably pass into the hands of those controlling the votes of thousands of illiterates. In this Division this illiterate vote is organized and its bosses admit it was organized to control First Division politics and openly boast they already control the balance of political power, can elect those who will bow to their will and defeat condidates who refuse to line up with them.

THIS TICKET PLEDGES ITSELF TO PUT A LITERACY TEST LAW ON THE TERRITORIAL STATUTES

Pledging themselves to work for enactment of a law requiring all voters to be able to read and write English understandingly and to be possessed of some knowledge of American government, the candidates named herein assert their conviction that the vast majority of white Alaskans, and those of Indian blood who have successfully labored to attain true citizenship, are opposed to boss domination of any kind, particularly of domination that is based upon the votes of those who can neither read nor write English, nor in most instances speak that the vast majority of white Alaskans, and those of Indian blood who have successfully labored to attain true citizenship, are opposed to boss domination of any kind, particularly of domination that is based upon the votes of those who can neither read nor write English, nor in most instances speak it, and are absolutely without knowledge of American principles of government and the ideals forming its foundation.

If you would maintain the white race's standard of government in this Territory, preserve its institutions, protect its industries from destructive taxation, and maintain the high standard of its schools, vote for this ticket.

DEMOCRATIC TICKET

For Delegate to Congress
FRANK A. BOYLE—Juneau

For Territorial Senator
N. R. Walker—Ketchikan

For Representatives
Chris Christensen—Petersburg
J. J. Connors—Juneau
N. O. Hardy—Juneau
James McCloskey—Juneau

FOR SANE GOVERNMENT

N. R. WALKER
Candidate for Senator

CHRIS CHRISTENSEN
Candidate for Representative

FIFTH MAN ON TICKET
JAMES McCLOSKEY
OF JUNEAU
VICE W. W. CASEY
DECEASED.
DON'T FORGET TO PUT HIS NAME ON BALLOT WITH STICKER

J. J. CONNORS
Candidate for Representative

N. O. HARDY
Candidate for Representative

A VOTE FOR THEM IS A VOTE TO SAFEGUARD OUR PUBLIC SCHOOLS

Figure 9.5 Advertisement during the 1924 election for a literacy test for voting in Alaska
This political advertisement ran in the *Alaska Daily Empire* on November 3, 1924, the day before the general election. The ad was directed at derailing the candidacy of Alaska Native William Paul for the territorial legislature.
Source: Reprinted with permission of the Alaska State Library, Alaska State Library Newspapers on Microfilm Collection.

Figure 9.6 Alaska Territorial House of Representatives, 1925
Seventh Alaska Territorial Legislature, House of Representatives, Juneau, Alaska, April 30, 1925. William Paul, the first Alaska Native elected to the legislature, is seated third from the left.
Source: Photo reprinted with permission of the Alaska State Library, Winter and Pond Photograph Collection, 1893-1943, ASL-PCA-87-2507.

vote but satisfied many proponents of a literacy test by excluding Natives in the rest of the state. It passed the House by a vote of 14 to 2 and unanimously in the Senate. As enacted, it provided that unless individuals had previously voted, they had to demonstrate that they were "able to read and write the English language" (Haycox 1986–1987: 17, 28–30).

For the next few years, supporters of a literacy test without exceptions took their campaign to Congress. The press touted that "A White Man's Party is Necessary," arguing that only whites could protect the interests of Alaska Natives (Paul 2006: 47–48; Landreth and Smith 2007: 90–91; Haycox 1986–1987: 30–32). The fight in Congress ultimately proved unsuccessful. When a federal law was enacted, it duplicated the territory's 1925 Act by including a grandfather clause for those Natives who voted in 1924 and earlier, tracking similar clauses that were included in seven of the 20 state literacy tests (Haycox 1986–1987: 32–35).[51]

The territorial legislature subsequently enacted a law providing that the literacy test was satisfied by "reading ten lines of the federal constitution chosen at random by the election judge and legibly

51 *See* Act of Mar. 3, 1927, c. 363, § 1, 44 Stat. 1392, 1393 (codified at 48 U.S.C. § 51) (repealed).

writing ten lines dictated by the judge."[52] Chapters 1 and 2 explore the manner in which similar literacy tests in other states were abused, particularly where administered by poll workers who could exercise discretion in whether and how to apply the test. High illiteracy rates in a majority of Native villages without schools undoubtedly prevented thousands of Natives outside southeastern Alaska from qualifying as voters under the literacy test, even when it was relaxed (Chapter 10).

Alaska's Constitutional Literacy Test

Alaska went further than many states in its literacy requirements for voting by including them in its state constitution. By the time the constitutional convention convened in 1955, Alaska had used a literacy test for 30 years. Although Native voter participation was greater than in 1925, it still lagged considerably behind white turnout. Continuing those practices after statehood was a logical extension of treatment of Native citizens which, regardless of any benign purpose, had a discriminatory impact on their voting.

On December 5, 1955, the Committee on Suffrage, Elections, and Apportionment reported out Article 5 of the constitution, which included a literacy test. It provided that qualifications for voting required, among other things, a citizen "who is able to read or speak the English language as prescribed by the Legislature." It also included a grandfather clause that tracked similar clauses in the 1925 state act and the 1927 federal act, providing that the "section shall not apply to any citizen who legally voted at the general election of November 4, 1924."[53] Delegate John Hellenthal of Anchorage, who was chairman of the committee, explained the exemption's purpose:

> In 1924 the Native people of Alaska were awarded citizenship for the first time. Prior to that they were not citizens of the United States. In 1924 they were granted this privilege, and at that time it was stated ... that every Native person who voted at that November 4 election in 1924 would automatically be qualified to vote thereafter ... That is the law today and that is the law that will exist up until the moment we become a state. That is an Act of Congress. I have never heard it criticized, only praised.[54]

Delegate Hellenthal did not mention that the grandfather clause was a compromise that Native leaders accepted to avoid total disenfranchisement of all illiterate Natives.

The most significant change from Alaska's existing territorial literacy test was that it could be satisfied by proof that the applicant could either "read or speak the English language." It was apparent that delegates would include some form of a literacy test in the constitution. Delegate Frank Peratrovich, a Tlingit leader and the only Native out of the convention's 55 delegates, adopted the same approach as William Paul in 1925; he agreed to the compromise language in an effort to avoid more oppressive restrictions. As Delegate Marvin "Muktuk" Marston explained, "The 'read or write' [language] was put in by a great statesman from Southeastern Alaska to save a lot of great people who live here." At that time, Tlingit and Haida voters who were the most assimilated Natives in Alaska, had much higher turnout than Natives in the rest of the territory.

---

52 Gordon S. Harrison, *Alaska's Constitutional "Literacy Test" and the Question of Voting Discrimination*, 22 ALASKA HIST. 23, 36 n.14 (Spring/Fall 2007).

53 State of Alaska, Report of the Committee on Suffrage, Elections, and Apportionment to the Hon. William A. Egan, President of the Alaska Constitutional Convention (Dec. 5, 1955).

54 State of Alaska, Minutes of the Alaska Constitutional Convention, Day 36 (Dec. 13, 1955). Unless otherwise noted, all references to the debates are from Day 36 of the Convention.

Even with the more relaxed standard, the literacy test had a discriminatory impact on Natives, particularly those outside southeastern Alaska. White citizens had full access to Alaska's public schools and low illiteracy rates; among those who were illiterate, nearly all spoke English fluently. On the other hand, Native adults not only suffered from high illiteracy rates because of Alaska's segregated schooling, but many in geographically isolated villages spoke little, if any, English. The present-day rates of illiteracy and lack of English proficiency are considerably lower than they were in 1955 but remain among the highest in the United States (Chapter 10).

Many delegates still were unsatisfied. Delegate Ralph E. Robertson, the former mayor of Juneau, introduced an amendment that would have required demonstration of both English reading and speaking abilities, contending that the convention already had "lowered the standards of education or qualifications as an elector." Robertson argued:

> I can't see how a person can intelligently vote by secret ballot if he is not able to read. I think to read and speak the English language is the very minimum of qualifications. We are not challenging the loyalty of the Eskimo or the Indians or anyone else. We are simply trying to put something into our law so a person can intelligently vote the secret ballot.

According to Delegate Victor Rivers of Anchorage, regardless of how intelligent voters were, if they were illiterate, "[T]hey could not carry out the mechanics of actually voting their wishes unless they were able to read what the ballot said." Delegate Maynard Londborg of Unalakleet proposed that instead of "lowering the voting standards," the convention should focus on "bringing the people up to the standards so they can vote intelligently." He pointed out that there were nearly 1,600 Native children without access to a school and suggested addressing that instead.

Several delegates opposed Robertson's amendment. Frank Peratrovich explained that although Natives "in the outlying and fringe areas" lacked "the advantages of civilization," they nevertheless were well-informed and capable of voting. Others agreed.[55] Echoing arguments that would be made in Congress 10 years later when the Voting Rights Act (VRA) was enacted, John Coghill of Nenana maintained that if the convention was "going to shut … off" Natives, "that will set that area back probably 20 years" until the educational problems could be addressed. Katherine Nordale of Juneau suggested, "I don't see any reason why an election board could not also assist a person who couldn't read but who could speak and very definitely make his wishes known in casting his vote." The Robertson amendment failed 18 to 36.[56] The requirement that applicants "read or speak the English language" was included in Alaska's Constitution.[57] The literacy requirement was ratified by voters on April 24, 1956, and became operative on January 3, 1959.[58] "[M]any Alaskans, Natives and non-Natives alike" viewed the literacy test as "an affront" with "its racist overtones" (Harrison 2007: 30).

Alaska did not repeal its constitutional literacy test until August 25, 1970, when Constitutional Amendment 2 was narrowly passed with 51.1 percent of the vote.[59] By that time, Alaska's literacy

55 *See* Day 36 Minutes 1955 (statement of Del. Smith); Day 36 Minutes (statement of Del. Stewart).

56 *See* Day 36 Minutes 1955. A separate amendment that would have required a voter to "read, speak, and write English" had been defeated earlier by a vote of 11 to 44. *See* State of Alaska, Minutes of the Alaska Constitutional Convention.

57 *See* Alaska Const. art. V, § 1 (1959).

58 *See* Alaska Statehood Act, Pub. L. No. 85–508, 72 Stat. 339 (July 7, 1958).

59 *See* H.J. Res. 51, 6th Leg., Reg. Sess. (Alaska 1970); State of Alaska, Office of the Lt. Gov., *Alaska Constitutional Amendment Summary*, *available at* http://ltgov.state.ak.us (providing the vote total on H.J. Res. 51).

test violated federal law. In June 1970, Congress had amended the VRA to ban all literacy tests nationwide.[60] The suspension of Alaska's literacy test marked an important step towards integrating Alaska Natives into the political process.

Alaska's Coverage under Sections 4(f)(4) and 203 in 1975

Congress was well aware of the impact of Alaska's discrimination when it amended the coverage formula in Section 4 of the VRA to add language minorities in 1975. The Senate Report described documentation of "discriminatory practices" against Alaska Natives as "substantial." The Report cited the *Hootch* litigation in Alaska as an example of unequal educational opportunities available to language minorities.[61]

Educational discrimination resulted in illiteracy rates among Natives rivaling rates of African-Americans in southern states already covered by Section 5 of the Act. According to 1960 Census data considered by Congress, 38.6 percent of Alaska's non-white population age 25 years and older failed to complete the fifth primary grade, rendering them illiterate.[62] Alaska's 1960 illiteracy rate was higher than the rates for African-Americans in Alabama, Florida, North Carolina, and Virginia. By 1970, the illiteracy rate of Natives had improved little. It stood at "approximately 36 percent," exceeding the illiteracy rate for African-Americans in every state covered by Section 5.[63]

Illiteracy was compounded by high LEP rates among Natives. In 1975, Alaska had at least 18 Native languages in use. The number of speakers included at least 1,000 each who spoke Tlingit, Tutchone, Suypiaq, or Siberian Yup'ik; 6,000 who spoke Inupiaq; and 15,000 who spoke Central Yup'ik (Gravel Testimony 1975: 531). Senator Mike Gravel testified he used an interpreter when traveling to Native villages in Alaska, especially when he spoke to tribal elders. He acknowledged that lack of English proficiency or literacy was an insufficient reason to disenfranchise Native voters. Senator Gravel explained, "I think that it is a very unfortunate criteria that is used, because certainly a person who cannot read or write English can make a decision" about issues that affected him or her (Gravel Testimony 1975: 526).

Senator Gravel also introduced evidence about Alaska's constitutional literacy test. He observed that "Alaska's Constitution contained within it, an English language literacy requirement for voting" (Gravel Testimony 1975: 529). He recognized the discriminatory purpose of the law by noting, "I do not think we have a great deal of discrimination in Alaska, but I think we do have some evidence of it by the fact that this provision did creep into law." Senator Gravel conceded that there was "the possibility of disenfranchising people" under Alaska's constitutional literacy test (Gravel Testimony 1975: 525–26).

Alaska's discrimination against Alaska Natives had a profound effect on their ability to participate in the state's English-only elections. Alaska was covered under Section 5 statewide in 1965 and again in certain areas in 1970 because voter turnout was below 50 percent in the 1964 and 1968 Presidential Elections, respectively (S. Rep. No. 94–295, 1975: 12–13). In the 1968 Presidential Election, Alaska's voter turnout rate was 49.9 percent, which was lower than

60 *See* Pub. L. No. 91–285, 84 Stat. 314 (signed into law by President Nixon on June 22, 1970). The 1970 amendments are discussed in more detail in Chapters 1–2.

61 S. Rep. No. 94–295 at 29, 31 (1975).

62 *See Extension of the Voting Rights Act of 1965: Hearings on S. 407, S, 903, S. 1297, S. 1409, and S. 1443 Before the Subcomm. on Const'l Rts. of the Senate Comm. on the Judiciary* (1975 Senate Hearings), 94th Cong., 1st Sess., at 664 (1975) (Ex. 23 to the testimony of J. Stanley Pottinger).

63 1975 Senate Hearings at 529 (statement of Sen. Gravel) ("Gravel Testimony").

every southern state except Georgia, South Carolina, and Texas. In the 1972 Presidential Election, Alaska's voter turnout rate decreased to 48.2 percent, comparable to the low participation rates experienced by southern states covered by Section 5.[64] The data showed that Natives "generally suffer from severe language barriers" because of their high rate of English illiteracy.[65] Congress was "obligated to intervene" on behalf of Natives and other language minorities because state and local election officials had been "disturbingly unresponsive" to voting barriers (S. Rep. No. 94–295, 1975: 39). Therefore, Alaska was covered by the language assistance provisions of the VRA in 1975 for the Alaska Native languages (Chapters 3–4).

Conclusion

Alaska's legacy of disenfranchisement remains manifest today in Natives who are the victims of segregated schooling and have been denied registration and voting opportunities because of their illiteracy and limited-English proficiency. Natives continue to encounter English-only election practices that impose the very sort of English literacy tests or devices that the VRA was intended to eradicate.[66] That contributed to Native voter turnout of just 44.8 percent in the 2004 election, compared to non-Native turnout of 68.4 percent.[67] Turnout in some Native villages was as low as 12 percent (Continued Need 2006: 1333). In the 2008 Presidential Election, turnout among Natives was just 47 percent,[68] nearly 20 percent lower than the statewide turnout rate of 66 percent.[69] Alaska is demonstrative of the congressional finding that without the continuation of the VRA's protections, "racial and language minority citizens will be deprived of the opportunity to exercise their right to vote, or will have their votes diluted, undermining the significant gains made by minorities in the last 40 years."[70] Alaska has proven to be a recalcitrant jurisdiction, failing to provide effective assistance for Alaska Natives for more than three decades before state officials were sued in 2007 (Chapter 10).

---

64 *See* 1975 Senate Hearings, at 717–18 (Ex. 40 to the testimony of J. Stanley Pottinger).

65 121 Cong. Rec. H4716 (daily ed. June 2, 1975) (statement of Rep. Edwards).

66 H.R. Rep. No. 109–478 at 52 (2006).

67 152 Cong. Rec. S7962 (daily ed. July 20, 2006) (statement of Sen. Specter).

68 *See* Nat'l Cong. of Am. Indians, *Election 2008: Impact in Indian Country* (Nov. 6, 2008), *available at* http://www.ncai.org/fileadmin/pdfElection2008AnalysisFINALCompatibilityMode.pdf.

69 *See* State of Alaska, Division of Elections, Official Results of the Nov. 4, 2008 General Election, *available at* http://www.elections.alaska.gov/08general/data/results.pdf.

70 VRARA § 2(b)(9), 120 Stat. 577, 578.

Chapter 10
Remedying Language Discrimination in the Bethel Census Area of Alaska

Among the jurisdictions required to provide language assistance, few demonstrate the continuing need for the federal bilingual voting mandate as much as Alaska. The state is home to thousands of Alaska Natives and American Indians and has the greatest number of indigenous languages in the country. LEP and illiteracy rates are among the highest of any jurisdiction covered by Section 203 of the Voting Rights Act (VRA). Native voters there continue to suffer the effects of past and present discrimination that block them from full and effective participation in the political process (Chapter 9).

Alaska has exacerbated those barriers through ideological resistance to bilingual elections and ongoing efforts to undermine tribal sovereignty. Some members of Alaska's congressional delegation led the opposition to language assistance for Alaska Native (Chapters 3–4). The Alaska Legislative Council, a constitutionally created body of the state legislature, distributes policy papers arguing that tribes do not exist in Alaska. Alaska's Bureau of Vital Statistics has refused to recognize adoptions over tribal member children adjudicated in tribal courts instead of through the state, despite the clear authority for the tribal governments to act under federal law.[1] In 1998, voters passed Ballot Measure 6, which required that only English be used for "all government functions and actions."[2] The policy was adopted in part to block the provision of bilingual materials and services to the state's non-English speaking population.[3] Alaska's highest court struck down the provision for violating the free speech guarantees of the state constitution.[4]

English-only policies have carried over to the administration of state-run elections. Alaska's initial steps to provide language assistance to LEP Alaska Native voters did not begin until 2008, shortly before a federal court in *Nick v. Bethel* directed election officials to comply with the VRA in the Bethel Census Area.[5] Demonstrating that resistance, the state's Director of Elections said that Alaska would not provide any bilingual voting assistance beyond what it was required to provide and had not even done that.[6] When U.S. Senate candidate Mark Begich offered to translate forms for voter registration and absentee voting into Native languages, Alaska's election officials refused to accept them.

---

1 *See* Order, *Kaltag Tribal Council et al. v. Jackson et al.*, case no. 3:06-cv-00211-TMB (D. Alaska Feb. 22, 2008) (concluding that the tribal courts have the authority to adjudicate adoptions under the Indian Child Welfare Act).

2 Alaska Stat. § 44.12.300 (1998).

3 *See* Susan Fischetti, *Official Language Practical, Reins in Bureaucracy*, Anchorage Daily News, Apr. 4, 2002, at B6.

4 *See Alaskans for a Common Language, Inc. v. Kritz*, 170 P.3d 183, 187–88 (Alaska 2007).

5 Preliminary Injunction, *Nick et al. v. City of Bethel et al.*, case no. 3:07-cv-0098-TMB (D. Alaska July 30, 2008).

6 *Nick* 2007: Pls.' Ex. 94, at STATE 209; Pls.' Ex. 191, Brewster Dep. 124:8–14. In contrast, many jurisdictions outside of Alaska routinely provide more language assistance than what is required by the VRA (Figure A.11).

The *Nick* litigation illustrates how English-only policies and violations of the language assistance provisions can disenfranchise LEP voters. The Bethel region is a particularly apt example because its coverage under both Sections 4(f)(4) and 203 of the VRA shows the importance of both provisions in remedying voting discrimination against language minorities. Alaska's failure to implement the federal bilingual elections and voter assistance mandate is a warning for other covered jurisdictions of practices that they should avoid.

Yup'ik Eskimos in the Bethel Region

The Bethel Census Area is a wild and beautiful region in southwest Alaska. It has a land area of nearly 41,000 square miles, approximately the size of Tennessee. Fifty-six villages of Yup'ik-speaking Eskimos are spread throughout the tundra and marshlands in the Yukon-Kuskokwim Delta. "The region is not accessible by road, so residents and visitors must travel to Bethel by water or air … People travel to the villages by air or boat along the waterways in the summer and by snow machine or all terrain vehicles on the frozen rivers and trails in the winter."[7]

The area is sparsely populated, with 16,006 persons and a population density of 0.4 persons per square mile, the 14th lowest population density of any county-level jurisdiction in the United States. More than 85 percent are American Indians and Alaska Natives (AIAN), the seventh highest percentage among county-level jurisdictions.[8] Bethel, located at the mouth of the Kuskokwim River 40 miles inland from the Bering Sea (400 air miles west of Anchorage), is the area's most populous municipality.

Yup'ik Eskimos are a proud people who are economically disadvantaged despite the region's rich abundance of natural resources. Nearly a quarter of Yup'ik families are below the poverty line. Their per capita income is $9,000 per year, less than half of the average rate in Alaska. Over a third of households receive public assistance. Almost half lack adequate plumbing facilities or kitchen facilities. Yup'iks account for nearly 95 percent of households in the region without basic telephone service. Most Yup'ik residents of the region rely upon subsistence fishing to survive. Increasingly, their lifestyle is threatened by state restrictions that favor sportsmen who bring tourist dollars to Alaska.

Yup'ik is the predominant language spoken in the region. The Bethel Census Area is one of just three county-level jurisdictions in which a majority of persons speak an AIAN language at home. The limited-English proficiency (LEP) rate is very high. Nearly 21 percent of eligible Yup'ik voters are LEP. In eight Yup'ik villages more than half of eligible voters are LEP. Ten villages have LEP rates between 20 to 50 percent, and six villages have LEP rates of 5 to 20 percent (Appendix C).

The Bethel region is home to five villages represented in the *Molly Hootch* case, which successfully challenged Alaska's failure to provide them with high schools until the 1980s (Chapter 9).[9] Because of that discrimination, 34.7 percent of Yup'ik voters have not graduated from high school, nearly 3.5 times the rate for non-Natives. Nearly one-fifth have less than a ninth-grade education, half of whom have less than a fifth-grade education. Yup'ik elders denied secondary schooling have the lowest rates of educational attainment. Among Yup'iks aged 60 and older, 91.7 percent lack a high school diploma and 86.3 percent have less than a ninth-grade education. Among

7 State of Alaska, Department of Commerce, Community, and Economic Development, Bethel Census Area: Tourism, "Transportation and Access."

8 U.S. Census Bureau, County and City Data Book: 2000, Tables B-1 and B-2.

9 The villages are Akiachak, Kongiganak, Kwigillingok, Mekoryuk, and Nunapitchuk.

Yup'iks aged 45 to 59 years, 40.7 percent lack a high school diploma, and 27.7 percent have less than a ninth-grade education.

That low educational attainment has contributed to a high illiteracy rate, defined as the failure to complete the fifth primary grade (Chapter 4). Among Yup'ik voters who are LEP, 21.5 percent are illiterate, nearly 16 times the national rate (Appendix C). Five villages have illiteracy rates of 40 percent or greater, with some as high as 100 percent. Nineteen villages have illiteracy rates of 15 percent or greater. About half of Yup'ik students are not proficient in English, making it likely "that the average reading level of Alaska Native voters in the Bethel Census Area is considerably lower than their grade level of educational attainment."[10]

As a result of the LEP and illiteracy rates among Yup'ik-speaking voters, the Bethel Census Area has been covered by Section 203 since 1975. The region also has been subject to the requirements of Section 4(f)(4) for Alaska Native languages since Alaska was covered statewide in 1975 (Chapter 9; Appendix B). Like much of rural Alaska, the region does not have an organized county-level government. Therefore, except for a handful of municipal elections, Alaska's Division of Elections is responsible for administering registration and voting activities. State officials have evaded their responsibilities and denied language assistance to LEP voters.

Characteristics of Alaska's Ineffective Language Assistance Program

Congress found that "where State and local officials conduct elections only in English, language minority citizens are excluded from participating in the electoral process."[11] Evidence from the Bethel region supports that conclusion. Between 2000 and 2006, the average turnout in the area's voting precincts was less than 44 percent, more than 13 percent lower than the statewide average of 57 percent. Low Yup'ik turnout was particularly pronounced in the 2004 Presidential Election, when it trailed the statewide average by more than 20 percent.[12] Alaska's election officials were dismissive of the region's lower turnout, which the state Director of Elections said "has been the trend of that area."[13] They did not look into causes of that "trend," which was attributable to the state's failure to provide Yup'ik language assistance.

In June 2007, Yup'ik voters and tribes in the Bethel area sought to reverse that pattern and compel the state to provide assistance in Yup'ik. Represented by the Native American Rights Fund (NARF) and the ACLU, they sued Alaska for violating the VRA's bilingual voting and voter assistance provisions. The four individual plaintiffs each spoke Yup'ik as their first and primary language and used very little English in their daily lives.

The lead plaintiff was Anna Nick, a petite woman whose quiet determination to help disenfranchised LEP Yup'ik voters overcome the state's English-only barriers evoked memories of Elizabeth Peratrovich (Chapter 9). Ms. Nick was a 69-year-old resident of Akiachak, a village of nearly 700 people located 18 miles northeast of Bethel along the Kuskokwim River. One-third of the village lacks basic plumbing and sewer facilities.[14] Because of state discrimination, Ms.

---

10 *Nick* 2007: Pls.' Ex. 174, Dybdahl Decl., at 25.

11 42 U.S.C. § 1973b(f)(1); *see also* 42 U.S.C. § 1973aa-1a(a) (stating similar legislative findings for Section 203 of the VRA).

12 *Nick* 2007: Pls.' Ex. 141; Pls.' Ex. 183, RFA 2 ¶¶ 113–150.

13 *Nick* 2007: Pls.' Ex. 191, Brewster Dep., 83:11–19.

14 Dan Berry, *This Land: Remote and Struggling, but Still a Bit of America*, N.Y. Times, Oct. 5, 2008, *available at* http://www.nytimes.com/2008/10/06/us/06land.html?_r=2&hp. Pictures of Akiachak are available at the *New York Times* webpage, including one of Anna Nick.

Nick only completed the fifth grade. She learned how to read and write through her church. She worked as a poll worker in state elections for eight years until she resigned because she could not translate voting materials from English to Yup'ik and did not understand many of the duties of her position due to the language barriers.

The remaining individual plaintiffs were three elderly Yup'ik voters who were LEP and illiterate because of educational discrimination: David O. David from Kwigillingok; Billy McCann, a resident of Bethel born in Tununak; and Arthur Nelson, a resident of Bethel born in Kwigillingok. Other plaintiffs included tribal councils from Kasigluk, Kwigillingok, Tuluksak, and Tuntutuliak. Each tribal plaintiff was a federally recognized government for LEP Yup'ik-speaking voters living in the Bethel area.[15]

The *Nick* plaintiffs identified neglect and ideological opposition by election officials to the bilingual voting mandate that resulted in Alaska's liability under the VRA.[16] State election officials took few, if any, steps characteristic of an effective language program (Chapters 4, 6). Instead, they engaged in several practices that should be avoided to comply with Section 203.

Habit 1: Don't Accept or Investigate Voter Complaints

In late 2005, NARF contacted Alaska's Division of Elections with complaints from Yup'ik voters about insufficient language assistance. NARF obtained the information as part of the efforts to reauthorize the expiring provisions of the VRA (Chapter 7). The NARF findings were included in the congressional record.[17] One of the report's authors, NARF attorney Natalie Landreth, testified before the Senate Judiciary Committee in May 2006.[18] That led to calls for further investigations of Alaska's voting discrimination by Senator Patrick Leahy and the U.S. Commission on Civil Rights,[19] among others.

Lieutenant Governor Loren Leman, who supervised the Alaska Division of Elections, dismissed the NARF report. Leman wrote a letter to Congressman Steve Chabot, chairman of the House subcommittee responsible for reauthorization, denouncing the report. He informed Chabot that Alaska was "in compliance" and "[h]appily so" with the VRA.[20] A federal court found otherwise in 2008, citing the state's lack of responsiveness in remedying discrimination against Alaska Natives. The U.S. Department of Justice also noted evidence of Alaska's violations. Later, Leman himself was concerned enough about the report to mention it to incoming Lieutenant Governor Sean Parnell during his transition.

---

15 *See* Amended Complaint, *Nick et al. v. City of Bethel et al.*, case no. 3:07-cv-0098-TMB (D. Alaska filed December 31, 2007).

16 The *Nick* case also included claims against the City of Bethel. This chapter focuses on claims against state election officials, who were responsible for most of the election activities in the Bethel area.

17 *See* Natalie Landreth and Moira Smith, *Voting Rights in Alaska 1982–2006*, 17 S. Cal. Rev. L. & Soc. Just. 79, 83–85 (2007).

18 *See Modern Enforcement of the Voting Rights Act: Hearing Before the S. Comm. on the Judiciary,* 109th Cong. 18 (testimony of Natalie Landreth, Staff Attorney, Native American Rights Fund).

19 *See* U.S. Comm'n on Civil Rts., Transcript, *Review of the Department of Justice's Plans to Monitor Voting Rights Enforcement for the 2008 U.S. Presidential Election* 56–57 (statement of Commissioner Melendez) (June 6, 2008), *available at* http://www.usccr.gov/calendar/trnscrpt/060608ccr1.pdf.

20 *Fannie Lou Hamer, Rosa Parks, and Coretta Scott King Voting Rights Reauthorization and Amendments Act of 2006 (Part II): Hearing on H.R. 9 Before the Subcomm. on the Const. of the House Comm. on the Judiciary*, 109th Cong., 2d Sess., at 115, 116 (2006) (letter from Alaska Lt. Gov. Loren Leman) (commenting on Landreth and Smith 2007).

Figure 10.1 The Native village of Akiachak, home to Anna Nick, June 2007
Akiachak is a typical Yup'ik village in the Bethel Census Area. In the foreground, Yup'ik residents of the village are fishing, building up their subsistence supplies for the long winter months ahead. The Yupiit School District offices and high school are pictured in the center of the photo. Like other native villages in the Bethel region, Alaska did not provide secondary schooling until it built high schools in the 1980s as a result of the *Molly Hootch* litigation (Chapter 9).
Source: Author's photograph.

Parnell did not take any steps to address the complaints after receiving Leman's assurance "that they had been addressed" and an assurance from the Elections Director that "we are in compliance with applicable federal law." Even after the *Nick* plaintiffs sued Parnell and other state election officials, Parnell still did not direct any elections officials to investigate their allegations. Rather, he asked the Director whether she believed the state's language assistance program "was in compliance and she expressed … that she believed that it was."[21]

During the *Nick* litigation, state election officials did not accept responsibility for their failure to identify and correct the problems. Instead, they blamed Yup'ik voters for not complaining about the lack of language assistance before filing their lawsuit, despite the NARF report. The officials admitted Alaska had done little to facilitate feedback from Yup'ik voters. The state did not post any information in polling places regarding how to contact the state with any complaints.[22] The regional supervisor said that providing that information was a "policy call" that she never thought to request.[23]

The Elections Director admitted it "would be a good idea" to have voter complaint forms in the polls on election day "because if there was an issue, they would have the ability right then and there to … write out … their complaint…" Although having complaint forms in the polls was something

21 *Nick* 2007: Pls.' Ex. 190, Parnell Dep., 15:8–16:9, 50:22–51:12, 53:12–22.
22 *Nick* 2007: Pls.' Ex. 191, Brewster Dep., 67:10–68:4; Pls.' Ex.159, Baker Dep., 80:8–12.
23 *Nick* 2007: Pls.' Ex.159, Baker Dep., 81:6–13.

that the state "could implement," it did not do so. The Director recognized the importance of having translators available at the polls to record complaints from LEP Yup'ik voters but acknowledged the state did not do that.[24] The absence of language assistance for voter complaints was attributable to the state's lack of assistance in Yup'ik for any registration and voting activities.

Covered jurisdictions like Alaska that do not solicit feedback from voters remove an important component of a successful language program: community involvement. A covered jurisdiction must actively monitor the effectiveness of its program by regularly communicating with language minorities. That prophylactic measure facilitates identification of areas where the jurisdiction's efforts fall short. Regular contact with LEP voters builds a partnership with them, instilling mutual trust and citizen involvement. Blaming voters for their complaints, as Alaska's election officials did, shuts down the lines of communication and makes litigation inevitable.

Habit 2: Ignore the Law or Treat It as a Low Priority

Alaska committed insufficient resources to providing Yup'ik language assistance. In 2007, election officials did not allocate any funds for language assistance and did not ask for any. Alaska had several million dollars in unspent federal Help America Vote Act (HAVA) funding available for language assistance (Chapter 8). However, in the four years that Alaska had received the HAVA funds, election officials spent less than $6,000 for all languages covered in the state, most of which was spent after the state was sued in 2007.[25]

Alaska's Division of Elections had just one election employee who worked on language assistance for all Alaska Native languages "about half" the time before she went on maternity leave and left her position vacant. The Director admitted that having a bilingual coordinator "would be a good idea." She did not start "thinking seriously" about having a full-time staff worker whose only responsibility was language assistance until she was "contacted by the … Department of Justice" in 2007 about the lack of audio translations on Alaska's voting machines.[26]

Even after it became apparent litigation was likely, Alaska treated the violations as a low priority. The Elections Director "started looking in April 2006" at improving the language assistance program. Nevertheless, election officials "put it aside as we were conducting our major statewide election as well as our [school board] election … and we picked it back up after the election and then we were hit with another statewide special election in April of 2007." The Director explained, "Language assistance is not the only assistance that the Division of Elections provides … We have … the demands of every voter in the state. I think it would [be] important to balance all of those needs and our resources to be able to make that determination."[27] Alaska's election officials viewed compliance with the VRA as optional, something extraneous to running an election rather than one of their core responsibilities. Section 203 requires language assistance be provided to covered LEP voters for every public election, not merely when it is administratively convenient (Chapter 4).

If a jurisdiction implements an effective language program when it becomes covered (or ideally, before it becomes covered) and maintains that program, compliance costs can be minimal (Chapters 4, 6, 8). When a jurisdiction like Alaska fails to make compliance a priority, the costs are much greater. The state's active opposition to language assistance made it difficult to build relationships with the Yup'ik community, increasing program expenses. The state also spent

24 *Nick* 2007: Pls.' Ex. 191, Brewster Dep., 52:20–54:17, 67:14–23.

25 *Nick* 2007: Pls.' Ex. 64, at STATE 722; Pls.' Ex. 190, Parnell Dep., 21:3–23; Pls.' Ex. 191, Brewster Dep., 205:10–207:16.

26 *Nick* 2007: Pls.' Ex. 191, Brewster Dep., at 22:24–23:19, 24:4–10, 24:16–18, 96:7–97:24.

27 *Nick* 2007: Pls.' Ex. 191, Brewster Dep., at 70:8–18, 80:25–81:2, 113:12–25.

hundreds of thousands of dollars on attorneys' fees and work-time of election officials to respond to the *Nick* litigation. Compliance would have been much cheaper.

Habit 3: Pass the Buck

Alaska's election officials attempted to shift their legal responsibilities under Section 203 to others. Except for two radio advertisements the state purchased in 2006, all public service announcements (PSAs) were in English. Election officials included a notation of "Local Native Language Requested" with their PSAs, requesting that print, radio, and television media provide translations for them. They left it to the media to determine when to broadcast any translated announcements. Officials took no steps to confirm whether the PSAs were aired in Yup'ik to provide clear, complete, and accurate translations.[28]

Alaska placed a similar burden on bilingual poll workers. The state made precinct chairs responsible for recruiting poll workers and providing language assistance. Election officials did not provide any election information in Yup'ik, whether in oral or written form, making poll workers responsible for translating English voting materials on-the-spot. Election officials left it to the poll workers to identify if their co-workers were providing effective translations.[29]

The state also imposed its duties on tribal governments. In 2006, election officials sent voter registration forms to some Native villages for the first time. The materials were only in English, with a request that tribal councils "provide as much assistance to the LEP applicants as needed."[30] Although state officials performed polling place accessibility assessments elsewhere, they placed that burden on the tribal governments for the precincts located in Yup'ik villages.[31]

Election officials even tried to shift their responsibility under the language assistance provisions to voters. They expected elderly LEP Yup'ik voters to get assistance from a family member who would deliver the voter a special-needs ballot or accompany them to the polling place. In a Catch-22, LEP Yup'ik voters were provided with English-only voter information pamphlets asking them to let the state know before the election whether they would need language assistance at the polls. Election officials assumed that LEP Yup'ik voters who could not read the English-only request "might" be told about it by a friend or family member. If an LEP voter failed to obtain that self-help, that person would be unable to register and vote.[32]

Section 203 makes it the duty of covered jurisdictions, not private citizens, to provide effective language assistance. The statute requires that "[w]henever any State or political subdivision ... provides ... materials or information relating to the electoral process ... *it shall provide them in the language of the applicable minority group as well as in the English language*."[33] That requirement has been described by an attorney retained by Alaska as "almost strict liability in nature: If you

28 *Nick* 2007: Pls.' Ex. 33, State Defs.' Response to Interrogatory No. 10; Pls.' Exs. 46, 49–50, 57; Pls.' Ex. 183, RFA 2 ¶ 213; Pls.' Ex. 191, Brewster Dep., 127:21–133:22, 145:19–147:21.

29 *Nick* 2007: Pls.' Ex. 33, State Defs.' Response to Interrogatory Nos. 8–9; Pls.' Exs. 47–48; Pls.' Ex. 94, at STATE 206–08; Pls.' Ex.159, Baker Dep., 26:1–5, 54:25–55:1, 76:6–77:5, 122:8–125:24; Pls.' Ex. 191, Brewster Dep., 33:3–7, 112:12–114:11, 118:17–119: 21.

30 *Nick* 2007: Pls.' Ex. 94, at STATE 205; Pls.' Ex. 191, Brewster Dep., 112:12–24.

31 *Nick* 2007: Pls.' Ex.159, Baker Dep., 22:3–25:17. Polling place accessibility assessments are required by the Voting Accessibility for the Elderly and Handicapped Act, 42 U.S.C. §§ 1973ee, *et seq.*, and the public accommodations provisions of the Americans with Disabilities Act.

32 *Nick* 2007: Pls.' Ex. 69; Pls.' Ex. 94, at STATE 206; Pls.' Ex.159, Baker Dep., 32:9–12; Pls.' Ex. 191, Brewster Dep., 141:1–25.

33 42 U.S.C. § 1973aa-1a(c) (emphasis added).

are a covered jurisdiction, you must provide language-based assistance."[34] Covered jurisdictions cannot escape liability for their noncompliance by passing the buck for their responsibilities.

Habit 4: Don't Engage in Community Outreach

Alaska's election officials acknowledged the importance of voter outreach. According to the Elections Director, "Working with the tribal governments seemed to be the most effective approach in reaching out to LEP voters in areas where Alaska Native languages are spoken."[35] The state's language assistance program required an "employee of the Division of Elections" to travel "to each locality to work with the interpreters in preparing" audio tapes with all the election information that Yup'ik voters need to participate effectively.[36] However, officials admitted "that has not happened." Rather, by late 2007, the state's outreach was limited to a single mailing of a voter registration form and instructions in English, with no follow-up mailings or phone calls.[37]

The regional election supervisor did not reach out to any community leaders in the four years she held her position.[38] She did not attend any tribal council meetings explaining, "My job is to conduct elections and … that's what I'm focused on. I'm not focused on attending tribal council meetings in all of these communities." She acknowledged that tribal council meetings "quite possibly may" provide a good opportunity to meet with local leaders about Yup'ik language assistance, "but I wouldn't know that unless I attended one."[39]

State officials also did not reach out to Native organizations. The Alaska Federation of Natives (AFN), Alaska Inter-Tribal Council (AITC), and Bureau of Indian Affairs regularly held meetings in Anchorage and Juneau attended by tribal leaders from all over Alaska, including the Bethel region. State officials ignored those opportunities even though "it would be helpful to have the opportunity to meet face-to-face with some of these leaders …"[40] Lieutenant Governor Parnell attended many of those meetings but never discussed language assistance with Native leaders.[41] Even when election officials took some steps to facilitate voting among tribal leaders, they did not include any information about language assistance.[42] An election supervisor employed by Alaska for nearly two decades admitted the state scheduled meetings with Yup'ik contacts and AFN and AITC members for the first time in 2008. Both meetings took place just a few weeks before oral arguments on the Motion for a Preliminary Injunction filed by the plaintiffs in the *Nick* litigation. Alaska officials scheduled the meeting only under threat of imminent judicial action.[43]

The state likewise did not attempt to reach out to LEP voters. Instead, Yup'ik voters received English-only information materials about polling place locations, sample ballots, early voting,

34 Bruce L. Adelson, *Minority-Language Election Rules and the Public Lawyer*, 15 PUB. LAWYER 1 (2007).

35 *Nick* 2007: Pls.' Ex. 94, at STATE 205; Pls.' Ex. 191, Brewster Dep., 90:17–20, 116:14–23.

36 *Nick* 2007: First Amended Complaint, Attach. B, at STATE 564.

37 *Nick* 2007: Pls.' Ex 191, Brewster Dep., at 86:9–19, 114:1–15, 117:20–118:13, 151:10–152:25; Fenumiai Dep., at 76:4–77:12; Growden Dep., at 37:19–40:12.

38 *Nick* 2007: Pls.' Ex. 191, Brewster Dep., 74:15–19, 79:14–80:24.

39 *Nick* 2007: Pls.' Ex.159, Baker Dep., 86:8–87:8.

40 *Nick* 2007: Pls.' Ex. 191, Brewster Dep., 91:12–93:22.

41 *Nick* 2007: Pls.' Ex. 190, Parnell Dep., 49:17–24.

42 *Nick* 2007: Pls.' Ex. 191, Brewster Dep., 92:20–93:14.

43 *Nick* 2007: Growden Dep., at 9:14–10:15, 132:16–133:1, 189:12–190:9.

instructions for using voting machines, marking ballots, and provisional voting procedures.[44] Even after Alaska implemented touch-screen voting units in 2006, officials did not explain to LEP voters how to use the new equipment. Although the regional supervisor visited the City of Bethel several times, she never considered conducting voter education meetings because "that would take a policy decision from the Director's office."[45]

Jurisdictions must engage in outreach with covered LEP voters to comply with Section 203. The Justice Department's regulations explain, "Announcements, publicity, and assistance should be given in oral form to the extent needed to enable members of the … language minority group to participate effectively in the electoral process."[46] Furthermore, "public notices and announcements of electoral activities" should be "handled in a manner that provides members of the … language minority group an effective opportunity to be informed about electoral activities."[47] A covered jurisdiction should publicize information including "the display of appropriate notices, in the minority language, at voter registration offices, polling places, etc., the making of announcements over minority language radio or television stations, the publication of notices in minority language newspapers, and direct contact with language minority group organizations."[48]

A Native language expert described four ways that Alaska failed to provide meaningful outreach: no in-person outreach, no "training materials or presentations on language assistance," no "written translations of voting materials," and "no audio (tape or radio) translations of any elections information." Native language groups require a "comprehensive" approach to outreach because "Natives have only been allowed to vote in many parts of the United States for less than 50 years. There isn't a long tradition of voting." Effective outreach includes traveling to Native villages, attending tribal council meetings and other public events, in-person voter registration, providing information about language assistance, and consulting with tribal councils about the language program.[49]

Where election officials have ignored outreach, qualified bilingual coordinators can turn things around. They can provide effective communication of election information. They also help recruit translators, including: confirming their ability to serve as translators; providing translator training in English and the covered Native language; preparing written and audio aids in the covered Native language to help ensure translations are clear, complete, and accurate; trouble-shooting language assistance issues on Election Day; and identifying areas where language assistance can be improved based upon feedback from election officials, translators, voters, and what they observe.

Outreach coordinators should be bilingual and fully fluent and literate in English and the covered Native language and be trained in providing language assistance. They must have sufficient resources.[50] Although bilingual coordinators are not required by the VRA, covered jurisdictions using them are more likely to comply with Section 203. That is why localities with large LEP populations tend to use bilingual coordinators or are directed by federal courts to hire them under comprehensive remedial orders (Chapter 6).

---

44 *Nick* 2007: Pls.' Ex. 94, at STATE 203–04, 207; Pls.' Ex. 101, Bethel Defs.' Response to Interrogatory Nos. 6, 9; Pls.' Ex.159, Baker Dep., 26:1–5, 54:25–55:1; Pls.' Ex. 191, Brewster Dep., 112:12–113:7, 114:1–11, 119:7–21.

45 *Nick* 2007: Pls.' Ex.159, Baker Dep., 26:6-27:2.

46 28 C.F.R. § 55.20(a).

47 28 C.F.R. § 55.18(b).

48 28 C.F.R. § 55.18(e).

49 *Nick* 2007: Pls.' Ex. 176, Yazzie Decl. ¶¶ 93–103.

50 *Nick* 2007: Pls.' Ex. 176, Yazzie Decl. ¶¶ 80–92.

Habit 5: Don't Provide Language Assistance for Voter Registration Activities

Lieutenant Governor Parnell agreed the most effective approach to providing language assistance during the voter registration process is to work with the local tribal governments.[51] That did not occur. Election officials never targeted the Bethel region for voter registration drives despite doing so in other parts of the state.[52]

Consistent with Alaska's opposition to bilingual election materials, voter registration forms were available only in English and Tagalog, with the latter forms added under threat of litigation by the Justice Department. In 2006, for the first time, the state sent out voter registration packets in English to some tribes in other parts of Alaska,but did not send them to all the tribal governments in the Bethel region. Election officials did not send registration information to any tribal governments in 2007, even though the state conducted two elections.[53]

When election officials conducted annual purges of voter registration rolls, all information provided to LEP Yup'ik voters being removed from the list was in English. The National Voter Registration Act (NVRA) requires that voters be notified that they are being purged to give them an opportunity to remain registered.[54] State officials had no information about whether any purge announcements or notices were translated by private citizens into Yup'ik, and if so, whether those translations were accurate and complete.[55]

In addition, oral Yup'ik assistance was not provided for any voter registration information. An election supervisor explained, "All our communications are done in English."[56] There was no dedicated telephone line that LEP voters could call to obtain information in Yup'ik.[57] Alaska did not hire a bilingual coordinator until July 2008, weeks before the *Nick* plaintiffs secured their injunction.[58] LEP Yup'ik voters were left to fend for themselves. Some purged elderly voters did not vote for decades because they thought that they had been permanently disenfranchised.

Language assistance was offered for registration on Election Day in some precincts with trained bilingual poll workers. State election officials designated Yup'ik poll workers as deputy voting registrars, authorizing them to assist unregistered eligible citizens in completing voter registration forms. However, a quarter of all bilingual poll workers did not know about that responsibility because of their lack of training. Although the state's language plan required that registration officials in the rural areas "speak the minority language spoken in that particular area," many registrars in the Bethel region did not.[59]

Covered jurisdictions must provide language assistance for voter registration. Registration activities must be "conducted in such a way that members of the ... language minority group have an effective opportunity to register." Ways to offer those opportunities include providing

51 *Nick* 2007: Pls.' Ex. 190, Parnell Dep., 47:12–23.

52 *Nick* 2007: Pls.' Exs. 79, 82; Pls.' Ex. 94, at STATE 205; Pls.' Ex. 191, Brewster Dep., 182:20–22, 188:18–189:6.

53 *Nick* 2007: Pls.' Ex. 94, at STATE 205; Pls.' Exs. 79, 82; Pls.' Ex.159, Baker Dep., 30:8–21, 50:15–17, 83:9–15; Pls.' Ex. 191, Brewster Dep., 32:22–33:2, 182:20–22.

54 *See* 42 U.S.C. § 1973gg-6(c).

55 *Nick* 2007: Pls.' Ex. 62; Pls.' Ex. 191, Brewster Dep., 148:9–149:17, 190:23–193:11.

56 *Nick* 2007: Pls.' Ex.159, Baker Dep., 28:24–29:4.

57 *Nick* 2007: Pls.' Ex. 94, at STATE 205; Pls.' Ex. 191, Brewster Dep., 64:7–65:5.

58 *Nick* 2007: Pls.' Ex. 33; State Defs.' Response to Interrogatory Nos. 1–2; Pls.' Ex. 39; Pls.' Ex. 191, Brewster Dep., 173:11–21.

59 *Nick* 2007: Pls.' Ex. 52, at STATE 562; Pls.' Ex. 177, Leonard Decl. ¶ 43, Attach. B; Pls.' Ex. 191, Brewster Dep., 29:16–30:25.

in the "minority language, all notices, forms and other materials … and to have only bilingual persons as registrars." Jurisdictions also should use "deputy registrars who are members of the … language minority group and the use of decentralized places of registration, with minority language materials available at places where persons who need them are most likely to come to register."[60] Election officials should travel to language minority communities and hold registration drives at convenient times and locations, such as at cultural events, scheduled school activities like football or basketball games, and tribal council meetings. Registration must be made accessible for LEP voters like Yup'ik voters in the Bethel region, who often lack transportation and encounter severe language barriers in routine daily activities.[61]

Habit 6: Don't Have Bilingual Poll Workers Where They Are Needed

Alaska did not have Yup'ik translators available for more than one-third of the elections it administered.[62] Only 12 of 32 precincts in the Bethel area had Yup'ik translators for every statewide election between 2000 and 2007, and just 14 of 32 had translators for every school board election. Overall, 13 of the 32 precincts for statewide elections and 12 of the 32 precincts for school board elections had not had a Yup'ik translator for four or more elections held during that seven-year period. Three voting precincts in the City of Bethel had not had a Yup'ik translator for nearly every statewide and school board election held between 2000 and 2007.[63]

Language assistance often was unavailable even when the state said it was. Nine of 89 poll workers identified as translators reported that they had not worked as translators. Four out of nine translators in the City of Bethel were not fluent in Yup'ik or had not worked as Yup'ik translators. Another three translators worked less than a full day, leaving gaps in language assistance coverage.[64] Election officials complained that many bilingual poll workers they recruited did not show up on Election Day.[65]

A covered jurisdiction violates Section 203 when it fails to have bilingual poll workers where needed. Election officials must "determine the number of helpers (i.e., persons to provide oral assistance in the minority language)" necessary for polling places measured under the basic standard of "effectiveness."[66] Jurisdictions can use targeting methods to identify the precincts where assistance is needed if they do not have a homogenous language minority population like the Bethel region (Chapters 4, 8). Decisions on where bilingual poll workers are to be placed should be revisited periodically, to accommodate changing demographics or the current needs of LEP voters.

Officials also must ensure that bilingual poll workers feel comfortable translating and agree to fulfill that role. They have to prepare for contingencies such as no-shows by recruiting stand-by workers who can step in at the last minute. Precincts without a translator because there are few voters there who need language assistance may accommodate LEP voters through audio translations or bilingual translators available by telephone. Such alternatives may be permissible for places with few LEP voters if they provide effective language assistance for the voter (Chapters 4, 8). Jurisdictions like Alaska cannot assume that liability will be avoided for the lack of language assistance if LEP voters do not complain about it.

60 28 C.F.R. § 55.18(c).

61 *Nick* 2007: Pls.' Ex. 176, Yazzie Decl. ¶ 99.

62 *Nick* 2007: Pls.' Ex. 178; Pls.' Ex. 183, RFA 2 ¶¶ 155–173.

63 *Nick* 2007: Pls.' Exs. 178 and 179; Pls.' Ex. 183, RFA 2 ¶¶ 155–197.

64 *Nick* 2007: Pls.' Ex. 177, Leonard Decl. ¶¶ 35, 38–39, 64–67, 80, Attach. B, L.

65 *Nick* 2007: Pls.' Ex.159, Baker Dep., 34:22–36:22.

66 28 C.F.R. § 55.20(c).

Habit 7: Don't Confirm Your Bilingual Poll Workers' Abilities

Alaska's Elections Director described the importance of translations using "the appropriate language and dialect for the precincts" provided "by someone who understands the language." She admitted that poll workers come "from every walk of life with all sorts of different abilities," and that the quality of Yup'ik translations would vary from translator to translator.[67] Yet, despite the differences in individual translator's skills, Alaska took no steps to ensure that all translators were capable of performing their responsibilities. As one election official explained, "I'm telling you now as an election supervisor and as somebody from the Division of Elections, we'll take anybody we can who is breathing who is a registered voter so we can have an election in that village on election day."[68] Language skills did not matter, despite Section 203's mandate.

When translators provide language assistance, it is important that they be able to communicate in the covered language. Translators must provide accurate translations about voter assistance, voter qualifications for closed primary elections, how to use a voting machine, the names and offices on the ballot, special instructions, and ballot questions, among others. Nevertheless, Alaska's election officials did not confirm the language abilities of Yup'ik poll workers. Their sole basis for designating translators as Yup'ik speakers was through a form that poll workers completed in English.[69] Their stereotypical assumption that all Yup'iks can translate proved unfounded. At least three election workers identified by the state as translators for elections in the Native villages did not speak Yup'ik fluently. Four of the nine election workers identified as translators for Bethel voting precincts also were not fluent in Yup'ik.[70]

Similarly, a regional election supervisor acknowledged "it's a good idea" for poll workers to be able to speak English and to perform their responsibilities. Native speakers often overstate their ability to understand spoken English, making it important to confirm their English language abilities (Chapter 4). That can be done by having a fluent bilingual speaker evaluate the translator's abilities by asking the translator to read a ballot question in English and translate it into the covered language. However, Alaska did not conduct any "specific evaluation" to see if poll workers "speak English."[71] Instead, LEP voters like Anna Nick were designated as Yup'ik translators, even though many needed language assistance themselves. That left several polling places without anyone capable of reading and translating English information.[72]

Election officials likewise did not identify the educational attainment of Yup'ik translators.[73] When plaintiffs interviewed 89 of the state's translators, 26 (29.2 percent) reported they had less than a high school education. Several Native villages had multiple election workers who never attended high school. In Lower Kalskag, one translator only completed the third grade. In Akiak, the only election worker identified as a translator reported that she only completed the eighth

67 *Nick* 2007: Pls.' Ex. 191, Brewster Dep., 18:15–23, 59:24–60:13.

68 *Nick* 2007: Growden Dep., at 114.

69 *Nick* 2007: Pls.' Exs. 67A, 67B; Pls.' Ex.159, Baker Dep., 53:17–55:11, 67:4–69:15; Pls.' Ex. 183, RFA 2 ¶ 211; Pls.' Ex. 191, Brewster Dep., 162:19–165:1.

70 *Nick* 2007: Pls.' Ex. 177, Leonard Decl. ¶¶ 36–37, 64–67, Attachs. B and L.

71 *Nick* 2007: Pls.' Ex.159, Baker Dep., 73:15–75:15, 133:9–11; Pls.' Ex. 176, Yazzie Decl. ¶¶ 17–21; Pls.' Ex. 191, Brewster Dep., 165:7–13.

72 *Nick* 2007: Pls.' Ex. 154, Nick Dep., 18:22–25, 36:25–37:8; Pls.' Ex. 185, Nick Decl. ¶¶ 17, 21.

73 *Nick* 2007: Pls.' Ex. 183, RFA 2 ¶¶ 208–209.

Figure 10.2 Polling place in the Native village of Atmautluk, November 2008
Like many Yup'ik villages in the Bethel region, the only polling place in Atmautluk is located in the tribal council office. Walking to the polling place in ice and snow can be especially hazardous for elderly voters who are denied special needs voting assistance in their homes.
Source: Author's photograph.

grade.[74] These poll workers were expected to translate complex ballot questions written at a college graduate (or 16th grade) level.[75]

Alaska also failed to confirm whether its bilingual poll workers were literate. Election officials admitted that poll workers also should be able to read English because "Everything that we provide them is in English." Therefore, "it would be difficult" for translators "if they didn't read English to be able to translate that ballot into Yup'ik." If a translator could not read a ballot written in English, a voter "[q]uite possibly" would not get an accurate translation of what is on the ballot.[76] That is why many states require that their poll workers be literate.[77]

Election officials assumed poll workers could understand English-only training materials based solely on poll workers "signing the documents, that they are agreeing that they understand, that they are attending training." They placed the burden on poll workers to "speak up" if they did not understand. A regional election supervisor acknowledged that talking with poll workers and asking them to read to her in English is something "that could be done," but she had not done it.

74 *Nick* 2007: Pls.' Ex. 177, Leonard Decl. ¶¶ 44–46, Attach. B.

75 *Nick* 2007: Pls.' Ex. 174, Dybdahl Decl., at 17–20.

76 *Nick* 2007: Pls.' Ex.159, Baker Dep., 75:16–23, 90:19–91:4, 132:5–8.

77 *See* U.S. Election Assistance Comm'n, Compendium of State Poll Worker Requirements (Aug. 2007).

Instead, she claimed, "I think it would be disenfranchising."[78] However, getting confirmation of a translator's English reading skills is not "some kind of literacy test that disenfranchised them … Election officials are hiring translators to perform a job, and demonstrating the ability to read, understand, and translate English voting materials into the covered native language is merely assessing them to see if they are capable of doing that job."[79]

Alaska's failure to confirm the Yup'ik language skills of their translators is one of the reasons that it failed to offer effective language assistance. Confirmation is essential to ensure that a bilingual poll worker is able to perform his or her responsibilities.

A good Native language translator must have four qualities: (a) fluency in the covered Native language; (b) a clear understanding of English and the covered Native language to be able to provide the same concept in the covered language, so the idea is apparent in the translation; (c) the ability to read and understand the English language well enough to provide that same information to LEP voters in the covered Native language; and (d) a complete understanding of the meaning of all election terms, as well as the proper translation of those terms into the covered Native language.

A simple role-playing exercise requiring a translator to translate a form or ballot question from English into the covered language allows a speaker fluent in both languages to confirm the translator's skills. Without such confirmation, it is unlikely LEP voters will receive accurate translations.[80]

Habit 8: Don't Train Your Poll Workers

Even qualified translators are ineffective if untrained. Most poll workers in the Bethel area received no training. Instead, state officials used optional training covering basic election responsibilities without any instruction on language or voter assistance.[81] One quarter of voting precincts in the Bethel area did not have trained poll workers for elections held between 2000 and 2007. Only 10 percent of the 726 poll workers used in the area's precincts received training. Among the 135 Yup'ik translators, less than a third received training.[82] Overall, poll workers only received training for 8.1 percent of all election shifts. Many poll workers worked several years without training.[83]

Yup'ik translators who attended training received "the same training as non-bilingual poll workers."[84] The state's regional supervisor herself never received any training on providing effective language assistance and had no idea of what to include.[85] Consequently, her training tracked the poll worker handbook, which did not include any information on providing language assistance.[86] Although other Section 203 covered jurisdictions offer separate translator training on

78 *Nick* 2007: Pls.' Ex.159, Baker Dep., 73:19–76:2, 88:12–89:10, 93:6–13, 132:9–23; Pls.' Ex. 183, RFA 2 ¶ 210; Pls.' Ex. 191, Brewster Dep., 36:16–41:12, 166:4–18.

79 *Nick* 2007: Pls.' Ex. 176, Yazzie Decl. ¶ 26.

80 *Nick* 2007: Pls.' Ex. 176, Yazzie Decl. ¶¶ 15–16, 25, 29–32.

81 *Nick* 2007: Pls.' Ex.159, Baker Dep., 60:10–20; Pls.' Ex. 176, Yazzie Decl. ¶¶ 41–44; Pls.' Ex. 191, Brewster Dep., 169:8–10, 170:9–11, 171:5–9.

82 *Nick* 2007: Pls.' Ex. 144; Pls.' Ex. 183, RFA 2 ¶¶ 198–99.

83 *Nick* 2007: Pls.' Ex. 48; Pls.' Ex. 180, Training Received and Number of Elections Worked.

84 *Nick* 2007: Pls.' Ex. 94, at STATE 206; Pls.' Ex.159, Baker Dep., 122:1–7; Pls.' Ex. 177, Leonard Decl. ¶ 75; Pls.' Ex. 191, Brewster Dep., 120:25–17.

85 *Nick* 2007: Pls.' Ex.159, Baker Dep., 14:11–22, 47:1–23.

86 *Nick* 2007: Pls.' Ex. 33, State Defs.' Response to Interrogatory No. 5; Pls.' Exs. 43 and 72; Pls.' Ex.159, Baker Dep., 96:1–100:1, 120:20–24, 121:11–12; Pls.' Ex. 189, Modigh Dep., 87:11–25, 90:2–6, 98:7–99:7.

language assistance lasting as much as a full day for each election, Alaska's optional training on all election procedures included just a few minutes on language assistance if there was any instruction at all. Bilingual poll workers did not practice providing language assistance or translating voting information, doing both for the first time on Election Day.[87]

Election officials also instructed poll workers to provide only "passive" language assistance; that is, "poll workers were instructed to wait until a voter asked for assistance before providing it." The officials said, "[T]he assumption is made that someone does not need assistance until they ask for it."[88] Passive assistance conflicted with the Yup'ik tradition of offering active assistance to their elders. Moreover, "'[P]assive language assistance is not language assistance at all'... The failure to offer active language assistance 'results in disenfranchisement of LEP voters who are confused about the voting process and are not sure what is on the ballot and whether they have voted how they intended.'"[89]

Covered jurisdictions must provide translators with training in language assistance. Some training on voting information should be in covered languages to ensure that effective language assistance is provided in the polls. Translators must be instructed on translations for election terms they will encounter. They also should be trained to provide active assistance, greeting voters and guiding them through the elections process. Other areas of instruction should include: review of all voting materials and especially each office and question that appears on the ballot, in both English and the Native language; making sure the translators understand the materials and will provide clear, complete, and accurate translations; role-playing in English and the Native language, to allow confirmation of translator's skills, to assess whether the translator wants to/feels comfortable translating, and to provide substantive instruction; and questions and answers in the language in which the translators feel most comfortable, which is usually their Native language.

Role-playing allows election officials to confirm that the poll worker is qualified to translate. "It also gives the trainer an opportunity to give pointers in the native language for better options of how to handle a situation or how to translate. Trainers can reinforce instruction through hands-on training that gives the translator the opportunity to practice their translation skills before the election."[90] Untrained or poorly trained bilingual poll workers can be just as bad as not having any translators at all.

Habit 9: Don't Do Any Quality Control

Alaska implemented no quality control measures in the Bethel region. Election officials did not confirm whether the available language assistance offered accurate, complete, and clear translations or was effective.[91] They did not ask for feedback from Yup'ik voters because they "haven't seen the need to do that."[92] No full-time election official was present in polling places on Election Day to

87 *Nick* 2007: *Nick* 2007: Pls.' Ex.159, Baker Dep., 106:1–107:12; Pls.' Ex. 176, Yazzie Decl. ¶¶ 49–59; Pls.' Ex. 189, Modigh Dep., 85:8–86:14, 100:25–101:3.

88 *Nick* 2007: Pls.' Ex. 33, State Defs.' Response to Interrogatory No. 14; Pls.' Ex. 94, at STATE 208; Pls.' Ex.159, Baker Dep., 104:17–19; Pls.' Ex. 191, Brewster Dep., 121:18–122:5.

89 *Nick* 2007: Pls.' Ex. 176, Yazzie Decl. ¶¶ 36–38, 40, 73.

90 *Nick* 2007: Pls.' Ex. 176, Yazzie Decl. ¶¶ 32–33, 49–61.

91 *Nick* 2007: Pls.' Ex. 94, at STATE 208; Pls.' Ex. 183, RFA 2 ¶ 235; Pls.' Ex. 191, Brewster Dep., 123:13–124:7.

92 *Nick* 2007: Pls.' Ex.159, Baker Dep., 84:5–10.

observe whatever assistance was offered. Nevertheless, the Elections Director concluded that her office was providing effective assistance without any factual basis for her conclusion.[93]

The Director admitted that providing translations "understandable to the people in that community" was important. For pre-recorded translations the state had to find "the voice talent to provide those translations and then testing those translations by someone who understands the language … making sure that it's understandable to the people in that community." In 2006, the state placed two radio ads intended to communicate information about voter registration, deadlines, the election date, Election Day procedures, and the availability of language assistance. However, Alaska did not verify the Yup'ik content or the accuracy of the translations.[94]

The *Nick* plaintiffs asked a Yup'ik expert to review the ads. One of the ads stated, "On August 22nd, from 7 in the morning until 8 o'clock in the evening there will be voting for leaders. When you vote [unknown, something like all your choices] are written in the Division of Elections. Also [unknown]. And be sure to bring your ID when you go to vote. For those who need more information, call 888–383–8683." The ads were given in an English diction, inflection, and intonation difficult for a Native speaker to understand. They were "almost useless" to any Yup'ik speakers who would have heard them.[95] The state also did not confirm whether any of its PSAs were broadcast in Yup'ik or whether any Yup'ik translations were accurate.[96]

Election officials acknowledged the importance of complete translations. For example, it "would be a problem" if a translator did not translate the candidate's party affiliation to a voter. Complicated ballot questions using terms that did not exist in the Yup'ik language, needed to be explained in a manner that voters could understand. Although it "would be possible" for the state to have asked Yup'ik tribes in the Bethel area about the accuracy of translations, election officials had not done that. They took no steps to assess whether clear, complete, and accurate translations of all voting materials were being provided in Yup'ik.[97]

Alaska's lack of training, absence of materials to assist bilingual poll workers, and failure to implement any quality control measures were manifested in the poor quality of Yup'ik translations. A translator in Bethel translated "Republican" as "Using those things of long ago, the words that were made, following them." He translated "Democrat" as "The new ones … that were made, that have to be followed." His translation of "voter registration" was "the voting [the English word "voting" was used in Yup'ik] place where they write their name where they are to be, making it known." The question, "Should this initiative become law," which appeared after the summary of each ballot question, was translated as "Should this one they are asking about become, (pause) these things that need to be followed, these, towards the laws."[98]

The quality of translations for ballot questions was even worse. The bilingual poll worker was asked to translate the following question that appeared on the ballot in the Alaska's November 5, 2002 general election:

> Initiative on Gas Pipeline Development Authority. This bill would create the Alaska Natural Gas Development Authority (Authority) as a public corporation of the State. The Authority would

93 *Nick* 2007: Pls.' Ex.159, Baker Dep., 70:18–73:14, 123–11:14; Pls.' Ex. 183, RFA 2 ¶ 207; Pls.' Ex. 191, Brewster Dep., 125:1–6.

94 *Nick* 2007: Pls.' Ex. 191, Brewster Dep., 18:15–19:22, 128:14–129:18, 147:7–21.

95 Nick 2007: Pls.' Ex. 177, Leonard Decl. ¶¶ 89, 92–93.

96 *Nick* 2007: Pls.' Exs. 46, 50; Pls.' Ex. 191, Brewster Dep., 131:12–133:22.

97 *Nick* 2007: Pls.' Ex. 183, RFA 2 ¶ 212; Pls.' Ex. 191, Brewster Dep., 18:15–19:22, 44:24–45:8, 54:23–57:1.

98 *Nick* 2007: Pls.' Ex. 177, Leonard Decl. ¶¶ 85–87, Attach. N.

> acquire and condition North Slope natural gas, and construct a pipeline to transport the gas. The Authority's powers would include buying property or taking it by eminent domain, and to issue state tax-exempt revenue bonds. The gasline route would be from Prudhoe Bay to tidewater on Prince William Sound and the spur line from Glennallen to the Southcentral gas distribution grid. The Authority would operate and maintain the gas pipeline, ship the gas, and market the gas. Should this initiative become law?

The poll worker provided the following translation, using English for the underlined words:

> This Initiative on Gas Pipeline Development Authority. This thing that needs to be made, this, that needs to be followed, this the path for the gas, this the gas, the one that is not water, but is a … gas in the stomach, that can be used to the point where it can become fire. This, to our big lands authority and to the whole population, it will get (pause). These leaders will be able to take and finish from the place to our North, this gas in the stomach, gas, they'll be able to take from there and take it to the place where it will be stored, where it will be its place. Those leaders power will include the purchase of land or (pause) it will take the things that are underground, they will take away from that person. They will work till completion, this our lands tax (pause) tax, tax, tax, will be non-taxable towards this thing. These things that will be gotten. The path of the pipeline, from the point on Prudhoe Bay to the beach, the sandy place, of Prince William Sound. And over the mountains from there, Glenallen to, through the mountains, its path, to the end of our ocean. (pause) Those leaders workers on the pipeline, and also the gas in the stomach, the gas, they will be able to oversee, that. Like this! They will take it out, work on it, store it (pause) and then they will take it to the place where they will sell it. All that, they are deeming it important to be completed.

Yup'ik voters therefore would have received a translation using the word for "'gas' meaning the bodily function rather than the natural resource."[99]

Effective language assistance cannot be provided without quality control. "It is essential that material provided in the language of a language minority group be clear, complete and accurate."[100] Translations must allow LEP voters to understand every part of the voting process, including voter registration requirements, the content of ballots, and how to use voting machines (Chapter 4). Election officials must ensure that "sufficient attention" is given "to the needs of language minority group members who cannot effectively read either English or the applicable minority language …"[101] Having bilingual poll workers is not enough. Election officials must actively monitor the quality of translations to ensure that LEP voters are getting the same information provided in English. Without quality control, a covered jurisdiction has no way of knowing about ineffective translations and correcting them.

Habit 10: Deny Voters Assistance from the Person of Their Choice

The absence of help in Yup'ik was worsened when Alaska denied LEP Yup'ik voters the right to receive assistance from the person of their choice. Section 208 provides that "Any voter who requires assistance to vote by reason of blindness, disability, or inability to read or write may be

99 *Nick* 2007: Pls.' Ex. 177, Leonard Decl. ¶¶ 85–87, Attachs. J, L-O.

100 28 C.F.R. § 55.19(b).

101 28 C.F.R. § 55.20(b).

Figure 10.3 Bilingual sticker given to Yup'ik voters in the November 2008 election

In 2008, as a result of the *Nick* litigation, the Alaska Division of Elections provided voters with one item in written Yup'ik: this bilingual "I voted" sticker superimposed over the state flag. However, the failure of elections officials to confirm the accuracy of even this simple translation with Yup'ik tribal leaders caused them to misspell the one Yup'ik word used, which should be "Cucuklillruunga."
Source: State of Alaska, Division of Elections (public document).

given assistance by a person of the voter's choice, other than the voter's employer or agent of that employer or officer or agent of the voter's union"[102] (Chapter 4).

Part of the problem was attributable to lack of training. Poll workers who received training were directed to limit assistance in violation of Section 208 (Chapter 6). A training pamphlet provided that "If requested, an election worker may assist the voter. The election workers should maintain a reasonable distance from the ballot box to ensure the secrecy of the voter's ballot ….[103] Blocking a translator from going "into the voting booth with a voter who wants language or voter assistance" is not assistance and results in "an uninformed voter who has no idea whether they are voting the way they intended."[104]

Alaska's erroneous instructions resulted in a variety of Section 208 violations. Poll workers in Akiachak provided translation assistance only at the voting table and did not go into the booth to assist voters. In Bethel, a Yup'ik voter was told that his vote had to be in private despite his request for assistance. A Yup'ik resident of Tuluksak "voted in an election where the poll worker told [her] that elders could not have help interpreting or reading the ballots, and that everyone had to be 50 feet away from the person voting." Poll workers in Kwigillingok barred translators from helping voters inside the voting booth. In Tuntutuliak, poll workers were told "not to help voters." Even though there were poll workers at some precincts who spoke Yup'ik, they did "not offer to help."[105]

102 42 U.S.C. § 1973aa-6.

103 *Nick* 2007: Pls.' Ex. 110, at B000093.

104 *Nick* 2007: Pls.' Ex. 176, Yazzie Decl. ¶¶ 63–70.

105 *Nick* 2007: Pls.' Ex. 153, McCann Dep., 26:25–27:3; Pls.' Ex. 154, Nick Dep. 19:17–20:12, 25:16–26:4; Pls.' Ex. 181, Gregory Decl. ¶ 8; Pls.' Ex. 185, Nick Decl. ¶¶ 19–21; Pls.' Ex. 186, McCann Decl. ¶ 24; Pls.' Ex. 192, Lupie Decl. ¶ 23; Pls.' Ex. 193, Alexie Decl. ¶ 23; Pls.' Ex. 195, Jimmie Decl. ¶ 22.

One voter explained, "No poll worker has ever offered to help translate my ballot. We vote like we are blind because we don't know what we are voting for."[106]

Accurate training on voter assistance is essential. "The translator needs to be where the voter they are assistance is voting … The translator needs to be in the voting booth to provide complete, clear and accurate translations of ballot questions." If a voter does not understand a ballot question, translators must be "trained to elaborate on the language of the question by giving analogies and presenting information in a way that the voter can understand."[107] Failure to provide that training makes Section 208 violations more likely.

Alaska's Violations of Section 5 of the VRA

Alaska has been covered statewide by Section 4(f)(4) for Alaska Native languages since 1975.[108] Alaska therefore not only is required to provide language assistance, but also must satisfy Section 5's requirements. Because Alaska's elections were conducted only in English when the state became covered, election officials had to change their procedures to comply with Section 203. Conducting bilingual elections for the first time would entail the administration of a "standard, practice, or procedure with respect to voting different from that in force or effect," making it a covered voting change under Section 5.[109] As a result, Alaska had to submit those changes for approval, or "preclearance," before they could be enforced (Chapter 3).[110]

Alaska did not submit its minority language program voluntarily. Six years after coverage, the state attorney general submitted changes in its election code to the Justice Department for preclearance. The Department noted "that the election code and its revisions do not make reference to bilingual procedures for language minorities." The Department responded with what is called a "Please Submit" letter, asking that Alaska submit for preclearance "the manner by which the state will, or plans to, comply with the language minority requirements" of the VRA.[111]

In 1981, Alaska submitted a language assistance program. The Elections Director claimed that the state's program included providing oral language assistance to LEP voters in six languages. In addition, she said her office appointed registrars who spoke Native languages and translated voter registration information. She contended that the state provided "a minority language interpreter" in every precinct where needed. She indicated that elections officials provided all voting information through public service announcements and short television programs in covered languages including Yup'ik. The content of that publicity was alleged to include the availability of minority language assistance for both voter registration and the Election Day procedures, filing deadlines, absentee balloting procedures and deadlines, requirements for identification at the polls, the types of identification required, and the frequency and length of time for voting in order to remain on the list of registered voters.

The Director said that audio and video publicity materials were prepared by trained Native linguists at the University of Alaska. She explained that elections officials traveled to each region of

106 *Nick* 2007: Pls.' Ex. 193, Alexie Decl. ¶ 24.

107 *Nick* 2007: Pls.' Ex. 176, Yazzie Decl. ¶¶ 63–70.

108 *See* 40 Fed. Reg. 49,422 (Oct. 22, 1975); Chapters 3, 9; Appendix B.

109 42 U.S.C. § 1973c.

110 *See* S. Rep. No. 94–295 at 47 (1975); 28 C.F.R. § 55.22 (2006).

111 Letter from Gerald Jones, Chief of the Voting Section, to Wilson L. Condon, Attorney General of Alaska (May 19, 1981).

the state to work with local interpreters in preparing recordings. If local facilities were unavailable, she asserted that the state paid for local translators to travel to locations outside their villages that had those facilities.[112]

When reviewing a submitted language plan like Alaska's, the Justice Department attempts to determine whether the provided information is accurate and the plan provides effective assistance. However, the Department's ability to investigate can be limited by two considerations. First, in a "typical year," the Department "receives between 4,500 and 5,500 Section 5 submissions, and reviews between 14,000 and 20,000 voting changes."[113] Second, the Department must complete its review within 60 days, unless the submitting jurisdiction has not provided all required information. Consequently, the Department relies upon the submitting jurisdiction to provide accurate information.

Where a submitting jurisdiction's submission proves inaccurate or its enforcement would be unlawful, the Department or private litigants may sue "to enjoin enforcement of such qualification, prerequisite, standard, or practice."[114] It is unclear whether the Department was able to conduct its own investigation into the language program Alaska submitted in 1981. Evidence suggests that it relied solely on the state's representations. In October 1981, the Department pre-cleared Alaska's language assistance program.[115]

The Department later determined in two separate lawsuit cases brought by Alaska that the state failed to implement its language program. In a 1978 case,[116] the Department determined "that Alaska had a voting discrimination problem with language minorities." That discrimination was manifested in a lack of assistance for LEP Alaska Native voters:

> The questioning by the federal attorneys ... centered on the impediment that English-only materials created for Natives whose first language was other than English ... They were told that bilingual assistance and oral translation of election materials would undoubtedly be helpful to some voters if such assistance [was] available ... It was revealed that the state election division had never conducted a formal survey or study to determine how many people were disadvantaged by not having bilingual election judges or election information broadcast in the local dialect.[117]

The Department made similar findings in a 1984 case.[118] Instead of responding to those concerns and remedying the Section 203 violations, Alaska dismissed both bailout lawsuits.[119] Nearly a quarter-century of neglect for the 1981 language plan followed.

---

112 Letter from Patty Ann Polley, Director of the Alaska Division of Elections, to Tom Jahnke, Assistant Attorney General of Alaska (July 30, 1981).

113 U.S. Dep't of Just., *About Section 5 of the Voting Rights Act* (July 25, 2008), *available at* http://www.usdoj.gov/crt/voting/sec_5/about.htm.

114 42 U.S.C. § 1973c(a).

115 Letter from Gerald Jones, Chief of the Voting Section, to Wilson L. Condon, Attorney General of Alaska (October 5, 1981).

116 *See Alaska v. United States*, case no. 78–0484 (D.D.C. 1978).

117 Gordon S. Harrison, *Alaska's Constitutional "Literacy Test" and the Question of Voting Discrimination*, 22 Alaska Hist. 23, 32, 34 (Spring/Fall 2007).

118 *See Alaska v. United States*, case no. 84–1362 (D.D.C. 1984); Paul F. Hancock and Lora L. Tredway, *The Bailout Standard of the Voting Rights Act: An Incentive to End Discrimination*, 17 Urb. Law. 379, 415 (1985).

119 Harrison 2007: 32; J. Gerald Hebert, *An Assessment of the Bailout Provisions of the Voting Rights Act*, *in* Voting Rights Act Reauthorization of 2006: Perspectives on Democracy, Participation, and Power 257, 261 (Ana Henderson ed. 2007).

Alaska's failure to implement the pre-cleared procedures resulted in voting changes covered by Section 5. As such, those changes had to be submitted to the Attorney General or federal court in Washington, D.C., for approval. However, Alaska made no further submissions of its language program until March 2008, following two events.[120] In November 2007, the Elections Director admitted in her deposition that the state failed to implement most of procedures identified in its 1981 submission. The *Nick* plaintiffs then filed an Amended Complaint adding a claim for the state's violations of Section 5. Alaska's election officials conceded that their new language procedures were covered voting changes, explaining they had "developed a new Minority Language Assistance Program to comply with the [VRA] … and its minority language obligations …"[121] Officials failed to explain why the state's 1981 plan was never implemented.

In May 2008, the Justice Department sent Alaska a "More Information Request" (MIR) letter, which is a request that the submitting authority "provide additional information about a proposed change in voting procedure or practice" because of questions raised by the submission. Through MIRs, the Department "may signal the submitting jurisdiction about the assessment of their proposed change," suggesting it might issue an objection to stop implementation of the change if the jurisdiction does not provide satisfactory answers. MIRs deter election practices "that could have a discriminatory effect." They frequently are a prelude to a jurisdiction withdrawing its submission or abandoning the discriminatory practices altogether.[122]

The Department's MIR focused on evidence that the 1981 plan had not been implemented. Department officials noted that discovery in the *Nick* litigation; "admissions by State elections officials," and assertions by officials in a letter withdrawing the changes indicated that "Alaska is not currently fully implementing the 1981 plan and is instead implementing new and different procedures." The Department requested that Alaska inform it of the action the state planned "to take regarding the changes affecting voting that have not been submitted for judicial review or preclearance." The Department asked the questions to decide whether the plan could serve as the existing "benchmark" of comparison with the submitted changes for purposes of evaluating whether those changes placed Alaska Natives in a worse position.[123] An election practice does not become a benchmark merely if it is pre-cleared. Instead, even a pre-cleared submission must be implemented to serve as a benchmark for subsequent Section 5 submissions.[124] Rather than answering those questions, Alaska withdrew its submission, criticizing "DOJ's questions on past practices" as "inappropriate."[125] Election officials recognized they had no explanation for the lack of language assistance throughout the Bethel region.

Alaska's failure to inform the Justice Department of changes to its language program highlights a limitation of Section 5. Congress found that the Attorney General has no "systematic way to monitor" jurisdictions to ensure submission of all voting changes. As a result, "[M]any

---

120 In 2002 and 2003, Alaska submitted a language program for Tagalog voters on Kodiak Island, after the Department opened an investigation of the state's failure to provide language assistance for them following the Census Bureau's Section 203 determinations in July 2002 (Chapter 5).

121 State of Alaska's Section 5 Submission letter, submission no. 2008–1726 (Mar. 18, 2008).

122 Luis Ricardo Fraga and Maria Lizet Ocampo, *More Information Requests and the Deterrent Effect of Section 5 of the Voting Rights Act*, *in* Henderson 2007: 47, 49–50, 65.

123 *Nick* 2007: Dkt. 292, Dep't of Justice More Information Request for submission number 2008–1726 (May 19, 2008).

124 *See* 28 C.F.R. § 51.54(b).

125 *Nick* 2007: Dkt. 292, State of Alaska's letter withdrawing submission number 2008–1726, at 9 n.19 (June 9, 2008).

defiant covered jurisdictions and … officials continue to enact and enforce changes to voting procedures without the Federal Government's knowledge." The burden falls on private citizens to enforce Section 5 to stop "discriminatory changes" before they "negatively affect" Alaska Natives.[126] That is precisely what the *Nick* litigants did in their Section 5 claim against Alaska. Because of the 2006 amendments to the VRA, private litigants can recover costs including expert witness fees they incur in bringing enforcement actions (Chapters 4 and 7).

Jurisdictions covered by Section 4(f)(4) can learn a lot from Alaska's mistakes. Unless a jurisdiction uses exactly the same practices at the time it became covered, election officials will need to change election procedures to comply with Section 203. Those changes must receive preclearance before being implemented. The jurisdiction cannot avoid its legal duty by failing to provide the required language assistance. It likewise must commit to providing the assistance that it has told the Department it is going to offer. If a covered jurisdiction does not do so, it may find itself liable not only for violating Section 203, but also Section 5.

Remedying the State's Language Discrimination

Alaska never provided effective language assistance in the Bethel region. In 2008, a federal court ordered state election officials to take several initial steps to remedy their violations of Section 203. In doing so, the court examined the meaning of the "historically unwritten" exception to the requirement for written voting materials. Although the court decided that Yup'ik fell within that proviso, it found that certain written Yup'ik materials were necessary.

Yup'ik as a Historically Written Language

Consistent with their ideological opposition to bilingual voting, state officials were unconcerned that LEP Yup'ik voters asked for written Yup'ik materials. According to those officials, "All of the Alaska Native languages listed are considered 'unwritten.'" *They* admitted they had no idea whether Yup'ik was historically written or if written Yup'ik materials would help Yup'ik voters. Rather, they made their determination on "precedent set by the State" of conducting English-only elections.[127] Alaska therefore asked the federal court to exempt it from providing written materials in Yup'ik.

Development of written Yup'ik Yup'ik is a single written language developed and improved upon, like other written languages.[128] Figure 10.4 summarizes that development. Yup'ik was written as early as July 1778, when Captain James Cook's expedition from Great Britain anchored in the Kuskokwim Bay.[129] James King, a member of Cook's party, prepared a written word list of Central Yup'ik words gathered from villages on the Norton Sound. King's list included 40 Yup'ik words

---

126 H.R. Rep. No. 109–478 at 4142 (2006).

127 *Nick* 2007: Pls.' Ex. 33, State Defs.' Response to Interrogatory Nos. 12, 14; Pls.' Ex. 94, at STATE 203; Pls.' Ex. 183, RFA 2 ¶ 234; Pls.' Ex. 190, Parnell Dep., 19:19–24; Pls.' Ex. 191, Brewster Dep., 107:18–22, 109:20–110:9.

128 *Nick* 2007: Dkt. 87, Jacobson Decl. ¶ 11.

129 *See* Murray Lundberg, *Captain James Cook in Alaska, available at* http://explorenorth.com/library/yafeatures/bl-Cook1.htm.

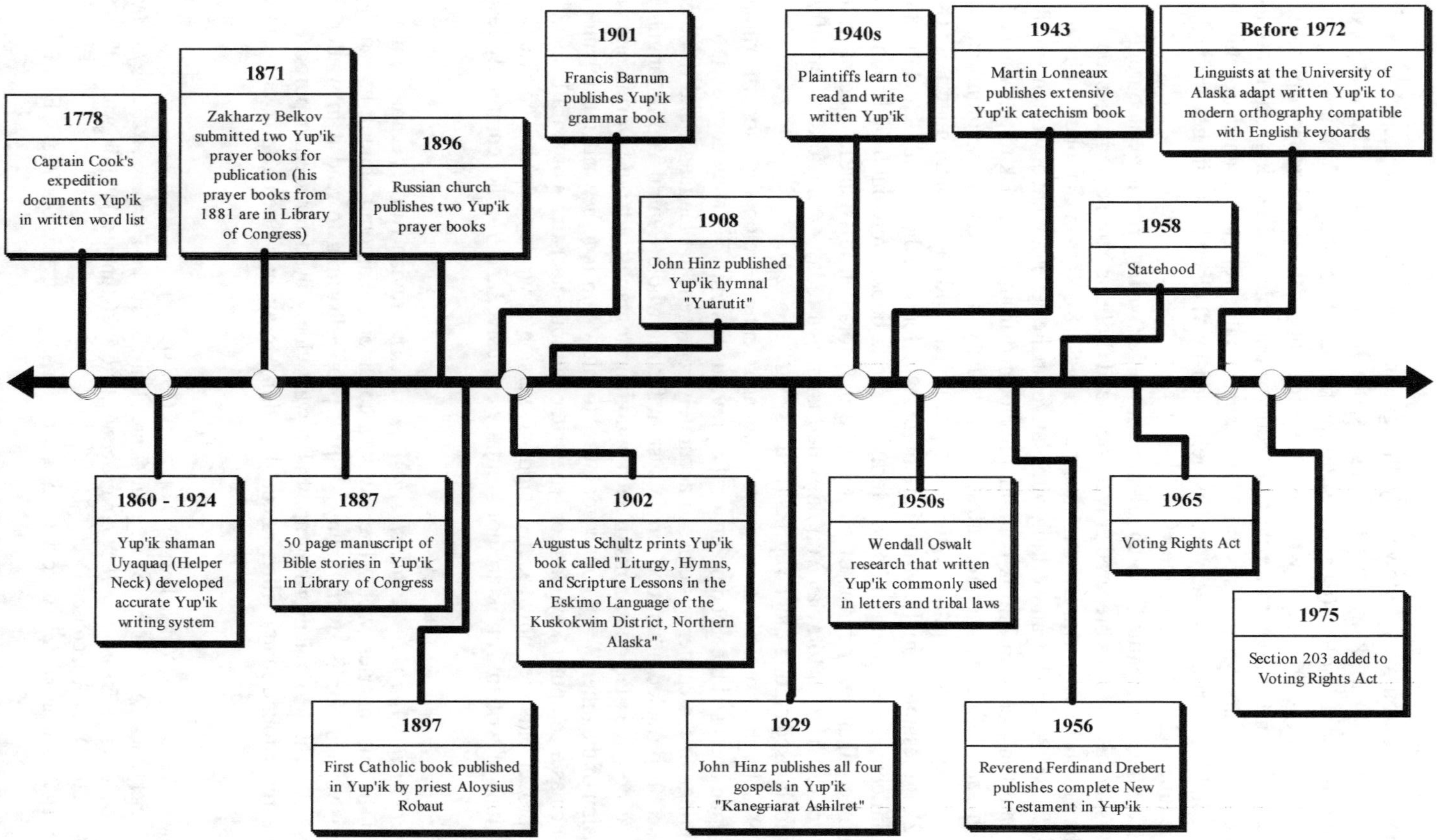

Figure 10.4 Key dates in the historical usage of written Yup'ik

and 10 numerals with their English translations. The list he prepared is the first written record of the Yup'ik language.[130]

The Cook expedition was followed by the gradual evolution of written Yup'ik into its modern form. Written Yup'ik was used through self-help in Bethel area villages to overcome state discrimination in schooling (Chapter 9). In the nineteenth century, a Yup'ik shaman named Uyaquq (Helper Neck) developed a writing system for Yup'ik that evolved from pictographs to symbols based on word sounds to a true alphabetic or phonological writing. Publications were never produced using that writing system, "but a considerable religious manuscript and literacy developed in it." The writing system was widely used by "helpers" in villages throughout the region by the time Helper Neck died in 1924.[131]

Also in the nineteenth century, church missionaries began writing Yup'ik to encourage religious learning. Russian missionaries prepared prayer books and Bibles in Yup'ik in villages located in the middle of the Yukon-Kuskokwim Delta (Krauss: 5–16 to 5–18). Roman Catholic Jesuits arrived in the Bethel area in 1886, and began working with Natives in the development of written Yup'ik. They had their greatest influence in Yup'ik communities located from Chefornak to St. Michael. They prepared "thousands of pages of grammatical and dictionary" manuscripts, "sermons, catechisms, Bible stories, lessons, hymns, prayers, and various liturgical and sacramental materials" (Krauss: 5–26 to 5–32). Protestants from the Moravian Church, who founded the City of Bethel in 1885, had the greatest influence. Beginning in 1889, Moravian Yup'ik books were published and distributed in larger numbers than other forms of written Yup'ik. Moravian missionaries had an extensive literacy program. Written Moravian Yup'ik, which is known today as the "old" form of written Yup'ik, is widely used among older Yup'iks (Krauss: 5–18 to 5–24).

Before 1972, linguists at the Alaska Native Language Center developed a "modern orthography [that] built upon and used the good points of the previous systems."[132] They devised it to "rectify the shortcomings of the earlier systems, to accurately represent the language, and to be easy to learn and use." It provided a "unified single system for the whole Central Yup'ik language area using as far as possible the good points of each church orthography without favoring one of them to the exclusion of the others."[133] Another goal was "to allow Yup'ik to be written using an English keyboard, such as a computer keyboard or typewriter, without diacriticals or extra letters."[134] The linguists' improvements are known as the "modern" version of written Yup'ik. The Moravian and modern versions of written Yup'ik are not mutually exclusive, and Yup'iks commonly read both versions.

Common use of written Yup'ik in the Bethel region Written Moravian Yup'ik became commonplace as a result of the missionaries' work. There was "a considerable amount of adult literacy" in that older form of written Yup'ik, with "many" Yup'ik people learning to read it in written Yup'ik religious texts.[135] The Moravian orthography also was widely used for secular purposes. In the 1950s, a researcher found many villagers could read in Moravian written Yup'ik only, observing

130 Steven A. Jacobson, Yup'ik Eskimo Dictionary (1984).

131 Michael Krauss, Alaska Native Language Center, Univ. of Alaska-Fairbanks, *Reading for ANL: 215 Alaska Native Languages: Eskimo and Aleut Languages* 5–24 to 5–26 (undated) (on file with author).

132 *Nick* 2007: Dkt. 87, Jacobson Decl. ¶ 11.

133 Steven A. Jacobson, A Practical Grammar of the Central Alaskan Yup'ik Eskimo Language 448 (1995).

134 *Nick* 2007: Dkt. 87, Jacobson Decl. ¶ 11.

135 *Nick* 2007: Dkt. 87, Jacobson Decl. ¶¶ 8–9.

that "between villagers, letters are commonly written in Yup'ik. The laws of the community and some of the council minutes are recorded in Eskimo."[136]

Elders in the *Nick* litigation are typical of Yup'iks who read the Moravian form of written Yup'ik. Alaska denied schooling to nearly all Yup'ik elders in the Bethel region, causing them to turn to missionaries for their education. Anna Nick began learning to read Moravian Yup'ik at church in the early 1940s when she was 6 years old. She wrote "in Yup'ik" and would "only write in English with the knowledge that I have, not very much."[137] David O. David learned to read Moravian Yup'ik in Bible school when he was a child. He did not read English "very much. Even if I look at English, I don't understand it."[138]

Written modern Yup'ik began to flourish when Alaska started providing education through high school in Bethel area villages beginning in the 1980s (Chapter 9). Today, there "are over 10,000 Yup'ik speakers in Alaska, and in approximately one quarter of the 68 villages children still grow up speaking and reading Yup'ik as their first language." Local schools have bilingual education programs and teach exclusively in written modern Yup'ik for the lowest grade levels, with both English and modern Yup'ik used for the higher grades. Hundreds of story books and educational materials are published in modern Yup'ik. Other documents are written "in Yup'ik, such as government publications, religious literature, story collections, works of fiction," as well as forms, like a loan application used by Key Bank.[139] Alaska state agencies, other than the Division of Elections, regularly disseminated publications in written modern Yup'ik.[140]

Interviews of Alaska's Yup'ik poll workers confirmed the common usage of written Yup'ik. Nearly all 89 interviewed Yup'ik translators reported that they read written Yup'ik. Seventy (78.7 percent) reported that they read written Yup'ik fluently, and an additional nine (10.1 percent) reported that they read some or a little Yup'ik. Just ten (11.2 percent) reported that they did not read written Yup'ik, which included four who were not fluent in Yup'ik or had not worked as translators and one who was illiterate in English. In 28 out of 29 village voting precincts, there was at least one translator who reported that written Yup'ik was read for every election between 2000 and 2007 in which a translator was available.[141] Of 79 translators who reported they read written Yup'ik, 71 (89.9 percent) read the modern form. Forty-eight translators (60.8 percent) read both the modern and Moravian Yup'ik, 23 (29.1 percent) read only the modern Yup'ik, and just seven (8.9 percent) read only Moravian Yup'ik.

Because of the common usage of written Yup'ik, translators asked for written Yup'ik voting materials.[142] Anna Nick explained, it would "help our Yup'ik speakers and the poll workers if the voting materials were translated into Yup'ik, then we would not need a proficient translator since the poll worker could read the translated information out loud in Yup'ik."[143] LEP Yup'ik voters who were literate could read Yup'ik materials on their own without assistance.

136 Wendell Oswalt, Napaskiak, An Alaskan Eskimo Community 111 (1963).

137 *Nick* 2007: First Am. Compl. ¶ 6; Pls.' Ex. 154, Nick Dep., 7:17–25, 9:11–10:4; Pls.' Ex. 185, Nick Decl. ¶¶ 5–7.

138 *Nick* 2007: First Am. Compl. ¶ 8; Pls.' Ex. 152, David Dep. 8:9–9:11, 11:2–6, 12:11–20; Pls.' Ex. 187, David O. David Decl. ¶¶ 5–7.

139 *Nick* 2007: Dkt. 87, Jacobson Decl. ¶¶ 12–13.

140 *Nick* 2007: Pls.' Ex. 151.

141 *Nick* 2007: Pls.' Ex. 177, Leonard Decl. ¶¶ 47–50, 72, Attachs. B, G, and L.

142 *Nick* 2007: Pls.' Ex. 177, Leonard Decl. ¶ 51, Attach. B.

143 *Nick* 2007: Dkt. 90, Nick Decl. ¶ 23.

The court's finding that Yup'ik is not historically written Chapter 4 describes how members of Alaska's congressional delegation sought to limit bilingual voting in Alaska. Senator Stevens explained, "[W]e do want to print our election materials in English only."[144] Consistent with that English-only legacy, Alaska sought to prevent the use of voting materials written in Yup'ik. In the *Nick* litigation, state officials asked the federal court to find that the "historically unwritten" exception to written voting materials was designed to exempt Alaska from all written language assistance requirements.[145]

The court declined to do so, relying upon Section 203's language and Justice Department regulations (Chapter 4). According to the court, "[T]he exemption from the VRA's written assistance requirement must be applied on a language-by-language basis. In other words, a language is only exempt if found to be 'historically unwritten,' whatever that term may mean in the context of the VRA."[146] There was no categorical exemption for written materials for covered Alaska Native and American Indian languages.

The court was vexed by the meaning of "historically unwritten," noting that no other court had interpreted the term:

> [I]t is difficult for the Court to pinpoint a precise date or year for dividing "historically unwritten" from simply "unwritten," or "historically written" from "written." Yet the emphasis on history strongly suggests that it is not enough for Yup'ik to be commonly written in modern times; if the written-assistance requirement is to apply, Yup'ik must also have been written during some earlier era. And if "history" refers to a chronology of the "life or development of a people or institution," the Court concludes that the dividing line between "historically unwritten" and simply "unwritten" must extend at least several generations into the past.

The court was not wholly comfortable with its own interpretation, noting that it was using "this lens, imprecise as it may be," to conduct its analysis.[147]

The court candidly recognized that its construction was not included in the language of Section 203, which left "historically unwritten" undefined.[148] The court did not examine the legislative history of the historically unwritten exception. That history demonstrated that no senator thought that "historically" meant more than 25 years; Senator Stevens, the author of the proviso, said it meant the language had to be written more than 15 years.[149] Nothing in the statute or the legislative history supported the court's conclusion that "historically" meant "at least several generations into the past" (Chapter 4). Indigenous language experts criticized the court's ruling. However, one commentator explained that despite his disagreement with the decision, it could not be regarded as "unfair" because of "the evidence before the court and the vagueness as to what exactly it means for a language to be 'historically unwritten.'"[150]

The combination of educational discrimination, its resulting illiteracy, and the delayed development of written Native languages until the nineteenth century could preclude all Native

---

144 121 Cong. Rec. S13655 (daily ed. July 24, 1975).

145 *Nick* 2007: Dkt. 136, Defs.' Motion for Summary Judgment 5.

146 *Nick* 2007: Dkt. 319, Order 7 (filed July 23, 2008).

147 *Nick* 2007: Dkt. 319, Order 10 (filed July 23, 2008).

148 *See* 42 U.S.C. § 1973aa-1a.

149 121 Cong. Rec. S13367 (daily ed. July 23, 1975) (statement of Sen. Stevens); 121 Cong. Rec. S13369 (daily ed. July 23, 1975) (statement of Sen. Tunney).

150 Bill Poser, Language Log, *Nick v. Bethel – Voting in Yup'ik* (July 24, 2008), *available at* http://languagelog.ldc.upenn.edu/nll/?p=396#more-396.

languages from meeting the court's definition. Such a result ignores the congressional purpose of only exempting languages developed by anthropologists that were not commonly used by the language minority voters. The pragmatic approach embodied in Section 203 recognized the truism that providing bilingual voting materials was ineffective if few, if any, voters or translators could read them. Where that was not the case, written materials had to be provided in the Native language (Chapter 4).

The federal court did "not examine or draw any conclusions on the extent to which written Yup'ik is commonly used today."[151] Instead, the court found that Yup'ik failed to meet its test of a "historically unwritten" language. Despite the widespread use of written Yup'ik among elders, particularly written Moravian Yup'ik that the *Nick* plaintiffs learned in the 1940s, the court concluded that written Yup'ik did not become "common or routine" until "after the modern version was developed in the late 1960s." Therefore, the court determined "that Yup'ik is a 'historically unwritten' language for purposes of the VRA." The court softened that blow by acknowledging that Alaska "may need to produce certain written materials in order to provide effective oral assistance to Yup'ik voters."[152] That ruling would prove to be critical for the state to cure its violations of Section 203.

Remedying Alaska's Language Discrimination

In early 2008, Alaska began taking initial steps to address some of its violations of the VRA. As a forthcoming judicial remedy increasingly became apparent, state election officials started to devise a Yup'ik language program in the Bethel region for the first time, a third of a century after becoming covered. Their belated efforts included what they believed would be the minimum they had to do to avoid an injunction.

Court findings and relief In July 2008, the court rejected Alaska's argument that relief should be denied because state officials were "in the midst of revamping" their language program. The court pointed to evidence that NARF informed officials of their violations in early 2006, but the officials did not begin their efforts "in earnest" until after the Nick litigation was filed in June 2007. Furthermore, the court cited the state's decision to put its new efforts on hold while it addressed other election issues. When officials resumed their efforts in 2008, they were "relatively new and untested" and their overhaul remained "a work in progress." The court likewise was struck by evidence of the state's consistent denial of voter assistance in many villages throughout the Bethel region. Consequently, the court found that injunctive relief was necessary to stop the state's violations of Sections 203 and 208 of the Act.[153]

The preliminary relief ordered in *Nick* was intended to get some measures in place for three state-run elections in 2008, the first of which was just weeks away. The state was required to provide training to all poll workers, including instructions "on the VRA's guarantees of language and voter assistance" and "the methods and tools available for providing complete and accurate translations." It had to hire a language assistance coordinator fluent in Yup'ik to serve as a liaison with voters and tribal councils to ensure that effective language assistance was provided. At least one translator fluent in English and Yup'ik had to be at every precinct in the Bethel region. Pre-election publicity had to be offered in Yup'ik, including information "that language assistance will

151 *Nick* 2007: Dkt. 319, Order 10 n.30 (filed July 23, 2008).

152 *Nick* 2007: Dkt. 319, Order 1–2, 12 (filed July 23, 2008).

153 *Nick* 2007: Dkt. 327, Order 8–10 (filed July 30, 2008).

be available at all polling locations ..." State election officials were directed to provide pre- and post-election progress reports, including verifiable information about their language efforts, such as a list of all Yup'ik translators by precinct.[154]

The court also was concerned about the ad hoc nature of the few oral Yup'ik translations offered, which varied depending upon the skills of the translator. The court found that election officials failed to "ensure that at least one poll worker at each precinct is fluent in Yup'ik and capable of translating ballot questions from English into Yup'ik." In the process, state officials had not ensured "that 'on the spot' oral translations of ballot questions are comprehensive and accurate."[155]

Although the court ruled that Yup'ik was historically unwritten, the state's failure to take steps to provide uniform and accurate oral translations required that the state use some written Yup'ik materials. The court ordered Alaska to provide sample ballots in written Yup'ik, with at least one such ballot "available at each precinct ... to aid poll workers in translating ballot materials and instructions" for LEP Yup'ik voters. Due to the lack of radio coverage for all villages in the region and the complexity of some voting information, the court directed that some pre-election publicity in Yup'ik would be "published in Yup'ik as well." In addition, the state had to provide a Yup'ik glossary of election terms to all poll workers and translators to assist them in their translations. Finally, the state had to ensure its translations were accurate by consulting with Yup'ik language experts before the translations were disseminated.[156]

Continuing violations of the VRA in the 2008 elections Election officials must accurately evaluate whether they are providing effective language assistance. Alaska failed to do so after the 2008 elections. Instead, election officials painted a picture of substantial compliance, trying to remove the state from judicial oversight. Although the officials made modest improvements in certain areas, their predominately English elections practices changed very little. Over three dozen tribal council members, poll workers, and voters in 17 Native villages detailed numerous violations of the court's injunction.

Alaska claimed to have trained "nearly all" of its poll workers.[157] However, the state's own training rosters revealed that just over half were trained, with that percentage decreasing in the general election when turnout was highest. Although officials conducted training in Bethel, only one of the city's three precincts had a trained translator to respond to more than 100 requests for language assistance.[158] Many polling places continued to lack translators, or if they did have them, they were not qualified or did not work the entire day, leaving gaps where no language assistance was available.[159]

The state's training failed to instruct the poll workers about providing complete and accurate translations, including an opportunity to practice the translations in advance. Language assistance instructions in the poll worker training materials were limited to a single page that simply restated the VRA's requirements without elaboration.[160] Some untrained poll workers did not use Yup'ik materials, resulting in incomprehensible translations that failed to provide any assistance to LEP Yup'ik voters. In some cases, frustrated translators who could not understand the English voting

154 *Nick* 2007: Dkt. 327, Order 10–11 (filed July 30, 2008).

155 *Nick* 2007: Dkt. 327, Order 7–8 (filed July 30, 2008).

156 *Nick* 2007: Dkt. 327, Order 10–11 (filed July 30, 2008).

157 *Nick* 2007: Dkt. 421, at 4.

158 *Nick* 2007: Pls.' Exs. 345–47; Dkt. 357–3, Ex. B, at 2–3; Dkt. 426–3, Attach 2 to Ex. E, Bates 12064–072.

159 *Nick* 2007: Dkt. 518, at 7–11.

160 *Nick* 2007: Dkt. 359–2, Baker Aff., Attach. A, at 34–35.

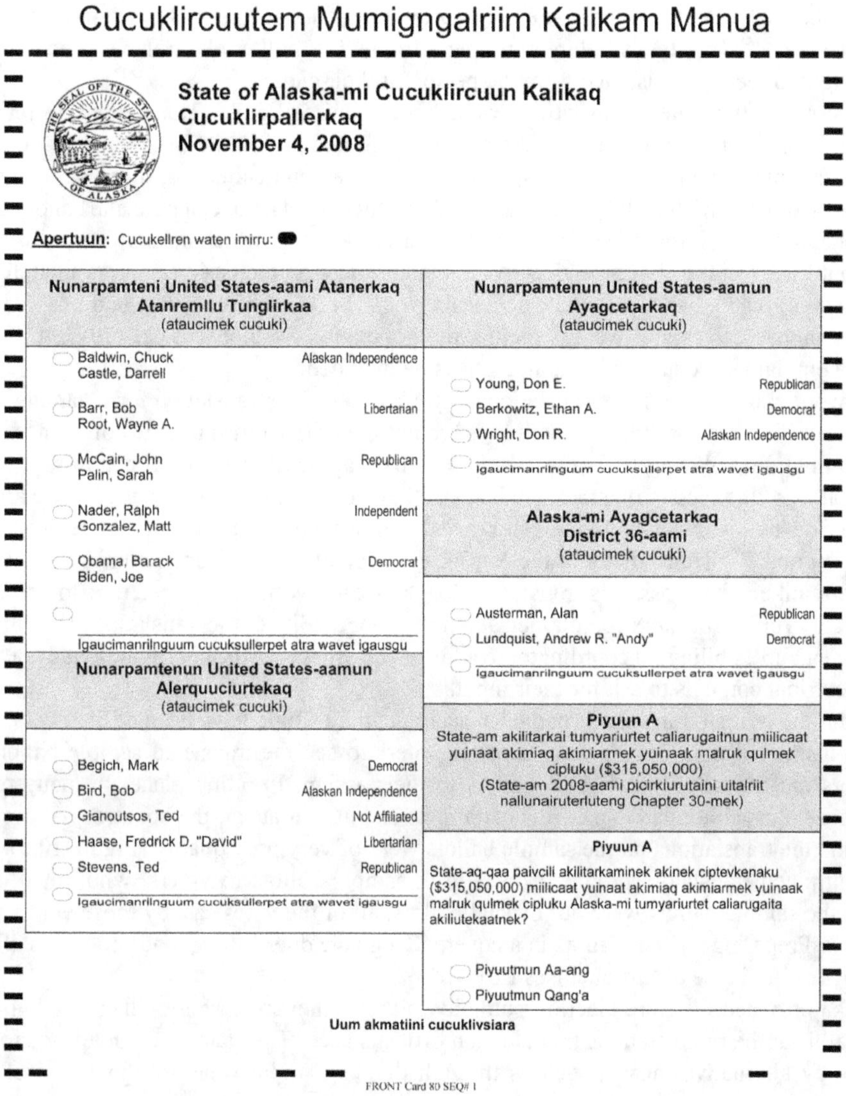

Cucuklircuutem Mumigngalriim Kalikam Manua

State of Alaska-mi Cucuklircuun Kalikaq
Cucuklirpallerkaq
November 4, 2008

Apertuun: Cucukellren waten imirru:

Nunarpamteni United States-aami Atanerkaq Atanremllu Tunglirkaa
(ataucimek cucuki)

Baldwin, Chuck / Castle, Darrell	Alaskan Independence
Barr, Bob / Root, Wayne A.	Libertarian
McCain, John / Palin, Sarah	Republican
Nader, Ralph / Gonzalez, Matt	Independent
Obama, Barack / Biden, Joe	Democrat
Igaucimanrilnguum cucuksullerpet atra wavet igausgu	

Nunarpamtenun United States-aamun Alerquuciurtekaq
(ataucimek cucuki)

Begich, Mark	Democrat
Bird, Bob	Alaskan Independence
Gianoutsos, Ted	Not Affiliated
Haase, Fredrick D. "David"	Libertarian
Stevens, Ted	Republican
Igaucimanrilnguum cucuksullerpet atra wavet igausgu	

Nunarpamtenun United States-aamun Ayagcetarkaq
(ataucimek cucuki)

Young, Don E.	Republican
Berkowitz, Ethan A.	Democrat
Wright, Don R.	Alaskan Independence
Igaucimanrilnguum cucuksullerpet atra wavet igausgu	

Alaska-mi Ayagcetarkaq District 36-aami
(ataucimek cucuki)

Austerman, Alan	Republican
Lundquist, Andrew R. "Andy"	Democrat
Igaucimanrilnguum cucuksullerpet atra wavet igausgu	

Piyuun A
State-am akilitarkai tumyariurtet caliarugaitnun miilicaat yuinaat akimiaq akimiarmek yuinaak malruk qulmek cipluku ($315,050,000)
(State-am 2008-aami picirkiurutaini uitalriit nallunairuterluteng Chapter 30-mek)

Piyuun A
State-aq-qaa paivcili akilitarkaminek akinek ciptevkenaku ($315,050,000) miilicaat yuinaat akimiaq akimiarmek yuinaak malruk qulmek cipluku Alaska-mi tumyariurtet caliarugaita akiliutekaatnek?

Piyuutmun Aa-ang
Piyuutmun Qang'a

Uum akmatiini cucuklivsiara

FRONT Card 80 SEQ# 1

Figure 10.5 Bilingual Yup'ik sample ballot prepared for the November 2008 election
In the *Nick* litigation, a federal court ordered the State of Alaska to use Yup'ik sample ballots in polling places in the Bethel Census Area to help provide clear, complete, accurate, and uniform translations to LEP voters. Although State election officials prepared the ballots and displayed them at public events, they directed poll workers not to share them with voters during the actual election. Some poll workers left them at home. Other poll workers found that the translations on the sample ballot were so poor, that they were essentially useless.
Source: State of Alaska, Division of Elections (public document).

materials themselves either did not attempt to provide any assistance or skipped translations of the ballot questions.[161] The state's failure to properly train all its poll workers also denied many voters of their right to receive assistance from the person of their choice.[162]

Furthermore, the state's translations were largely unintelligible. Translations were prepared by a Yup'ik speaker who had no professional training and had limited time to work on them.[163] The translations contained numerous spelling errors, grammatical errors, dialectical bias, with a "jumbled" word order. They did not account for different dialects. For example, the ballot translation for a predator control initiative used the Yup'ik word "takukaq," which means "brown bear" in one dialect but "seal" in the coastal dialect. As a result, voters on the coast (a predominately Yup'ik-speaking area) read a ballot that indicated seals would be shot because they had been consuming too many moose calves and were depleting the population – a nonsensical prospect. Some poll workers complained, requesting that all dialects be included.[164]

The word choice on written translations also was poor. The translation for a gaming initiative used the Yup'ik word for "playing with toys" rather than the word for games of chance. That led voters to think that playing with toys would now be regulated by a special commission. Another translation was "the second one that will be used they don't want to happen, those who are pulling up metal from below the land, digging, not to let them, what they have dug up the remnants of stuff that is not good."[165] Translations in the Yup'ik glossary of election terms confused poll workers and voters alike. The glossary's translation for "absentee voting" was referred to as "the gone machine."[166] Yup'ik speakers complained about the poor quality of the translations.[167] Although the state hired a Yup'ik bilingual coordinator to address the problems, the coordinator had not bothered to contact tribal councils to ask for their input.[168]

Even if the written translations had been accurate, they would have been of little help. Election officials instructed poll workers not to allow voters to see the translated sample ballots. Some translators did not bring the sample ballots to their assigned polling place. In many precincts, Yup'ik translators continued to provide incomplete and inaccurate on-the-spot translations because they found the translations on the sample ballots were of very poor quality (Figure 10.5). In some cases, untrained translators provided the Yup'ik sample ballots to voters, who voted on them. Because the sample ballots were not official ballots, all of the votes cast by those voters were not counted.[169] Preparing written ballots in a covered language does little good if no one is allowed to use them or if their use disenfranchises LEP voters.

Alaska provided little pre-election publicity in the Bethel area. Many villages did not receive the signal from the radio stations that election officials used. The state made no efforts to provide publicity by alternative means, such as through the VHF radios that are the principal form of

161 *Nick* 2007: John Decl. ¶ 12; Berlin Decl. ¶ 12; N. Nicholai Decl. ¶¶ 11, 19; Sharp Decl. ¶ 12; Chaliak Decl. ¶ 10; Alexie Decl. ¶ 12; Jimmy Decl. ¶ 10; Nicholas Decl. ¶ 12; Phillip Decl. ¶ 10; Jacobs Decl. ¶ 11; A. Nelson Decl. ¶¶15–16.

162 *Nick* 2007: John Decl. ¶¶ 2, 7; Lincoln Decl. ¶ 9; Panruk Decl. ¶ 6; Nicholas Decl. ¶ 7; Jimmy Decl. ¶ 6.

163 *Nick* 2007: Dkt. 362, Wassilie Aff. ¶ 10.

164 *Nick* 2007: Meade Decl. ¶¶ 20, 25, 36.

165 *Nick* 2007: Meade Decl. ¶¶ 27, 46.

166 *Nick* 2007: Meade Second Decl. ¶ 7.

167 *Nick* 2007: Dkt. 518, at 7–11.

168 *Nick* 2007: Lincoln Decl. ¶ 11; Sharp Decl. ¶ 18; N. Nicholai Decl. ¶¶ 28–29; E. Chimiugak Decl. ¶ 16; John Decl. ¶ 17.

169 *Nick* 2007: Evon Decl. ¶ 12; Friend Decl. ¶ 10; Phillip Decl. ¶¶ 6–7. Panruk Decl. ¶ 10.

communication in all of the villages. Election information such as voter registration deadlines, polling place hours, and summaries of ballot questions and candidates, was not provided anywhere. Tribal councils resorted to self-help to disseminate certain information. No publicity was aired about the regional school board elections, which many Yup'ik voters consider to be the most important because of the control the boards exercise over school curriculum and budgets. Several voters complained that they did not find out about the elections until after they were over.[170]

The common observation among Yup'ik voters in the Bethel area was that "[t]he way things were on November 4, 2008 was not any better than they were before" the *Nick* litigation. A tribal leader explained, "[T]he elders and people like me who speak mostly Yup'ik do not understand the ballot any better than we did before. We still vote without full understanding."[171] Court oversight will be needed for many years to come.

Conclusion

Violations of the bilingual voting mandate can be difficult to cure overnight. When English-only ideology is pervasive among election officials responsible for providing language assistance, compliance with the VRA is even less likely. Alaska's failure to comply with the Act's bilingual voting mandate in the Bethel region demonstrates that while our nation has come a long way towards providing equal access to the electoral process, we still have far to go. Sections 4(f)(4) and 203 of the VRA will continue to be needed as long as covered jurisdictions like Alaska implement obstructionist election practices or neglect their obligations to protect the rights of LEP voters to cast effective and informed ballots. Election officials ignore the lessons from the Bethel region at their own peril and at the risk of expensive, time-consuming litigation and the bad publicity and ill will among language minority voters that accompany it.

170 *Nick* 2007: Dkt. 518, at 14–16.

171 Lincoln Decl. ¶ 21; E. Chimiugak Decl. ¶ 15; C. Chimiugak Decl. ¶ 13; John Decl. ¶ 15; Charlie Decl. ¶ 13; Alexie Decl. ¶¶ 10, 14; Jimmie Decl. ¶¶ 10, 12.

PART VI
Commentaries and Appendices

Chapter 11
Essays on Language Assistance under the VRA

This chapter includes five essays about language assistance by commentators who have enforced the VRA's bilingual elections mandate, lobbied on its extension, and proposed changes to its scope to be more inclusive. In the first essay, Terry Ao examines barriers to LEP Asian American voters and how language assistance under the VRA makes voting more accessible to those voters with the assistance of advocacy groups such as the Asian American Justice Center (AAJC). But not every group that needs language assistance gets it, as Jocelyn Friedrichs Benson details in the second essay about LEP Arab American U.S. citizens who are not covered by Section 203. In the third essay, Ana Henderson offers a perspective from the field as a litigator at the U.S. Department of Justice's Voting Section, detailing her observations of how jurisdictions have implemented the bilingual elections mandate. Glenn Magpantay follows in the fourth essay by discussing several exit surveys of LEP Asian American voters by the Asian American Legal Defense and Education Fund (AALDEF). John Tanner completes the essays with his discussion of his experience as Chief of the Voting Section, overseeing more enforcement actions under the language assistance provisions than any of his predecessors.

Impact of Section 203 on Asian American Voters

Terry M. Ao[1]

The Voting Rights Act of 1965 (VRA) has been hailed as a true instrument of change for the political and civic empowerment of African American and Latino American communities. This has also been the case for the Asian American community. In particular, Section 203 of the Act has been vital to increasing access for Asian American voters to the ballot by mandating that covered jurisdictions provide language assistance during the election process. This essay explores barriers to Asian American political participation and describes the impact of Section 203 on removing those barriers.

Barriers to Asian American Voters

The history of Asian Americans and exclusion from voting stretches back many centuries. Dating back to 1790, Asian Americans were considered "aliens ineligible for citizenship." Chinese Americans were expressly prohibited from naturalizing as citizens in the late 1800s. By 1924, virtually all Asian immigrants (except Filipinos) were prohibited from naturalizing and thereby denying them the right to vote, with Filipinos being similarly denied by 1935. The last of these restrictions was not ended until 1965, finally giving all Asian American citizens the right to vote.

However, another obstacle to meaningful voter participation became clear once all Asian American citizens were finally granted the right to vote – the lack of assistance at the polls needed to address language barriers. Although many Asian Americans were born in this country, a majority of Asian Americans immigrated and many of those have not had adequate opportunities to learn English. Forty percent of Asian Americans nationwide over the age of 18 are limited English proficient (LEP) – or, more simply put, are not fluent in English and have some difficulty with the language – and more than three-quarters of the population speaks a language other than English in their homes. Certain Asian American groups have LEP rates well above the national average, such as 67 percent of Vietnamese Americans and 60 percent of Laotians, Cambodians, and Hmongs. Coupled with the lack of English as a Second Language (ESL) programs, some Asian Americans are effectively precluded from learning English.

For Asian American citizens who speak some English but are not fluent, the voting process can be quite daunting. They can have difficulty understanding complex voting materials and procedures

1 Terry M. Ao, American University Washington College of Law, J.D., *cum laude*, 2002; University of Chicago, B.A. 1997. Ms. Ao is the Director of Census & Voting Programs at the Asian American Justice Center, 1140 Connecticut Avenue, NW, Suite 1200; Washington, DC 20036; www.advancingequality.org; 202–296–2300. Founded in 1991, AAJC is a national non-partisan, non-profit organization that works to advance the human and civil rights of Asian Americans through advocacy, public policy, public education, and litigation.

and can end up feeling intimidated by the process. These feelings of intimidation and unfamiliarity with the mechanisms of voting can lead many to bypass the entire political process. By providing Asian American citizens with equal access to voting, Section 203 gives Asian American citizens power to influence the policies that impact their community.

The Role of Section 203 in Removing Voting Barriers

Section 203 has served to increase significantly voter turnout and participation in covered jurisdictions when implemented properly. Once Asian American voters are given information in their own language about the voting process – that is, how to register and vote, where to vote, ballots that they can understand, and how they can get help if needed, among other components – they turn out to vote. In San Diego County, voter registration among Filipinos rose by over 20 percent after the U.S. Department of Justice (DOJ) filed a lawsuit against the county for Section 203 noncompliance. DOJ was also able to secure voluntary language assistance for Vietnamese voters in San Diego, resulting in a 40 percent increase in Vietnamese registrations. Similarly, in Harris County, Texas, Vietnamese voters doubled their turnout following efforts by DOJ in 2004 after the county failed to comply with Section 203. That same year, Harris County elected the first Vietnamese American to the Texas state legislature after the county began fully complying with Section 203. Finally, more than 10,000 Vietnamese American voters registered in Orange County in 2004, which helped lead to the election of the first Vietnamese American to California's state legislature.

Although Asian Americans are still underrepresented in government, they have experienced substantial gains in electoral representation since the adoption of Section 203 in 1975. Studies show a sharp rise in the number of Asian American elected officials in federal, state, and local offices. In 2004 the total number was 346, up from 120 in 1978. Of the 346 total elected officials, 260 serve at the local level, up from 52 in 1978. Approximately 75 Asian American officials serve at the state legislative level.[2] Those gains followed large increases in voter registration and turnout, often as the result of the greater availability of language assistance.

Section 203 has played a significant role in these gains. For example, three-quarters of the Asian American elected officials were elected in Section 203-covered jurisdictions. Section 203-covered jurisdictions account for 65 percent of Asian Americans elected to state legislatures, 79 percent elected to city councils, and 84 percent of those serving on school boards. In California, the increase has been particularly dramatic. In 1990, California had no Asian American state legislators; it now has nine, which can be directly attributed to Section 203. Eight of the nine Californian Asian American state legislators represent legislative districts located in counties that are covered under Section 203 for at least one Asian language.[3] Every county in California covered under Section 203 for an Asian language has at least one Asian American legislator. It is clear that, by increasing voter registration and turnout among Asian American voters, Section 203 is ensuring that their political voices are heard, often for the first time.

2 Carol Hardy–Fanta, Christine Marie Sierra, Pei–te Lien, Dianne M. Pinderhughes, and Wartyna L. Davis, *Race, Gender and Descriptive Representation: An Exploratory View of Multicultural Elected Leadership in the United States*, available at http://www.allacademic.com/meta/p41324_index.html.

3 These legislators are California State Assembly members Judy Chu (Los Angeles), Carol Liu (Los Angeles), Ted Lieu (Los Angeles), Van Tran (Orange), Shirley Horton (San Diego), Wilma Chan (Alameda), Alberto Torrico (Alameda, Santa Clara), and Leland Yee (San Francisco, San Mateo).

Continuing Vigilance of Section 203 Compliance

As we move forward, Section 203 can continue to serve as an instrument for increasing civic participation and ensuring the political will of Asian Americans is carried out. As our nation continues to diversify, and Asian Americans continue to move to new areas of the country, the need and utility for Section 203 will only continue to increase. However, we must be vigilant about Section 203 compliance by jurisdictions and take action against noncompliance if the potential of Section 203 is to be fully realized.

Section 203 noncompliance can come in different forms and can occur with varying degrees. Noncompliance includes the failure to fully translate and provide multilingual materials, as well as the failure to provide bilingual poll workers at polling sites. Even when multilingual materials are available, they are frequently hidden from sight so that voters are unable to see or reach them. Ballots and other materials are hidden in boxes under tables, or hidden under other materials. Sometimes ballots are simply not taken out of their original packaging, or placed behind poll workers where voters cannot reach them.

Bilingual poll workers can be equally inaccessible. Because many counties have no system to target where to recruit and place bilingual poll workers, they are often placed in locations where they are not needed or helpful to Asian American voters. Even if bilingual poll workers are where they are actually needed, they frequently are inadequately utilized due to the lack of signs indicating availability of interpreters, lack of identification of bilingual poll workers in a polling site, inconsistent quality in oral bilingual assistance, and an unwillingness of monolingual poll workers to utilize the bilingual poll workers across polling sites.

Inadequate training on proper translation and treatment of Asian American voters also can make bilingual poll workers ineffective to LEP voters even when they are available. Poll workers have frequently been reluctant to help Asian American voters with language needs, were unaware of how to help, and were suspicious of bilingual poll workers or Asian American voters with language needs. It is clear that these poll workers did not understand why language assistance was needed, often manifesting itself in talking down to voters, berating them, or simply treating these voters generally as lesser voters. Even more problematic are poll workers who are openly hostile and discriminate against language minority voters and voters of color. For example, poll workers at a polling site in Boston segregated Asian American voters from "English-speaking" voters, allegedly to speed up the voting process for monolingual voters. Poll workers ended up being yet another barrier for Asian American voters to overcome.

Conclusion

Section 203 has helped to break down barriers for Asian American voters since its inception in 1975. As we look forward to the future, with conscientious efforts by jurisdictions to comply and vigilant monitoring by interested parties to ensure compliance, Section 203 will continue to make voting more accessible for Asian American voters.

Expanding the Language Protections of the Voting Rights Act to Additional Communities

Jocelyn Friedrichs Benson[1]

Section 203 of the Voting Rights Act (VRA) requires that jurisdictions with significant concentrations of limited-English proficient (LEP) U.S. citizens provide election materials in the native languages of those citizens. Currently, Section 203's protections only extend to Hispanic, Asian, American Indian, and Alaska Native voters. Absent from this list are other groups of English-learning or LEP citizens, such as Haitian-Americans and Arab Americans, who may face similar barriers but are not afforded similar coverage under federal law. Some localities seek to fill these gaps. Miami-Dade County in Florida requires that ballots be available in Creole in precincts where a significant portion of the electorate is Haitian-American.[2] Voters in Maine who speak French as their primary language can, through their local clerk, request ballot instructions in French from the Maine Secretary of State.[3]

But many groups of citizens who are learning English or are LEP fall outside the coverage of Section 203 or state or local language assistance requirements, even though they arguably experience barriers to voting that mirror those in covered communities. In fact, enough evidence exists to suggest the need for more extensive research into whether Section 203 in particular should be broadened to reach other sectors of LEP citizens in order to ensure the provision continues to reflect and achieve its original goals. This essay describes evidence supporting the extension of Section 203 to other communities of LEP voters, such as Arab Americans, to make the VRA's language assistance mandate more inclusive.

Congressional Intent in Its Identification of Covered Language Groups

When Section 203 was enacted in 1975, the decision to limit the provision to four language groups was based on three factors: (1) evidence that members of the groups encountered discriminatory barriers to participation in electoral politics; (2) qualitative and anecdotal educational disparities correlating with high levels of illiteracy; and (3) data indicating comparatively low turnout and registration rates. The last of these factors, low turnout and participation rates, was particularly central to Congress's decision to set the four language minority groups apart from others for Section 203 coverage.

---

1 Jocelyn Friedrichs Benson is an Assistant Professor of Law at Wayne State University Law School and a member of the American Bar Association's Standing Committee on Election Law. She received her Juris Doctorate from Harvard Law School, her Master's in Philosophy from Oxford University, and her Bachelor of Arts from Wellesley College.

2 Metropolitan Dade County, Florida, Sec. 12–16, Ord. No. 99–160, §§ 1–4, 11–16–99 (1999).

3 ME. REV. STAT. ANN. 21-A § 603(5) (2005).

Both the House and Senate Judiciary Committee reports from 1975 acknowledge that other groups of LEP citizens – such as German or Polish citizens – could suffer from racial and ethnic discrimination. However, Congress received little to no evidence that members of those groups actually experienced voting difficulties or low turnout and registration rates. To the contrary, 85.7 percent of eligible Russian citizens had registered to vote in the 1972 Presidential election, as compared with only 44.4 percent of eligible Latino citizens. As such, Congress concluded then – and rightfully so – that groups of citizens who could not demonstrate that they faced language-based barriers to voting should not be entitled to language-based protections on the federal level.

High LEP Rates of Arab Americans

Today, however, there is evidence that suggests Arab American citizens in particular experience low voter participation rates, electoral barriers, and educational disparities that mirror similar problems afflicting Asian American and Latino communities throughout the United States. A 2004 survey of 1,016 Arab Americans in Michigan conducted by the University of Michigan's Institute for Social Research found that two-thirds of Arab Americans are U.S. citizens, though 75 percent were born outside of the United States.[4] In addition to this high rate of citizenship, the report revealed that nearly 90 percent of Arab Americans over the age of 5 speak Arabic at home (Detroit Arab American Study 2004: 6–7).[5] The high rate of Arabic speakers is particularly compelling considering Census figures that estimate nearly 35 percent of all individuals who speak Arabic at home speak English "less than very well."[6]

The ability to speak English less than "very well" is crucial to coverage under Section 203. Data from the 2000 Census also reveal that 40.6 percent of Latino respondents and 39.5 percent of Asian American respondents over the age of five speak English "less than very well."[7] Alaska Natives and American Indians over the age of five responded with even higher rates of English proficiency; only 11 percent of both groups indicated that they speak English less than "very well."[8] Thus with approximately 34.4 percent of Arab Americans over the age of five indicating that they speak English "less than very well," the language proficiency of the Arab American community is at relatively similar levels to that of most Section 203 covered communities.

4 University of Michigan Institute for Social Research, *Preliminary Results: Detroit Arab American Study* (2004), available at http://www.umich.edu/news/Releases/2004/Jul04/daas.pdf (The study surveyed 1,016 Arabs and Chaldeans and 508 members of the general population in Wayne, Oakland, and Macomb counties in 2003).

5 The survey also revealed that 56 percent of Arab American respondents reported that they received some of their news and information from Arabic broadcasts (Detroit Arab American Study 2004: 27).

6 U.S. Census Bureau, Language Use and English Speaking Ability: 2000 (2003) at 4 (citing Census 2000 Summary File 3). Census figures also show that Arabic is one of the ten languages most frequently spoken at home in the United States, other than English and Spanish. *Id.* at 2, Fig. 3.

7 U.S. Census Bureau, Language Use and English-Speaking Ability: 2000 (2003) at 2.

8 U.S. Census 2000, Summary File 3. There are some local areas, however, where the percentage is much higher (Appendix C).

Low Educational Attainment Rates of Arab Americans

Similar parallels between Arab Americans and the four covered language minority groups appear in the realm of educational attainment and literacy. In all but one of the six counties in the United States with more than 10,000 Arab American voting-age population (AVAP), illiteracy rates among Arab Americans are higher than the national rate of 2.2 percent.[9] Arab Americans residing in the two counties with the highest number of AVAP in the country – Los Angeles County, California, and Wayne County, Michigan, – experience some of the worst rates of educational achievement in the country. For while nationally 2.64 percent of all Arab Americans are functionally illiterate (close to the national rate of 2.20 percent), nearly 4 percent of all Arab Americans in Los Angeles County (3.41 percent) are functionally illiterate. This figure is close to the percentage of Asian Americans in Los Angeles County who are functionally illiterate (5.37 percent).

In Wayne County, Michigan, Arab Americans (citizens and non-citizens) have lower rates of educational attainment than *any* covered language minority group in the county. Nearly 12 percent of Arab Americans in Wayne County are functionally illiterate – almost double the rate of Latinos (6.95 percent) and Asian Americans (5.83 percent) and almost three times that of American Indians and Alaska Natives (3.36 percent). Compounding these disparities are blatant instances of discriminatory treatment of Arab American students in Wayne County schools. In March 2004, for example, a teacher in the Dearborn Public Schools referred to a group of unruly students, which included some Arab Americans, as "terrorists," and several of the teacher's colleagues and staff members applauded.[10]

Discrimination and Its Impact on Arab American Voting

These incidents, predictably, spill over into the world of political participation. One striking incident of electoral discrimination against Arab Americans in Wayne County occurred in 1999 in Hamtramck, Michigan.[11] In what one local newspaper called "one of the ugliest shows of bigotry in Hamtramck since the racial conflicts of the 1960s,"[12] a citizen group calling itself "Citizens for a Better Hamtramck" (CCBH) registered with the city clerk to provide challengers for the November 1999 city elections. On Election Day, CCBH challengers challenged the citizenship of more than 40 voters with distinctly Arabic-sounding names. Some voters were challenged upon their arrival to the polling location based on physical appearance alone, while others were challenged after they had revealed their names, often distinctly Arabic, and signed their applications to vote. In some instances, citizens of Arabic descent recall poll workers handing them a sheet of paper and asking them to read an oath of allegiance to the United States.

The implications of these incidents stretched beyond those who showed up to vote. As word of the discriminatory challenges spread throughout the Arab community in Hamtramck, some citizens decided not to vote and risk being "subjected to the embarrassment of being challenged as non-citizens." The United States Department of Justice filed suit in federal court alleging violations of Section 2 of the VRA. A federal court supported their claims. That led to a consent decree

9 The national illiteracy rate for U.S. citizens of voting age, the standard used for Section 203 determinations, was 1.35 percent in the 2002 Census determinations.

10 Gregg Krupa, *Teacher's Remark Irks Rights Group*, The Detroit News, Mar. 28, 2004, at 4B.

11 *See* Complaint, *United States. v. Hamtramck*, No. 0073541 (E.D. Mich. 2000).

12 Cecil Angel, *Now They Call him Councilman Ahmed; First Bangladeshi American Wins Hamtramck Office*, Detroit Free Press, Nov. 8, 2003, at 3A.

that enjoined Hamtramck from discriminating against voters in future elections and, among other things, required the placement of at least one bilingual poll worker at every polling location in Hamtramck on Election Day.

Correlating with these examples of barriers to electoral participation are quantifiable turnout disparities similar to those Congress in 1975 found for the groups covered by Section 203. An examination of the participation patterns of Arab Americans in Dearborn, Michigan, suggests that Arab Americans participate in elections at much lower rates than the general population in that city. In the 2004 General Election, for example, the average turnout of registered voters in east Dearborn, the area with the highest concentration of Arab American voting-age population (citizen and non-citizen) was 53.5 percent, while the average turnout of registered voters in precincts located in west Dearborn was ten percentage points higher: 63.2 percent. Similar 10-point gaps occurred in the 2004 Primary Election (17.4 percent to 26.6 percent) and the 2000 General Election (49.4 percent to 59.1 percent).

Conclusion

In 1975, the House and Senate reports implied that if Congress had received evidence of disparities from other language minority groups, they also would have been covered by Section 203. Members indicated that they did not intend to preclude the addition of other groups in the future.[13] The arguments in this essay suggest that it may be time for Congress to consider additional language minority groups that would be well served by inclusion under the language protections in Section 203.

The data discussed above also suggest that further research could uncover additional language minorities that, under the standards established by Congress in 1975, should arguably also receive language assistance. Congress could, at the very least, provide funding and mandates for additional research into this area, perhaps to be conducted by the U.S. Election Assistance Commission. Such research has proven costly and prohibitive for advocacy groups, but support from Congress could ensure that no group is left behind in Section 203 coverage.

13 S. Rep. No. 94–295, at 30 (1975).

Section 203 in Action: Lessons from the Field

Ana Henderson[1]

During my time as a trial attorney in the Voting Section at the U.S. Department of Justice, Civil Rights Division, I investigated several jurisdictions for compliance with Sections 203 and 4(f)(4) of the Voting Rights Act (VRA), and where necessary took action to enforce these requirements. My investigations focused on jurisdictions in the Northeast, Southeast, Northwest, Southwest and Alaska, encompassing all of Section 203's language groups.

Throughout the course of these investigations, I was in frequent contact with local community members and advocates, local (and sometimes state) election officials and limited-English proficient (LEP) voters in a variety of communities. In a typical investigation, I would: (a) contact election officials and community advocates in a covered jurisdiction to find out more about the language minority community's needs and the jurisdiction's efforts at providing language assistance; (b) observe elections in the polls to see how the jurisdiction's language program worked on election day; and (c) provide feedback and consult with election officials about how to design and implement a successful language program. Often, jurisdictions would institute a language assistance program or improve their existing language assistance efforts, and I would see a more or less voluntary (since there was always a threat of potential litigation) process of compliance. In a minority of my investigations, litigation was ultimately necessary to enforce the VRA's language assistance mandate.

This essay draws on my experience "in the field." It illustrates some common themes in election administrators' initial responses to Section 203 requirements and describes the impact that the lack of effective assistance had on covered LEP voters. Next, it explores election officials' explanations and concerns about Section 203 compliance. Finally, the essay concludes with a brief discussion of the political involvement of language minority voters after the institution of a language assistance program.

Initial Responses to Section 203

When I first met with election officials in a covered jurisdiction, I usually found that they were taking some minimal action to respond to Section 203, but usually not enough to provide effective assistance. I often found that they had very limited familiarity with the language minority citizens and communities within their jurisdiction. In most jurisdictions, there were no election staff members who were members of the language minority community or who spoke the covered language. In several

---

1 Ana Henderson is Director of Opportunity and Inclusion at the Chief Justice Earl Warren Institute on Race, Ethnicity, and Diversity and Lecturer-in-Residence at the University of California, Berkeley, School of Law; A.B., *summa cum laude*, Dartmouth College, 1995, J.D., Harvard Law School, 1999. Former Trial Attorney at the United States Department of Justice Civil Rights Division, Housing and Civil Enforcement and Voting Sections (1999–2005).

jurisdictions, elections officials were surprised by Census data showing a large LEP citizen population in their midst.

Election officials often had not reached out to or learned more about the covered language communities within their jurisdiction. This frequently led to a lack of effective language assistance for covered LEP voters. Officials in an Alaska jurisdiction covered for Filipino voters were unaware that more than one language is spoken in the Philippines and that the most commonly-spoken language for LEP voters within their jurisdiction was not Tagalog. As a result, the jurisdiction's Tagalog translations were of limited utility to the voters. In a Mississippi county, an election official insisted that no election assistance in Choctaw was needed because all Indians spoke English and merely pretended not to understand when it was convenient for them. However, tribal leaders confirmed that several elders would benefit from Choctaw assistance in the covered counties. In a jurisdiction in New Mexico, an election administrator informed me that Navajo elders would find Spanish translations already being provided by the state sufficient and did not need Navajo translation; the local Navajo chapter president disputed this claim. In another New Mexico county, the elections administrator contended that the local Pueblo government would not permit a polling place on its territory without ever consulting with the Pueblo leadership about this issue. In a Washington jurisdiction, the election administrator assumed that providing Spanish language assistance would offend LEP voters, because it presumed that they could not speak English; this assumption was not based on any input from the community.

Lack of Effective Language Assistance

In addition to election officials' lack of familiarity with the needs of language minority populations, I often found they did not know how to run an effective language assistance program. Many translations were of poor quality. Sometimes this occurred because jurisdictions asked county employees who happened to speak the covered language, but were neither trained nor hired to be interpreters, to translate official documents.[2] In a jurisdiction in Washington state, for example, election officials used ballot translations prepared by an employee who spoke Spanish but was not an interpreter and did not have any elections experience or knowledge of election terms. The resulting Spanish language ballot asked voters to respond to a bond measure increasing "tax rats" rather than "tax rates." Some jurisdictions did not ensure that poll workers possessed sufficient language skills to provide assistance or provide training to poll workers about how to provide language assistance. In a jurisdiction in Arizona, a monolingual English speaker wore a badge identifying her in Spanish as the official translator. In a New Mexico jurisdiction, a "bilingual" poll worker was unable to understand and respond to my questions in Spanish. In a Washington state jurisdiction, a fluent bilingual poll worker lacked the ability to translate basic election terminology into Spanish, such as how to say "ballot."

Some jurisdictions have developed election terminology dictionaries that can help bilingual poll workers. Just as speaking a language does not mean that one can translate official documents, being bilingual does not mean that one will possess technical vocabulary. This point is poignantly clear in the case of many Alaska Native and American Indian languages, where direct cognates of

2 Translation is a difficult process and merely speaking a language does not ensure that one can produce a correct and understandable translation, especially of a complex government document. As a result, bilingual employees, particularly those with no experience with election terminology, are placed in a difficult position when directed to produce a translation of an official ballot.

terms such as "Tax Assessor" simply do not exist, and the concept must be explained through other words. However, many jurisdictions do not provide the tools necessary for an effective language assistance program until they are compelled to do so under the threat of litigation.

Non-compliance and LEP Voter Participation

I found that participation of language minority communities in jurisdictions with ineffective language programs was very low. In the polls on Election Day, I observed that a surprisingly low number of LEP voters (and sometimes non-LEP co-ethnic voters) voted compared to their numbers in the local population. For some jurisdictions covered for Spanish, a Spanish-surname analysis[3] of voter rolls suggested that Latino registration was disparately low compared with the Latino citizen voting-age population. Reports from community advocates confirmed that participation was generally low, often due to a history of discrimination or neglect by government officials. For example, in a New Mexico jurisdiction, Navajo leaders reported that their members' requests to the county for assistance were often rebuffed, sometimes on the grounds that "Indians don't pay taxes." In Mississippi, Choctaw leaders reported a tension between county officials and tribal members. In Washington and Arizona, I heard reports of Latino voters being mistreated at the polls. In Alaska, Arizona, and Washington, Anglo poll workers complained to me, in the polling place during voting hours, about having to provide information and assistance in languages other than English.

These situations could have been avoided by obtaining good translations, assessing the language skills of designated bilingual poll workers, training all poll workers on how to provide effective language assistance, and providing election terminology to bilingual poll workers. Election officials have to work with members of the local language minority communities to identify what language assistance is most effective. They also must evaluate their language program regularly to determine whether it is meeting the needs of LEP voters, and adjust it if it does not.

Reactions of Election Officials to Section 203 and Identified Violations

When confronted with Section 203 requirements, election officials I met frequently had similar reactions. The most common objection to Section 203 requirements was the lack of funding for language programs and how to pay for a language program out of an already strapped budget. While many of the expenses can be absorbed into the normal election budget – such as hiring bilingual staff to serve as poll workers – this is not always the case. In a New York county, where poll workers are appointed by the political parties in a one-to-one ratio, officials stated that finding one Democrat and one Republican bilingual poll worker for each polling place where needed would be very difficult, and it would require them to hire interpreters. In a county in Arizona, election officials worried about how to train poll workers on language assistance when their budget

3 Spanish-surname analysis uses a list of names determined by the Census Bureau to have a high correlation with an individual self-identifying as Latino. It is not a perfect measure as some non-Latinos have Spanish surnames and some Latinos do not have Spanish surnames. I believe it is a tool best used for preliminary analysis of voter registration rolls, in this context, as it can provide an approximation of Latino population where no racial/ethnic data are available.

allowed them to pay for only one hour of training, which was entirely taken up with instruction on voting machines and polling place administration.[4]

Some election officials also cited hostility from non-LEP voters as a reason for concern, or even inaction. Election officials recounted how they had received complaints about providing bilingual voting materials, such as phone calls or letters objecting, sometimes in vulgar terms, to election materials in any language other than English. This hostility was a particular concern for election officials who are elected to office, such as some county registrars or auditors. Although administering elections is often just one of the tasks their offices entail, they viewed opposition to bilingual ballots as a potential liability in upcoming elections. That is, they were afraid to do "too much" for LEP voters, anger the non-LEP majority of voters, and risk their re-election.

The Impact of Effective Language Assistance Programs

Despite the challenges election officials face or fear, language assistance programs can have real positive effects for LEP voters. A key benefit of an effective language program is enabling LEP voters to understand the process well enough to cast a meaningful vote. The high level of complexity on many ballots, when complicated ballot initiatives, bond issues, and constitutional amendments can take up several pages, requires a sophisticated knowledge of English that far exceeds day-to-day conversational proficiency.[5] Providing good language assistance gives the voter the opportunity to make a reasoned, meaningful decision.

Equally important, effective language assistance allows an LEP voter to cast a secret ballot, without anyone else helping, watching or influencing his decision. The ability to cast a secret ballot is powerful and an important part of voting ignored by those who claim Section 203 can be replaced by private voter assistance. I saw this most poignantly when I met an elderly voter outside a polling place in Washington state in the first election where bilingual ballots were provided. When I asked her in Spanish what she thought of the bilingual ballot, she told me with tears in her eyes that it was the first time she was able to vote on her own; that in every other election, her daughter had to go into the voting booth with her to tell her what was on the ballot, but this time she was able to do it herself. This was a momentous occasion for this voter to do what most voters in the U.S. take for granted: cast a secret ballot.

An ancillary, but I believe important, effect of language assistance programs is to help incorporate LEP and co-ethnic English speakers, who have often been politically isolated and excluded, into the larger political community. It is important to remember that Section 203 is a not just about "bilingual ballots," although bilingual ballots get most of the attention. Section 203 requires that all election-related information provided to the public in English also be provided in the covered language. The most successful programs empower language minority and LEP voters to participate in the electoral system by providing election-related information in new and different ways. This means more than simply translating documents; it means conducting outreach and education in ways that more effectively reach LEP citizens. For example, after instituting a program and hiring a bilingual coordinator, officials in a Washington state jurisdiction started attending and providing information at Latino-centered public events. An Arizona jurisdiction abandoned its practice of

4 Some of these budget constraints would be addressed if local officials used a portion of the Help America Vote Act funds they receive for providing language assistance. However, most election administrators I met used or plan to use their HAVA disbursements to purchase new voting technology.

5 *See* Ana Henderson, *English Language Naturalization Requirements and the Bilingual Assistance Provisions of the Voting Rights Act* (2006) (unpublished article on file with author).

"complying" with Section 203 by printing Spanish versions of election announcements in the local English language newspaper and started placing them in Spanish-language media instead.

Moreover, due to their language skills, language minority citizens become parts of the electoral system, such as serving as poll workers. I met newly hired bilingual poll workers in several jurisdictions who were enthusiastic to play such an important role in the electoral process and to use their language skills to help LEP citizens maneuver the polling place. Small moves like these can make a big difference to LEP and language minority citizens who have been disenfranchised. They can also increase participation. In a Washington jurisdiction, Latino registration increased by about 24 percent after the county instituted its language assistance program.[6]

Conclusion

Although Section 203 can pose some challenges to covered jurisdictions, the potential benefits to language minority voters are many. In my experience, election officials expressed concern about how to pay for language assistance out of already-stretched election budgets, and some election officials feared hostility or backlash from non-LEP voters who dislike bilingual voting. I found that effective language assistance programs were able to increase awareness and participation among LEP and language minority voters. Section 203 is an important tool for opening the electoral process up to those who have been excluded.

6 *Voting Rights Act: Section 203 – Bilingual Election Requirements (Part I): Hearing Before the Subcomm. on the Constitution of the H. Comm. on the Judiciary*, 109th Cong. 4 (2005) (statement of Bradley J. Schlozman, Acting Assistant Att'y Gen., Civil Rights Div., Dep't of Justice).

Asian Americans and Barriers to Voting

Glenn D. Magpantay[1]

Asian Americans are one of the fastest-growing minority groups in the nation, estimated to number almost 12 million.[2] More and more are becoming naturalized U.S. citizens and registering to vote. Asian citizens of voting age numbered 3.9 million in 1996 and rose from 4.7 million in 2000 to 6.7 million in 2004. Asian American voter turnout is also steadily increasing, from 1.7 million in 1996, to nearly 3 million in 2004.[3] Almost half (43 percent) of all Asian Americans over 18 are limited-English proficient (LEP)[4] and 81 percent speak a language other than English in their homes. Sixty-six percent of Asian Americans are citizens; yet most (53 percent) acquired citizenship through naturalization.[5]

Since 1988, the Asian American Legal Defense and Education Fund (AALDEF) has conducted nonpartisan multilingual exit polls of Asian American voters and monitored elections to document instances of anti-Asian voter disenfranchisement.[6] In the November 2008 Presidential Election, AALDEF's 1,500 volunteer attorneys, law students, and community activists covered 113 poll sites in 39 cities in 11 states and Washington, DC. AALDEF surveyed 16,665 Asian American voters.[7] It was the largest survey of its kind. Thirty-one percent of respondents reported that the November 2008 elections were the first U.S. elections in which they had voted. Seventy-nine percent of respondents were foreign-born naturalized citizens, and 21 percent had no formal education in the United States. Only 20 percent identified English as their native language. Thirty-five percent were LEP.

AALDEF's surveys have documented the tremendous need for language assistance among Asian American voters. Asian American citizens want to vote, but they are often unfamiliar with the American electoral process. Many come from Asian countries with very different political

1 Glenn D. Magpantay, New England School of Law, J.D., *cum laude*, 1998; State University of New York at Stony Brook, BA 1992. Mr. Magpantay is a Staff Attorney at the Asian American Legal Defense and Education Fund, 99 Hudson Street, 12th Floor; New York, NY 10013; info@aaldef.org; www.aaldef.org; 212–966–5932. AALDEF, founded in 1974, is a national organization that protects and promotes the legal rights of Asian Americans through litigation, legal advocacy, and community education.

2 Census 2000 identified 11,898,828 individuals who are of Asian heritage. Asian American growth since 1990 is 72.2 percent (for those who only identified themselves as Asian alone or in combination with another race). U.S. Census Bureau, Census 2000 PHC-T-1 (Apr. 2, 2001) (Tables 3, 4).

3 *Voting Rights Act: Section 203 – Bilingual Election Requirements (Part I): Hearing Before the Subcomm. on the Constitution of the H. Comm. on the Judiciary* (Nov. 8, 2005) (statement of Margaret Fung, Exec. Dir., AALDEF) (Fung 2005).

4 Limited English proficiency is determined by one's ability to read English less than "very well." Letter from Robert Kominski, U.S. Census Bureau, Population Division, to Paul Siegel, Chief of Education & Social Stratification Branch, U.S. Census Bureau, Population Division (Feb. 4, 1985) (on file with author).

5 U.S. Census Bureau, Census 2000 Summary File 3, PCT62D and PCT63D.

6 For a full review of AALDEF's exit poll and election monitoring activities, see Glenn D. Magpantay, *Ensuring Asian American Access to Democracy in New York City*, 2 AAPI Nexus, Asian Am. & Pac. Is. Pol'y, Prac. & Comm. 87 (2004).

7 AALDEF, The Asian American Vote 2008: A Report on the Multilingual Exit Poll in the 2008 Presidential Election (forthcoming).

systems or which may even lack a tradition of voting. They do not understand basic political procedures, such as the need to register to vote by a certain date or to enroll in a political party to vote in a primary or how to operate voting machines.[8] Special efforts are needed to prepare Asian American voters to fully participate in elections. This essay highlights why the Voting Rights Act continues to be necessary to help Asian American voters overcome these barriers to political participation.

Anti-Asian Voting Discrimination

AALDEF's election monitoring efforts over the years documented several instances of Asian American voter disenfranchisement.[9] In elections before 2008, poll workers made inappropriate or racially disparaging remarks about Asian American and LEP voters:

- Poll workers called Asian American voters "terrorists" in New York City.
- A poll worker in Edison, New Jersey, said that when a Gujarati- or Hindi-speaking voter appeared, she would "send them to the nearest gas station."[10]
- In Queens, New York, one poll worker said, "I'll talk to [Asian voters] the way they talk to me when I call to order Chinese food," which was then followed with random English phrases with a mock Chinese accent. Another poll worker blamed Asian American voters for holding up the lines saying, "You Oriental guys are taking too long to vote."
- A poll worker in Brooklyn, New York, asked, "How does one tell the difference between Chinese and Japanese?" and brought her fingers to each side of her eyes and moved her skin up and down.

Elected officials, white voters, and others were hostile toward Asian American voters and engaged in efforts to harass and intimidate them:

- A New York City Councilwoman representing the largely Asian American neighborhood of Flushing, Queens, New York, described Asian immigrants as "colonizers" and "marauding invaders."[11]
- In Fort Lee, New Jersey, a losing candidate for school board charged that Korean American voters illegally voted because they did not live in Fort Lee or were not U.S. citizens. He

---

8 *Language Assistance Provisions of the Voting Rights Act, Hearing on S. 2236 Before the Subcomm. on Civil and Constitutional Rts. of the H. Comm. on the Judiciary*, 102 Cong. at 1 (Apr. 1, 1992) (statement of Margaret Fung, Exec. Dir., AALDEF); Senate Report 102–315, Calendar No. 537 July 2, 1992, at 12.

9 *Diaz v. Silver*, 978 F. Supp. 96, 101 (E.D.N.Y. 1997), *aff'd mem.*, 118 S. Ct. 36 (1997) (citing Affidavit of Michael Shen at ¶¶ 25 for Defendant-Intervenor) (Shen Affidavit 1997); Asian American Legal Defense and Education Fund, Asian American Access to Democracy in the 2004 Elections: Local compliance with the Voting Rights Act and Help America Vote Act (HAVA) in NY, NJ, MA, RI, MI, IL, PA, VA (Aug. 2005) (AALDEF Report 2004); Asian American Access to Democracy in the 2003 Elections in NYC: An Assessment of New York City Compliance with the Language Provisions of the Voting Rights Act (May 2004).

10 Fung 2005: 4; Jerry Barca, *Feds to Watch Edison Vote*, New Brunswick Home News Trib., Nov. 2, 2005.

11 Celia W. Dugger, *Queens Old-Timers Uneasy As Asian Influence Grows*, N.Y. Times, Mar. 31, 1996, at A1.

persuaded the local sheriff to issue subpoenas to the voters at their Fort Lee addresses, in the early morning hours, and forced them to present passports and naturalization certificates. Voters complained that they felt punished for voting.

- In Edison, New Jersey, local talk radio hosts made several racist remarks, speaking in an incoherent, mock Asian accent, about a Korean American candidate for mayor. In response to a caller's statement that "Indians have taken over Edison," they responded, "It's like you're a foreigner in your country, isn't it?"

Elderly Asian American voters in many cities were treated differently from white voters or were taken advantage of due to their limited English proficiency. In Boston, poll workers at one site segregated voters and made minority voters form one line and white voters form another line in order to vote. They claimed that separate but equal lines for LEP voters would speed up the voting process for others. At another Boston polling place, poll workers took the ballots of Asian American voters and completed the ballots for them without the voters' approval because the voters did not read English well.[12] In Annandale, Virginia, a bilingual partisan campaign worker encouraged Korean American voters to apply for absentee ballots, promising to help them since the ballots were in English. The voters did not hear back and so on Election Day when they came to vote at their poll site, they were told that their ballots were already cast. In Palisades Park, New Jersey, Korean American voters complained that they felt unduly rushed to vote.

Asian American voters also encountered a number of other voting difficulties compounding these inappropriate and racist remarks. Just like the encounters of African American and Latino voters in Florida in 2000, many Asian Americans were turned away because their names were missing from lists of registered voters located at poll sites. This barrier often was due to the faulty processing or mishandling of voter registration forms by election administrators. Although the Help America Vote Act allows voters whose names do not appear on voter registration lists to vote by provisional ballots, election officials did not offer those ballots or denied them when voters asked.[13] Voters were simply turned away without being able to cast a ballot.

Identification checks are not typically required to vote in most jurisdictions, except for a very narrow category of first-time voters.[14] Nevertheless, poll workers in some jurisdictions racially profiled Asian American voters and required them to prove their identity, verify their addresses, and sometimes even produce naturalization certificates.

Asian American voters also complained that they were given inadequate notice of their poll sites or found that their poll sites were suddenly changed. On Election Day, voters were often redirected, sometimes wrongly, to other poll sites and were sent back to their original sites. Because of direct disenfranchisement and other barriers to voting, special efforts are needed to ensure that Asian Americans have fair and equal access to the ballot.[15]

---

12 Decl. of Lydia Lowe, Chinese Progressive Assoc., Decl. of Siu Tsang (voter), in *U.S. v. City of Boston, MA*, Civ. 05–11598 WGY (D. Mass. 2005).

13 HAVA Section 302, 42 U.S.C. § 15482.

14 HAVA Section 303, 42 U.S.C. §§ 15483(b), (d).

15 Voting Rights Language Assistance Act of 1992, H.R. Rep. 102–655, 1992 U.S.C.C.A.N. 766, 771 (July 8, 1992); S. Rep. 102–315, at 5–6 (July 2, 1992) (both discussing the history of discrimination against Asian Americans).

The Impact of the Voting Rights Act

The language assistance provisions of the Voting Rights Act (VRA), codified at Section 203,[16] have opened up the political process to tens of thousands of Asian American citizens. After the 2000 Census, 16 counties in seven states were required to provide assistance in one or more Asian languages. These include counties in Alaska, California, Hawaii, Illinois, New York, Texas, and Washington for Chinese, Korean, Filipino, Vietnamese, or Japanese language assistance.[17]

At the most fundamental level, translated ballots have enabled Asian American voters to exercise their right to vote independently and privately inside the voting booth. The mandate for interpreters in poll sites was instrumental for Asian American voters who were not fully proficient in English (Fung 2005: 2). In 1992, when three counties in New York City were first covered under Section 203, more than 54,000 Chinese Americans in Manhattan and Queens benefited from the availability of Chinese language materials (Shen Affidavit 1997: ¶ 24). Community exit polls then and now documented that the main beneficiaries were first-time voters, newly-naturalized citizens, and voters with no formal U.S. education or less than a high school education (AALDEF Report 2004: 14–15).

According to AALDEF's 2008 multilingual exit poll of almost 16,665 Asian American voters in 11 states and Washington, DC, a third of all voters needed some form of language assistance in order to vote. In jurisdictions covered for bilingual ballots, more than half of the covered language minority groups were LEP.

Section 203 has also aided grassroots efforts to increase Asian American voter registration. From 2001 to 2004, multilingual voter registration forms required under Section 203 helped to increase Asian American voter registration by 40 percent.[18] AALDEF's 2008 exit poll confirmed the impact of the multilingual forms, with a third of responding Asian American voters reporting that they were voting for the first time.

Most importantly, Section 203 has contributed to Asian American electoral success. In New York City, up until 2001, no Asian American had ever been elected to the City Council, State Legislature, or Congress, notwithstanding a population of over 800,000. Following coverage and increased enforcement of Section 203, more Asian Americans have run for political office. In 2001, 13 Asian American candidates ran for New York City Council, and one was finally elected. In 2004, the first Asian American was elected to the New York State Assembly. In the same year, the first-ever Vietnamese American was elected to the State Legislature from Harris County, Texas, after it became covered for Vietnamese Americans under Section 203 (Fung 2005: 2).

Asian American Voters' Continuing Need for the Voting Rights Act

Although Section 203 has made the vote more accessible for Asian American voters, AALDEF's election monitoring has uncovered numerous violations in covered jurisdictions for bilingual voting materials. During the 2000 Presidential Elections in New York City, ballots flipped the translated party headings so that Republican candidates were listed as Democrats and Democrats as Republicans.[19] In several elections in New York City, in New York and Los Angeles, and in Orange, San Francisco, and Alameda Counties in California, poll workers kept translated materials hidden and unavailable

16 42 U.S.C. § 1973aa-1a (2004).

17 67 Fed. Reg. No. 144, 48871–77 (July 26, 2002) (Notices).

18 Sandy Endo, *Asian-American Voters Could Swing Mayoral Election*, NY1 News, Feb. 9, 2005.

19 William Murphy, Mae Cheng, Herbert Lowe, *Spirit Willing, System Weak*, Newsday (Nov. 8, 2000) at A10; *Bungled Ballots in Chinatown*, N.Y. Times (Jan. 1, 2001) (Editorial).

to voters.[20] On a number of occasions, poll workers never even bothered to open the kit containing translated materials. Translated signs were posted in obscure locations or not posted at all.

Voters have also complained about too few interpreters or interpreters who spoke the wrong language or dialect. At a poll site in Queens, New York, a Chinese American voter who asked for language assistance was directed to a Korean interpreter who could not help. At another site, a poll worker who was asked about translated materials sarcastically replied, "What, are we in China? It's ridiculous." Far too often, election officials do not make any effort to provide oral language assistance for Asian voters in jurisdictions covered by Section 203. The U.S. Department of Justice has dispatched federal attorneys to monitor for Section 203 compliance. The Department has filed several lawsuits to remedy these deficiencies.[21] Both have more forcefully ensured that jurisdictions fully comply with Section 203.

Another notable mechanism for enforcement has been Section 5 of the Voting Rights Act.[22] Under Section 5, jurisdictions with a history of voter discrimination must obtain "preclearance" before any change to any voting procedure or practice can be implemented. Some jurisdictions, such as parts of New York City, are covered under both Sections 5 and 203; Section 5 requires that Section 203 compliance plans, or changes to current language assistance plans, must be precleared. In preclearance, the public may review the submission and make comments, oftentimes in opposition to preclearance.[23] Here, community groups have real opportunities to shape meaningful language assistance programs.

Community input under Section 5 made a real difference when New York was first covered under Section 203 in 1992. The Board of Elections claimed that New York's mechanical-lever voting machines did not have space for the candidates' names in Chinese. AALDEF pressed the Board to transliterate the candidates' names into Chinese. Asian American voters typically know the candidates by their transliterated names, which appear in candidate literature and Asian-language media outlets.[24] In 2004, AALDEF found that 36 percent of Asian American voters surveyed got their news about politics and community issues from the Asian-language press, rather than mainstream media outlets. Candidate names are the most important pieces of information for voters.

Political and media advocacy only went so far. More than a hundred Asian Americans packed a meeting of the Board of Elections, carrying placards and Chinese-language signs demanding fully translated bilingual ballots. A *New York Times* editorial described the Board's inaction saying, "That sounds like the foot-dragging bureaucratic arguments that have been raised all over America at one time or another against giving minorities their rights. It is no excuse for not obeying the law."[25] Ultimately, it was the denial of preclearance of the Board of Election language assistance program under Section 5 that forced the Board to provide fully translated ballots with candidates' names in Chinese. Section 5, through comments to the Justice Department, gave community groups the power to ensure that language minorities have full access to the vote.

20 Glenn D. Magpantay, *Asian American Access to the Vote: The Language Assistance Provisions (Section 203) of the Voting Rights Act and Beyond*, 11 Asian L. J. 31, 40–42 (2004).

21 28 C.F.R. §§ 55.2 (b) (1)–(2). *See, e.g., U.S. v. City of Rosemead* (C.D. Cal. 2005); *U.S. v. San Diego County* (S.D. Cal 2004); *U.S. v. City of Boston* (D. Mass. 2005). For a full listing of cases filed by the U.S. Department of Justice, Voting Section, go to http://www.usdoj.gov/crt/voting/litigation/caselist.htm.

22 42 U.S.C. § 1973c.

23 28 C.F.R. § 51.29.

24 28 C.F.R. § 55.20.

25 Fung 2005: 5 (citing Editorial, N.Y. Times (Aug. 19, 1999)).

Conclusion

Asian Americans political participation has surged throughout the United States. Asian Americans are becoming citizens and attempting to participate in the nation's political franchise, but they have encountered many voting barriers. The Voting Rights Act has helped to expand access to the vote, but shortcomings in local compliance remain. Aggressive enforcement is needed to ensure that all Americans fully enjoy the right to vote.

Federal Enforcement of the Language Assistance Provisions

John Tanner[1]

Enforcement of the minority language assistance provisions of the Voting Rights Act (VRA) is crucial to the equal participation in the political process of millions of American citizens. There is a widespread misperception that English fluency is a prerequisite of citizenship, and that those who cannot speak English must not be citizens. In fact, literally millions of citizens who were born here in the United States cannot speak English fluently. The 2000 Census determined that more than four million Spanish speakers, individuals who could not speak English well enough to participate in the political process, had been born here. The same is true of many Asian Americans and, of course, of virtually all Native Americans and Alaska Natives. Today 87 jurisdictions are covered under Section 203 for Native Languages under the reservation formula, because many descendants of the First Americans continue to rely on languages used by their ancestors long before anyone on this continent uttered a word in English; indeed, long before English was a language.

The dependence of minority languages within various communities is remarkable, and far from limited to more recent Hispanic immigrants who have been vilified by some commentators. The Acadians were ejected from Canada in 1755, and more than 350 years later there are still several Louisiana Cajun parishes in where more than 5 percent of the population speak French and do not speak English well enough to participate in the political process in English. Many Germans, having been lured to Russia by Catherine the Great in 1763, subsequently moved to the steppes of North Dakota, and today many of their descendants – enough to meet the 5 percent threshold in at least three counties (if European languages were covered by the VRA) – rely on the German language. In the tiny New Mexico Pueblos like Jemez, Zia, and San Felipe, none with as many as 2,100 residents, more than 40 percent of the population is dependent upon one of the Pueblo languages.

The detachment of the visceral and ingrained link between language and citizenship reached its peak for me when, while I was prosecuting a minority language case on behalf of Native American voters, an election official told me, "They should have learned English before they came here." Some cannot accept that all of these citizens have and deserve the same rights as their fellow Americans to register and vote with materials and ballots that they can understand.

The importance of bilingual elections for those who cannot speak or read English fluently has been illustrated by recent litigation to enforce the VRA's minority language provisions. Following the July 2002 determinations of those jurisdictions to be covered under Section 203 of the Act, the U.S. Department of Justice led a rising surge in enforcement of Section 203 and the other minority language assistance provisions. The cases included the Department's first cases on behalf of Filipino, Vietnamese, and Korean voters. The Department's minority language enforcement also expanded for the first time to areas whose Hispanic population was predominated by Mexican

1 John Tanner is a former Chief of the Voting Section of the U.S. Department of Justice's Civil Rights Division. Denison University, B.A. 1971; Washington College of Law, J.D. 1980.

Americans, by far the largest Hispanic group in the United States. Indeed, the Department filed a majority of all language cases it has brought in the 42-year history of the VRA in the four years from 2004 through 2007.[2] This essay describes some of the evidence of discrimination in those cases, and the impact that enforcement of the VRA had on the political access of language minority voters.

Discrimination against Language Minority Voters

Since most of the cases brought by the U.S. Department of Justice between 2004 and 2007 were settled by consent decree or other agreement rather than fully litigated, the full investigative basis for the lawsuits is not always included in the public record. The scanty public record does, however, provide the outlines of truly appalling treatment of American citizens on the basis of their minority language status, race, or ethnicity. In Westchester County, New York, for example, poll workers actually stood in front of the voting booth – in the schoolhouse door, as it were – to block Spanish-speaking voters from receiving necessary assistance. At least one of those voters was visually impaired. English-speaking voters were allowed to receive assistance from persons of their choice. Poll workers displayed open hostility to Hispanic voters who needed assistance.

The record in *United States v. Springfield, Massachusetts* includes the declarations of numerous individual victims of discrimination. A sample from the Department's filing illustrates the experience that voters who cannot speak English face at the polls:

- Jaime Dominguez Almena, who has trouble with more complicated English, spent three hours searching for a polling place in November 2004 because poll workers could not correctly determine where he was supposed to vote and bounced him from polling place to polling place. He was not offered assistance in Spanish.
- Delia Benitez asked for bilingual assistance at the Mason Square Fire Station in Ward 4, but an English-speaking poll worker … pointed to the presidential candidates on the sample ballot and told her, "here and here," but then left before explaining more. Ms. Benitez had wanted to vote the entire ballot, but because she did not understand, she did not complete it. Ms. Benitez was discouraged by this experience, which she described as rushed, uncomfortable, and unpleasant. As a result, she did not vote in the November 2005 election.
- Maria Melendez, an LEP voter who had a seventh-grade education in Puerto Rico, went to vote for the first time in the 2004 presidential election. There was no one to assist her at the Independence House polling place, and she filled out her ballot without knowing which candidate she was marking. The experience was so discouraging that she said, "I won't ever vote again."
- Maria Idali Torres witnessed a group of Hispanic voters in November 2004 speaking to each other in Spanish at Our Lady of Hope polling place … The voters were visibly confused, but rather than getting assistance in Spanish from poll workers (which was not available), a white poll worker told them in a loud and hostile voice "We are in America."

2 A list of the Department's cases and selected pleadings are available online at http://www.usdoj.gov/crt/voting/litigation/caselist.htm#sec203cases. In addition to these cases, during the 2004–2007 period, the Voting Section also obtained out-of-court formal agreements with Broward County (Ft. Lauderdale), Florida; Harris County (Houston), Texas; the City of Los Angeles, California; and Maricopa County (Phoenix), Arizona. During that period, the Department also obtained extensions of consent decrees in Cibola County and Sandoval County in New Mexico.

- In the late 1990s, Carlos Gonzalez was translating for an elderly Hispanic man, when an older white female poll worker overheard them speaking Spanish and said, in a rude and degrading way to the voter, "You can't speak English!"
- Jose Molina, a bilingual poll worker in Ward 1, witnessed a police officer stationed at the polling place and the lead worker say, "[W]e are in America and you should speak English" in front of the Spanish-speaking workers. The police officer also became "furious" with Hispanic voters who spoiled their ballot and requested a new one.
- Carlos Gonzalez witnessed a Spanish-speaking voter become frustrated when a police officer prevented him from receiving help from Mr. Gonzalez. The voter [who could not speak English] shouted in Spanish, "I'm leaving and I'm never voting again."

Discriminatory conduct is all too widespread. Consider the declaration from *United States v. City of Philadelphia*, where a citizen of the United States describes her experience when she went to the polls with her young daughter:

> The poll workers were laughing at the fact that I could not speak English. My daughter told the poll worker in broken English that I needed help in Spanish. They could not help me in Spanish. I became very upset at being laughed at and being made fun of, that I started crying. I was frustrated that there was no one there to assist me and I walked out of the polling place … I am very happy to be an American and to live in this country. I pay attention to what goes on in this neighborhood and I know that I am not the only person who has struggled. Here, people do not complain, but they struggle. It is our right to vote.

And the quintessentially American reaction of another voter elsewhere in Philadelphia: "Our people are good enough to fight in any war … And now when it is [our] right to vote as United States citizen, we're laughed at, pushed, I don't understand it. If we're good enough to die for the United States, are we not good enough to vote?"

Such mistreatment – and worse – is not confined to areas subject to the Act's minority language assistance provisions. The complaint in *United States v. City of Boston* recounts that Chinese and Vietnamese citizens with limited English proficiency actually had their ballots taken from them and mismarked. The complaint in *United States v. Long County, Georgia*, details abusive challenges to the county's relatively small handful of Hispanic voters, who were required to attend a hearing to affirmatively establish their citizenship and eligibility to vote despite the complete and utter lack of evidence that they were not citizens of the United States. They were challenged solely because they were Hispanic. At least three of the challenged voters were on active duty in the United States Army. Similar spurious challenges against Vietnamese American citizens in Bayou la Batre, Alabama, ultimately were thwarted after Justice Department intervention.

The Impact of the Department's Enforcement Actions

Voting discrimination against language minorities can be addressed effectively and with remarkable results. Effective bilingual procedures transform the voting experience for millions of Americans. The relief provided in *United States v. San Diego County, California*, immediately provided bilingual ballots (including bilingual accessible ballots for persons with disabilities) and added more than 1,000 bilingual poll workers able to serve Hispanic, Filipino, and Vietnamese citizens. The change in the voting experience was not simply in form and personnel, however. A

Vietnamese voter, thrilled to find a Vietnamese-speaking poll worker, exclaimed that "America is the greatest country in the world! I'm going to tell everyone!" The voter later brought more Vietnamese voters to the polls. At the other end of the spectrum, when a white poll worker began asking for identification and questioning the citizenship of Hispanic voters, the poll worker was promptly fired and removed from the polls.

Witness also the sharp increase in participation by previously excluded citizens once the language barrier is removed. In San Diego County, Hispanic and Filipino voter registration rose by more than 21 percent during the six-month period after resolution of the lawsuit, and Vietnamese registration rose by more than 37 percent during the same period. In the very different rural setting of Yakima County, Washington, the number of Hispanic registered voters among a largely farm worker population increased by more than 24 percent within six months of resolution of the Justice Department's Section 203 lawsuit against that county.

Increases in minority voter registration and assistance, as well as the dramatic improvement in the election experience for minority language citizens ripple beyond the polling place. They can determine the outcome of elections. Following a successful Section 203 lawsuit in Passaic, New Jersey, the Department of Justice withdrew its Section 2 challenge to the at-large election system there. The doubling of Vietnamese turnout in Harris County, Texas, led to the election of the first Vietnamese candidate in history to the Texas legislature. That candidate, Hubert Vo, actually defeated the incumbent Chair of the House Appropriations Committee by 16 votes out of more than 40,000 cast for the first Democratic gain of a seat in the Texas House since at least 1972. The five-fold increase in bilingual poll workers in Boston was followed by the election of Sam Woo to the City Council.

Conclusion

The election of candidates to public office, however, is only ancillary to the language assistance provisions' most simple and direct function: bilingual elections let citizens of the United States participate in the life of the country freely and equally. The issue is less about winning elections or the representation of racial and ethnic groups in elected bodies – although both sometimes come, too – than about the dignity of the individual. The provisions eliminate the last literacy test for voters, and free Hispanic, Asian American, Alaska Native, and American Indian citizens to vote with the same information and independence that African Americans first enjoyed in the early months after passage of the Act. Like all citizens, they deserve no less. Ultimately, the language assistance provisions of the VRA make our nation more just by helping to fulfill the self-evident truth that governments derive their just powers from the consent of the governed.

Appendix A

Examples of Bilingual Voting Materials

Section 203 requires that with some narrow exceptions, all voting materials provided in English also must be provided in the language of the applicable minority groups or sub-groups that triggered coverage. According to the U.S. Department of Justice, bilingual voting materials shall encompass "voter registration through activities related to conducting elections, including, for example, the issuance, at any time during the year, of notifications, announcements, or other informational materials concerning the opportunity to register, the deadline for voter registration, the time, places and subject matters of elections, and the absentee voting process."[1] It includes materials provided by mail, public notices, registration materials, polling place activities and materials, and publicity concerning the availability of minority language materials.[2] The Justice Department recommends that the definition of voting materials "be broadly construed to apply to all stages of the electoral process"[3] (Chapter 4).

This Appendix provides examples of bilingual voting materials. It is illustrative of some of the materials that generally must be provided in the covered languages. Bilingual materials must offer LEP voters effective assistance and equal access to the same registration and voting opportunities as English-speaking voters. A covered jurisdiction and its election officials are responsible for meeting that standard.

1 28 C.F.R. § 55.15.

2 28 C.F.R. § 55.18.

3 28 C.F.R. § 55.15.

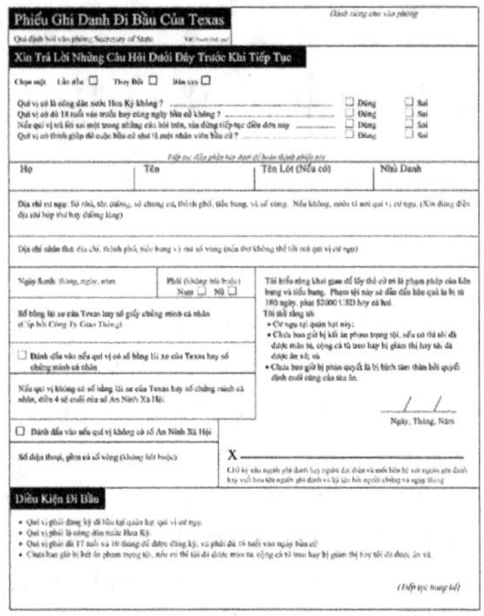

Figure A.1 Bilingual voter registration forms
A voter registration form does an LEP voter little good if he or she cannot read it. The State of New York provides voter registration forms in several languages, including Korean (left). The State of Texas provides bilingual voter registration forms such as this one in Vietnamese (right), which is offered because of the coverage of Harris County (Houston) for Vietnamese (Appendices B–C).

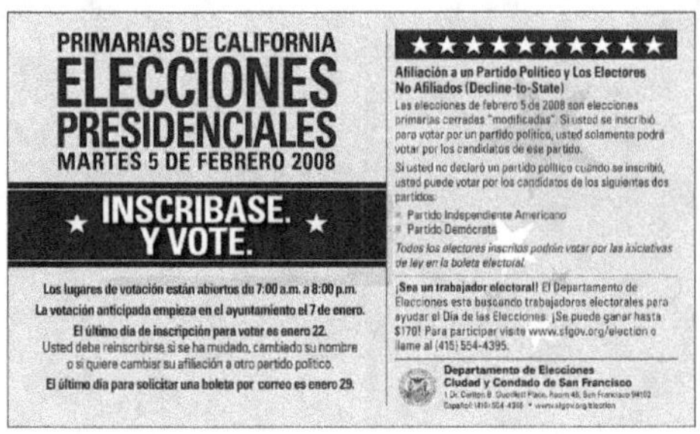

Figure A.2 Spanish publicity about election deadlines
All announcements about election information published in English also should be provided in the covered language. Passaic County, New Jersey, advertised voter registration deadlines and locations in Spanish for the 2000 election (left). San Francisco County, California, advertised information about the February 2008 presidential primary in Spanish, including a request for Spanish-speaking poll workers (right).

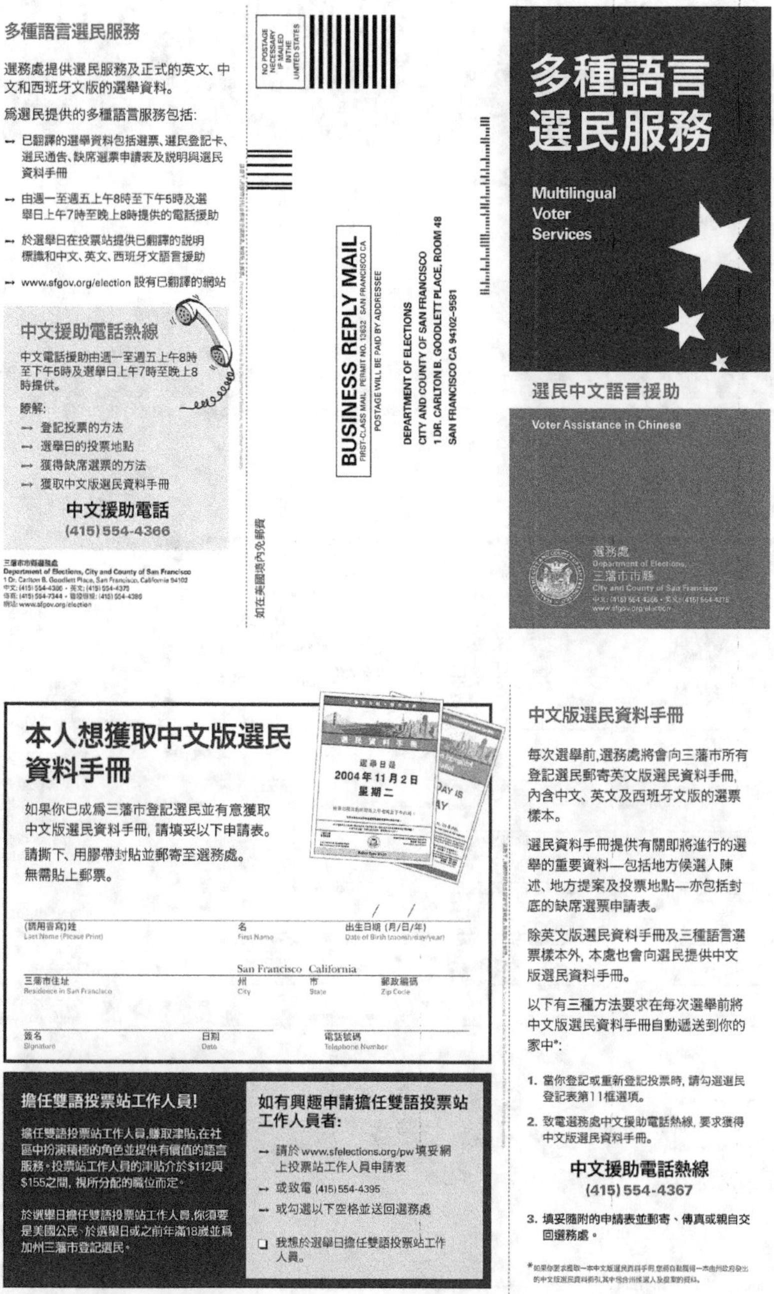

Figure A.3 Chinese brochure about language assistance services for voters

Language assistance does voters little good if they do not know about it. San Francisco County, California, distributes brochures with information about its language services for registration and voting activities in several languages, including Chinese (above).

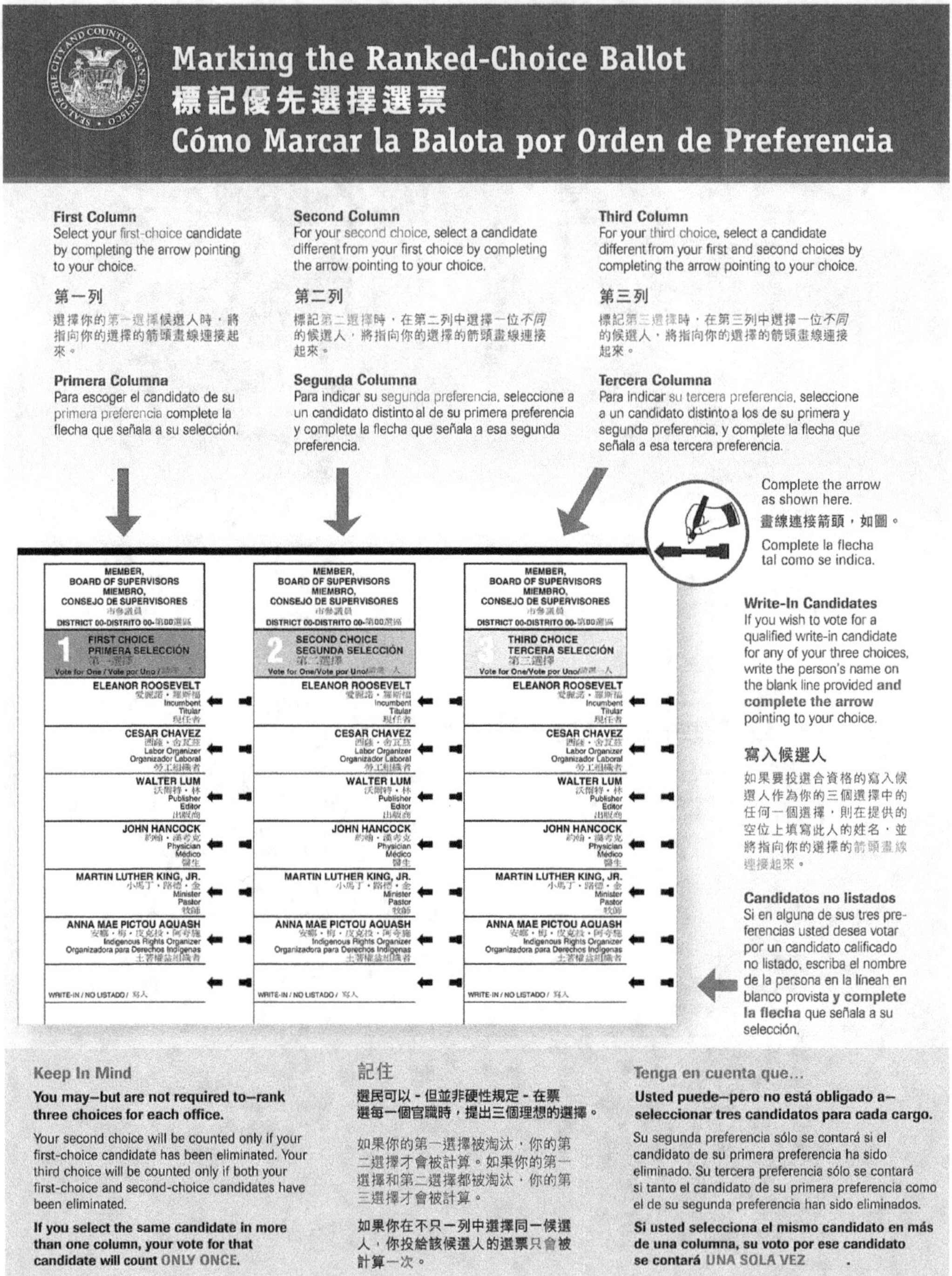

Marking the Ranked-Choice Ballot
標記優先選擇選票
Cómo Marcar la Balota por Orden de Preferencia

First Column
Select your first-choice candidate by completing the arrow pointing to your choice.

第一列
選擇你的第一選擇候選人時，將指向你的選擇的箭頭畫線連接起來。

Primera Columna
Para escoger el candidato de su primera preferencia complete la flecha que señala a su selección.

Second Column
For your second choice, select a candidate different from your first choice by completing the arrow pointing to your choice.

第二列
標記第二選擇時，在第二列中選擇一位*不同*的候選人，將指向你的選擇的箭頭畫線連接起來。

Segunda Columna
Para indicar su segunda preferencia, seleccione a un candidato distinto al de su primera preferencia y complete la flecha que señala a esa segunda preferencia.

Third Column
For your third choice, select a candidate different from your first and second choices by completing the arrow pointing to your choice.

第三列
標記第三選擇時，在第三列中選擇一位*不同*的候選人，將指向你的選擇的箭頭畫線連接起來。

Tercera Columna
Para indicar su tercera preferencia, seleccione a un candidato distinto a los de su primera y segunda preferencia, y complete la flecha que señala a esa tercera preferencia.

Complete the arrow as shown here.
畫線連接箭頭，如圖。
Complete la flecha tal como se indica.

Write-In Candidates
If you wish to vote for a qualified write-in candidate for any of your three choices, write the person's name on the blank line provided **and complete the arrow** pointing to your choice.

寫入候選人
如果要投選合資格的寫入候選人作為你的三個選擇中的任何一個選擇，則在提供的空位上填寫此人的姓名，並將指向你的選擇的箭頭畫線連接起來。

Candidatos no listados
Si en alguna de sus tres preferencias usted desea votar por un candidato calificado no listado, escriba el nombre de la persona en la líneah en blanco provista **y complete la flecha** que señala a su selección.

Keep In Mind
You may—but are not required to—rank three choices for each office.

Your second choice will be counted only if your first-choice candidate has been eliminated. Your third choice will be counted only if both your first-choice and second-choice candidates have been eliminated.

If you select the same candidate in more than one column, your vote for that candidate will count ONLY ONCE.

記住
選民可以 - 但並非硬性規定 - 在票選每一個官職時，提出三個理想的選擇。

如果你的第一選擇被淘汰，你的第二選擇才會被計算。如果你的第一選擇和第二選擇都被淘汰，你的第三選擇才會被計算。

如果你在不只一列中選擇同一候選人，你投給該候選人的選票只會被計算一次。

Tenga en cuenta que…
Usted puede—pero no está obligado a—seleccionar tres candidatos para cada cargo.

Su segunda preferencia sólo se contará si el candidato de su primera preferencia ha sido eliminado. Su tercera preferencia sólo se contará si tanto el candidato de su primera preferencia como el de su segunda preferencia han sido eliminados.

Si usted selecciona el mismo candidato en más de una columna, su voto por ese candidato se contará UNA SOLA VEZ.

Figure A.4 Multilingual publicity about casting a ranked-choice ballot
Changes in the method of casting a ballot, such as the use of new voting equipment, often are overlooked by jurisdictions when they prepare bilingual voter information materials. This San Francisco County, California, publicity flyer provides instructions in English, Chinese, and Spanish on how to mark a ranked-order ballot.

Figure A.5 Multilingual directions to the polling place
All English language signs at polling places should be provided in the covered languages, including signs directing voters to the polling place. This multilingual sign in English, Spanish, and Chinese is used by San Francisco County, California.

Figure A.6 Multilingual poll worker and voter stickers
Poll worker nametags can facilitate the availability, use, and effectiveness of language assistance at polling places. Name tags allow LEP voters to identify poll workers who are bilingual in their language and available to offer language assistance. They can break the ice with LEP voters by making them feel welcomed in the polling place. If a poll worker engages in misconduct or a designated translator is unable to offer language assistance, name tags allow the voter, federal observers, or other election officials to readily identify the poll worker or translator and take appropriate corrective measures. The four name tags on the top are used by San Francisco County, California, and are provided, clockwise from the top left, in Russian, English, Spanish, and Chinese.

Simple gestures, such as providing "I voted" stickers in the covered language promote pride in LEP voters. The "I registered" (bottom left) and "I voted" (bottom right) stickers are used by San Francisco County, California, and are written in English, Chinese, and Spanish.

We can assist you in English, Mandarin, Cantonese and Spanish!

If a bilingual pollworker is not available, there is an Election Official who speaks your language who will assist you by phone. If you need a phone to make this call, ask a pollworker or point to the red phone on this sign.

(?) Information (including polling place location): 415-554-4375

我們能用國語或粵語協助你！

如果雙語投票站工作人員不能提供你所需的語言協助, 你可由會講你的語言的選務處職員以電話溝通來協助你。如果你需要使用電話機打這個電話，請詢問投票站工作人員或用手指向此標牌上的紅色電話機圖案。

本投票站的雙語工作人員是:

__________ __________ __________

(?) 中文協助電話：415-554-4367

¡Podemos asistirle en español!

Si no hay un trabajador electoral bilingüe disponible, un funcionario electoral podrá asistirle en español por teléfono. Si necesita un teléfono para hacer esta llamada, pídale uno a un trabajador electoral o señale el teléfono rojo de este rótulo.

Los trabajadores electorales bilingües en este lugar de votación son:

__________ __________ __________

(?) Asistencia en español: 415-554-4366

Figure A.7 Sign advertising availability of language assistance by telephone
Sometimes a polling place might not have a poll worker bilingual in English and the covered language. Where that occurs, a bilingual or multilingual sign advertising the availability of language assistance by telephone is particularly useful, with one caveat. A covered jurisdiction will violate Section 203 if it fails to staff polling places with a sufficient number of bilingual poll workers where they are needed. This sign is used by San Francisco County, California, and is written in English, Chinese, and Spanish.

U.S. Election Assistance Commission

C

- **call an election:** 選挙を求める
- **calling special elections:** 特別選挙を求める
- **campaign:** 選挙運動

  See also: running for office, candidate
- **campaign contributions:** 選挙運動寄付金
- **campaign disclosure:** 選挙運動開示
- **campaign expense report:** 選挙運動費報告
- **campaign finance:** 選挙運動資金
- **campaign finance disclosure:** 選挙運動資金の開示
- **campaign finance disclosure statements:** 選挙運動財務の開示報告書
- **campaign finance laws:** 選挙資金法
- **campaign finance report:** 選挙運動資金報告
- **campaign finance reporting requirements:** 選挙運動報告条件
- **campaign financing:** 選挙運動資金調達
- **campaign materials:** 選挙運動資材
- **campaign signs:** 選挙運動のサイン
- **campaign spending:** 選挙運動資金の用途
- **cancel:** 取り消す、取り消し
- **cancellation:** 取り消し

  See also: cancellation notices, cancellation of registration
- **cancellation notices:** 取り消し通知
- **cancellation of registration:** 登録取り消し
- **candidacy:** 立候補
- **candidate:** 候補者

  See also: candidate registration, running for office, acceptance of candidacy

  Definition: Person contending in a contest for office. A candidate may be explicitly presented as one of the choices on the ballot or may be a write-in candidate.
- **candidate committee:** 候補者委員会
- **candidate nomination procedures:** 候補者指名手順
- **candidate petitions:** 候補者陳情
- **candidate registration:** 候補者登録

  See also: running for office, candidate, acceptance of candidacy
- **candidate roster:** 候補者名簿
- **candidate statement:** 候補者声明
- **candidate withdrawal periods:** 候補撤回期間
- **candidates list:** 候補者リスト
- **candidate's profile:** 候補者のプロフィール
- **canvass :** 勧誘する、遊説する、開票点検する

  Definition: Compilation of election returns and validation of the outcome that forms the basis of the official results by political subdivision.

GLOSSARY OF KEY ELECTION TERMS • *English-Japanese* 18

U.S. Election Assistance Commission

- **運転免許証:** driver's license
- **運輸省:** Department of Transportation

え

- **永久障害証書:** certificate of permanent disability
- **衛星位置:** satellite location
- **衛星投票ステーション:** satellite voting stations
- **永続事前投票者:** permanent advance voter

  説明: 時には永続不在投票者と呼ばれる。
- **永続的:** permanent
- **永続的に病気あるいは身体障害を持つ:** permanently ill or disabled
- **永続不在投票の申し込み:** permanent absentee application
- **永続不在投票者:** permanent absentee voter
- **永続不在投票者の地位:** permanent absentee voter status
- **選ぶ:** choose, elect, select

  参照: 選択する、選別、選択

  例: 投票したい候補者の名を選びます。*(Example: Select the name of the candidate you wish to vote for.)*
- **延長時間:** extended hours, extension

  説明: 例として「延長期間」または「投票時間の延長」。
- **エントリー:** entry

お

- **オーディオ投票:** audio ballot

  説明: 一連の公職に対する投票選択が書面でなく、口頭で示されたもの。
- **オーバルに書き込む:** fill in the oval
- **オペレーティング·システム:** operating system
- **オンライン投票:** e-voting
- **オンライン投票者登録:** EZ Voter Registration

  参照: 投票民登録、投票登録をする

  例: 投票者登録により、個人がオンライン投票の登録ができるようになる。*(Example: The new EZ Voter Registration allows individuals to register to vote online)*
- **穏健派の:** moderate

か

- **ガイドライン:** guidelines

  参照: 方針

  例: 州が選挙事務遂行のために一般的なガイドラインを出す。*(Example: The state provides general guidelines for administering elections.)*
- **会員寄付:** member contributions
- **会議:** convention

主要選挙用語集 • 日本語 - 英語 78

Figure A.8 Bilingual glossary of election terms

Election materials and information can contain some very technical terms that are difficult for bilingual translators to accurately translate on-the-spot. One of the keys to effective language assistance is to make available to bilingual translators, others offering assistance to LEP voters, and the LEP voters themselves the tools necessary to obtain clear, complete, and accurate translations from English into the covered language, and vice versa. Bilingual glossaries of common election terms increasingly are used by covered jurisdictions as one of those tools.

Figure A.8 includes excerpts from two pages of a bilingual Japanese-English glossary of election terms prepared by the U.S. Election Assistance Commission (EAC). The EAC provides its bilingual glossaries in two parts. The first part defines election terms in English and translates them into the covered language, in this case Japanese (left). The second part does the same thing in the covered language, in this case Japanese, and translates the terms back into English (right).

As of 2008, the EAC offered its bilingual election glossaries in six languages covered by Section 203 of the VRA. Five are in Asian languages: Chinese, Japanese, Korean, Tagalog (Filipino), and Vietnamese. The sixth glossary is available in Spanish. Those glossaries are available at http://www.eac.gov/voter/language-accessibility-program-1. At an EAC meeting in Albuquerque, New Mexico, in June 2008, EAC officials discussed the possibility of providing the bilingual election glossaries in other languages, including Alaska Native and American Indian languages.

Several jurisdictions covered by Alaska Native or American Indian languages offer or are preparing to offer their own bilingual election glossaries. Counties encompassing the Navajo Nation in Arizona, New Mexico, and Utah use a Navajo glossary. Maricopa County, Arizona, uses a bilingual election glossary for the Tohono O'odham language. *See* http://recorder.maricopa.gov/pdf/TohonoGlossaryFall2006.pdf. Certain counties in South Dakota reportedly are developing a bilingual election glossary in the Lakota dialect of the Sioux language. The State of Alaska currently is developing a bilingual election glossary in the Yup'ik (Alaska Native) language, in response to the preliminary injunction entered against it in *Nick v. City of Bethel* (Chapter 10).

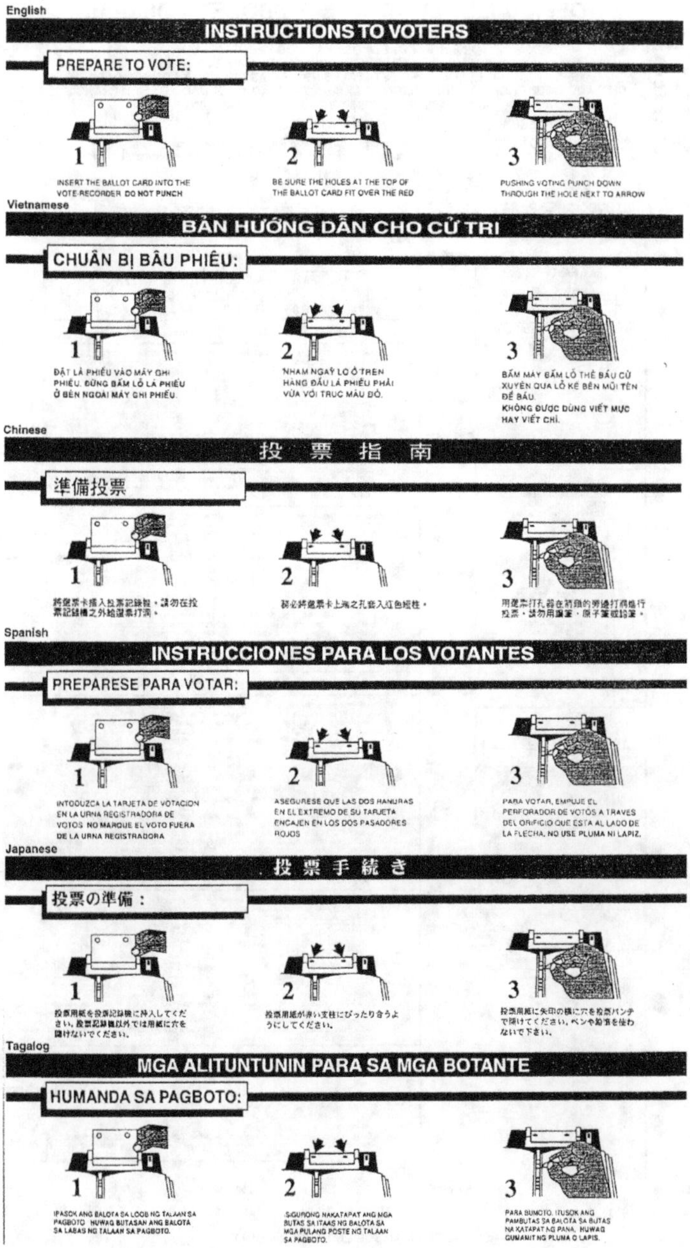

Figure A.9 Multilingual instructions on how to use a voting machine

When a covered jurisdiction provides written instructions in English on how to use a voting machine, it also should provide those written instructions in each covered language. Los Angeles County, California, provided these voting machine instructions in English and five other languages before the July 2002 Census determinations, when it also became covered for the Korean language (Appendix B).

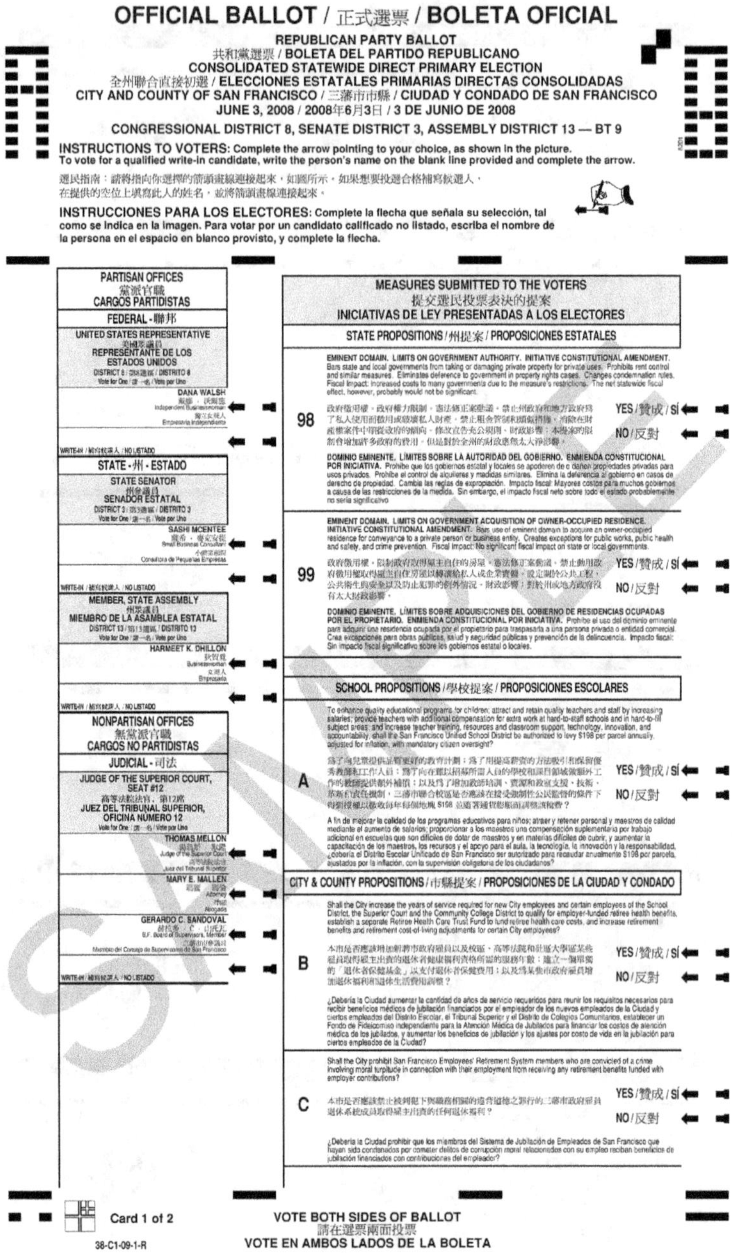

OFFICIAL BALLOT / 正式選票 / BOLETA OFICIAL

REPUBLICAN PARTY BALLOT
共和黨選票 / BOLETA DEL PARTIDO REPUBLICANO
CONSOLIDATED STATEWIDE DIRECT PRIMARY ELECTION
全州聯合直接初選 / ELECCIONES ESTATALES PRIMARIAS DIRECTAS CONSOLIDADAS
CITY AND COUNTY OF SAN FRANCISCO / 三藩市市縣 / CIUDAD Y CONDADO DE SAN FRANCISCO
JUNE 3, 2008 / 2008年6月3日 / 3 DE JUNIO DE 2008

CONGRESSIONAL DISTRICT 8, SENATE DISTRICT 3, ASSEMBLY DISTRICT 13 — BT 9

INSTRUCTIONS TO VOTERS: Complete the arrow pointing to your choice, as shown in the picture. To vote for a qualified write-in candidate, write the person's name on the blank line provided and complete the arrow.

INSTRUCCIONES PARA LOS ELECTORES: Complete la flecha que señala su selección, tal como se indica en la imagen. Para votar por un candidato calificado no listado, escriba el nombre de la persona en el espacio en blanco provisto, y complete la flecha.

PARTISAN OFFICES / 黨派官職 / CARGOS PARTIDISTAS

FEDERAL - 聯邦

UNITED STATES REPRESENTATIVE / REPRESENTANTE DE LOS ESTADOS UNIDOS

DANA WALSH

STATE - 州 - ESTADO

STATE SENATOR / SENADOR ESTATAL

SASHI MCENTEE

MEMBER, STATE ASSEMBLY / MIEMBRO DE LA ASAMBLEA ESTATAL

HARMEET K. DHILLON

NONPARTISAN OFFICES / 無黨派官職 / CARGOS NO PARTIDISTAS

JUDICIAL - 司法

JUDGE OF THE SUPERIOR COURT, SEAT #12 / JUEZ DEL TRIBUNAL SUPERIOR, OFICINA NUMERO 12

THOMAS MELLON

MARY E. MALLEN

GERARDO C. SANDOVAL

MEASURES SUBMITTED TO THE VOTERS / 提交選民投票表決的提案 / INICIATIVAS DE LEY PRESENTADAS A LOS ELECTORES

STATE PROPOSITIONS / 州提案 / PROPOSICIONES ESTATALES

98 YES / 贊成 / SÍ NO / 反對

99 YES / 贊成 / SÍ NO / 反對

SCHOOL PROPOSITIONS / 學校提案 / PROPOSICIONES ESCOLARES

A YES / 贊成 / SÍ NO / 反對

CITY & COUNTY PROPOSITIONS / 市縣提案 / PROPOSICIONES DE LA CIUDAD Y CONDADO

B YES / 贊成 / SÍ NO / 反對

C YES / 贊成 / SÍ NO / 反對

Card 1 of 2

VOTE BOTH SIDES OF BALLOT
請在選票兩面投票
VOTE EN AMBOS LADOS DE LA BOLETA

38-C1-09-1-R

Figure A.10 Multilingual ballot

Covered jurisdictions should provide ballots, like other written registration and voting materials, in the languages that triggered coverage. This multilingual ballot in English, Chinese, and Spanish, was used by San Francisco County, California, in the statewide Republican primary in June 2008. Note that all of the ballot propositions also are translated into each of the covered languages.

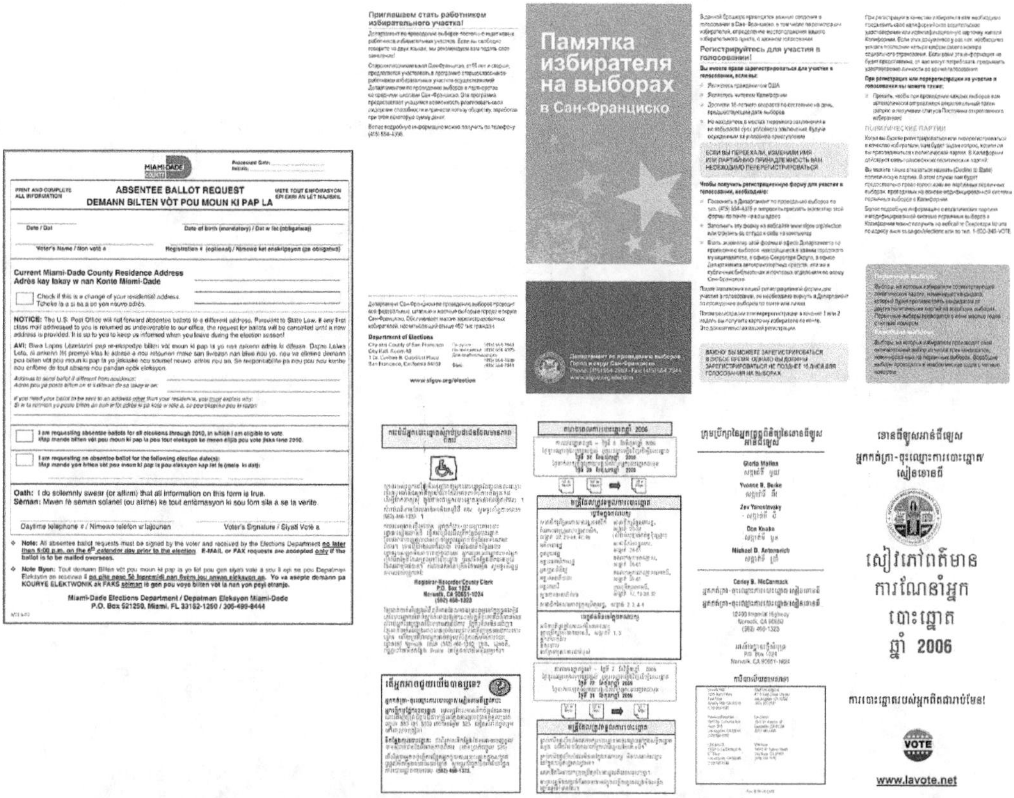

Figure A.11 Voting materials in languages not covered by Section 203
Many jurisdictions around the United States offer written language assistance in languages that are not covered by Section 203. These examples include, clockwise from the left: an absentee ballot application written in Creole used by Miami-Dade County, Florida; a voter information pamphlet written in Russian disseminated by San Francisco County, California; and a voter information pamphlet written in Cambodian that is distributed by Los Angeles County, California.

Appendix B

Jurisdictions Covered under Sections 4(f)(4) and 203 of the Voting Rights Act, by State, Political Subdivision, Language, and Year of Census Determination

This Appendix summarizes the bilingual voting coverage determinations made by the Director of the Census between 1975 and 2002 (Chapters 3–5). For each covered jurisdiction, it identifies the language covered and the year the coverage determination was made. The four languages groups are identified as follows: Alaska Native is "AN"; American Indian is "AI"; Asian American is "AS"; and Spanish is "SP." The numbers in parentheses that are after the language group identify the specific languages that are covered for that group. For example, Los Angeles County, California, lists the following for the 2002 determinations: "AS (1, 2, 3, 4, 5), SP", which indicates that for the 2002 Census determinations, Los Angeles County was covered for five Asian languages (Chinese, Filipino/Tagalog, Japanese, Korean, and Vietnamese) and for Spanish. The complete list of numbers used to identify each specific language is at the end of this Appendix, organized by language groups.

A symbol next to the language group denotes the section of the VRA that triggered coverage. If there is no symbol, that language group is only covered under Section 203 of the Act. For example, California lists "SP" for the 2002 coverage determinations, indicating statewide coverage for Spanish under Section 203 only. A cross "†" indicates that the language is covered only under Section 4(f)(4). For example, Alaska lists "AN†" for the 1975–1977 coverage determinations, indicating statewide coverage for Alaska Native languages that is only under Section 4(f)(4). An asterisk "*" indicates that the language is covered under both Section 4(f)(4) and Section 203. For example, Apache County, Arizona, lists "AI*" for the 1975–1977 coverage determinations, indicating coverage for American Indian languages under both Section 4(f)(4) and Section 203.

Initial determinations under Section 4(f)(4) of the Act were made following the enactment of that section in 1975. There have been no further determinations under that section. In some cases, jurisdictions that were covered for minority languages under Section 4(f)(4) have bailed out; where that has occurred, a footnote is provided with information about the bailout. For all other Section 4(f)(4) covered jurisdictions, the determinations remain in effect. Jurisdictions that continue to be covered by Section 4(f)(4) today are identified with the covered language in bold type. For example, the entry for Jackson County, North Carolina, is "**AI***", which indicates that the county continues to be covered by Section 4(f)(4) for American Indian languages. More information about coverage determinations under Section 4(f)(4) is provided in Chapter 3.

The Section 203 coverage determinations were made during four different time periods. The table illustrates how coverage for the four language groups evolved and changed between Census determinations. There are several reasons for those changes. In some cases, Census terminology or data groupings for particular languages changed. For example, American Indian languages such as Hopi and Zuni, which were separately identified in the 1992 determinations, were grouped together as "Pueblo" American Indian languages in 2002. In other cases, Census terminology for geographic areas changed; the most dramatic changes in geographic terminology came in Alaska, as explained below in the note accompanying the state's summary of determinations. Demographic changes also explain some of the differences between the determinations. But one of the most significant causes of the changes is attributable to amendments to the Section 203 coverage formula in 1982 and 1992, which are described in Chapter 4.

The first Section 203 determinations occurred between 1975 and 1977, immediately following the enactment of the section. Those initial determinations were made on several different occasions during that two-year period. In some cases, jurisdictions or particular languages in jurisdictions were inadvertently excluded from earlier determinations, resulting in their addition later on. In other cases, certain jurisdictions were removed as a result of later corrections, as identified in the table. For example, Manhomen County, Minnesota, includes the following for the 1975–1977 determinations: "AI (deleted Aug. 4, 1976)." That indicates that the county initially was identified for coverage of American Indian languages, but was later deleted on the specified date. One jurisdiction originally covered under Section 203 bailed out: in 1979, the United States consented to the bailout of Maui County, Hawaii, for Japanese because the illiteracy rate for that language group no longer exceeded the national average. *Doi v. Bell*, the case that led to Maui County's bailout for Japanese, is discussed in Chapter 4.

The coverage determinations for 1984 were made shortly after Congress reauthorized Section 203 for ten years in 1982, using 1980 Census data. The coverage determinations for 1992 were made using 1990 Census data, almost immediately after Section 203 was reauthorized for 15 years in 1992. The 2002 determinations, which are described in greater detail in Chapter 5, were made following the release of data from the 2000 decennial Census. Appendix C includes the Census data used for the 2002 determinations. Summary tables depicting changes in coverage by state and by language group are provided in Chapters 4 and 5.

ALASKA

Political Subdivision Covered 1975–1977		
State of Alaska	**AN**†	**Note:** Alaska has no counties, and the names, boundaries, and designations of the political subdivisions have changed since the U.S. Census Bureau made its first Section 203 determinations in the 1970s. In the Section 203 determinations made in 1975–1977, the U.S. Census Bureau used the 22 Election Districts created by the State of Alaska as a result of the 1970 reapportionment. The boundaries of these Election Districts corresponded roughly to those of the 29 Census Divisions used to tabulate data for Alaska in the 1970 Census. The names are provided in parentheses to the left. Beginning with the 1980 Census, the U.S. Census Bureau tabulated data in Alaska according to geographic areas designated as Boroughs for the more populous regions or as Census Areas for more sparsely populated rural areas. As a result, the Section 203 determinations for Alaska in the 1970s are treated separately from those of the other Section 203 determinations, which used different geographical boundaries. Despite these differences in geographic boundaries, it is still possible to make some comparisons between the 1970 determinations and subsequent determinations. Almost every county-level political subdivision of the State of Alaska was independently covered for Alaska Native languages, with the exception of eight urban Election Districts: Election District 6 (Palmer) and Election Districts 7–12 (Anchorage).
Election District 1 (Ketchikan – Prince of Wales)	AN	
Election District 2 (Wrangell – Petersburg)	AN	
Election District 3 (Sitka)	AN	
Election District 4 (Juneau – Lynn Canal)	AN	
Election District 5 (Cordova – Valdez – Seward)	AN	
Election District 13 (Kenai – Cook Outlet)	AN	
Election District 14 (Kodiak)	AN	
Election District 15 (Aleutian Chain)	AN	
Election District 16 (Bristol Bay)	AN	
Election District 17 (Bethel)	AN	
Election District 18 (Wade Hampton)	AN	
Election District 19 (Yukon – Tanana)	AN	
Election District 21 (Barrow – Kobuk)	AN	
Election District 22 (Nome)	AN	

Political Subdivision Covered	**1984**	**1992**	**2002**
Aleutians East Borough		AN (8)	
Aleutians West Census Area		AN (6)	AN (6)
Bethel Census Area	AN (8)	AN (8), AI (9, 13)	AN (8), AI (51, 52)
Bristol Bay Borough		AN (8)	
Denali Borough			AN (7)
Dillingham Census Area	AN (8)	AN (8)	AN (8, 10), AI (51)
Kenai Peninsula Borough		AN (8)	AN (6), AI (52)
Kobuk Census Area	AN (8)		
Kodiak Island Borough		AN (6, 8)	AS (2)
Lake and Peninsula Borough		AN (6, 8), AI (13)	AN (6, 7, 8)
Nome Census Area	AN (8)	AN (8)	AN (8)
North Slope Borough	AN (8)	AN (8)	AN (8), AI (52)
Northwest Arctic Borough		AN (8)	AN (8, 10)
Skagway-Yakutat-Angoon Census Area		AI (41)	
Southeast Fairbanks Census Area		AI (13)	AN (7, 10)
Valdez-Cordova Census Area		AI (13)	AN (7)
Wade Hampton Census Area	AN (8)	AN (8)	AN (8), AI (16, 52)
Yukon-Koyukuk Census Area	AI (13)	AN (8), AI (13, 27)	AN (7, 8), AI (51)

ARIZONA				
Political Subdivision Covered	**1975–1977**	**1984**	**1992**	**2002**
State of Arizona	**SP**†			
Apache County	**AI***, SP	AI (31)	AI (12, 31, 49)	AI (12, 31, 35)
Cochise County	SP	SP		SP
Coconino County	**AI***, SP	AI (31)	AI (23, 24, 31)	AI (31, 35)
Gila County	AI, SP		AI (12)	AI (12)
Graham County	AI, SP	SP	AI (12)	AI (12)
Greenlee County	SP	SP	SP	SP
Maricopa County	SP		AI (34, 47), SP	AI (42), SP
Mohave County	SP			
Navajo County	**AI***, SP	AI (31)	AI (12, 24, 31)	AI (12, 31, 35)
Pima County	SP		AI (34), SP	AI (42, 46), SP
Pinal County	**AI***, SP	SP	AI (12, 34)	AI (12, 42)
Santa Cruz County	SP	SP	SP	SP
Yavapai County	SP			
Yuma County	SP	SP	AI (20, 48), SP	AI (48), SP

CALIFORNIA				
Political Subdivision Covered	**1975–1977**	**1984**	**1992**	**2002**
State of California				SP
Alameda County	SP		AS (1), SP	AS (1), SP
Amador County	SP			
Colusa County	SP		AI (45)	SP
Contra Costa County	SP			SP
Fresno County	SP	SP	SP	SP
Imperial County	SP	SP	SP	AI (48, 50), SP
Inyo County	AI		AI (39)	
Kern County	SP	SP	SP	SP
Kings County	**SP***	SP	SP	SP
Lake County			AI (39)	
Lassen County	SP			
Los Angeles County	SP		AS (1, 2, 3, 5), SP	AS (1, 2, 3, 4, 5), SP
Madera County	SP	SP		SP
Merced County	**SP***			SP
Monterey County	SP		SP	SP
Napa County	SP			
Orange County	SP		AS (5), SP	AS (1, 4, 5), SP
Placer County	SP			
Riverside County	SP		SP	AI (50), SP
Sacramento County	SP			SP
San Benito County	SP	SP	SP	SP
San Bernardino County	SP		SP	SP
San Diego County	SP		SP	AS (2), SP
San Francisco County	AS (1), SP		AS (1)	AS (1), SP
San Joaquin County	SP			SP

CALIFORNIA (Continued)				
Political Subdivision Covered	**1975–1977**	**1984**	**1992**	**2002**
San Luis Obispo County	SP			
San Mateo County	SP			AS (1), SP
Santa Barbara County	SP			SP
Santa Clara County	SP		SP	AS (1, 2, 5), SP
Santa Cruz County	SP			
Sierra County	SP			
Solano County	SP			
Sonoma County	SP			
Stanislaus County	SP			SP
Sutter County	SP			
Tulare County	SP	SP	SP	SP
Tuolumne County	SP			
Ventura County	SP		SP	SP
Yolo County	SP			
Yuba County	**SP***			

COLORADO				
Political Subdivision Covered	**1975–1977**	**1984**	**1992**	**2002**
Adams County	SP			
Alamosa County	SP	SP	SP	SP
Archuleta County	SP	SP	SP	
Bent County	SP	SP	SP	
Boulder County	SP			
Chafee County	SP			
Clear Creek County	SP			
Conejos County	SP	SP	SP	SP
Costilla County	SP	SP	SP	SP
Crowley County	SP			SP
Delta County	SP			
Denver County	SP			SP
Eagle County	SP			
El Paso County	SP*[1]			
Fremont County	SP			
Huerfano County	SP	SP		
Jackson County	SP			
Lake County	SP			
La Plata County	SP		SP	AI (31, 43)
Las Animas County	SP	SP	SP	

1 El Paso County, Colorado, was removed from Section 4(f)(4) coverage after bringing a successful bailout action in 1984. *See Board of County Comm'rs v. United States*, case no. 84–1626 (D.D.C. 1984). El Paso County had dropped an earlier bailout lawsuit it filed in 1977. In the 1984 case, the county presented a community study that showed "a substantial majority of its citizens of Spanish origin were fluent in English and that an effective bilingual election program had been implemented to meet the voting needs of the citizens who had difficulty with the English language." The United States consented to bailout based upon the county's demonstration that it had not used English-only elections in the preceding ten years to disenfranchise language minority voters. Paul F. Hancock & Lora L. Tredway, *The Bailout Standard of the Voting Rights Act: An Incentive to End Discrimination*, 17 Urb. Law. 379, 414–15 (1985).

COLORADO (Continued)				
Political Subdivision Covered	**1975–1977**	**1984**	**1992**	**2002**
Mesa County	SP			
Moffat County	SP			
Montezuma County	AI, SP		AI (43)	AI (31, 43)
Montrose County	SP			
Morgan County	SP			
Otero County	SP	SP	SP	SP
Prowers County	SP			
Pueblo County	SP	SP		
Rio Grande County	SP	SP	SP	SP
Saguache County	SP	SP	SP	SP
San Juan County	SP			
San Miguel County	SP			
Sedgwick County	SP			
Weld County	SP			

CONNECTICUT				
Political Subdivision Covered	**1975–1977**	**1984**	**1992**	**2002**
Bridgeport (Fairfield County)	SP	SP	SP	SP
Hartford (Hartford County)		SP	SP	SP
Meriden (New Haven County)				SP
New Britain (Hartford County)			SP	SP
New Haven (New Haven County)				SP
Waterbury (New Haven County)				SP
Windham (Windham County)			SP	SP

FLORIDA				
Political Subdivision Covered	**1975–1977**	**1984**	**1992**	**2002**
Broward County			AI (28, 30), SP	AI (36), SP
Collier County	**SP***		AI (28)	AI (36)
Glades County	AI		AI (30)	AI (36)
Hardee County	**SP***	SP	SP	SP
Hendry County	**SP***		AI (28, 30)	SP
Hillsborough County	**SP***		SP	SP
Miami-Dade County (Dade County)	SP	SP	AI (28), SP	SP
Monroe County	**SP***			
Orange County			SP	SP
Osceola County				SP
Palm Beach County				SP

HAWAII				
Political Subdivision Covered	**1975–1977**	**1984**	**1992**	**2002**
State of Hawaii	AS (1, 2)			
Hawaii County	AS (2, 3)	AS (3)		

HAWAII (Continued)				
Political Subdivision Covered	**1975–1977**	**1984**	**1992**	**2002**
Honolulu County	AS (1, 2)[2]		AS (2, 3)	AS (1, 2, 3)
Kauai County	AS (2, 3)	AS (3)	AS (2)	
Maui County	AS (2, 3) (3 was deleted on July 26, 1979)[3]	AS (3)	AS (2)	AS (2)

IDAHO				
Political Subdivision Covered	**1975–1977**	**1984**	**1992**	**2002**
Bannock County			AI (37)	AI (51)
Bingham County	AI		AI (37)	AI (51)
Caribou County				AI (51)
Cassia County	SP			
Minidoka County		SP		
Owyhee County			AI (37)	AI (51)
Power County			AI (37)	AI (51)

ILLINOIS				
Political Subdivision Covered	**1975–1977**	**1984**	**1992**	**2002**
Cook County			SP	AS (1), SP
Kane County				SP

IOWA				
Political Subdivision Covered	**1975–1977**	**1984**	**1992**	**2002**
Tama County			AI (21)	

KANSAS				
Political Subdivision Covered	**1975–1977**	**1984**	**1992**	**2002**
Finney County	SP			SP
Ford County				SP
Grant County	SP			SP
Haskell County				SP

2 Honolulu County, Hawaii, was covered under Section 5 of the VRA, but not as a result of the language minority trigger in Section 4(f)(4) of the Act. Instead, the county was covered under the trigger in the original 1965 Act because Hawaii used a literacy test and the county's voter registration or participation was below 50 percent in the November 1964 Presidential Election (Hancock and Tredway 1985: 388–89). Honolulu County filed a bailout lawsuit in 1984. *See Waihee v. United States*, case no. 84–1694 (D.D.C. 1984). The United States consented to the bailout after the county established "that the English or Hawaiian language literacy test contained in … the Hawaii Constitution was not applied" in the county before or after it was repealed in 1968. In addition, Hawaii "demonstrated that Asian Americans who were unable to read English were able to register and vote" prior to and after the VRA was enacted in 1965 (Hancock and Tredway 1985: 415).

3 Japanese coverage in Maui County, Hawaii, under Section 203 of the Act was deleted on July 26, 1979. Coverage for Filipino/Tagalog in the county remained unaffected by that deletion. *See* 44 FED. REG. 43,719 (July 26, 1979). The United States consented to the bailout of Maui County, Hawaii, for Japanese because the illiteracy rate for that language group no longer exceeded the national average. Hawaii failed to make a similar showing for Filipino/Tagalog, which is why it remained covered in Maui County. *See Doi v. Bell*, 449 F. Supp. 267 (D. Haw. 1978). *Doi* is discussed in Chapter 4.

KANSAS (Continued)				
Political Subdivision Covered	**1975–1977**	**1984**	**1992**	**2002**
Kearny County				SP
Seward County				SP
Wichita County	SP			

LOUISIANA				
Political Subdivision Covered	**1975–1977**	**1984**	**1992**	**2002**
Allen Parish				AI (51)
Avoyelles Parish			AI (22)	
St. Bernard Parish	SP			

MAINE				
Political Subdivision Covered	**1975–1977**	**1984**	**1992**	**2002**
Passamaquoddy Pleasant Point Indian Reservation (Washington County)	AI			
Perry Town (Washington County)	AI (deleted Aug. 4, 1976)			

MARYLAND				
Political Subdivision Covered	**1975–1977**	**1984**	**1992**	**2002**
Montgomery County				SP

MASSACHUSETTS				
Political Subdivision Covered	**1975–1977**	**1984**	**1992**	**2002**
Boston (Suffolk County)			SP	SP
Chelsea (Suffolk County)		SP	SP	SP
Holyoke (Hampden County)		SP	SP	SP
Lawrence (Essex County)		SP	SP	SP
Southbridge (Worcester County)				SP
Springfield (Hampden County)			SP	SP

MICHIGAN				
Political Subdivision Covered	**1975–1977**	**1984**	**1992**	**2002**
Adrian City (Lenawee County)	SP			
Buena Vista Township (Saginaw County)	**SP***			
Clyde Township (Allegan County)	**SP***	SP	SP	SP
Colfax Township (Oceana County)			SP	
Fennville City (Allegan County)		SP		
Grant Township (Newaygo County)	SP	SP		
Imlay Township (LaPeer County)	SP			

MICHIGAN (Continued)				
Political Subdivision Covered	**1975–1977**	**1984**	**1992**	**2002**
Madison Township (Lenawee County)	SP			
Orangeville Township (Barry County)	SP			
Saginaw City (Saginaw County)	SP			
Sugar Island Township (Chippewa County)	AI			
Zilwaukee Township (Saginaw County)			SP	

MINNESOTA				
Political Subdivision Covered	**1975–1977**	**1984**	**1992**	**2002**
Beltrami County	AI			
Cass County	AI			
Mahnomen County	AI (deleted Aug. 4, 1976)			

MISSISSIPPI				
Political Subdivision Covered	**1975–1977**	**1984**	**1992**	**2002**
Attala County				AI (17)
Jackson County				AI (17)
Jones County			AI (17)	AI (17)
Kemper County			AI (17)	AI (17)
Leake County			AI (17)	AI (17)
Neshoba County	AI		AI (17)	AI (17)
Newton County			AI (17)	AI (17)
Scott County				AI (17)
Winston County			AI (17)	AI (17)

MONTANA				
Political Subdivision Covered	**1975–1977**	**1984**	**1992**	**2002**
Big Horn County				AI (15)
Blaine County	AI			
Glacier County	AI			
Hill County	AI			
Lake County	AI			
Roosevelt County	AI			
Rosebud County	AI	AI (15)		AI (15)
Valley County	AI			

NEBRASKA				
Political Subdivision Covered	**1975–1977**	**1984**	**1992**	**2002**
Colfax County				SP
Scotts Bluff County	SP			
Sheridan County				AI (38)
Thurston County	AI			

NEVADA				
Political Subdivision Covered	**1975–1977**	**1984**	**1992**	**2002**
Clark County				SP
Elko County	AI, SP		AI (37)	AI (37, 51)
Humboldt County			AI (33)	AI (51)
Lyon County				AI (33)
Mineral County	AI			
Nye County	SP			AI (37)
White Pine County	SP			AI (37)

NEW JERSEY				
Political Subdivision Covered	**1975–1977**	**1984**	**1992**	**2002**
Bergen County				SP
Cumberland County				SP
Essex County			SP	SP
Hudson County		SP	SP	SP
Middlesex County			SP	SP
Passaic County		SP	SP	SP
Union County			SP	SP

NEW MEXICO				
Political Subdivision Covered	**1975–1977**	**1984**	**1992**	**2002**
State of New Mexico	AI, SP			SP
Bernalillo County	SP	SP	AI (26, 31, 40), SP	AI (31, 35), SP
Catron County	SP			AI (35)
Chaves County	SP	SP	SP	SP
Cibola County		AI (26), SP	AI (26, 31, 49), SP	AI (31, 35)
Colfax County	SP	SP		
Curry County	SP*[4]			
De Baca County	SP	SP		SP
Dona Ana County	SP	SP	SP	SP
Eddy County	SP	SP	SP	SP
Grant County	SP	SP	SP	SP
Guadalupe County	SP	SP	SP	SP
Harding County	SP	SP	SP	SP
Hidalgo County	SP	SP	SP	SP
Lea County	SP		SP	SP
Lincoln County	SP	SP		
Los Alamos County	SP			
Luna County	SP	SP	SP	SP
McKinley County	AI*, SP*[5]	AI (31), SP	AI (31, 49)	AI (31, 35)
Mora County	SP	SP	SP	SP

4 Curry County, New Mexico, was removed from Section 4(f)(4) coverage after bringing a successful bailout action in 1976. *See New Mexico v. United States*, case no. 76–0067 (D.D.C. July 30, 1976). It remained covered by Section 203 under the 1975–1977 determinations.

5 McKinley County, New Mexico, was removed from Section 4(f)(4) coverage after bringing a successful bailout action in 1976. *See New Mexico v. United States*, case no. 76–0067 (D.D.C. July 30, 1976). It remained covered by Section 203 under the 1975–1977 determinations.

NEW MEXICO (Continued)				
Political Subdivision Covered	**1975–1977**	**1984**	**1992**	**2002**
Otero County	SP*[6]			
Quay County	SP	SP	SP	
Rio Arriba County	AI, SP	SP	AI (25, 31), SP	AI (31), SP
Roosevelt County	SP	SP	SP	SP
San Juan County	AI, SP	AI (31)	AI (31)	AI (31, 43)
San Miguel County	SP	SP	SP	SP
Sandoval County	AI, SP	AI (26), SP	AI (25, 26, 31, 40)	AI (31, 35)
Santa Fe County	SP	SP	SP	AI (35), SP
Sierra County	SP			
Socorro County	SP	AI (31), SP	AI (31), SP	AI (31, 35), SP
Taos County	AI, SP	SP	AI (40), SP	AI (35), SP
Torrance County	SP	SP	SP	SP
Union County	SP		SP	SP
Valencia County	AI, SP	SP	AI (26, 40), SP	AI (35), SP

NEW YORK				
Political Subdivision Covered	**1975–1977**	**1984**	**1992**	**2002**
Bronx County	**SP***	SP	SP	SP
Franklin County			AI (29)	
Kings County	**SP***	SP	AS (1), SP	AS (1), SP
Nassau County				SP
New York County	SP	SP	AS (1), SP	AS (1), SP
Queens County			AS (1), SP	AS (1, 4), SP
Suffolk County			SP	SP
Westchester County			SP	SP

NORTH CAROLINA				
Political Subdivision Covered	**1975–1977**	**1984**	**1992**	**2002**
Hoke County	AI			
Jackson County	**AI***			
Robeson County	AI			
Swain County	AI			

NORTH DAKOTA				
Political Subdivision Covered	**1975–1977**	**1984**	**1992**	**2002**
Benson County	AI		AI (19)	
Dunn County	AI			
Eddy County			AI (19)	
McKenzie County	AI			
Mountrail County	AI			
Ramsey County			AI (19)	
Richland County				AI (38)
Rolette County	AI	AI (18)		

6 Otero County, New Mexico, was removed from Section 4(f)(4) coverage after bringing a successful bailout action in 1976. *See New Mexico v. United States*, case no. 76–0067 (D.D.C. July 30, 1976). It remained covered by Section 203 under the 1975–1977 determinations.

NORTH DAKOTA (Continued)				
Political Subdivision Covered	**1975–1977**	**1984**	**1992**	**2002**
Sargent County				AI (38)
Sioux County		AI (19)		

OKLAHOMA				
Political Subdivision Covered	**1975–1977**	**1984**	**1992**	**2002**
Adair County	AI	AI (14)	AI (14)	
Blaine County	AI			
Caddo County	AI			
Cherokee County	AI			
Choctaw County	AI*[7]			
Coal County	AI			
Craig County	AI			
Delaware County	AI			
Harmon County	SP			SP
Hughes County	AI			
Johnston County	AI			
Latimer County	AI			
Mayes County	AI			
McCurtain County	AI*[8]			
McIntosh County	AI			
Okfuskee County	AI			
Okmulgee County	AI			
Osage County	AI			
Ottawa County	AI			
Pawnee County	AI			
Pushmataha County	AI			
Rogers County	AI			
Seminole County	AI			
Sequoyah County	AI			
Texas County				SP
Tillman County	SP			

OREGON				
Political Subdivision Covered	**1975–1977**	**1984**	**1992**	**2002**
Jefferson County	AI			
Malheur County	SP		AI (33)	AI (51)

7 Choctaw County, Oklahoma, was deleted from the list of Section 4(f)(4) covered jurisdictions on July 26, 1979. *See* 44 Fed. Reg. 43,719 (July 26, 1979). Choctaw County was removed from Section 4(f)(4) coverage after bringing a successful bailout action in 1978. *See Choctaw and McCurtain Counties v. United States*, case no. 78–0484 (D.D.C. May 10, 1979).

8 McCurtain County, Oklahoma, was deleted from the list of Section 4(f)(4) covered jurisdictions on July 26, 1979. *See* 44 Fed. Reg. 43,719 (July 26, 1979). McCurtain County was removed from Section 4(f)(4) coverage after bringing a successful bailout action in 1978. *See Choctaw and McCurtain Counties v. United States*, case no. 78–0484 (D.D.C. May 10, 1979).

PENNSYLVANIA				
Political Subdivision Covered	**1975–1977**	**1984**	**1992**	**2002**
Philadelphia County			SP	SP

RHODE ISLAND				
Political Subdivision Covered	**1975–1977**	**1984**	**1992**	**2002**
Central Falls (Providence County)			SP	SP
Providence (Providence County)				SP

SOUTH DAKOTA				
Political Subdivision Covered	**1975–1977**	**1984**	**1992**	**2002**
Bennett County	AI			AI (38)
Buffalo County		AI (19)		
Charles Mix County	AI			
Codington County				AI (38)
Corson County	AI			
Day County				AI (38)
Dewey County		AI (19)	AI (19)	AI (38)
Grant County				AI (38)
Gregory County			AI (19)	AI (38)
Haakon County				AI (38)
Jackson County				AI (38)
Lyman County	AI		AI (19)	AI (38)
Marshall County				AI (38)
Meade County				AI (15, 38)
Mellette County	AI		AI (19)	AI (38)
Roberts County				AI (38)
Shannon County	**AI***	AI (19)		AI (38)
Stanley County				AI (38)
Todd County	**AI†**	AI (19)	AI (19)	AI (38)
Tripp County			AI (19)	AI (38)
Washabaugh County	AI			
Ziebach County			AI (19)	AI (38)

TEXAS				
Political Subdivision Covered	**1975–1977**	**1984**	**1992**	**2002**
State of Texas	**SP†**			SP
Andrews County	SP	SP	SP	SP
Aransas County	SP	SP		
Atascosa County	SP	SP	SP	SP
Bailey County	SP	SP	SP	SP
Bandera County	SP			
Bastrop County	SP			
Bee County	SP	SP	SP	SP
Bell County	SP			
Bexar County	SP	SP	SP	SP

TEXAS (Continued)				
Political Subdivision Covered	**1975–1977**	**1984**	**1992**	**2002**
Blanco County	SP			
Borden County	SP			SP
Brazoria County	SP			
Brazos County	SP			
Brewster County	SP	SP	SP	SP
Briscoe County	SP	SP		
Brooks County	SP	SP	SP	SP
Burleson County	SP			
Burnet County	SP			
Caldwell County	SP	SP	SP	SP
Calhoun County	SP	SP	SP	SP
Cameron County	SP	SP	SP	SP
Castro County	SP	SP	SP	SP
Cochran County	SP	SP	SP	SP
Coke County	SP			
Colorado County	SP			
Comal County	SP	SP	SP	
Concho County	SP	SP	SP	SP
Coryell County	SP			
Cottle County	SP	SP		
Crane County	SP	SP		SP
Crockett County	SP	SP	SP	SP
Crosby County	SP	SP	SP	SP
Culberson County	SP	SP	SP	SP
Dallam County	SP			
Dallas County			SP	SP
Dawson County	SP	SP	SP	SP
Deaf Smith County	SP	SP	SP	SP
DeWitt County	SP	SP	SP	SP
Dickens County	SP	SP	SP	
Dimmit County	SP	SP	SP	SP
Duval County	SP	SP	SP	SP
Ector County	SP	SP	SP	SP
Edwards County	SP	SP	SP	SP
Ellis County	SP			
El Paso County	SP	SP	AI (39), SP	AI (35), SP
Falls County	SP			
Fisher County	SP	SP		SP
Floyd County	SP	SP	SP	SP
Foard County	SP			
Fort Bend County	SP	SP		
Frio County	SP	SP	SP	SP
Gaines County	SP	SP	SP	SP
Galveston County	SP			
Garza County	SP	SP	SP	SP
Gillespie County	SP			

TEXAS (Continued)				
Political Subdivision Covered	**1975–1977**	**1984**	**1992**	**2002**
Glasscock County	SP		SP	SP
Goliad County	SP	SP	SP	SP
Gonzales County	SP	SP	SP	SP
Grimes County	SP			
Guadalupe County	SP	SP	SP	SP
Hale County	SP	SP	SP	SP
Hall County	SP	SP		SP
Hansford County	SP			SP
Harris County	SP		SP	AS (5), SP
Haskell County	SP	SP		
Hays County	SP	SP	SP	
Hidalgo County	SP	SP	SP	SP
Hockley County	SP	SP	SP	SP
Howard County	SP	SP	SP	SP
Hudspeth County	SP	SP	SP	SP
Irion County		SP	SP	SP
Jackson County	SP	SP		
Jeff Davis County	SP	SP	SP	SP
Jim Hogg County	SP	SP	SP	SP
Jim Wells County	SP	SP	SP	SP
Jones County	SP	SP		
Karnes County	SP	SP	SP	SP
Kendall County	SP			
Kenedy County	SP	SP	SP	SP
Kent County			SP	
Kerr County	SP			
Kimble County	SP			
Kinney County	SP	SP	SP	SP
Kleberg County	SP	SP	SP	SP
Knox County	SP	SP		SP
La Salle County	SP	SP	SP	SP
Lamb County	SP	SP	SP	SP
Lampasas County	SP			
Live Oak County	SP	SP	SP	SP
Loving County		SP		SP[9]
Lubbock County	SP	SP	SP	SP
Lynn County	SP	SP	SP	SP
Madison County	SP			SP
Martin County	SP	SP	SP	SP
Mason County	SP	SP		
Matagorda County	SP	SP		SP
Maverick County	SP	SP	SP	AI (51), SP

9 Loving County, Texas, was identified as being covered for Spanish by the Census Bureau in its 2002 coverage determinations. The Census data used to make the 2002 determinations indicates Loving County is only flagged for statewide coverage for Spanish and is not separately covered under Section 203.

TEXAS (Continued)				
Political Subdivision Covered	**1975–1977**	**1984**	**1992**	**2002**
McCulloch County	SP	SP	SP	
McLennan County	SP			
McMullen County	SP	SP	SP	SP
Medina County	SP	SP	SP	SP
Menard County	SP	SP	SP	SP
Midland County	SP		SP	SP
Milam County	SP			
Mitchell County	SP	SP	SP	SP
Moore County	SP		SP	SP
Nolan County	SP	SP	SP	SP
Nueces County	SP	SP	SP	SP
Parmer County	SP	SP	SP	SP
Pecos County	SP	SP	SP	SP
Polk County			AI (11)	
Potter County	SP			
Presidio County	SP	SP	SP	SP
Reagan County	SP	SP	SP	SP
Real County	SP	SP		
Reeves County	SP	SP	SP	SP
Refugio County	SP	SP	SP	SP
Robertson County	SP			
Runnels County	SP	SP	SP	SP
San Patricio County	SP	SP	SP	SP
San Saba County	SP			
Schleicher County	SP	SP	SP	SP
Scurry County	SP	SP	SP	SP
Sherman County	SP			
Starr County	SP	SP	SP	SP
Sterling County	SP	SP		SP
Sutton County	SP	SP	SP	SP
Swisher County	SP	SP	SP	SP
Tarrant County			SP	SP
Taylor County	SP			
Terrell County	SP	SP	SP	SP
Terry County	SP	SP	SP	SP
Throckmorton County	SP			
Titus County				SP
Tom Green County	SP	SP	SP	SP
Travis County	SP		SP	SP
Upton County	SP	SP	SP	SP
Uvalde County	SP	SP	SP	SP
Val Verde County	SP	SP	SP	SP
Victoria County	SP	SP	SP	SP
Ward County	SP	SP	SP	SP
Webb County	SP	SP	SP	SP
Wharton County	SP	SP	SP	SP

TEXAS (Continued)				
Political Subdivision Covered	**1975–1977**	**1984**	**1992**	**2002**
Willacy County	SP	SP	SP	SP
Williamson County	SP			
Wilson County	SP	SP	SP	SP
Winkler County	SP	SP	SP	SP
Yoakum County	SP	SP	SP	SP
Zapata County	SP	SP	SP	SP
Zavala County	SP	SP	SP	SP

UTAH				
Political Subdivision Covered	**1975–1977**	**1984**	**1992**	**2002**
Carbon County	SP			
San Juan County	AI	AI (31)	AI (31, 43)	AI (31, 43)
Tooele County	SP			
Uintah County	AI			

VIRGINIA				
Political Subdivision Covered	**1975–1977**	**1984**	**1992**	**2002**
Charles City County	AI			

WASHINGTON				
Political Subdivision Covered	**1975–1977**	**1984**	**1992**	**2002**
Adams County	SP			SP
Columbia County	SP			
Ferry County	AI (deleted Aug. 4,1976)			
Franklin County				SP
Grant County	SP			
King County				AS (1)
Okanogan County	AI			
Yakima County	SP			SP

WISCONSIN				
Political Subdivision Covered	**1975–1977**	**1984**	**1992**	**2002**
Bovina Town (Outagamie County)	SP			
Couderay Town (Sawyer County)		AI (44)		
Curtiss Village (Clark County)			SP	
Hayward City (Sawyer County)	AI			
Komensky Town (Jackson County)		AI (32)		
Nashville County (Forest County)	AI			
Oneida Town (Outagamie County)	AI			
Pine Grove Town (Portage County)		SP		

WYOMING				
Political Subdivision Covered	**1975–1977**	**1984**	**1992**	**2002**
Carbon County	SP			
Fremont County	AI			
Laramie County	SP			
Sweetwater County	SP			
Washakie County	SP			

Numbers used to identify covered languages, by language group

Number	Asian Languages
1	Chinese
2	Filipino / Tagalog
3	Japanese
4	Korean
5	Vietnamese

Number	Alaska Native Languages
6	Aleut
7	Alaska Athabascan
8	Eskimo
9	Tanaina
10	Other Alaska Native

Number	American Indian Languages
11	Alabama
12	Apache
13	Athapascan
14	Cherokee
15	Cheyenne
16	Chickasaw
17	Choctaw
18	Cree
19	Dakota
20	Delta River Yuma
21	Fox
22	French (American Indian)
23	Havasupai
24	Hopi
25	Jicarilla
26	Keres
27	Kuchin
28	Mikasuki
29	Mohawk
30	Muskogee
31	Navajo
32	Ojibwa
33	Paiute
34	Pima
35	Pueblo

Number	American Indian Languages (Continued)
36	Seminole
37	Shoshone
38	Sioux
39	Spanish (American Indian)
40	Tiwa
41	Tlinglit
42	Tohono O'Odham
43	Ute
44	Winnebago
45	Wintun
46	Yaqui
47	Yavapai
48	Yuma/Yuman
49	Zuni
50	Latin American Indian
51	Other American Indian
52	American Indian (Tribe not specified)

Appendix C
Census Data Used to Make the Section 203 Coverage Determinations in 2002

Figures C.1 through C.4 were compiled from sampled data used by the Census Bureau to make its July 26, 2002, determinations under Section 203 of the Voting Rights Act. According to the Voting Rights Output File Documentation, the determination data were created from sampled weights of data from the Census 2000 long forms (Summary Table Files 3 and 4). The file contains records for the entire United States, including all states and political subdivisions, which are defined as "counties for all states except for Connecticut, Maine, Massachusetts, Michigan, New Hampshire, Rhode Island, Vermont, and Wisconsin," where political subdivisions are minor civil divisions (MCDs) or MCD equivalents. There are 62 records in the file, including one each for total population and Spanish/Hispanic/Latino, one for American Indian/Alaska Native and 42 for American Indian/Alaska Native tribal groups, one for Asian and 16 for Asian groups.

The Census Bureau has suppressed data for jurisdictions indicated by an asterisk (*) to avoid disclosure of specific persons. According to Census documentation, "This means that data in a record are suppressed if the unweighted count of voting age citizens for a record is less than 50 and the weighted population count for the record is not 0 or the unweighted population count for the record is not 0." The Census Bureau rounded data that have not been suppressed. Section 203 determinations are based on data prior to rounding and prior to suppression.

"LEP Number (N)" refers to the number of voting-age citizens in the identified language group who are limited-English proficient, or LEP. A person is LEP if he or she speaks English less than "very well."

"LEP Percent (P)" refers to the percentage of voting-age citizens in the identified language group who are LEP.

"Illiteracy Rate" refers to the percent of voting-age citizens in the identified language group who are LEP and illiterate. According to the Census Bureau, "voting age limited-English proficient illiteracy" refers to all voting-age citizens who are limited-English proficient and who have completed less than fifth grade. Jurisdictions are covered if they meet one of the population triggers and have an illiteracy rate among voting-age citizens in a single language minority group that exceeds the national illiteracy rate of all voting-age citizens of 1.35 percent.

"Coverage basis" refers to the population trigger resulting in Section 203 coverage. There are four different bases for coverage: "N" if the number of LEP voting age citizens in a single language group is more than 10,000; "P" if the percentage of LEP voting age citizens in a single language group is more than 5 percent of all voting age citizens; "RW" if an Alaska Native or American Indian reservation is wholly located within the jurisdiction and the percentage of LEP voting-age citizens in a single language group is more than 5 percent of all voting-age citizens on that reservation; and "RP" if an Alaska Native or American Indian reservation is partially located within the jurisdiction and the percentage of LEP voting-age citizens in a single language group is more than 5 percent of all voting age citizens on that reservation. A jurisdiction can be covered for a single language group by multiple population triggers.

Figure C.1 Jurisdictions covered by Section 203 for Spanish heritage, by state

ARIZONA				
Covered Jurisdiction	**Number LEP (N)**	**Percent LEP (P)**	**Illiteracy Rate**	**Coverage Basis**
Cochise County	4325	5.36	14.34	P
Greenlee County	315	5.52	4.76	P
Maricopa County	53385	2.70	12.71	N
Pima County	23220	3.97	12.36	N
Santa Cruz County	5585	29.68	8.59	P
Yuma County	7440	8.23	15.79	P

CALIFORNIA				
Covered Jurisdiction	**Number LEP (N)**	**Percent LEP (P)**	**Illiteracy Rate**	**Coverage Basis**
State of California[1]	1003995	5.02	16.36	P
Alameda County	22010	2.45	13.90	N
Colusa County	805	8.31	31.06	P
Contra Costa County	13115	2.14	11.55	N
Fresno County	32195	7.21	24.13	N, P
Imperial County	16110	21.64	20.17	N, P
Kern County	23285	6.04	23.34	N, P
Kings County	5080	6.36	17.13	P
Los Angeles County	428580	8.58	15.92	N, P
Madera County	4380	6.13	23.29	P
Merced County	8500	7.73	23.00	P
Monterey County	16935	7.80	22.91	N, P
Orange County	64385	3.95	15.89	N
Riverside County	49495	5.39	15.83	N, P
Sacramento County	13440	1.69	14.32	N
San Benito County	2540	8.36	21.85	P
San Bernardino County	56250	5.69	13.50	N, P
San Diego County	65520	3.66	12.80	N
San Francisco County	14645	2.65	13.21	N
San Joaquin County	14630	4.42	17.19	N
San Mateo County	15365	3.46	12.50	N
Santa Barbara County	10595	4.20	16.66	N
Santa Clara County	33520	3.44	14.53	N
Stanislaus County	12035	4.53	19.53	N
Tulare County	15505	8.00	23.44	N, P
Ventura County	24505	5.35	18.87	N, P

COLORADO				
Covered Jurisdiction	**Number LEP (N)**	**Percent LEP (P)**	**Illiteracy Rate**	**Coverage Basis**
Alamosa County	565	5.37	15.04	P
Conejos County	680	12.24	14.71	P
Costilla County	490	18.85	16.33	P

1 All 58 counties and their political subdivisions are covered as a result of statewide coverage of California.

COLORADO (Continued)

Covered Jurisdiction	Number LEP (N)	Percent LEP (P)	Illiteracy Rate	Coverage Basis
Crowley County	245	5.49	10.20	P
Denver County	10880	2.92	14.20	N
Otero County	840	5.91	19.64	P
Rio Grande County	535	6.22	15.89	P
Saguache County	250	6.74	34.00	P

CONNECTICUT

Covered Jurisdiction	Number LEP (N)	Percent LEP (P)	Illiteracy Rate	Coverage Basis
Bridgeport (Fairfield County)	9585	11.28	12.36	P
Hartford (Hartford County)	12400	16.69	14.44	N, P
Meriden (New Haven County)	2600	6.24	8.46	P
New Britain (Hartford County)	4140	8.62	8.57	P
New Haven (New Haven County)	5090	6.08	10.61	P
Waterbury (New Haven County)	5045	6.91	11.60	P
Windham (Windham County)	1180	7.17	12.29	P

FLORIDA

Covered Jurisdiction	Number LEP (N)	Percent LEP (P)	Illiteracy Rate	Coverage Basis
Broward County	35780	3.42	5.14	N
Hardee County	900	5.52	35.00	P
Hendry County	1430	7.32	21.33	P
Hillsborough County	27480	3.99	9.04	N
Miami-Dade County	273975	23.53	8.27	N, P
Orange County	30935	5.10	6.24	N, P
Osceola County	11375	9.99	5.45	N, P
Palm Beach County	20020	2.52	9.24	N

ILLINOIS

Covered Jurisdiction	Number LEP (N)	Percent LEP (P)	Illiteracy Rate	Coverage Basis
Cook County	131530	3.84	12.61	N
Kane County	10055	4.12	13.53	N

KANSAS

Covered Jurisdiction	Number LEP (N)	Percent LEP (P)	Illiteracy Rate	Coverage Basis
Finney County	1420	6.72	9.86	P
Ford County	990	5.62	15.15	P
Grant County	305	6.36	21.31	P
Haskell County	140	5.34	14.29	P
Kearny County	135	5.04	25.93	P
Seward County	1160	9.90	11.64	P

MARYLAND

Covered Jurisdiction	Number LEP (N)	Percent LEP (P)	Illiteracy Rate	Coverage Basis
Montgomery County	10055	1.86	8.20	N

MASSACHUSETTS				
Covered Jurisdiction	**Number LEP (N)**	**Percent LEP (P)**	**Illiteracy Rate**	**Coverage Basis**
Boston (Suffolk County)	11820	3.04	11.59	N
Chelsea (Suffolk County)	2160	12.91	15.51	P
Holyoke (Hampden County)	3840	14.10	16.67	P
Lawrence (Essex County)	6410	18.02	10.92	P
Southbridge (Worcester County)	930	7.45	17.20	P
Springfield (Hampden County)	9560	9.33	17.05	P

MICHIGAN				
Covered Jurisdiction	**Number LEP (N)**	**Percent LEP (P)**	**Illiteracy Rate**	**Coverage Basis**
Clyde Township, Allegan County	75	5.47	33.33	P

NEBRASKA				
Covered Jurisdiction	**Number LEP (N)**	**Percent LEP (P)**	**Illiteracy Rate**	**Coverage Basis**
Colfax County	385	6.15	15.58	P

NEVADA				
Covered Jurisdiction	**Number LEP (N)**	**Percent LEP (P)**	**Illiteracy Rate**	**Coverage Basis**
Clark County	27020	3.03	12.12	N

NEW JERSEY				
Covered Jurisdiction	**Number LEP (N)**	**Percent LEP (P)**	**Illiteracy Rate**	**Coverage Basis**
Bergen County	12885	2.19	3.76	N
Cumberland County	5685	5.44	11.70	P
Essex County	23065	4.56	9.73	N
Hudson County	47440	13.49	8.83	N, P
Middlesex County	14200	2.94	10.07	N
Passaic County	24270	8.20	8.67	N, P
Union County	17235	5.22	5.98	N, P

NEW MEXICO				
Covered Jurisdiction	**Number LEP (N)**	**Percent LEP (P)**	**Illiteracy Rate**	**Coverage Basis**
State of New Mexico[2†]	74855	6.08	13.21	P
Bernalillo County	18140	4.65	8.30	N
Chaves County	3220	8.10	19.25	P
De Baca County	160	9.55	21.88	P
Dona Ana County	13770	13.08	19.79	N, P
Eddy County	2715	7.62	24.31	P
Grant County	2015	8.96	13.15	P
Guadalupe County	440	12.83	10.23	P
Harding County	65	10.24	15.38	P
Hidalgo County	460	12.33	21.74	P
Lea County	2330	6.60	23.61	P
Luna County	1610	11.01	15.53	P
Mora County	985	26.09	11.17	P

2 All 33 counties and their political subdivisions are covered as a result of statewide coverage of New Mexico.

NEW MEXICO (Continued)				
Covered Jurisdiction	**Number LEP (N)**	**Percent LEP (P)**	**Illiteracy Rate**	**Coverage Basis**
Rio Arriba County	4025	14.16	10.06	P
Roosevelt County	765	6.11	20.26	P
San Miguel County	2900	13.58	9.83	P
Santa Fe County	5060	5.59	7.71	P
Socorro County	870	7.11	12.07	P
Taos County	2395	10.90	5.01	P
Torrance County	600	5.25	18.33	P
Union County	200	6.70	17.50	P
Valencia County	2980	6.78	12.58	P

NEW YORK				
Covered Jurisdiction	**Number LEP (N)**	**Percent LEP (P)**	**Illiteracy Rate**	**Coverage Basis**
Bronx County	119365	16.21	11.67	N, P
Kings County	84760	6.13	13.51	N, P
Nassau County	14820	1.62	9.99	N
New York County	80140	7.76	13.55	N, P
Queens County	84460	6.87	7.99	N, P
Suffolk County	16685	1.71	8.45	N
Westchester County	16305	2.77	9.14	N

OKLAHOMA				
Covered Jurisdiction	**Number LEP (N)**	**Percent LEP (P)**	**Illiteracy Rate**	**Coverage Basis**
Harmon County	145	6.04	31.03	P
Texas County	720	5.83	16.67	P

PENNSYLVANIA				
Covered Jurisdiction	**Number LEP (N)**	**Percent LEP (P)**	**Illiteracy Rate**	**Coverage Basis**
Philadelphia County	25660	2.39	13.33	N

RHODE ISLAND				
Covered Jurisdiction	**Number LEP (N)**	**Percent LEP (P)**	**Illiteracy Rate**	**Coverage Basis**
Central Falls (Providence County)	1305	13.80	8.81	P
Providence (Providence County)	7395	7.11	10.55	P

TEXAS				
Covered Jurisdiction	**Number LEP (N)**	**Percent LEP (P)**	**Illiteracy Rate**	**Coverage Basis**
State of Texas[3*]	818185	6.15	19.46	P
Andrews County	585	7.22	29.91	P
Atascosa County	3985	15.62	25.35	P
Bailey County	330	8.26	21.21	P
Bee County	3335	13.58	21.44	P
Bexar County	98165	10.65	15.22	N, P
Borden County	•	•	•	P

3 All 254 counties and their political subdivisions are covered as a result of statewide coverage of Texas.

* Loving County was included by the Census Bureau in its coverage determination. Census data indicates it is only flagged for statewide coverage. Therefore, it is excluded from this table.

TEXAS (Continued)				
Covered Jurisdiction	**Number LEP (N)**	**Percent LEP (P)**	**Illiteracy Rate**	**Coverage Basis**
Brewster County	620	9.48	31.45	P
Brooks County	1540	29.39	24.03	P
Caldwell County	1790	8.06	21.51	P
Calhoun County	935	6.79	27.81	P
Cameron County	46875	26.84	25.05	N, P
Castro County	620	12.34	35.48	P
Cochran County	295	12.66	32.20	P
Concho County	265	8.14	24.53	P
Crane County	210	8.64	19.05	P
Crockett County	415	15.34	15.66	P
Crosby County	580	12.17	29.31	P
Culberson County	420	22.52	38.10	P
Dallas County	53985	4.17	17.42	N
Dawson County	1270	11.64	40.16	P
Deaf Smith County	1650	14.66	30.61	P
DeWitt County	890	5.94	34.83	P
Dimmit County	1950	29.84	34.87	P
Duval County	2500	27.65	22.40	P
Ector County	6775	8.75	18.97	P
Edwards County	230	15.70	32.61	P
El Paso County	85400	23.12	16.00	N, P
Fisher County	185	5.70	43.24	P
Floyd County	555	10.85	32.43	P
Frio County	2360	21.17	25.42	P
Gaines County	895	10.94	30.17	P
Garza County	365	10.80	10.96	P
Glasscock County	45	5.45	33.33	P
Goliad County	350	6.99	31.43	P
Gonzales County	1085	8.85	29.03	P
Guadalupe County	3540	5.79	20.34	P
Hale County	2625	10.97	27.43	P
Hall County	130	5.06	23.08	P
Hansford County	180	5.41	22.22	P
Harris County	107915	5.49	14.97	N, P
Hidalgo County	75255	27.86	26.04	N, P
Hockley County	1285	8.29	33.07	P
Howard County	1945	8.08	17.74	P
Hudspeth County	355	23.13	22.54	P
Irion County	75	5.88	33.33	P
Jeff Davis County	170	10.97	26.47	P
Jim Hogg County	1025	29.50	27.80	P
Jim Wells County	5530	20.99	19.26	P
Karnes County	1505	12.85	30.56	P
Kenedy County	90	33.33	22.22	P
Kinney County	365	15.77	38.36	P
Kleberg County	3430	15.64	16.18	P

TEXAS (Continued)				
Covered Jurisdiction	**Number LEP (N)**	**Percent LEP (P)**	**Illiteracy Rate**	**Coverage Basis**
Knox County	210	7.05	38.10	P
La Salle County	1170	28.92	28.63	P
Lamb County	1135	11.52	33.92	P
Live Oak County	815	8.64	28.83	P
Lubbock County	9285	5.26	25.20	P
Lynn County	495	11.47	33.33	P
Madison County	540	5.50	6.48	P
Martin County	320	10.88	40.63	P
Matagorda County	1385	5.64	31.77	P
Maverick County	8530	41.87	19.87	P
McMullen County	60	9.68	25.00	P
Medina County	2920	10.75	23.46	P
Menard County	145	8.41	44.83	P
Midland County	4290	5.62	21.21	P
Mitchell County	765	10.06	21.57	P
Moore County	940	8.67	23.94	P
Nolan County	625	5.54	39.20	P
Nueces County	26190	12.18	20.41	N, P
Parmer County	655	11.47	32.82	P
Pecos County	1850	16.88	33.51	P
Presidio County	955	29.25	30.37	P
Reagan County	175	9.51	20.00	P
Reeves County	2110	25.65	29.15	P
Refugio County	540	9.52	35.19	P
Runnels County	525	6.46	24.76	P
San Patricio County	5740	12.68	29.18	P
Schleicher County	230	11.86	34.78	P
Scurry County	660	5.52	35.61	P
Starr County	10050	44.47	24.08	N, P
Sterling County	75	8.11	46.67	P
Sutton County	375	14.34	29.33	P
Swisher County	430	7.44	32.56	P
Tarrant County	25350	2.71	16.33	N
Terrell County	70	9.66	21.43	P
Terry County	900	10.32	35.00	P
Titus County	1005	5.98	29.85	P
Tom Green County	4180	5.65	21.53	P
Travis County	19195	3.54	15.37	N
Upton County	260	11.85	36.54	P
Uvalde County	3245	19.99	29.43	P
Val Verde County	5740	23.07	24.22	P
Victoria County	3915	6.78	25.03	P
Ward County	785	10.84	24.84	P
Webb County	33000	36.03	14.91	N, P
Wharton County	1450	5.22	29.66	P
Willacy County	3875	30.96	32.26	P

TEXAS (Continued)				
Covered Jurisdiction	**Number LEP (N)**	**Percent LEP (P)**	**Illiteracy Rate**	**Coverage Basis**
Wilson County	1675	7.45	22.69	P
Winkler County	460	10.53	36.96	P
Yoakum County	390	9.08	25.64	P
Zapata County	1940	29.24	23.97	P
Zavala County	2860	40.92	30.42	P

WASHINGTON				
Covered Jurisdiction	**Number LEP (N)**	**Percent LEP (P)**	**Illiteracy Rate**	**Coverage Basis**
Adams County	745	8.76	28.19	P
Franklin County	1840	7.53	20.38	P
Yakima County	6950	5.36	28.92	P

Figure C.2 Jurisdictions covered by Section 203 for Alaska Native languages

Covered Jurisdiction	Covered Language	Indian Reservation	Number LEP	Percent LEP	Illiteracy Rate	Coverage Basis
Aleutians West Census Area	Aleut	Atka ANVSA	0	*	*	RP
	Aleut	Nikolski ANVSA	0	*	*	RP
	Aleut	St. Paul ANVSA	40	11.94	10	RP
Bethel Census Area	Eskimo		1980	20.82	21.46	P
	Eskimo	Akiachak ANVSA	75	23.44	26.67	RP
	Eskimo	Akiak ANVSA	25	17.24	40	RP
	Eskimo	Aniak ANVSA	15	6.98	66.67	RP
	Eskimo	Atmautluak ANVSA	105	51.22	19.05	RP
	Eskimo	Bethel ANVSA	195	9.31	20.51	RP
	Eskimo	Chefornak ANVSA	105	58.33	19.05	RP
	Eskimo	Goodnews Bay ANVSA	45	32.14	22.22	RP
	Eskimo	Kalskag ANVSA	0	*	*	RP
	Eskimo	Kasigluk ANVSA	105	38.89	14.29	RP
	Eskimo	Kipnuk ANVSA	170	45.95	14.71	RP
	Eskimo	Kwethluk ANVSA	90	25.71	27.78	RP
	Eskimo	Kwigillingok ANVSA	65	39.39	15.38	RP
	Eskimo	Mekoryuk ANVSA	20	16.67	75	RP
	Eskimo	Napakiak ANVSA	50	27.03	8	RP
	Eskimo	Napaskiak ANVSA	110	44.9	22.73	RP
	Eskimo	Newtok ANVSA	95	52.78	15.79	RP
	Eskimo	Nightmute ANVSA	0	*	*	RP
	Eskimo	Nunapitchuk ANVSA	105	43.75	14.29	RP
	Eskimo	Oscarville ANVSA	0	*	*	RP
	Eskimo	Platinum ANVSA	0	*	*	RP
	Eskimo	Toksook Bay ANVSA	180	65.45	16.67	RP
	Eskimo	Tuluksak ANVSA	70	25.45	28.57	RP
	Eskimo	Tuntutuliak ANVSA	80	50	31.25	RP
	Eskimo	Tununak ANVSA	100	60.61	15	RP
Denali Borough	Alaskan Athabascan	Cantwell ANVSA	0	*	*	RP
Dillingham Census Area	Eskimo		310	10.32	45.16	P
	Eskimo	Aleknagik ANVSA	0	*	*	RP
	Eskimo	Clark's Point ANVSA	0	*	*	RP
	Eskimo	Dillingham ANVSA	55	6.47	36.36	RP
	Eskimo	Manokotak ANVSA	0	*	*	RP
	Eskimo	New Koliganek ANVSA	0	*	*	RP
	Eskimo	New Stuyahok ANVSA	50	18.87	50	RP
	Eskimo	Togiak ANVSA	100	24.39	45	RP
	Eskimo	Twin Hills ANVSA	0	*	*	RP
	Other Alaska Native	Manokotak ANVSA	0	*	*	RP
Kenai Peninsula Borough	Aleut	Port Graham ANVSA	0	*	*	RP

Covered Jurisdiction	Covered Language	Indian Reservation	Number LEP	Percent LEP	Illiteracy Rate	Coverage Basis
Lake and Peninsula Borough	Alaskan Athabascan	Newhalen ANVSA	0	*	*	RP
	Aleut	Igiugig ANVSA	0	*	*	RP
	Aleut	Port Heiden ANVSA	0	*	*	RP
	Eskimo	Newhalen ANVSA	0	*	*	RP
Nome Census Area	Eskimo		360	6.26	12.50	P
	Eskimo	Brevig Mission ANVSA	15	11.54	26.67	RP
	Eskimo	Gambell ANVSA	75	22.39	5.33	RP
	Eskimo	Shishmaref ANVSA	40	12.7	10	RP
	Eskimo	Stebbins ANVSA	20	7.02	20	RP
	Eskimo	Teller ANVSA	10	7.41	40	RP
	Eskimo	Unalakleet ANVSA	30	7.5	13.33	RP
North Slope Borough	Eskimo		525	11.86	22.86	P
	Eskimo	Barrow ANVSA	350	21.21	21.43	RP
	Eskimo	Kaktovik ANVSA	20	14.81	50	RP
	Eskimo	Nuiqsut ANVSA	25	11.9	80	RP
	Eskimo	Point Hope ANVSA	65	17.57	15.38	RP
	Eskimo	Wainwright ANVSA	50	15.63	8	RP
Northwest Arctic Borough	Eskimo		335	7.98	13.43	P
	Eskimo	Kiana ANVSA	60	37.5	6.67	RP
	Eskimo	Kotzebue ANVSA	125	9.62	12	RP
	Eskimo	Noatak ANVSA	15	6.67	26.67	RP
	Eskimo	Noorvik ANVSA	35	9.09	11.43	RP
	Eskimo	Shungnak ANVSA	60	42.86	33.33	RP
	Other Alaska Native	Selawik ANVSA	80	21.33	5	RP
Southeast Fairbanks Census Area	Alaskan Athabascan	Northway ANVSA	0	*	*	RP
	Alaskan Athabascan	Tanacross ANVSA	0	*	*	RP
	Alaskan Athabascan	Tetlin TDSA	0	*	*	RP
	Other Alaska Native	Tetlin TDSA	0	*	*	RP
Valdez-Cordova Census Area	Alaskan Athabascan	Chistochina ANVSA	0	*	*	RP
Wade Hampton Census Area	Eskimo		570	15.24	36.84	P
	Eskimo	Alakanuk ANVSA	55	15.94	54.55	RP
	Eskimo	Algaacig ANVSA	35	18.92	28.57	RP
	Eskimo	Andreafsky ANVSA	0	*	*	RP
	Eskimo	Chevak ANVSA	20	6.06	50	RP
	Eskimo	Emmonak ANVSA	85	22.37	23.53	RP

Covered Jurisdiction	Covered Language	Indian Reservation	Number LEP	Percent LEP	Illiteracy Rate	Coverage Basis
Wade Hampton Census Area (Continued)	Eskimo	Hooper Bay ANVSA	100	20.2	45	RP
	Eskimo	Kotlik ANVSA	45	15.25	22.22	RP
	Eskimo	Marshall ANVSA	30	16.67	50	RP
	Eskimo	Mountain Village ANVSA	65	18.31	38.46	RP
	Eskimo	Nunam Iqua ANVSA	0	*	*	RP
	Eskimo	Pilot Station ANVSA	65	24.07	46.15	RP
	Eskimo	Pitkas Point ANVSA	0	*	*	RP
	Eskimo	Russian Mission ANVSA	20	14.81	75	RP
Yukon-Koyukuk Census Area	Alaskan Athabascan	Allakaket ANVSA	0	*	*	RP
	Alaskan Athabascan	Chalkyitsik ANVSA	0	*	*	RP
	Alaskan Athabascan	Fort Yukon ANVSA	25	6.58	16	RP
	Alaskan Athabascan	Galena ANVSA	15	5.56	26.67	RP
	Alaskan Athabascan	Nikolai ANVSA	0	*	*	RP
	Eskimo	Nikolai ANVSA	0	*	*	RP
	Eskimo	Stevens Village ANVSA	0	*	*	RP

Figure C.3 Jurisdictions covered by Section 203 for American Indian languages, by state

ALASKA

Covered Jurisdiction	Covered Language	Indian Reservation (RP or RW)	Number LEP (L)	Percent LEP (P)	Illiteracy Rate	Coverage Basis
Bethel Census Area	American Indian	Eek ANVSA	80	53.33	5	RP
	American Indian	Kongiganak ANVSA	35	14	42.86	RP
	American Indian	Kwinhagak ANVSA	175	53.03	20	RP
	American Indian	Lower Kalskag ANVSA	10	7.14	100	RP
	American Indian	Sleetmute ANVSA	0	*	*	RP
	Other American Indian	Kwigillingok ANVSA	0	*	*	RP
Dillingham Census Area	Other American Indian	Manokotak ANVSA	0	*	*	RP
Kenai Peninsula Borough	American Indian	Port Graham ANVSA	0	*	*	RP
North Slope Borough	American Indian	Anaktuvuk Pass ANVSA	30	18.75	33.33	RP
Wade Hampton Census Area	American Indian	Nunam Iqua ANVSA	0	*	*	RP
	American Indian	Scammon Bay ANVSA	45	20.45	22.22	RP
	Chickasaw	Chevak ANVSA	45	13.64	33.33	RP
Yukon-Koyukuk Census Area	Other American Indian	Hughes ANVSA	0	*	*	RP

ARIZONA

Covered Jurisdiction	Covered Language	Indian Reservation (RP or RW)	Number LEP (L)	Percent LEP (P)	Illiteracy Rate	Coverage Basis
Apache County	Apache	Fort Apache Reservation	15	10	0	RP
	Navajo		11245	26.52	25.43	N, P
	Navajo	Navajo Nation Reservation and Off-Reservation Trust Land	11175	36.11	25.37	RP
	Pueblo	Zuni Reservation and Off Reservation Trust Land	0	0	0	RP
Coconino County	Navajo		5405	6.74	26.64	P
	Navajo	Navajo Nation Reservation and Off-Reservation Trust Land	4555	35.41	29.75	RP
	Pueblo	Hopi Reservation and Off-Reservation Trust Land	90	14.75	0	RP

ARIZONA (Continued)

Covered Jurisdiction	Covered Language	Indian Reservation (RP or RW)	Number LEP (L)	Percent LEP (P)	Illiteracy Rate	Coverage Basis
Gila County	Apache	Fort Apache Reservation	270	32.53	1.48	RP
	Apache	San Carlos Reservation	570	22.01	2.63	RP
	Apache	Tonto Apache Reservation	0	*	*	RP
Graham County	Apache	San Carlos Reservation	715	29.24	0.56	RP
Maricopa County	Tohono O'Odham	Tohono O'odham Reservation and Off-Reservation Trust Land	190	62.3	28.95	RP
Navajo County	Apache	Fort Apache Reservation	1620	29.54	2.78	RP
	Navajo		7185	11.58	30.48	P
	Navajo	Navajo Nation Reservation and Off-Reservation Trust Land	6515	43.16	32.46	RP
	Pueblo	Hopi Reservation and Off-Reservation Trust Land	815	23.55	3.68	RP
Pima County	Tohono O'Odham	Tohono O'odham Reservation and Off-Reservation Trust Land	1670	31.48	9.28	RP
	Yaqui	Pascua Yaqui Reservation	280	18.24	10.71	RP
Pinal County	Apache	San Carlos Reservation	0	0	0	RP
	Tohono O'Odham	Maricopa (Ak Chin) Reservation	45	11.84	8.89	RP
	Tohono O'Odham	Tohono O'odham Reservation and Off-Reservation Trust Land	170	39.08	14.71	RP
Yuma County	Yuman	Cocopah Reservation	80	20.78	37.5	RP
	Yuman	Fort Yuma Reservation	0	*	*	RP

CALIFORNIA

Covered Jurisdiction	Covered Language	Indian Reservation (RP or RW)	Number LEP (L)	Percent LEP (P)	Illiteracy Rate	Coverage Basis
Imperial County	Latin American Indian	Torres-Martinez Reservation	0	0	0	RP
	Yuman	Fort Yuma Reservation	50	6.29	8	RP
Riverside County	Latin American Indian	Torres-Martinez Reservation	0	*	*	RP

COLORADO

Covered Jurisdiction	Covered Language	Indian Reservation (RP or RW)	Number LEP (L)	Percent LEP (P)	Illiteracy Rate	Coverage Basis
La Plata County	Navajo	Ute Mountain Reservation and Off-Reservation Trust Land	0	0	0	RP
	Ute	Ute Mountain Reservation and Off-Reservation Trust Land	0	0	0	RP

COLORADO (Continued)						
Covered Jurisdiction	**Covered Language**	**Indian Reservation (RP or RW)**	**Number LEP (L)**	**Percent LEP (P)**	**Illiteracy Rate**	**Coverage Basis**
Montezuma County	Navajo	Ute Mountain Reservation and Off-Reservation Trust Land	0	*	*	RP
	Ute	Ute Mountain Reservation and Off-Reservation Trust Land	200	23.67	10	RP

FLORIDA						
Covered Jurisdiction	**Covered Language**	**Indian Reservation (RP or RW)**	**Number LEP (L)**	**Percent LEP (P)**	**Illiteracy Rate**	**Coverage Basis**
Broward County	Seminole	Hollywood Reservation	35	11.29	57.14	RP
Collier County	Seminole	Immokalee Reservation	0	*	*	RP
Glades County	Seminole	Brighton Reservation	0	*	*	RP

IDAHO						
Covered Jurisdiction	**Covered Language**	**Indian Reservation (RP or RW)**	**Number LEP (L)**	**Percent LEP (P)**	**Illiteracy Rate**	**Coverage Basis**
Bannock County	Other American Indian	Fort Hall Reservation and Off-Reservation Trust Land	55	7.69	7.27	RP
Bingham County	Other American Indian	Fort Hall Reservation and Off-Reservation Trust Land	80	5.8	5	RP
Caribou County	Other American Indian	Fort Hall Reservation and Off-Reservation Trust Land	0	0	0	RP
Owyhee County	Other American Indian	Duck Valley Reservation	0	*	*	RP
Power County	Other American Indian	Fort Hall Reservation and Off-Reservation Trust Land	0	*	*	RP

LOUISIANA						
Covered Jurisdiction	**Covered Language**	**Indian Reservation (RP or RW)**	**Number LEP (L)**	**Percent LEP (P)**	**Illiteracy Rate**	**Coverage Basis**
Allen Parish	Other American Indian	Coushatta Reservation	0	*	*	RP

MISSISSIPPI						
Covered Jurisdiction	**Covered Language**	**Indian Reservation (RP or RW)**	**Number LEP (L)**	**Percent LEP (P)**	**Illiteracy Rate**	**Coverage Basis**
Attala County	Choctaw	Mississippi Choctaw Reservation and Off-Reservation Trust Land	0	0	0	RP
Jackson County	Choctaw	Mississippi Choctaw Reservation and Off-Reservation Trust Land	0	0	0	RP
Jones County	Choctaw	Mississippi Choctaw Reservation and Off-Reservation Trust Land	0	*	*	RP

MISSISSIPPI						
Covered Jurisdiction	**Covered Language**	**Indian Reservation (RP or RW)**	**Number LEP (L)**	**Percent LEP (P)**	**Illiteracy Rate**	**Coverage Basis**
Kemper County	Choctaw	Mississippi Choctaw Reservation and Off-Reservation Trust Land	0	*	*	RP
Leake County	Choctaw	Mississippi Choctaw Reservation and Off-Reservation Trust Land	0	*	*	RP
Neshoba County	Choctaw	Mississippi Choctaw Reservation and Off-Reservation Trust Land	620	38.39	16.13	RP
Newton County	Choctaw	Mississippi Choctaw Reservation and Off-Reservation Trust Land	0	*	*	RP
Scott County	Choctaw	Mississippi Choctaw Reservation and Off-Reservation Trust Land	0	0	0	RP
Winston County	Choctaw	Mississippi Choctaw Reservation and Off-Reservation Trust Land	0	*	*	RP

MONTANA						
Covered Jurisdiction	**Covered Language**	**Indian Reservation (RP or RW)**	**Number LEP (L)**	**Percent LEP (P)**	**Illiteracy Rate**	**Coverage Basis**
Big Horn County	Cheyenne	Northern Cheyenne Reservation and Off-Reservation	55	7.14	0	RP
Rosebud County	Cheyenne	Northern Cheyenne Reservation and Off-Reservation	170	11.6	2.35	RP

NEBRASKA						
Covered Jurisdiction	**Covered Language**	**Indian Reservation (RP or RW)**	**Number LEP (L)**	**Percent LEP (P)**	**Illiteracy Rate**	**Coverage Basis**
Sheridan County	Sioux	Pine Ridge Reservation and Off-Reservation	0	*	*	RP

NEVADA						
Covered Jurisdiction	**Covered Language**	**Indian Reservation (RP or RW)**	**Number LEP (L)**	**Percent LEP (P)**	**Illiteracy Rate**	**Coverage Basis**
Elko County	Other American Indian	Duck Valley Reservation	95	18.45	10.53	RP
	Shoshone	Elko Colony	40	9.64	10	RP
Humboldt County	Other American Indian	Fort McDermitt Reservation	60	31.58	6.67	RP
Lyon County	Paiute	Yerington Colony	0	*	*	RP
Nye County	Shoshone	Duckwater Reservation	0	*	*	RP
White Pine County	Shoshone	Ely Reservation	0	*	*	RP

NEW MEXICO						
Covered Jurisdiction	**Covered Language**	**Indian Reservation (RP or RW)**	**Number LEP (L)**	**Percent LEP (P)**	**Illiteracy Rate**	**Coverage Basis**
Bernalillo County	Navajo	Navajo Nation Reservation and Off-Reservation Trust Land	265	31.55	26.42	RP
	Pueblo	Laguna Pueblo and Off-Reservation Trust Land	0	0	0	RP
Catron County	Pueblo	Acoma Pueblo and Off-Reservation Trust Land	0	0	0	RP
	Pueblo	Zuni Reservation and Off-Reservation Trust Land	0	0	0	RP
Cibola County	Navajo	Navajo Nation Reservation and Off-Reservation Trust Land	465	38.43	29.03	RP
	Pueblo	Acoma Pueblo and Off-Reservation Trust Land	300	16.9	3.33	RP
	Pueblo	Laguna Pueblo and Off-Reservation Trust Land	430	17.48	2.33	RP
	Pueblo	Zuni Reservation and Off-Reservation Trust Land	0	0	0	RP
McKinley County	Navajo		8510	18.58	25.91	P
	Navajo	Navajo Nation Reservation and Off-Reservation Trust Land	6640	34.35	27.41	RP
	Pueblo	Zuni Reservation and Off-Reservation Trust Land	1310	27.93	1.91	RP
Rio Arriba County	Navajo	Navajo Nation Reservation and Off-Reservation Trust Land	0	*	*	RP
San Juan County	Navajo		6730	8.95	25.33	P
	Navajo	Navajo Nation Reservation and Off-Reservation Trust Land	5325	32.13	27.98	RP
	Navajo	Ute Mountain Reservation and Off-Reservation Trust Land	0	0	0	RP
	Ute	Ute Mountain Reservation and Off-Reservation Trust Land	0	0	0	RP
Sandoval County	Navajo	Navajo Nation Reservation and Off-Reservation Trust Land	795	50.64	35.22	RP
	Pueblo	Jemez Pueblo	525	42	1.9	RP
	Pueblo	Laguna Pueblo and Off-Reservation Trust Land	0	0	0	RP
	Pueblo	San Felipe Pueblo	600	38.71	4.17	RP
	Pueblo	Santo Domingo Pueblo	425	22.14	3.53	RP
	Pueblo	Zia Pueblo and Off-Reservation Trust Land	180	47.37	2.22	RP

NEW MEXICO (Continued)						
Covered Jurisdiction	**Covered Language**	**Indian Reservation (RP or RW)**	**Number LEP (L)**	**Percent LEP (P)**	**Illiteracy Rate**	**Coverage Basis**
Santa Fe County	Pueblo	Santo Domingo Pueblo	0	0	0	RP
	Pueblo	Tesuque Pueblo and Off-Reservation Trust Land	20	6.9	20	RP
Socorro County	Navajo	Navajo Nation Reservation and Off-Reservation Trust Land	575	62.84	13.04	RP
	Pueblo	Acoma Pueblo and Off-Reservation Trust Land	0	0	0	RP
Taos County	Pueblo	Taos Pueblo and Off-Reservation Trust Land	160	16.16	2.5	RP
Valencia County	Pueblo	Laguna Pueblo and Off-Reservation Trust Land	0	0	0	RP

NORTH DAKOTA						
Covered Jurisdiction	**Covered Language**	**Indian Reservation (RP or RW)**	**Number LEP (L)**	**Percent LEP (P)**	**Illiteracy Rate**	**Coverage Basis**
Richland County	Sioux	Lake Traverse Reservation	0	0	0	RP
Sargent County	Sioux	Lake Traverse Reservation	0	*	*	RP
Shannon County	Sioux		400	5.86	3.75	P
	Sioux	Pine Ridge Reservation and Off-Reservation Trust Land	400	6.38	3.75	RP
Stanley County	Sioux	Cheyenne River Reservation and Off-Reservation Trust Land	0	0	0	RP
Todd County	Sioux		265	5.25	1.51	P
	Sioux	Rosebud Reservation and Off-Reservation Trust Land	265	6.48	1.51	RW
Tripp County	Sioux	Rosebud Reservation and Off-Reservation Trust Land	0	*	*	RP
Ziebach County	Sioux		105	7.02	3.81	P
	Sioux	Cheyenne River Reservation and Off-Reservation Trust Land	105	10.94	3.81	RP

TEXAS						
Covered Jurisdiction	**Covered Language**	**Indian Reservation (RP or RW)**	**Number LEP (L)**	**Percent LEP (P)**	**Illiteracy Rate**	**Coverage Basis**
El Paso County	Pueblo	Ysleta Del Sur Pueblo and Off-Reservation Trust Land	40	24.24	10	RP

TEXAS (Continued)						
Covered Jurisdiction	**Covered Language**	**Indian Reservation (RP or RW)**	**Number LEP (L)**	**Percent LEP (P)**	**Illiteracy Rate**	**Coverage Basis**
Maverick County	Other American Indian	Kickapoo (TX) Reservation	145	59.18	86.21	RP

UTAH						
Covered Jurisdiction	**Covered Language**	**Indian Reservation (RP or RW)**	**Number LEP (L)**	**Percent LEP (P)**	**Illiteracy Rate**	**Coverage Basis**
San Juan County	Navajo		1660	19.12	25.60	P
	Navajo	Navajo Nation Reservation and Off-Reservation Trust Land	1510	42.24	26.82	RP
	Navajo	Ute Mountain Reservation and Off-Reservation Trust Land	0	*	*	RP
	Ute	Ute Mountain Reservation and Off-Reservation Trust Land	15	8.82	66.67	RP

Figure C.4 Jurisdictions covered by Section 203 for Asian languages, by state

ALASKA

Covered Jurisdiction	Covered Asian Languages	Number LEP (N)	Percent LEP (P)	Illiteracy Rate	Coverage Basis
Kodiak Island Borough	Filipino	470	5.58	12.77	P

CALIFORNIA

Covered Jurisdiction	Covered Asian Languages	Number LEP (N)	Percent LEP (P)	Illiteracy Rate	Coverage Basis
Alameda County	Chinese (including Taiwanese)	28280	3.15	10.98	N
Los Angeles County	Chinese (including Taiwanese)	95700	1.92	10.71	N
	Filipino	34985	0.7	4.46	N
	Japanese	12510	0.25	2.88	N
	Korean	42390	0.85	2.67	N
	Vietnamese	30340	0.61	10.42	N
Orange County	Chinese (including Taiwanese)	14805	0.91	4.36	N
	Korean	12240	0.75	2.37	N
	Vietnamese	45730	2.8	6.9	N
San Diego County	Filipino	17155	0.96	4.58	N
San Francisco County	Chinese (including Taiwanese)	58735	10.61	16.89	N, P
San Mateo County	Chinese (including Taiwanese)	11780	2.65	6.24	N
Santa Clara County	Chinese (including Taiwanese)	24895	2.56	5.12	N
	Filipino	11245	1.15	3.65	N
	Vietnamese	31265	3.21	5.76	N

HAWAII

Covered Jurisdiction	Covered Asian Languages	Number LEP (N)	Percent LEP (P)	Illiteracy Rate	Coverage Basis
Honolulu County	Chinese (including Taiwanese)	12640	2.07	13.49	N
	Filipino	24815	4.06	10.44	N
	Japanese	13865	2.27	5.27	N
Maui County	Filipino	5350	6.09	13.08	P

ILLINOIS

Covered Jurisdiction	Covered Asian Languages	Number LEP (N)	Percent LEP (P)	Illiteracy Rate	Coverage Basis
Cook County	Chinese (including Taiwanese)	11645	0.34	9.36	N

NEW YORK

Covered Jurisdiction	Covered Asian Languages	Number LEP (N)	Percent LEP (P)	Illiteracy Rate	Coverage Basis
Kings County	Chinese (including Taiwanese)	33635	2.43	13.32	N
New York County	Chinese (including Taiwanese)	21070	2.04	21.33	N
Queens County	Chinese (including Taiwanese)	37865	3.08	8.05	N
	Korean	11835	0.96	6.46	N

TEXAS					
Covered Jurisdiction	**Covered Asian Languages**	**Number LEP (N)**	**Percent LEP (P)**	**Illiteracy Rate**	**Coverage Basis**
Harris County	Vietnamese	16970	0.86	7.81	N

WASHINGTON					
Covered Jurisdiction	**Covered Asian Languages**	**Number LEP (N)**	**Percent LEP (P)**	**Illiteracy Rate**	**Coverage Basis**
King County	Chinese	10535	0.86	9.35	N

Selected Bibliography

The Language Assistance Provisions of the Voting Rights Act

Background

Ancheta, Angelo. *Language Accommodation and the Voting Rights Act*, *in* VOTING RIGHTS ACT REAUTHORIZATION OF 2006: PERSPECTIVES ON DEMOCRACY, PARTICIPATION, AND POWER 293 (Ana Henderson ed., 2007).

Benson, Jocelyn Friedrichs. *¡Su Voto Es Su Voz! Incorporating Voters of Limited English Proficiency into American Democracy*, 48 B.C. L. REV. 251 (2007).

Benson, Jocelyn Friedrichs. *One Person, One Vote: Protecting Access to the Franchise through the Effective Administration of Election Procedures and Protections*, 40 URB. LAW. 269 (2008).

Cartagena, Juan. *Latinos and Section 5 of the Voting Rights Act: Beyond Black and White*, 18 NAT'L BLACK L.J. 201 (2004–05).

Culliton-González, Katherine. *Time to Revive Puerto Rican Voting Rights*, 19 BERKELEY LA RAZA L.J. 27 (2008).

Del Valle, Sandra. *Fulfilling the Promise of Citizenship: English Literacy, Naturalization, and Voting Rights*, *in* LANGUAGE RIGHTS AND THE LAW IN THE UNITED STATES 97–116 (2003).

Guerra, Sandra. Student Note, *Voting Rights and the Constitution: The Disenfranchisement of Non-English Speaking Citizens*, 97 YALE L.J. 1419 (1988).

Hill, Josh, Devin Ross, and Brad Serafine. *Watch Your Language! The Kansas Law Review Survey of Official-English and English-Only Laws and Policies*, 57 UNIV. KAN. L. REV. 669 (2009).

Magpantay, Glenn D. *Asian American Access to the Vote: The Language Assistance Provisions (Section 203) of the Voting Rights Act and Beyond*, 11 ASIAN L.J. 31 (2004).

Magpantay, Glenn D. and Nancy W. Yu. *Asian Americans and Reauthorization of the Voting Rights Act*, 19 NAT'L BLACK L.J. 1 (2005).

McCool, Dan, Susan Olson and Jennifer L. Robinson. *On Account of Race or Color: The Development of the Voting Rights Act*, *in* NATIVE VOTE: AMERICAN INDIANS, THE VOTING RIGHTS ACT, AND THE RIGHT TO VOTE 21–44 (2007).

Narasaki, Karen K. and Terry M. Ao. *Meeting the demand of a growing language-minority voting populate*, *in* AMERICA VOTES! A GUIDE TO MODERN ELECTION LAW AND VOTING RIGHTS (Benjamin E. Griffith ed., Feb. 2008).

Overton, Spencer. STEALING DEMOCRACY: THE NEW POLITICS OF VOTER SUPPRESSION 121–47 (2006).

Pew Center on the States. *Translating the Vote: The Impact of the Language Minority Provision of the Voting Rights Act*, electionline.org (Oct. 2006).

Rodríguez, Cristina M. Book Review, *From Litigation, Legislation: A Review of Brian Landsberg's* FREE AT LAST TO VOTE: THE ALABAMA ORIGINS OF THE 1965 VOTING RIGHTS ACT, 117 YALE L.J. 1132 (2008).

Sutherland, Brian J. *The Patchwork of State and Federal Language Assistance for Minority Voters and a Proposal for Model State Legislation*, 64 ANN. SURV. AM. L. issue 4 (forthcoming 2009).

Tanner, John. *Effective Monitoring of Polling Places*, 61 BAYLOR L. REV. 50 (2009).

Trasviña, John. *Bilingual Ballots: Their History and a Look Forward*, *in* LANGUAGE LOYALTIES: A SOURCE BOOK ON THE OFFICIAL ENGLISH CONTROVERSY 258–64 (James Crawford ed., 1992).
Tucker, James Thomas. *Enfranchising Language Minority Citizens: The Bilingual Election Provisions of the Voting Rights Act*, 10 N.Y.U. J. LEGIS. & PUB. POL'Y 195 (2006).
Tucker, James Thomas. *The Politics of Persuasion: Passage of the Voting Rights Act Reauthorization Act of 2006*, 33 J. LEGIS. 205 (2007).
Tucker, James Thomas. *The Battle over Bilingual Ballots Shifts to the Courts: A Post-*Boerne *Assessment of Section 203 of the Voting Rights Act*, 45 HARV. J. ON LEGIS. 507 (2008).
Tucker, James Thomas. *The Case for Language Assistance under the Voting Rights Act*, *in* THE MOST FUNDAMENTAL RIGHT: THE 2006 REAUTHORIZATION OF THE VOTING RIGHTS ACT (Dan McCool ed., forthcoming 2010).
Tucker, James Thomas and Rodolfo Espino. *Government Effectiveness and Efficiency? The Minority Language Assistance Provisions of the VRA*, 12 TEX. J. C.L. & C.R. 163, 215 (2007).
U.S. Comm'n on Civil Rts. A CITIZEN'S GUIDE TO UNDERSTANDING THE VOTING RIGHTS ACT (1984).
U.S. Comm'n on Civil Rts. VOTING RIGHTS ENFORCEMENT AND REAUTHORIZATION (May 2006).
U.S. Comptroller Gen. VOTING RIGHTS ACT – ENFORCEMENT NEEDS STRENGTHENING (Feb. 6, 1978).
U.S. Dep't of Just. *Minority Language Citizens: Section 203 of the Voting Rights Act* (Aug. 1992) (pamphlet).
U.S. Dep't of Just, Civil Rights Div., Voting Section, *Minority Language Citizens: Section 203 of the Voting Rights Act* (2002), *available at* http:www.usdoj.gov/crt/voting/sec_203/203_brochure.htm.

Constitutionality of

Ancheta, Angelo. *Language Accommodation and the Voting Rights Act*, *in* VOTING RIGHTS ACT REAUTHORIZATION OF 2006: PERSPECTIVES ON DEMOCRACY, PARTICIPATION, AND POWER 293 (Ana Henderson ed., 2007).
Fuentes-Rohwer, Luis. *Legislative Findings, Congressional Powers, and the Future of the Voting Rights Act*, 82 IND. L.J. 99 (2007).
Guerra, Sandra. Student Note, *Voting Rights and the Constitution: The Disenfranchisement of Non-English Speaking Citizens*, 97 YALE L.J. 1419 (1988).
Magpantay, Glenn D. and Nancy W. Yu. *Asian Americans and Reauthorization of the Voting Rights Act*, 19 NAT'L BLACK L.J. 1 (2005).
Pitts, Michael J. *The Voting Rights Act and the Era of Maintenance*, 59 ALA. L. REV. 903 (2008).
Takaji, Daniel P. *Intent and its Alternatives: Defending the New Voting Rights Act*, 58 ALA. L. REV. 349 (2006).
Tucker, James Thomas. *The Battle over Bilingual Ballots Shifts to the Courts: A Post-*Boerne *Assessment of Section 203 of the Voting Rights Act*, 45 HARV. J. ON LEGIS. 507 (2008).
Tucker, James Thomas. *The Case for Language Assistance under the Voting Rights Act*, *in* THE MOST FUNDAMENTAL RIGHT: THE 2006 REAUTHORIZATION OF THE VOTING RIGHTS ACT (Dan McCool ed., forthcoming 2010).

Cost and Effectiveness of

Benson, Jocelyn Friedrichs. *Towards Full Participation: Solutions for Improvements to the Federal Language Assistance Laws*, American Constitution Society for Law and Policy paper (Sept. 2007).

Benson, Jocelyn Friedrichs. *One Person, One Vote: Protecting Access to the Franchise through the Effective Administration of Election Procedures and Protections*, 40 URB. LAW. 269 (2008).

Guerra, Sandra. Student Note, *Voting Rights and the Constitution: The Disenfranchisement of Non-English Speaking Citizens*, 97 YALE L.J. 1419 (1988).

Henderson, Ana and Christopher Edley, Jr. *Voting Rights Act Reauthorization: Research-Based Recommendations to Improve Voting Access* (2006), *reprinted in Fannie Lou Hamer, Rosa Parks, and Coretta Scott King Voting Rights Act Reauthorization and Amendments Act of 2006 (Part I): Hearing on H.R. 9 Before the Subcomm. on the Const. of the H. Comm. on the Judiciary*, 109th Cong. 166 (2006).

Ichinose, Daniel Kikuo. Asian Pacific American Legal Center, *Reauthorization of Section 203 of the Voting Rights Act: The Impact of Modifying Coverage Thresholds on Asian and Spanish Language Minority Groups and Political Subdivisions Subject to the Law* (Dec. 15, 2005).

Jones-Correa, Michael. *Language Provisions Under the Voting Rights Act: How Effective Are They?*, 86 SOC. SCI. Q. 549 (Sept. 2005).

Jones-Correa, Michael and Karthick Ramakrishnan. *Studying the Effects of Language Provisions Under the Voting Rights Act.*

Jones-Correa, Michael and Israel Waismel-Manor. *Verifying Implementation of Language Provisions in the Voting Rights Act*, *in* VOTING RIGHTS ACT REAUTHORIZATION OF 2006: PERSPECTIVES ON DEMOCRACY, PARTICIPATION, AND POWER 161 (Ana Henderson ed., 2007).

Narasaki, Karen K. and Terry M. Ao. *Meeting the demand of a growing language-minority voting populate*, *in* AMERICA VOTES! A GUIDE TO MODERN ELECTION LAW AND VOTING RIGHTS (Benjamin E. Griffith ed., Feb. 2008).

Pew Center on the States. *Translating the Vote: The Impact of the Language Minority Provision of the Voting Rights Act*, electionline.org (Oct. 2006).

Tucker, James Thomas. *Enfranchising Language Minority Citizens: The Bilingual Election Provisions of the Voting Rights Act*, 10 N.Y.U. J. LEGIS. & PUB. POL'Y 195 (2006).

Tucker, James Thomas and Rodolfo Espino. *Government Effectiveness and Efficiency? The Minority Language Assistance Provisions of the VRA*, 12 TEX. J. C.L. & C.R. 163, 215 (2007).

Tucker, James Thomas, Rodolfo Espino, et al. MINORITY LANGUAGE ASSISTANCE PRACTICES IN PUBLIC ELECTIONS (2006), *reprinted in Voting Rights Act: Evidence of Continued Need: Hearing before the Subcomm. on the Const. of the H. Comm. on the Judiciary*, 109th Cong. 2124 (2006).

U.S. Comptroller Gen. VOTING RIGHTS ACT – ENFORCEMENT NEEDS STRENGTHENING (Feb. 6, 1978).

U.S. Gen. Acct. Off. BILINGUAL VOTING ASSISTANCE: COSTS OF AND USE DURING THE 1984 GENERAL ELECTION (1986).

U.S. Gen. Acct. Off. BILINGUAL VOTING ASSISTANCE: ASSISTANCE PROVIDED AND COSTS (1997).

U.S. Govt. Acct. Off. BILINGUAL VOTING ASSISTANCE: SELECTED JURISDICTIONS' STRATEGIES FOR IDENTIFYING NEEDS AND PROVIDING ASSISTANCE (2008).

Vigil-Giron, Rebecca. Secretary of State of New Mexico, Testimony before the Subcomm. on the Const. of the H. Comm. on the Judiciary, *Voting Rights Act: Section 203 – Bilingual Election Requirements (Part I)*, H. HRG. 109–83 (Nov. 8, 2005).

Wright, Deborah. Acting Assistant Registrar-Recorder in Los Angeles County, Cal., Testimony before the Senate Jud. Comm., *Continuing Need for Section 203's Provisions for Limited English Proficient Voters*, S. HRG. 109–669 (June 13, 2006).

Federal Observer Coverage to Promote Enforcement of

Tanner, John. *Effective Monitoring of Polling Places*, 61 BAYLOR L. REV. 50 (2009).

Tucker, James Thomas. *The Power of Observation: The Role of Federal Observers under the Voting Rights Act*, 13 MICH. J. RACE & LAW 227 (Fall 2007).

Weinberg, Barry H. and Lyn Utrecht. *Problems in America's Polling Places: How They Can Be Stopped*, 11 TEMP. POL. & CIV. RTS. L. REV. 401 (2002).

Legislative History of

Ao, Terry M. *When the Voting Rights Act Became Un-American: The Misguided Vilification of Section 203*, 58 ALA. L. REV. 377 (2006).

Benson, Jocelyn Friedrichs. *Language Assistance Provisions of the Voting Rights Act and the 2006 Reauthorization, in* AMERICA VOTES! A GUIDE TO MODERN ELECTION LAW AND VOTING RIGHTS (Benjamin E. Griffith ed., Feb. 2008).

Benson, Jocelyn Friedrichs. *One Person, One Vote: Protecting Access to the Franchise through the Effective Administration of Election Procedures and Protections*, 40 URB. LAW. 269 (2008).

Cartagena, Juan. *Latinos and Section 5 of the Voting Rights Act: Beyond Black and White*, 18 NAT'L BLACK L.J. 201 (2004–05).

Chiu, Lucy. Student Note, *The Emerson English Language Empowerment Act: The House's "Straw Man" Bill*, 23 J. LEGIS. 231 (1997).

Hunter, David H. *The 1975 Voting Rights Act and Language Minorities*, 25 CATH. U. L. REV. 250 (1976).

McCool, Dan, Susan Olson, and Jennifer L. Robinson. *On Account of Race or Color: The Development of the Voting Rights Act, in* NATIVE VOTE: AMERICAN INDIANS, THE VOTING RIGHTS ACT, AND THE RIGHT TO VOTE 21–44 (2007).

Mexican Am. Legal Def. and Educ. Fund. *Redressing Impediments to Voting Language Minorities: The Need to Reauthorize and Expand Section 203 of the Voting Rights Act* 46–71, *reprinted in S. 2236 Hearings*, 102d Cong., 2d Sess., S. HRG. 102–1066, at 454–71 (1992).

Persily, Nathaniel. *The Promise and Pitfalls of the New Voting Rights Act*, 117 YALE L.J. 174 (2007).

Rodríguez, Cristina M. Book Review, *From Litigation, Legislation: A Review of Brian Landsberg's* FREE AT LAST TO VOTE: THE ALABAMA ORIGINS OF THE 1965 VOTING RIGHTS ACT, 117 YALE L.J. 1132 (2008).

Tucker, James Thomas. *Enfranchising Language Minority Citizens: The Bilingual Election Provisions of the Voting Rights Act*, 10 N.Y.U. J. LEGIS. & PUB. POL'Y 195 (2006).

Tucker, James Thomas. *The Politics of Persuasion: Passage of the Voting Rights Act Reauthorization Act of 2006*, 33 J. LEGIS. 205 (2007).

Criticism of the Language Assistance Provisions

Enforcement of

Adelson, Bruce. *Minority-Language Election Rules and the Public Lawyer*, 15 PUB. LAW. 1 (Sept. 2007).

Blum, Edward. *Se Habla Lawsuit?*, THE WKLY. STANDARD (Mar. 26, 2007).

Requirements of

Betsch, Michael L. *Bilingual Ballots are "Loco" Say Conservatives*, CyberCast News Service (Aug. 2, 2002), *available at* http://www.cnsnews.com/ViewCulture.asp?Page=%5CCulture%5Carchive%5C200208%5CCUL20020802d.html.

Boulet, Jim Jr. *Lost in Translation: Bilingual Voting and the South Dakota Senate Race*, NAT'L REV. ONLINE (Oct. 22, 2002), *available at* http://www.nationalreview.com/comment/comment-boulet102202.asp.

Chavez, Linda. OUT OF THE BARRIO, TOWARD A NEW POLITICS OF HISPANIC ASSIMILATION (1991).

Chavez, Linda. President of the Center for Equal Opportunity, Testimony before the Subcomm. on the Const. of the House Jud. Comm. (Apr. 18, 1996).

Chavez, Linda. *Let Bilingual Voting Requirements of Voting Rights Act Die*, HUMAN EVENTS, Nov. 14, 2005.

Clegg, Roger. *203 Mistakes: A Bilingual Flaw in the Voting Rights Act*, NAT'L REV. ONLINE, July 27, 2006, *available at* http://article.nationalreview.com.

Diamond, Stanley. Chairman of the Board, U.S. English, Inc., Testimony before the Senate Jud. Comm., *S. 2236 Hearings*.

English First Foundation. *Bilingual Ballots: Election Fairness or Fraud?* (2000), *available at* http://www.englishfirst.org/eff/efbb.htm.

English First Foundation. *Resources on Bilingual Ballots* (Feb. 1, 2007), *available at* http://www.englishfirst.org/ballots/ballots.htm.

English Language Political Action Committee, *Language in America: Declaring English the Official Language of the United States Government – A Candidate's Briefing Paper* (5th ed. 2000), *available at* http://www.workings.com/LIA_BB.htm.

Kirsanow, Peter. *Bilingual Bailout: Making sense of bilingual voting requirements*, NAT'L REV. ONLINE, June 21, 2006, *available at* http://article.nationalreview.com.

Miller, John J. *English Is Broken Here: Bilingual Ballots Are Bad for Democracy*, 79 POL'Y REV. 54 (1996).

ProEnglish. *A Nation Divided: The Consequences of Bilingual Ballots. Five Reasons Why Congress Should Not Renew the Bilingual Voting Provisions of the Voting Rights Act*, *available at* http://www.proenglish.org/issues/ballots/fivereasons.html.

Schlafly, Phyllis. *Foreign Language Ballots Are A Bad Idea* (Aug. 28, 2002), *at* http://www.eagleforum.org/column/2002/aug02/02-08-28.shtml.

Thernstrom, Abigail, WHOSE VOTES COUNT? (1987).

U.S. English. *Official English: Facts and Figures* (2008), *available at* http://www.usenglish.org/view/24.

Will, George. *A Vote for English*, WASH. POST, May 25, 2006, at A29.

Will, George. *Discomforting Truths About Bilingual Ballots*, 6 THE SOC. CONT. 262 (Summer 1996).

Reauthorization of the Language Assistance Provisions in 2006

Lobby Materials

Asian American Justice Center (AAJC). Lobby packet on behalf of Asian-American voters, *available at* http://65.36.162.215/files/vra_kit.pdf.

Asian American Legal Defense and Education Fund (AALDEF). *Language Access to the Vote for Asian Americans*, *available at* http://www.aaldef.org/docs/LanguageAccesstotheVote_VRA203.pdf.

California Voter Empowerment Circle. Various materials and resources, *available at* http://www.calvec.org.

Leadership Conference on Civ. Rts., *Interactive Map: States Affected by VRA Reauthorization*, *available at* http://www.renewthevra.org/interactive_map.

Leadership Conference on Civ. Rts. *Protect Voting Rights: Renew the VRA, A Handbook for Voting Rights Activists*, *available at* http://www.renewthevra.org/act_now/.

National Council of La Raza (NCLR). *Language Assistance for Limited-English-Proficient Voters*, *available at* http://65.36.162.215/files/vra_kit.pdf.

Tucker, James Thomas. *Debunking Common Myths Cited by Opponents of the Language Assistance Provisions of the Voting Rights Act* (2005), *available at* http://www.votingrights.org/resources/index.php#Section203.

Voting Rts. Project of the Am. Civ. Liberties Union, *Scope of Coverage of the Language Assistance Provisions of the Federal Voting Rights Act*, *available at* http://www.votingrights.org/states/.

Voting Rts. Project of the Am. Civ. Liberties Union, *State Language Assistance Grid* (2004), *available at* http://www.votingrights.org/resources/index.php#Section203.

Witnesses Opposing

Chavez, Linda. President of One Nation Indivisible, Testimony before the Subcomm. on the Const. of the H. Comm. on the Judiciary, *Voting Rights Act: Section 203 – Bilingual Election Requirements (Part I)*, H. Hrg. 109–83 (Nov. 8, 2005).

Chavez, Linda. President of One Nation Indivisible, Testimony before the Senate Jud. Comm., *Continuing Need for Section 203's Provisions for Limited English Proficient Voters*, S. Hrg. 109–669 (June 13, 2006).

Clegg, Roger. General Counsel of the Center for Equal Opportunity, Testimony before the Subcomm. on the Const. of the H. Comm. on the Judiciary, *Voting Rights Act: Section 203 – Bilingual Election Requirements (Part I)*, H. Hrg. 109–83 (Nov. 8, 2005).

Kirsanow, Peter N. Member, United States Civil Rights Commission (June 13, 2006), Testimony before the Senate Jud. Comm., *The Continuing Need for Section 203's Provisions for Limited English Proficient Voters*, S. Hrg. 109–669 (June 13, 2006).

McAlpin, K.C. Exec. Dir. of ProEnglish, Testimony before the Subcomm. on the Const. of the House Jud. Comm., *Voting Rights Act: Section 203 – Bilingual Election Requirements (Part II)*, H. Hrg. 109–78 (Nov. 9–10, 2005).

Mujica, Mauro E. Chairman of the Board of U.S. English, Inc., Testimony before the Senate Jud. Comm., *Continuing Need for Section 203's Provisions for Limited English Proficient Voters*, S. Hrg. 109–669 (June 13, 2006).

Norby, Chris. Supervisor on the Orange County, Cal. Board of Supervisors, Testimony before the Subcomm. on the Const. of the House Jud. Comm., *Fannie Lou Hamer, Rosa Parks, and Coretta Scott King Voting Rights Act Reauthorization and Amendments Act of 2006 (Part II)*, H. Hrg. 109–119 (May 4, 2006).

Witnesses Supporting

Cartagena, Juan. General Counsel, Community Service Society, Testimony before the Subcomm. on the Const. of the H. Comm. on the Judiciary, *Voting Rights Act: Section 203 – Bilingual Election Requirements (Part I)*, H. HRG. 109–78 (Nov. 9–10, 2005).

Cartagena, Juan. General Counsel, Community Service Society, Testimony before the Senate Jud. Comm., *Modern Enforcement of the Voting Rights Act*, S. HRG. 109–75 (May 10, 2006).

Comisac, Rena. Principal Deputy Assistant Attorney General for the Civil Rights Division of the U.S. Department of Justice, Testimony before the Subcomm. on the Const. of the House Jud. Comm., *Fannie Lou Hamer, Rosa Parks, and Coretta Scott King Voting Rights Act Reauthorization and Amendments Act of 2006 (Part II)*, H. HRG. 109–119 (May 4, 2006).

Fung, Margaret. Executive Director of the Asian American Legal Defense and Education Fund (AALDEF), Testimony before the Subcomm. on the Const. of the H. Comm. on the Judiciary, *Voting Rights Act: Section 203 – Bilingual Election Requirements (Part I)*, H. HRG. 109–83 (Nov. 8, 2005).

Fung, Margaret. Executive Director of the Asian American Legal Defense and Education Fund (AALDEF), Testimony before the Senate Jud. Comm., *Continuing Need for Section 203's Provisions for Limited English Proficient Voters*, S. HRG. 109–669 (June 13, 2006).

Johnson, Jacqueline. Executive Director of the National Congress of American Indians, Testimony before the Subcomm. on the Const. of the H. Comm. on the Judiciary, *Voting Rights Act: Section 203 – Bilingual Election Requirements (Part I)*, H. HRG. 109–78 (Nov. 9–10, 2005).

Kim, Wan J. Assistant Attorney General for the Civil Rights Division of the U.S. Department of Justice, Testimony before the Senate Jud. Comm., *Modern Enforcement of the Voting Rights Act*, S. HRG. 109–75 (May 10, 2006).

Landreth, Natalie A. Staff Attorney for the Native American Rights Fund (NARF), Testimony before the Senate Jud. Comm., *Modern Enforcement of the Voting Rights Act*, S. HRG. 109–75 (May 10, 2006).

Narasaki, Karen. President and Executive Director of the Asian American Justice Center (AAJC), Testimony before the Subcomm. on the Const. of the House Jud. Comm., *Fannie Lou Hamer, Rosa Parks, and Coretta Scott King Voting Rights Act Reauthorization and Amendments Act of 2006 (Part II)*, H. HRG. 109–19 (May 4, 2006).

Schlozman, Bradley J. Acting Assistant Attorney General of the Civil Rights Division of the U.S. Department of Justice, Testimony before the Subcomm. on the Const. of the H. Comm. on the Judiciary, *Voting Rights Act: Section 203 – Bilingual Election Requirements (Part I)*, H. HRG. 109–83 (Nov. 8, 2005).

Trasviña, John. Interim President and General Counsel of the Mexican American Legal Defense and Education Fund (MALDEF), Testimony before the Senate Jud. Comm., *Continuing Need for Section 203's Provisions for Limited English Proficient Voters*, S. HRG. 109–669 (June 13, 2006).

Tucker, James Thomas. Shareholder, Ogletree Deakins, Testimony before the Subcomm. on the Const. of the H. Comm. on the Judiciary, *Voting Rights Act: Section 203 – Bilingual Election Requirements (Part I)*, H. HRG. 109–78 (Nov. 9–10, 2005).

Tucker, James Thomas. Voting Rights Consultant for the National Association of Latino Elected and Appointed Officials (NALEO) Educational Fund, Testimony before the Subcomm. on the Const. of the House Jud. Comm., *Fannie Lou Hamer, Rosa Parks, and Coretta Scott King Voting Rights Act Reauthorization and Amendments Act of 2006 (Part II)*, H. HRG. 109–19 (May 4, 2006).

Tucker, James Thomas. Voting Rights Consultant for the National Association of Latino Elected and Appointed Officials (NALEO) Educational Fund, Written testimony before the Senate Jud. Comm., *The Continuing Need for Federal Examiners and Observers to Ensure Electoral Integrity*, S. Hrg. 109–669 (June 13, 2006).

Vigil-Giron, Rebecca. Secretary of State of New Mexico, Testimony before the Subcomm. on the Const. of the H. Comm. on the Judiciary, *Voting Rights Act: Section 203 – Bilingual Election Requirements (Part I)*, H. Hrg. 109–83 (Nov. 8, 2005).

Wright, Deborah. Acting Assistant Registrar-Recorder in Los Angeles County, Cal., Testimony before the Senate Jud. Comm., *Continuing Need for Section 203's Provisions for Limited English Proficient Voters*, S. Hrg. 109–669 (June 13, 2006).

Yazzie, Alfred. Written testimony before the Senate Jud. Comm., *The Continuing Need for Federal Examiners and Observers to Ensure Electoral Integrity*, S. Hrg. 109–669 (June 13, 2006).

Limited-English Proficiency among Language Minorities (2000 Census)

Bureau of the Census, Economics and Statistics Admin., U.S. Dep't of Commerce, The Native Hawaiian and Other Pacific Islander Population: 2002 (Dec. 2001).

Bureau of the Census, U.S. Dep't of Commerce. *Voting Rights Act Amendments of 1992, Determinations Under Section 203*, 67 Fed. Reg. 48,871 (July 26, 2002) (to be codified at 28 C.F.R. Pt. 55).

Bureau of the Census, U.S. Dep't of Commerce. The American Indian and Alaska Native Population: 2000 (2002).

Bureau of the Census, U.S. Dep't of Commerce. Language Use and English-Speaking Ability: 2000 (2003).

Bureau of the Census, U.S. Dep't of Commerce, *Voting Rights Output File Documentation* (Sept. 2, 2004).

Bureau of the Census, U.S. Dep't of Commerce. We the People: Asians in the United States (2004).

Bureau of the Census, U.S. Dep't of Commerce. We the People: Hispanics in the United States (2004).

Bureau of the Census, U.S. Dep't of Commerce. We the People: Pacific Islanders in the United States (2005).

Bureau of the Census, U.S. Dep't of Commerce. We the People: American Indians and Alaska Natives in the United States (2006).

Siegal, Paul et al., U.S. Census Bureau, *Language Use and Linguistic Isolation: Historical Data and Methodological Issues* 6–8 (Feb. 12, 2001).

Educational Barriers to Language Minority Voters (By Language Group or Ethnicity)

Alaska Natives

Alaska Advisory Comm. to the U.S. Comm'n on Civil Rts. Racism's Frontier: The Untold Story of Discrimination and Division in Alaska 17–26 (Apr. 2002).

Alton, Thomas. *Politics, Economics, and the Schools: Roots of Alaska Native Language Loss Since 1867*, 20 Alaska Hist. 18 (Fall 2005).

Bureau of Indian Affairs. *Answers to Your Questions on Alaska Native Service Educational Activities* (Feb. 1950), *in* Ray, *infra*, at Appendix A.

Cotton, Stephen E. *Alaska's "Molly Hootch Case": High Schools and the Village Voice*, 8 EDUC. RES. Q. 30 (1984).

Cotton, Stephen E. *Thirty Years Later: The Molly Hootch Case*, SHARING OUR PATHWAYS vol. 9, issue 4, at 4 (Sept./Oct. 2004).

Haycox, Stephen. *Desegregation in Alaska's Schools: Alaska Yesterday*, ANCHORAGE TIMES, Jan. 26, 1986.

Landreth, Natalie and Moira Smith. *Voting Rights in Alaska: 1982–2006*, 17 S. CAL. REV. L. & SOC. SCI. 79 (2007).

Olthuis, Diane. *The Molly Hootch Case: 1972, Emmonak, in* IT HAPPENED IN ALASKA 125 (2006).

Ray, Charles K. *Alaskan Native Education: An Historical Perspective* (Oct. 1973).

State of Alaska, Governor's Comm. on Educ. *An Overall Education Plan for Rural Alaska* (rev. Feb. 26, 1966), *available in* Ray, *supra*, at Appendix E.

U.S. Comm'n on Civ. Rts, Alaska Advisory Comm. ALASKAN NATIVES AND OTHER MINORITIES IN THE SPECIAL EDUCATION PROGRAMS OF FOUR ALASKAN SCHOOL DISTRICTS (June 1999).

U.S. Dep't of Interior, *Organization of School Districts on Indian Reservations in Alaska*, 63 Interior Dec. 333 (Sept. 17, 1956).

American Indians

Adams, David Wallace. EDUCATION FOR EXTINCTION: AMERICAN INDIANS AND THE BOARDING SCHOOL EXPERIENCE, 1875–1928 (1995).

Brown, Alison McKinney. *Native American Education: A System in Need of Reform*, 2 KAN. J. L. & PUB. POL'Y 105 (1993).

Child, Brenda J. BOARDING SCHOOL SEASONS: AMERICAN INDIAN FAMILIES: 1900–1940 (1998).

Hoxie, Frederick E. A FINAL PROMISE: THE CAMPAIGN TO ASSIMILATE THE INDIANS, 1880–1920 (1984).

Kuhn, Tom. *Phoenix Indian School: Segregation*, THE NEW TIMES WKLY, Vol. 11, No. 23 (Jan. 2, 1980).

McDonald, Laughlin, Janine Pease and Richard Guest. *Voting Rights in South Dakota 1982–2006*, 17 S. CAL. REV. L. & SOC. JUST. 195 (2007).

Reyhner, Jon and Jeanne Eder. AMERICAN INDIAN EDUCATION: A HISTORY (2004).

Riney, Scott. THE RAPID CITY INDIAN SCHOOL, 1893–1933 (1999).

Rosenfelt, Daniel M. *Indian Schools and Community Control*, 25 STAN. L. REV. 489 (1973).

Special Subcomm. on Indian Educ., Comm. on Labor and Pub. Welfare. INDIAN EDUCATION: A NATIONAL TRAGEDY – A NATIONAL CHALLENGE, S. REP. NO. 91–501 (1969).

Szasz, Margaret Connell. *Listening to the Native Voice: American Indian Schooling in the Twentieth Century, in* THE AMERICAN INDIAN, PAST AND PRESENT 267 (5th ed. Roger L. Nichols ed., 1999).

Trennert, Jr., Robert A. THE PHOENIX INDIAN SCHOOL: FORCED ASSIMILATION IN ARIZONA, 1891–1935 (1988).

U.S. Comm'n on Civ. Rts, Iowa Advisory Comm. RACE RELATIONS IN TAMA COUNTY (Aug. 1981).

U.S. Comm'n on Civ. Rts, Minnesota Advisory Comm. BRIDGING THE GAP: A REASSESSMENT (June 1978).

U.S. Comm'n on Civ. Rts, North Dakota Advisory Comm. NATIVE AMERICAN STUDENTS IN NORTH DAKOTA SPECIAL EDUCATION PROGRAMS (April 1993).

U.S. Dep't of Educ. INDIAN NATIONS AT RISK: AN EDUCATIONAL STRATEGY FOR ACTION (1991).

Asian Americans

Ancheta, Angelo N. RACE, RIGHTS, AND THE ASIAN AMERICAN EXPERIENCE (1998).
U.S. Comm'n on Civ. Rts. SUCCESS OF ASIAN AMERICANS: FACT OR FICTION? (Sept. 1980).
U.S. Comm'n on Civ. Rts. CIVIL RIGHTS ISSUES FACING ASIAN AMERICANS IN THE 1990S (Feb. 1992).
U.S. Comm'n on Civ. Rts, California Advisory Comm. ASIAN AMERICANS AND PACIFIC PEOPLES: A CASE OF MISTAKEN IDENTITY (Feb. 1975).
U.S. Comm'n on Civ. Rts, Illinois Advisory Comm. CIVIL RIGHTS ISSUES FACING ASIAN AMERICANS IN METROPOLITAN CHICAGO (May 1995).
Wollenberg, Charles. ALL DELIBERATE SPEED: SEGREGATION AND EXCLUSION IN CALIFORNIA SCHOOLS, 1855–1975 (1996).

Spanish Heritage

Fraga, Luis Ricardo, Kenneth J. Meier, and Robert E. England. *Hispanic Americans and Educational Policy: Limits to Equal Access*, *in* PURSUING POWER: LATINOS AND THE POLITICAL SYSTEM 279–85 (F. Chris Garcia ed., 1997).
Hakimzadeh, Shirin and D'Vera Cohn, Pew Hispanic Center. *English Usage among Hispanics in the United States* (Nov. 2007).
Johnson, Kevin R. and George A. Martínez. *Discrimination by Proxy: The Case of Proposition 227 and the Ban on Bilingual Education*, 33 U. CAL.-DAVIS L. REV. 1227 (2002).
Muñoz, Laura K. *Separate But Equal? A Case Study of Romo v. Laird and Mexican American Education*, 15 ORG. AM. HISTORIANS MAG. OF HIST. 28 (Winter 2001).
Perea, Juan F. *Buscando América: Why Integration and Equal Protection Fail to Protect Latinos*, 117 HARV. L. REV. 1420 (2004).
Pew Hispanic Center. *Fact Sheet: Hispanic Attitudes Towards Learning English* (June 7, 2006).
Rangel, Jorge C. and Carlos M. Alcala. *Project Report: De Jure Segregation of Chicanos in Texas Schools*, 7 HARV. C.R.-C.L. L. REV. 307 (1972).
Rochmes, Daniel Aaron. Student Note, *Blinded by the White: Latino School Desegregation and the Insidious Allure of Whiteness*, 13 TEX. HISP. J. L. & POL'Y 7 (2007).
Rolstad, Kellie, Kate S. Mahoney, and Gene V. Glass. *Weighing the Evidence: A Meta-Analysis of Bilingual Education in Arizona*, 29 BILINGUAL RES. J. 43 (2005).
Salinas, Lupe S. and Dr. Robert H. Kimball. *The Equal Treatment of Unequals: Barriers Facing Latinos and the Poor in Texas Public Schools*, 14 GEO. J. ON POVERTY L. & POL'Y 215 (2007).
U.S. Comm'n on Civil Rts. ETHNIC ISOLATION OF MEXICAN AMERICANS IN THE PUBLIC SCHOOLS OF THE SOUTHWEST, Report I of the Mexican American Education Study (Apr. 1971).
U.S. Comm'n on Civil Rts. THE UNFINISHED EDUCATION: OUTCOMES FOR MINORITIES IN THE FIVE SOUTHWESTERN STATES, Report II of the Mexican American Education Study (Oct. 1971).
U.S. Comm'n on Civil Rts. THE EXCLUDED STUDENT: EDUCATIONAL PRACTICES AFFECTING MEXICAN AMERICANS IN THE SOUTHWEST, Report III of the Mexican American Education Study (May 1972).
U.S. Comm'n on Civ. Rts. MEXICAN AMERICAN EDUCATION IN TEXAS: A FUNCTION OF WEALTH, Report IV of the Mexican American Education Study (1972).
U.S. Comm'n on Civil Rts. TEACHERS AND STUDENTS: DIFFERENCES IN TEACHER INTERACTION WITH MEXICAN AMERICAN STUDENTS AND ANGLO STUDENTS, Report V of the Mexican American Education Study (Mar. 1973).

U.S. Comm'n on Civil Rts. TOWARD QUALITY EDUCATION FOR MEXICAN AMERICANS, Report VI of the Mexican American Education Study (Feb. 1974).

U.S. Comm'n on Civ. Rts, Colorado Advisory Comm. HISPANIC STUDENT DROPOUT PROBLEM IN COLORADO (June 1987).

Valencia, Richard R. CHICANO SCHOOL FAILURE AND SUCCESS 35 (Richard R. Valencia ed., 1991).

Wollenberg, Charles. ALL DELIBERATE SPEED: SEGREGATION AND EXCLUSION IN CALIFORNIA SCHOOLS, 1855–1975 (1996).

Multiple Groups

Fernández, Alberto T. *Legal Support for Bilingual Education and Language-Appropriate Related Services for Limited English Proficient Students with Disabilities*, 16 BILINGUAL RES. J. 117 (1992).

Henderson, Ana. *English Language Naturalization Requirements and the Bilingual Assistance Provisions of the Voting Rights Act* 3 (2006) (on file with author).

Kominski, Robert. U.S. Census Bureau, Population Division, *How Good is "How Well"? An Examination of the Census English-Speaking Ability Question 1* (1989).

SERVE. ENGLISH LANGUAGE LEARNERS IN THE SOUTHEAST: RESEARCH, POLICY & PRACTICE (2004).

Tucker, James Thomas. *Enfranchising Language Minority Citizens: The Bilingual Election Provisions of the Voting Rights Act*, 10 N.Y.U. J. LEGIS. & PUB. POL'Y 195 (2006).

Tucker, James Thomas. *The ESL Logjam: Waiting Times for ESL Classes and the Impact on English Language Learners*, 96 NAT'L CIVIC REV. 30 (Mar. 2007).

Tucker, James Thomas. *The Battle over Bilingual Ballots Shifts to the Courts: A Post-*Boerne *Assessment of Section 203 of the Voting Rights Act*, 45 HARV. J. ON LEGIS. 507 (2008).

Tucker, James Thomas. *The Case for Language Assistance under the Voting Rights Act*, *in* THE MOST FUNDAMENTAL RIGHT: THE 2006 REAUTHORIZATION OF THE VOTING RIGHTS ACT (Dan McCool ed., forthcoming 2010).

Tucker, James Thomas. NALEO Educational Fund, *The ESL Logjam: Waiting Times for ESL Classes and the Impact on English Language Learners* (Sept. 2006), *at* http://www.naleo.org/downloads/ESLReportLoRes.pdf.

U.S. Comm'n on Civil Rts. INEQUALITY IN SCHOOL FINANCING: THE ROLE OF LAW (Aug. 1972).

U.S. Comm'n on Civil Rts. A GENERATION DEPRIVED: LOS ANGELES SCHOOL DESEGREGATION (May 1977).

U.S. Comm'n on Civil Rts. EQUAL EDUCATIONAL OPPORTUNITY PROJECT SERIES VOL I (Dec. 1996).

U.S. Comm'n on Civ. Rts, California Advisory Comm. STATE ADMINISTRATION OF BILINGUAL EDUCATION – ¿SI O NO? (June 1976).

U.S. Department of Education, Office of English Language Acquisition (OELA), LANGUAGE ENHANCEMENT AND ACADEMIC ACHIEVEMENT FOR LIMITED ENGLISH PROFICIENT STUDENTS, SURVEY OF THE STATES' LIMITED ENGLISH PROFICIENT STUDENTS AND AVAILABLE EDUCATIONAL PROGRAMS AND SERVICES (Oct. 2002).

Discrimination against Language Minority Voters (By Language Group or Ethnicity)

Alaska Natives

Cole, Terrence M. *Jim Crow in Alaska: The Passage of the Alaska Equal Rights Act of 1945*, *in* AN ALASKA ANTHOLOGY: INTERPRETING THE PAST 314–35 (Stephen W. Haycox and Mary Childers Mangusso eds., 1996).

Cent. Council of Tlingit and Haida Indian Tribes of Alaska (CCTHITA). *A Recollection of Civil Rights Leader Elizabeth Peratrovich, 1911-1958* (1991).

Comm'n on Wartime Relocation and Internment of Civilians. PERSONAL JUSTICE DENIED (1997).

Harrison, Gordon S. *Alaska's Constitutional 'Literacy Test' and the Question of Voting Discrimination*, 22 ALASKA HIST. 23 (Spring/Fall 2007).

Haycox, Stephen W. *William Paul, Sr., and the Alaska Voters' Literacy Act of 1925*, 2 ALASKA HIST. 16 (Winter 1986–1987).

Jones, Preston. *Yankees in Parkas: Native Influence at Nome, 1900–1920*, 20 ALASKA HIST. 42 (Fall 2005).

Landreth, Natalie and Moira Smith. *Voting Rights in Alaska: 1982–2006*, 17 S. CAL. REV. L. & SOC. SCI. 79 (2007).

Paul, Fred. THEN FIGHT FOR IT!: THE LARGEST PEACEFUL REDISTRIBUTION OF WEALTH IN THE HISTORY OF MANKIND (2006).

Philip, Kenneth R. *The New Deal and Alaskan Natives: 1936–1945*, *in* AN ALASKA ANTHOLOGY: INTERPRETING THE PAST 267–86 (Stephen W. Haycox and Mary Childers Mangusso eds., 1996).

U.S. Dep't of Interior. *Status of Alaskan Natives*, 53 Interior Dec. 593 (Feb. 24, 1932).

American Indians

Allen, John H. *Denial of Voting Rights to Reservation Indians*, 5 UTAH L. REV. 247 (1956).

Dussias, Allison M. *Waging War with Words: Native Americans' Continuing Struggle Against the Suppression of their Languages*, 60 OHIO ST. L.J. 901 (1999).

Inter-Tribal Council of Arizona, Inc. DVD: *The History of Indian Voting in Arizona* (2004).

Jackson, Danna R. *Eighty Years of Indian Voting: A Call to Protect Indian Voting Rights*, 65 MONT. L. REV. 269 (2004).

McCool, Dan, Susan Olson, and Jennifer L. Robinson. NATIVE VOTE: AMERICAN INDIANS, THE VOTING RIGHTS ACT, AND THE RIGHT TO VOTE (2007).

McDonald, Laughlin. *The Voting Rights Act of Indian Country: South Dakota, A Case Study*, 29 AM. INDIAN L. REV. 43 (2004–2005).

McDonald, Laughlin, Janine Pease, and Richard Guest. *Voting Rights in South Dakota: 1982–2006*, 17 S. CAL. REV. L. & SOC. SCI. 195 (2007).

Phelps, Glenn A. *Representation without Taxation: Citizenship and Suffrage in Indian Country*, 9 AM. INDIAN Q. 135 (1985).

Phelps, Glenn A. *Mr. Gerry Goes to Arizona: Electoral Geography and Voting Rights in Navajo Country*, 15 AM. INDIAN CULTURE & RES. J. 63 (1991).

Rollings, Willard Hughes. *Citizenship and Suffrage: The Native American Struggle for Civil Rights in the American West, 1830–1965*, 5 NEV. L.J. 126 (2004).

Svingen, Orlan J. *Jim Crow, Indian Style*, 11 AM. INDIAN Q. 275 (1987).

Wolfley, Jeanette. *Jim Crow, Indian Style: The Disenfranchisement of Native Americans*, 16 AM. INDIAN L. REV. 368 (1990).

Asian Americans

Ancheta, Angelo N. RACE, RIGHTS, AND THE ASIAN AMERICAN EXPERIENCE (1998).

Aoki, Keith. *A Tale of Three Cities: Thoughts on Asian American Electoral and Political Power after 2000*, 8 ASIAN-PAC. AM. L.J. 1 (2002).

Asian American Justice Center (AAJC) (formerly known as the Nat'l Asian Pacific American Legal Consortium, or NAPALC). *Sound Barriers: Asian Americans and Language Access in Election 2004* (2005), *available at* http://65.36.162.215/files/sound_barriers.pdf.

Asian American Legal Defense and Education Fund (AALDEF). *The Asian American Vote: A Report on the AALDEF Multilingual Exit Poll in the 2004 Presidential Election* (2005), *available at* http://www.aaldef.org/articles/2005-04-20_67_TheAsianAmeric.pdf.

Asian American Legal Defense and Education Fund (AALDEF). *Asian Americans and the Voting Rights Act: The Case for Reauthorization* (2006), *available at* http://www.aaldef.org/docs/AALDEF-VRAReauthorization-2006.pdf.

Asian American Legal Defense and Education Fund (AALDEF). *The Asian American Vote in the 2006 Midterm Elections* (2007), *available at* http://www.aaldef.org/docs/AALDEF2006ExitPollReportMay2007.pdf.

Asian American Legal Defense and Education Fund (AALDEF). *Asian American Access to Democracy in the 2008 Elections* (2009), *available at* http://aaldef.org/docs/AALDEF_Election_2008_Report.pdf.

Collet, Christian. *Bloc Voting, Polarization and the Panethnic Hypothesis: The Case of Little Saigon*, 67 J. OF POL. 907 (August 2005).

Comm'n on Wartime Relocation and Internment of Civilians. PERSONAL JUSTICE DENIED (1997).

Inada, Lawson Fusao. ONLY WHAT WE COULD CARRY: THE JAPANESE AMERICAN INTERNMENT EXPERIENCE (2000).

Lien, Pei-te. *The Participation of Asian Americans in U.S. Elections: Comparing Elite and Mass Patterns in Hawaii and Mainland States*, 8 ASIAN-PAC. AM. L.J. 55 (2002).

Magpantay, Glenn D. *Asian American Voting Rights and Representation: A Perspective from the Northeast*, 28 FORDHAM URB. L.J. 739 (2001).

Magpantay, Glenn D. *Asian American Access to the Vote: The Language Assistance Provisions (Section 203) of the Voting Rights Act and Beyond*, 11 ASIAN L.J. 31 (2004).

Magpantay, Glenn D. *Ensuring Asian American Access to Democracy in New York City*, 2 AAPI NEXUS: ASIAN AMER. AND PAC. IS. POLICY, PRACTICE, AND COMMUNITY 87 (2004) (UCLA Asian American Studies Center).

Magpantay, Glenn D. and Nancy W. Yu. *Asian Americans and Reauthorization of the Voting Rights Act*, 19 NAT'L BLACK L.J. 1 (2005).

Olaya, Philip A., et al. *Asian Americans and the Voting Rights Act: The Case for Reauthorization* (Asian American Legal Defense and Educ. Fund 2006), *reprinted in Continuing Need for Section 203's Provisions for Limited English Proficient Voters: Hearing Before the S. Comm. on the Judiciary*, 109th Cong. 229 (2006).

Haitian Americans

Newman, JoNel. *Unfinished Business: The Case for Continuing Special Voting Rights Act Coverage in Florida*, 61 MIAMI L. REV. 1 (2006).

Newman, JoNel. *Ensuring that Florida's Language Minorities Have Access to the Ballot*, 36 STETSON L. REV. 329 (2007).

Spanish Heritage

Absoch, Yishaiya, et al. *An Assessment of Racially Polarized Voting Both For and Against Latino Candidates*, address at Voting Rights Act Research Roundtable (Feb. 9, 2006), *reprinted in Voting Rights Act: Evidence of Continued Need: Hearing Before the Subcomm. on the Const. of the H. Comm. on the Judiciary*, 109th Cong. 2415 (2006).

Bedoya, Alvaro. *The Unforeseen Effects of* Georgia v. Ashcroft *on the Latino Community*, 115 YALE L.J. 2112 (2006).

Newman, JoNel. *Unfinished Business: The Case for Continuing Special Voting Rights Act Coverage in Florida*, 61 MIAMI L. REV. 1 (2006).

Newman, JoNel. *Ensuring that Florida's Language Minorities Have Access to the Ballot*, 36 STETSON L. REV. 329 (2007).

Perea, Juan F. *Buscando América: Why Integration and Equal Protection Fail to Protect Latinos*, 117 HARV. L. REV. 1420 (2004).

Tucker, James Thomas. NALEO Educational Fund, *"I Was Asked If I Was A Citizen": Latino Elected Officials Speak Out On the Voting Rights Act* (Sept. 2006), *available at* http://www.naleo.org/downloads/NALEO_VRA_Report.pdf.

Multiple Groups

Clarke, Kristen. *The Congressional Record Underlying the 2006 Voting Rights Act: How Much Discrimination Can the Constitution Tolerate?*, 43 HARV. C.R.-C.L. L. REV. 385 (2008).

Comptroller General of the United States. VOTING RIGHTS ACT: ENFORCEMENT NEEDS STRENGTHENING (1978).

Fraga, Luis Ricardo and Maria Lizet Ocampo. *More Information Requests and the Deterrent Effect of Section 5 of the Voting Rights Act*, *in* VOTING RIGHTS ACT REAUTHORIZATION OF 2006: PERSPECTIVES ON DEMOCRACY, PARTICIPATION, AND POWER 47-82 (Ana Henderson ed., 2007).

Katz, Ellen, et al. *Documenting Discrimination in Voting: Judicial Findings under Section 2 of the Voting Rights Act Since 1982*, 39 U. MICH. J. L. REFORM 643 (2006).

Keyssar, Alexander. THE RIGHT TO VOTE: THE CONTESTED HISTORY OF DEMOCRACY IN THE UNITED STATES (2000).

Lopez, Caroline D. Comment, *Beyond the Old Paradigms: The Continuum Theory of Asian, Black and Latino Voting Coalitions*, 13 ASIAN PAC. AM. L.J. 24 (2007–2008).

Nat'l Comm'n on the Voting Rts. Act. PROTECTING MINORITY VOTERS: THE VOTING RIGHTS ACT AT WORK, 1982–2005 (2006), *reprinted in Voting Rights Act: Evidence of Continued Need: Hearing Before the Subcomm. on the Const. of the H. Comm. on the Judiciary*, 109th Cong. (2006).

Sowell, Thomas. ETHNIC AMERICA: A HISTORY (1981).

Tucker, James Thomas. *Enfranchising Language Minority Citizens: The Bilingual Election Provisions of the Voting Rights Act*, 10 N.Y.U. J. LEGIS. & PUB. POL'Y 195 (2006).

Tucker, James Thomas. *The Battle over Bilingual Ballots Shifts to the Courts: A Post-*Boerne *Assessment of Section 203 of the Voting Rights Act*, 45 HARV. J. ON LEGIS. 507 (2008).

Tucker, James Thomas. *The Case for Language Assistance under the Voting Rights Act*, *in* THE MOST FUNDAMENTAL RIGHT: THE 2006 REAUTHORIZATION OF THE VOTING RIGHTS ACT (Dan McCool ed., forthcoming 2010).

Tucker, James Thomas and Rodolfo Espino. *Government Effectiveness and Efficiency? The Minority Language Assistance Provisions of the VRA*, 12 TEX. J. C.L. & C.R. 163, 215 (2007).

U.S. Comm'n on Civil Rts. REPORT OF THE U.S. COMM'N ON CIVIL RIGHTS (1959).

U.S. Comm'n on Civil Rts. THE VOTING RIGHTS ACT: TEN YEARS AFTER (1975).

U.S. Comm'n on Civil Rts. THE VOTING RIGHTS ACT: UNFULLFILLED GOALS (1981).

Voting Rts. Project of the Am. Civ. Liberties Union. VOTE: THE CASE FOR EXTENDING AND AMENDING THE VOTING RIGHTS ACT, VOTING RIGHTS LITIGATION 1982–2005 (2006), *reprinted in Voting Rights Act: Evidence of Continued Need*, H.R. REP NO. 109–103, at 378 (2006).

Weinberg, Barry H. and Lyn Utrecht. *Problems in America's Polling Places: How They Can Be Stopped*, 11 TEMP. POL. & CIV. RTS. L. REV. 401 (2002).

Language Assistance in Voting (By Language Group or Ethnicity)

Alaska Natives

Landreth, Natalie and Moira Smith. *Voting Rights in Alaska: 1982–2006*, 17 S. CAL. REV. L. & SOC. SCI. 79 (2007).

American Indians

McCool, Dan, Susan Olson, and Jennifer L. Robinson. NATIVE VOTE: AMERICAN INDIANS, THE VOTING RIGHTS ACT, AND THE RIGHT TO VOTE (2007).

Native Am. Rts. Fund and Nat'l Cong. of Am. Indians. *Joint Statement on S. 2236 Reauthorizing Section 203 of the Voting Rights Act, reprinted in S. 2236 Hearings*, 102d Cong., 2d Sess., S. HRG. 102–1066, at 309–340 (1992).

Tucker, James Thomas, Rodolfo Espino, et al. *Voting Rights in Arizona: 1982–2006*, 17 S. CAL. REV. L. & SOC. JUST. 283 (2008).

Arab Americans

Abdelall, Brenda Fathy. Student Note, *Not Enough of a Minority? Arab Americans and the Language Assistance Provisions (Section 203) of the Voting Rights Act*, 38 U. MICH. J. L. REFORM 911 (2005).

Benson, Jocelyn Friedrichs. *Language Protections for All? Extending and Expanding the Language Protections of the Voting Rights Act*, *in* VOTING RIGHTS ACT REAUTHORIZATION OF 2006: PERSPECTIVES ON DEMOCRACY, PARTICIPATION, AND POWER 327 (Ana Henderson ed., 2007).

Asian Americans

Asian American Justice Center (AAJC) (formerly known as the Nat'l Asian Pacific American Legal Consortium, or NAPALC). *Sound Barriers: Asian Americans and Language Access in Election 2004* (2005), *available at* http://65.36.162.215/files/sound_barriers.pdf.

Asian American Legal Defense and Education Fund (AALDEF). *The Asian American Vote: A Report on the AALDEF Multilingual Exit Poll in the 2004 Presidential Election* (2005), *available at* http://www.aaldef.org/articles/2005-04-20_67_TheAsianAmeric.pdf.

Asian American Legal Defense and Education Fund (AALDEF). *Asian Americans and the Voting Rights Act: The Case for Reauthorization* (2006), *available at* http://www.aaldef.org/docs/AALDEF-VRAReauthorization-2006.pdf.

Asian American Legal Defense and Education Fund (AALDEF). *The Asian American Vote in the 2006 Midterm Elections* (2007), *available at* http://www.aaldef.org/docs/AALDEF2006ExitPollReportMay2007.pdf.

Asian American Legal Defense and Education Fund (AALDEF). *Asian American Access to Democracy in the 2008 Elections* (2009), *available at* http://aaldef.org/docs/AALDEF_Election_2008_Report.pdf.

Avila, Joaquin G., Eugene Lee, and Terry M. Ao. *Voting Rights in California: 1982–2006*, 17 S. Cal. Rev. L. & Soc. Sci. 131 (2007).

Cartegna, Juan, *Voting Rights in New York: 1982–2006*, 17 S. Cal. Rev. L. & Soc. Just. 501 (2008).

Lee, Eugene. Statement on behalf of the Voting Rts. Project of the Asian Pacific Am. Ctr. before the Nat'l Comm'n on Voting Rts. Act, Western Regional Hr'g (Sept. 27, 2005).

Magpantay, Glenn D. *Asian American Access to the Vote: The Language Assistance Provisions (Section 203) of the Voting Rights Act and Beyond*, 11 Asian L.J. 31 (2004).

Magpantay, Glenn D. *Ensuring Asian American Access to Democracy in New York City*, 2 AAPI Nexus: Asian Amer. and Pac. Is. Policy, Practice, and Community 87 (2004) (UCLA Asian American Studies Center).

Magpantay, Glenn D. *Two Steps Forward, One Step Back, and a Side Step: Asian Americans and the Federal Help America Vote Act*, 10 Asian L.J. 31 (2005).

Magpantay, Glenn D. and Nancy W. Yu. *Asian Americans and Reauthorization of the Voting Rights Act*, 19 Nat'l Black L.J. 1 (2005).

Haitian Creoles

Newman, JoNel. *Unfinished Business: The Case for Continuing Special Voting Rights Act Coverage in Florida*, 61 Miami L. Rev. 1 (2006).

Newman, JoNel. *Ensuring that Florida's Language Minorities Have Access to the Ballot*, 36 Stetson L. Rev. 329 (2007).

Puerto Ricans

Cartagena, Juan. *Latinos and Section 5 of the Voting Rights Act: Beyond Black and White*, 18 Nat'l Black L.J. 201 (2004–2005).

Cartegena, Juan, Gabe Kaimowitz and Ignacio Pérez, *United States Language Policy: Where Do We Go From Here?*, 18 Rev. Jurídica U. Inter. P.R. 527 (1984).

Culliton-González, Katherine. *Time to Revive Puerto Rican Voting Rights*, 19 Berkeley La Raza L.J. 27 (2008).

Spanish Heritage

Avila, Joaquin G., Eugene Lee, and Terry M. Ao. *Voting Rights in California: 1982–2006*, 17 S. Cal. Rev. L. & Soc. Sci. 131 (2007).

Cartagena, Juan. *Latinos and Section 5 of the Voting Rights Act: Beyond Black and White*, 18 Nat'l Black L.J. 201 (2004–05).

Cartegna, Juan. *New Jersey's Multi-Member Legislative Districts and Latino Political Power*, 7 Rutgers Race & L. Rev. 13 (2005).

Cartegna, Juan, *Voting Rights in New York: 1982–2006*, 17 S. Cal. Rev. L. & Soc. Just. 501 (2008).

Culliton-González, Katherine. *Time to Revive Puerto Rican Voting Rights*, 19 Berkeley La Raza L.J. 27 (2008).

Mahoney, Martha R. *"Democracy Begins at Home" – Notes from the Grassroots on Inequality, Voters, and Lawyers*, 63 Miami L. Rev. 1 (2008).

Mexican Am. Legal Def. & Educ. Fund. *Bilingual Elections: Latinos, Language and Voting Rights* (1992), *reprinted in S. 2236 Hearings*, 102d Cong., 2d Sess., S. Hrg. 102–1066, at 32–87 (1992).

Nat'l Council of La Raza. *State of Hispanic America 1991: An Overview* (1992), *reprinted in S. 2236 Hearings*, 102d Cong., 2d Sess., S. Hrg. 102–1066, at 88–132 (1992).

Newman, JoNel. *Unfinished Business: The Case for Continuing Special Voting Rights Act Coverage in Florida*, 61 Miami L. Rev. 1 (2006).

Newman, JoNel. *Ensuring that Florida's Language Minorities Have Access to the Ballot*, 36 Stetson L. Rev. 329 (2007).

Perales, Nina, Luis Figueroa, and Criselda G. Rivas. *Voting Rights in Texas: 1982–2006*, 17 S. Cal. Rev. L. & Soc. Just. 713 (2008).

Tucker, James Thomas. *The Power of Observation: The Role of Federal Observers under the Voting Rights Act*, 13 Mich. J. Race & Law 227 (Fall 2007).

Tucker, James Thomas, Rodolfo Espino, et al. *Voting Rights in Arizona: 1982–2006*, 17 S. Cal. Rev. L. & Soc. Just. 283 (2008).

Multiple Groups

Tanner, John. *Effective Monitoring of Polling Places*, 61 Baylor L. Rev. 50 (2009).

Tucker, James Thomas. *Enfranchising Language Minority Citizens: The Bilingual Election Provisions of the Voting Rights Act*, 10 N.Y.U. J. Legis. & Pub. Pol'y 195 (2006).

Tucker, James Thomas. *The Case for Language Assistance under the Voting Rights Act*, *in* The Most Fundamental Right: The 2006 Reauthorization of the Voting Rights Act (Dan McCool ed., forthcoming 2010).

Weinberg, Barry H. and Lyn Utrecht. *Problems in America's Polling Places: How They Can Be Stopped*, 11 Temp. Pol. & Civ. Rts. L. Rev. 401 (2002).

Language Assistance in Voting (By State)

Alaska

Landreth, Natalie and Moira Smith. *Voting Rights in Alaska: 1982–2006*, 17 S. Cal. Rev. L. & Soc. Sci. 79 (2007).

Arizona

Tucker, James Thomas, Rodolfo Espino, et al. *Voting Rights in Arizona: 1982–2006*, 17 S. Cal. Rev. L. & Soc. Just. 283 (2008).

California

Avila, Joaquin G., Eugene Lee, and Terry M. Ao. *Voting Rights in California: 1982–2006*, 17 S. CAL. REV. L. & SOC. SCI. 131 (2007).

Hall, Thad E. *Public Participation in Election Management: The Case of Language Minority Voters*, 33 AM. REV. PUB. ADMIN. 407–22 (2003).

Hall, Thad E. *Delivering Political Power to Language Minorities: Voting, Elections, and the Rights of Language Minorities*, 27 INT'L JOURNAL OF PUB. ADMIN. 127 (2004).

Narasaki, Karen K. and Terry M. Ao. *Meeting the demand of a growing language-minority voting populate*, *in* AMERICA VOTES! A GUIDE TO MODERN ELECTION LAW AND VOTING RIGHTS (Benjamin E. Griffith ed., Feb. 2008).

Florida

Hall, Thad E. *Public Participation in Election Management: The Case of Language Minority Voters*, 33 AM. REV. PUB. ADMIN. 407–22 (2003).

Hall, Thad E. *Delivering Political Power to Language Minorities: Voting, Elections, and the Rights of Language Minorities*, 27 INT'L JOURNAL OF PUB. ADMIN. 127 (2004).

Mahoney, Martha R. *"Democracy Begins at Home" – Notes from the Grassroots on Inequality, Voters, and Lawyers*, 63 MIAMI L. REV. 1 (2008).

Newman, JoNel. *Unfinished Business: The Case for Continuing Special Voting Rights Act Coverage in Florida*, 61 MIAMI L. REV. 1 (2006).

Newman, JoNel. *Ensuring that Florida's Language Minorities Have Access to the Ballot*, 36 STETSON L. REV. 329 (2007).

Pritchard, Claudius H. *Counties Must Publish and Disseminate Electoral Pamphlets in the Language of Minority Groups within the Community*, 23 STETSON L. REV. 558 (1994).

Georgia

Kengle, Robert A. *Voting Rights in Georgia: 1982–2006*, 17 S. CAL. REV. L. & SOC. JUST. 367 (2008).

Michigan

Abdelall, Brenda Fathy. Student Note, *Not Enough of a Minority? Arab Americans and the Language Assistance Provisions (Section 203) of the Voting Rights Act*, 38 U. MICH. J. L. REFORM 911 (2005).

Benson, Jocelyn Friedrichs. *Language Protections for All? Extending and Expanding the Language Protections of the Voting Rights Act*, *in* VOTING RIGHTS ACT REAUTHORIZATION OF 2006: PERSPECTIVES ON DEMOCRACY, PARTICIPATION, AND POWER 327 (Ana Henderson ed., 2007).

New Jersey

Cartegna, Juan. *New Jersey's Multi-Member Legislative Districts and Latino Political Power*, 7 RUTGERS RACE & L. REV. 13 (2005).

Tucker, James Thomas. *The Power of Observation: The Role of Federal Observers under the Voting Rights Act*, 13 MICH. J. RACE & LAW 227 (Fall 2007).

New York

Cartagena, Juan. *Latinos and Section 5 of the Voting Rights Act: Beyond Black and White*, 18 NAT'L BLACK L.J. 201 (2004–05).

Cartegna, Juan, *Voting Rights in New York: 1982–2006*, 17 S. CAL. REV. L. & SOC. JUST. 501 (2008).

Magpantay, Glenn D. *Ensuring Asian American Access to Democracy in New York City*, 2 AAPI NEXUS: ASIAN AMER. AND PAC. IS. POLICY, PRACTICE, AND COMMUNITY 87 (2004) (UCLA Asian American Studies Center).

South Dakota

McDonald, Laughlin, Janine Pease, and Richard Guest. *Voting Rights in South Dakota: 1982–2006*, 17 S. CAL. REV. L. & SOC. SCI. 195 (2007).

Texas

Perales, Nina, Luis Figueroa, and Criselda G. Rivas. *Voting Rights in Texas: 1982–2006*, 17 S. CAL. REV. L. & SOC. JUST. 713 (2008).

Utah

McCool, Dan, Susan Olson, and Jennifer L. Robinson. *It's Our Turn: Indian Voting in San Juan County, Utah*, *in* NATIVE VOTE: AMERICAN INDIANS, THE VOTING RIGHTS ACT, AND THE RIGHT TO VOTE 90–110 (2007).

Virginia

Earls, Anita S., Kara Millonzi, Oni Seliski, and Torrey Dixon. *Voting Rights in Virginia: 1982–2006*, 17 S. CAL. REV. L. & SOC. JUST. 761 (2008).

Hall, Thad E. *Delivering Political Power to Language Minorities: Voting, Elections, and the Rights of Language Minorities*, 27 INT'L JOURNAL OF PUB. ADMIN. 127 (2004).

Four or More States

Asian American Justice Center (AAJC) (formerly known as the Nat'l Asian Pacific American Legal Consortium, or NAPALC). *Sound Barriers: Asian Americans and Language Access in Election 2004* (2005), *available at* http://65.36.162.215/files/sound_barriers.pdf.

Asian American Legal Defense and Education Fund (AALDEF). *The Asian American Vote: A Report on the AALDEF Multilingual Exit Poll in the 2004 Presidential Election* (2005), *available at* http://www.aaldef.org/articles/2005-04-20_67_TheAsianAmeric.pdf.

Asian American Legal Defense and Education Fund (AALDEF). *Asian Americans and the Voting Rights Act: The Case for Reauthorization* (2006), *available at* http://www.aaldef.org/docs/AALDEF-VRAReauthorization-2006.pdf.

Asian American Legal Defense and Education Fund (AALDEF). *The Asian American Vote in the 2006 Midterm Elections* (2007), *available at* http://www.aaldef.org/docs/AALDEF2006ExitPollReportMay2007.pdf.

Asian American Legal Defense and Education Fund (AALDEF). *Asian American Access to Democracy in the 2008 Elections* (2009), *available at* http://aaldef.org/docs/AALDEF_Election_2008_Report.pdf.

Culliton-González, Katherine. *Time to Revive Puerto Rican Voting Rights*, 19 BERKELEY LA RAZA L.J. 27 (2008).

Magpantay, Glenn D. *Asian American Access to the Vote: The Language Assistance Provisions (Section 203) of the Voting Rights Act and Beyond*, 11 ASIAN L.J. 31 (2004).

Pew Center on the States. *Translating the Vote: The Impact of the Language Minority Provision of the Voting Rights Act*, electionline.org (Oct. 2006).

Sutherland, Brian J. *The Patchwork of State and Federal Language Assistance for Minority Voters and a Proposal for Model State Legislation*, 64 ANN. SURV. AM. L. issue 4 (forthcoming 2009).

Tucker, James Thomas and Rodolfo Espino. *Government Effectiveness and Efficiency? The Minority Language Assistance Provisions of the VRA*, 12 TEX. J. C.L. & C.R. 163, 215 (2007).

Weinberg, Barry H. and Lyn Utrecht. *Problems in America's Polling Places: How They Can Be Stopped*, 11 TEMP. POL. & CIV. RTS. L. REV. 401 (2002).

Political Participation of Language Minority Voters

Aoki, Keith. *A Tale of Three Cities: Thoughts on Asian American Electoral and Political Power after 2000*, 8 ASIAN-PAC. AM. L.J. 1 (2002).

De la Garza, Rodolfo O. and Louis DeSipio. *Reshaping the Tub: The Limits of the VRA for Latino Electoral Politics*, *in* THE FUTURE OF THE VOTING RIGHTS ACT 139 (David Epstein et al. eds., 2006).

De la Garza, Rodolfo O. and Louis DeSipio. *Save the Baby, Change the Bathwater, and Scrub the Tub: Latino Electoral Participation After Seventeen Years of Voting Rights Act Coverage*, 71 TEX. L. REV. 1479 (1993).

Epstein, David and Sharyn O'Halloran. *Trends in Minority Representation, 1974 to 2000*, *in* THE FUTURE OF THE VOTING RIGHTS ACT 61 (David Epstein et al. eds., 2006).

First Am. Educ. Project. NATIVE VOTE 2004: A NATIONAL SURVEY AND ANALYSIS OF EFFORTS TO INCREASE THE NATIVE VOTE IN 2004 AND THE RESULTS ACHIEVED (2005).

Hardy-Fanta, Carol, Pei-te Lien, Dianne M. Pinderhughes, and Christine Marie Sierra. 2006. *Gender, Race, and Descriptive Representation in the United States: Findings from the Gender and Multicultural Leadership Project*. 28 J. of Women, Pol. & Pol'y (Issues 3-4): 7-41.

Lehman, Russ and First Am. Educ. Project. THE EMERGING ROLE OF AMERICAN INDIANS IN THE AMERICAN ELECTORAL PROCESS (2003), *available at* http://www.centerforcivicparticipation.org/resources/libraryresearch/electoralprocess-1.attachment/302077/ElectorP.pdf.

Lien, Pei-te. *The Participation of Asian Americans in U.S. Elections: Comparing Elite and Mass Patterns in Hawaii and Mainland States*, 8 ASIAN-PAC. AM. L.J. 55 (2002).

Lien, Pei-te, Dianne M. Pinderhughes, Carol Hardy-Fanta, and Christine M. Sierra. *The Voting Rights Act and the Election of Nonwhite Officials*, 40 POL. SCI. & POL. 489 (July 2007).

National Ass'n of Latino Elected and Appointed Officials (NALEO) Educational Fund. *2008 Latino Election Handbook* (2008), *available at* http://www.naleo.org/downloads/NALEO_LEH_2008_final.pdf.

New California Media, Executive Summary, *Poll of Asian Pacific Islanders on the 2004 Presidential Election* (Sept. 14, 2004).

Pew Hispanic Center, Fact Sheet: The Hispanic Electorate in 2004, http://pewhispanic.org/files/factsheets/8.pdf.

Index

Index of Cases

For Product Safety Concerns and Information please contact our EU
representative GPSR@taylorandfrancis.com
Taylor & Francis Verlag GmbH, Kaufingerstraße 24, 80331 München, Germany

www.ingramcontent.com/pod-product-compliance
Lightning Source LLC
Chambersburg PA
CBHW081306100626
62CB00005B/473

9780754675723